exploring
behavior
and
experience

READINGS IN
GENERAL PSYCHOLOGY

EDITED BY

Robert M. Stutz
UNIVERSITY OF CINCINNATI

William N. Dember
UNIVERSITY OF CINCINNATI

James J. Jenkins
UNIVERSITY OF MINNESOTA

Prentice-Hall, Inc., Englewood Cliffs, N.J.

exploring

behavior

and

experience

READINGS IN
GENERAL PSYCHOLOGY

EXPLORING BEHAVIOR AND EXPERIENCE:
Readings in General Psychology

Edited by Robert M. Stutz, William N. Dember,
and James J. Jenkins

Copyright © 1971 by Prentice-Hall, Inc., Englewood Cliffs, New Jersey. All rights reserved. No part of this book may be reproduced in any form or by any means without permission in writing from the publisher. *Printed in the United States of America.* 13–296368–X. Library of Congress Catalog Card Number: 75–135022.

Current printing (last digit): 10 9 8 7 6 5 4 3 2 1

PRENTICE-HALL INTERNATIONAL, INC., *London*
PRENTICE-HALL OF AUSTRALIA PTY. LTD., *Sydney*
PRENTICE-HALL OF CANADA LTD., *Toronto*
PRENTICE-HALL OF INDIA PRIVATE LIMITED, *New Delhi*
PRENTICE-HALL OF JAPAN, INC., *Tokyo*

To Rochelle, Cynthia, and Jerry

contents

UNIT

 III

learning and memory

UNIT

social psychology

preface

The articles reprinted in this volume were selected, in large part, because of their exceptional readability and/or because of the intrinsic interest the chosen topics have for the beginning psychology student. Most of the articles describe broad programs of research of personal concern to the author, and many were first presented as talks. We hope that such articles will offer the student more of the flavor of the processes involved in formulating and solving selected theoretical, methodological, and, sometimes, ethical problems than can be obtained either from highly technical reports of individual experiments or from the impersonal, condensed research reviews provided by even the best of our textbooks.

The topics discussed in the papers which appear in this collection are not meant to be fully representative of the countless subareas within the broad field of psychology. In general, we are biased in favor of issues which are of contemporary concern to academic psychologists, but we have also included articles that focus directly on the application of psychological knowledge and methods to the solution of practical problems. Quite remarkably, several of the articles serve both ends.

We have tried to preserve each article as close as possible to its original form. In a few instances this meant retaining some rather esoteric references and terminology, as well as statistical analyses, which the beginning student typically is not prepared to fully understand. Nevertheless it should be possible to gloss over these spots without losing the main thrust of the presentation. We have also chosen not to restyle the bibliographic references to make them conform to a single mold. This will pose no impediment to the casual reader, and the serious student might just as well learn that different journals have different styles.

We are pleased to express our sincere thanks to the many authors who have generously allowed us to reprint their articles. The credit for whatever is good in this volume certainly belongs to them. We are also grateful for the helpful suggestions and criticisms offered by our colleagues and students, and for the heroic secretarial efforts of Mrs. Lynn Pierce, Mrs. Barbara Aiduk, and Miss Diane Burkhart.

Robert M. Stutz
William N. Dember
James J. Jenkins

September, 1970

exploring
behavior
and
experience

READINGS IN
GENERAL PSYCHOLOGY

UNIT

I

methods and models

1　Extensory *Extrasensory perception (ESP), or the ability to receive information from another individual via routes other than the "normal" sense organs, has not been accepted as a valid phenomenon by many scientists. R. A. McConnell is a biophysicist who has become interested in research on ESP. In the article which follows, he discusses some of the attitudes of scientists which have led them to reject or to discredit parapsychological findings.*

McConnell draws a possible historical parallel between the current status of ESP research and an earlier scientific phenomenon that was initially discounted but was later accepted as a real event. He then presents some examples of ESP demonstrations which he finds convincing.

ESP and credibility in science [1]

R. A. MC CONNELL

In discussing extrasensory perception (ESP) before psychology students, it is not uncommon to stress the credulity of the public. Perhaps, instead, we ought to examine the credibility of scientists—including those on both sides of the controversy.

In ESP research whom shall we trust? One can rather easily imagine experimental precautions to keep participating subjects from cheating. But how do we know whether the experimenter is deliberately deceiving us? And in a world where people believe all kinds of nonsense, how can we be sure that the experimenter is not deceiving himself?

Let us suppose that 10 experimenters independently get the same result. Can we

[1] An invited lecture to the introductory psychology classes at Carnegie-Mellon University, December 18 and 19, 1967.

accept it? Ten is not a large number. There are about 150,000 names in *American Men of Science*. We may reasonably assume that at least 10,000 of these hold beliefs about the nature of reality that the majority of scientists would regard as wholly without foundation. Thus, on a subject like ESP, where there are no recognized authorities, why should we accept the word of 10 experimenters—or, for that matter, a thousand? Are we not, all of us, creatures of our culture? Is there any way we can be sure that a scientist in any field is as rational as he pretends to be?

Questions concerning the credibility of scientists are rarely asked in our classrooms. I have wondered why. Perhaps it makes us uncomfortable to consider the possibility of incompetence, dishonesty, or mental illness among professional people. Whatever the reason, this is forbidden territory for study.

Once in a long while, these embarrassing ideas do come to the surface. Someone, a little bolder or a little more eccentric than the rest of us, may write an article that slips

3

by the editorial censor. When that happens, we have a chance to learn what people really think.

When I accepted this invitation to talk to you, I was told I could give you an advance reading assignment. I asked that you read an eight-page article on ESP by G. R. Price (1955) that appeared in *Science* together with several letters to the editor (Soal; Rhine; Meehl and Scriven; Bridgman; Price; Rhine, 1956) written in reply to Price. These papers are currently available as part of the Bobbs-Merrill reprint series that is widely used for teaching psychology, and they have thus acquired a quasi-official status as source documents to which the very young may be exposed.

I also suggested that you read an analysis of Price's article (McConnell, 1955) that appeared in the *Journal of Parapsychology* and that was not included in the Bobbs-Merrill series. I hope that most of you have had a chance to study these references, which I shall now discuss briefly.

Price, a chemist by profession, presented a well-supported argument showing that existing experimental evidence constitutes conclusive proof of ESP if one accepts the good faith and sanity of the experimenters. But he went on to say that all of the otherwise convincing evidence for ESP can be easily explained away if one assumes that experimenters, working in collaboration with their witnesses, have intentionally faked their results.

Perhaps the most interesting thing about this unsubstantiated suggestion of fraud is that it was published on the first page of the most influential scientific journal in the United States. I will not say whether Price intended what he wrote as a joke. That is a riddle that I leave to you to answer. The important question is not whether Price took himself seriously, but whether you and I ought to do so.

I believe, as apparently does Price, that all kinds of fraud, even by highly placed sicentists, are possible and that it is con-

ceivable that there might be collaboration between two scientists in perpetuating a scientific hoax. Nevertheless, I think that those who accept Price's argument fail to understand two important things about science as a social enterprise.

First, they fail to realize that the way to tell whether a number of scientists are collaborating in a hoax is to consider the intricate web of public and private motivation, belief, and retribution that determines the behavior of professional people in our culture. Price suggested that scientists, university teachers, medical doctors, and intellectually prominent persons who have assisted in the investigation of ESP may have engaged in conscious collusive fraud. Price answered the question of how one might get such people to become willing accomplices by saying: "In recruiting, I would appeal not to desire for fame or material gain but to the noblest motives, arguing that much good to humanity could result from a small deception designed to strengthen religious belief." An experienced lawyer or even a politician would laugh at this explanation of a supposed conspiracy among well-educated and fully engaged members of our society, but evidently quite a few scientists find it plausible.

Second, those scientists who take Price seriously do not understand scientific method. Price suggested that the way to establish the scientific truth of ESP is to carry out a fraudproof experiment. In his words: "What is needed is one completely convincing experiment." He described in specific detail how this might be done by using prominent scientists and stage magicians as witnesses, backed up by motion pictures of the entire proceedings, plus photomicrographs of welded seals, and so on. This is nonsense because it assumes that scientific proof is of the same nature as legal proof. On the contrary, the acceptance of a scientific principle does not, and never can, depend upon the honesty of individual scientists.

I wish I had time to pursue with you the subtle psychological question of the nature of scientific proof and of how the method of science deals with individual experimenter error as well as mass irrationality. Those of you who are especially interested may wish to read a book by T. S. Kuhn (1962) titled *The Structure, of Scientific Revolutions*.[2] Here today, I can only say that in my opinion, wittily or unwittingly, Price's article is a hoax about hoaxes and about the nature of science.

If you were to ask: "What does it signify that Price successfully placed his article in our most important journal of science?" I would answer as follows: There is a facade of respectability and belief that covers all of the activities of society and makes it possible for men to work together and for society to exist. Most people—including those who are well educated—are unaware of this false front and lose their equilibrium when they are forced by circumstances to penetrate behind it. On the other hand, those of you who are intellectually alienated from our culture understand quite well that this pretense exists. I hope that some day you will also understand why it is necessary and that it is not the contrivance of a group of evil men but reflects what existential philosophers refer to as "the human condition."

This curtain of propriety and convention exists in science also, where it allows us to believe that all is well with our knowledge system. ESP or any other revolutionary discovery may seem to threaten science. From time to time, when such a challenge is offered, the stagehands nervously fumble, the curtain slips, and we see a little of the normally concealed machinery. We get a glimpse of underlying reality, a glimpse of the ignorance and fear that govern the inner affairs of the mind of man. Such was the case when *Science* published Price's

[2] For a condensation of this book see McConnell (1968b).

critique of ESP. That is why his article is important.

evidence and belief

Then, what about ESP? If laboratory scientists lack sophistication about human nature and even about the methodology of science, how do we decide for ourselves whether ESP is real or imaginary, true or false?

Before we try to answer so difficult a question, let us go back to the beginning. I shall give you an operational definition of ESP that you may find a bit confusing. Then I shall describe a test for ESP that I hope will make the matter clear to you.

The definition goes this way: "Extrasensory perception is a response to an unknown event not presented to any known sense." I shall not try to explain it. Instead, let me describe the test.

I have brought with me a deck of ESP cards. These cards have five different kinds of symbols printed on them: a circle, a square, a plus, a star, and wavy lines. Altogether, there are 25 cards, 5 of each kind.

Suppose I shuffle these cards, hide them, and ask you to guess them. By the theory of chance probability, the number you would most often get right is five. Sometimes you would get four or six or seven. Only once in a long while would you get 15 right out of 25. In fact, if you got more than 10 right very often, you would begin to suspect that it was not just good luck. It might even be ESP.

Of course, you could not be sure. It might be luck—or it might be something else. If you look closely at the backs of these cards, sometimes you can see the symbol showing through. Perhaps in this way you recognized some of the cards when I shuffled them. Or again, every time I asked whether you were ready for your next guess, perhaps I gave you a hint without knowing it. Perhaps, unconsciously, I raised the tone of my voice just a little when I came to each star—because I think of stars as being "higher" than the other symbols, or for some other trivial reason.

You can see that there are many subtle ways for information to leak through by sight or by sound. No serious scientist would try to conduct an ESP experiment in this fashion. My only purpose in showing you these cards is to let you know how some of the early tests for ESP were done at Duke University 35 years ago. I regard these cards as a museum piece, although they are a lot of fun and can be used in preliminary testing.

The experiments that are carried out today are often so complex that one cannot evaluate them without advanced training in statistics, physics, and psychology. For this reason, and because the field is too large to describe in one lecture, I have prepared a list of reading materials. Some of these are intended to show the scope of the subject (Heywood, 1964; Langdon-Davies, 1961; McConnell, 1966; Murphy and Dale, 1961); others are experimental reports (Anderson and McConnell, 1961; McConnell and Forwald, 1967a,b, 1968; McConnell, Snowdon, and Powell, 1955; Sinclair, 1962; Soal and Bateman, 1954).

You will notice that I have listed only my own journal articles. For this I offer my apology along with the following explanation. In any frontier field of science there are experimental hazards. If someone questions the soundness of what I recommend to you as evidence, I can probably do a better job of explaining if I have chosen research with which I am most familiar. I also want to convey the idea that there has been a large amount of work done in this field. If you study my papers and cannot find anything wrong with them, you ought to remember that there have been perhaps a hundred other investigators who have found substantial evidence for ESP under controlled experimental conditions.

ESP is a controversial idea in psychology. Nevertheless, the psychologists whom I know personally agree with me on many things. I am sure we agree on what constitutes good quality experimental laboratory research. We also agree that there is a sizable body of high-grade evidence for ESP in the literature.

In 1947 I visited Duke University in North Carolina where a man by the name of Rhine was doing experiments on ESP. I wanted to get acquainted with Rhine and with the people who were working under him. Even more important, I wanted to talk to those faculty members who rejected Rhine's work. I rented a dormitory room, and during four weeks I interviewed everyone I could, beginning with the President of the University and working down to assistant professors in various departments. I shall not have time to describe that adventure, but I will tell you what I was told by one professor of psychology in a private interview.

He said that he was familiar with the experimental literature of ESP and that, in his opinion, if it were anything else *but* ESP, one-tenth of the published evidence would already have established the phenomenon. He also explained that he would not accept ESP himself because, as he put it, he found "a world without ESP a more comfortable place in which to live."

That trip to Duke University was part of a larger investigation that made me decide to leave engineering electronics, in which I had acquired some experience, and to devote my life to the investigation of ESP and related effects.

That was 20 years ago. What has happened in this field since then? Among other things, there has been time to publish 20 more volumes of the *Journal of Parapsychology*. That comes to about 4,000 pages of research. There have been several thousand additional pages in the *Journal of the American Society for Psychical Research* and in the English and Continental journals. You might think that the argument would be settled by now.

Only recently, a brilliant young psychologist, who is here on your campus, gave a lecture on ESP in which he said "I tend to believe the evidence is as good as it is for many of our other psychological phenomena." He also said that "Psychologists will not be interested in ESP until there is a repeatable experiment."

Where my psychologist friends and I disagree, is that I believe that the available evidence for ESP is sufficient to establish its reality beyond all reasonable doubt. My psychologist friends think that the evidence is not yet conclusive. I do not regard this difference of opinion as very important. I am happy to allow anyone the privilege of doubt.

How else does the position of professional psychologists whom I know differ from my own? Perhaps the main difference—the really important difference—lies in our interpretation of the history and methodology of science—in what today we call the philosophy of science.

For one thing, my friends seem to believe that the only good evidence for ESP must come from controlled experimentation in a laboratory. My own belief is that all available evidence must be weighed, taking into account its source and the conditions under which it was gathered.

Perhaps it will clarify the problem if I say that there are only two important kinds of scientific evidence in this world: our own evidence and someone else's. Since most of us are not in a position to gather evidence of ESP, my remarks apply especially to other people's evidence.

The first thing to remember is that, no matter how reputable the scientific journal, someone else's evidence is always suspect. And if the matter is important, we ought to be *aggressively* skeptical about it.

Whether we are listening to a tale of a ghost in a haunted house or reading the tightly edited *Journal of Experimental Psychology*, we have to concern ourselves with two questions: what is the content of the report and what are the competence and motivation of the observer?

What I am suggesting is that our attitude toward *all* supposedly scientific reports must be that of the psychologist in receiving an introspective account from a human subject in a laboratory experiment —for it must be remembered that, as far as the reader is concerned, a journal article by a distant scientist is in some ways even less dependable than what psychologists, often condescendingly, refer to as a "verbal report."

From a study of the history of science, I have come to two conclusions in this connection: (a) the evidence presented in scientific journals by professional scientists for all kinds of ordinary phenomena is not as good as commonly supposed, and (b) on a controversial subject where the professionals do not agree, the evidence of the layman may have considerable scientific value. As corollaries, I suggest that the textbooks of science are often wrong and that contrary popular opinion is sometimes right. Let us examine these ideas.

storehouses of knowledge?

Textbooks are the storehouses of man's knowledge. They are presumed to contain all of the things we know to be true. If you are becoming a scientist, you will spend at least 18 years studying from books. It would be not entirely unfair to call most of this training a "brainwashing" process. Nearly everything you learn as factual reality must be accepted upon the word of some recognized authority and not upon your own firsthand experience. It should be a matter of concern to you whether you have been told the truth for those 18 years. Just how bad are the textbooks we use? Let me take an example from the field of geology.

Did you know that until the year 1800 the highest scientific authorities thought that there was no such thing as a meteorite? After all, there are no stones in the sky; so stones cannot fall out of the sky. Only a superstitious person would believe in meteorites.

Many of you are familiar with the work of Lavoisier. He was the founder of modern chemistry. He discovered that burning is the combining of oxygen with other things, and he helped to show that the formula for water is H_2O. He was one of the great scientists of all time.

In 1772 Lavoisier signed a report to the French Academy of Science in which he said he had examined a stone that was believed to have fallen from the sky in a great blaze of light. Lavoisier said in his report that this was just an ordinary stone that had been struck by lightning and had melted partly into glass while lying on the ground.

Eventually, of course, the leaders of science decided that meteorites do come from outer space, and they revised the textbooks accordingly. But in doing so, they forgot to mention that there had ever been any argument about the matter. So here we are, living in the space age, without realizing how hard it is to discover the truth about even a simple thing like meteorites, which can be seen as meteors in the sky on any clear night, and which have been found upon the surface of the earth since the dawn of history.

Even worse, as students, we have no way of estimating how many arguments are still going on in science and how many mistakes—truly serious mistakes—there are in the textbooks from which we study. It is my guess that we can safely believe nearly all of what is said in the physics and chemistry books. But we ought to believe only half of the ideas in the biological sciences—although I am not sure which half. And we should accept as final very little in the social sciences, which try to explain why groups of people behave as they do.

Our subject today is extrasensory perception, which belongs in psychology, one of the biological sciences. ESP is something about which the "authorities" are in error. Most psychology textbooks omit the subject entirely as unworthy of serious atten-

tion. But these books are mistaken, because ESP is a real psychological phenomenon.

Of course, I am only giving you my individual opinion about ESP. I do not want you to base your belief upon what I tell you. When you have studied advanced psychology and statistics, and when you come to realize that your professors cannot be expected to teach you everything you wish to know, then I hope you will go to the scientific journals and study the experiments that have been done and decide for yourself.

mental radio

I have already discussed the credibility of experts and the errors we find in science textbooks. I would like to turn next to the other half of my thesis, namely, that evidence from a layman may sometimes have scientific value.

Most of you are familiar with the name Upton Sinclair, who was a socialist reformer and a writer active in the first half of the twentieth century. He died in 1968 at the age of 90. In his time he wrote nearly 90 books. One of the best known of these, published in 1906, was called *The Jungle*. It told about the cruel and unsanitary conditions in the processing of beef in the Chicago stock yards. As a result of that book, laws were passed, and today the situation is much improved. In a very real sense, all of us are indebted to this man.

Sinclair discovered that his wife had an unusual amount of what was then known as "psychic ability." (That was before the beginning of the ESP controversy.) After three years of serious experimentation, he wrote a book about it: *Mental Radio* (1962, orig. publ. 1930).

In his experiments, Sinclair, or someone else, would draw a secret picture and ask Mrs. Sinclair to draw another picture to match it. Some of the pairs of pictures are presented in the following examples.[3] The one on the left is always the original picture, and the one on the right is what Mrs. Sinclair got by ESP.

Sometimes the pictures were made as far apart as 40 miles. At another times the target picture was held by Mrs. Sinclair in her hand—without looking, of course—while she concentrated before drawing her matching picture. The degree of success did not seem to depend upon distance.

Let us examine some of the pictures. In Example 1 we see an almost perfect ESP

example 1

response. It is a knight's helmet. Notice that for every important line in the left-hand picture there is a corresponding line on the right.

Compare that with Example 2. Here, the

example 2

response on the right is not quite the same as the target on the left, but the idea is the same.

. . . [N]ext . . . is Example 3. Sinclair drew a football as a target. Mrs. Sinclair made the drawing on the right, but she thought it was "a baby calf with a belly

[3] Illustrations from *Mental Radio* by Upton Sinclair are reproduced by permission of the publisher, Charles C Thomas, Springfield, Illinois.

example 3

band." Why did her ESP make this mistake? We cannot be sure, but we think it had something to do with the fact that in her childhood she had known a queer old man who raised calves as parlor pets and dressed them in embroidered belly bands.

Example 4 is another instance of the

example 4

right shape with a wrong interpretation. Upton Sinclair drew a volcano, and Mrs. Sinclair drew what she called a black beetle. The beetle is upside down. If you turn the example over, you can more easily recognize its antennae and legs.

In Example 5 Sinclair drew a fish hook,

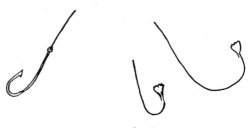

example 5

which turned into two flowers.

Example 6 shows a fragmentary response. Sinclair drew a balloon. The response on the right is what his wife received

example 6

example 9

by "mental radio." She was not sure what it was, so she wrote beside the picture: "Shines in sunlight, must be metal, a scythe hanging among vines or strings."

Example 7 on the left is a swastika. Mrs.

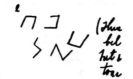

example 7

Sinclair drew the response on the right. She did not know what it meant, but she wrote beside it, "These things somehow belong together, but won't get together." You can see some of her words which were accidentally included when the printer made the book. Here is the beginning of "These" and "belong" and "but won't" and "together."

Example 8 is a pair of drawings in which

example 8

a stick man became a skull and crossbones.

Notice that in Example 9, Mrs. Sinclair left out some of the stars and added a moon instead.

In Example 10 Sinclair drew an umbrella. His wife responded with this curious

picture, which she described in writing beside it as follows: "I feel that it is a snake crawling out of something—vivid feeling of snake, but it looks like a cat's tail." I might mention that she had a special fear of snakes, having grown up on a plantation in a Mississippi swamp.

example 10

The last example is the American flag and a response to it that could hardly be called a chance coincidence (Example 11).

example 11

You have seen a selection of 11 pictures out of a total of 290 trials made by Mrs. Sinclair. Perhaps 4 of the 11 would be called direct target hits. The rest are partial hits. Out of the 290 tries, 23 per cent were rated by Upton Sinclair as hits, 53 per cent were partial hits, and 24 per cent were failures.

Of course, before you can be sure that these pictures were made by ESP, many questions must be answered. Because Upton Sinclair and his wife were laymen, you will have to pay particular attention to their competence and motivation. On the other hand, one important feature of Sinclair's book is that you do not have to be a scientist to understand it. Even though you may not have studied statistics and psychology, you can read the book yourself and make up your mind as to its' value on the basis of common sense. When you do, I think you will arrive at the same conclusion that many scientists have reached by entirely different kinds of experiments. I think you will decide that extrasensory perception is a reality regardless of the skepticism of the psychological profession.

a matter of interest

I have been told by my friends that psychologists will not be interested in ESP until someone discovers a repeatable experiment. Upton Sinclair repeated his experiments over a period of three years. In London, a mathematician by the name of Soal (Soal and Bateman, 1954) repeated certain card-guessing experiments again and again over a period of six years using two subjects and many different witnesses. What do psychologists mean by a repeatable experiment?

Evidently, they mean an experiment that is "repeatable by prescription." They want a standard experimental procedure that can be described on paper by which any qualified person—or at least some qualified persons—can guarantee to produce ESP upon demand. I must confess that we have not yet reached that stage in ESP research. And, until we do, I can sympathize with my skeptical friends. I can see why they, as busy individuals with other interests, are unwilling to reach a firm position about the reality of ESP.

What I cannot understand is why they say: "Psychologists will not be *interested* in ESP until there is a repeatable experiment."

It is a statement of fact that psychologists are *not* interested in ESP. Recently, I had occasion to examine a number of psychology textbooks. Only one of them mentioned ESP—that book, by Hilgard and Atkinson (1967). After reading the four pages which these authors devote to ESP, I have only two minor critical observations to offer.

The first is that the authors have given too much space to finding fault with unimportant papers. They go back 25 years to a journal article in which they accuse an ESP experimenter of overanalyzing his data. I am sure that comparable examples of weak statistical method could be found in any one of the quantitative journals of the APA—and we would not need to go back a generation in time to do it.

My second comment is that Hilgard and Atkinson may have tended to damage their own scholarly reputations by recommending as a "scholarly review" a book by C. E. M. Hansel (1966) titled *ESP: A Scientific Evaluation*. This book has been reviewed by S. S. Stevens of Harvard, who regards ESP as a Rabelaisian joke and who gave Hansel his unqualified approval. If you like amusing book reviews, I suggest that you read Stevens (1967). I regret that I do not have time here today to document for you the basis of my unfavorable opinion of Hansel's book.[4]

I have wandered over many facets of ESP. I shall now summarize what I think are the most important ideas. Since the scientific study of ESP was begun by the London Society for Psychical Research in 1882, there have been hundreds and perhaps thousands of experiments done with a care typical of the journals of the APA. Many psychologists of high repute admit that the evidence is as good as that for other phenomena that are accepted by their profession.

Surprising though it may seem, most of this research on ESP has been done by

---

[4] This has since been done. See McConnell (1968a).

people who were not psychologists. From this fact and from the usual psychology textbook treatment of the subject as well as from private discussion, we know that psychologists are *not* interested in ESP. This raises a question—a very mysterious question that I invite you to try to answer: Why are psychologists not interested in ESP? [5]

REFERENCES

ANDERSON, M. L., and R. A. McCONNELL. Fantasy testing for ESP in a fourth and fifth grade class. *Journal of Psychology,* 1961, **52,** 491–503.

CLARK, K. E., ET AL. The scientific and professional aims of psychology. *American Psychologist,* 1967, **22,** 49–76.

HANSEL, C. E. M. *ESP: A scientific evaluation.* New York: Scribner's, 1966.

HEYWOOD, R. *ESP: A personal memoir.* New York: Dutton, 1964.

HILGARD, E. R., and R. C. ATKINSON. *Introduction to psychology.* New York: Harcourt Brace Jovanovich, 1967.

KUHN, T. S. *The structure of scientific revolutions* (Vol. II, No. 2, of the *International Encyclopedia of Unified Science*). Chicago: University of Chicago Press, 1962.

LANGDON-DAVIES, J. *On the nature of man.* New York: New American Library Corporation, 1961.

LINDER, R. Light one candle. *American Psychologist,* 1967, **22,** 804–805.

McCONNELL, R. A. Price in *Science. Journal of Parapsychology,* 1955, **19,** 258–261.

———. ESP research at three levels of method. *Journal of Parapsychology,* 1966 **30,** 195–207.

———. The ESP scholar. *Contemporary Psychology,* 1968a, **13,** 41.

———. The structure of scientific revolutions: An epitome. *Journal of the American Society for Psychical Research,* 1968b, **62,** 321–327.

———. *ESP Curriculum Guide for Secondary Schools and Colleges.* Department of Biophysics, University of Pittsburgh. In press.

———, and H. FORWALD. Psychokinetic placement: I. A re-examination of the Forwald-Durham experiment. *Journal of Parapsychology,* 1967a, **31,** 51–69.

———. Psychokinetic placement: II. A factorial study of successful and unsuccessful series. *Journal of Parapsychology,* 1967b, **31,** 198–213.

———. Psychokinetic placement: III. Cube-releasing devices. *Journal of Parapsychology,* 1968, **32,** 9–38.

McCONNELL, R. A., R. J. SNOWDON, and K. F. POWELL. Wishing with dice. *Journal of Experimental Psychology,* 1955, **50,** 269–275.

MURPHY, G., and L. A. DALE. *Challenge of psychical research.* New York: Harper, 1961.

PRICE, G. R. Science and the supernatural. *Science,* 1955, **122,** 359–367.

SINCLAIR, U. *Mental radio.* Springfield, Ill.: Charles C Thomas, 1962.

SOAL, S. G., and F. BATEMAN. *Modern experiments in telepathy.* London: Faber & Faber, 1954.

SOAL, S. G.; RHINE, J. B.; MEEHL, P. E., and M. SCRIVEN; BRIDGMAN, P. W.; PRICE, G. R.; RHINE, J. B. (Letters to the editor in rejoinder to G. R. Price.) *Science,* 1956, **123,** 9–19.

STEVENS, S. S. The market for miracles. *Contemporary Psychology,* 1967, **12,** 1–3.

---

[5] Those who wish to answer this question might start their odyssey by visiting Clark et al. (1967) and Linder (1967).

2

S. S. Stevens has spent most of his career studying how man extracts information from the environment by using the various sensory systems. The following selection by Stevens is a review of a book which critically evaluated the ESP literature published before 1966.* Although this article was written a few years before the McConnell paper appeared (see Chapter 1), Stevens cogently presents some of the major arguments that have been raised in questioning the validity of several parapsychological demonstrations. He also makes some interesting comments about some possible reasons for the general public's uncritical "acceptance" of ESP.

It is important for the student to realize that Stevens and McConnell are probably in complete agreement on at least one point—that ESP should be carefully studied by scientists. McConnell's scientific interest revolves around a better understanding of the phenomenon which, he believes, has been adequately demonstrated. Stevens contends that ESP has not yet been reliably demonstrated, although he would probably encourage the search for some solid data.

* The book is C. E. M. Hansel's *ESP: A Scientific Evaluation.* New York: Charles Scribner's Sons, 1966.

the market for miracles

S. S. STEVENS

What is there left to say about a book that has already had its merits applauded by reviewers of fine perceptive phrase and skillful pen? Both Hansel's book and the reviews that I have seen make engaging reading, especially the review within the book itself—the Introduction by E. G. Boring, a gay and galloping account of faith, chance, and scientific credulity. But what can be expected from a reviewer with the wrong credentials, a sensory psychophysicist by trade, when he addresses the

Reprinted from *Contemporary Psychology*, 1967, 12: 1–3, by permission of the author and publisher. Copyright © 1967 by the American Psychological Association.

extra-sensory, the meta-esthesis, the *res mirabilis?* If I venture to tread the boggy mire of evidence for inputs without sensors, the excuse can be offered that we are all in this thing together. Man is the believing animal. Creatures in saucers are not likely to stop their visitations upon us as long as they can home in on the glowing beacon of human faith. Perhaps it is too much to say that man believes without evidence, but the evidence, as Hansel so clearly demonstrates, may often be flimsy indeed.

Will Hansel's careful, methodical analysis of the potentials for fraud and error in many of the classical ESP experiments alter anyone's belief? The odds are against it. True, it may reinforce the nonbelief of the nonbelievers (if their convictions needed reinforcement) and it may comfort those who may have felt vaguely uneasy about rumors of staunch statistical evidence for sensing without benefit of sensors and communication among persons tuned directly to the wavelength of thought itself. Hansel reassures those who like to postulate an orderly universe, but will his care and diligence in the sifting of evidence put an end to the counter claims of the faithful? It seems unlikely. Perhaps casuistry for the cause of ESP may suffer a temporary blockage, but the will to believe can surely find a loophole to squeeze itself through. The evidence of things hoped for has a persistent way of turning up when faith is threatened.

Those who discount the supernatural give many different reasons (rationalizations?) for their negative views. My own indifference to ESP is simple enough to state—however complex may be the crosscurrents that swirl in the turbulence of my unconscious. The signal-to-noise ratio for ESP is simply too low to be interesting. When telepathy, clairvoyance, precognition, or psychokinesis can be produced on demand, under conditions of aseptic control of the kind that would satisfy a man like Hansel, then I will "believe in it," as I believe, for example, in the migration of holes in a semiconductor, a mysterious but demonstrable phenomenon.

My indifference has a long history. Back in what Hansel calls the "salad days at Duke University," a reporter from the Harvard Crimson wandered into my office and said he wanted to write an article about ESP.

"What," he asked, "is the Psychology Department doing about it?"

I told him that departments are mere committees and that only people do research.

"Then who at Harvard is doing research on ESP?" he asked.

"No one, so far as I know," I said.

The reporter was indignant that a department of psychology could neglect a subject so revolutionary and challenging, especially a department in the university of William James, William McDougall, and the many other Harvard people who have concerned themselves with the occult. Even J. B. Rhine touched base at Harvard. And with its special endowment funds for the conduct of psychic research, Harvard has had the makings and tradition of a spook center, if ever there was one.

"Why aren't *you* working on ESP?" the reporter finally asked.

"Because I am studying a much more interesting phenomenon," I told him.

He shifted his notebook and asked, "What is that?"

"If you put a wire in your ear and fill the ear with salt water," I told him, "you can listen to a radio program without using a loudspeaker."

That did it. The reporter scooped up the details and ran the story in the student paper. The national press then picked it up and gave it space, complete with cartoon strips, and for a brief interlude ESP was knocked out of the headlines.

The scientist in this age is bombarded daily with insistent claims on his belief and interest. He sees so many tainted experiments in his own specialty, so many claims of "significant" results from insignificant studies, so much noise generated by the penchant of experimenters to believe their own data, and so many poorly controlled investigations with their spurious verdicts that he hardly needs the further distraction of miraculous demonstrations based on far-out odds in the percipient responses of rare and sensitive subjects. It is not that telepathy is a priori impossible. Most scientists who have lived long enough and have stayed loose will no doubt have changed their minds with sufficient frequency to retain little credence in any assertion of impossibility. But the possible must be demonstrated—the conditions of its occurrence must be specified in terms that are positive rather than negative. "Look, ma, no hands" is hardly a prescription for the repeatable realization of anything.

In the course of a day's work, the typical scientist must ignore many disclosures of sensational results, including those made by colleagues he both knows and trusts. Unless the revelation touches his own personal research, his survival in the world of scientific specialization requires that he leave to the discipline concerned the task of sifting and checking and certifying. The scientific community has waited a long time for a Hansel to do for ESP what gets done as a matter of course in other areas where experimental findings are offered for attention. Now, perhaps, the case can rest. A demonstration has been made that, in the transmission of the telepathic message, deception is as likely as reception. Until some new development occurs, science can put aside its concern for the furtive manifestations of psychic forces and return to the bewildering behavior of other forces, such as those that tie the particles within the nucleus, or those that move men to acts of violence.

Hansel may have cleared the air from the point of view of the objective scholar, but he will have done little, I predict, to attenuate the fervor of the supernaturalists. They will read Hansel with an acute singleness of purpose, namely, to detect the flaws in his argument, to trip him up on whatever points he may have muffed, and to fasten their own faith more firmly to the idol of their convictions. In many ways the arresting phenomenon is not the calling of cards with hits that exceed expectations; it is the spectacle of the human believer, the seeker after signs and manifestations, the cultist and his reverence for a hyperphysics. Down through the ages the awestruck believer has created a market for miracles, and, where there is a demand, someone will usually step forward to fill it. A priesthood arises to play oracle to those who cannot tolerate the vacuum of the de-ferred decision, the unanswered query, the enduring wherefore. If a bit of deception is involved, who can say that the trumpery is not for the believer's own good?

Believing holds many attractions. Believing is easy, even lazy. Furthermore, it fills many people with a warm glow of satisfaction. And when two or more believers are gathered together in common conviction, there wells up the buoyant emotion of zeal. It is cozy, comforting, contagious. The very universality of the phenomenon has been cited to support the thesis that believing is an act of virtuous achievement—a thesis that the uncommitted mind will view with high skepticism.

Despite their entrapment in most of the normal human foibles, many scientists have surmounted belief to a remarkable degree. The capacity to cultivate doubt is not given to all men, but it should be cherished and nurtured by those who know its price and its value. The substitution of one intense conviction for another does not count here, for true doubt is calm, dispassionate, disinterested. Never mind the argument that every man must perforce have faith—faith that the sun will rise, faith that the seed will grow, faith that order will prevail. The accomplished doubter may even place those beliefs in tentative jeopardy, but his main concern will address itself to the arduous and exacting task of maintaining vigilance regarding the foundations of all beliefs, so that he can know when not to believe. The standard of consistent scientific skepticism may be only an unattainable ideal, but, like honesty itself, it is a virtue to be cultivated.

Hansel's book stands forth as an exercise in honest skepticism. It is addressed to and will be appreciated by those engaged in what I shall call the schemapiric endeavor, the task of mapping the universe into a consistent model, the devising of formal systems for the depicting of empirical events, in other words, the scientific preoccupation. The essence of the schemapiric activity is the creation of a schema to serve to some degree as an isomorphic representation of the empirical experiment. Alternative schemas are usually possible, which gives rise, of course, to competing hypotheses. The clash of competing hypotheses provides the pervasive theme in Hansel's evaluation of ESP. One hypothesis says that the Welsh schoolboys identified the cards at better than chance expectation by sending thoughts back and forth. Another hypothesis says that they signaled each other through normal sensory channels, perhaps, as Hansel showed to be possible in his own experiments, by sound frequencies in the range audible to children but not to adults. Of course, the failure to find a trick in a supernatural manifestation does not mean that none was played. Nor does the detection of trickery prove that in other instances the phenomenon was not honest. The universal negative can be proved by neither disputant in this endless debate.

In his 17 chapters Hansel ranges over the history and recent status of ESP as well as such related topics as strange coincidences, spiritualism, and mental mediums. It makes for fascinating reading, much of it like a detective story. The aim, however, is not to entertain but to investigate. Here in Hansel's words is the spirit that animates his opus.

Scientists in general have been little influenced by philosophers who strive to inform them about the methodology and logic of their subject. Science has a basic methodological principle that is self-generating. It was not formulated by anybody, but it has the same empirical basis and underlying logic as the principle of natural selection in evolution. Investigators are continually producing reports of their experimental findings, which may be classified, for convenience, as good and bad. The bad ones are forgotten because they cannot be confirmed. Science advances through a process of natural selection. New findings become targets for criticism, and a finding must be confirmed by critics under their own experimental conditions; it then soon becomes clear when it is to be rejected.

If anyone invents a pseudoscience in which this principle ceases to operate, the result soon becomes apparent, for the new "science" fails to have predictive value and leads to more and more findings and theories that are incompatible with orthodox science. This is what has happened in parapsychology [pp. 236–237].

3

In many types of psychological research the subject is kept uninformed (and sometimes even misinformed) about the real purpose of the experiment in which he is participating. Often, this is to prevent the subject from biasing his responses in order to "help the experimenter." According to Robert Rosenthal, it is unfortunate that the experimenter himself is generally aware of the purpose of the experiment since his expectations may, quite innocently, affect the final outcome. Although the mechanisms by which such "experimenter expectancies" operate are not mystical, they can be quite subtle. In the following paper, Rosenthal discusses his research on this problem and some of the consequences of his findings for situations occurring outside the pychology laboratory.

teacher expectation and pupil learning [1]

ROBERT ROSENTHAL

The primary purpose of the present paper is to consider the proposition that a teacher's expectation about her pupils' performance can come to serve as a significant determinant of that performance. Later in this paper we shall examine the evidence

[1] Preparation of this chapter and much of the research summarized here was supported by research grants (G–17685, G–24826, GS–177, GS–714, and GS–1741) from the Division of Social Sciences of the National Science Foundation. Much of the research summarized here has also been summarized elsewhere but in the context of a more technical exposition (Rosenthal, 1969). Readers interested in the more technical details of the experiments summarized only briefly in the present chapter will want to refer to the more extensive bibliography of that paper.

for and some implications of this proposition but first we shall want to provide an appropriate historical and conceptual perspective. The goal of this perspective is to show that there is in fact, nothing very special about the "effects of teacher expectations." These effects may be seen to be only a specific instance of the operation of a far more general principle, a principle that holds that often in the course of interpersonal relationships, one person's expectation for the behavior of another person can come to be a significant determinant of that other person's behavior.

Most of the systematic evidence to support the idea of what we may call interpersonal self-fulfilling prophecies comes from experiments conducted not with teachers but with psychological experimenters. Simply to extend the generality of the principle of interpersonal self-fulfilling prophecies, any other group of persons might have served equally well. But the social situation which comes into being when a behavioral scientist encounters his research subject is a situation of both general and unique importance to the field of education and to the other behavioral sciences. Its general importance derives from the fact that the interaction of experimenter and subject, like other hierarchically ordered two-person interactions, may be investigated empirically with a view to teaching us more about such dyadic interactions in general. Its unique importance derives from the fact that the interaction of experimenter and subject, unlike other dyadic interactions, is a major source of our knowledge in the field of education and in the other behavioral sciences.

experimenter expectations

The particular expectation a scientist has of how his experiment will turn out is variable, depending on the experiment being conducted, but the presence of some expectation is virtually a constant in science. The variables selected for study by the scientist are not chosen by means of a table of random numbers. They are selected because the scientist expects a certain relationship to appear among them. Even in those less carefully planned examinations of relationships called "fishing expeditions" or, more formally, "exploratory analyses," the expectation of the scientist is reflected in the selection of the entire set of variables chosen for examination. Exploratory analyses of data, like real fishing ventures, do not take place in randomly selected pools.

These expectations of the scientist are likely to affect the choice of the experimental design and procedure in such a way as to increase the likelihood that his expectation or hypothesis will be supported. That is as it should be. No scientist would select intentionally a procedure likely to show his hypothesis in error. If he could too easily think of procedures that would show this, he would be likely to revise his hypothesis.

If the selection of a research design or procedure is regarded by another scientist as too "biased" to be a fair test of the hypothesis, he can test the hypothesis employing oppositely biased procedures or less biased procedures by which to demonstrate the greater value of his hypothesis. The designs and procedures employed are, to a great extent, public knowledge, and it is this public character that permits relevant replications to serve the required corrective function.

The major concern of this section will be with the effects of the experimenter's expectation on the responses he obtains from his subjects. The consequences of such an expectancy bias can be quite serious. Expectancy effects on subjects' responses are not public matters. It is not only that other scientists cannot know whether such effects occurred in the experimenter's interaction with his subjects; the investigator himself may not know whether these effects have occurred. Moreover, there is the likelihood that the experimenter has not even considered the possibility of such unintended effects on his subject's response. That is not so different from the situations wherein the subject's response is affected by any attribute of the experimenter. Later, the problem will be discussed in more detail. For now it is enough to note that while other attributes of the experimenter may affect the subject's response, they do not necessarily affect these responses differentially as a function of the subject's treatment condition. Expectancy effects, on the other hand, always do. The sex of the experimenter does not change as a function of the subject's treatment condition in an experiment. The experimenter's expectancy of how the subject will respond does change as a function of the subject's experimental treatment condition.

That one person's expectation about another person's behavior may contribute to a determination of what that behavior will actually be has been suggested by various theorists. Merton (1948) elaborated the very useful concept of "self-fulfilling prophecy." One prophesies an event and the expectation of the event then changes the behavior of the prophet in such a way as to make the prophesied event more likely. The late Gordon Allport (1950) applied the concept of interpersonal expectancies to an analysis of the causes of war. Nations expecting to go to war affect the behavior of their opponents-to-be by the behavior which reflects their expectations of armed conflict. Nations who expect to remain out of wars at least sometimes manage to avoid entering into them.

Drawn from the general literature, and the literatures of the healing professions, survey research, and laboratory psychology, there is considerable suggestive evidence for the operation of interpersonal self-fulfilling prophecies. The literatures referred to have been reviewed elsewhere (Rosenthal, 1964a,b, 1965, 1966; Rosenthal and Jacobson, 1968) but it may be of interest here to give one illustration from the literature of experimental psychology. The case is one known generally to psychologists as a case study of an artifact in animal research. It is less well known, however, as a case study of the effect of experimenter expectancy. While the subject sample was small, the experimenter sample was very large indeed. The case, of course, is that of Clever Hans (Pfungst, 1911). Hans, it will be remembered, was the horse of Mr. von Osten, a German mathematics teacher. By means of tapping his foot, Hans was able to add, subtract, multiply, and divide. Hans could spell, read, and solve problems of musical harmony. To be sure, there were other clever animals at the time, and Pfungst tells about them. There was "Rosa," the mare of Berlin, who performed similar feats in vaudeville, and there was the dog of Utrecht, and the reading pig of Virginia. All these other clever animals were highly trained performers who were, of course, intentionally cued by their trainers.

Mr. von Osten, however, did not profit from his animal's talent, nor did it seem at all likely that he was attempting to perpetrate a fraud. He swore he did not cue the animal, and he permitted other people to question and test the horse even without his being present. Pfungst and his famous colleague, Stumpf, undertook a program of systematic research to discover the secret of Hans' talents. Among the first discoveries made was that if the horse could not see the questioner, Hans was not clever at all. Similarly, if the questioner did not himself know the answer to the question, Hans could not answer it either. Still, Hans was able to answer Pfungst's questions as long as the investigator was present and visible. Pfungst reasoned that the questioner might in some way be signaling to Hans when to begin and when to stop tapping his foot. A forward inclination of the head of the questioner would start Hans tapping, Pfungst observed. He tried then to incline his head forward without asking a question and discovered that this was sufficient to start Hans' tapping. As the experimenter straightened up, Hans would stop tapping. Pfungst then tried to get Hans to stop tapping by using very slight upward motions of the head. He found that even the raising of his eyebrows was sufficient. Even the dilation of the questioner's nostrils was a cue for Hans to stop tapping.

When the questioner bent forward more, the horse would tap faster. This added to the reputation of Hans as brilliant. That is, when a large number of taps was the correct response, Hans would tap very, very rapidly until he approached the region of correctness, and then he began to slow down. It was found that questioners typically bent forward more when the answer was a long one, gradually straightening up as Hans got closer to the correct number.

For some experiments, Pfungst discovered that auditory cues functioned additively with visual cues. When the experimenter was silent, Hans was able to respond correctly 31 per cent of the time in picking one of many placards with different words written on it, or cloths of different colors. When auditory cues were added, Hans responded correctly 56 per cent of the time.

Pfungst himself then played the part of Hans, tapping out responses to questions with his hand. Of 25 questioners, 23 unwittingly cued Pfungst as to when to stop tapping in order to give a correct response. None of the questioners (males and females of all ages and occupations) knew the intent of the experiment. When errors occurred, they were usually only a single tap from being correct. The subjects of this study, including an experienced psychologist, were unable to discover that they were unintentionally emitting cues.

Hans' amazing talents, talents rapidly acquired too by Pfungst, serve to illustrate the power of the self-fulfilling prophecy. Hans' questioners, even skeptical ones, expected Hans to give the correct answers to their queries. Their expectation was reflected in their unwitting signal to Hans that the time had come for him to stop his tapping. The signal cued Hans to stop, and the questioner's expectation became the reason for Hans' being, once again, correct.

Not all of Hans' questioners were equally good at fulfilling their prophecies. Even when the subject is a horse, apparently, the attributes of the experimenter make a considerable difference in determining the response of a subject. On the basis of his studies, Pfungst was able to summarize the characteristics of those of Hans' questioners who were more successful in their covert and unwitting communication with the horse. Among the characteristics of the more successful unintentional influencers were those of tact, an air of dominance, attention to the business at hand, and a facility for motor discharge. Pfungst's observations of 60 years ago seem not to have suffered excessively for the lack of more modern methods of scaling observations. To anticipate some of the research findings turned up much later, it must be said that Pfungst's description seems also to fit those

experimenters who are more likely to affect their human subject's responses by virtue of their experimental hypothesis.

In summarizing his difficulties in learning the nature of Clever Hans' talents, Pfungst felt that he had been too long off the track by "looking for in the horse, what should have been sought in the man." Perhaps, too, when we conduct research in the behavioral sciences we are sometimes caught looking at our subjects when we ought to be looking at ourselves. It was to this possibility that much of the research to be summarized here was addressed.

ANIMAL LEARNING

A good beginning might have been to replicate Pfungst's research, but with horses hard to come by, rats were made to do (Rosenthal and Fode, 1963a).

A class in experimental psychology had been performing experiments with human subjects for most of a semester. Now they were asked to perform one more experiment, the last in the course, and the first employing animal subjects. The experimenters were told of studies that had shown that maze-brightness and maze-dullness could be developed in strains of rats by successive inbreeding of the well- and the poorly-performing maze-runners. Sixty laboratory rats were equitably divided among the 12 experimenters. Half the experimenters were told that their rats were maze-bright while the other half were told their rats were maze-dull. The animal's task was to learn to run to the darker of two arms of an elevated T-maze. The two arms of the maze, one white and one gray, were interchangeable; and the "correct" or rewarded arm was equally often on the right as on the left. Whenever an animal ran to the correct side he obtained a food reward. Each rat was given 10 trials each day for five days to learn that the darker side of the maze was the one which led to the food.

Beginning with the first day and continuing on through the experiment, animals believed to be better performers became better performers. Animals believed to be brighter showed a daily improvement in their performance while those believed to be dull improved only to the third day and then showed a worsening of performance. Sometimes an animal refused to budge from his starting position. This happened 11 per cent of the time among the allegedly bright rats; but among allegedly dull rats it happened 29 per cent of the time. When animals did respond and correctly so, those believed to be brighter ran faster to the rewarded side of the maze than did even the correctly responding rats believed to be dull.

When the experiment was over, all experimenters made ratings of their rats and of their own attitudes and behavior vis-à-vis their animals. Those experimenters who had been led to expect better performance viewed their animals as brighter, more pleasant, and more likable. These same experimenters felt more relaxed in their contacts with the animals and described their behavior toward them as more pleasant, friendly, enthusiastic, and less talkative. They also stated that they handled their rats more and also more gently than did the experimenters expecting poor performance.

So far we have given only one example of the results of studies of expectancy effect and the subjects were animals. Most of the research available, however, is based on human subjects and it is those results we now consider. In this set of experiments at least 20 different specific tasks have been employed but some of these tasks seemed sufficiently related to one another that they could reasonably be regarded as a family of tasks or a research area. These areas include human abilities, psychophysical judgments, reaction time, inkblot tests, structured laboratory interviews, and per-son perception. We have space, however, only to consider some examples.

HUMAN ABILITIES

Especially instructive for its unusual within-subject experimental manipulation was an experiment by Larrabee and Kleinsasser (1967). They employed five experimenters to administer the Wechsler Intelligence Scale for Children (WISC) to 12 sixth-graders of average intelligence. Each subject was tested by two different experimenters, one administering the even-numbered items and the other administering the odd-numbered items. For each subject, one of the experimenters was told the child was of above average intelligence while the other experimenter was told the child was of below average intelligence. When the child's experimenter expected superior performance the total IQ earned was over 7 points higher on the average than when the child's experimenter expected inferior performance. When only the performance subtests of the WISC were considered, the advantage to the children of having been expected to do well was less than three IQ points and could easily have occurred by chance. When only the verbal subtests of the WISC were considered, the advantage of having been expected to do well, however, exceeded 10 IQ points. The particular subtest most affected by experimenters' expectancies was Information. The results of this study are especially striking in view of the very small sample size (12) of subjects employed.

The other experiment to be mentioned in this section is of special importance because of the elimination of plausible alternatives to the hypothesis that it is the subject's response that is affected by the experimenter's expectancy. In his experiment, Johnson (1967) employed the Stevenson marble-dropping task. Each of the 20 experimenters was led to believe that marble-dropping rate was related to intelligence. More intelligent subjects were alleged to show a greater increase in rate of marble-dropping over the course of six trials. Each experimenter then contacted eight subjects half of whom were alleged to be brighter than the remaining subjects.

The recording of the subject's response was by means of an electric counter and the counter was read by the investigator who was blind to the subject's expectancy condition. The results of this study, one of the best controlled in this area, were the most dramatic. Experimenters expecting a greater increase in marble-dropping rate obtained a much greater increase than they did when expecting a lesser increase.

INKBLOT TESTS

In one of the most recent of the inkblot experiments, Marwit (1968) employed 20 graduate students in clinical psychology as his experimenters and 40 undergraduate students of introductory psychology as his subjects. Half the experimenters were led to expect some of their subjects to give many Rorschach responses and especially a lot of animal responses. Half the experimenters were led to expect some of their subjects to give few Rorschach responses but proportionately a lot of human responses. Results showed that subjects who were expected to give more responses gave more responses and that subjects who were expected to give a greater number of animal relative to human responses did so. Marwit also found trends for the first few responses to have been already affected by the experimenter's expectancy and for later-contacted subjects to show greater effects of experimenter expectancy than earlier contacted subjects.

STRUCTURED LABORATORY INTERVIEWS

A number of experiments have been conducted in which the experimenters conducted a structured interview with their research subjects. One of these, an experiment by Raffetto (1968), was addressed to the question of whether the experimenter's expectation for greater reports of hallucinatory behavior might be a significant determinant of such reports.

Raffetto employed 96 paid, female students from a variety of less advanced undergraduate courses to participate in an experiment on sensory restriction. Subjects were asked to spend one hour in a small room that was relatively quite free from light and sound. Eight more advanced students of psychology served as the experimenters, with each one interviewing 12 of the subjects before and after the sensory restriction experience. The pre-experimental interview consisted of factual questions such as age, college major, and college grades. The postexperimental interview was relatively well-structured, including questions to be answered by "yes" or "no" as well as more open-ended questions, e.g., "Did you notice any particular sensations or feelings?" Postexperimental interviews were tape recorded.

Half the experimenters were led to expect high reports of hallucinatory experiences and half were led to expect low reports of hallucinatory experiences. Obtained scores of hallucinatory experiences ranged from zero to 32 with a grand mean of 5.4. Of the subjects contacted by experimenters expecting more hallucinatory experiences, 48 per cent were scored above the mean of these experiences. Of the subjects contacted by experimenters expecting fewer hallucinatory experiences, only 6 per cent were scored above the mean.

PERSON PERCEPTION

Although a good many experiments on the effects of experimenter expectancy have been conducted in the area of .person perception, the basic paradigm of these investigations has been sufficiently uniform that we need only an illustration (Rosenthal and Fode, 1963b).

Ten advanced undergraduates and graduate students of psychology served as the experimenters. All were enrolled in an advanced course in experimental psychology and were already involved in conducting research. Each student-experimenter was assigned as his subjects a group of about 20 students of introductory psychology. The experimental procedure was for the experimenter to show a series of ten photographs of people's faces to each of his subjects individually. The subject was to rate the degree of success or failure shown in the face of each person pictured in the photos. Each face could be rated as any value from −10 to +10 with −10 meaning extreme failure and +10 meaning extreme success. The 10 photos had been selected so that, on the average, they would be seen as neither successful nor unsuccessful, but quite neutral, with an average numerical score of zero.

All 10 experimenters were given identical instructions on how to administer the task to their subjects and were given identical instructions to read to their subjects. They were cautioned not to deviate from these instructions. The purpose of their participation, it was explained to all experimenters, was to see how well they could duplicate experimental results which were already well-established. Half the experimenters were told that the "well-established" finding was such that their subjects should rate the photos as of successful people (ratings of +5) and half the experimenters were told that their subjects should rate the photos as being of unsuccessful people (ratings of −5). Results showed that experimenters expecting higher photo ratings obtained higher photo ratings than did experimenters expecting lower photo ratings.

Subsequent experiments in the program of research launched with the experiment just described were designed not so much to demonstrate the effects of the investigator's expectancy as to learn something about the conditions which increase, decrease or otherwise modify these effects. It was learned, for example, that the subject's expectations about what would constitute behavior appropriate to the role of "experimental subject" could alter the extent to which they were influenced by the effects of the experimenter's hypothesis.

Through the employment of accomplices, serving as the first few subjects, it was learned that when the responses of the first few subjects confirmed the experimenter's hypothesis, his behavior toward his subsequent subjects was affected in such a way that these subjects tended to confirm further the experimenter's hypothesis. When accomplices, serving as the first few subjects, intentionally disconfirmed the expectation of the experimenter, the real subjects subsequently contacted were affected by a change in the experimenter's behavior so as also to disconfirm his experimental hypothesis. It seems possible, then, that the results of behavioral research can, by virtue of the early data returns, be determined by the performance of just the first few subjects.

In some of the experiments conducted, it was found that when experimenters were offered a too-large and a too-obvious incentive to affect the results of their research, the effects of expectancy tended to diminish. It speaks well for the integrity of our student-experimenters that when they felt bribed to get the data we led them to expect, they seemed actively to oppose us. There was a tendency for those experimenters to "bend over backward" to avoid the biasing effects of their expectation, but with the bending so far backward that the results of their experiments tended to be significantly opposite to the results they had been led to expect.

Individual differences among experimenters in the degree to which they obtain results consistent with their hypothesis have been discovered. The evidence comes both from additional experiments and from the analysis of sound motion pictures of experimenters interacting with their experimental subjects. Those experimenters who show greater expectancy effects tend to be of higher status in the eyes of their subjects and they seem to conduct their experiments in a more professional, more competent manner. They are judged more likable and more relaxed, particularly in their movement patterns, while avoiding an overly personal tone of voice that might interfere with the business at hand. It is interesting to note that, although the influence of an experimenter's expectancy is quite unintentional, the characteristics of the more successful influencer are very much the same ones associated with more effective influencers when the influence is intentional. The more successful agent of social influence may be the same person whether the influence be as overt and intentional as in the case of outright persuasion attempts, or as covert and unintentional as in the case of the experimenter's subtly communicating his expectancy to his research subject.

experimenter expectations: a summary

There have been 103 experiments testing the effects on subjects' responses of their experimenter's expectations and these studies can be classified into seven different research domains. Table 1 shows the number of studies conducted in each of these seven areas and the percentage of the studies in each area obtaining results with an associated probability of 10 per cent or less. Table 1 also shows the number of principal investigators that conducted one or more studies in each of the seven areas and the percentage of these investigators in each area who obtained results with an associated p of 10 per cent or less. By chance we expect only about 10 per cent of the experiments or the investigators to obtain results "significant" at the 10 per cent level.

table 1

***experimenter expectancy effects
in seven research areas***

	by experiments		by investigators	
research area	*number of studies*	*percentage of studies at* p ≤ .10 [a]	*number of investigators*	*percentage of studies at* p ≤ .10 [a]
Animal Learning	9	100	5	100
Human Abilities [b]	10	40	9	44
Psychophysics [b]	9	33	6	33
Reaction Time	3	67	3	67
Inkblot Tests	5	80	4	75
Laboratory Interviews [c]	6	83	6	83
Person Perception [b, c]	64	36	22	27
Total [d]	103	48	52	50

[a] One-tail.
[b] Indicates a single experiment or investigator represented in each of three areas by the same subject sample.
[c] Indicates another experiment or investigator represented in two areas by the same subject sample.
[d] Three entries were non-independent with respect to their subject samples and the mean standard normal deviate across areas was computed to obtain the independent p level entries.

In fact, we find about five times that number of experiments or investigators obtaining results at that level. The probability of this many positive results occurring by chance is infinitely small.

Because so much of the business of the behavioral sciences is transacted at a number of particular levels of probability, an additional summary is provided. Table 2

table 2

experimenter expectancy effects obtained
at various p levels

p (one-tail)	I experi- ments	II investi- gators [a]	III labora- tories
< .10	48%	50%	58%
< .05	34%	37%	48%
< .01	17%	27%	36%
< .001	12%	19%	27%
< .0001	5%	10%	18%
N	103	52	33
Grand Sum z	+100.86	+69.75	+57.86
$\sqrt{}$ Number of units	$\sqrt{103}$	$\sqrt{52}$	$\sqrt{33}$
Combined z [b]	+ 9.94	+ 9.67	+10.08
Null Replicates [c]	3,656	1,746	1,204

[a] Principal investigators may be represented in more than one research area. Entries in Column III, however, are entirely independent with type of research area disregarded.
[b] Standard normal deviate associated with overall p for experiments, investigators, and laboratories.
[c] Number of additional experiments, investigators, and laboratories obtaining perfectly null results ($z = 0.00$, exactly) required to bring overall combined p to .05.

shows for 103 experiments, for 52 investigators, and for 33 laboratories, the percentage obtaining results at five different levels of p.

Tables 1 and 2 tell us that the effects of experimenters' expectancies are "real" but they do not tell us whether they are large in magnitude in a given experiment. On the basis of analyses reported elsewhere (Rosenthal, 1969) it can be estimated that about two out of three research subjects and about two out of three experimenters

will give or obtain responses in the direction of the experimenter's expectancy.

Though we have been able to arrive at some estimate, however crude, of the magnitude of expectancy effects, we will not know quite how to assess this magnitude until we have comparative estimates from other areas of behavioral research. Such estimates are not easy to come by, but it seems worthwhile for us to try to obtain such estimates in the future. Although in individual studies, investigators occasionally give the proportion of variance accounted for by their experimental variable, it is more rare that systematic reviews of bodies of research literature give estimates of the overall magnitude of effects of the variable under consideration. It does not seem an unreasonable guess, however, to suggest that in the bulk of the experimental literature of the behavioral sciences, the effects of the experimental variable are not impressively "larger," either in the sense of magnitude of obtained ps or in the sense of proportion of subjects affected, than the effects of experimenter expectancy. The best support for such an assertion would come from experiments in which the effects of experimenter expectancy are compared directly, in the same experiment, with the effects of some other experimental variable believed to be a significant determinant of behavior. Fortunately, there are two such experiments to shed light on the question.

The first of these was conducted by Burnham (1966). He had 23 experimenters each run one rat in a T-maze discrimination problem. About half the rats had been lesioned by removal of portions of the brain, and the remaining animals had received only sham surgery which involved cutting through the skull but no damage to brain tissue. The purpose of the study was explained to the experimenters as an attempt to learn the effects of lesions on discrimination learning. Expectancies were manipulated by labeling each rat as lesioned or nonlesioned. Some of the really lesioned rats were labeled accurately as lesioned but some were falsely labeled as unlesioned. Some of the really unlesioned rats were labeled accurately as unlesioned but some were falsely labeled as lesioned. The results showed that animals that had been lesioned did not perform as well as those that had not been lesioned and animals that were believed to be lesioned did not perform as well as those that were believed to be unlesioned. What makes this experiment of special interest is that the effects of experimenter expectancy were actually greater than the effects of the removal of brain tissue.

The first of the experiments to compare directly the effects of experimenter expectancy with some other experimental variable employed animal subjects. The next such experiment to be described employed human subjects. Cooper, Eisenberg, Robert, and Dohrenwend (1967) wanted to compare the effects of experimenter expectancy with the effects of effortful preparation for an examination on the degree of belief that the examination would actually take place.

Each of ten experimenters contacted ten subjects; half of the subjects were required to memorize a list of 16 symbols and definitions that were claimed to be essential to the taking of a test that had a 50–50 chance of being given, while the remaining subjects, the "low effort" group, were asked only to look over the list of symbols. Half of the experimenters were led to expect that "high effort" subjects would be more certain of actually having to take the test, while half of the experimenters were led to expect that "low effort" subjects would be more certain of actually having to take the test.

Results showed that there was a very slight tendency for subjects who had exerted greater effort to believe more strongly that they would be taking the test. Surprising in its magnitude was the finding that experimenters expecting to obtain responses of greater certainty obtained such responses to a much greater degree than did experimenters expecting responses of

lesser certainty. The effects of the experimenters' expectancies were more than 10 times greater than the effects of preparatory effort.

experimenter expectations: mediating processes

How are we to account for the results of the experiments described? What are the processes by which an experimenter unintentionally informs his subject just what response is expected of him?

We know that the process whereby the experimenter communicates his expectancy to his subject is a subtle one. We know that it is subtle because for six years we have tried to find in sound films the unintended cues the experimenter gives the subject—and for six years we have failed, at least partly. But there are some things about the unintentional communication of expectancies that have been learned.

We know that if a screen is placed between experimenter and subject there will be a reduction of the expectancy effect, so visual cues from the experimenter are probably important (Rosenthal and Fode, 1963; Zoble, 1968). But the interposed screen does not eliminate expectancy effects completely, so auditory cues also seem to be important. Just how important auditory cues may be has been dramatically demonstrated by the work of Adair and Epstein (1968). They first conducted a study which was essentially a replication of the basic experiment on the self-fulfilling effects of experimenters' prophecies. Results showed that, just as in the original studies, experimenters who prophesied the perception of success by their subjects fulfilled their prophecies as did the experimenters who had prophesied the perception of failure by their subjects.

During the conduct of this replication experiment, Adair and Epstein tape-recorded the experimenters' instructions to their subjects. The second experiment was then conducted not by experimenters at all, but by tape-recordings of experimenters' voices reading standard instructions to their subjects. When the tape-recorded instructions had originally been read by experimenters expecting success perception by their subjects, the tape-recordings evoked greater success perceptions from their subjects. When the tape-recorded instructions had originally been read by experimenters expecting failure perception by their subjects, the tape-recordings evoked greater failure perceptions from their subjects. Self-fulfilling prophecies, it seems, can come about as a result of the prophet's voice alone. Since, in the experiment described, all prophets read standard instructions, self-fulfillment of prophecies may be brought about by the tone in which the prophet prophesies.

Early in the history of the research program on self-fulfilling prophecies in the behavioral sciences it had been thought that a process of operant conditioning might be responsible for their operation (Rosenthal, 1966). It was thought that perhaps every time the subject gave a response consistent with the experimenter's expectancy, the experimenter might look more pleasant, or smile, or glance at the subject approvingly, even without the experimenter's being aware of his own reinforcing responses. The experimenter, in other words, might unwittingly have taught the subject what responses were the desired ones. Several experiments were analyzed to see whether this hypothesis of operant conditioning might apply. If it did apply, we would expect that the subjects' responses gradually would become more like those prophesied by the experimenter—that there would be a learning curve for subjects, but no learning curve was found. On the contrary, it turned out that the subjects' very first responses were about as much affected by their experimenters' expectancies as were their very last responses. Since the very first response, by definition, cannot follow any unwitting reinforcement by the experi-

menter, the mechanism of operant conditioning can be ruled out as necessary to the communication of experimenters' expectancies.

True, there was no learning curve for subjects, but there seemed to be a learning curve for experimenters. Several studies showed that expected results became more likely as more subjects were contacted by each experimenter (Rosenthal, 1966, 1969). In fact, there was very little expectancy effect in evidence for just the very first-seen subjects. If the experimenter were indeed learning to increase the unintended influence of his prophecy, who would be the teacher? Probably the subject. It seems reasonable to think of a subject's responding in the direction of the experimenter's hypothesis as a reinforcing event. Therefore, whatever the covert communicative behavior of the experimenter that preceded the subject's reinforcement, it will be more likely to recur. Subjects, then, may quite unintentionally shape the experimenter's unintended communicative behavior. Not only does the experimenter influence his subjects to respond in the expected manner, but his subjects may well evoke just that unintended behavior that will lead them to respond increasingly as prophesied. Probably neither subject nor experimenter "knows" just exactly what the unintended communication behavior is—and neither do we.

experimenter expectations: methodological implications

The implications of the research on the effects of the experimenter's expectancy on the results of his research are of two general kinds: those that are primarily methodological and those that are more substantive. Our focus in this paper is more on some of the substantive implications but brief mention may be made of some implications for how we conduct research in the behavioral sciences.

To the extent that the results of behavioral research are affected by the expectation of the experimenter, we can only place a lessened confidence in these results. But to say that our confidence is weakened in the results of many experiments as they are actually conducted is not to say that our confidence is weakened in the basic logic of the experimental method. We must simply take those, only sometimes inconvenient, extra precautions required to prevent or reduce expectancy effects or those procedures designed to permit us to assess whether they have or have not affected the results of our research.

It is possible for research investigators to employ, as data collectors, research assistants who have not been told the purpose of the research. As long as the investigator's expectation can be kept from these data collectors, there should be no effects attributable to the investigator's expectation. There are some experiments in which the experimenter need have no direct contact with the subjects and, in such studies, automated data collection systems should be employed to reduce any possibility of the unintended influence of the experimenter's expectation. When a human data collector is required and that is often the case, at least the amount of contact between experimenter and subject can be reduced in order to minimize any opportunity for unintended communication.

Not only because of the danger of expectancy effects but also because of the general nature of other experimenter effects, it would be desirable to employ larger numbers of experimenters for each study than are now routinely employed. That would permit the assessment of the extent to which different experimenters obtained different results and, in any area of psychological research, that is a fact worth knowing.

Only one final technique for the control of expectancy effects can be mentioned here and that is the employment of special control groups known as "expectancy controls."

In any experiment employing an experimental (treatment) and a control (no treatment) condition, two extra groups are added. In one of these added groups, the data collector is led to believe that no treatment has been administered when, in fact, it has. In the other added group, the data collector is led to believe that the treatment has been administered when, in fact, it has not. Such a research design permits the assessment of the effects in which the investigator is primarily interested as well as the assessment of the magnitude or complicating effect of the experimenter's expectancy (Rosenthal, 1966). It may be noted that the important studies by Burnham (1966) and by Cooper et al. (1967), both described earlier, were the first to employ this basic research paradigm.

teacher expectations

Most of what has been said so far may seem to be not very directly related to the title of this chapter and of this section. Yet what has been said is a necessary introduction to this section, an introduction designed to emphasize that there is nothing very special about the idea that a teacher's expectation about her pupils' performance can come to serve as a partial determinant of those pupils' performance. If rats can become brighter when expected to by their experimenter, it can hardly be thought to be far-fetched to suppose that children could also become brighter when expected to by their teacher. Kenneth Clark (1963), in any case, has presented the view for some time that culturally disadvantaged children are the unfortunate victims of teachers' educational self-fulfilling prophecies. The following experiment, then, was simply an extension of the earlier work on interpersonal expectations (Rosenthal and Jacobson, 1968).

All of the children in an elementary school serving a lower socio-economic status neighborhood were administered a nonverbal test of intelligence. The test was disguised as one that would predict intellectual "blooming." There were 18 classrooms in the school, three at each of the six grade levels. Within each grade level the three classrooms were composed of children with about average ability, average ability, and below average ability, respectively. Within each of the 18 classrooms approximately 20 per cent of the children were chosen at random to form the experimental group. Each teacher was given the names of the children from her class who were in the experimental condition. The teacher was told that these children had scored on the "test for intellectual blooming" such that they would show remarkable gains in intellectual competence during the next eight months of school. The difference between the experimental group and the control group children, then, was in the mind of the teacher.

At the end of the school year, eight months later, all the children were retested with the same IQ test. This intelligence test, while relatively nonverbal in the sense of requiring no speaking, reading or writing, was not entirely nonverbal. Actually there were two subtests, one requiring a greater comprehension of English—a kind of picture vocabulary test. The other subtest required less ability to understand any spoken language but more ability to reason abstractly. For shorthand purposes we refer to the former as a "verbal" subtest and to the latter as a "reasoning" subtest. The pretest correlation between these subtests was +.42.

For the school as a whole, the children of the experimental group showed only a slightly greater gain in verbal IQ (2 points) than did the control group children. However, in total IQ (4 points) and especially in reasoning IQ (7 points), the experimental group children gained appreciably more than did the control group children.

When educational theorists have discussed the possible effects of teachers' expectations, they have usually referred to the children at lower levels of scholastic achievement. It was interesting, therefore, to find that in the present study, children of the highest level of achievement showed as great a benefit as did the children of the lowest level of achievement of having their teachers expect intellectual gains.

At the end of the school year of this study, all teachers were asked to describe the classroom behavior of their pupils. Those children from whom intellectual growth was expected were described as having a significantly better chance of becoming successful in the future, as significantly more interesting, curious, and happy. There was a tendency, too, for these children to be seen as more appealing, adjusted, and affectionate and as lower in the need for social approval. In short, the children from whom intellectual growth was expected became more intellectually alive and autonomous or at least were so perceived by their teachers.

We have already seen that the children of the experimental group gained more intellectually so that perhaps it was the fact of such gaining that accounted for the more favorable ratings of these children's behavior and aptitude. But a great many of the control group children also gained in IQ during the course of the year. We might expect that those who gained more intellectually among these undesignated children would also be rated more favorably by their teachers. Such was not the case. The more the control group children gained in IQ the more they were regarded as less well-adjusted, as less interesting, and as less affectionate. From these results it would seem that when children who are expected to grow intellectually do so, they are considerably benefited in other ways as well. When children who are not especially expected to develop intellectually do so, they seem either to show accompanying undesirable behavior or at least are perceived by their teachers as showing such undesirable behavior. If a child is to show intellectual gain it seems to be better for his real or perceived intellectual vitality and for his real or perceived mental health if his teacher has been expecting him to grow intellectually. It appears worthwhile to investigate further the proposition that there may be hazards to unpredicted intellectual growth.

A closer analysis of these data, broken down by whether the children were in the high, medium, or low ability tracks or groups, showed that these effects of unpredicted intellectual growth were due primarily to the children of the low ability group. When these slow track children were in the control group so that no intellectual gains were expected of them, they were rated more unfavorably by their teachers if they did show gains in IQ. The greater their IQ gains, the more unfavorably were they rated, both as to mental health and as to intellectual vitality. Even when the slow track children were in the experimental group, so that IQ gains were expected of them, they were not rated as favorably relative to their control group peers as were the children of the high or medium track, despite the fact that they gained as much in IQ relative to the control group children as did the experimental group children of the high group. It may be difficult for a slow track child, even one whose IQ is rising, to be seen by his teacher as a well-adjusted child, and as a potentially successful child, intellectually.

The effects of teacher expectations had been most dramatic when measured in terms of pupils' gains in reasoning IQ. These effects on reasoning IQ, however, were not uniform for boys and girls. Although all the children of this lower socioeconomic status school gained dramatically in IQ, it was only among the girls that greater gains were shown by those who were expected to bloom compared to the children of the control group. Among the boys, those who were expected to bloom gained less than did the children of the control group.

In part to check this finding, the experiment originally conducted on the West Coast was repeated in a small Midwestern town (Rosenthal and Evans, 1968). This time the children were from substantial middle-class backgrounds, and this time the results were completely and significantly reversed. Now it was the boys who showed the benefits of favorable teacher expectations. Among the girls, those who were expected to bloom intellectually gained less in reasoning IQ than did the girls of the control group. Just as in the West Coast experiment, however, all the children showed substantial gains in IQ. These results, while they suggest the potentially powerful effects of teacher expectations, also indicate the probable complexity of these effects as a function of pupils' sex, social class, and, as time will no doubt show, other variables as well.

In both the experiments described, IQ gains were assessed after a full academic year had elapsed. However, the results of another experiment suggest that teacher expectations can significantly affect students' intellectual performance in a period as short as two months (Anderson and Rosenthal, 1968). In this small experiment, the 25 children were mentally retarded boys with an average pretest IQ of 46. Expectancy effects were significant only for reasoning IQ and only in interaction with membership in a group receiving special remedial reading instruction in addition to participating in the school's summer day camp program. Among these specially tutored boys those who were expected to bloom showed an expectancy disadvantage of nearly 12 IQ points; among the untutored boys who were participating only in the school's summer day camp program, those who were expected to bloom showed an expectancy advantage of just over three IQ points. (For verbal IQ, in contrast, the expectancy disadvantage of the tutored boys was less than one IQ point, while the expectancy advantage for the untutored boys was over two points.)

The results described were based on

post-testing only two months after the initiation of the experiment. Follow-up testing was undertaken seven months after the end of the basic experiment. In reasoning IQ, the boys who had been both tutored and expected to bloom intellectually made up the expectancy disadvantage they had shown after just two months. Now, their performance change was just like that of the control group children, both groups showing an IQ loss of four points over the nine-month period. Compared to these boys who had been given both or neither of the two experimental treatments, the boys who had been given either tutoring or the benefit of favorable expectations showed significantly greater gains in reasoning IQ scores. Relative to the control group children, those who were tutored showed a 10 point advantage while those who were expected to bloom showed a 12 point advantage. While both tutoring and a favorable teacher expectation were effective in raising relative IQ scores, it appeared that when these two treatments were applied simultaneously, they were ineffective in producing IQ gains over the period from the beginning of the experiment to the nine-month follow-up. One possible explanation of this finding is that the presence of both treatments simultaneously led the boys to perceive too much pressure. The same pattern of results reported for reasoning IQ was also obtained when verbal IQ and total IQ were considered, though the interaction was significant only in the case of total IQ.

In the experiment under discussion, a number of other measures of the boys' behavior were available as were observations of the day-camp counselors' behavior toward the boys. Preliminary analysis suggests that boys who had been expected to bloom intellectually were given less attention by the counselors and developed a greater degree of independence compared to the boys of the control group.

Another study, this time conducted in an East Coast school with upper middle-class pupils, again showed the largest effect of teachers' expectancies to occur when the measure was of reasoning IQ (Conn, Edwards, Rosenthal, and Crowne, 1968). In this study, both the boys and girls who were expected to bloom intellectually showed greater gains in reasoning IQ than did the boys and girls of the control group and the magnitude of the expectancy effect favored the girls very slightly. Also in this study, we had available a measure of the children's accuracy in judging the vocal expressions of emotion of adult speakers. It was of considerable theoretical interest to find that greater benefits of favorable teacher expectations accrued to those children who were more accurate in judging the emotional tone expressed in an adult female's voice. These findings, taken together with the research of Adair and Epstein (1968) and others (Rosenthal, 1969) described earlier, give a strong suggestion that vocal cues may be important in the covert communication of interpersonal expectations in both teachers and psychological experimenters.

In all the experiments described so far, the same IQ measure was employed, the Flanagan (1960) Tests of General Ability. Also employing the same instrument, Claiborn (1968) found among first-graders a tendency for children he designated as potential bloomers to gain less in IQ than the children of the control group (two-tail $p < .15$). A similar tendency was obtained by Rosenthal and Anderson (1969) employing somewhat older children (two-tail, $p < .17$).

With fifth-grade boys as his subjects and males as teachers, Pitt (1956) found no effect on achievement scores of arbitrarily adding or subtracting ten IQ points to the children's records. In her study, Heiserman (1967) found no effect of teacher expectations on her seventh-graders' stated levels of occupational aspiration.

There have been two studies in which teachers' expectations were varied not for specific children within a classroom but rather for classrooms as a whole (Biegen, 1968; Flowers, 1966). In both cases the performance gains were greater for those classrooms expected by their teachers to show the better performance.

A radically different type of performance measure was employed in the research by Burnham (1968): not intelligence or scholastic achievement this time but swimming ability. His subjects were boys and girls aged 7–14 attending a summer camp for the disadvantaged. None of the children could swim at the beginning of the two-week experimental period. Half the children were alleged by the camp staff to have shown unusual potential for learning to swim as judged from a battery of psychological tests. Children were, of course, assigned to the "high potential" group at random. At the end of the two-week period of the experiment all the children were retested on the standard Red Cross Beginner Swimmer Test. Those children who had been expected to show greater improvement in swimming ability showed greater improvement than did the children of the control group.

In their experiment, Meichenbaum, Bowers, and Ross (1968) also employed a very different type of criterion variable: appropriateness of classroom behavior. The choice of this variable was itself particularly appropriate in view of the fact that these workers employed as their research population a sample of institutionalized adolescent female offenders. Two weeks before the beginning of this experiment, classroom observers, who knew nothing of the experimental manipulations to come, began to record the behavior of both the girls and their teachers. These observations continued through the entire experiment, which remarkably enough lasted only two weeks. Within two weeks after teachers were given the names of the "potential bloomers," the designated children already showed a significantly greater improvement in classroom behavior than did the children of the control group. This experiment was

particularly important in suggesting that the benefits of favorable teacher expectations were associated with an increase in the teachers' positively toned attention to the designated children.

We may conclude now with the brief description of just one more experiment, this one conducted by W. Victor Beez (1968) who kindly made his data available for the analyses to follow. This time the pupils were 60 pre-schoolers from a summer Headstart program. Each child was taught the meaning of a series of symbols by one teacher. Half the 60 teachers had been led to expect good symbol-learning and half had been led to expect poor symbol-learning. Most (77 per cent) of the children alleged to have better intellectual prospects learned five or more symbols but only 13 per cent of the children alleged to have poorer intellectual prospects learned five or more symbols. In this study the children's actual performance was assessed by an experimenter who did not know what the child's teacher had been told about the child's intellectual prospects. Teachers who had been given favorable expectations about their pupil tried to teach more symbols to their pupil than did the teachers given unfavorable expectations about their pupil. The difference in teaching effort was dramatic. Eight or more symbols were taught by 87 per cent of the teachers expecting better performance, but only 13 per cent of the teachers expecting poorer performance tried to teach that many symbols to their pupil.

These results suggest that a teacher's expectation about a pupil's performance may sometimes be translated not into subtle vocal nuances or general increases in positively toned attention but rather into overt and even dramatic alterations in teaching style. The magnitude of the effect of teacher expectations found by Beez is also worthy of comment. In all the earlier studies described, one group of children had been singled out for favorable expectations while nothing was said of the remaining children of the control group. In Beez' short-term experiment it seemed more justified to give negative as well as positive expectations about some of the children. Perhaps the very large effects of teacher expectancy obtained by Beez were due to the creation of strong equal but opposite expectations in the minds of the different teachers. Since strong negative expectations doubtless exist in the real world of classrooms, Beez' procedure may give the better estimate of the effects of teacher expectations as they occur in everyday life.

In the experiment by Beez it seems clear that the dramatic differences in teaching style accounted at least in part for the dramatic differences in pupil learning. However, not all of the obtained differences in learners' learning was due to the differences in teachers' teaching. Within each condition of teacher expectation, for example, there was no relationship between number of symbols taught and number of symbols learned. In addition, it was also possible to compare the performances of just those children of the two conditions who had been given an exactly equal amount of teaching benefit. Even holding teaching benefits constant, the difference favored significantly the children believed to be superior though the magnitude of the effect was now diminished by nearly half.

. . .

This paper began its discussion of interpersonal expectancy effects by suggesting that the expectancy of the behavioral researcher might function as a self-fulfilling prophecy. This unintended effect of the research hypothesis itself must be regarded as a potentially damaging artifact. But interpersonal self-fulfilling prophecies do not operate only in laboratories and while, when there, they may act as artifacts, they are more than that. Interpersonal expectancy effects occur also among teachers and there seems no reason to doubt it, among others as well. What started life as an arti-

fact continues as an interpersonal variable of theoretical and practical importance.

some implications

The implications of the research described in this paper are of several kinds. There are methodological implications for the conduct of education research, and these have been discussed elsewhere in detail (Rosenthal, 1966; Rosenthal and Jacobson, 1968). There are implications for the further investigation of unintentional influence processes, especially when these processes result in interpersonal self-fulfilling prophecies, and some of these have been discussed. Finally, there are some possible implications for the educational enterprise, and some of these will be suggested briefly.

Over time, our educational policy question has changed from "who ought to be educated" to "who is capable of being educated." The ethical question has been traded in for the scientific question. For those children whose educability is in doubt there is a label. They are the educationally, or culturally, or socio-economically deprived children and, as things stand now, they appear not to be able to learn as do those who are more advantaged. The advantaged and the disadvantaged differ in parental income, in parental values, in scores on various tests of achievement and ability, and often in skin color and other phenotypic expressions of genetic heritage. Quite inseparable from these differences between the advantaged and the disadvantaged are the differences in their teachers' expectations for what they can achieve in school. There are no experiments to show that a change in pupils' skin color will lead to improved intellectual performance. There are, however, the experiments described in this paper to show that change in teacher expectation can lead to improved intellectual performance and related behaviors.

In none of the relevant experiments was anything done directly for the "disadvantaged" child. There were no crash programs to improve his school achievement, no trips to museums or art galleries. There was only the belief that the children bore watching, that they had intellectual competencies that would in due course be revealed. What was done in these programs of educational change was done directly for teachers, only indirectly for their pupils. Perhaps, then, it is the teacher to whom we should direct more of our research attention. If we could learn how she is able to effect dramatic improvement in her pupils' competence without formal changes in her teaching methods, then we could teach other teachers to do the same. If further research shows that it is possible to select teachers whose untrained interactional style does for most of their pupils what teachers did for the allegedly special children described in this paper, it may be possible to combine sophisticated teacher selection and placement with teacher training to optimize the learning of all pupils.

As teacher training institutions begin to teach the possibility that teachers' expectations of their pupils' performance may serve as self-fulfilling prophecies, there may be a new expectancy created. The new expectancy may be that children can learn more than had been believed possible, an expectation held by many educational theorists, though for quite different reasons (e.g., Bruner, 1960; Skinner, 1968). The new expectancy, at the very least, will make it more difficult when they encounter the educationally disadvantaged, for teachers to shrug and say or think, "Well, after all, what can you expect?" As Lenore Jacobson has said:

The man on the street may be permitted his opinions and prophecies of the unkempt children loitering in a dreary schoolyard. The teacher in the schoolroom may need to learn that those same prophecies within her may be fulfilled; she is no casual passer-by. Perhaps Pygmalion in the classroom is more her role.

REFERENCES

ADAIR, J. G., and J. S. EPSTEIN. Verbal cues in mediation of experimenter bias. *Psychological Reports*, 1968, **22**, 1045–1053.

ALLPORT, G. W. The role of expectancy, in H. Cantril (Ed.), *Tensions that cause wars*. Urbana, Ill.: University of Illinois Press, 1950, pp. 43–78.

ANDERSON, D. F., and R. ROSENTHAL. Some effects of interpersonal expectancy and social interaction on institutionalized retarded children, *Proceedings of the 76th Annual Convention of the American Psychological Association*, 1968, 479–480.

BEEZ, W. V. Influence on biased psychological reports on teacher behavior and pupil performance, *Proceedings of the 76th Annual Convention of the American Psychological Association*, 1968, 605–606.

BIEGEN, D. A. Unpublished data, University of Cincinnati, 1968.

BRUNER, J. S. *The process of education*. Cambridge, Mass.: Harvard University Press, 1960.

BURNHAM, J. R. Experimenter bias and lesion labeling, unpublished manuscript, Purdue University, 1966.

———. Effects of experimenter's expectancies on children's ability to learn to swim, unpublished master's thesis, Purdue University, 1968.

———, and D. M. HARTSOUGH. Effect of experimenter's expectancies ("the Rosenthal effect") on children's ability to learn to swim, Paper presented at the meeting of the Midwestern Psychological Association, Chicago, May, 1968.

CLAIBORN, W. L. An investigation of the relationship between teacher expectancy, teacher behavior and pupil performance, unpublished doctoral dissertation, Syracuse University, 1968.

CLARK, K. B. Educational stimulation of racially disadvantaged children, in A. H. Passow (Ed.), *Education in depressed areas*. New York: Teachers College Press, 1963, pp. 142–162.

CONN, L. K., C. N. EDWARDS, R. ROSENTHAL, and D. CROWNE. Perception of emotion and response to teachers' expectancy by elementary school children, *Psychological Reports*, 1968, **22**, 27–34.

COOPER, J., L. EISENBERG, J. ROBERT, and B. S. DOHRENWEND. The effect of experimenter expectancy and preparatory effort on belief in the probable occurrence of future events, *Journal of Social Psychology*, 1967, **71**, 221–226.

FLANAGAN, J. C. *Test of general ability: technical report*. Chicago: Science Research Associates, 1960.

FLOWERS, C. E. Effects of an arbitrary accelerated group placement on the tested academic achievement of educationally disadvantaged students, unpublished doctoral dissertation, Teachers College, Columbia University, 1966.

HEISERMAN, M. S. The relationship between teacher expectations and pupil occupational aspirations, unpublished master's thesis, Iowa State University, Ames, 1967.

JOHNSON, R. W. Subject performance as affected by experimenter expectancy, sex of experimenter, and verbal reinforcement, unpublished master's thesis, University of New Brunswick, 1967.

LARRABEE, L. L., and L. D. KLEINSASSER. The effect of experimenter bias on WISC performance, unpublished manuscript. St. Louis: Psychological Associates, 1967.

MARWIT, S. J. An investigation of the communication of tester-bias by means of modeling, unpublished doctoral dissertation, State University of New York at Buffalo, 1968.

MEICHENBAUM, D. H., K. S. BOWERS, and R. R. ROSS. A behavioral analysis of teacher expectancy effect, unpublished manuscript, University of Waterloo, 1968.

MERTON, R. K. The self-fulfilling prophecy, *Antioch Review*, 1948, **8**, 193–210.

PFUNGST, O. *Clever Hans (the horse of Mr. von Osten): a contribution to experimental, animal, and human psychology* (Trans. C. L. Rahn). New York: Holt, 1911. Republished by Holt, Rinehart & Winston, 1965.

PITT, C. C. V. An experimental study of the effects of teachers' knowledge or incorrect knowledge of pupil IQ's on teachers' attitudes and practices and pupils' attitudes and achievements, unpublished doctoral dissertation, Columbia University, 1956.

RAFFETTO, A. M. Experimenter effects on subjects' reported hallucinatory experiences under visual and auditory deprivation, Paper presented at the meeting of the Midwestern Psychological Association, Chicago, May, 1968.

ROSENTHAL, R. The effect of the experimenter on the results of psychological research, in B. A. Maher (Ed.), *Progress in experimental personality research*. Vol. I. New York: Academic Press, 1964a, pp. 79–114.

————. Experimenter outcome-orientation and the results of the psychological experiment. *Psychological Bulletin*, 1964b, **61**, 405–412.

————. Clever Hans: a case study of scientific method, Introduction to O. Pfungst, *Clever Hans: (the horse of Mr. von Osten)*. New York: Holt, Rinehart & Winston, 1965, pp. ix–xlii.

————. *Experimenter effects in behavioral research*. New York: Appleton-Century-Crofts, 1966.

————. Interpersonal expectations: effects of the experimenter's hypothesis, in R. Rosenthal and R. L. Rosnow (Eds.), *Artifact in behavioral research*. New York: Academic Press, 1969, pp. 181–277.

————, and D. F. ANDERSON. Teacher behavior and the mediation of teacher expectancy effects, unpublished data, Harvard University, 1969.

ROSENTHAL, R., and J. EVANS. Unpublished data, Harvard University, 1968.

ROSENTHAL, R., and K. L. FODE. The effect of experimenter bias on the performance of the albino rat, *Behavioral Science*, 1963a, **8**, 183–189.

————. Three experiments in experimenter bias, *Psychological Reports*, 1963b, **12**, 491–511.

ROSENTHAL, R., and L. JACOBSON. *Pygmalion in the classroom: Teacher expectation and pupils' intellectual development*. New York: Holt, Rinehart & Winston, 1968.

SKINNER, B. F. Teaching science in high school: What is wrong? *Science*, 1968, **159**, 704–710.

ZOBLE, E. J. Interaction of subject and experimenter expectancy effects is a tone length discrimination task, unpublished AB thesis, Franklin and Marshall College, 1968.

4

Clinical psychologists often use the case history method to obtain information about an individual's past in order to better understand the significance of his present behavior. In the next paper, Professor B. F. Skinner, who has been a major force in shaping modern psychological thought, discusses the events which led to some of his early discoveries and which helped to determine his particular approach to psychological research. This is one of the best "behind the scenes" pictures of the experimental psychologist at work.

a case history in scientific method [1]

B. F. SKINNER

It has been said that college teaching is the only profession for which there is no professional training, and it is commonly argued that this is because our graduate schools train scholars and scientists rather than teachers. We are more concerned with the discovery of knowledge than with its dissemination. But can we justify ourselves quite so easily? It is a bold thing to say that we know how to train a man to be a scientist. Scientific thinking is the most complex and probably the most subtle of all human activities. Do we actually know how to shape up such behavior, or do we simply mean that some of the people who attend our graduate schools eventually become scientists?

Except for a laboratory course which acquaints the student with standard ap-

[1] Address of the President at the Eastern Psychological Association meetings in Philadelphia, April 1955.

Reprinted from *American Psychologist*, 1956, **11**: 221–223, by permission of the author and publisher. Copyright © 1956 by the American Psychological Association.

paratus and standard procedures, the only explicit training in scientific method generally received by a young psychologist is a course in statistics—not the introductory course, which is often required of so many kinds of students that it is scarcely scientific at all, but an advanced course which includes "model building," "theory construction," and "experimental design." But it is a mistake to identify scientific practice with the formalized constructions of statistics and scientific method. These disciplines have their place, but it does not coincide with the place of scientific research. They offer *a* method of science but not, as is so often implied, *the* method. As formal disciplines they arose very late in this history of science, and most of the facts of science have been discovered without their aid. It takes a great deal of skill to fit Faraday with his wires and magnets into the picture which statistics gives us of scientific thinking. And most current scientific practice would be equally refractory, especially in the important initial stages. It is no wonder that the laboratory scientist is puzzled and often dismayed when he discovers how his behavior has been reconstructed in the formal analyses of scientific method. He is likely to protest that this is not at all a fair representation of what he does.

But his protest is not likely to be heard. For the prestige of statistics and scientific methodology is enormous. Much of . it is borrowed from the high repute of mathematics and logic, but much of it derives from the flourishing state of the art itself. Some statisticians are professional people employed by scientific and commercial enterprises. Some are teachers and pure researchers who give their colleagues the same kind of service for nothing—or at most a note of acknowledgement. Many are zealous people who, with the best of intentions, are anxious to show the nonstatistical scientist how he can do his job more efficiently and assess his results more accurately. There are strong professional societies devoted to the advancement of statistics, and hundreds of technical books and journals are published annually.

Against this, the practicing scientist has very little to offer. He cannot refer the young psychologist to a book which will tell him how to find out all there is to know about a subject matter, how to have the good hunch which will lead him to devise a suitable piece of apparatus, how to develop an efficient experimental routine, how to abandon an unprofitable line of attack, how to move on most rapidly to later stages of his research. The work habits which have become second nature to him have not been formalized by anyone, and he may feel that they possibly never will be. As Richter (5) has pointed out, "Some of the most important discoveries have been made without any plan of research," and "there are researchers who do not work on a verbal plane, who cannot put into words what they are doing."

If we are interested in perpetuating the practices responsible for the present corpus of scientific knowledge, we must keep in mind that some very important parts of the scientific process do not now lend themselves to mathematical, logical, or any other formal treatment. We do not know enough about human behavior to know how the scientist does what he does. Although statisticians and methodologists may seem to tell us, or at least imply, how the mind works—how problems arise, how hypotheses are formed, deductions made, and crucial experiments designed—we as psychologists are in a position to remind them that they do not have methods appropriate to the empirical observation or the functional analysis of such data. These are aspects of human behavior, and no one knows better than we how little can at the moment be said about them.

Some day we shall be better able to express the distinction between empirical analysis and formal reconstruction, for we shall have an alternative account of the behavior of Man Thinking. Such an account will not only plausibly reconstruct what a particular scientist did in any given case, it will permit us to evaluate practices and, I believe, to teach scientific thinking. But that day is some little distance in the future. Meanwhile we can only fall back on examples.

Some time ago the director of Project A of the American Psychological Association asked me to describe my activities as a research psychologist. I went through a trunkful of old notes and records and, for my pains, reread some of my earlier publications. This has made me all the more aware of the contrast between the reconstructions of formalized scientific method and at least one case of actual practice. Instead of amplifying the points I have just made by resorting to a generalized account which is not available, I should like to discuss a case history. It is not one of the case histories we should most like to have, but what it lacks in importance is perhaps somewhat offset by accessibility. I therefore ask you to imagine that you are all clinical psychologists—a task which becomes easier and easier as the years go by—while I sit across the desk from you or stretch out upon this comfortable leather couch.

The first thing I can remember happened when I was only twenty-two years old. Shortly after I had graduated from college Bertrand Russell published a series of articles in the old *Dial* magazine on the epistemology of John B. Watson's Behaviorism. I had had no psychology as an undergraduate but I had had a lot of biology, and two of the books which my biology professor had put into my hands were Loeb's *Physiology of the Brain* and the newly published Oxford edition of Pavlov's *Conditioned Reflexes*. And now here was Russell extrapolating the principles of an objective formulation of behavior to the problem of knowledge! Many years later when I told Lord Russell that his articles were responsible for my interest in behavior, he could only exclaim, "Good Heavens! I had always supposed that those articles had demolished Behaviorism!" But at any rate he had taken Watson seriously, and so did I.

When I arrived at Harvard for graduate study, the air was not exactly full of behavior, but Walter Hunter was coming in once a week from Clark University to give a seminar, and Fred Keller, also a graduate student, was an expert in both the technical details and the sophistry of Behaviorism. Many a time he saved me as I sank into the quicksands of an amateurish discussion of "What is an image?" or "Where is red?" I soon came into contact with W. J. Crozier, who had studied under Loeb. It had been said of Loeb, and might have been said of Crozier, that he "resented the nervous system." Whether this was true or not, the fact was that both these men talked about animal behavior without mentioning the nervous system and with surprising success. So far as I was concerned, they cancelled out the physiological theorizing of Pavlov and Sherrington and thus clarified what remained of the work of these men as the beginnings of an independent science of behavior. My doctoral thesis was in part an operational analysis of Sherrington's syn-

apse, in which behavioral laws were substituted for supposed states of the central nervous system.

But the part of my thesis at issue here was experimental. So far as I can see, I began simply by looking for lawful processes in the behavior of the intact organism. Pavlov had shown the way; but I could not then, as I cannot now, move without a jolt from salivary reflexes to the important business of the organism in everyday life. Sherrington and Magnus had found order in surgical segments of the organism. Could not something of the same sort be found, to use Loeb's phrase, in "the organism as a whole"? I had the clue from Pavlov: control your conditions and you will see order.

It is not surprising that my first gadget was a silent release box, operated by compressed air and designed to eliminate disturbances when introducing a rat into an apparatus. I used this first in studying the way a rat adapted to a novel stimulus. I built a soundproofed box containing a specially structured space. A rat was released, pneumatically, at the far end of a darkened tunnel from which it emerged in exploratory fashion into a well-lighted area. To accentuate its progress and to facilitate recording, the tunnel was placed at the top of a flight of steps, something like a functional Parthenon (Figure 1). The rat would peek out from the tunnel, perhaps glancing suspiciously at the one-way window through which I was watching it, then stretch itself cautiously down the steps. A soft click (carefully calibrated, of course) would cause it to pull back into the tunnel and remain there for some time. But repeated clicks had less and less of an effect. I recorded the rat's advances and retreats by moving a pen back and forth across a moving paper tape.

The major result of this experiment was that some of my rats had babies. I began to watch young rats. I saw them right themselves and crawl about very much like the decerebrate or thalamic cats and rabbits of Magnus. So I set about studying

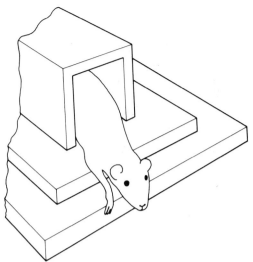

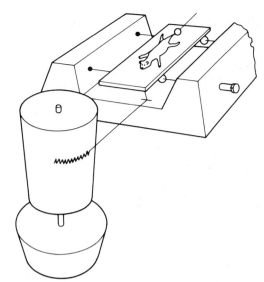

figure 1

figure 2

the postural reflexes of young rats. Here was a first principle not formally recognized by scientific methodologists: When you run onto something interesting, drop everything else and study it. I tore up the Parthenon and started over.

If you hold a young rat on one hand and pull it gently by the tail, it will resist you by pulling forward and then, with a sudden sharp spring which usually disengages its tail, it will leap out into space. I decided to study this behavior quantitatively. I built a light platform covered with cloth and mounted it on tightly stretched piano wires (Figure 2). Here was a version of Sherringon's torsion-wire myograph, originally designed to record the isometric contraction of the *tibialis anticus* of a cat, but here adapted to the response of a whole organism. When the tail of the young rat was gently pulled, the rat clung to the cloth floor and tugged forward. By amplifying the fine movements of the platform, it was possible to get a good kymograph record of the tremor in this motion and then, as the pull against the tail was increased, of the desperate spring into the air (Figure 3).

Now, baby rats have very little future, except as adult rats. Their behavior is literally infantile and cannot be usefully extrapolated to everyday life. But if this

technique would work with a baby, why not try it on a mature rat? To avoid attaching anything to the rat, it should be possible to record, not a pull against the substrate, but the ballistic thrust exerted as the rat runs forward or suddenly stops in response to my calibrated click. So, in-

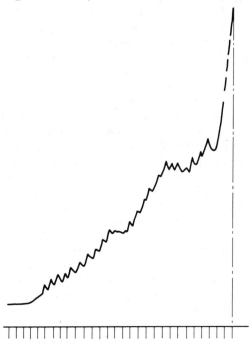

figure 3

39

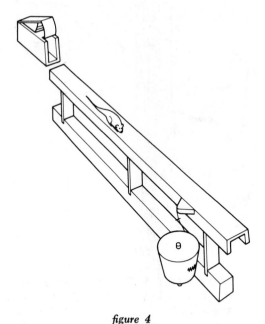

figure 4

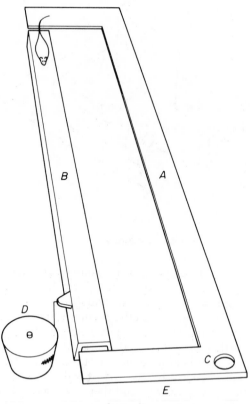

figure 5

voking the first principle of scientific practice again, I threw away the piano-wire platform, and built a runway, eight feet long. This was constructed of light wood, in the form of a U girder, mounted rigidly on vertical glass plates, the elasticity of which permitted a very slight longitudinal movement (Figure 4). The runway became the floor of a long tunnel, not shown, at one end of which I placed my soundless release box and at the other end myself, prepared to reinforce the rat for coming down the runway by giving it a bit of wet mash, to sound a click from time to time when it had reached the middle of the runway, and to harvest kymograph records of the vibrations of the substrate.

Now for a second unformalized principle of scientific practice: Some ways of doing research are easier than others. I got tired of carrying the rat back to the other end of the runway. A back alley was therefore added (Figure 5). Now the rat could eat a bit of mash at point C, go down the back alley A, around the end as shown, and back home by runway B. The experimenter

at E could collect records from the kymograph at D in comfort. In this way a great many records were made of the forces exerted against the substratum as rats ran down the alley and occasionally stopped dead in their tracks as a click sounded (Figure 6).

There was one annoying detail, however. The rat would often wait an inordinately long time at C before starting down the back alley on the next run. There

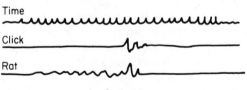

figure 6

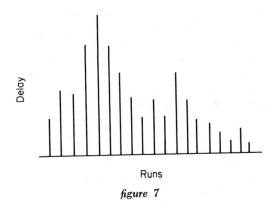

Delay

Runs

figure 7

seemed to be no explanation for this. When I timed these delays with a stop watch, however, and plotted them, they seemed to show orderly changes (Figure 7). This was, of course, the kind of thing I was looking for. I forgot all about the movements of the substratum and began to run rats for the sake of the delay measurements alone. But there was now no reason why the runway had to be eight feet long and, as the second principle came into play again, I saw no reason why the rat could not deliver its own reinforcement.

A new apparatus was built. In Figure 8 we see the rat eating a piece of food just after completing a run. It produced the food by its own action. As it ran down the back alley A to the far end of the rectangular runway, its weight caused the whole runway

to tilt slightly on the axis C and this movement turned the wooden disc D, permitting a piece of food in one of the holes around its perimeter to drop through a funnel into a food dish. The food was pearl barley, the only kind I could find in the grocery stores in reasonably uniform pieces. The rat had only to complete its journey by coming down the home stretch B to enjoy its reward. The experimenter was able to enjoy *his* reward at the same time, for he had only to load the magazine, put in a rat, and relax. Each tilt was recorded on a slowly moving kymograph.

A third unformalized principle of scientific practice: Some people are lucky. The disc of wood from which I had fashioned the food magazine was taken from a store room of discarded apparatus. It happened to have a central spindle, which fortunately I had not bothered to cut off. One day it occurred to me that if I wound a string around the spindle and allowed it to unwind as the magazine was emptied (Figure 9), I would get a different kind of record. Instead of a mere report of the up-and-down movement of the runway, as a series of pips as in a polygraph, I would get a *curve*. And I knew that science made great use of curves, although, so far as I could discover, very little of pips on a polygram. The difference between the old type of record at A (Figure 10) and the new at B may not seem great, but as it turned out the curve revealed things in the rate of responding, and in changes in that rate, which would certainly otherwise have been missed. By allowing the string to unwind rather than to wind, I had got my curve in an awkward Cartesian quadrant, but that was easily remedied. Psychologists have adopted cumulative curves only very slowly, but I think it is fair to say that they have become an indispensable tool for certain purposes of analysis.

Eventually, of course, the runway was seen to be unnecessary. The rat could simply reach into a covered tray for pieces of food, and each movement of the cover

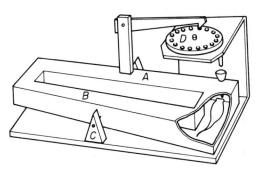

figure 8

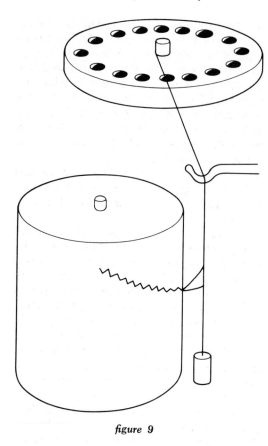

figure 9

could operate a solenoid to move a pen one step in a cumulative curve. The first major change in rate observed in this way was due to ingestion. Curves showing how the rate of eating declined with the time of eating comprised the other part of my thesis. But a refinement was needed. The

behavior of the rat in pushing open the door was not a normal part of the ingestive behavior of *Rattus rattus*. The act was obviously learned but its status as part of the final performance was not clear. It seemed wise to add an initial conditioned response connected with ingestion in a quite arbitrary way. I chose the first device which came to hand—a horizontal bar or lever placed where it could be conveniently depressed by the rat to close a switch which operated a magnetic magazine. Ingestion curves obtained with this initial response in the chain were found to have the same properties as those without it.

Now, as soon as you begin to complicate an apparatus, you necessarily invoke a fourth principle of scientific practice: Apparatuses sometimes break down. I had only to wait for the food magazine to jam to get an extinction curve. At first I treated this as a defect and hastened to remedy the difficulty. But eventually, of course, I deliberately disconnected the magazine. I can easily recall the excitement of that first complete extinction curve (Figure 11). I had made contact with Pavlov at last! Here was a curve uncorrupted by the physiological process of ingestion. It was an orderly change due to nothing more than a special contingency of reinforcement. It was pure behavior! I am not saying that I would not have got around to extinction curves without a breakdown in the apparatus; Pavlov had given too strong

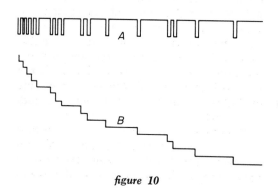

figure 10

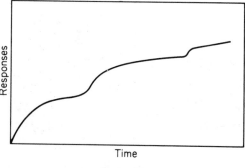

figure 11

a lead in that direction. But it is still no exaggeration to say that some of the most interesting and surprising results have turned up first because of similar accidents. Foolproof apparatus is no doubt highly desirable, but Charles Ferster and I in recently reviewing the data from a five-year program of research found many occasions to congratulate ourselves on the fallibility of relays and vacuum tubes.

I then built four soundproofed ventilated boxes, each containing a lever and a food magazine and supplied with a cumulative recorder, and was on my way to an intensive study of conditioned reflexes in skeletal behavior. I would reinforce every response for several days and then extinguish for a day or two, varying the number of reinforcements, the amount of previous magazine training, and so on.

At this point I made my first use of the deductive method. I had long since given up pearl barley as too unbalanced a diet for steady use. A neighborhood druggist had shown me his pill machine, and I had had one made along the same lines (Figure 12). It consisted of a fluted brass bed across which one laid a long cylinder of stiff paste (in my case a MacCollum formula for an adequate rat diet). A similarly fluted cutter was then lowered onto the cylinder and rolled slowly back and forth, converting the paste into about a dozen spherical pellets. These were dried for a day or so before use. The procedure was

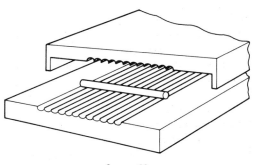

figure 12

painstaking and laborious. Eight rats eating a hundred pellets each per day could easily keep up with production. One pleasant Saturday afternoon I surveyed my supply of dry pellets, and, appealing to certain elemental theorems in arithmetic, deduced that unless I spent the rest of that afternoon and evening at the pill machine, the supply would be exhausted by ten-thirty Monday morning.

Since I do not wish to deprecate the hypothetico-deductive method, I am glad to testify here to its usefulness. It led me to apply our second principle of unformalized scientific method and to ask myself why *every* press of the lever had to be reinforced. I was not then aware of what had happened at the Brown laboratories, as Harold Schlosberg later told the story. A graduate student had been given the task of running a cat through a difficult discrimination experiment. One Sunday the student found the supply of cat food exhausted. The stores were closed and so, with a beautiful faith in the frequency-theory of learning, he ran the cat as usual and took it back to its living cage unrewarded. Schlosberg reports that the cat howled its protest continuously for nearly forty-eight hours. Unaware of this I decided to reinforce a response only once every minute and to allow all other responses to go unreinforced. There were two results: (*a*) my supply of pellets lasted almost indefinitely and (*b*) each rat stabilized at a fairly constant rate of responding.

Now, a steady state was something I was familiar with from physical chemistry, and I therefore embarked upon the study of periodic reinforcement. I soon found that the constant rate at which the rat stabilized depended upon how hungry it was. Hungry rat, high rate; less hungry rat, lower rate. At that time I was bothered by the practical problem of controlling food deprivation. I was working half time at the Medical School (on chronaxie of subordination!) and could not maintain a good schedule in working with the rats. The rate of responding under periodic reinforcement suggested a scheme for keeping a rat at a constant level of deprivation. The argument went like this: Suppose you reinforce the rat, not at the end of a given period, but when it has completed the number of responses ordinarily emitted in that period. And suppose you use substantial pellets of food and give the rat continuous access to the lever. Then, except for periods when the rat sleeps, it should operate the lever at a constant rate around the clock. For, whenever it grows slightly hungrier, it will work faster, get food faster, and become less hungry, while whenever it grows slightly less hungry, it will respond at a lower rate, get less food, and grow hungrier. By setting the reinforcement at a given number of responses it should even be possible to hold the rat at any given level of deprivation. I visualized a machine with a dial which one could set to make available, at any time of day or night, a rat in a given state of deprivation. Of course, nothing of the sort happens. This is "fixed-ratio" rather than "fixed-interval" reinforcement and, as I soon found out, it produces a very different type of performance. This is an example of a fifth unformalized principle of scientific practice, but one which has at least been named. Walter Cannon described it with a word invented by Horace Walpole: *serendipity*—the art of finding one thing while looking for something else.

This account of my scientific behavior up to the point at which I published my results in a book called *The Behavior of Organisms* is as exact in letter and spirit as I can now make it. The notes, data, and publications which I have examined do not show that I ever behaved in the manner of Man Thinking as described by John Stuart Mill or John Dewey or in reconstructions of scientific behavior by other philosophers of science. I never faced a Problem which was more than the eternal problem of finding order. I never attacked a problem by constructing a Hypothesis. I never deduced Theorems or submitted them to Experi-

mental Check. So far as I can see, I had no preconceived Model of behavior—certainly not a physiological or mentalistic one, and, I believe, not a conceptual one. The "reflex reserve" was an abortive, though operational, concept which was retracted a year or so after publication in a paper at the Philadelphia meeting of the APA. It lived up to my opinion of theories in general by proving utterly worthless in suggesting further experiments. Of course, I was working on a basic Assumption—that there was order in behavior if I could only discover it—but such an assumption is not to be confused with the hypotheses of deductive theory. It is also true that I exercised a certain Selection of Facts but not because of relevance to theory but because one fact was more orderly than another. If I engaged in Experimental Design at all, it was simply to complete or extend some evidence of order already observed.

Most of the experiments described in *The Behavior of Organisms* were done with groups of four rats. A fairly common reaction to the book was that such groups were too small. How did I know that other groups of four rats would do the same thing? Keller, in defending the book, countered with the charge that groups of four were too *big*. Unfortunately, however, I allowed myself to be persuaded of the contrary. This was due in part to my association at the University of Minnesota with W. T. Heron. Through him I came into close contact for the first time with traditional animal psychology. Heron was interested in inherited maze behavior, inherited activity, and certain drugs—the effects of which could then be detected only through the use of fairly large groups. We did an experiment together on the effect of starvation on the rate of pressing a lever and started the new era with a group of sixteen rats. But we had only four boxes, and this was so inconvenient that Heron applied for a grant and built a battery of twenty-four lever-boxes and cumulative recorders. I supplied an attachment which would record, not only the mean performance of all twenty-four rats in a single averaged curve, but mean curves for four subgroups of twelve rats each and four subgroups of six rats each (3). We thus provided for the design of experiments according to the principles of R. A. Fisher, which were then coming into vogue. We had, so to speak, mechanized the latin square.

With this apparatus Heron and I published a study of extinction in maze-bright and maze-dull rats using *ninety-five* subjects. Later I published mean extinction curves for groups of twenty-four, and W. K. Estes and I did our work on anxiety with groups of the same size. But although Heron and I could properly voice the hope that "the possibility of using large groups of animals greatly improves upon the method as previously reported, since tests of significance are provided for and properties of behavior not apparent in single cases may be more easily detected," in actual practice that is not what happened. The experiments I have just mentioned are almost all we have to show for this elaborate battery of boxes. Undoubtedly more work could be done with it and would have its place, but something had happened to the natural growth of the method. You cannot easily make a change in the conditions of an experiment when twenty-four apparatuses have to be altered. Any gain in rigor is more than matched by a loss in flexibility. We were forced to confine ourselves to processes which could be studied with the baselines already developed in earlier work. We could not move on to the discovery of other processes or even to a more refined analysis of those we were working with. No matter how significant might be the relations we actually demonstrated, our statistical Leviathan had swum aground. The art of the method had stuck at a particular stage of its development.

Another accident rescued me from mechanized statistics and brought me back to an even more intensive concentration on the single case. In essence, I suddenly found myself face to face with the engineering problem of the animal trainer. When you have the responsibility of making absolutely sure that a given organism will engage in a given sort of behavior at a given time, you quickly grow impatient with theories of learning. Principles, hypotheses, theorems, satisfactory proof at the .05 level of significance that behavior at a choice point shows the effect of secondary reinforcement—nothing could be more irrelevant. No one goes to the circus to see the average dog jump through a hoop significantly oftener than untrained dogs raised under the same circumstances, or to see an elephant demonstrate a principle of behavior.

Perhaps I can illustrate this without giving aid and comfort to the enemy by describing a Russian device which the Germans found quite formidable. The Russians used dogs to blow up tanks. A dog was trained to hide behind a tree or wall in low brush or other cover. As a tank approached and passed, the dog ran swiftly alongside it, and a small magnetic mine attached to the dog's back was sufficient to cripple the tank or set it afire. The dog, of course, had to be replaced.

Now I ask you to consider some of the technical problems which the psychologist faces in preparing a dog for such an act of unintentional heroism. The dog must wait behind the tree for an indefinite length of time. Very well, it must therefore be intermittently reinforced for waiting. But what schedule will achieve the highest probability of waiting? If the reinforcement is to be food, what is the absolutely optimal schedule of deprivation consistent with the health of the dog? The dog must run to the tank—that can be arranged by reinforcing it with a practice tank—but it must start instantly if it is to overtake a swift tank, and how do you differentially reinforce short reaction times, especially in counteracting the reinforcement for sitting and waiting? The dog must react only to tanks, not to a refugee driving his oxcart along the road, but what are the defining properties of a tank so far as a dog is concerned?

I think it can be said that a functional analysis proved adequate in its technological application. Manipulation of environmental conditions alone made possible a wholly unexpected practical control. Behavior could be shaped up according to specifications and maintained indefinitely almost at will. One behavioral technologist who worked with me at the time (Keller Breland) is now specializing in the production of behavior as a salable commodity and has described this new profession in the *American Psychologist* (2).

There are many useful applications within psychology itself. Ratliff and Blough have recently conditioned pigeons to serve as psychophysical observers. In their experiment a pigeon may adjust one of two spots of light until the two are equally bright or it may hold a spot of light at the absolute threshold during dark adaptation. The techniques which they have developed to induce pigeons to do this are only indirectly related to the point of their experiments and hence exemplify the application of a behavioral science (4). The field in which a better technology of behavior is perhaps most urgently needed is education. I cannot describe here the applications which are now possible, but perhaps I can indicate my enthusiasm by hazarding the guess that educational techniques at all age levels are on the threshold of revolutionary changes.

The effect of a behavioral technology on scientific practice is the issue here. Faced with practical problems in behavior, you necessarily emphasize the refinement of *experimental* variables. As a result, some of the standard procedures of statistics appear to be circumvented. Let me illustrate. Suppose that measurements have been made on two groups of subjects differing in some detail of experimental treatment. Means and standard deviations for the two groups are determined, and any difference

due to the treatment is evaluated. If the difference is in the expected direction but is not statistically significant, the almost universal recommendation would be to study larger groups. But our experience with practical control suggests that we may reduce the troublesome variability by changing the conditions of the experiment. By discovering, elaborating, and fully exploiting every relevant variable, we may eliminate *in advance of measurement* the individual differences which obscure the difference under analysis. This will achieve the same result as increasing the size of groups, and it will almost certainly yield a bonus in the discovery of new variables which would not have been identified in the statistical treatment.

The same may be said of smooth curves. In our study of anxiety, Estes and I published several curves, the reasonable smoothness of which was obtained by averaging the performances of 12 rats for each curve. The individual curves published at that time show that the mean curves do not faithfully represent the behavior of any one rat. They show a certain tendency toward a change in slope which supported the point we were making, and they may have appeared to justify averaging for that reason.

But an alternative method would have been to explore the individual case until an equally smooth curve could be obtained. This would have meant, not only rejecting the temptation to produce smoothness by averaging cases, but manipulating all relevant conditions as we later learned to manipulate them for practical purposes. The individual curves which we published at that time do not point to the need for larger groups but for improvement in experimental technique. Here, for example, is a curve the smoothness of which is characteristic of current practice. Such curves were shown in the making in a demonstration which Ferster and I arranged at the Cleveland meeting of the American Psychological Association (Figure 13). Here,

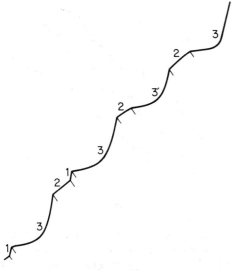

figure 13

what some critics have described as a *folie à deux* or group neurosis.

An early application of the method to the behavior of avoidance and escape was made by Keller in studying the light aversion of the rat. This was brilliantly extended by Murray Sidman in his shock-avoidance experiments. It is no longer necessary to describe avoidance and escape by appeal to "principles," for we may *watch* the behavior develop when we have arranged the proper contingencies of reinforcement, as we later watch it change as these contingencies are changed.

Hunt and Brady have extended the use of a stable rate in the study of anxiety-producing stimuli and have shown that the depression in rate is eliminated by electroconvulsive shock and by other measures which are effective in reducing anxiety in human patients. O. R. Lindsley has found the same thing for dogs, using insulin-shock therapy and sedatives. Brady has refined the method by exploring the relevance of various schedules of reinforcement in tracing the return of the conditioned depression after treatment. In these experiments you *see* the effect of a treatment as directly as you see the constriction of a capillary under the microscope.

Early work with rats on caffeine and Benzedrine has been extended by Lindsley with dogs. A special technique for evaluating several effects of a drug in a single short experimental period yields a record of behavior which can be read as a specialist reads an electrocardiogram. Dr. Peter Dews of the Department of Pharmacology at the Harvard Medical School is investigating dose-response curves and the types and effects of various drugs, using pigeons as subjects. In the Psychological Laboratories at Harvard additional work on drugs is being carried out by Morse, Herrnstein, and Marshall, and the technique is being adopted by drug manufacturers. There could scarcely be a better demonstration of the experimental treatment of variability. In a *single* experimen-

in a single organism, three different schedules of reinforcement are yielding corresponding performances with great uniformity under appropriate stimuli alternating at random. One does not reach this kind of order through the application of statistical methods.

In *The Behavior of Organisms* I was content to deal with the over-all slopes and curvature of cumulative curves and could make only a rough classification of the properties of behavior shown by the finer grain. The grain has now been improved. The resolving power of the microscope has been increased manyfold, and we can see fundamental processes of behavior in sharper and sharper detail. In choosing rate of responding as a basic datum and in recording this conveniently in a cumulative curve, we make important temporal aspects of behavior *visible*. Once this has happened, our scientific practice is reduced to simple looking. A new world is opened to inspection. We use such curves as we use a microscope, X-ray camera, or telescope. This is well exemplified by recent extensions of the method. These are no longer part of my case history, but perhaps you will permit me to consult you about tal session with a *single* organism one observes the onset, duration, and decline of the effects of a drug.

The direct observation of *defective* behavior is particularly important. Clinical or experimental damage to an organism is characteristically unique. Hence the value of a method which permits the direct observation of the behavior of the individual. Lindsley has studied the effects of near-lethal irradiation, and the effects of prolonged anesthesia and anoxia are currently being examined by Thomas Lohr in co-operation with Dr. Henry Beecher of the Massachusetts General Hospital. The technique is being applied to neurological variables in the monkey by Dr. Karl Pribram at the Hartford Institute. The pattern of such research is simple: establish the behavior in which you are interested, submit the organism to a particular treatment, and then look again at the behavior. An excellent example of the use of experimental control in the study of *motivation* is some work on obesity by J. E. Anliker in collaboration with Dr. Jean Mayer of the Harvard School of Public Health, where abnormalities of ingestive behavior in several types of obese mice can be compared by direct inspection.

There is perhaps no field in which behavior is customarily described more indirectly than psychiatry. In an experiment at the Massachusetts State Hospital, under the sponsorship of Dr. Harry Solomon and myself, O. R. Lindsley is carrying out an extensive program which might be characterized as a quantitative study of the temporal properties of psychotic behavior. Here again it is a question of making certain characteristics of the behavior visible.

The extent to which we can eliminate sources of variability before measurement is shown by a result which has an unexpected significance for comparative psychology and the study of individual differences. Figure 14 shows tracings of three curves which report behavior in response to a multiple fixed-interval fixed-ratio

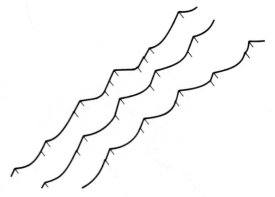

figure 14

schedule. The hatches mark reinforcements. Separating them in some cases are short, steep lines showing a high constant rate on a fixed-ratio schedule and, in others, somewhat longer "scallops" showing a smooth acceleration as the organism shifts from a very low rate just after reinforcement to a higher rate at the end of the fixed interval. The values of the intervals and ratios, the states of deprivation, and the exposures to the schedules were different in the three cases, but except for these details the curves are quite similar. Now, one of them was made by a *pigeon* in some experiments by Ferster and me, one was made by a *rat* in an experiment on anoxia by Lohr, and the third was made by a *monkey* in Karl Pribram's laboratory at the Hartford Institute. Pigeon, rat, monkey, which is which? It doesn't matter. Of course, these three species have behavioral repertoires which are as different as their anatomies. But once you have allowed for differences in the ways in which they make contact with the environment, and in the ways in which they act upon the environment, what remains of their behavior shows astonishingly similar properties. Mice, cats, dogs, and human children could have added other curves to this figure. And when organisms which differ as widely as this nevertheless show similar properties of behavior, differences between members of the same species may be viewed more hopefully. Difficult problems of idiosyncrasy or individuality will always arise as products of biological and cultural processes, but it is the very business of the experimental analysis of behavior to devise techniques which reduce their effects except when they are explicitly under investigation.

We are within reach of a science of the individual. This will be achieved, not by resorting to some special theory of knowledge in which intuition or understanding takes the place of observation and analysis, but through an increasing grasp of relevant conditions to produce order in the individual case.

A second consequence of an improved technology is the effect upon behavior theory. As I have pointed out elsewhere, it is the function of learning theory to create an imaginary world of law and order and thus to console us for the disorders we observe in behavior itself. Scores on a T maze or jumping stand hop about from trial to trial almost capriciously. Therefore we argue that if learning is, as we hope, a continuous and orderly process, it must be occurring in some other system of dimensions —perhaps in the nervous system, or in the mind, or in a conceptual model of behavior. Both the statistical treatment of group means and the averaging of curves encourage the belief that we are somehow going behind the individual case to an otherwise inaccessible, but more fundamental, process. The whole tenor of our paper on anxiety, for example, was to imply that the change we observed was not necessarily a property of behavior, but of some theoretical state of the organism ("anxiety") which was merely *reflected* in a slight modification of performance.

When we have achieved a practical control over the organism, theories of behavior lose their point. In representing and managing relevant variables, a conceptual model is useless; we come to grips with behavior itself. When behavior shows order and consistency, we are much less likely to be concerned with physiological or mentalistic causes. A datum emerges which takes the place of theoretical fantasy. In the experimental analysis of behavior we address ourselves to a subject matter which is not only manifestly the behavior of an individual and hence accessible without the usual statistical aids but also "objective" and "actual" without recourse to deductive theorizing.

Statistical techniques serve a useful function, but they have acquired a purely honorific status which may be troublesome. Their presence or absence has become a shibboleth to be used in distinguishing between good and bad work. Because measures of behavior have been highly variable, we have come to trust only results obtained from large numbers of subjects. Because some workers have intentionally or unconsciously reported only selected favorable instances, we have come to put a high value on research which is planned in advance and reported in its entirety. Because measures have behaved capriciously, we have come to value skillful deductive theories which restore order. But although large groups, planned experiments, and valid theorizing are associated with significant scientific results, it does not follow that nothing can be achieved in their absence. Here are two brief examples of the choice before us.

How can we determine the course of dark adaptation in a pigeon? We move a pigeon from a bright light to a dark room. What happens? Presumably the bird is able to see fainter and fainter patches of light as the process of adaptation takes place, but how can we follow this process? One way would be to set up a discrimination apparatus in which choices would be made at specific intervals after the beginning of dark adaptation. The test patches of light could be varied over a wide range, and the percentages of correct choices at each value would enable us eventually to locate the threshold fairly accurately. But hundreds of observations would be needed to establish only a few points on the curve and to prove

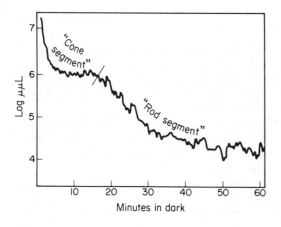

figure 15

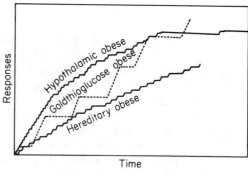

figure 16

that these show an actual change in sensitivity. In the experiment by Blough already mentioned, the pigeon holds a spot of light close to the threshold throughout the experimental period. A single curve, such as the one sketched in Figure 15, yields as much information as hundreds of readings, together with the means and standard deviations derived from them. The information is more accurate because it applies to a single organism in a single experimental session. Yet many psychologists who would accept the first as a finished experiment because of the tables of means and standard deviations would boggle at the second or call it a preliminary study. The direct evidence of one's senses in observing a process of behavior is not trusted.

As another example, consider the behavior of several types of obese mice. Do they all suffer from a single abnormality in their eating behavior or are there differences? One might attempt to answer this with some such measure of hunger as an obstruction apparatus. The numbers of crossings of a grid to get to food, counted after different periods of free access to food, would be the data. Large numbers of readings would be needed, and the resulting mean values would possibly not describe the behavior of any one mouse in any experimental period. A much better picture may be obtained with one mouse of each

kind in single experimental sessions, as Anliker has shown (1). In an experiment reported roughly in Figure 16, each mouse was reinforced with a small piece of food after completing a short "ratio" of responses. The hypothalamic-obese mouse shows an exaggerated but otherwise normal ingestion curve. The hereditary-obese mouse eats slowly but for an indefinite length of time and with little change in rate. The gold-poisoned obese mouse shows a sharp oscillation between periods of very rapid responding and no responding at all. These three individual curves contain more information than could probably ever be generated with measures requiring statistical treatment, yet they will be viewed with suspicion by many psychologists because they are single cases.

It is perhaps natural that psychologists should awaken only slowly to the possibility that behavioral processes may be directly observed, or that they should only gradually put the older statistical and theoretical techniques in their proper perspective. But it is time to insist that science does not progress by carefully designed steps called "experiments" each of which has a well-defined beginning and end. Science is a continuous and often a disorderly and accidental process. We shall not do the young psychologist any favor if we agree to reconstruct our practices to fit the pattern demanded by current scientific methodology. What the statistician means by the design of experiments is design which yields the kind of data to which *his* techniques are applicable. He does not mean the behavior of the scientist in his laboratory devising research for his own immediate and possibly inscrutable purposes.

The organism whose behavior is most extensively modified and most completely controlled in research of the sort I have described is the experimenter himself. The point was well made by a cartoonist in the Columbia *Jester* (Figure 17). The caption

figure 17

read: "Boy, have I got this guy conditioned! Every time I press the bar down he drops in a piece of food." The subjects we study reinforce us much more effectively than we reinforce them. I have been telling you simply how I have been conditioned to behave. And of course it is a mistake to argue too much from one case history. My behavior would not have been shaped as it was were it not for personal characteristics which all psychologists fortunately do not share. Freud has had something to say about the motivation of scientists and has given us some insight into the type of person who achieves the fullest satisfaction from precise experimental design and the intricacies of deductive systems. Such a person tends to be more concerned with his success as a scientist than with his subject matter, as is shown by the

fact that he often assumes the role of a roving ambassador. If this seems unfair, let me hasten to characterize my own motivation in equally unflattering terms. Several years ago I spent a pleasant summer writing a novel called *Walden Two*. One of the characters, Frazier, said many things which I was not yet ready to say myself. Among them was this:

I have only one important characteristic, Burris: I'm stubborn. I've had only one idea in my life—a true *idée fixe* . . . to put it as bluntly as possible, the idea of having my own way. "Control" expresses it, I think. The control of human behavior Burris. In my early experimental days it was a frenzied, selfish desire to dominate. I remember the rage I used to feel when a prediction went awry. I could have shouted at the subjects of my experiments, "Behave, damn you, behave as you ought!" Eventually I realized that the subjects were always right. They always behaved as they ought. It was I who was wrong. I had made a bad prediction.

(In fairness to Frazier and the rest of myself, I want to add his next remark: "And what a strange discovery for a would-be tyrant, that the only effective technique of control is unselfish." Frazier means, of course, positive reinforcement.)

We have no more reason to say that all psychologists should behave as I have behaved than that they should all behave like R. A. Fisher. The scientist, like any organism, is the product of a unique history. The practices which he finds most appropriate will depend in part upon this history. Fortunately, personal idiosyncrasies usually leave a negligible mark on science as public property. They are important only when we are concerned with the encouragement of scientists and the prosecution of research. When we have at last an adequate empirical account of the behavior of Man Thinking, we shall understand all this. Until then, it may be best not to try to fit all scientists into any single mold.

REFERENCES

1. Anliker, J. E. Personal communication.
2. Breland, K., and Marion Breland. A field of applied animal psychology. *Amer. Psychologist*, 1951, **6**, 202–204.
3. Heron, W. T., and B. F. Skinner. An apparatus for the study of behavior. *Psychol. Rec.*, 1939, **3**, 166–176.
4. Ratliff, F., and D. S. Blough. Behavioral studies of visual processes in the pigeon. Report of Contract N5ori–07663, Psychological Laboratories, Harvard University, September 1954.
5. Richter, C. P. Free research versus design research. *Science*, 1953, **118**, 91–93.

UNIT

perception

5

Although the sense receptors of two or more individuals may be exposed to identical physical stimulation, considerable differences may occur in the perception or organization of such stimulation. Expectations, physiological and psychological needs, previous experiences, and attitudes may all affect what a person actually "sees." That our perception may be selective and distorted is readily apparent to anyone who has heard conflicting courtroom testimony from several eyewitnesses to an event, although the inaccuracies may be due to unusual circumstances under which the original observations were made. However, it may surprise you to learn that the same distortions may tend to occur even when the witnesses are allowed to see a re-play of the original event. This is the subject of the next article by Hastorf and Cantril.

they saw a game: a case study

ALBERT H. HASTORF

HADLEY CANTRIL

On a brisk Saturday afternoon, November 23, 1951, the Dartmouth football team played Princeton in Princeton's Palmer Stadium. It was the last game of the season for both teams and of rather special significance because the Princeton team had won all its games so far and one of its players, Kazmaier, was receiving All-American mention and had just appeared as the cover man on *Time* magazine, and was playing his last game.

A few minutes after the opening kick-off, it became apparent that the game was going to be a rough one. The referees were kept busy blowing their whistles and penalizing both sides. In the second quarter,

Reprinted from *The Journal of Abnormal and Social Psychology*, 1954, **29**: 129–134, by permission of the authors and publisher. Copyright 1954 by the American Psychological Association.

Princeton's star left the game with a broken nose. In the third quarter, a Dartmouth player was taken off the field with a broken leg. Tempers flared both during and after the game. The official statistics of the game, which Princeton won, showed that Dartmouth was penalized 70 yards, Princeton 25, not counting more than a few plays in which both sides were penalized.

Needless to say, accusations soon began to fly. The game immediately became a matter of concern to players, students, coaches, and the administrative officials of the two institutions, as well as to alumni and the general public who had not seen the game but had become sensitive to the problem of big-time football through the recent exposures of subsidized players, commercialism, etc. Discussion of the game continued for several weeks.

One of the contributing factors to the extended discussion of the game was the extensive space given to it by both campus and metropolitan newspapers. An indication of the fervor with which the discussions were carried on is shown by a few excerpts from the campus dailies.

For example, on November 27 (four days after the game), the *Daily Princetonian* (Princeton's student newspaper) said:

This observer has never seen quite such a disgusting exhibition of so-called "sport." Both teams were guilty but the blame must be laid primarily on Dartmouth's doorstep. Princeton, obviously the better team, had no reason to rough up Dartmouth. Looking at the situation rationally, we don't see why the Indians should make a deliberate attempt to cripple Dick Kazmaier or any other Princeton player. The Dartmouth psychology, however, is not rational itself.

The November 30th edition of the *Princeton Alumni Weekly* said:

But certain memories of what occurred will not be easily erased. Into the record books will go in indelible fashion the fact that the last game of Dick Kazmaier's career was cut short by more than half when he was forced out with a broken nose and a mild concussion, sustained from a tackle that came well after he had thrown a pass.

This second-period development was followed by a third quarter outbreak of roughness that was climaxed when a Dartmouth player deliberately kicked Brad Glass in the ribs while the latter was on his back. Throughout the often unpleasant afternoon, there was undeniable evidence that the losers' tactics were the result of an actual style of play, and reports on other games they have played this season substantiate this.

Dartmouth students were "seeing" an entirely different version of the game through the editorial eyes of the *Dartmouth* (Dartmouth's undergraduate newspaper). For example, on November 27 the *Dartmouth* said:

However, the Dartmouth-Princeton game set the stage for the other type of dirty football. A type which may be termed as an unjustifiable accusation.

Dick Kazmaier was injured early in the game. Kazmaier was the star, an All-American. Other stars have been injured before, but Kazmaier had been built to represent a Princeton idol. When an idol is hurt there is only one recourse—the tag of dirty football. So what did the Tiger Coach Charley Caldwell do? He announced to the world that the Big Green had been out to extinguish the Princeton star. His purpose was achieved.

After this incident, Caldwell instilled the old see-what-they-did-go-get-them attitude into his players. His talk got results. Gene Howard and Jim Miller were both injured. Both had dropped back to pass, had passed, and were standing unprotected in the backfield. Result: one bad leg and one leg broken.

The game was rough and did get a bit out of hand in the third quarter. Yet most of the roughing penalties were called against Princeton while Dartmouth received more of the illegal-use-of-the-hands variety.

On November 28 the *Dartmouth* said:

Dick Kazmaier of Princeton admittedly is an unusually able football player. Many Dartmouth men traveled to Princeton, not expecting to win—only hoping to see an All-American in action. Dick Kazmaier was hurt in the second period, and played only a token part in the remainder of the game. For this, spectators were sorry.

But there were no such feelings for Dick Kazmaier's health. Medical authorities have confirmed that as a relatively unprotected passing and running star in a contact sport, he is quite liable to injury. Also, his particular injuries—a broken nose and slight concussion—were no more serious than is experienced almost any day in any football practice, where there is no more serious stake than playing the following Saturday. Up to the Princeton game, Dartmouth players suffered about 10 known nose fractures and face injuries, not to mention several slight concussions.

Did Princeton players feel so badly about losing their star? They shouldn't have. During the past undefeated campaign they stopped several individual stars by a concentrated effort, including such mainstays as Frank Hauff of Navy, Glenn Adams of Pennsylvania and Rocco Calvo of Cornell.

In other words, the same brand of football condemned by the *Prince*—that of stopping the big man—is practiced quite successfully by the Tigers.

Basically, then, there was disagreement as to what had happened during the "game." Hence we took the opportunity presented by the occasion to make a "real life" study of a perceptual problem.[1]

procedure

Two steps were involved in gathering data. The first consisted of answers to a questionnaire designed to get reactions to the game and to learn something of the climate of opinion in each institution. This questionnaire was administered a week after the game to both Dartmouth and Princeton undergraduates who were taking introductory and intermediate psychology courses.

The second step consisted of showing the same motion picture of the game to a sample of undergraduates in each school and having them check on another questionnaire, as they watched the film, any infraction of the rules they saw and whether these infractions were "mild" or "flagrant."[2] At Dartmouth, members of two fraternities were asked to view the film on December 7; at Princeton, members of two undergraduate clubs saw the film early in January.

The answers to both questionnaires were carefully coded and transferred to punch cards.[3]

[1] We are not concerned here with the problem of guilt or responsibility for infractions, and nothing here implies any judgment as to who was to blame.

[2] The film shown was kindly loaned for the purpose of the experiment by the Dartmouth College Athletic Council. It should be pointed out that a movie of a football game follows the ball, is thus selective, and omits a good deal of the total action on the field. Also, of course, in viewing only a film of a game, the possibilities of participation as spectator are greatly limited.

[3] We gratefully acknowledge the assistance of Virginia Zerega, Office of Public Opinion Research, and J. L. McCandless, Princeton University, and E. S. Horton, Dartmouth College, in the gathering and collation of the data.

results

Table 1 shows the questions which received different replies from the two student populations on the first questionnaire.

Questions asking if the students had friends on the team, if they had ever played football themselves, if they felt they knew the rules of the game well, etc., showed no differences in either school and no relation to answers given to other questions. This is not surprising since the students in both schools come from essentially the same type of educational, economic, and ethnic background.

Summarizing the data of Tables 1 and 2, we find a marked contrast between the two student groups.

Nearly all *Princeton* students judged the game as "rough and dirty"—not one of them thought it "clean and fair." And almost nine-tenths of them thought the other side started the rough play. By and large they felt that the charges they understood were being made were true; most of them felt the charges were made in order to avoid similar situations in the future.

When Princeton students looked at the movie of the game, they saw the Dartmouth team make over twice as many infractions as their own team made. And they saw the Dartmouth team make over twice as many infractions as were seen by Dartmouth students. When Princeton students judged these infractions as "flagrant" or "mild," the ratio was about two "flagrant" to one "mild" on the Dartmouth team, and about one "flagrant" to three "mild" on the Princeton team.

As for the *Dartmouth* students, while the plurality of answers fell in the "rough and dirty" category, over one-tenth thought the game was "clean and fair" and over a third introduced their own category of "rough and fair" to describe the action. Although a third of the Dartmouth students felt that Dartmouth was to blame for starting the rough play, the majority of Dartmouth students thought both sides

table 1

data from first questionnaire

question	Dart-mouth students (N = 163) %	Prince-ton students (N = 161) %	question	Dart-mouth students (N = 163) %	Prince-ton students (N = 161) %
1. Did you happen to see the actual game between Dartmouth and Princeton in Palmer Stadium this year?			(Combined answers to questions 3 and 4 above)		
			Clean and fair	13	0
			Rough and dirty	42	93
Yes	33	71	Rough and fair *	39	3
No	67	29	Don't know	6	4
2. Have you seen a movie of the game or seen it on television?			5. From what you saw in the game or the movies, or from what you have read, which team do you feel started the rough play?		
Yes, movie	33	2			
Yes, television	0	1			
No, neither	67	97			
3. (Asked of those who answered "yes" to either or both of above questions.) From your observations of what went on at the game, do you believe the game was clean and fairly played, or that it was unnecessarily rough and dirty?			Dartmouth started it	36	86
			Princeton started it	2	0
			Both started it	53	11
			Neither	6	1
			No answer	3	2
Clean and fair	6	0	6. What is your understanding of the charges being made? †		
Rough and dirty	24	69	Dartmouth tried to get Kazmaier	71	47
Rough and fair *	25	2	Dartmouth intentionally dirty	52	44
No answer	45	29	Dartmouth unnecessarily rough	8	35
4. (Asked of those who answered "no" on both of the first questions.) From what you have heard and read about the game, do you feel it was clean and fairly played, or that it was unnecessarily rough and dirty?			7. Do you feel there is any truth to these charges?		
			Yes	10	55
			No	57	4
			Partly	29	35
			Don't know	4	6
Clean and fair	7	0	8. Why do you think the charges were made?		
Rough and dirty	18	24			
Rough and fair *	14	1	Injury to Princeton star	70	23
Don't know	6	4	To prevent repetition	2	46
No answer	55	71	No answer	28	31

* This answer was not included on the checklist but was written in by the percentage of students indicated.

† Replies do not add to 100% since more than one charge could be given.

table 2

data from second questionnaire checked while seeing film

group	N	total number of infractions checked against			
		Dartmouth team		Princeton team	
		mean	SD	mean	SD
Dartmouth students	48	4.3 *	2.7	4.4	2.8
Princeton students	49	9.8 *	5.7	4.2	3.5

* Significant at the .01 level.

were to blame. By and large, Dartmouth men felt that the charges they understood were being made were not true, and most of them thought the reason for the charges was Princeton's concern for its football star.

When Dartmouth students looked at the movie of the game they saw both teams make about the same number of infractions. And they saw their own team make only half the number of infractions the Princeton students saw them make. The ratio of "flagrant" to "mild" infractions was about one to one when Dartmouth students judged the Dartmouth team, and about one "flagrant" to two "mild" when Dartmouth students judged infractions made by the Princeton team.

It should be noted that Dartmouth and Princeton students were thinking of different charges in judging their validity and in assigning reasons as to why the charges were made. It should also be noted that whether or not students were spectators of the game in the stadium made little difference in their responses.

interpretation: the nature of a social event [4]

It seems clear that the "game" actually was many different games and that each

[4] The interpretation of the nature of a social event sketched here is in part based on discussions with Adelbert Ames, Jr., and is being elaborated in more detail elsewhere.

version of the events that transpired was just as "real" to a particular person as other versions were to other people. A consideration of the experiential phenomena that constitute a "football game" for the spectator may help us both to account for the results obtained and illustrate something of the nature of any social event.

Like any other complex social occurrence, a "football game" consists of a whole host of happenings. Many different events are occurring simultaneously. Furthermore, each happening is a link in a chain of happenings, so that one follows another in sequence. The "football game," as well as other complex social situations, consists of a whole matrix of events. In the game situation, this matrix of events consists of the actions of all the players, together with the behavior of the referees and linesmen, the action on the sidelines, in the grandstands, over the loud-speaker, etc.

Of crucial importance is the fact that an "occurrence" on the football field or in any other social situation does not become an experiential "event" unless and until some significance is given to it: an "occurrence" becomes an "*event*" only when the happening has significance. And a happening generally has significance only if it reactivates learned significances already registered in what we have called a person's assumptive form-world (1).

Hence the particular occurrences that different people experienced in the football game were a limited series of events from the total matrix of events *potentially* available to them. People experienced those occurrences that reactivated significances they brought to the occasion; they failed to experience those occurrences which did not reactivate past significances. We do not need to introduce "attention" as an "intervening third" (to paraphrase James on memory) to account for the selectivity of the experiential process.

In this particular study, one of the most interesting examples of this phenomenon was a telegram sent to an officer of Dartmouth College by a member of a Dartmouth alumni group in the Midwest. He had viewed the film which had been shipped to his alumni group from Princeton after its use with Princeton students, who saw, as we noted, an average of over nine infractions by Dartmouth players during the game. The alumnus, who couldn't see the infractions he had heard publicized, wired:

PREVIEW OF PRINCETON MOVIES INDICATES CONSIDERABLE CUTTING OF IMPORTANT PART PLEASE WIRE EXPLANATION AND POSSIBLY AIR MAIL MISSING PART BEFORE SHOWING SCHEDULED FOR JANUARY 25 WE HAVE SPLICING EQUIPMENT.

The "same" sensory impingements emanating from the football field, transmitted through the visual mechanism to the brain, also obviously gave rise to different experiences in different people. The significances assumed by different happenings for different people depend in large part on the purposes people bring to the occasion and assumptions they have of the purposes and probable behavior of other people involved. This was amusingly pointed out by the New York *Herald Tribune's* sports columnist, Red Smith, in describing a prize fight between Chico Vejar and Carmine Fiore in his column of December 21, 1951. Among other things, he wrote:

You see, Steve Ellis is the proprietor of Chico Vejar, who is a highly desirable tract of Stamford, Conn., welterweight. Steve is also a radio announcer. Ordinarily there is no conflict between Ellis the Brain and Ellis the Voice because Steve is an uncommonly substantial lump of meat who can support both halves of split personality and give away weight on each end without missing it.

This time, though, the two Ellises met head-on, with a sickening, rending crash. Steve the Manager sat at ringside in the guise of Steve the Announcer broadcasting a dispassionate, unbiased, objective report of Chico's adventures in the ring. . . .

Clear as mountain water, his words came

through, winning big for Chico. Winning? Hell, Steve was slaughtering poor Fiore.

Watching and listening, you could see what a valiant effort the reporter was making to remain cool and detached. At the same time you had an illustration of the old, established truth that when anybody with a preference watches a fight, he sees only what he prefers to see.

That is always so. That is why, after any fight that doesn't end in a clean knockout, there always are at least a few hoots when the decision is announced. A guy from, say, Billy Graham's neighborhood goes to see Billy fight and he watches Graham all the time. He sees all the punches Billy throws, and hardly any of the punches Billy catches. So it was with Steve.

"Fiore feints with a left," he would say, honestly believing that Fiore hadn't caught Chico full on the chops. "Fiore's knees buckle," he said, "and Chico backs away." Steve didn't see the hook that had driven Chico back. . . .

In brief, the data here indicate that there is no such "thing" as a "game" existing "out there" in its own right which people merely "observe." The "game" "exists" for a person and is experienced by him only in so far as certain happenings have significances in terms of his purpose. Out of all the occurrences going on in the environment, a person selects those that have some significance for him from his own egocentric position in the total matrix.

Obviously in the case of a football game, the value of the experience of watching the game is enhanced if the purpose of "your" team is accomplished, that is, if the happening of the desired consequence is experienced—i.e., if your team wins. But the value attribute of the experience can, of course, be spoiled if the desire to win crowds out behavior we value and have come to call sportsmanlike.

The sharing of significances provides the links except for which a "social" event would not be experienced and would not exist for anyone.

A "football game" would be impossible except for the rules of the game which we bring to the situation and which enable us to share with others the significances of various happenings. These rules make possible a certain repeatability of events such as first downs, touchdowns, etc. If a person is unfamiliar with the rules of the game, the behavior he sees lacks repeatability and consistent significance and hence "doesn't make sense."

And only because there is the possibility of repetition is there the possibility that a happening has a significance. For example, the balls used in games are designed to give a high degree of repeatability. While a football is about the only ball used in games which is not a sphere, the shape of the modern football has apparently evolved in order to achieve a higher degree of accuracy and speed in forward passing than would be obtained with a spherical ball, thus increasing the repeatability of an important phase of the game.

The rules of a football game, like laws, rituals, customs, and mores, are registered and preserved forms of sequential significances enabling people to share the significances of occurrences. The sharing of sequential significances which have value for us provides the links that operationally make social events possible. They are analogous to the forces of attraction that hold parts of an atom together, keeping each part from following its individual, independent course.

From this point of view it is inaccurate and misleading to say that different people have different "attitudes" concerning the same "thing." For the "thing" simply is *not* the same for different people whether the "thing" is a football game, a presidential candidate, Communism, or spinach. We do not simply "react to" a happening or to some impingement from the environment in a determined way (except in behavior that has become reflexive or habitual). We behave according to what we bring to the occasion, and what each of us brings to the occasion is more or less unique. And except for these significances which we bring to the occasion, the happenings around us would be meaningless occurrences, would be "inconsequential."

From the transactional view, an attitude is not a predisposition to react in a certain way to an occurrence or stimulus "out there" that exists in its own right with certain fixed characteristics which we "color" according to our predisposition (2). That is, a subject does not simply "react to" an "object." An attitude would rather seem to be a complex of registered significances reactivated by some stimulus which assumes its own particular significance for us in terms of our purposes. That is, the object as experienced would not exist for us except for the reactivated aspects of the form-world which provide particular significance to the hieroglyphics of sensory impingements.

REFERENCES

1. CANTRIL, H. *The "why" of man's experience.* New York: Macmillan, 1950.
2. KILPATRICK, F. P. (Ed.) *Human behavior from the transactional point of view.* Hanover, N.H.: Institute for Associated Research, 1952.

6

Experimental and theoretical analyses of the concept of attention have been useful in formulating models of how the nervous system processes information. However, research in this area has much broader significance. In the next article, for example, Jerome Kagan discusses how an analysis of the determinants of attention may help us to understand the development of cognitive functioning in children. Kagan also briefly discusses the implications of his recent findings for the educational process.

the determinants of attention in the infant [1]

JEROME KAGAN

The evolution of a science is recorded in what are usually gradual but are sometimes abrupt changes in the central question asked, the concepts preferred, and the subject judged convenient for study. Nineteenth-century physiologists asked how sensory events were transferred from receptor surface to brain, conceived of a process requiring energy transmission, and studied animal forms with accessible afferent nerves. Physiologists now believe they know how a flash of light travels from the retina inward but remain puzzled over what happens when afferent nerves release their information at the end of the journey. This question has generated the concepts of inhibition and arousal and has attracted

investigators to organisms whose brains are accessible to surgery and electrical recording.

Psychology too has experienced a dramatic shift in preferred question, process, and organism. Until recently behavioral scientists wanted to understand how an animal learned a new habit, be it running a maze or pressing a bar with its paw. The solution seemed to require theoretical and empirical inquiry into the phenomena surrounding motivation, reinforcement, and the hypothetical connections between external stimulus and response. This conception of the problem led naturally to the selection of small mammals which allowed close control of experimental conditions. Psychologists have recently redirected their interest from the puzzle of response acquisition to the mystery of mental processes. This shift is due to several factors. Neurophysiologists have found that the brain's electrical activity covaries more closely with states of attention than with patterns of behavior. The psycholinguists have reminded psychology of the profound

[1] Preparation of this paper was supported in part by research grant HD04299 from NICHD, United States Public Health Service, and a grant from the Carnegie Corporation of New York.

chasm between knowing and acting: the young child understands sentences long before he utters them, and all of us possess the competence to generate many more rules than we will ever use. Piaget's life-time effort to outline a developmental history of the stages of human reasoning has catalyzed inquiry into the structure of thought in the child.

These lines of investigation have been supplemented by events in other sectors. Existentialism, drug experience, and popularizations of psychopathology have aroused interest in the quality of inner feelings at the expense of concern with the pragmatic outcome of action. Public recognition that the majority of school failures are poor children has led public and private institutions to increase their support of scientific exploration of children's thought. And the concept of critical period, an idea born in experimental embryology and nurtured in comparative psychology, has prompted scientists to examine more carefully the early months of human development. These diverse forces have found a common aim in study of the mental processes of the young child.

A six-month-old infant displays a remarkable ability to focus his attention on interesting events, and he will maintain prolonged orientations to the face of a stranger, the movement of a leaf, or a lively conversation. He seems to be quietly absorbing information and storing it for future use. Since acquiring knowledge about the environment depends so intimately upon how the infant distributes his attention, and for how long, it is important to ask what governs these processes. This question has stimulated fruitful research from which an outline of preliminary principles is emerging.

early determinants of fixation time: contrast and movement

The most obvious index of attentiveness to visual events is the length of orientation to an object—called fixation time. Like any response it has multiple determinants; the relative power of each seems to change as the infant grows. Ontogenetically, the earliest determinant of length of orientation to a visual event derives from the basic nature of the central nervous system. The infant is predisposed to attend to events that possess a high rate of change in their physical characteristics. Stimuli that move or possess light-dark contrast are most likely to attract and hold a newborn's attention. A two-day-old infant is more attentive to a moving or intermittent light than to a continuous light source; to a design with a high degree of black-white contrast than to one of homogeneous hue (Fantz, 1966; Fantz and Nevis, 1967; Haith, 1966; Salapatek and Kessen, 1966). These facts come from experiments in which stimuli varying, for example, in degree of black-white contrast (e.g., a black triangle on a white background versus a totally gray stimulus) are presented to infants singly or in pairs while observers or cameras record the length of orientation to each of the stimuli. In general, the newborn's visual search behavior seems to be guided by the following rules: (1) If he is alert and the light is not too bright, his eyes open. (2) Seeing no light, he searches. (3) Seeing light but no edges, he keeps searching. (4) Finding contour edges, his eyes focus on and cross them (Haith, 1968).

The attraction to loci of maximal contrast and movement is in accord with knowledge about ganglion potentials in the retinas of vertebrates. Some ganglion cells respond to a light going on; others to its going off; still others to both. Since an object moving across a visual field stimulates a set of cells for a short period, it creates onset and offset patterns similar to those of an intermittent light. Figures that contain dark lines on light backgrounds serve better as onset stimuli than do solid patterns because the change in stimulation created by the border of dark on light elicits more frequent firing of nerve cells,

figure 1   One of a set of random designs shown to four-month infants.

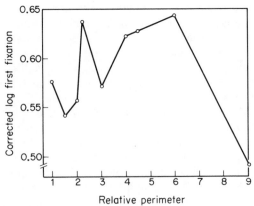

figure 2   Relation between fixation time and approximate area of random design in four-month infants.

and this phenomenon may facilitate sustained attention (Kuffler, 1952, 1953).

The preference for attending to objects with high contrast is dependent, however, on the size of the figure; there seems to be an optimal area that maintains fixation at a maximum. Four-month-old infants shown designs of varying areas (Figure 1) were most attentive to the moderately large designs (Figure 2) (McCall and Kagan, 1967). Similarly there is a nonlinear relation between the total amount of black-white edge in a figure and attention. Consider a series of black-and-white checkerboards of constant area but varying numbers of squares. The total number of inches at which black borders white increases as the number of squares increases. Karmel (1966) has suggested, on the basis of studies with young infants, that the longest fixations are devoted to figures with a moderate amount of edge.

Although indices of attention to auditory events are more ambiguous than those to visual ones, intermittent tones, which have a high rate of change, elicit more sustained interest, as evidenced by motor quieting, than continuous tones (Brackbill et al., 1966; Eisenberg, 1964). Nature has apparently awarded the newborn an initial bias in his processing of experience. He does not have to learn what he should examine, as the nineteenth-century empiricists argued. The preferential orientation to change is clearly adaptive, for the source of change is likely to contain the most information about the presence of his mother or danger.

the role of discrepancy from schema

The initial disposition to attend to events with a high rate of change soon competes with a new determinant based on experience. The child's encounters with events result, inevitably, in some mental representation of the experience, called a schema. A schema is defined as an abstraction of a sensory event that preserves the spatial or temporal pattern of the distinctive elements of the event. A schema is to be regarded as a functional property of mind that permits an organism to recognize and retrieve information. The schema does not necessarily involve a motor response. It is neither a detailed copy of the event nor synonymous with the language label for the event. An example from a recent experiment may be useful here.

A four-year-old looked through a set of 50 magazine pictures illustrating objects, people, or scenes, many of which he had never seen before and could not name when asked. He spent only a few seconds on each picture and flipped through the 50 in less than three minutes. He was then shown 50 pairs of pictures; one of each pair was the picture he saw earlier, the other was new. He was asked to point to the picture he saw before. Although he could recall spontaneously only three or four, the average four-year-old recognized over 45 of the 50 pictures. Some children recognized them all. Since some of the pictures showed objects the child had never seen (say, a lathe or a slide rule), it is unlikely that his performance can be totally explained by assuming that each picture elicited a language label or a fragmentary motor response. What hypothetical entity shall we invoke to explain the child's ability to recognize over 90 percent of the scenes? If we use the concept schema to refer to the processes that permitted recognition, we can say that each picture contained a unique configuration of salient elements, and the schema preserved that configuration, without necessarily preserving an exact spatial analogue of the event. Some psychologists might use the older term memory engram to convey the meaning we attribute to schema. The schema for a visual event is not a photographic copy, for minor changes in the scenes viewed initially do not produce changes in the child's performance. Nor is the schema synonymous with a visual image, for the child is also able to recognize a series of different melodies or sound patterns after brief exposure to each. Early twentieth-century biologists used the concept of the gene to explain demonstrated properties of cells and nuclear material, though no one knew the gene's structure. We use the concept of

schema to account for properties of mind, even though we cannot specify its structure.

The notion of schema helps to explain the older infant's distribution of attention. Toward the end of the second month, fixation time is influenced by the degree to which the child's memory for a particular class of events resembles the specific external event encountered originally. Thus the length of orientation to a picture of a strange face is dependent on the child's schema for the faces he has seen in the past. Events which are moderately discrepant from his schema elicit longer fixations than very familiar events or ones that are completely novel and bear no relation to the schema. The relation of fixation time to magnitude of discrepancy between schema and event is assumed to be curvilinear; this assumption is called the discrepancy hypothesis.

The neurophysiologist describes this attentional phenomenon in slightly different language.

The prepotent role of novelty in evoking the orienting reflex suggests that this response is not initiated directly by a stimulus, in the customary sense of the term, but rather by a change in its intensity, pattern or other parameters. A comparison of present with previous stimulation seems of prime significance, with an orienting reflex being evoked by each point of disagreement. The concept of a cortical neuronal model . . . accounts for this induction of the orienting reflex by stimuli whose characteristic feature is their novelty. This model preserves information about earlier stimuli, with which aspects of novel stimulation may be compared. The orienting reflex is evoked whenever the parameters of the novel stimulus do not coincide with those of the model [Magoun, 1969, p. 180].

Although an orienting reflex can often be produced by any change in quality or intensity of stimulation, duration of sustained attention seems to be influenced by the degree of discrepancy between event and related schema. Consider some empirical support for the discrepancy hypothesis. One- or two-week-old infants look equally long at a black-and-white outline of a regular face (upper right, Figure 3) and a

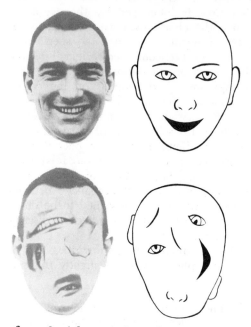

figure 3   Achromatic faces shown to infants.

meaningless design, for contrast is still the major determinant of attention at this early age. Even the eight-week-old attends equally long to a three-dimensional model of a head and an abstract three-dimensional form (Carpenter, 1969). But four-month-old infants show markedly longer fixations to the two regular faces in Figure 3 than to the design in Figure 1 (McCall and Kagan, 1967). The four-month-old has acquired a schema for a human face, and the achromatic illustrations are moderately discrepant from that schema. However, if the face is highly discrepant from the schema, as occurs when the components are rearranged (the lower faces in Figure 3), fixation time is reduced (Haaf and Bell, 1967; Wilcox, 1969). The moderately discrepant face elicits more sustained attention than

the extremely discrepant form at 16 weeks, but not during the first eight weeks of life (Fantz and Nevis, 1967; Lewis, 1969; Wilcox, 1969). The differences in length of fixation to a normal face and to an equally complex but distorted face is greatest between three and six months of age, when infants normally display long fixations to faces. After six months fixation times to photographs of faces drop by over 50 percent and are equally long for both regular and irregular faces (Lewis, 1969).

This developmental pattern confirms the discrepancy hypothesis. Prior to two months, before the infant has a schema for a human face, photographs of either regular or irregular faces are treated as nonsense designs and elicit equal periods of attention. Between two and four months the schema for a human face is established, and a photograph of a strange face is optimally discrepant from that schema. During the latter half of the first year, the schema for a face becomes so firmly established that photographs of regular or irregular faces, though discriminable, elicit short and equal fixations.

A second source of support for the discrepancy hypothesis comes from experiments in which an originally meaningless stimulus is presented repeatedly (usually 5 to 10 times), and afterward a variation of the original stimulus is shown to the infant. Fixation time typically decreases with repetitions of the first stimulus; but when the variation is presented, fixation times increase markedly (McCall and Melson, 1969). In one experiment four-month-old infants were shown a stimulus containing three objects (a doll, a bow, and a flower) for five 30-second presentations. On the sixth trial the infants saw a stimulus in which one, two, or all three objects were replaced with new ones. Most infants showed significantly longer fixations to the changed stimulus than to the last presentation of the original (McCall and Kagan, 1970).

The most persuasive support for the

curvilinear hypothesis comes from an experiment in which a new schema was established experimentally (Super, Kagan, Morrison, Haith, and Weiffenbach, unpublished). Each of 84 firstborn Caucasian infants, four months old, was shown the same three-dimensional stimulus composed of three geometric forms of different shape and hue for 12 half-minute periods (Figure 4). Each infant was then randomly assigned to one of seven groups. Six of these groups were exposed at home to a stimulus that was of varying discrepancy from the standard viewed in the laboratory. The mother showed the stimulus, in the form of a mobile, to the child 30 minutes a day for 21 days. The seven experimental groups were as follows (Figure 5):

Group 1: Control standard. These infants were exposed to the same stimulus they saw in the laboratory at four months.

Group 2: Subtraction. These infants were shown a four-element stimulus constructed by adding a fourth element to the three-element standard seen in the laboratory. ("Subtraction" referred to the later labora-

tory session [see below], which used only three elements.)

Group 3: Serial rearrangement. Infants exposed to a stimulus in which the three elements of the original standard were rearranged in the horizontal plane.

Group 4: Asymmetric rearrangement. Infants shown the three-element stimulus rearranged in an asymmetric form.

Group 5: Ninety-degree rotation. Infants shown a stimulus in which the three horizontal elements in the standard were rearranged in a vertical plane.

Group 6: Extreme discrepancy. Infants shown a mobile consisting of many more elements of different shapes and colors than those of the standard.

Group 7: No-mobile control. Infants exposed to no stimulus during the 21-day experimental period.

Three weeks later each subject was brought back to the laboratory and shown the same stimulus viewed initially at four months. The major dependent variable was the change in fixation time between the first and second test sessions. Figure 6 illustrates

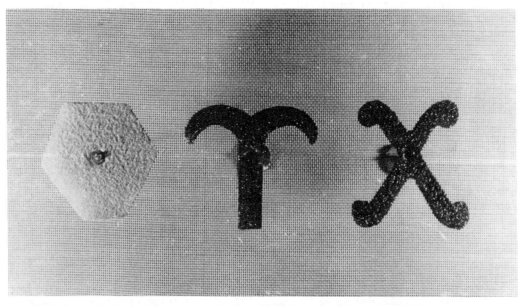

figure 4   One of the two standard mobiles shown to infants in the laboratory.

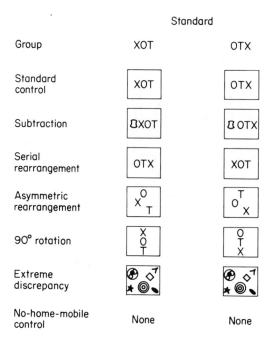

figure 5 Schematic illustrations of the mobiles infants saw at home for 21 days.

these change scores for total fixation time across the first six trials of each session.

The infants who saw no stimulus at home are the referent group to which all the other groups are to be compared. These infants showed no change in fixation time

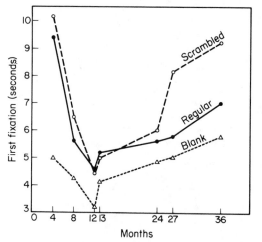

figure 6 Change in fixation time for each of the experimental groups.

across the three weeks, indicating that the laboratory stimulus was as attractive on the second visit as on the first. The infants who developed a schema for the asymmetric and vertical rotation mobiles (moderate discrepancy) showed the smallest drop in interest across the three weeks. By contrast, the infants who experienced a minimal (groups 2 and 3) or major discrepancy (group 6) showed the greatest drop in interest. (Analysis of variance for total fixation time across the first six trials yielded an F ratio of 5.29 and a probability value of less than .05.) There was a curvilinear relation between attention and stimulus-schema discrepancy. Although the existing data are still not conclusive, they clearly support the discrepancy hypothesis.

The onset of a special reaction to discrepancy between two and three months is paralleled by other physiological and behavioral changes in the infant. Temporal characteristics of the cortical evoked potential to a visual stimulus approach adult form, growth of occipital neurons levels off, and the alpha rhythm of the electroencephalogram becomes recognizable (Ellingson, 1967). The Moro reflex—the spreading and coming together of the arms when the head is suddenly dropped a few inches—begins to disappear, crying decreases, babbling increases, decreased attention to repeated presentations of a visual event becomes a reliable phenomenon (Dreyfus-Brisac, 1958; Ellingson, 1967), and three-dimensional representations of objects elicit longer fixations than two-dimensional ones (Fantz, 1966). Perhaps the infant's capacity to react to discrepancy at this age reflects the fact that the brain has matured enough to permit the establishment of long-term memories and their activation by external events.

the effect of the infant's hypotheses

As the child approaches the end of the first year he acquires a new kind of cognitive structure which we call hypotheses. A hypothesis is an interpretation of some experience accomplished by mentally transforming an unusual event to the form the child is familiar with. The "form he is familiar with" is the schema. The cognitive structure used in the transformation is the hypothesis. Suppose a five-year-old notes a small bandage on his mother's face; he will attempt to find the reason for the bandage and may activate the hypothesis, "She cut her face." A five-month-old will recognize his mother in spite of the bandage but will not try to explain its presence.

To recognize that a particular sequence of sounds is human speech, rather than a telephone, requires a schema for the quality of a human voice. Interpretation of the meaning of the speech, on the other hand, requires the activation of hypotheses, in this case linguistic rules. The critical difference between a schema and a hypothesis resembles the difference between recognition and interpretation. Recognition is the assimilation of an event as belonging to one class rather than another. The performance of the four-year-old in the experiment with 50 pictures illustrates the recognition process. The child requires only a schema for the original event in order to answer correctly. Interpretation involves the additional process of activating hypotheses that change the perception of an event so that it can be understood. It is assumed that the activation of hypotheses to explain discrepant events is accompanied by sustained attention. The more extensive the repertoire of hypotheses—the more knowledge the child has—the longer he can work at interpretation and the more prolonged his attention. The child's distribution of attention at an art museum provides a final analogy. He may be expected to study somewhat unusual pictures longer than extremely realistic ones or surrealistic ones because he is likely to have a richer set of hypotheses for the moderately discrepant scenes. The richer the repertoire of hypotheses, holding discrepancy of event constant, the longer the child will persist at interpretation.

There is as yet no body of empirical proof for these ideas, but data that we shall consider agree with these views.

In sum, three factors influence length of fixation time in the infant. High rate of change in physical aspects of the stimulus is primary during the opening weeks, discrepancy becomes a major factor at two months, and activation of hypotheses becomes influential at around 12 months. These three factors supplement each other; and a high-contrast, discrepant event that activates many hypotheses should elicit longer fixation times from an 18-month-old than a stimulus with only one or two of these attributes.

Two parallel investigations attest to the potential usefulness of the complementary principles of discrepancy and activation of hypotheses. In the first, one-, two-, and three-year-old children of middle-class families in Cambridge, Massachusetts, and of peasant Indian families from a village in the Yucatán peninsula were shown color prints of male faces—Caucasian for the American children and Indian for the Mexican children (Finley, 1967). Fixation time to the faces increased with age. The largest increase between two and three years of age occurred to the discrepant, scrambled face rather than to the nondiscrepant, regular face; the former required the activation of more hypotheses in order to be assimilated.

In the second study 180 white, firstborn boys and girls from the Cambridge area viewed the clay faces in Figure 7 repeatedly at 4, 8, 13, and 27 months of age. There was a U-shaped relation between age and fixation time. Fixation decreased from 4 to 13 months but increased between 13 and 27 months. The longer fixations at 4 months reflect the fact that these stimuli were discrepant from the infant's acquired schema for his parents' faces. Fixations decreased at 8 and 13 months because these masks were less discrepant but did not yet activate a long train of hypotheses in the service of assimilation. Between one and

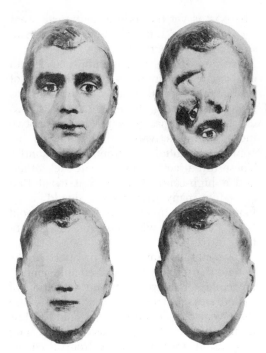

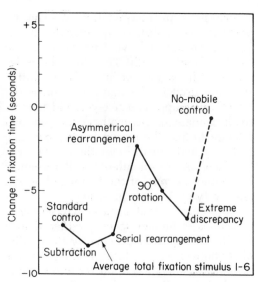

figure 8   Relation between fixation time to faces and age of child.

figure 7   Clay masks shown to children at 4, 8, 13, and 27 months.

two years fixations rose because the child was activating hypotheses to resolve the discrepancy.

As with the first study, the largest increase in fixation time, between 13 and 27 months, occurred to the scrambled face. The children's spontaneous comments indicated that they were trying to understand how a face could be so transformed. "What happened to his nose? Who hit him in the nose?" asked a two-year-old. And, "Who that, Mommy? A monster, Mommy?" said another.

The function resulting from combining the data of the two studies is illustrated in Figure 8. The U-shaped relation between fixation time and age is concordant with the theoretical argument given earlier.

social class and fixation time

The number of hypotheses surrounding a class of events should covary, in part, with

language competence. Hence any experiences that promote acquisition of language should be associated with longer fixation times toward the end of the first year. The positive correlation between parental educational level and the child's linguistic competence is well known and well documented (see, for example, Cazden, 1966). Thus a positive relation between parental education and fixation time should appear toward the end of the first year and grow with time. The data on 180 firstborns indicated that parental education was not highly related to fixation time to faces at 4 and 8 months but was moderately related (correlation coefficient [r] = about 0.4) at 13 and 27 months, and this relation was slightly stronger for girls than for boys. Since the majority of infants either increased in fixation time or showed no essential change between 13 and 27 months, we computed the change in first fixation between 13 and 27 months for each child and correlated that change with parental educational level as well as independent indexes of verbal ability at 27 months. There was a positive relation between increase in fixation time and parents' educational level for the girls (r = .31) but not for boys (r = −.04); 27-month-old girls with the highest vocabulary scores showed the largest increases in fixation time.

It is not clear why the relation between parental education and sustained attention should be stronger for girls than for boys. Other investigators have also reported closer covariation in girls than boys between social class and various indexes of cognitive development including IQ scores and school grades. Moss and Robson (1968) studied the relation between amount of face-to-face interaction mother and infant had in the home and the three-month-old infant's fixation time to photographs of faces in the laboratory. The association was positive for girls (r = .61, p < .01) and close to zero for boys. Hess, Shipman, Brophy, and Bear (1968, 1969) and Werner (1969) have reported more substantial correlations for girls than boys between maternal education or verbal ability, on the one hand, and the child's IQ or level of reading achievement on the other. There seems to be a general tendency for indexes of maternal intellectual ability and, by inference, maternal concern with the child's mental development, to be better predictors of cognitive development in daughters than sons.

One interpretation of this puzzling phenomenon rests on the fact that girls are biologically less variable than boys (Acheson, 1966). This implies that fewer infant girls would display extreme degrees of irritability, activity, or attentiveness. Let us assume the following principle: the more often the mother attempts to interest her child in an event the stronger the child's tendency to develop a general sensitivity to change and a capacity for sustained attention to discrepancy. This principle is likely to be less valid for infants who temperamentally have a tendency toward apathy or hyper-vigilance. There are many functional relations in nature that lose their validity when one of the variables assumes an extreme value, and this may be another instance of that phenomenon.

An alternative explanation of the stronger covariation for girls than boys between maternal intelligence and the child's mental development assumes greater differences between well and poorly educated mothers in their treatment of daughters than of sons, especially in maternal actions that promote attention and language acquisition. A mother seems more likely to project her motives, expectations, and self-image on her daughter than on her son, and is more likely to assume that her daughter will come to resemble her. Many poorly educated mothers feel less competent than the college graduate and have greater doubts about their daughters' potential for intellectual accomplishment. Such a mother may set or supply lower standards and less enthusiastic as well as less consistent encouragement to her infant girl to learn new skills. The well-educated mother sets higher aspirations and acts as though she held the power to catalyze her child's development.

The situation with sons is somewhat different. Most mothers, regardless of class background, believe their sons will have to learn how to support a family and achieve some degree of independence. Hence mothers of all classes may be more alike in energizing the cognitive development of sons. The restricted range of acceleration of sons, compared with daughters, would result in closer covariation for girls between social class and indexes of cognitive development.

This argument finds support in observations of the mother-child interaction in the home. Well-educated mothers are more likely to talk to their four-month-old daughters than mothers with less than a high school education. But this class difference in maternal "talkativeness" does not occur for sons. Observations of an independent sample of 60 mother-daughter pairs at 10 months of age (Tulkin, unpublished) also indicates that middle-, in contrast to lower-, class mothers spend significantly more time in face-to-face contact with their daughters, vocalize more often to them, and more frequently reward their attempts to crawl and stand. A final source of data is the home observations on some of the 180 children at 27 months. The observer noted each instance in which the mother reproved the child for disobeying a rule. Mothers of all social classes were more likely to reprove sons than daughters. However, reproval for incompetence at a task was most frequently meted out by the well-educated mothers of daughters; there was no comparable class difference for mothers of sons.

Thus, independent and complementary evidence supports the idea that differential pressures toward intellectual competence are more likely to covary with social class for mother-daughter than for mother-son pairs. It has usually been assumed that the girl is more concerned with acceptance by parents and teachers than the boy, and that this particular motive for intellectual accomplishment covaries with social class; but intellectual achievement among boys is spurred by more varied motives, including hostility, power, and identification with competent male figures—motives less closely linked to social class. However valid these propositions, they are not operative during the first year of life.

implications

The influence of contrast, discrepancy, and activation of hypotheses on distribution of attention is probably not limited to the first two years of life. Schools implicitly acknowledge the validity of these principles for older children by using books with contrasting colors and unusual formats and by emphasizing procedures whose aim is to ensure that the child has a relevant hypothesis available when he encounters a new problem. A child who possesses no hypothesis for solution of a problem is likely to withdraw from the task. Many children regard mathematics as more painful than English or social studies because they have fewer strategies to use with a difficult problem in arithmetic than for one in history or composition. The school might well give children more help in learning to generate

hypotheses with which to solve problems, and put less pressure on them to accumulate facts.

The principles discussed in this paper are also related to the issue of incentives for acquiring new knowledge. The behaviorist, trying to preserve the theoretical necessity of the concept of reinforcement, has been vexed by the fact that the child acquires new knowledge in the absence of any demonstrable external reward. However, the process of assimilating a discrepant event to a schema has many of the characteristics of a pleasant experience and therefore is in accord with the common understanding of a reward. The central problem in educating children is to attract and maintain focused attention. The central theoretical problem in understanding mental growth is to discern the factors that are continually producing change in schema and hypothesis. Solution of these two problems is not to be found through analyses of the environment alone. We must decipher the relation between the perceiver and the space in which he moves, for that theme, like Ariadne's thread, gives direction to cognitive growth.

REFERENCES

ACHESON, R. N. 1966. Maturation of the skeleton. In F. Falkner, ed. *Human development*. Philadelphia: W. B. Saunders, pp. 465–502.

BRACKBILL, Y., G. ADAMS, D. H. CROWELL, and M. C. GRAY. 1966. Arousal level in newborns and preschool children under continuous auditory stimulation. *J. Exp. Child Psychol.*, 3:176–88.

CARPENTER, G. C. Feb. 1969. Differential visual behavior to human and humanoid faces in early infancy. Presented at Merrill-Palmer Infancy Conference, Detroit, Mich.

CAZDEN, C. B. 1966. Subcultural differences in child language. *Merrill-Palmer Quart.*, 12:185–219.

DREYFUS-BRISAC, C., D. SAMSON, C. BLANC, and N. MONOD, 1958. L'électroencéphlograme de l'enfant normal de moins de trois ans. *Etudes néo-natales*, **7**:143–75.

EISENBERG, R. B., E. J. GRIFFIN, D. B. COURSIN, and M. A. HUNTER. 1964. Auditory behavior in the neonate. *J. Speech and Hearing Res.*, **7**:245–69.

ELLINGSON, R. J. 1967. Study of brain electrical activity in infants. In L. P. Lipsitt and C. C. Spiker, eds. *Advances in child development and behavior*. New York: Academic Press, pp. 53–98.

FANTZ, R. L. 1966. Pattern discrimination and selective attention as determinants of perceptual development from birth. In A. H. Kidd and J. J. Rivoire, eds. *Perceptual development in children*. New York: International Universities Press.

———, and S. NEVIS. 1967. Pattern preferences in perceptual cognitive development in early infancy. *Merrill-Palmer Quart.*, **13**:77–108.

FINLEY, G. E. 1967, Visual attention, play, and satiation in young children: a cross cultural study. Unpublished doctoral dissertation, Harvard Univ.

HAAF, R. A., and R. Q. BELL. 1967. A facial dimension in visual discrimination by human infants. *Child Devel.* **38**:893–99.

HAITH, M. M. 1966. Response of the human newborn to visual movement. *J. Exp. Child Psychol.*, **3**:235–43.

———. March 1968. Visual scanning in infants. Paper presented at regional meeting of Society for Research in Child Development. Clark Univ., Worcester, Mass.

HESS, R. D., V. C. SHIPMAN, J. E. BROPHY, and R. M. BEAR. 1968 and (follow-up phase) 1969. The cognitive environments of urban preschool children. Report to the Graduate School of Education, Univ. of Chicago.

KARMEL, B. Z. 1966. The effect of complexity, amount of contour, element size and element arrangement on visual preference behavior in the hooded rat, domestic chick, and human infant. Unpublished doctoral dissertation, George Washington Univ., Washington, D.C.

KUFFLER, S. W. 1952. Neurons in the retina: Organization, inhibition, and excitation problems. *Cold Spring Harbor Symposium in Quantitative Biology*, **17**:281–92.

———. 1953. Discharge patterns and functional organization of mammalian retina. *J. Physiol.*, **16**:37–68.

LEWIS, M. 1969. Infants' responses to facial stimuli during the first year of life. *Devel. Psychol.*, no. 2, pp. 75–86.

McCALL, R. B., and J. KAGAN. 1967. Attention in the infant: effects of complexity, contour, perimeter, and familiarity. *Child Devel.*, **38**:939–52.

———. 1970. Individual differences in the infant's distribution of attention to stimulus discrepancy. *Developmental Psychology*, **2**:90–98.

McCALL, R. B., and W. H. MELSON. March 1969. Attention in infants as a function of the magnitude of discrepancy and habituation rate. Paper presented at meeting of the Society for Research in Child Development. Santa Monica, Calif.

MAGOUN, H. W. 1969. Advances in brain research with implications for learning. In K. H. Pribram, ed., *On the biology of learning*. New York: Harcourt Brace Jovanovich, pp. 171–90.

MOSS, H. A. 1967. Sex, age and state as determinants of mother-infant interaction. *Merrill-Palmer Quart.*, **13**:19–36.

———, and K. S. ROBSON. 1968. Maternal influences on early social-visual behavior. *Child Devel.*, **39**:401–8.

SALAPATEK, P., and W. KESSEN. 1966. Visual scanning of triangles by the human newborn. *J. Exp. Child Psychol.*, **3**:113–22.

SUPER, C., J. KAGAN, F. MORRISON, and M. HAITH. An experimental test of the discrepancy hypothesis. Unpublished.

TULKIN, S. Social class differences in mother-child interaction. Unpublished.

WERNER, E. E. 1969. Sex differences in correlations between children's IQs and measure of parental ability and environment ratings. *Devel. Psychol.*, **1**:280–85.

WILCOX, B. M. 1969. Visual preferences of human infants for representations of the human face. *J. Exp. Child Psychol.*, **7**:10–20.

7

*It seems perfectly obvious that we must all learn to walk and to talk.
However, those of us with normal eyesight find it difficult even to
consider the possibility that we must also learn to use our eyes. In the next
article, Ivan London describes observations made on some Russian patients
shortly after the surgical removal of congenital cataracts. (Prior to this operation, the visual experience of these patients was probably limited to what you
would see if your eyes were continually covered with translucent parchment or
ping pong balls.) Although technical problems make interpretation of these
data somewhat difficult, the observations raise some important theoretical and
practical questions concerning the developmental nature of perceptual functioning.*

a Russian report on
the postoperative newly seeing

IVAN D. LONDON

Surgical acquirement of vision by the congenitally blind has always excited great
interest. Not only are the accounts of how
these people "learn to see" provocative, but
the theoretical implications of the process
discerned are of considerable significance.[1]
Authentic instances of cases where the congenitally or near-congenitally blind have
been rendered seeing are not many,[2] and
those that have been reported have been
the subject of dispute and interpretive dis-

agreement.[3] For this reason, any addition
to the literature reporting on restoration of
vision to the congenitally blind supplements
the meager stock of data extant and is,
therefore, welcome.

In 1953 an article describing several cases
of visual restoration appeared in *Vestnik
Oftalmologii* [*Herald of Ophthalmology*], a
Soviet journal.[4] While the account leaves
much to be desired, it is unusual in some
of its detail and also in that the writer of
the article himself, A. I. Pokrovskiĭ, Director of the Eye Clinic of the Voronezh Medical Institute, performed the surgery and

[1] D. O. Hebb, *The Organization of Behavior*,
1949, 1–335.

[2] M. von Senden, *Raum- und Gestaltauffassung
bei operierten Blindgeborenen vor und nach der
Operation*, 1932, 1–303.

Reprinted from *American Journal of Psychology*, 1960, 73: 478–482, by permission of the author and publisher. Copyright © 1960 by the
University of Illinois Press.

[3] M. Wertheimer, Hebb and Senden on the
role of learning in perception, *Amer. J. Psych.*, 64,
1951, 133–137.

[4] A. I. Pokrovskii, On the development of visual
perceptions and judgments in the postoperative
newly seeing in the light of the works of I. P.
Pavlov, *Vestn. Oftal.*, 32 (6), 1953, 6–17.

conducted the postoperative studies and observations. In other words, the account is not second-hand, but stems from direct personal encounter with the cases reported.

Pokrovskiĭ first reports on the cases of two children, born with mild cataracts which, while sight-depriving, permitted reaction to light. Pokrovskiĭ records the age of one of the children as 10 years at the time of operation, but fails to mention the age of the other. He reports the following of their progress toward visual perception:

1. After the operation both children were completely unable to recognize and name objects in their surroundings for some time, the duration of which varied for each. Their usual reaction was that they saw "something," but what it was, they did not know.
2. Both quickly and easily recognized and named objects on running their fingers over them if these objects were of a kind frequently encountered in their home surroundings and, hence, familiar.
3. If they looked [at] and simultaneously touched objects not ordinarily encountered in their home environment, but possessing forms and certain properties, tactilely discriminable and reminiscent of some familiar object or other, the children, on the basis of tactile contact, applied to the former names apropriate to the latter.
4. For both children forms of objects were not visually discriminated, but were tactilely determined.
5. Size and bulk of objects were similarly determined.
6. The children were unable by vision alone to determine distance or, more exactly, the distance of the nearest objects. When walking, they collided with these objects and in the beginning employed the customary method of the blind to avoid them, putting their hands out in front and touching the objects in their way.
7. Both children were completely unable by vision alone to determine the number of objects presented to them, but could do so by touch.
8. Nor did they determine colors as such, distinguishing them only by brightness

and naming one darker and another lighter.
9. They possessed no conception of perspective, and their conceptions of extent and space, developed through touch and movement, were very limited in comparison with the same conceptions in normal children of the same age.
10. In these newly seeing children, all the processes for discriminating objects, their form, size, etc., based in the beginning chiefly on the tactile-muscular analyzers [which include the receptors to the cortical termini], were without question carried out more slowly than in normal children operating by vision alone.

Pokrovskiĭ then considers the cases of two children who became blind in their early years and who had sight restored to them after an interval of five years. After stating that their postoperative progress to full vision was similar to that of the two cases reported on above, Pokrovskiĭ notes the following differences.

1. Although the children did not recognize objects and reacted to them with "I see something," they did distinguish the size of this "something" in comparison with an object of different size.
2. They distinguished the colors of objects, though not too descriptively, and correctly named them.
3. The most noteworthy feature of progress to fuller vision in comparison with that of the 2 born blind was its duration which was considerably shorter than in the case of the latter.

Pokrovskiĭ reports the following of the first case—a 9-year-old girl blinded at the age of five.

She said that she saw everything, but in the beginning—and of this one can be easily convinced—she did not perceive what she saw; without question she did not recognize by vision alone the familiar objects of her surroundings, though she could quickly recognize and name these objects on running her fingers over them. In other words, she had to compare the visual sensations, which after long blindness were new to her, with the tactile-motor perceptions customary for the blind in order immediately to recognize and, one may say, "see" the familiar object.

When she was shown a kitten, she said. "I see something gray; since I was a baby I have not seen anything like that." On touching it, she exclaimed joyfully—"a kitten!" She did not recognize a dog, but said, "I see something yellow." On stroking the dog's back with her hand, she immediately named it. On seeing a cow, she said, "I see something big, red and white." On seeing a horse, she said, "I see something big, gray and white." She looked long at this and the other animal, listened to the particular sound of their breathing, and after some prying questions about animals' tails, faces, and the like, said "horse?" When she looked at a flower, she said, "I see something green." On touching the flower, she correctly named it as a flower.

She did not recognize buckets of various sizes and color, but on handling them she correctly named them and correctly judged their differences in size and color.

The girl could not judge the form of objects merely on the basis of sight, but on touching them did distinguish their forms. She distinguished the color and size of 2 little containers presented to her—one round, the other four-cornered—but she correctly determined their respective forms only by manipulating them.

In the beginning the girl could not determine the distances to objects closest to her. All objects in front of her appeared very near to her. When requested to grasp any particular object, she extended her hand in the proper direction, but as a rule failed when trying to grasp even objects very near to her.

The girl walked about her room during the first postoperative days very uncertainly, stumbling and knocking against objects standing in her way. But after several days she began to walk with steadily increasing confidence and after 2 weeks was already leading other patients around. Only when she found herself in unfamiliar surroundings, did she move around more circumspectly.

She began rather quickly to recognize the objects about her, and at the time of discharge from the hospital, after 3 weeks, had begun without tactile intercession to utilize her vision, not in full, but in sufficient measure.

Pokrovskiĭ also refers to a second case—

a girl of 8 years, who was blinded at the age of three. He reports that the progress toward visual perception was similar to that above, but very much slower. She was kept in the hospital for 2½ months and at the time of her discharge was not as advanced as the other girl although, as long as her surroundings were of the familiar kind, she was able to see and recognize things in her environment.

Pokrovskiĭ concludes by citing the cases of two patients who were blinded in their very early years and who were restored to sight much later in life—16 and 54 years, respectively.

The 16 year old boy distinguished only light and grew up blind in a village as a member of a poor family living under very unfavorable conditions. Nobody had anything to do with him, and his mental development lagged greatly behind that of his seeing peers. His judgments of the surrounding world were elementary in the extreme. His behavior with respect to his surroundings before the operation reminded one of those born blind, and after a successful operation his development of visual perception also proceeded in accordance with that typical of the latter, but very slowly. While he recognized objects by fingering them, he was for a very long time unable to recognize them by sight alone. He did not have visual conceptions of size, form, bulk, color of objects, or their distance from him. He was unable to grasp an object in his visual field and erred many times in repeated attempts to accomplish this.

The patient was in the hospital for 2½ months after the operation and during this time learned to orient himself somewhat in his surroundings and to walk without stumbling against objects. He began to distinguish to some degree the form and size of objects and to distinguish their color not only by brightness but as more darkly or more brightly colored. However, even at the time of his discharge the visual perception of the patient was by no means as far advanced as in others with restored sight. From a letter, received from the patient 8 months after the operation, it was learned that he now goes about everywhere alone and distinguishes all colors of objects and that his vision has improved.

Concerning the patient who was blinded at the age of 2 or 3 years and who underwent surgery at the age of 54, Pokrovskiĭ then has this to report:

Before the operation he saw only light and did not distinguish color. He recognized his children and grandchildren by voice. Development of visual perception proceeded even more slowly than in the case just cited. Utilizing vision, he began to walk in the hospital with great difficulty and uncertainty. He was poor in recognizing people around him and, evidently, had frequent recourse to auditory cues in accordance with his previous wont. He would look for a long time at the face of his visiting son without recognizing him, but did so immediately at the sound of his voice. Unfortunately, it was not possible to keep track of this patient after discharge from the hospital.

Pokrovskiĭ discusses all of the above 6 cases in terms of Pavlovian theory and gives no indication of awareness of the differential importance of his observations and data for alternate theories. Pokrovskiĭ states that he and others have personally dealt with a number of other such cases, but restricts his account to the above six as representative. Direct communication with the author on his report, though attempted, has not yet been established.

8

*Subliminal perception refers to the influence on our behavior of phys-
ical stimuli of which we are unaware. In the next article McConnell,
Cutler, and McNeil consider some of the research dealing with this problem. In
addition to evaluating some of the methodological issues involved in demonstrations of subliminal perception, the authors discuss some of the ethical considerations which this phenomenon, if valid, may raise for psychologists.*

subliminal stimulation: an overview

JAMES V. MC CONNELL

RICHARD L. CUTLER

ELTON B. MC NEIL

Seldom has anything in psychology caused such an immediate and widespread stir as the recent claim that the presentation of certain stimuli below the level of conscious awareness can influence people's behavior in a significant way. The controversy was precipitated primarily by a commercial firm which claimed that the subliminal presentation of the words "Eat Popcorn" and "Drink Coca-Cola" fantastically stimulated the respective sales of these products among the motion picture audiences who received the stimulation. Despite the fact that detailed reports of the experiment have not been made directly available in any published form, this technique was seized upon as the newest of the "new look" promises of the application of psychology to advertising. While such claims and demonstrations will be considered in greater detail below, it is important to note here that they have given rise to a series of charges and

Reprinted from *American Psychologist*, 1958, 13: 229–242, by permission of the authors and publisher. Copyright © 1958 by the American Psychological Association.

countercharges, the effects of which have reached the United States Congress and the Federal Communications Commission (7, 117).

Rarely does a day pass without a statement in the public press relating to the Utopian promise or the 1984 threat of the technique (8, 17, 29, 37, 42, 45, 118, 132). Since the process of choosing up sides promises to continue unabated, it appears wise to provide the potential combatants with a more factual basis for arriving at their positions than presently seems available. Meanwhile, the present writers have cautiously sought to avoid aligning themselves behind either of the barricades.

Obviously, the notion that one may influence the behavior of another individual without the individual's knowing about it is a fascinating one. It is of extreme interest, not only to psychologists and advertisers, but also to politicians, psychiatrists, passionate young men, and others, whose motives would be considered more or less sacred by the larger society. Equally obvious is the need for a clarification of the issues surrounding the application of sub-liminal perception. This clarification must involve the assessment of available scientific evidence, the answering of a series of tech-nical questions, and the examination of what, if any, levels of behavior may indeed be influenced. Finally, a series of extremely complex ethical issues needs to be explored. It is the purpose of the present paper to undertake this task, in the hope of pro-viding information upon which possible de-cisions involving its application may be based.

recent history of the technique

The custom of providing a chronological review of the literature will be violated in this paper, inasmuch as three separate threads of investigation seem worth tracing: (a) the recent demonstrations by adver-tisers which first aroused large-scale public interest in subliminal perception, (b) sys-tematic research by psychologists relating directly to the influencing of behavior with-out the individual's awareness that he is being influenced, and (c) psychological re-search concerned primarily with the influ-ence of inner states of the organism upon the threshold for conscious recognition of certain stimuli.

RECENT ADVERTISING DEMONSTRATIONS

While the advertising possibilities of subliminal stimulation were recognized by Hollingworth (59) as early as 1913, the intensive work in its application to this area has been carried out within the past two years. In 1956, BBC-TV, in conjunction with one of its regular broadcasts, trans-mitted the message "Pirie Breaks World Record" at a speed assumed to be sublimi-nal (85). At the conclusion of the regular program, viewers were asked to report whether they had noticed "anything un-usual" about the program. While no re-liable statistical data are available, it seems

possible that those few viewers responding to the message possessed sufficiently low thresholds so that for them the message was supraliminal.

A demonstration by the commercial en-terprise which has been most vocal in its claims for the advertising promise of the technique consisted of projecting, during alternate periods, the words "Eat Popcorn" and "Drink Coca-Cola" during the regular presentation of a motion picture program. As a result of this stimulation, reports con-tend,[1] popcorn sales rose more than 50 percent and Coca-Cola sales 18 percent, as compared to a "previous period." Despite the likelihood of serious methodological and technical defects (exposure time was reported as 1/3,000 sec., far faster than any previously reported stimulation), this dem-onstration has been the one which has caused the most stir in both the fields of advertising and psychology. There were no reports, however, of even the most rudi-mentary scientific precautions, such as ade-quate controls, provision for replication, etc., which leaves the skeptical scientist in a poor position to make any judgment about the validity of the study.

In a later demonstration for the press, technical difficulties permitted the viewers to become consciously aware of the fact that they were being stimulated. Although described as a purposeful and prearranged part of the demonstration, it left many of the reporters present unconvinced that the technical difficulties inherent in the tech-nique have been surmounted.

The FCC, turning its attention to the problem, has reported that one TV station (WTWO, Bangor, Maine) has experi-mented with the transmission of public service announcements at subliminal levels, with "negative results" (117).

[1] The essential facts of this study have not been reported in any journal. The discussion of this ex-periment and the findings reported by the com-mercial enterprise responsible for the study is based on reports in several general news accounts appearing in the popular press (7, 8, 16, 17, etc.).

The uncontrolled and unsystematic nature of the demonstrations reported above makes very difficult the task of reaching a trustworthy conclusion about the effectiveness of subliminal stimulation in advertising. Whether the technique represents a promising means of communicating with the individual at a level of his unconsciousness or whether it reflects only the hyperenthusiasm of an entrepreneurial group remains an unanswered question.

RESEARCH ON BEHAVIOR WITHOUT AWARENESS

In the hope of providing a more substantial foundation upon which to base judgments of the validity of advertising claims for subliminal stimulation, a systematic review of relevant scientific work was undertaken. While we believe that our review was comprehensive, we have decided not to provide an extensive critical discussion of the various studies, choosing instead to present summative statements and conclusions based upon what seems to be sufficient evidence and consensus in the literature.[2]

The work of experimental psychologists in subliminal stimulation dates from Suslowa (119) in 1863, as reported by Baker (5). Suslowa's experiments concerned the effect of electrical stimulation upon subjects' ability to make two-point threshold discriminations. He found that, even when the intensity of the electrical stimulation was so low that the subjects were not aware of its presence, their ability to discriminate one- from two-point stimulation was somewhat reduced.

In 1884, Pierce and Jastrow (94) were able to show that subjects could discriminate differences between weights significantly better than chance would allow, even though the differences were so small they

[2] The reader who wishes a more complete technical critique of studies in the field is referred to reviews by Adams (1), Collier (27), Coover (28), Lazarus and McCleary (76), and Miller (90).

had no confidence whatsoever in their judgments.

Numerous experimenters have relied upon this criterion of "zero confidence" to establish that discrimination of stimuli presented below the level of conscious awareness is possible. For example, Sidis (107) showed that subjects could reliably distinguish letters from numbers, even when the stimuli were presented at such a distance from them that the subjects thought they were relying on pure guesswork for their judgments.

In what was essentially a replication of Sidis' research, Stroh, Shaw, and Washburn (116) found evidence to support his conclusions. They found similar results when auditory stimuli (whispers) were presented at a distance such that the subjects were not consciously aware that they were hearing anything.

Several experiments have provided further support for Peirce and Jastrow's initial conclusions (44, 127). Baker (5) found subjects able to discriminate diagonal from vertical crossed lines, and a dot-dash from a dash-dot auditory pattern. Miller (88) presented five geometric figures at four different levels of intensity below the threshold and found that, while subjects could discriminate which was being presented a significant proportion of the time, their ability to discriminate was reduced as the intensity of stimulation was further reduced. More recently, a series of studies by Blackwell (11) has shown that subjects can reliably identify during which of four time periods a subliminal spot of light is presented upon a homogeneous field. Blackwell, however, stresses that reliability of discrimination decreases as the intensity of the stimulus is further lowered. Several other supporting studies are available (28, 97, 130) which show essentially the same results, namely, that even when subjects have zero confidence in their judgments, they can discriminate reliably (though not perfectly) between stimuli.

In his review, Adams (1) points out certain general weaknesses inherent in studies of this type, but agrees with the present authors that discrimination can occur under certain circumstances. However, it is interesting to note that, in nearly all studies reporting relevant data, the reliability of the subjects' judgments increases directly with the intensity of the stimuli. If a valid extrapolation can be drawn from this finding, it would be that accuracy of perception increases as the stimulation approaches a supraliminal level.

A second series of studies has involved presenting subjects with variations of the Mueller-Lyer illusion, in which the angular lines have differed, subliminally, in hue or brightness from the background. The first of these studies, reported by Dunlap in 1909 (36), gave clear evidence that the subjects were influenced in their judgments of line length, even though they could not "see" the angular lines. Several replications of this study have been carried out, and while at least three have found partial support for Dunlap's conclusions (14, 59, 86), others have failed to find the phenomenon (123). In another experiment conducted by Sidis in 1898 (107), subjects asked to fixate on a number series in the center of a card, and then asked to pick a number from this series, systematically chose that number which was written in the periphery of the card, even though they were not consciously aware of its presence. Coover (28) in 1917 showed essentially the same results by asking subjects to pick a number at random while they were fixating on a letter in the upper right portion of a card. He found that subjects tended to pick the number printed in the lower left of the card, even though they did not *usually* know it was there. In similar experiments, Collier (27) and Perky (95) showed that subjects could be made to produce drawings, even though they were not aware that they were being influenced in their actions. While these studies are not unequivocal in their findings, nor generally rigorous in their methodology, they too seem to support the contention that behavior of a sort can be influenced by subliminal means.

However, they require cautious interpretation, since the degree of the subject's attention to the stimuli seems clearly to be a factor. Further, as contrasted to those studies where the subject is actually aware in advance of at least the general nature of the stimulation, these studies reveal a somewhat less pronounced effect of subliminal stimulation upon the subject's behavior.

While the studies reported above seem to indicate that discrimination without awareness may occur, it may reasonably be asked whether stimulation below the level of conscious awareness can produce any but the most simple modifications in behavior. A series of studies (24, 26, 73, 109), beginning with Newhall and Sears in 1933 (92), have attempted to show that it is possible to condition subjects to subliminal stimuli. Newhall and Sears found it possible to establish a weak and unstable conditioned response to light presented subliminally, when the light had been previously paired with shock. Baker (6) in 1938 reported the successful conditioning of the pupillary reflex to a subliminal auditory stimulus, but later experimenters have failed to replicate his results (57, 128). In a now classic experiment, McCleary and Lazarus (79) found that nonsense syllables which had previously been associated with shock produced a greater psychogalvanic reflex when presented tachistoscopically at subliminal speeds than did nonshock syllables. Deiter (34) confirmed the McCleary and Lazarus findings and showed further that, when verbal instructions were substituted for the shock, no such differences were produced. Bach and Klein (4) have recently reported that they were able to influence subjects' judgments of whether the line drawing of a face (essentially neutral in its emotional expression) was "angry" or "happy" by projecting the appropriate words at subliminal speeds upon the drawing.

A series of related studies (58, 65, 89, 99, 105, 121, 122) have shown that, even when the subject is not aware that any cue is being given, certain responses can be learned or strengthened during the experimental process. For example, Cohen, Kalish, Thurston, and Cohen (25) showed that, when the experimenter said "right" to any sentence which the subject started with "I" or "We," the number of such sentences increased significantly. Klein (69) was able to produce both conditioning and extinction without awareness, using the Cohen et al. technique.

Several experimenters have used subliminal or "unnoticed" reward-punishment techniques to modify subjects' responses in a variety of situations, including free or chained association tasks, performance on personality tests, and interview elicited conversation (35, 41, 50, 56, 72, 78, 93, 120, 125, 126). Typical is the work of Greenspoon (48), who reinforced the use of plural nouns by saying "mm-humm" after each plural mentioned by the subject. He found that, even though none of his subjects could verbalize the relationship between their response and his reinforcement, their use of plural nouns doubled. Sidowski (108) demonstrated essentially the same thing using a light, of which the subject was only peripherally aware, as a reinforcer for the use of plural words. Weiss (129), however, failed to find any increase in the frequency of "living things" responses, using a right-wrong reinforcement to free associations by the subjects.

This evidence suggests that subjects may either (*a*) "learn" certain subliminally presented stimuli or (*b*) make use of subliminal reinforcers either to learn or strengthen a previously learned response. Again, the critical observations of Adams (1) and the introduction of other possible explanations by Bricker and Chapanis (15) make necessary a cautious interpretation of these results.

EFFECTS OF INNER STATES UPON THRESHOLDS

Whatever the possibility that subliminal stimulation may significantly alter behavior, there is excellent evidence that certain inner states of the organism, as well as externally induced conditions, may significantly alter the recognition threshold of the individual. This, of course, has important implications for the susceptibility of the individual to the effects of subliminal stimulation. It is well known that physiological factors, such as fatigue, visual acuity, or satiation, may change the threshold of an individual for various kinds of stimuli.

Recent evidence has accumulated to show that, in addition to these physiological factors, certain "psychological states," such as psychological need, value, conflict, and defense, may also significantly influence thresholds, as well as other aspects of the perceptual process. Early work in this area is reported by Sanford (102, 103) who showed that subjects who had been deprived of food were more prone to produce "food-relevant" responses to a series of ambiguous stimuli. McClelland and Atkinson (80) showed that levels of the hunger drive were systematically related to the ease with which food responses were made when no words were presented on the screen.

While a complete review of the experimental work on "perceptual defense" and "selective vigilance" would take us too far afield, it seems wise to indicate, by example, some of the inner state factors which allegedly produce variations in recognition threshold. Bruner and Postman (19, 20, 21) and Bruner and Goodman (18) were able to show that such factors as symbolic value, need, tension and tension release, and emotional selectivity were important in the perceptual process. Ansbacher (3) had earlier demonstrated that the perception of numerosity was significantly affected by the monetary value of the stimuli. Rees and Israel (101) called attention to the fact that the mental set of the organism was an important factor in the perceptual process. Beams and Thompson (9) showed that emotional factors were important determiners of the perception of the magnitude of need-relevant objects. Other studies bearing upon the issue of inner state determiners of perception are reported by Carter and Schooler (23), Cowen and Beier (31, 32), and Levine, Chein, and Murphy (77).

More specifically related to the issue of altered recognition thresholds is a study by McGinnies (82) in which he demonstrated that emotionally toned words had generally higher thresholds than neutral words. Blum (13) has shown that subjects tend to be less likely to choose conflict-relevant stimuli from a group presented at subliminal speeds than to choose neutral stimuli. Lazarus, Ericksen, and Fonda (75) have shown that personality factors are at least in part determiners of the recognition threshold for classes of auditory stimuli. Reece (100) showed that the association of shock with certain stimuli had the effect of raising the recognition threshold for those stimuli.

While many writers have contended that the variations in threshold can be accounted for more parsimoniously than by introducing "motivational" factors such as need and value (60, 61, 111), and while the issue of the degree to which need states influence perception is still unresolved (22, 39, 40, 62, 74, 83), it is apparent that the recognition threshold is not a simple matter of intensity nor speed of presentation. Recent work by Postman and others (47, 96, 98), which has sought to illuminate the prerecognition processes operating to produce the apparent changes in threshold, does not alter the fact that individual differences in the perceptual process must be taken into account in any further work on the effects of subliminal stimulation.

unanswered methodological questions

Having now concluded that, under certain conditions, the phenomenon of subliminal perception does occur, we turn our attention next to the many unanswered questions which this conclusion raises. For example, what kinds of behavior can be influenced by subliminal stimulation? What types of stimuli operate best at subthreshold intensities? Do all subliminal stimuli operate at the same "level of unconscious-

ness," or do different stimuli (or modes of stimulation) affect different levels of unconsciousness? What characteristics of the perceiver help determine the effectiveness of subliminal stimulation? All of these questions, as well as many others of a technological nature, will be discussed in the ensuing paragraphs.

A few words of caution concerning the word "subliminal" seem in order, however. It must be remembered that the psychological limen is a statistical concept, a fact overlooked by far too many current textbook writers. The common definition of the limen is "that stimulus value which gives a response exactly half the time" (44, p. 111). One of the difficulties involved in analyzing the many studies on subliminal perception is the fact that many experimenters have assumed that, because the stimuli which they employed were below the statistical limen for a given subject, the stimuli were therefore never consciously perceivable by the subject. This is, of course, not true. Stimuli slightly below the statistical limen might well be consciously perceivable as much as 49 per cent of the time. Not only this, but thresholds vary from moment to moment, as well as from day to day. All this is not to deny that stimuli which are so weak that they are never consciously reportable under any circumstances may not indeed influence behavior. We simply wish to make the point that the range of stimulus intensities which are in fact "subliminal" may be smaller than many experimenters in the past have assumed. It has been commonly assumed that the several methods of producing subliminal stimuli, i.e., reducing intensity, duration, size, or clarity, are logically and methodologically equivalent. While this may be true, it remains to be demonstrated conclusively.

TYPES OF BEHAVIOR INFLUENCED BY SUBLIMINAL STIMULATION

One of the first questions that springs to mind concerns the types of response which can be elicited with subliminal stimulation. Let us assume for the moment that the below-threshold advertisements used in commercial demonstrations were the sole cause of increased popcorn buying among the movie audiences subjected to the ads. How did this come about? Did the stimulus "Eat Popcorn" elicit an already established response in some members of the audience? Or did the frequent repetitions of the stimulus message cause a shift in attitude towards popcorn eating which eventually resulted in the purchase of popcorn at the first opportunity the audience had? Did the ads merely raise an already existing, presumably learned, but weak need for popcorn to an above the action-threshold level, or did the ads actually create a need for popcorn where no need had existed beforehand? Did members of the audience rise like automatons during the course of the movie and thus miss part of the feature in order to satisfy a sudden craving for popcorn or in order to respond to a suddenly evoked stimulus-response connection? Or did they wait until a "rest period" to do their purchasing? How many patrons bought popcorn only after they had seen the film and were heading home? How many people purchased popcorn on their way *in* to see the next movie they attended? How many of those who purchased popcorn did so for the first time in their lives, or for the first time in recent memory? What if the message presented had been "Buy Christmas Seals," which are available only in one season? How many people failed to buy popcorn at the theater, but purchased it subsequently at the local supermarket?

Unfortunately, these pertinent questions have yet to be answered. Let us tentatively accept this demonstration that impulse buying of inexpensive items such as popcorn and Coca-Cola can be influenced by subliminal advertising, without yet knowing what the mechanism involved is. It remains to be demonstrated, however, that such ads could make a person of limited means wreck himself financially by purchasing a Cadillac merely because the ads told him to do so. Nor do we know if deep-seated, strongly emotional attitudes or long established behavior patterns can be shifted one way or another as a result of subliminal stimulation. The answers to these questions must come from further experimentation.

As we have already seen, people can make use of subthreshold stimuli in making difficult perceptual judgments in situations where they are required to call up images of various objects (95) and in situations where they are asked to "read the experimenter's mind" (88). Kennedy (68) believes that some extrasensory-perception (ESP) experimenters may have obtained positive results because the "senders" unconsciously transmitted slight auditory and visual cues to their "receivers," and offers many experimental findings to back up his belief. Kennedy's studies also point up the difficult dilemma faced by people who object to subliminal stimulation as being an immoral or illegal attempt to influence other people. All of us, apparently, are constantly attempting to influence the people around us by means of sounds and movements we are unconscious of making. Correspondingly, all of us make some unconscious use of the cues presented to us by the people around us.

It also seems fairly clear that learning can take place when the stimuli to which the organism must respond are presented subliminally. Hankin (51) learned to predict changes in the flight of birds by utilizing wing-tip adjustments which were too slight to be consciously (reportably) noticeable. As we stated previously, Baker (6) obtained a conditioned pupillary response to subliminal auditory stimuli, although other investigators failed to replicate his findings. Miller (89) had subjects look at a mirror while trying to guess geometrical forms in an ESP-type experiment. Stimuli far below the statistical limen were projected on a mirror from behind. When the subjects were rewarded by praise for correct guesses and punished by electric shock for wrong guesses, learning took place. It is interesting to note that neither punishment alone nor reward alone was sufficient to produce learning.

Whether different types of learning than those reported above can take place using subliminal stimulation, and indeed how broad a range of human behavior can be influenced in any way whatsoever by subliminal stimulation, are questions which remain unanswered.

LEVELS OF UNCONSCIOUSNESS AFFECTED BY SUBLIMINAL STIMULATION [3]

We must now differentiate between stimuli which a subject cannot bring to awareness under any conditions (completely subliminal stimuli) and those stimuli of which he is merely not aware at the moment but could be made aware of should his set be changed. At any given moment, a vast conflux of stimuli impinges upon a subject's receptors. Few of the sensations arising from this stimulation ever enter the focus of attention. As Dallenbach was fond of reminding his Freshman classes: "Until I mentioned it, you were quite unaware that your shoes are full of feet." A great many experimenters have demonstrated that subjects could make use of stimuli well above the threshold of awareness but which could not be consciously reported on. Thus in one phase of her experiment, Perky (95) raised the intensity of the visual stimuli she was using to such a level that other psychologists who had not participated in the study apparently refused to believe that the subjects had not been aware of the stimuli. Perky's subjects, however, operating under a set to call up "images" of the stimuli presented, did not notice even relatively intense stimuli. Correspondingly, Newhall

and Dodge (91) presented visual stimuli first at below-threshold intensities, then increased the intensities so slowly that the subjects were not aware of them even when the stimuli were well above threshold. When the stimuli were turned off suddenly, however, the subjects experienced afterimages. Thus certain stimuli may be well above threshold and yet be "subliminal" in the sense that they cannot be reported on under certain experimental conditions.

There are other levels of "unconsciousness" which are deserving of our attention, however. Much work has been done at the animal level in which conditioning has been attempted upon animals with various parts of the brain removed (33, 43). The same is true of animals under various types of anesthesia (106, 115). Miller, in summarizing the experimental data dealing with conditioning and consciousness, concludes:

a. That conditioning can take place in other parts of the nervous system than the cortex —even in the spinal cord;

b. That, if conditioned responses are evidences of consciousness, then consciousness is not mediated solely by the cortex;

c. That it may be possible to develop conditioning . . . at more than one level of the nervous system at the same time;

d. And that . . . animals are conditionable even when anesthetized [90, p. 100].

The nervous system has many levels of anatomical integration. Should we be surprised to discover that incoming stimuli may have an effect on a lower level and not on a higher and that under certain conditions this effect can later be demonstrated in terms of behavioral changes? We shall not be able to speak clearly of the effects of subliminal stimulation upon the various "levels of unconsciousness" until we have some better method of specifying exactly what these levels are and by what parts of the nervous system they are mediated. Experimentation is badly needed in this area.

---

[3] For an excellent review of the many meanings of the word "unconsciousness," readers are referred to Miller's book of the same name (90).

TECHNOLOGICAL PROBLEMS INVOLVED IN
STIMULATING SUBJECTS SUBLIMINALLY

The paucity of data presented by those dealing with subliminal perception on a commercial basis, as well as the equivocal nature of their results, suggests that there are many technological problems yet to be solved by these and other investigators. For example, during a two-hour movie (or a one-hour television show), how many times should the stimulus be repeated to make sure that the "message" gets across to the largest possible percentage of the audience? Should the stimulus be repeated every second, every five seconds, only once a minute? Is the effect cumulative, or is one presentation really enough? Is there a satiation effect, such that the audience becomes "unconsciously tired" of the stimulation, and "unconsciously blocks" the incoming subliminal sensations? Should the stimuli be presented "between frames" of the movie (that is, when the shutter of the film projector is closed and the screen momentarily blank as it is 24 times each second), or should the message be presented only when the screen already has a picture on it? How close to the threshold (statistical or otherwise) should the stimuli be? How many words long can the message be? If the message must be short, could successive stimulations present sequential parts of a longer advertisement? How much of the screen should the stimuli fill? Should the stimuli be presented only during "happier" moments in the film, in order to gain positive affect? Does any affect transfer at all from the film to the ad? Should one use pictures, or are words best? Must the words be familiar ones? And what about subliminal auditory, cutaneous, and olfactory stimulation?

As we have stated before, there has been so much talk and so little experimentation, and much of what experimentation has been done is so inadequately reported, that we can merely hazard guesses based on related but perhaps not always applicable studies.

To begin with, we can state with some assurance that, the closer to the threshold of awareness the stimuli are, the more effect they are likely to have. Study after study has reported increased effectiveness with increased intensity of stimulation (5, 14, 88, 97, 104). The main difficulty seems to be that thresholds vary so much from subject to subject (112), and from day to day (114), that what is subliminal but effective for one person is likely to be subliminal but ineffective for a second, and supraliminal for a third. As is generally the case, anyone who wishes to use the technique of subliminal stimulation must first experiment upon the specific group of people whom he wishes to influence before he can decide what intensity levels will be most efficacious.

Somewhat the same conclusion holds for the question of how many times the stimuli should be presented. While under some conditions subliminal stimuli which did not influence behavior when presented only once seemed to "summate" when presented many times (10, 66), Bricker and Chapanis (15) found that one presentation of a stimulus slightly below the (statistical) limen was enough to increase the likelihood of its being recognized on subsequent trials. We interpret this to mean that too many presentations may well raise the "subliminal" stimuli above the limen of awareness if the stimuli themselves are not carefully chosen.

As for the physical properties of the message itself, we can but guess what the relevant issues are. Both verbal and pictorial presentations apparently are effective in the visual modality, but no one has tested the relative effectiveness of these two types of stimulation. Quite possibly subsequent experimentation will show that words are best for some situations (such as direct commands), while pictures are best for others.[4] It can be stated unequivocally, however, that advertisers should look to their basic English when writing their sub-liminal commercials. Several studies have shown that, the more familiar a subject is with the stimulus he is to perceive, the more readily he perceives it (22, 54, 63, 110). We interpret these studies to mean that unfamiliar stimuli may be ineffective when presented subliminally, even though familiar messages may "get through."

The exact length the message should be, its composition, and the background in which it should be presented are variables upon which no work has been done and about which no conclusions can presently be drawn. Suffice it to say, however, that a message which would be short enough to be perceived by one person might be too long for another person to perceive under any conditions.

Which modalities are most useful for subliminal stimulation? While most of the work has been done on the visual modality, Vanderplas and Blake (124) and Kurland (71) have found subthreshold auditory stimuli to be effective, and earlier in this paper we have reported similar studies with cutaneous stimulation. Advertisers who wish to "sneak up on" their patrons by presenting subliminal stimuli in one mo-dality while the patrons are attending to supraliminal stimuli from another modality are probably doomed to failure, however. Collier (27) presented subliminal geo-metric forms simultaneously to both the visual and the cutaneous modalities and found little, if any, lowering of thresholds. Correspondingly, it should be remembered that Hernández-Peón et al. (55) found that some part of the nervous system acts as a kind of gating mechanism, and when an organism is attending strongly to one mo-dality, the other modalities are probably "shut off" to most incoming stimuli.

Even if experimenters succeed in finding answers to many of the questions raised above concerning the physical characteris-tics of the stimuli to be employed, it is quite probable that they will have suc-ceeded in discovering the source of only a small part of the variance operant in sub-liminal perception. For, as always, the major source of variance will come from the perceiver himself.

CHARACTERISTICS OF THE PERCEIVER WHICH AFFECT SUBLIMINAL PERCEPTION

The following section of this paper might well be considered a plea for the recog-nition that individual differences exist and that they must be taken into account by anyone who wishes to deal with individ-uals. We know next to nothing about the relationships between such factors as age, sex, social class, etc., and subliminal per-ception. Perhaps only one study is relevant: Perky (95) found that children were as much influenced by subthreshold visual stimulation as were naive adults. It is quite likely that many differences in the percep-tion of subliminal stimuli do exist between individuals of differing classes, ages, and sexes. As always, only experimentation can determine what these differences are.

We do have some idea, however, of how what might be called "personality factors" influence subliminal perception. First and foremost, there seems little doubt but that a high need state affects perception. Gil-christ and Nesberg (46) found that the greater the need state, the more their sub-jects tended to overestimate the brightness of objects relevant to that need. It should be noted that they were dealing with dif-ference limens, not absolute limens, but other studies to be quoted later show the same effect for absolute limens. It should be noted also that Gilchrist and Nesberg apparently overlooked evidence in their

---

[4] Perhaps much of the work on sensory precon-ditioning is applicable here. When Ellson (38) presented his subjects with both a light and a buzzer for many trials, then presented the light alone, subjects "heard" the buzzer too.

own data that a strong need affects judgments of non-need-related objects in the same direction (but not as much) as it does need-related objects. Wispé and Drambarean, dealing with visual duration thresholds, concluded that "need-related words were recognized more rapidly as need increased" (131, p. 31). McClelland and Lieberman (81) found that subjects with high need achievement scores had lower visual thresholds for "success" words than did subjects not scoring as high on need achievement. Do all of these findings mean that subliminal ads will work only when some fairly strong need (of any kind) is present in the viewers? Only experimentation can answer this question.

What about abnormalities of personality? What effect do they have? Kurland (71) tested auditory recognition thresholds using emotional and neutral words. He found that hospitalized neurotics perceived the emotional words at significantly lower thresholds than did a group of normal subjects. Does this mean that neurotics are more likely to respond to low-intensity subliminal commands than normals? Should advertisers take a "neurotic inventory" of their audiences?

A more pertinent problem is posed by the findings of Krech and Calvin (70). Using a Wechsler Vocabulary Score of 30.5 as their cutting point, they found that almost all college students above this score showed better visual discriminations of patterns presented at close to liminal values than did almost all students scoring below the cutting point. Does this mean that the higher the IQ, the better the subliminal perception? What is the relationship between the value of the absolute limen and intelligence? Will advertisers have to present their messages at such high intensities (in order that the "average man" might perceive the message) that the more intelligent members of the audience will be consciously aware of the advertising?

One further fascinating problem is posed by Huntley's work (64). He surreptitiously obtained photographs of the hands and profiles of his subjects, as well as handwriting samples and recordings of their voices. Six months later each subject was presented with the whole series of samples, among which were his own. Each subject was asked to make preference ratings of the samples. Huntley reports evidence of a significant tendency for subjects to prefer their own forms of expression above all others, even though in most cases they were totally unaware that the samples were their own and even though many subjects were unable to identify their own samples when told they were included in the series. If an advertiser is making a direct appeal to one specific individual, it would seem then that he should make use of the photographs and recordings of that individual's behavior as the subliminal stimuli. If an advertiser is making an appeal to a more general audience, however, it might be that he would find the use of pictures and recordings of Hollywood stars, etc., more efficacious than mere line drawings, printed messages, and unknown voices.

Nor can the advertiser afford to overlook the effects of set and attention. Miller (88), Perky (95), and Blake and Vanderplas (12), among others, discovered that giving the subject the proper set lowered the recognition threshold greatly. In fact, in many cases the stimulus intensity which was subliminal but effective for sophisticated subjects was far too subliminal to have much, if any, effect upon naive subjects. Thus advertisers might do well to tell their audiences that subliminal messages were being presented to them, in order to bring all members of that audience closer to a uniform threshold. Does this not, however, vitiate some of the effect of subliminal advertising?

As for attentional effects, we have presented evidence earlier (46) that strong needs seem to have an "alerting" effect upon the organism, lowering recognition thresholds for *all* stimuli, not just need-related stimuli. In addition to this, two studies by Hartmann (52, 53), as well as two by Spencer (113, 114), lead us to the belief that subliminal stimuli might best be presented when either the television or movie screen was blank of other pictures. Perhaps, then, subliminal commercials in movie houses should be shown between features; while on television the commercials should consist of an appropriate period of apparent "visual silence," during which the audience would not be aware of the subliminal stimulation presented, but might react to it later.

One fact emerges from all of the above. Anyone who wishes to utilize subliminal stimulation for commercial or other purposes can be likened to a stranger entering into a misty, confused countryside where there are but few landmarks. Before this technique is used in the market place, if it is to be used at all, a tremendous amount of research should be done, and by competent experimenters.

the ethics of subliminal influence

From its beginnings as a purely academic offshoot of philosophy, psychology has, with ever increasing momentum, grown in the public perception as a practical and applied discipline. As psychologists were called upon to communicate and interpret their insights and research findings to lay persons, it was necessary to make decisions about what constituted proper professional behavior, since it was evident that the misuse of such information would reflect directly on the community of psychologists. As a growing number of our research efforts are viewed as useful to society, the problem of effective and honest communication becomes magnified, although its essential nature does not change. Recently, to our dismay, the announcement of a commercial application of long established psychological principles has assumed nightmarish qualities, and we find ourselves unwillingly cast in the role of invaders of personal

privacy and enemies of society. A kind of guilt by association seems to be occurring, and, as future incidents of this kind will, it threatens to undermine the public relations we have built with years of caution and concern for the public welfare. The highly emotional public reaction to the "discovery" of sublimal perception should serve as an object lesson to our profession, for in the bright glare of publicity we can see urgent ethical issues as well as an omen of things to come. When the theoretical notion $E = MC^2$ became the applied reality of an atom bomb, the community of physicists became deeply concerned with social as well as scientific responsibility. Judging from the intensity of the public alarm when confronted with a bare minimum of fact about this subliminal social atom, there exists a clear need for psychologists to examine the ethical problems that are a part of this era of the application of their findings.

The vehemence of the reaction to the proposed use of a device to project subliminal, or from the public's point of view "hidden," messages to viewers indicates that the proposal touches a sensitive area. One of the basic contributors to this reaction seems to be the feeling that a technique which avowedly tampers with the psychological status of the individual ought to be under the regulation or control of a trusted scientific group. As a professional group, psychologists would fit this description, for in the *Ethical Standards of Psychologists* (2) there is a clear statement of their motives and relationship to society:

Principle 1.12–1   The psychologist's ultimate allegiance is to society, and his professional behavior should demonstrate an awareness of his social responsibilities. The welfare of the profession and of the individual psychologist are clearly subordinate to the welfare of the public. . . .

Both this statement and the long record of responsible behavior of the members of the profession would certainly seem to be sufficient to reduce any anxiety the public might have over the possible unscrupulous use of this or any other device. It is precisely the fact that the public *is* aware that decisions about the use of subliminal perception devices rest not with psychologists but with commercial agencies that may be distressing to the public. The aura of open-for-business flamboyance and the sketchily presented percentages in the first public announcement tended to reinforce existing apprehensions rather than allay them.

Although subliminal perception happens now to be the focus of a great deal of reaction, it is merely the most recent in a succession of perturbing events to which the public has been exposed. It has become the focus of, and is likely to become the whipping boy for, a host of techniques which now occupy the twilight zone of infringement of personal psychological freedom. It must be remembered that to the lay person the notion of an unconscious part of the "mind" is eerie, vague, and more than a little mysterious. Unable fully to comprehend the systematic and theoretical aspects of such a concept, he must be content with overly popularized and dramatic versions of it. In every form of mass media the American public has been exposed to convincing images of the bearded hypnotist (with piercing eye) who achieves his nefarious ends by controlling the unconscious of his victim. It has been treated to the spectacle of the seeming reincarnation of Bridey Murphy out of the unconscious of an American housewife and, in *Three Faces of Eve*, to complex multiple personalities hidden in the psychic recesses of a single individual. With such uncanny and disturbing images as an emotional backdrop, the appearance of *The Hidden Persuaders* on the best seller lists formed the indelible impression of the exploitation of the unconscious for purposes of profit and personal gain. In combination, this growth of emotionally charged attitudes toward the unconscious and the suspicions about commercial morality came to be a

potentially explosive set of tensions which was triggered off by the first commercial use of subliminal techniques.

What is to be the psychologist's position in regard to future developments with subliminal perception? The apparent discrepancy between the claims being made for the technique and the available research evidence suggests a need for considerable scientific caution as well as extensive investigation. The responsibility of psychologists in this instance is clearly indicated in the code of ethics:

Principle 2.12–1   The psychologist should refuse to suggest, support, or condone unwarranted assumptions, invalid applications, or unjustified conclusions in the use of psychological instruments or techniques.

The flurry of claim and opinion about the effectiveness of subliminal methods seems to be based more on enthusiasm than controlled scientific experimentation, and it is here that psychology can be of service. Until acceptable scientific answers are forthcoming, we believe psychologists should guard against a premature commitment which might jeopardize public respect for them. The course of scientific history is strewn with the dessicated remains of projects pursued with more vigor than wisdom.

Scientific caution is essential, but it falls short of meeting the ethical issue raised by the nature of subliminal perception itself. The most strident public objections have been directed toward the possibility that suggestions or attempts to influence or persuade may be administered without the knowledge or consent of the audience. Assurances that widespread adoption of this technique would provide increased enjoyment through the elimination of commercial intrusions, or that the users will establish an ethical control over the content of the messages presented, can only fail to be convincing in light of past experience. The suggestion that the public can be taught means of detecting when it is being exposed to a planned subliminal stimulation is far from reassuring since such a suggestion implies that the ability to defend oneself warrants being attacked. A captive audience is not a happy audience, and even the plan to inform the viewers in advance concerning the details of what is to be presented subliminally may not prevent the public from reacting to this technique as a demand that it surrender an additional degree of personal freedom. Fresh from similar encounters, the public may not allow this freedom to be wrested from it.

Finally, the argument that a great deal of our normal perception occurs on the fringe of conscious awareness and that subliminal events are no more effective than weak conscious stimuli rests on opinion and not fact. This seems particularly dangerous clinical ground on which to tread since the effect, on behavior, of stimuli which may possibly be inserted directly into the unconscious has yet to be explored. Assurances that this technique can only "remind" a person of something he already knows or "support" a set of urges already in existence but cannot establish a completely new set of urges or needs are reckless assertions having no evidence to support them. So it seems that the aspect of subliminal projection which is marked by the greatest potential risk to the individual's emotional equilibrium is the aspect about which the least is scientifically known.

The psychologist's ethical quandary, then, stems directly from the inescapable implication of deviousness in the use of such a technique. The appropriate guidelines for conduct are provided in this ethical statement:

Principle 2.62–2 It is unethical to employ psychological techniques for devious purposes, for entertainment, or for other reasons not consonant with the best interests of a client or with the development of psychology as a science.

It is obvious that "devious purposes" and "the best interests . . . of psychology as a science" are not self-defining terms and must be interpreted by the individual psychologist in light of the circumstances of each situation. It is a trying and complex decision to make. If in his mature judgment the intended uses of the principles of subliminal perception do not meet acceptable ethical standards, the psychologist is obligated to diassociate himself from the endeavor and to labor in behalf of the public welfare to which he owes his first allegiance. In this respect, the responsibility of the social scientist must always be that of watchdog over his own actions as well as the actions of those to whom he lends his professional support.

The furor which promises to accompany the further application of a variety of devices involving subliminal perception is certain to embroil psychology in a dispute not of its own choosing. The indiscriminate and uncontrolled application of psychological principles is increasing at a fearsome rate in the form of motivation research, propaganda, public relations, and a host of other "useful" practices based on the work of psychologists. In a very real sense this era of applied psychology will be a test of the workability of the psychologist's code of ethics and promises to stimulate the profession to give further consideration to its responsibility for assisting society to use its findings wisely.

REFERENCES

1. ADAMS, J. K. Laboratory studies of behavior without awareness. *Psychol. Bull.,* 1957, **54**, 383–405.
2. AMERICAN PSYCHOLOGICAL ASSOCIATION, Committee on Ethical Standards for Psychology. *Ethical standards of psychologists.* Washington: APA, 1953.
3. ANSBACHER, H. Perception of number as affected by the monetary value of the objects. *Arch. Psychol.,* 1937, **30**, No. 215.
4. BACH, S., and G. S. KLEIN. Conscious effects of prolonged subliminal exposures

of words. *Amer. Psychologist,* 1957, **12,** 397. (Abstract)

5. BAKER, L. E. The influence of subliminal stimuli upon verbal behavior. *J. exp. Psychol.,* 1937, **20,** 84–100.

6. ———. The pupillary response conditioned to subliminal auditory stimuli. *Psychol. Monogr.,* 1938, **50,** No. 3 (Whole No. 223).

7. Ban on subliminal ads, pending FCC probe, is urged. *Adv. Age,* 1957, **28,** No. 45.

8. BATTELLE, PHYLLIS. The lady objects to id tampering. *Publishers Auxiliary,* 1957, **92,** No. 40.

9. BEAMS, H. L., and G. G. THOMPSON. Affectivity as a factor in the perception of the magnitude of food objects. *Amer. Psychologist,* 1952, **7,** 323. (Abstract)

10. BEITEL, R. J., JR. Spatial summation of subliminal stimuli in the retina of the human eye. *J. gen. Psychol.,* 1934, **10,** 311–327.

11. BLACKWELL, H. R. Personal communication, 1958.

12. BLAKE, R. R., and J. M. VANDERPLAS. The effects of prerecognition hypotheses on veridical recognition thresholds in auditory perception. *J. Pers.,* 1950–1951, **19,** 95–115.

13. BLUM, G. S. Perceptual defense revisited. *J. abnorm. soc. Psychol.,* 1955, **56,** 24–29

14. BRESSLER, J. Illusion in the case of subliminal visual stimulation. *J. gen. Psychol.,* 1931, **5,** 244–250.

15. BRICKER, P. D., and A. CHAPANIS. Do incorrectly perceived tachistoscopic stimuli convey some information? *Psychol. Rev.,* 1953, **60,** 181–188.

16. BRITT, S. H. Subliminal advertising—fact or fantasy? *Adv. Age,* 1957, **28,** 103.

17. BROOKS, J. The little ad that isn't there. *Consumer Rep.,* 1957, **23,** No. 1.

18. BRUNER, J. S., and C. C. GOODMAN. Value and need as organizing factors in perception. *J. abnorm. soc. Psychol.,* 1947, **42,** 33–44.

19. BRUNER, J. S., and L. POSTMAN. Emotional selectivity in perception and action. *J. Pers.,* 1947, **16,** 69–77.

20. ———. Tension and tension-release as organizing factors in perception. *J. Pers.,* 1947, **16,** 300–308.

21. ———. Symbolic value as an organizing factor in perception. *J. soc. Psychol.* 1948, **27,** 203–208.

22. ———. Perception, cognition, and behavior. *J. Pers.,* 1949, **18,** 14–31.

23. CARTER, L. F., and K. SCHOOLER. Value, need, and other factors in perception. *Psychol. Rev.,* 1949, **56,** 200–207.

24. CASON, H., and NAOMI KATCHER. An attempt to condition breathing and eyelid responses to a subliminal electric stimulus. *J. exp. Psychol.,* 1934, **16,** 831–842.

25. COHEN, B. D., H. I. KALISH, J. R. THURSTON, and E. COHEN. Experimental manipulation of verbal behavior. *J. exp. Psychol.,* 1954, **47,** 106–110.

26. COHEN, L. H., E. R. HILGARD, and G. R. WENDT. Sensitivity to light in a case of hysterical blindness studied by reinforcement-inhibition and conditioning methods. *Yale J. Biol. Med.,* 1933, **6,** 61–67.

27. COLLIER, R. M. An experimental study of the effects of subliminal stimuli. *Psychol. Monogr.,* 1940, **52,** No. 5 (Whole No. 236).

28. COOVER, J. E. Experiments in psychical research. *Psychical Res. Monogr.,* 1917, No. 1.

29. COUSINS, N. Smudging the subconscious. *Saturday Rev.,* 1957, **40,** No. 40.

30. COWEN, E. L., and E. G. BEIER. The influence of "threat-expectancy" on perception. *J. Pers.,* 1950–1951, **19,** 85–94.

31. ———. A further study of the "threat-expectancy" variable in perception. *Amer. Psychologist,* 1952, **7,** 320–321. (Abstract)

32. ———. Threat-expectancy, word frequencies, and perceptual prerecognition hypotheses. *J. abnorm. soc. Psychol.,* 1954, **49,** 178–182.

33. CULLER, E., and F. A. METTLER. Conditioned behavior in a decorticate dog. *J. comp. Psychol.,* 1934, **18,** 291–303.

34. DEITER, J. The nature of subception. Unpublished doctoral dissertation, Univer. of Kansas, 1953.

35. DIVEN, K. Certain determinants in the conditioning of anxiety reactions. *J. Psychol.,* 1937, **3,** 291–308.

36. DUNLAP, K. Effect of imperceptible shadows on the judgments of distance. *Psychol. Rev.,* 1900, **7,** 435–453.

JAMES V. MC CONNELL / RICHARD L. CUTLER / ELTON B. MC NEIL **93**

37. DuSHANE, G. The invisible word, or no thresholds barred. *Science,* 1957, **126,** 681.

38. ELLSON, D. G. Hallucinations produced by sensory conditioning. *J. exp. Psychol.,* 1941, **28,** 1–20.

39. ERIKSEN, C. W. The case for perceptual defense. *Psychol. Rev.,* 1954, **61,** 175–182.

40. ———. Subception: Fact or artifact? *Psychol. Rev.,* 1956, **63,** 74–80.

41. ———, and J. L. KUETHE. Avoidance conditioning of verbal behavior without awareness: A paradigm of repression. *J. abnorm. soc. Psychol.,* 1956, **53,** 203–209.

42. FINK, A. A. Questions about subliminal advertising. New York: Author, 1957.

43. FOLEY, J. P., JR. The cortical interpretation of conditioning. *J. gen. Psychol.,* 1933, **9,** 228–234.

44. FULLERTON, G. S., and J. McK. CATTELL. On the perception of small differences. *Univer. Penn. Publ., Philos. Ser.,* 1892, No. 2.

45. "Ghost" ads overrated. *Sci. Newsltr.,* 1957, **72,** No. 17.

46. GILCHRIST, J. C., and L. S. NESBERG. Need and perceptual change in need-related objects. *J. exp. Psychol.,* 1952, **44,** 369–376.

47. GOODNOW, JACQUELINE J., and L. POSTMAN. Probability learning in a problem-solving situation. *J. exp. Psychol.,* 1955, **49,** 16–22.

48. GREENSPOON, J. The reinforcing effect of two spoken sounds on the frequency of two responses. *Amer. J. Psychol.,* 1955, **68,** 409–416.

49. GUILFORD, J. P. *Psychometric methods.* New York: McGraw-Hill, 1936.

50. HAGGARD, E. A. Experimental studies in affective processes: I. Some effects of cognitive structure and active participation on certain autonomic reactions during and following experimentally induced stress. *J. exp. Psychol.,* 1943, **33,** 257–284.

51. HANKIN, H. *Common sense.* New York: Dutton, 1926.

52. HARTMANN, G. W. I. The increase of visual acuity in one eye through the illumination of the other. *J. exp. Psychol.,* 1933, **16,** 383–392.

53. ———. II. Changes in visual acuity through simultaneous stimulation of other sense organs. *J. exp. Psychol.,* 1933, **16,** 393–407.

54. HENLE, MARY. An experimental investigation of past experience as a determinant of visual form perception. *J. exp. Psychol.,* 1942, **30,** 1–21.

55. HERNÁNDEZ-PEÓN, R., H. SCHERRER, and J. MICHEL. Modification of electrical activity of cochlear nucleus during "attention" in unanesthetized cats. *Science,* 1955, **123,** 331–332.

56. HILDUM, D. C., and R. W. BROWN. Verbal reinforcement and interviewer bias. *J. abnorm. soc. Psychol.,* 1956, **53,** 108–111.

57. HILGARD, E. R., J. MILLER, and J. A. OHLSON. Three attempts to secure pupillary conditioning to auditory stimuli near the absolute threshold. *J. exp. Psychol.,* 1941, **29,** 89–103.

58. HILGARD, E. R., and G. R. WENDT. The problem of reflex sensitivity to light studied in a case of hemianopsia. *Yale J. Biol. Med.,* 1933, **5,** 373–385.

59. HOLLINGWORTH, H. L. *Advertising and selling.* New York: Appleton, 1913.

60. HOWES, D. A statistical theory of the phenomenon of subception. *Psychol. Rev.,* 1954, **61,** 98–110.

61. ———. On the interpretation of word frequency as a variable affecting speed of recognition. *J. exp. Psychol.,* 1954, **48,** 106–112.

62. ———, and R. L. SOLOMON. A note on McGinnies' "Emotionality and perceptual defense." *Psychol. Rev.,* 1950, **57,** 235–240.

63. ———. Visual duration threshold as a function of word probability. *J. exp. Psychol.,* 1951, **41,** 401–410.

64. HUNTLEY, C. W. Judgments of self based upon records of expressive behavior. *J. abnorm. soc. Psychol.,* 1953, **48,** 398–427.

65. IRWIN, F. W., K. KAUFMAN, G. PRIOR, and H. B. WEAVER. On "Learning without awareness of what is being learned." *J. exp. Psychol.,* 1934, **17,** 823–827.

66. KARN, H. W. The function of intensity in the spatial summation of subliminal stimuli in the retina. *J. gen. Psychol.,* 1935, **12,** 95–107.

67. KENNEDY, J. L. Experiments on "unconscious whispering." *Psychol. Bull.*, 1938, **35**, 526. (Abstract)

68. ———. A methodological review of extrasensory perception. *Psychol. Bull.*, 1939, **36**, 59–103.

69. KLEIN, G. S., D. MEISTER, and H. J. SCHLESINGER. The effect of personal values on perception: An experimental critique. *Amer. Psychologist*, 1949, **4**, 252–253. (Abstract)

70. KRECH, D., and A. CALVIN. Levels of perceptual organization and cognition. *J. abnorm. soc. Psychol.*, 1953, **48**, 394–400.

71. KURLAND, S. H. The lack of generality in defense mechanisms as indicated in auditory perception. *J. abnorm. soc. Psychol.*, 1954, **49**, 173–177.

72. LACEY, J. I., and R. L. SMITH. Conditioning and generalization of unconscious anxiety. *Science*, 1954, **120**, 1045–1052.

73. ———, and A. GREEN. Use of conditioned autonomic responses in the study of anxiety. *Psychosom. Med.*, 1955, **17**, 208–217.

74. LAZARUS, R. S. Subception: Fact or artifact? A reply to Eriksen. *Psychol. Rev.*, 1956, **63**, 343–347.

75. ———, C. W. ERIKSEN, and C. P. FONDA. Personality dynamics and auditory perceptual recognition. *J. Pers.*, 1950–1951, **19**, 471–482.

76. LAZARUS, R. S., and R. A. McCLEARY. Autonomic discrimination without awareness: A study of subception. *Psychol. Rev.*, 1951, **58**, 113–122.

77. LEVINE, R., I. CHEIN, and G. MURPHY. The relation of the intensity of a need to the amount of perceptual distortion. *J. Psychol.*, 1942, **13**, 283–293.

78. LYSAK, W. The effects of punishment upon syllable recognition thresholds. *J. exp. Psychol.*, 1954, **47**, 343–350.

79. McCLEARY, R. A., and R. S. LAZARUS. Autonomic discrimination without awareness: An interim report. *J. Pers.*, 1949, **18**, 171–179.

80. McCLELLAND, D. C., and J. W. ATKINSON. The projective expression of needs: I. The effect of different intensities of the hunger drive on perception. *J. Psychol.*, 1948, **25**, 205–222.

81. McCLELLAND, D. C., and A. M. LIEBER-

MAN. The effect of need for achievement on recognition of need-related words. *J. Pers.*, 1949, **18**, 236–251.

82. McGINNIES, E. Emotionality and perceptual defense. *Psychol. Rev.*, 1949, **56**, 244–251.

83. ———. Discussion of Howes' and Solomon's note on "Emotionality and perceptual defense." *Psychol. Rev.*, 1950, **57**, 229–234.

84. MANDLER, G., and W. K. KAPLAN. Subjective evaluation and reinforcing effect of a verbal stimulus. *Science*, 1956, **124**, 582–583.

85. MANNES, MARYA. Ain't nobody here but us commercials. *Reporter*, 1957, **17**, No. 6.

86. MANRO, H. M., and M. F. WASHBURN. Effect of imperceptible lines on judgment of distance. *Amer. J. Psychol.*, 1908, **19**, 242–243.

87. Michigan State prof. tells weaknesses of invisible commercials. *Publishers Auxiliary*, 1957, **92**, No. 40.

88. MILLER, J. G. Discrimination without awareness. *Amer. J. Psychol.*, 1939, **52**, 562–578.

89. ———. The role of motivation in learning without awareness. *Amer. J. Psychol.*, 1940, **53**, 229–239.

90. ———. *Unconsciousness*. New York: Wiley, 1942.

91. NEWHALL, S. M., and R. DODGE. Colored afterimages from unperceived weak chromatic stimulation. *J. exp. Psychol.*, 1927, **10**, 1–17.

92. NEWHALL, S. M., and R. R. SEARS. Conditioning finger retraction to visual stimuli near the absolute threshold. *Comp. psychol. Monogr.*, 1933, **9**, No. 43.

93. NUTHMANN, ANNE M. Conditioning of a response class on a personality test. *J. abnorm. soc. Psychol.*, 1957, **54**, 19–23.

94. PEIRCE, C. S., and J. JASTROW. On small differences of sensation. *Mem. Nat. Acad. Sci.*, 1884, **3**, 73–83.

95. PERKY, C. W. An experimental study of imagination. *Amer. J. Psychol.*, 1910, **21**, 422–452.

96. PHILBRICK, E. B., and L. POSTMAN. A further analysis of "learning without awareness." *Amer. J. Psychol.*, 1955, **68**, 417–424.

97. PILLAI, R. P. B. K. A study of the thresh-

old in relation to the investigations on subliminal impressions and allied phenomena. *Brit. J. educ. Psychol.*, 1939, **9**, 97–98.

98. POSTMAN, L., and R. F. JARRETT. An experimental analysis of "learning without awareness." *Amer. J. Psychol.*, 1952, **65**, 244–255.

99. RAZRAN, G. Stimulus generalization of conditioned responses. *Psychol. Bull.*, 1949, **46**, 337–365.

100. REECE, M. M. The effect of shock on recognition thresholds. *J. abnorm. soc. Psychol.*, 1954, **49**, 165–172.

101. REES, H. J., and H. E. ISRAEL. An investigation of the establishment and operation of mental sets. *Psychol. Monogr.*, 1935, **46**, No. 6 (Whole No. 210).

102. SANFORD, R. N. The effects of abstinence from food upon imaginal processes: A preliminary experiment. *J. Psychol.*, 1936, **2**, 129–136.

103. ———. The effects of abstinence from food upon imaginal processes: A further experiment. *J. Psychol.*, 1937, **3**, 145–159.

104. SCHAFER, T. H. Influence of the preceding item on units of the noise masked threshold by a modified constant method. *J. exp. Psychol.*, 1950, **40**, 365–371.

105. SEARS, R. R., and L. H. COHEN. Hysterical anesthesia, analgesia, and astereognosis. *Arch. Neurol. Psychiat.*, 1933, **29**, 260–271.

106. SETTLAGE, T. The effect of sodium amytal on the formation and elicitation of conditioned reflexes. *J. comp. Psychol.*, 1936, **22**, 339–343.

107. SIDIS, B. *The psychology of suggestion.* New York: Appleton, 1898.

108. SIDOWSKI, J. B. Influence of awareness of reinforcement on verbal conditioning. *J. exp. Psychol.*, 1954, **48**, 355–360.

109. SILVERMAN, A., and L. E. BAKER. An attempt to condition various responses to subliminal electrical stimulation. *J. exp. Psychol.*, 1935, **18**, 246–254.

110. SMOKE, K. L. An objective study of concept formation. *Psychol. Monogr.*, 1932, **42**, No. 4 (Whole No. 191).

111. SOLOMON, R. L., and D. H. HOWES. Word frequency, personal values, and visual duration thresholds. *Psychol. Rev.*, 1951, **58**, 256–270.

112. SOLOMON, R. L., and L. POSTMAN. Frequency of usage as a determinant of recognition thresholds for words. *J. exp. Psychol.*, 1952, **43**, 195–201.

113. SPENCER, L. T. The concept of the threshold and Heymans' law of inhibition: I. Correlation between the visual threshold and Heymans' coefficient of inhibition of binocular vision. *J. exp. Psychol.*, 1928, **11**, 88–97.

114. ———, and L. H. COHEN. The concept of the threshold and Heymans' law of inhibition: II. *J. exp. Psychol.*, 1928, **11**, 194–201.

115. STERLING, K., and J. G. MILLER. Conditioning under anesthesia. *Amer. J. Psychol.*, 1941, **54**, 92–101.

116. STROH, M., A. M. SHAW, and M. F. WASHBURN. A study in guessing. *Amer. J. Psychol.*, 1908, **19**, 243–245.

117. Subliminal ad okay if it sells: Lessler; FCC peers into subliminal picture on TV. *Adv. Age*, 1957, **28**, No. 48.

118. Subliminal ads wash no brains, declare Moore, Becker, developers of precon device. *Adv. Age*, 1957, **28**, No. 48.

119. SUSLOWA, M. Veranderungen der Hautgefule unter dem Einflusse electrischer Reizung. *Z. Rationelle Med.*, 1863, **18**, 155–160.

120. TAFFEL, C. Anxiety and the conditioning of verbal behavior. *J. abnorm. soc. Psychol.*, 1955, **51**, 496–501.

121. THORNDIKE, E. L. *The fundamentals of learning.* New York: Teachers College, Columbia Univer., 1932.

122. ———, and R. T. ROCK. Learning without awareness of what is being learned or intent to learn it. *J. exp. Psychol.*, 1934, **17**, 1–19.

123. TITCHNER, E. B., and W. H. PYLE. Effect of imperceptible shadows on the judgment of distance. *Proc. Amer. phil. Soc.*, 1907, **46**, 94–109.

124. VANDERPLAS, J. M., and R. R. BLAKE. Selective sensitization in auditory perception. *J. Pers.*, 1949, **18**, 252–266.

125. VERPLANCK, W. S. The control of the content of conversation: Reinforcement of statements of opinion. *J. abnorm. soc. Psychol.*, 1955, **51**, 668–676.

126. ———. The operant conditioning of human motor behavior. *Psychol. Bull.*, 1956, **53**, 70–83.

127. VINACKE, W. E. The discrimination of color and form at levels of illumination below conscious awareness. *Arch. Psychol.*, 1942, 38, No. 267.

128. WEDELL, C. H., F. V. TAYLOR, and A. SKOLNICK. An attempt to condition the pupillary response. *J. exp. Psychol.*, 1940, 27, 517–531.

129. WEISS, R. L. The influence of "set for speed" on "learning without awareness."

Amer. J. Psychol., 1955, 68, 425–431.

130. WILLIAMS, A. C. Perception of subliminal visual stimuli. *J. Psychol.*, 1938, 6, 187–199.

131. WISPÉ, L. G., and N. C. DRAMBAREAN. Physiological need, word frequency, and visual duration threshold. *J. exp. Psychol.*, 1953, 46, 25–31.

132. WOOLF, J. D. Subliminal perception is nothing new. *Adv. Age*, 1957, 28, No. 43.

UNIT

learning and memory

9

The experiment reported in the next paper by John B. Watson (the father of behaviorism) and Rosalie Rayner is perhaps the most famous in American psychology. It represents one of the first attempts to investigate the role of classical conditioning in the acquisition of fear by infants. The experiment also demonstrated the importance of stimulus generalization ("transfer") in fear conditioning. Although Watson and Rayner missed the opportunity to attempt to extinguish or eliminate the conditioned fear response, the methods and principles they suggested are amazingly similar to those successfully used by many contemporary behaviorally oriented psychotherapists.

conditioned emotional reactions

JOHN B. WATSON

ROSALIE RAYNER

In recent literature various speculations have been entered into concerning the possibility of conditioning various types of emotional response, but direct experimental evidence in support of such a view has been lacking. If the theory advanced by Watson and Morgan [1] to the effect that in infancy the original emotional reaction patterns are few, consisting so far as observed of fear, rage and love, then there must be some simple method by means of which the range of stimuli which can call out these emotions and their compounds is greatly increased. Otherwise, complexity in adult response could not be accounted for. These authors without adequate experimental evidence advanced the view that this range was increased by means of conditioned reflex factors. It was suggested

there that the early home life of the child furnishes a laboratory situation for establishing conditioned emotional responses. The present authors have recently put the whole matter to an experimental test.

Experimental work has been done so far on only one child, Albert B. This infant was reared almost from birth in a hospital environment; his mother was a wet nurse in the Harriet Lane Home for Invalid Children. Albert's life was normal: he was healthy from birth and one of the best developed youngsters ever brought to the hospital, weighing twenty-one pounds at nine months of age. He was on the whole stolid and unemotional. His stability was one of the principal reasons for using him as a subject in this test. We felt that we could do him relatively little harm by carrying out such experiments as those outlined below.

At approximately nine months of age we ran him through the emotional tests that have become a part of our regular

[1] "Emotional Reactions and Psychological Experimentation," *American Journal of Psychology*, April, 1917, Vol. 28, pp. 163–174.

Reprinted from *Journal of Experimental Psychology*, 1920, 3: 1–14.

routine in determining whether fear reactions can be called out by other stimuli than sharp noises and the sudden removal of support. Tests of this type have been described by the senior author in another place.[2] In brief, the infant was confronted suddenly and for the first time successively with a white rat, a rabbit, a dog, a monkey, with masks with and without hair, cotton, wool, burning newspapers, etc. A permanent record of Albert's reactions to these objects and situations has been preserved in a motion picture study. Manipulation was the most usual reaction called out. *At no time did this infant ever show fear in any situation.* These experimental records were confirmed by the casual observations of the mother and hospital attendants. No one had ever seen him in a state of fear and rage. The infant practically never cried.

Up to approximately nine months of age we had not tested him with loud sounds. The test to determine whether a fear reaction could be called out by a loud sound was made when he was eight months, twenty-six days of age. The sound was that made by striking a hammer upon a suspended steel bar four feet in length and three-fourths of an inch in diameter. The laboratory notes are as follows:

One of the two experimenters caused the child to turn its head and fixate her moving hand; the other, stationed back of the child, struck the steel bar a sharp blow. The child started violently, his breathing was checked and the arms were raised in a characteristic manner. On the second stimulation the same thing occurred, and in addition the lips began to pucker and tremble. On the third stimulation the child broke into a sudden crying fit. This is the first time an emotional situation in the laboratory has produced any fear or even crying in Albert.

We had expected just these results on account of our work with other infants brought up under similar conditions. It is

[2] *Psychology from the Standpoint of a Behaviorist* (Philadelphia: Lippincott, 1919), p. 202.

worthwhile to call attention to the fact that removal of support (dropping and jerking the blanket upon which the infant was lying) was tried exhaustively upon this infant on the same occasion. It was not effective in producing the fear response. This stimulus is effective in younger children. At what age such stimuli lose their potency in producing fear is not known. Nor is it known whether less placid children ever lose their fear of them. This probably depends upon the training the child gets. It is well known that children eagerly run to be tossed into the air and caught. On the other hand it is equally well known that in the adult fear responses are called out quite clearly by the sudden removal of support, if the individual is walking across a bridge, walking out upon a beam, etc. There is a wide field of study here which is aside from our present point.

The sound stimulus, thus, at nine months of age, gives us the means of testing several important factors. I. Can we condition fear of an animal, *e.g.*, a white rat, by visually presenting it and simultaneously striking a steel bar? II. If such a conditioned emotional response can be established, will there be a transfer to other animals or other objects? III. What is the effect of time upon such conditioned emotional responses? IV. If after a reasonable period such emotional responses have not died out, what laboratory methods can be devised for their removal?

I. The establishment of conditioned emotional responses. At first there was considerable hesitation upon our part in making the attempt to set up fear reactions experimentally. A certain responsibility attaches to such a procedure. We decided finally to make the attempt, comforting ourselves by the reflection that such attachments would arise anyway as soon as the child left the sheltered environment of the nursery for the rough and tumble of the home. We did not begin this work until Albert was eleven months, three days of age. Before attempting to set up a conditioned response we, as before, put him through all of the regular emotional tests. *Not the slightest sign of a fear response was obtained in any situation.*

The steps taken to condition emotional responses are shown in our laboratory notes.

11 MONTHS 3 DAYS

1. White rat suddenly taken from the basket and presented to Albert. He began to reach for rat with left hand. Just as his hand touched the animal the bar was struck immediately behind his head. The infant jumped violently and fell forward, burying his face in the mattress. He did not cry, however.
2. Just as the right hand touched the rat the bar was again struck. Again the infant jumped violently, fell forward and began to whimper.

In order not to disturb the child too seriously no further tests were given for one week.

11 MONTHS 10 DAYS

1. Rat presented suddenly without sound. There was steady fixation but no tendency at first to reach for it. The rat was then placed nearer, whereupon tentative reaching movements began with the right hand. When the rat nosed the infant's left hand, the hand was immediately withdrawn. He started to reach for the head of the animal with the forefinger of the left hand, but withdrew it suddenly before contact. It is thus seen that the two joint stimulations given the previous week were not without effect. He was tested with his blocks immediately afterwards to see if they shared in the process of conditioning. He began immediately to pick them up, dropping them, pounding them, etc. In the remainder of the tests the blocks were given frequently to quiet him and to test his general emotional state. They were always removed from sight when the process of conditioning was under way.
2. Joint stimulation with rat and sound. Started, then fell over immediately to right side. No crying.

3. Joint stimulation. Fell to right side and rested upon hands, with head turned away from rat. No crying.
4. Joint stimulation. Same reaction.
5. Rat suddenly presented alone. Puckered face, whimpered and withdrew body sharply to the left.
6. Joint stimulation. Fell over immediately to right side and began to whimper.
7. Joint stimulation. Started violently and cried, but did not fall over.
8. Rat alone. *The instant the rat was shown the baby began to cry. Almost instantly he turned sharply to the left, fell over on left side, raised himself on all fours and began to crawl away so rapidly that he was caught with difficulty before reaching the edge of the table.*

This was as convincing a case of a completely conditioned fear response as could have been theoretically pictured. In all seven joint stimulations were given to bring about the complete reaction. It is not unlikely had the sound been of greater intensity or of a more complex clang character that the number of joint stimulations might have been materially reduced. Experiments designed to define the nature of the sounds that will serve best as emotional stimuli are under way.

II. When a conditioned emotional response has been established for one object, is there a transfer? Five days later Albert was again brought back into the laboratory and tested as follows:

11 MONTHS 15 DAYS

1. Tested first with blocks. He reached readily for them, playing with them as usual. This shows that there has been no general transfer to the room, table, blocks, etc.
2. Rat alone. Whimpered immediately, withdrew right hand and turned head and trunk away.
3. Blocks again offered. Played readily with them, smiling and gurgling.
4. Rat alone. Leaned over to the left side as far away from the rat as possible, then fell over, getting up on all fours and scurrying away as rapidly as possible.

5. Blocks again offered. Reached immediately for them, smiling and laughing as before.

The above preliminary test shows that the conditioned response to the rat had carried over completely for the five days in which no tests were given. The question as to whether or not there is a transfer was next taken up.

6. Rabbit alone. The rabbit was suddenly placed on the mattress in front of him. The reaction was pronounced. Negative responses began at once. He leaned as far away from the animal as possible, whimpered, then burst into tears. When the rabbit was placed in contact with him he buried his face in the mattress, then got up on all fours and crawled away, crying as he went. This was a most convincing test.

7. The blocks were next given him, after an interval. He played with them as before. It was observed by four people that he played far more energetically with them than ever before. The blocks were raised high over his head and slammed down with a great deal of force.

8. Dog alone. The dog did not produce as violent a reaction as the rabbit. The moment fixation occurred the child shrank back and as the animal came nearer he attempted to get on all fours but did not cry at first. As soon as the dog passed out of his range of vision he became quiet. The dog was then made to aproach the infant's head (he was lying down at the moment). Albert straightened up immediately, fell over to the opposite side and turned his head away. He then began to cry.

9. The blocks were again presented. He began immediately to play with them.

10. Fur coat (seal). Withdrew immediately to the left side and began to fret. Coat put close to him on the left side, he turned immediately, began to cry and tried to crawl away on all fours.

11. Cotton wool. The wool was presented in a paper package. At the end the cotton was not covered by the paper. It was placed first on his feet. He kicked it away but did not touch it with his hands. When his hand was laid on the wool he immediately withdrew it but did not show the

shock that the animals or fur coat produced in him. He then began to play with the paper, avoiding contact with the wool itself. He finally, under the impulse of the manipulative instinct, lost some of his negativism to the wool.

12. Just in play W. put his head down to see if Albert would play with his hair. Albert was completely negative. Two other observers did the same thing. He began immediately to play with their hair. W. then brought the Santa Claus mask and presented it to Albert. He was again pronouncedly negative.

11 MONTHS 20 DAYS

1. Blocks alone. Played with them as usual.

2. Rat alone. Withdrawal of the whole body, bending over to left side, no crying. Fixation and following with eyes. The response was much less marked than on first presentation the previous week. It was thought best to freshen up the reaction by another joint stimulation.

3. Just as the rat was placed on his hand the rod was struck. Reaction violent.

4. Rat alone. Fell over at once to left side. Reaction practically as strong as on former occasion but no crying.

5. Rat alone. Fell over to left side, got up on all fours and started to crawl away. On this occasion there was no crying, but strange to say, as he started away he began to gurgle and coo, even while leaning far over to the left side to avoid the rat.

6. Rabbit alone. Leaned over to left side as far as possible. Did not fall over. Began to whimper but reaction not so violent as on former occasions.

7. Blocks again offered. He reached for them immediately and began to play.

All of the tests so far discussed were carried out upon a table supplied with a mattress, located in a small, well-lighted dark-room. We wished to test next whether conditioned fear responses so set up would appear if the situation were markedly altered. We thought it best before making this test to freshen the reaction both to the rabbit and to the dog by showing them at the moment the steel bar was struck. It will be recalled that this was the first time any effort had been made to directly condition response to the dog and rabbit. The experimental notes are as follows:

8. The rabbit at first was given alone. The reaction was exactly as given in test (6) above. When the rabbit was left on Albert's knees for a long time he began tentatively to reach out and manipulate its fur with forefingers. While doing this the steel rod was struck. A violent fear reaction resulted.
9. Rabbit alone. Reaction wholly similar to that on trial (6) above.
10. Rabbit alone. Started immediately to whimper, holding hands far up, but did not cry. Conflicting tendency to manipulate very evident.
11. Dog alone. Began to whimper, shaking head from side to side, holding hands as far away from the animal as possible.
12. Dog and sound. The rod was struck just as the animal touched him. A violent negative reaction appeared. He began to whimper, turned to one side, fell over and started to get up on all fours.
13. Blocks. Played with them immediately and readily.

On this same day and immediately after the above experiment Albert was taken into the large well-lighted lecture room belonging to the laboratory. He was placed on a table in the center of the room immediately under the skylight. Four people were present. The situation was thus very different from that which obtained in the small dark room.

1. Rat alone. No sudden fear reaction appeared at first. The hands, however, were held up and away from the animal. No positive manipulatory reactions appeared.
2. Rabbit alone. Fear reaction slight. Turned to left and kept face away from the animal but the reaction was never pronounced.
3. Dog alone. Turned away but did not fall over. Cried. Hands moved as far away from the animal as possible. Whimpered as long as the dog was present.
4. Rat alone. Slight negative reaction.
5. Rat and sound. It was thought best to freshen the reaction to the rat. The sound was given just as the rat was presented. Albert jumped violently but did not cry.
6. Rat alone. At first he did not show any negative reaction. When rat was placed

nearer he began to show negative reaction by drawing back his body, raising his hands, whimpering, etc.
7. Blocks. Played with them immediately.
8. Rat alone. Pronounced withdrawal of body and whimpering.
9. Blocks. Played with them as before.
10. Rabbit alone. Pronounced reaction. Whimpered with arms held high, fell over backward and had to be caught.
11. Dog alone. At first the dog did not produce the pronounced reaction. The hands were held high over the head, breathing was checked, but there was no crying. Just at this moment the dog, which had not barked before, barked three times loudly when only about six inches from the baby's face. Albert immediately fell over and broke into a wail that continued until the dog was removed. The sudden barking of the hitherto quiet dog produced a marked fear response in the adult observers!

From the above results it would seem that emotional transfers do take place. Furthermore it would seem that the number of transfers resulting from an experimentally produced conditioned emotional reaction may be very large. In our observations we had no means of testing the complete number of transfers which may have resulted.

III. The effect of time upon conditioned emotional responses. We have already shown that the conditioned emotional response will continue for a period of one week. It was desired to make the time test longer. In view of the imminence of Albert's departure from the hospital we could not make the interval longer than one month. Accordingly no further emotional experimentation was entered into for thirty-one days after the above test. During the month, however, Albert was brought weekly to the laboratory for tests upon right- and left-handedness, imitation, general development, etc. No emotional tests whatever were given and during the whole month his regular nursery routine was maintained in the Harriet Lane Home. The notes on the test given at the end of this period are as follows:

1 YEAR 21 DAYS

1. Santa Claus mask. Withdrawal, gurgling, then slapped at it without touching. When his hand was forced to touch it, he whimpered and cried. His hand was forced to touch it two more times. He whimpered and cried on both tests. He finally cried at the mere visual stimulus of the mask.
2. Fur coat. Wrinkled his nose and withdrew both hands, drew back his whole body and began to whimper as the coat was put nearer. Again there was the strife between withdrawal and the tendency to manipulate. Reached tentatively with left hand but drew back before contact had been made. In moving his body to one side his hand accidentally touched the coat. He began to cry at once, nodding his head in a very peculiar manner (this reaction was an entirely new one). Both hands were withdrawn as far as possible from the coat. The coat was then laid on his lap and he continued nodding his head and whimpering, withdrawing his body as far as possible, pushing the while at the coat with his feet but never touching it with his hands.
3. Fur coat. The coat was taken out of his sight and presented again at the end of a minute. He began immediately to fret, withdrawing his body and nodding his head as before.
4. Blocks. He began to play with them as usual.
5. The rat. He allowed the rat to crawl towards him without withdrawing. He sat very still and fixated it intently. Rat then touched his hand. Albert withdrew it immediately, then leaned back as far as possible but did not cry. When the rat was placed on his arm he withdrew his body and began to fret, nodding his head. The rat was then allowed to crawl against his chest. He first began to fret and then covered his eyes with both hands.
6. Blocks. Reaction normal.
7. The rabbit. The animal was placed directly in front of him. It was very quiet. Albert showed no avoiding reactions at first. After a few seconds he puckered up his face, be-

gan to nod his head and to look intently at the experimenter. He next began to push the rabbit away with his feet, withdrawing his body at the same time. Then as the rabbit came nearer he began pulling his feet away, nodding his head, and wailing "da da." After about a minute he reached out tentatively and slowly and touched the rabbit's ear with his right hand, finally manipulating it. The rabbit was again placed in his lap. Again he began to fret and withdrew his hands. He reached out tentatively with his left hand and touched the animal, shuddered and withdrew the whole body. The experimenter then took hold of his left hand and laid it on the rabbit's back. Albert immediately withdrew his hand and began to suck his thumb. Again the rabbit was laid in his lap. He began to cry, covering his face with both hands.
8. Dog. The dog was very active. Albert fixated it intensely for a few seconds, sitting very still. He began to cry but did not fall over backwards as on his last contact with the dog. When the dog was pushed closer to him he at first sat motionless, then began to cry, putting both hands over his face.

These experiments would seem to show conclusively that directly conditioned emotional responses as well as those conditioned by transfer persist, although with a certain loss in the intensity of the reaction, for a longer period than one month. Our view is that they persist and modify personality throughout life. It should be recalled again that Albert was of an extremely phlegmatic type. Had he been emotionally unstable probably both the directly conditioned response and those transferred would have persisted throughout the month unchanged in form.

IV. "Detachment" or removal of conditioned emotional responses. Unfortunately Albert was taken from the hospital the day the above tests were made. Hence the opportunity of building up an experimental technique by means of which we could remove the conditioned emotional responses was denied us. Our own view, expressed above, which is possibly not very well grounded, is that these responses in the home environment are likely to persist indefinitely, unless an accidental method for removing them is hit upon. The importance of establishing some method must be apparent to all. Had the opportunity been at hand we should have tried out several methods, some of which we may mention. (1) Constantly confronting the child with those stimuli which called out the responses in the hopes that habituation would come in corresponding to "fatigue" of reflex when differential reactions are to be set up. (2) By trying to "recondition" by showing objects calling out fear responses (visual) and simultaneously stimulating the erogenous zones (tactual). We should try first the lips, then the nipples and as a final resort the sex organs. (3) By trying to "recondition" by feeding the subject candy or other food just as the animal is shown. This method calls for the food control of the subject. (4) By building up "constructive" activities around the object by imitation and by putting the hand through the motions of manipulation. At this age imitation of overt motor activity is strong, as our present but unpublished experimentation has shown.

incidental observations

(a) Thumb sucking as a compensatory device for blocking fear and noxious stimuli. During the course of these experiments, especially in the final test, it was noticed that whenever Albert was on the verge of tears or emotionally upset generally he would continually thrust his thumb into his mouth. The moment the hand reached the mouth he became impervious to the stimuli producing fear. Again and again while the motion pictures were being made at the end of the thirty-day rest period, we had to remove the thumb from his mouth before the conditioned response could be obtained. This method of blocking noxious and emotional stimuli (fear and rage) through

erogenous stimulation seems to persist from birth onward. Very often in our experiments upon the work adders with infants under ten days of age the same reaction appeared. When at work upon the adders both of the infants' arms are under slight restraint. Often rage appears. They begin to cry, thrashing their arms and legs about. If the finger gets into the mouth crying ceases at once. The organism thus apparently from birth, when under the influence of love stimuli, is blocked to all others.[3] This resort to sex stimulation when under the influence of noxious and emotional situations, or when the individual is restless and idle, persists throughout adolescent and adult life. Albert, at any rate, did not resort to thumb sucking except in the presence of such stimuli. Thumb sucking could immediately be checked by offering him his blocks. These invariably called out active manipulation instincts. It is worthwhile here to call attention to the fact that Freud's conception of the stimulation of erogenous zones as being the expression of an original "pleasure" seeking principle may be turned about and possibly better described as a compensatory (and often conditioned) device for the blockage of noxious and fear and rage producing stimuli.

(b) Equal primacy of fear, love and possibly rage. While in general the results of our experiment offer no particular points of conflict with Freudian concepts, one fact out of harmony with them should be emphasized. According to proper Freudians sex (or in our terminology, love) is the principal emotion in which conditioned responses arise which later limit and distort personality. We wish to take sharp issue

[3] The stimulus to love in infants according to our view is stroking of the skin, lips, nipples and sex organs, patting and rocking, picking up, etc. Patting and rocking (when not conditioned) are probably equivalent to actual stimulation of the sex organs. In adults of course, as every lover knows, vision, audition and olfaction soon become conditioned by joint stimulation with contact and kinaesthetic stimuli.

with this view on the basis of the experimental evidence we have gathered. Fear is as primal a factor as love in influencing personality. Fear does not gather its potency in any derived manner from love. It belongs to the original and inherited nature of man. Probably the same may be true of rage although at present we are not so sure of this.

The Freudians twenty years from now, unless their hypotheses change, when they come to analyze Albert's fear of a seal skin coat—assuming that he comes to analysis at that age—will probably tease from him the recital of a dream which upon their analysis will show that Albert at three years of age attempted to play with the pubic hair of the mother and was scolded violently for it. (We are by no means denying that this might in some other case condition it.) If the analyst has sufficiently prepared Albert to accept such a dream when found as an explanation of his avoiding tendencies, and if the analyst has the authority and personality to put it over, Albert may be fully convinced that the dream was a true revealer of the factors which brought about the fear.

It is probable that many of the phobias in psychopathology are true conditioned emotional reactions either of the direct or the transferred type. One may possibly have to believe that such persistence of early conditioned responses will be found only in persons who are constitutionally inferior. Our argument is meant to be constructive. Emotional disturbances in adults cannot be traced back to sex alone. They must be retraced along at least three collateral lines—to conditioned and transferred responses set up in infancy and early youth in all three of the fundamental human emotions.

10

*In recent years, we have seen an increased tendency by edu-
cators to supplement traditional types of instruction by employing teaching machines or programmed instructional devices. Although
most college students have probably had contact with some type of "teaching
machine," they are often surprised to learn that the devices were designed on
the basis of principles of learning developed in laboratory research largely on
rats and pigeons. In the next article, James Holland discusses some of these
basic concepts. The effective user of teaching machines must know as much
about learning principles as he does about the subject he is trying to teach.*

teaching machines: an application of principles from the laboratory [1]

JAMES G. HOLLAND

Much has been said of teaching machines recently—but the emphasis has tended to be on the gadgets rather than on the much more significant development of a new technology of education initiated by B. F. Skinner (1954, 1958). The technology does use a device called a teaching machine, which presents a finely graded series of problems and provides immediate "reward" or reinforcement for the student's correct answers. But emphasis on machines has tended to obscure the more important facets

of the new technology based on application of principles from the laboratory. The machines of today are not necessarily better than those of yesterday. Indeed, adequate machines could have been built hundreds of years ago. The movement today is not simply the mechanization of teaching, but instead the development of a new technology—a behavioral engineering of teaching procedures.

The history of unsuccessful teaching machines illustrates the relatively greater importance of the technique as opposed to the gadgets. The first teaching machine was patented 93 years ago. There have since been a series of patents and a promising burst of activity initiated by Sidney Pressey (1926) in the 1920's. None of these early efforts really caught hold. But during this period in which the idea of mechanized teaching has been latent, the science of behavior has developed principles which permit extremely precise control of behavior. This new technology is not only the so-

[1] This article was previously presented before the 1959 Invitational Conference on Testing Problems sponsored by the Educational Testing Service, and appears in the *Proceedings of the Invitational Conference on Testing Problems* of 1960. The work discussed in this paper has been supported by grants from the Carnegie Corporation and the Ford Foundation.

Reprinted from *Journal of the Experiment Analysis of Behavior*, 1960, 3: 275–287, by permission of the author and publisher. Copyright © 1960 by the Society for the Experimental Analysis of Behavior, Inc.

called automation of teaching, but is an attempt to obtain the kind of behavioral control shown possible in the laboratory.

We have, of course, seen other practical applications of scientific psychology. We are all familiar with the development of a technology of testing, which permits placing an individual in situations suited to his abilities. We are also familiar with another technology called human engineering, which fits machines and jobs to the capacities of man. One places a man in a job that suits him; the other alters the job to suit the man; *neither* attempts to alter or control man's behavior.

For years in the laboratory we have controlled the behavior of experimental subjects—both animal and human—by a widening array of principles and techniques. The new technology of education is the application of behavioral laws in modifying or controlling behavior. Such a technology became possible with the realization that we are actually referring to a verbal repertoire (Skinner, 1957) controlled by the same laws as other behavior. The old, defunct explanatory concepts of knowledge, meaning, mind, or symbolic processes have never offered the possibility of manipulation or control; but behavior, verbal or otherwise, can be controlled with ease and precision.

While machines are not the essential or defining aspect of this technology, they do play an important role in providing some of this fine control the technology requires. We will now examine several machines and notice the advantages they offer.

At Harvard there is a self-instruction room with ten booths, each containing a machine such as the one shown in Figure 1. The student gets one set of material from the attendant and places it in the machine. He closes the machine and begins his studies.

This machine presents one item of material at a time. The subject reads the statement, which has one or more words missing, and he completes it by writing in the answer

figure 1   *Student working at a write-in teaching machine.*

space. He then raises the lever and a small shutter opens, revealing the correct answer. Simultaneously, his answer is moved under glass, where it can be read and compared with the now-exposed correct answer. After comparing his answer with the correct answer, the student indicates to the machine, with an appropriate movement of the lever, whether his answer was correct or incorrect, and the next item appears in the window. He repeats all items answered wrong after he completes the set of items. He does not repeat correctly answered items.

A critical feature of the machine is that it provides immediate reinforcement for correct answers. Being correct is known to be a reinforcer for humans. In machine teaching, reinforcement is immediate. We know from laboratory work (Perin, 1943) that a delay between a response and its reinforcement of a few seconds will greatly reduce the effectiveness of the reinforcement. Adult human subjects can sustain at least small delays; nevertheless, any delay makes reinforcement less effective.

Although other techniques such as programmed workbooks (Homme and Glaser, 1959) and flashcards are sometimes used in this new behavioral technology, they offer less control. Teaching machines eliminate undesirable forms of responses which would also be successful in obtaining the right answer. For example, the teaching machine insures that the student answers before peeking at the indicated answer. There is a strong temptation to glance ahead with only a poorly formulated, unwritten answer when programmed workbooks or flashcards are used.

turns the crank, and the next item appears immediately, so that immediate reinforcement is provided.

Both of the machines we have seen thus far require the student to compose the answer. Figure 2 shows a machine for a less mature organism who cannot yet compose an answer. This machine can be used for teaching preschool children.[2] There is a large top window and three small windows. In the large window, there is some sort of problem; and in the three smaller windows, there are three alternative choices. For example, in the machine as seen in the picture, the subject chooses one of the three alternatives which has the same form as the sample, independent, in this case, of

figure 2   Child working on the preverbal machine. In the upper rectangular window is a sample which is to be matched with a figure in one of the three lower windows. If the child presses the correct lower window, the material advances to the next frame. In this case, the match is in terms of form, with size and color irrelevant.

This write-in machine is a prototype of the most common machine. There is another machine used for teaching young children material which consistently has a single possible answer. In the machine the constructed answer is automatically compared with the true answer. The child is presented a problem, perhaps a statement such as $2 + 2 =$ ___, and he must provide the 4. By moving a slider appropriately, he can insert the 4 into the answer space. He then

color or size. When the correct choice is made, the next frame is presented.

A teaching machine for a still lower organism is shown in Figure 3.

This pigeon, with the aid of a teaching machine, has learned to hit the name plaque appropriate for a color projected

[2] Hively, W. An exploratory investigation of an apparatus for studying and teaching visual discrimination using preschool children. (In preparation.)

figure 3 A pigeon "naming colors." The pigeon pecks the color name corresponding to the color of the light projected above him.

above him. The principal difference between this and the other machines is that food reinforcement is used. With humans, simply being correct is sufficient reinforcement—pigeons will not work for such meager gains.

Enough of machines. They should not be allowed to obscure the truly important feature of the new technology, namely, the application of methods for behavioral control in developing programs for teaching. We need to say no more about the well-known principle of immediate reinforcement. Our second principle is also well known. Behavior is learned only when it is *emitted* and reinforced. But in the classroom, the student performs very little, verbally. However, while working with a machine, the student necessarily emits appropriate behavior, and this behavior is usually reinforced because the material is

so designed that the student is usually correct. Not only is reinforcement needed for learning, but a high density of correct items is necessary because material which generates errors is punishing. Laboratory experiments (Azrin, 1956) have shown that punishment lowers the rate of the punished behavior. In our experience with teaching machines, we have also observed that students stop work when the material is so difficult that they make many errors. Furthermore, they become irritated, almost aggressive, when errors are made.

The third important principle is that of gradual progression to establish complex repertoires. A visitor once asked if Skinner had realized that pigeons were so smart before he began using them as subjects. The answer given by a helpful graduate student was that they weren't so smart before Skinner began using them. And indeed they weren't. The behavior developed in many experiments is like that developed in the classroom. Both are complex operants. Both require a careful program of gradual progression. We cannot wait for a student to describe the content of a psychology course before reinforcing the performance; nor can we wait for a pigeon to emit such an improbable bit of behavior as turning a circle, facing a disk on the wall, pecking it if lit, and then bending down to a now-exposed food tray and eating. When developing a complex performance in a pigeon, we may first reinforce simply the behavior of approaching the food tray when it is presented with a loud click. Later, the pigeon learns to peck a key which produces the click and the food tray. Still later, he may learn to peck this key only when it is lit, the peck being followed by the loud click and approach to the food tray. In the next step, he may learn to raise his head or hop from one foot to another, or walk a figure eight, in order to produce the lighted key which he then pecks; the click follows, and he approaches the food tray. This principle of gradual progression runs through many of the teaching-machine techniques.

Both human and avian scholars deserve the same careful tutorage. The teaching-machine program moves in very finely graded steps, working from simple to an ever-higher level of complexity. Such a gradual development is illustrated in Table 1 by a few items taken from a psychology program.[3]

The principle of gradual progression serves not simply to make the student correct as often as possible, but it is also the fastest way to develop a complex repertoire. In fact, a new complex operant may never

[3] This program, prepared by J. G. Holland and B. F. Skinner, is entitled A *self-tutoring introduction to a science of behavior*.

appear except through separately reinforcing members of a graded series (Keller and Schoenfeld, 1950). Only this way can we quickly create a *new pattern* of behavior. The pigeon would not have learned the complex sequence necessary to receive the food if it had not learned each step in its proper order. Obviously, a child can't begin with advanced mathematics, but neither can he begin with $2 + 2 = 4$—even this is too complex and requires a gradual progression.

Our fourth principle is, in a sense, another form of gradual progression—one which involves the gradual withdrawal of stimulus support. This we shall call fading. This method will be illustrated with some

table 1

items from the psychology program (11).
these items illustrate the gradual development of a new concept

item	correct answer	percentage of students giving the answer
1. Performing animals are sometimes trained with "rewards." The behavior of a hungry animal can be "rewarded" with _____.	Food	96
2. A technical term for "reward" is reinforcement. To "reward" an organism with food is to _____ it with food.	Reinforce	100
3. *Technically* speaking, a thirsty organism can be _____ with water.	Reinforced	100
. . . .		
50. A school teacher is likely, whenever possible, to dismiss a class when her students are rowdy because she has been _____ by elimination of the stimuli arising from a rowdy class.	Reinforced	92
51. The teacher who dismisses a class when it is rowdy causes the frequency of future rowdy behavior to (1) _____, since dismissal from class is probably a(n) (2) _____ for rowdy children.	(1) Increase (2) Reinforcement	86
. . . .		
54. If an airplane spotter never sees the kind of plane he is to spot, his frequency of scanning the sky (1) _____. In other words his "looking" behavior is (2) _____.	(1) Decreases (2) Extinguished (or: Not Reinforced)	94

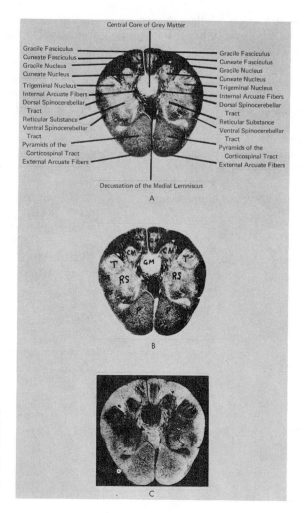

figure 4   An illustration of the technique of fading. Section A is in front of the student while he is working on the earliest items of a neuroanatomy program; Section B is in front of the student for later items; and Section C, for still later items.

neuroanatomy material.[4] Figure 4*a* is a fully labelled cross-section of the medulla oblongata. This is placed before the student while he works with a large set of items pertaining to the spatial arrangement of the various structures. For example, "posterior to the cuneate nuclei are the _____." The answer is the "cuneate fasciculi." After many such items, he begins another set and has another picture

4 This material has been prepared by D. M. Brethower in collaboration with the present author, and it is being used at Harvard for research purposes.

(Figure 4*b*); but now the structures before him are labelled only with initials. A new set of items again asks a long series of questions pertaining to the spatial position of the various structures. For example, "between the gracile and the trigeminal nuclei are _____." The answer is the "cuneate nuclei." After many more items, he proceeds to a new set and the next picture. This time (Figure 4*c*), the picture is unlabelled. Again, he goes through a series of new items, not simple repetitions of the previous ones, but items pertaining to the same problem of the spatial location of the different structures. This set is followed by still another but with no picture at all. He is now able to discuss the spatial position of the structures without any visual representations of the structures before him. In a sense, he has his own private map of the medulla. He may further demonstrate his newly acquired ability by accurately drawing the medulla. The neuroanatomy example is an elaborate example of fading. Fading is also applied in a more simple form in constructing verbal programs without pictorial displays. A single item may in one sentence give a definition or a general law and in a second sentence in that same item, an example in which a key word is omitted. This would be followed by a new example in the next frame, but with the definition or law lacking.

This brings us to our fifth principle: control of the student's observing and echoic behavior. In the classroom the student is often treated as though he were some kind of passive receiver of information, who can sop up information spoken by the teacher, written on the blackboard, or presented by films. But all of these are effective only insofar as the student has some behavior with respect to the material. He must listen carefully, or read carefully, thus engaging in usually covert echoic behavior. Ineffectiveness of classroom techniques is often credited to "inattention" or poor "concentration." It has been shown (Reid, 1953; Wyckoff, 1952) that if a discrimination is to be learned, adequate observing behavior must first be established. We have further found that observing behavior, or speaking loosely, "attention," is subject to the same forms of control as other behavior (Holland, 1958). This control of observing behavior is of prime importance. When the student becomes very "inattentive" in the classroom, the teaching material flows on; but with a machine, he moves ahead only as he finishes an item. Lapses in active participation result in nothing more than the machine sitting idle until the student continues. There is, however, a more subtle aspect to the control of observing behavior than this obvious mechanical one. In many of the examples we have seen, success in answering the problem depends only on the student's careful observation of the material in front of him at the moment. This may be illustrated by more material from the psychology program. A graph showing stimulus-generalization data is in front of the student while he works on the machine. In the program he may complete a statement: "As the wave length changes in either direction from the wave length present during reinforcement, the number of responses _____." The answer is "decreases." The item serves only to control the behavior of observing the data. Of course, many more such items are used to discuss the same data.

This principle of controlled observation extends to the details of writing a single item. For example, "Two events may have a common effect. An operant reinforced with two reinforcers appropriate to different deprivations will vary with _____ deprivations." The answer is "two" or "both." Here, the programmer's choice of the omission serves to insure a careful reading of the item. *Only* those parts of an item which must be read to correctly complete a blank can safely be assumed to be learned.

Our sixth principle deals with discrimination training. In learning spoken languages, for example, it is necessary to be able to identify the speech sounds. A student may listen to a pair of words on a special phonograph which repeats the passage as many times as he desires. The visual write-in machine instructs him to listen to a specific passage. For example, the student may hear two words such as: "sit, set." He listens as many times as he needs and then writes the phonetic symbols in the write-in machine. He then operates the machine, thereby exposing the true answer and providing immediate reinforcement for his correct discrimination.

However, little academic education is *simple* discrimination. More often, it is abstraction or concept formation. An abstraction is a response to a single isolated property of a stimulus. Such a property cannot exist alone. Redness is an abstraction. Anything that is red has other properties as well—size, shape, position in space, to name a few. There are red balls, red cars, red walls. The term red applies to all of them, but not to green balls, blue cars, or yellow walls. To establish an abstraction (Hovland, 1952, 1953), we must provide many examples. Each must have the common property, but among the various examples there must be a wide range of other properties. This is best illustrated by examples from the preverbal machine shown in Figure 5.

These are from a program [5] which teaches a child to respond to the abstract property of form. In each item, the upper figure is the sample and the lower three are the alternatives. While developing a program for establishing an abstraction, we remember our earlier principles and move

[5] This program was prepared by B. F. Skinner.

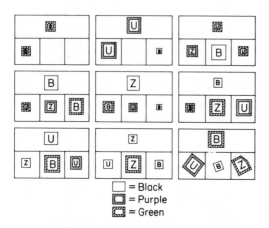

☐ = Black
☐ = Purple
☐ = Green

figure 5 Selected items from a program which teaches young children to respond in terms of the abstract property of form. The upper rectangle in each of the frames is the sample. The child must pick the alternative which corresponds to the sample in form. The color of each letter, as it appeared in the program, is indicated by the various shaded areas.

through a gradual progression. The first several items would be like the first one; here, there is a sample and a single match, the other two being blank. The sample and its match are exactly alike at this stage. After many such items, we would begin to have others like the next one, in which the sample and its match again correspond in size, color, and form—but an additional incorrect alternative has been added which differs from the sample in all these aspects. Later, we move on to frames with three choices; again, the sample and its match correspond exactly. Next, the sample and the match may differ in some property such as color, in the case of the next item shown, or size in the next. It is essential that the program contain many items among which the sample and correct match differ in all properties except the one providing the basis for the abstraction. Otherwise, the abstraction will be incomplete because the extraneous property will share some of the control over the abstract response. As we move on with additional examples, the sample and the correct match differ both in color and in size, and the incorrect alternatives are beginning to share some of the extraneous properties with the sample. The student continues with many such problems in which the only common property between the sample and the correct match is the shape, regardless of size and color. Even now our abstraction may be incomplete. We have kept the figures in only one orientation. Therefore, we also have a series in which the samples are rotated as in the next item. A great deal of academic education consists of trying to teach abstractions. Concepts such as force, reinforcement, supply and demand, freedom, and many, many other possible examples are all abstractions. Furthermore, in the academic setting, the student seldom adequately forms abstractions. The trigonometry student commonly uses triangles with the right angle as one of the two lower angles. If the triangle is rotated 90°, so that the right angle is upward, the student often does not recognize it as a right triangle. Neither is an abstraction developed simply by learning a definition. The psychology student who learns the definition of reinforcement in formal terms and is acquainted with a laboratory example of food reinforcement may not realize the horrible consequences of sending his girl friend flowers to end an argument. Thus, in the psychology program, we follow the pattern in the preverbal example to develop a new concept. Wide ranges of examples are analyzed which differ in as many aspects as possible, each still having the common property which characterizes the concept.

The last principle I shall discuss is really a question of a methodology which has served so well in the laboratory. This principle is to let the student write the program. A few years ago, the cartoon shown in Figure 6 was published in the *Columbia Jester*.

The rat leaning on the bar is saying to the other rat: "Boy, do we have this guy conditioned. Every time I press the bar down, he drops a pellet in." Although said in jest, it is true that the rat controls the experimenter's behavior. When interesting things are observed about the rat's behavior, the control circuits are rewired to investigate the interesting new facet of behavior. In a sense, the rat is wiring the control circuit. Similarly, the behavioral engineer who prepares good teaching-machine material must be under the control of the student's responses. When the student has trouble with part of a program, the programmer must correct this. The student's answers reveal ambiguities in items; they reveal gaps in the program and erroneous assumptions as to the student's background. The answers will show when the program is progressing too rapidly, when additional prompts are necessary, or when the programmer should try new techniques. When unexpected errors are made, they indicate deficiencies *not* in the student but in the program.

The most extensive experience with this principle of modifying the program to fit the student has been at Harvard with the psychology program. In 1958, we had a program consisting of 48 disks or lessons of 29 frames each. After using the program and making a detailed, item-by-item analysis of the students' answers, we diagnosed the particular deficiencies in the program and revised it accordingly. The program was also extended to cover a larger amount of subject matter; and in 1959, it consisted of 60 disks. You have already seen a few items from the course. After using the revised material in 1959, we evaluated the extent of its improvement. The next figure [Table 2] shows the percentage of errors on the first 20 disks for each of the 2 years.

The revision eliminated about half the

"Boy, do we have this guy conditioned. Every time I press the bar down he drops a pellet in."

figure 6

table 2

a comparison of the students' errors in using the revised (1959) and unrevised (1958) program in psychology

	percentage of errors	percentage of items improperly scored by students
1958	20.1	3.6
1959	11.0	1.4

errors. The last column of the table gives percentage of improper self-scoring by the students. Revision also cut these scoring errors approximately in half. Furthermore, the revision decreased the time required to complete the material. Although the second year's material had more disks—60 as opposed to 48—it actually required the average student about 1 hour less to complete the work than the shorter, first version had done. Frequency distributions on the median times in minutes for completion of the various disks are shown in Figure 7. These are the times required for the median student to move through each set of material answering every item once and to repeat items answered incorrectly. Notice the considerable time required for many disks in the first year's material. Primarily, this was because students repeated the larger number of items missed in the first cycle.

But the improved material provided faster performance, even when the delay due to repetition of incorrectly answered items is not considered. The frequency distributions for the first cycle only are provided in Figure 8. These data exclude the time used in repeating items. Here too, the

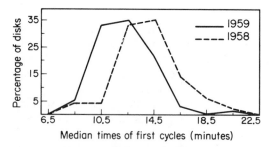

figure 8   Frequency distributions for the median times to complete only the first cycles for the revised (1959) and unrevised (1958) psychology program. Raw frequencies were converted to percentages to equate the area under the curves.

revision produced slightly more rapid progress.

Such careful tailoring of material to fit the student is impossible with most teaching techniques. With teaching machines, as in no other teaching technique, the programmer is able to revise his material in view of the student's particular difficulties. The student can write the program; he cannot write the textbook.

We have seen that the principles evolved from the laboratory study of behavior have provided the possibility for the behavioral engineering of teaching. This new technology is thoroughly grounded in some of the better-established facts of behavioral control. The future of education is bright if persons who prepare teaching-machine programs appreciate this, and appropriately educate themselves in a special, but truly *not* esoteric, discipline. But it is vital that we continue to apply these techniques in preparing programs. The ill-advised efforts of some of our friends, who automatize their courses without adopting the new technology, have an extremely good chance of burying the whole movement in an avalanche of teaching-machine tapes.

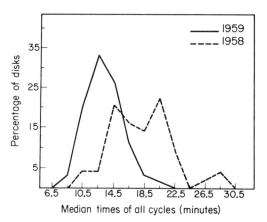

figure 7   Frequency distributions for the median times to complete the disks or "lessons" for the revised (1959) and unrevised (1958) psychology program. Raw frequencies were converted to percentages to equate the area under the curves.

REFERENCES

AZRIN, H. H. Some effects of two intermittent schedules of immediate and non-immediate punishment. *J. Psychol.*, 1956, **42**, 3–21.

HOLLAND, J. G. Human viligance. *Science*, 1958, **129**, 61–67.

HOMME, L. E., and R. GLASER. Relationships between programmed textbook and teaching machines. In E. Galanter (Ed.), *Automatic teaching*. New York: John Wiley, 1959, pp. 103–107.

HOVLAND, C. I. A "communication analysis" of concept learning. *Psychol. Rev.*, 1952, **59**, 461–472.

––––––. A set of flower designs for experiments in concept formation. *Amer. J. Psychol.*, 1953, **66**, 140–142.

KELLER, F. S., and W. N. SCHOENFELD. *Principles of psychology*. New York: Appleton-Century-Crofts, 1950.

PERIN, C. T. The effect of delayed reinforcement upon the differentiation of bar responses in white rats. *J. exp. Psychol.*, 1943, **32**, 95–109.

PRESSEY, S. L. Simple apparatus which gives tests and scores and teaches. *Sch. and Soc.*, 1926, **23**, 373–376.

REID, L. S. The development of noncontinuity behavior through continuity learning. *J. exp. Psychol.*, 1953, **46**, 107–112.

SKINNER, B. F. The science of learning and the art of· teaching. *Harvard educ. Rev.*, 1954, **29**, 86–97.

––––––. *Verbal behavior*. New York: Appleton-Century-Crofts, 1957.

––––––. Teaching machines. *Science*, 1958, **128**, 969–977.

WYCKOFF, L. B. The role of observing responses in discrimination learning. *Psychol. Rev.*, 1952, **59**, 431–442.

11

The experiments described in the next article by J. V. McConnell are responsible for much heated controversy concerning the physiological bases of learning and memory. The possibility that RNA and DNA protein molecules may constitute the physiochemical substrate of these processes is exciting in itself. The further possibility that memory may be biochemically transferred between organisms (by cannibalism) is almost unbelievable. Although the physiological bases of memory are still unknown, the experiments reported by McConnell and his associates have been powerful stimulants to further research.

memory transfer through cannibalism in planarians [1]

JAMES V. MC CONNELL

The research that I am going to outline . . . had its start several years ago, and I trust you will allow me to give you a few of the pertinent background details, if only to convince you that our work is more serious than it sometimes sounds, and of sufficient scope at least to approach respectability.[2] It was in 1953, when I was a graduate student at the University of Texas, that a fellow student, Robert Thompson, suggested to me that we attempt to condition a planarian, or common flatworm. Having avoided the rigors of introductory zoology up to that point, my only prior experience with worms had been at the business end of a fishing pole. I soon discovered, however, that fishing worms are round, while planarians are flat. Planarians are also usually less than an inch in length, and rather interesting in their own right.

Flatworms occupy a unique niche on the phylogenetic scale, being the lowest organisms to possess bilateral symmetry, a rude form of encephalization, and a human, synaptic-type nervous system. According to some psychological theories—the ones that postulate that learning is a matter of reshuffling connections among neurons—the planarian should be the lowest organism to be able to demonstrate "true" learning. As far as we knew in 1953, no one had ever demonstrated unequivocally that these organisms could indeed be trained. Since then, of course, we have discovered the usual obscure reference that antedates our work by 30 years—it appears in Dutch and

[1] *Acknowledgements:* Much of the research reported in the paper was supported by grants from the National Institute of Mental Health and from the Atomic Energy Commission.

[2] For an excellent survey of the history of worm running, see the paper by Allan L. Jacobson, "Learning in Flatworms and Annelids," *Psychol. Bull.*, 1963, 60: 74–94.

Reprinted from *Journal of Neuropsychiatry,* 1962, 3: Supplement No. 1, 42–48, by permission of the author and publisher. Copyright © 1962 by Behavioral Neuropsychiatry.

was published in a little-read European journal [3]—but I am not at all sure that even this knowledge would have deterred us. At any rate, Thompson and I set out in 1953 to attempt classical conditioning in planarians.

Imagine a trough gouged out of plastic, 12 inches in length, semi-circular in cross-section, and filled with pond water. At either end are brass electrodes attached to a power source. Above the trough are two electric light bulbs. Back and forth in the trough crawls a single flatworm, and in front of the apparatus sits the experimenter, his eye on the worm, his hands on two switches. When the worm is gliding smoothly in a straight line on the bottom of the trough, the experimenter turns on the lights for 3 seconds. After the light has been on for two of the three seconds, the experimenter adds one second of electric shock, which passes through the water and causes the worm to contract. The experimenter records the behavior of the worm during the two-second period after the light has come on but before the shock has started. If the animal gives a noticeable turning movement or a contraction prior to the onset of the shock, this is scored as a "correct" or "conditioned" response.[4]

From this brief description of the experimental paradigm, many of you will recognize that Thompson and I were attempting to establish a form of Pavlovian conditioning in our experimental animals (Group E), and according to our data, we were successful. Planarians occasionally give a mild and presumably innate response to the onset of the light even when it has not been previously paired with shock, so we ran a control group that received just trials of photic (light) stimulation (Group LC); we also ran a control group that re-

[3] P. Van Oye, *Natuurwetenschappelijk Tijdschrift*, 1920, **2**: 1–9.
[4] James V. McConnell, P. R. Cornwell, and Margaret L. Clay, *Amer. J. Psychol.*, 1960, **73**: 618–622.

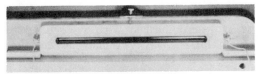

The original apparatus.

ceived just shock, occasionally interpersing a test trial of light alone (Group SC). All animals were given 150 trials. Over that period of time, as Tables 1 and 2 show, the experimental animals, which received light paired with shock, showed a significant increase in responsivity, while the control groups showed either no change at all or a significant decline.

table 1

mean turns, contractions, and combined responses on the first 50 and last 50 trials for groups E (experimental) and LC (light control)

group response	first 50 trials	last 50 trials	diff.	p
E				
Turns	12.6	16.6	4.0	.01
Contractions	1.2	5.0	3.8	.01
Combined	13.8	21.6	7.8	.01
LC				
Turns	11.7	7.6	−4.1	.01
Contractions	0.6	2.1	1.5	
Combined	12.3	9.7	−2.6	

table 2

mean turns, contractions, and combined responses on the first 15 and last 15 test trials for group SC (shock control)

response	first 15 test trials	last 15 test trials	diff.*
Turns	5.4	4.2	−1.2
Contractions	0.2	0.4	0.2
Combined	5.6	4.6	−1.0

* None of the differences is significant at the .05 level of confidence.

Hence Thompson and I concluded that we had accomplished what we set out to accomplish—namely, we had proven that worms could be conditioned.[5]

Those of you who have ever chopped up a planarian in a zoology course will know that these animals have enormous powers of regeneration. A large specimen may be cut into perhaps 50 pieces, each of which will eventually regenerate into a complete organism. It was while we were running that first experiment that Thompson and I wondered aloud, feeling rather foolish as we did so, what would happen if we conditioned a flatworm, then cut it in two and let both halves regenerate. Which half would retain the memory? As it happened, we never got around to performing that experiment at Texas, for Thompson received his doctorate soon after we finished our first study and went on to Louisiana State University and bigger and better things— namely, rats. When I went to the University of Michigan in 1956, however, I was faced with the difficult problem that in the academic world, one must publish or perish. The only thing I knew much about was flatworms, so I talked two bright young students, Allan Jacobson and Daniel Kimble, into performing the obvious experiment on learning and regeneration.

Kimble, Jacobson and I did the follow-

[5] Robert Thompson and James V. McConnell, *J. Comp. Physiol. Psychol.*, 1955, **48**: 65–68.

ing. We took our experimental animals and trained them to a criterion of 23 responses out of any block of 25 trials. When they had reached this criterion, we assumed that they were properly conditioned and immediately cut them in half across the middle. Head and tail sections were then put in individual bowls and allowed about 4 weeks to regenerate. At the end of this period, these experimental animals (Group E) were re-trained to the same criterion and savings scores calculated. We also ran a group of worms which were cut, allowed to regenerate, and then were conditioned for the first time—this to tell us if cutting and subsequent regeneration in any way sensitized the animals to conditioning (Group RC). Another control group was conditioned, then allowed to rest uncut for a month before being retested (Group TC) —this to tell us how much forgetting we could expect in our experimental animals had we not cut them in half.

In all honesty I must admit that we did not obtain the results we had expected. We had assumed that the regenerated heads would show fairly complete retention of the response for, after all, the head section retained the primitive brain and "everybody knows" that the brain is where memories are located. And, as Tables 3, 4, and 5 indicate, the heads did show just as much retention as did the uncut control animals. We had also hoped, in our heart of hearts, that perhaps the tails would show a slight

table 3

number of trials to criterion for group E (experimental)

S	original training	retest head	retest tail
E1	99	50	51
E2	191	37	24
E3	97	48	72
E4	83	35	44
E5	200	30	25
M	134	40	43.2

table 4

*number of trials to criterion for group RC
(regeneration control)*

S	head	tail
RC1	134	150
RC2	188	179
RC3	276	85
RC4	395	300
RC5	250	325
M	248.6	207.8

table 5

number of trials for group TC (time control)

S	original training	retest
TC1	123	24
TC2	153	25
TC3	195	62
TC4	131	43
TC5	325	45
M	185.4	39.8

but perhaps significant retention of some kind, merely because we thought this would be an interesting finding. We were astounded, then, to discover that the tails not only showed as much retention as did the heads, but in many cases did much better than the heads and showed absolutely no forgetting whatsover. Obviously memory, in the flatworm, was being stored throughout the animal's body, and as additional proof of this we found that if we cut the worm into three or even more pieces, each section typically showed clearcut retention of the conditioned response.[6]

It was at this time that we first postulated our theory that conditioning caused some chemical change throughout the worm's body, and it was also about then that Reeva Jacobson came along to help us test what

seemed at the time to be rather an odd hypothesis. She took planarians, cut off their tails, and conditioned the heads before any regeneration could take place. Then she let her animals grow new tails. She next removed these new tails and let them grow new heads, ending up with apparently completely reformed organisms. These total regenerates, as we called them, were then tested for any "savings" of the original conditioning. By now we knew what to expect from planarians, and so we weren't too surprised when Reeva's regenerated flatworms showed a significant retention of what the original organism had learned. True, as Table 6 suggests, these

table 6

*number of trials to criterion for totally
regenerated animals*

S	original training	retest after total regeneration
1	200	166
2	325	143
3	300	220
4	327	51
5	75	62
6	381	94
mean	268	122.7
SD	102	60

total regenerates did not demonstrate the complete retention that our original animals had shown, but they did remember enough so that our hypothesis seemed vindicated.[7]

By now, worms were in the *Zeitgeist*. Edward Ernhart, working with Carl Sherrick at Washington University, demonstrated not only that flatworms could learn a two-unit T-maze, but also that this maze habit was retained by their animals following cutting and regeneration. Again, the tails remembered at least as much as

---

[6] James V. McConnell, A. L. Jacobson, and D. P. Kimble, *J. Comp. Physiol. Psychol.*, 1959, **52**: 1–5.

[7] James V. McConnell, Reeva Jacobson, and D. M. Maynard, *Amer. Psychologist*, 1959, **14**: 410 (abstract).

did the heads.[8] Ernhart is perhaps most famous, however, for a more recent study of his. If one takes a flatworm and splits the head straight down the middle, time and time again, the two halves will not heal together but will each regenerate into a complete head. One ends up, then, with a two-headed worm. Ernhart compared the length of time it took two-headed animals to be conditioned with the length of time it took one-headed (or normal) animals to reach the same criterion and found that he had validated an old aphorism—two heads are indeed better than one.[9]

Roy John and William Corning, working at the University of Rochester, became quite interested in the chemical theory of learning about this time, and undertook one of the most spectacular pieces of research yet to come from any worm laboratory. John reasoned that learning in flatworms had to be mediated, at least in part, by some molecular change within the organism's cells. Since Hydén had found changes in RNA in nerve cells as a result of experience,[10] John believed that RNA might be implicated in learning and retention in planarians. So he and Corning conditioned a number of flatworms, cut them in half, and let them regenerate in a weak solution of ribonuclease, which breaks up RNA. When they compared their experimental animals with a number of controls, they found evidence that the experimental heads were relatively unaffected by the ribonuclease, while the tails showed complete forgetting. The tails could be retrained, but it took approximately as long the second time as it had the first.[11]

Ralph Gerard, the noted neurophysiologist, interprets the data as follows: There are probably two distinct but related physiological mechanisms for learning in planarians. The first such mechanism is the familiar one of neural interconnections which are reshuffled in the brain due to the animal's experiences—the so-called circuit-diagram model, if I may be permitted the analogy. Structural changes in the neural pathways in the brain would presumably not be altered by ribonuclease, which accounts for the fact that the Rochester head-regenerates showed no real forgetting. The second type of memory mechanism, however, involves a change in the coding of the RNA molecules in the cells throughout the worm's body. Presumably whenever the animal learns, the RNA is altered appropriately so that when regeneration takes place, the altered RNA builds the memory into the regenerated animal right from the start. If the RNA were destroyed by the ribonuclease, it is likely that the DNA in the cells would replace the lost RNA, but this replacement RNA would not carry the changed code since the DNA was presumably unaffected by the learning.[12]

If all of this sounds rather complex, you must forgive me. I am not at all sure that at this early date we have more than the vaguest notion just how learning could affect RNA nor how, much less why, this altered RNA might build the memory into the regenerating tissue. The important thing to remember is that John's hunch that RNA might be involved in memory seems to have been substantiated.

Before further discussing RNA and memory, I should like to detail, briefly, some other research that Roy John and Bill Corning, at Rochester, and my own group of worm runners at the University of Michigan and at the Britannica Center in Palo Alto have been pursuing jointly. In 1957, when we got our first results on re-

[8] E. N. Ernhart and C. Sherrick, Jr., "Retention of a maze habit following regeneration in planaria (*D. maculata*)," Paper read at Midwestern Psychological Association, St. Louis, May 1959.

[9] E. N. Ernhart, *Worm Runner's Digest*, 1960, 2: 92–94.

[10] Holgar Hydén, in Farber, Seymour M., and Wilson, Roger H. L. (eds.), *Control of the Mind* (New York: McGraw-Hill, 1961).

[11] W. C. Corning and E. R. John, *Science*, 1961, 134: 1363–1365.

[12] Ralph Gerard, Personal communication, 1961.

tention of learning following regeneration, and came up with our chemical hypothesis, it seemed to us that we might be able to transfer a memory from a trained animal to an untrained animal if we could somehow get the right chemicals out of the first worm and into the second. We spent several years trying to test this admittedly wild notion without much success. First we tried grafting the head of a trained animal onto the tail of an untrained planarian, but this never worked very well. If one reads introductory zoology texts, one often gets the notion that this little operation is most easy to perform. Sadly enough, the best average on record is three successes out of 150 attempts [13] and we simply did not have 150 trained heads to waste. We tried grinding the trained worms up and injecting the pieces into untrained animals, but we never could master the injection techniques. It was only some time after we began this work that it occurred to us that we could let the animals do the transferring for us. For, under the proper conditions, one worm will eat another. And since planarians have but the most rudimentary of digestive tracts, there seemed an excellent chance that the tissue from the food worm would pass into the body of the cannibal relatively unchanged.

So, with Barbara Humphries as our chief experimenter, we conditioned a number of worms, chopped them into small pieces and hand-fed the pieces to untrained cannibals. We also took the precaution of feeding a number of untrained worms to untrained cannibals for a control or comparison group. Our first pilot study gave us such unbelievable results that we immediately instituted several changes in our procedure and repeated the study not once, but four times. And each time the results were quite significant—and still rather unbelievable. I should mention before going any further that the chief procedural change we made was the institution of a "blind" running technique which helped guard against ex-

[13] Roman Kenk, *J. Exp. Zool.*, 1941, 87: 55–69.

perimenter bias. Under this blind procedure, the person actually training the worms never knows anything about the animals he runs—we follow an elaborate coding system in which each animal's code letter is changed daily. The experimenter then doesn't know which animal is in which group, nor even which animal is which from day to day. Thus, as far as we could tell, we could not have unconsciously tampered with the data.

The results of this work, as Table 7

table 7

number of responses in first 25 training trials for cannibals fed conditioned planarians (experimentals) and for canibals fed unconditioned planarians (controls)

experimentals	controls
4	1
6	1
7	3
8	4
8	4
8	4
9	5
10	5
10	5
10	6
11	6
12	6
13	6
14	7
14	7
15	10
15	10
15	11
15	11
17	16
18	22
19	
mean 11.73	7.14

shows, were somewhat startling. In all five studies, it was clear that the cannibals which had fed on trained worms gave approximately half again as many conditioned responses during the first days of training as did the cannibals which had fed on untrained worms. In our studies, the differences between the two groups tended to disappear after the first few days as the control animals approached criterion. The experimental animals were presumably so close to criterion right from the start that the slope of their learning curve was much less than that of the controls.[14, 15]

I would also like to mention a couple of fortunate mistakes we made which do not prove anything but which are interesting evidence in their own right. One time our elaborate coding system broke down and a control animal was fed a piece of conditioned worm. For several days prior to this feeding, the control animal had been responding at an average of 2 or 3 times out of any 25 trials. Immediately following this inadvertent meal of conditioned tissue, the animal performed at criterion level, giving 23 responses out of the next 25 trials. Then there was one group of cannibals which we accidentally fed animals that had been given a number of conditioning trials, but which were not even close to criterion when we cut them up. The cannibals which ate these trained but not-yet-conditioned worms showed absolutely no transfer effect at all.

Now, if we had been the only ones to have obtained such results, our findings might be dismissed as the achievement of crackpots. Luckily for us, Corning, Karpick, and John instituted their own program of cannibalism shortly after we did and so far have run two large and very well-controlled studies, both using the blind technique, and have obtained results which are essentially identical to ours.[16]

And, as if this were not enough, our work has just been replicated by a high school student. Let me quote briefly from the Washington *Post* of 25 March, 1962.

A 17-year-old girl's rather startling answer to a rather startling question—"Is Knowledge Edible?"—brought her one of the two top prizes in a Northern Virginia Science Fair yesterday. Tentatively, Ruth Ann Ziegler's answer is "yes."

What Miss Ziegler found was that a worm who eats an educated worm learns things twice as fast as his brother who eats an uneducated worm. Hence her title, "Is Knowledge Edible?"

By electrical shocks she taught flatworms to respond to light. An ordinary flatworm needs about 260 shocks before he responds without one. He is then "conditioned."

Experiments taught Miss Ziegler that a worm fed the head of an unconditioned worm needs an average of 264 shocks. A worm fed an unconditioned tail needs 269.

But a worm fed a conditioned tail takes only 168 shocks and a worm fed a conditioned head a mere 140 shocks.

This experiment was part of Miss Ziegler's effort to see if conditioned learning is affected by chemicals and, if it is, if it can be passed on through regeneration and ingestion. It's apparently "yes" all the way.

Frankly, we are not quite sure where all of this work leaves us—except that we are most definitely out on a limb of some kind. At the moment, a number of laboratories around the country are starting investigations into the biochemistry of learning, using planarians as their tools. Specifically, several of us are attempting to extract RNA, DNA and other biochemicals from conditioned worms to feed to untrained cannibals. If we can show, for example, that RNA and only RNA causes the memory transfer, we can surely hope to determine the subtle molecular differences between "trained" and "untrained" RNA. If this could be done, we would be one step closer to cracking the problem of the molecular properties of memory—perhaps a giant step closer at that, particularly if it turns out that teaching the animals different sorts of habits causes different sorts of changes in

[14] Barbara M. Humphries and Reeva Jacobson, *Worm Runner's Digest*, 1961, 3: 165–169.

[15] James V. McConnell, Reeva Jacobson, and Barbara M. Humphries, *Worm Runner's Digest*, 1961, 3: 41–47.

[16] W. C. Corning, R. Karpick, and E. R. John, Personal communication from E. R. John, 1961.

the RNA molecules. But perhaps that is too much to hope for at the present.

Now, in conclusion, let me attempt to tie all of this research together. We have shown that planarians are capable of learning, that this learning survives cutting and regeneration, that the memory storage mechanism has a biochemical component (probably RNA) which is widely distributed throughout the animal's body, and that learning seems to be transferable from one animal to another via cannibalistic ingestion. If memory in higher organisms is also mediated via biochemical changes, and if these changes are specific to the habits learned, we might eventually discover a substance (probably RNA with a deliberately modified structure) which would facilitate learning if it were incorporated into animal or human bodies. If so, the research we have been doing with our lowly flatworms may have practical consequences we never dreamed of when we began our work some nine years ago.

12

A large number of experimental psychologists are investigating the topic of memory, but very few seem to be "doing anything about it." Most work in this area has been oriented toward physiological and/or theoretical problems. So-called "memory experts" have not been loath to peddle their pet procedures, but systematic applied research on memory improvement techniques ("mnemonics") has only recently been initiated. In the next selection, R. J. Senter discusses some of his initial personal explorations into the use of mnemonic devices. The simplicity of the system is amazing (as you will discover if you attempt to replicate Senter's demonstration) although many of the phenomena which he mentions cannot be accommodated within current theories of learning. Clearly, the theories will have to be modified to take account of these phenomena.

review of mnemonics and mnemonotechnics for improved memory

section I: introduction

The name *mnemonics* can be applied to any technique which is intended to improve the efficiency of memory. The majority of the references covering the subject matter of mnemonics are not contained in the conventional literature of the psychological profession, but rather in what publishers call "trade books," i.e., nonfiction published for general public consumption. There appears to be considerable public demand for books devoted to memory and

Reprinted from Aerospace Medical Research Laboratories–Tr–65–180, Aerospace Medical Division, Air Force Systems Command, Wright-Patterson Air Force Base, Dayton, Ohio (December, 1965), by permission of the author and the Air Force Human Resources Laboratory. This report represents a portion of the program of the Training Research Division, Wright-Patterson Air Force Base, Ohio 45433.

memory training. There are two major reasons for making such a judgment: (1) there is a remarkably large number of books devoted to memory and memory training indexed in the public libraries (see selected bibliography) and (2) at any point in time, it is extremely difficult to procure any one of these books from such lending establishments because they seem perpetually already on loan with a lengthy list of potential borrowers awaiting their return.

Many of these texts are similar in content. They frequently form the core of commercial "memory training courses" which are available via mail order. Contemporary popular magazines abound in advertisements for such mail order courses. It is perhaps this element of commercialism which deters academic psychologists from indulging in serious formal study of these techniques. The most common beginning point in these expositions of mnemonics is to point out a fact which often comes as a surprise to the layman. This fact centers around the fallacy that most of us regard the phrase "poor memory" as being synonymous with "inadequate storage capacity." The modern psychologist would probably agree that the storage capacity of the normal human brain is large, finite, and as yet unmeasured. The average layman, however, is unaware of his own enormous capacity and tends to be aware only of numerous instances in which "his memory fails him." Most of the texts exposing mnemonic techniques, and the courses centering around these texts, base their technology on one major premise. This premise acknowledges the enormous storage capacity existing in the human brain and points out initially that defects in memory are usually not the result of inadequate storage capacity, but rather come about through misuse of the capability by improper input to, and/or improper retrieval from, that storage. With this primary premise, memory training proceeds, not with an exposure of methods for increasing memory storage capacity, but rather with fairly elaborate and detailed instruction in input and retrieval methods.

The lines of instruction in different books vary in emphasis according to the orientation of the author. These, however, can be divided basically into three general categories as follows:

1. Exposure to the application of the few principles of human learning which are familiar to any college sophomore having a course in introductory psychology.
2. Simple mnemonics which are devices having very limited application and which are invoked to recall *specific content* (e.g., resistor color code, the cranial nerves of the dogfish, etc.).
3. Mnemonotechnics or complex mnemonics are fairly elaborate systems which have general application to the recollection of almost any content material. The term "complex" is not meant to imply "complicated" but

rather that mnemonotechnics are "systems" in which one simple mnemonic device is developed into a whole series of interrelated devices.

section II: improved memory through better learning

In exposing the fundamental principles of learning (the first of the above three categories) most authors simply point out a number of principles which are common knowledge to any psychologist, but which people simply fail to use in their everyday interactions. Many theoreticians have made the point that there is a profound difference between learning and performance. They indicate that, even in the absence of motivation, exposure to an event can ultimately lead to alterations of performance, but incidental learning and passive conditioning are quite ineffectual from the standpoint of immediate or profound alterations in behavior. A major point in the presentation of these basic learning principles is simply the exposure of the truth that the human brain does not absorb information like a sponge simply by being plunged into the midst of it. The principal cause of faulty memory is faulty learning—most things that appear to be forgotten are not really forgotten at all but fail to appear in recollection because they were never learned in the first place. This dearth of learning is generally attributed to the supposition that the learner was passive. Strong emphasis is placed on the self-evident truth that in order for any content material to be remembered it must first be learned. The first principle in mnemonic training, then, is that *an intention or motivation to learn is the first requisite for remembering.*

A second admonition to the student wishing to improve his memory is that *attention* is as necessary as is *intention* in the learning situation. Numerous psychological studies show that the presence of distracting stimuli reduces human learning effectiveness. The potential learner must select from the stimulus complex those elements germane to the material he wishes to learn and he must disregard, or minimize, those elements which are irrelevant.

The third important principle of learning emphasized by the teachers of mnemonics is that people generally ignore, in their everyday functioning, the all-important role of *rehearsal*. Even if the learner has been motivated and has attended to the salient cues, a bit of overlearning, in the form of reviewing newly formed associations, reduces the slope of the forgetting curve and therefore enhances retention.

In addition to the basic formula "intenreviewing newly formed associations, retention," several authors review (though rarely by name) such phenomena as retroactive inhibition, negative transfer of training, distributed learning, and other basic elements so common in the psychological laboratory.

section III: improved memory through simple mnemonics

The second general category of memory training is the so-called *simple mnemonics*. The use of simple mnemonics is without doubt familiar to all of us who have been exposed to formal academic training. It is simply the process of imposing upon unordered material some logical or meaningful order from our past experience. To the grammar school student who is trying to remember the date of the discovery of America, the digits 1, 4, 9, and 2, comprising 1492, have no more reasonable order than if they were arranged 1, 9, 4, and 2. An example of a very simple mnemonic which is used to recall the date of Columbus' discovery is, "A Crew Discovers Us," in which the number of letters in each word corresponds to each successive digit in the year 1492. Many electronic technicians use a simple mnemonic to remember the numbers represented by colors on

resistors. One such mnemonic is, "Beyond Brown's rose orchard you glimpse blue violets growing wild." This mnemonic represents the colors and their associated numbers: black – 0, brown – 1, red – 2, orange – 3, yellow – 4, green – 5, blue – 6, violet – 7, grey – 8 and white – 9. Any student of comparative anatomy has encountered some modification of the mnemonic, "On Old Olympus' Towering Tops A Fop And Glutton Vended Some Hops," where the first letter of each word is the same as the first letter of each cranial nerve beginning with the first nerve and working back (Optic, Olfactory, Oculomotor, etc.). Another familiar mnemonic is "ROY G. BIV" for the colors of the spectrum.

section IV: improved memory through mnemonic systems

Perhaps less well known are the *mnemonic systems*, or mnemonotechnics. These consist, essentially, of a standard set of mnemonic devices which are prelearned and which can be applied, through association, to the recollection of many and diverse materials. This technique differs from the simple mnemonic in the scope of applicability. Several such systems are presented by the various authors, but one is mentioned and expounded upon in great detail by nearly all writers in the field. This is called the "hook" or "peg" system. According to Lorayne (1957) the hook system was first developed in the early 18th century and has undergone study and modification by various relatively obscure people since that time.

The so-called hook system involves three basic steps. The first of these is a phonetic translation of the digital number system in which a consonant sound is used to represent each of the ten digits used in our number system. The only part of the entire mnemonic system which must be rigidly memorized is this digital-phonetic translation. The second principle in the hook system is the creation and ordering of the list of standard words conforming to this phonetic-digital translation. The third and final step is the use of this standard set of words as mnemonic "hooks" or "pegs" onto which new material may be "hung" and through which recall may be expedited. This final step is made through association with visual mental images. The entire sequence, then, begins with the ten symbols of the digital numbering system translated to sounds, the sounds are incorporated into words, the words into images, and the images are then associated with new material to be learned.

Although there is some variation in the preferences of different authorities, the basic digital-phonetic translation is as follows:

Digits	Phonetic Translation
1	The consonant sound "t"
2	The consonant sound "n"
3	The consonant sound "m"
4	The consonant sound "r"
5	The consonant sound "l"
6	The consonant sound "j," "sh," or soft "g"
7	The consonant sound "k," hard "ch," or hard "g"
8	The consonant sound "f"
9	The consonant sound "p"
0	The consonant sound "z"

It might be pointed out that most authors even give a mnemonic for remembering this mnemonic. The letter "t" has *one* vertical downstroke. The letter "n" has *two* vertical downstrokes. The letter "m" has *three* points on the bottom. The letter "r" is the *fourth* letter of the word *four*. The letter "l" is the Roman numeral for 50 (hence 5). The letter "j" is a little like a backward *six*. The numeral 7 is *crooked*, hence the hard "k" sound. A script letter "f" has two loops similar to the numeral 8. The numeral 9 is a backward "p." The numeral 0 has as its initial consonant sound the "z."

Now, by using these basic consonant sounds in combination, words can be made

which correspond to numbers as large as needed. For the purpose of application of this mnemonotechnic device, each potential user must make for himself a list of words which phonetically translate into numbers. Since we have a phonetic sound for each digit, words corresponding to numbers may be made simply by tacking the sounds together. Most authors give a suggested list of common nouns (which are the best since they can be fairly readily represented as mental images) which can be used as mnemonics. I have discovered, however, that particular mnemonic words appear to be highly idiosyncratic and that a given word which works well for one person will not be so effective for another. Regardless of what authoritative text is being used for reference, any potential user of the hook method should create for himself a satisfactory list of nouns. Each noun in the mnemonic list must have consonant sounds so arranged as to translate into the corresponding number. For example, the noun corresponding to the number 11 must have two "t" sounds but no other consonant sounds. The word corresponding to the number 8 must have an "f" sound but no other consonant sound. And so forth. In conjunction with his text, Dr. Bruno Furst (1958) includes a dictionary of 1000 appropriate nouns corresponding to the numbers 1 through 1000.

I have developed for my own use the following set of words which is a modification of that suggested by Young and Gibson (1962):

1. hat	14. tar	27. neck	40. rose
2. hen	15. tail	28. knife	41. rat
3. ham	16. tissue	29. nap	42. rain
4. hair	17. tack	30. maze	43. ram
5. hail	18. taffy	31. mitt	44. rare
6. shoe	19. tap	32. men	45. rail
7. hook	20. nose	33. mum	46. rash
8. hoof	21. net	34. mare	47. rake
9. hoop	22. nun	35. mail	48. roof
10. toes	23. name	36. mash	49. rope
11. tot	24. Nair	37. Mack	50. lose
12. tin	25. nail	38. muff	
13. tam	26. Nash	39. mop	

Each word in the list translates according to the phonetic formula given above into the number corresponding. The fact that 8 of the first 9 words begins with the letter "h" is a matter which I have found convenient. For the first 9 digits, any words having only the appropriate consonant sounds will do. One authority suggests the word "tea" as the representative of the digit 1; the name "Noah," having only the consonant sound "n," as the representative of the digit 2, and so forth. I have found it more convenient to use the words listed above. Once the list of words has been established, a consistent mental picture corresponding to each word must be developed. Some of the images corresponding to the words are self-evident. In general, the more bizarre the mental picture created for each word, the better its ultimate use as a mnemonic will be. Once a convenient mental image has been associated with each word to the point where the word immediately brings forth the mental image, the mnemonic is ready for use.

section V: general use of mnemonic systems

The most common use of the hook system is probably in show business. Many professional mnemotists will allow an audience to shout, randomly, as many as 100 words (preferably common nouns). When the list is complete, the mnemotist can recite the list either forward or backward. He can give the number (order of presentation) for any word in the list, or can give the word corresponding to any number. The process by which this is done sounds so unbelievably simple that the reader may accept it with disbelief. Each time the performer receives a noun from the audience he simply pictures the object named by the noun in some relationship to the mnemonic which he has previously committed to memory. For example, if the first word is "baloney" he will form a mental picture of baloney stuffed into a hat.[1] If the second word is "automobile" he may conjure a picture of a large hen driving an automobile. The user of this mnemonic system very rapidly develops a "feel" for a satisfactory association of mental images. Once a satisfactory association has been achieved for a given pair (mnemonic word and new word), he may proceed to receive the next word and form an association with the next mnemonic word. Again, let it be emphasized that the more bizarre and exaggerated these mental associations are, the better they will serve in the mnemonic process.

A beginner should try to remember 10 or 15 words at first. His success will probably amaze him. When the associations have been made, the process of recall simply involves a mental review of his mnemonics. For example, he wishes to recall the first word, which was given above as "baloney." He simply remembers the numeral 1 which gives rise to the mnemonic equivalent "hat." To the astonishment of the beginner with the hook system, not only does the word "hat" revive the previouly stored mental image of a hat but also the previously associated picture of a hat filled with baloney. He then proceeds to the numeral 2 which elicits the mnemonic word "hen." The image of a gigantic hen appears and associated with it is the automobile, and so forth through the list.

section VI: subjective experience and analysis

I have found that the reliability and consistency with which recalling the mnemonic automatically recalls the new word previously associated with it is truly remarkable. I am frankly at a loss to account, in terms of known psychological principles, for the vividness and firmness of the so

---

[1] The examples cited make use of the author's set of words listed above.

casually formed associative bonds. Should the order of events in which the recollection is formed be reversed, the vividness with which the mental images reoccur is striking. For example, if the word "baloney" is mentioned, the reconstruction of a mental image of baloney will simultaneously produce the mental image of hat, and the word "hat" has previously been stored as a mnemonic form of the numeral 1, thus "baloney" corresponds to the first word listed.

In actually practicing with the hook system I served as my own subject (à la Ebbinghaus), and have made some of the following observations. The first of these has been mentioned before. This is the subjective feeling of utter amazement that such quickly formed associative bonds can actually exist with considerable durability. When the process of associating mental images for several mnemonic-word pairs has been completed, there is the disappointing subjective feeling that not *one single word* has been committed to memory. However, when the learner reviews each mnemonic word in its proper order, the appropriate mental images seem to "pop" abruptly and vividly into consciousness. The use of the hook system seems to necessitate almost total dependency on the mnemonic mediating process. I am convinced that not one word could be recalled, after initial exposure, without resorting to the appropriate mnemonic sequence.

A second interesting observation is that the traditional serial position effect appears not to exist when using the hook system. There appears to be no tendency for the first and/or last words in a sequence to be recalled any better than those in the middle of the sequence. Also, the effectiveness of recall seems virtually independent of the number of items committed to memory. It is true that it is more difficult to learn 20 items than to learn 10 items, but not much more difficult. With a little practice, I have found that I can commit 50 items to memory with almost as much ease as 10 items.

The phrase, "little practice," means just that, only four or five attempts.

Both from references and from talking to people who had used the hook system, it was quite clear that the major practical use to which this system has been put in the past is in the entertainment field. Many professional mnemotists use it nightly in night club acts. A few professional teachers with whom I am acquainted have mastered this technique for classroom demonstration. Both the entertainers and the teachers have reported that when they had finished working with a given list and then learned a second list, the first one is simply dismissed from memory and the new mnemonic associations replace them.

Out of pure intellectual curiosity I decided to indulge in a crude investigation of the role of retroaction and intrusion while using the hook method. After committing a short list of random nouns to memory (10 items) I requested another list of 10 items. Both of these sets of items were associated with the same mnemonic words. Thus, we have a situation in which, in essence, a different "response member" is being associated with the same "stimulus member," the word being learned constituting the response member and the mnemonic constituting the stimulus member. According to many classic studies in psychology the association of a new response member to an old stimulus should result in considerable retroactive inhibition. I found that the amount of retroaction that occurred when using the hook system was negligible. I could store one list of 10 mnemonic-word pairs, receive a new list using the same mnemonics with new words, and recall, with virtually no difficulty, any member of either list with neither appreciable retroaction nor intrusion. Labeling the two lists with the name of the person who had originally generated them seemed to be adequate information for sorting any given number of either list. It seemed an unbelievably simple matter to remember that "balloon" was the sixth member of Tom's list but "Andromeda" was the sixth member of David's list.

section VII: a major example

The ease with which the associations were formed and recalled and the apparent dearth of retroaction and intrusion between lists caused me to wonder if the ordinary use of the hook system, i.e., temporary recall long enough to finish a performance, is not a grossly wasteful application of the useful memory technique. I speculated as to the possibility of using the hook system for fairly permanent storage of meaningful and orderly material rather than for temporary storage of random material emitted by an audience. In our modern academic system we hold a hearty disdain for rote memory but yet require students to do a great deal of it. Is it possible that the hook system could be used as a practical device, allowing students to commit to fairly permanent storage lists of rote material acquired with minimum effort and minimum time expenditure?

Again using myself as a subject, I decided to commit to memory something that could possibly be required of a student of American history. I located a list of the 50 states of the United States in order of their admission to the Union and began com-

mitting these to memory through the use of the mnemonics of the hook system. To my amazement I found that I had associated each state with a mnemonic in less than 30 minutes. On attempting to recall the entire list from beginning to end, the first recall trial resulted in two errors which were immediately corrected by one rehearsal. The process of association, one rehearsal (without reference to the original list), review of the items missed, and total recall of the list required only about 45 minutes. Subsequent to this 45 minutes of study I could recall any state from any part of the list, associated with its appropriate number, or could associate any number with its appropriate state. Another interesting subjective impression is that even though the mnemonics are originally constructed from number to mnemonic word to response word, the latency in recall seems to be less when remembering from response word to mnemonic to number. For example, in the list of states it seems to take longer to recall "Delaware" if the number "1" is given than it takes to recall "1" if the state "Delaware" is given. In order to exemplify the process which is necessary for the use of the hook system, and to show the highly idiosyncratic nature of the associations, I will attempt to reproduce here the "mental process" which I used in committing the 50 states to memory.

Order of Admission	State	Mnemonic Association [2]
1	Delaware	From the author's childhood there remains the memory of a soft drink called "Delaware Punch" of which he was quite fond. The soft drink had a distinctively shaped bottle. The mnemonic association is a *hat* with the characteristically shaped bottle sitting in it.
2	Pennsylvania	The mnemonic word for "2" is "hen." The association is of a very large fluffy hen pecking furiously at a fountain pen. "Pen" engenders the recollection of the state "Pennsylvania."

[2] At the moment of this writing it has been approximately 3 weeks since the initial learning. The list has been recited either in its entirety or as individual stimulus-response members about six times. In the past 2 weeks there has been only one rehearsal which yielded about three errors necessitating prompting. The list printed here is, at the moment, being dictated from memory without reference to the original list.

Order of Admission	State	Mnemonic Association
3	New Jersey	The mnemonic word is "ham." The association is of a cow being milked and the milk, instead of falling into a pail, is splattering aginst the ham. The breed of cow is, of course, Jersey, calling forth the state of New Jersey.
4	Georgia	The mnemonic word is "hair." Georgia is the Peach State; thus, the mnemonic association of a peach with very long "hairy" fuzz.
5	Connecticut	The mnemonic is of a convict ("con") caught in a *hail* storm. "Con" is a contraction for Connecticut.
6	Massachusetts	The mnemonic is a shoe; the association is of a priest holding Mass in a shoe ("mass" equals Massachusetts).
7	Maryland	The mnemonic word is hook; the association is of a statue of the Virgin Mary hanging from a hook; "Mary" engenders Maryland.
8	S. Carolina	The mnemonic word is hoof; the association is of a close-up picture of horses' hoofs running down a dirt road. The hoofprints, instead of being in the traditional horseshoe shape, are shaped on the left like an "S" and on the right like a "C," thus "S. C.," South Carolina.
9	New Hampshire	The mnemonic word is hoop; the image is of a large hog twirling a "Hula Hoop"; the hog is of the Hampshire breed.
10	Virginia	The mnemonic is toes; the association is very obscure; a picture of toes with a hand sprinkling ginger on them as though being used as foot powder. Ginger, a contraction of the girl's name, Virginia.
11	New York	Tot; a huge baby in a diaper playing atop the Empire State Building.
12	N. Carolina	Tin; the image of a soldier in a Union Civil War uniform standing in a huge tin can singing Christmas carols. The blue uniform makes him "northern"; the hymnbook which he is holding is labeled on the binder, "Carols." He is a "northern caroler," thus North Carolina.
13	Rhode Island	The mnemonic is "tam"; the association, an island with a road running down the middle and a tam perched atop the island.
14	Vermont	Tar; the image is a mountain scene in Vermont familiar to the author. The mountain is capped in black tar rather than snow.
15	Kentucky	"Tail"; a monkey with a long tail which is wrapped around the head of a stereotyped mustached Kentucky colonel.
16	Tennessee	The mnemonic is "tissue"; tissues are scattered about in great abundance on a tennis court; tennis produces the association with Tennessee.
17	Ohio	The mnemonic is tack; this is one of the few associations involving the actual outline of a state map. The outline of the state of Ohio, "Ohio" is written across the map and a huge tack is driven in to dot the "i."

Order of Admission	State	Mnemonic Association
18	Louisiana	The mnemonic is taffy; again a state map of Louisiana with strings of sticky taffy being pulled from it.
19	Indiana	Tap; an Indian head in full war bonnet being held under a water tap.
20	Mississippi	This is one of the rare cases in which no mnemonic is necessary. Mississippi is the author's home state and was recalled as being associated with the 20th admission on the first trial without the mediating mnemonic.
21	Illinois	Net; the image of a person unconscious, wrapped in bandages, obviously *ill*, being carried away in a net (ill equals Illinois).
22	Alabama	The mnemonic is nun, the association a nun holding a bottle of ale; ale is almost "ala," which is the abbreviation for Alabama.
23	Maine	Name is the mnemonic; the author sees the nameplate on his desk with a lion's mane growing from it.
24	Missouri	The only successful mnemonic for the author for 24 is simply an image of two large red letters "n" and "r" (phonetic 2 and 4); between these two letters is a large battleship, "The Big Mo," calling to mind the state of Missouri.
25	Arkansas	A picture of Noah's *Ark* with a huge nail penetrating the side (phonetic 25 is nail).
26	Michigan	A very obscure but bizarre and consequently effective association; the mnemonic is Nash. The image is of a particular Nash from the author's experience. It is of a convertible. There is a person leaning out of the convertible who is making various gestures and grimaces reminiscent of the stereotype of the silent movie madman. He is "crazy." The Yiddish word for crazy is "meshugenah" which sounds like Michigan.
27	Florida	The mnemonic is neck; vegetation is growing on the neck; vegetation is flora, thus Florida.
28	Texas	The mnemonic is knife; the state map of Texas has a characteristic shape; a knife is slicing the state map in half.
29	Iowa	The mnemonic is nap; the image of a man taking a nap but with one very large eye open; "eye" recalls Iowa.
30	Wisconsin	The mnemonic is maze; the image is a large multiple T-maze (as used in rat learning experiments) with a huge wheel of cheese rolling through the alleys. Wisconsin is noted for being a dairy state and cheese brings the association "dairy," hence Wisconsin.
31	California	The mnemonic is "mitt"; a picture of a catcher catching, instead of a baseball, a cauliflower; cauliflower vaguely sounds like California.
32	Minnesota	The mnemonic is "men" which is almost the abbreviation for the state Minnesota.
33	Oregon	The mnemonic is mum, a contraction of chrysanthemum; the image is a chrysanthemum with an oar lying across it; "Ore." is a contraction of Oregon.

Order of Admission	State	Mnemonic Association
34	Kansas	The mnemonic is mare; the association is a mare with a large tin can on each ear; "can" equals Kan. equals Kansas.
35	W. Virginia	An extremely obscure association; the tenth state, Virginia, was remembered by using a can of ginger; the mnemonic for 35 is "mail"; the association is a can of ginger wearing a western ten-gallon hat, making it "western ginger," being stuffed into an envelope.
36	Nevada	The mnemonic is mash; the association is a slot machine being mashed in a punchpress. Legal gambling in Nevada brings to mind the slot machine.
37	Nebraska	The mnemonic is Mack (Mack truck); the cab of a Mack truck with a large wicker basket on top, a tag indicating that it has just been purchased, consequently is a *new basket*, having a sound similar to Nebraska.
38	Colorado	"Muff" is the mnemonic; a large fluffy fur muff with a Crayola crayon protruding from it. Crayola sounds, again vaguely, like Colorado.
39	Montana	A mountain, rugged, unlike the one used for the Vermont mnemonic, more like a rocky mountain such as would be in Montana, with a mop (39) protruding from its "peak."
40	N. and S. Dakota	These were the only two states admitted to the Union on the same day. This unusual event allowed them to be committed to memory without mnemonic (the numbers associated with the states following still represent their rank order of admission).
41	Washington	A rat (41) scrubbing clothes on a *wash*board.
42	Idaho	The mnemonic is "rain"; the association a large potato (Idaho potato) holding an umbrella to keep the rain off.
43	Wyoming	A ram (43) butting a large letter "Y" reminding of the state Wyoming.
44	Utah	The mnemonic word is "rare"; the association is of a steak with a wooden tag reading "rare" stuck in it. The word "Utah" is branded on the steak.
45	Oklahoma	A railroad train (the mnemonic word is rail); the wheels are shaped like the letters "O" and "K"; the first two letters signifying Oklahoma.
46	Arizona	The mnemonic is "rash"; the association is of a person with a severe rash on one arm treating it by spraying from an aerosol can, "aerosol" equals Arizona.
47	New Mexico	The mnemonic is "rake"; the association a baby in diapers wearing a sombrero making him a *new Mexican*. He is holding a rake.
48	Alaska	The mnemonic is roof; an Eskimo in fur is sitting on a roof shivering.
49	Hawaii	The mnemonic is rope; the association is a hula girl. Her skirt is made of rope strands rather than grass.

As a test for interference, intrusion, and retroaction, about two days subsequent to the learning of the list of states, I attempted to commit to memory the Presidents of the United States in order of their election. The learning process seemed to take about the same time. The initial exposure was approximately 20 minutes. The same stimulus members of the mnemonic pair (i.e., the mnemonic words) were the same. New associations, however, were made. For example, the 18th President was U. S. Grant; the mnemonic is taffy; the association is of 50-dollar bills bearing Grant's picture, stuck in a mass of taffy. The second President was John Adams; the mnemonic association is a huge hen pecking the electrons out of orbit in an enormous atom (atom: Adams). I found that learning the list of Presidents resulted in virtually no retroactive inhibition for the list of states. Immediately after recalling the list of Presidents, with no prompting at all, I tried to recall the list of states. I made only two errors. At this writing, both lists have been retained with very little rehearsal for a period of approximately 3 weeks. The retention has not been perfect but I have observed in attempting to recall both lists only five errors. The appropriate mnemonic associations can be reinstated at a glance and apparently are quite firmly embedded in memory after that brief review.

section VIII: general evaluation and recommendation

From these rather superficial introspective observations and "self-experimentation" I am convinced that research into the possibility of the use of the hook system, or some modification of it, toward the aim of developing techniques for quick, efficient, and reasonably permanent storage of rote material, would be fruitful. I believe that the use of such a method would significantly decrease the time necessary to commit such material to memory and increase the effec-

tiveness with which all, or any part, of that material could be recalled to consciousness. The use of such a technique would be immediately adaptable to many aspects of subject matter, such as geography, history, literature (involving names and dates), and other subject matters which include the necessity for memorizing lists of either orderly or unstructured items. It is also conceivable that routine checkout procedures, such as preflight checkouts, troubleshooting routines, routine maintenance tasks, and so forth, could also be committed to relatively permanent memory by the use of a system such as the hook system.

Further research to test the validity of my introspective judgment would clearly be desirable. Should these observations be confirmed, parametric studies determining the possible scope and extensions of the hook system to the retention of more or less meaningful and, perhaps, practically useful information would be indicated.

REFERENCES

Furst, B. *The Practical Way to a Better Memory*. New York: Grosset & Dunlap, 1944.

Lorayne, H. *How to Develop a Super-Power Memory*. New York: F. Fell, 1957.

Young, M. N., and W. B. Gibson. *How to Develop an Exceptional Memory*. Philadelphia: Chilton, 1962.

SELECTED BIBLIOGRAPHY OF MNEMONOTECHNICAL TRAINING METHODS

Brothers, J. D., and E. P. F. Eagen. *10 Days to a Successful Memory*. Englewood Cliffs, N. J.: Prentice-Hall, Inc., 1957.

Byrne, B. *Three Weeks to a Better Memory*. J. C. Winston Co., 1951.

Fletcher, A. L. *How to Train and Improve Your Memory*. Halcyon House, 1948.

FURST, B. *The Practical Way to a Better Memory.* New York: Grosset & Dunlap, 1944.

————. *Stop Forgetting: How to Develop Your Memory and Put It to Practical Use.* Garden City, N. Y.: Doubleday & Company, Inc., 1949, 1958.

HAMILTON, F. S. *Mastering Your Memory.* New York: Crown Publishers, 1947.

HUNTER, I. M. L. *Memory, Facts and Fallacies.* Baltimore: Penguin Books, 1957.

LAIRD, D. A., and E. C. LAIRD. *Techniques for Efficient Remembering.* New York: McGraw-Hill Book Company, 1960.

LOGAN, A. I. *Remembering Made Easy.* New York: Arco Publishing Co., 1955, 1959.

LORAYNE, H. *How to Develop a Super-Power Memory.* New York: F. Fell, 1957.

NUTT, R. H. *How to Remember Names and Faces.* New York: Simon and Schuster, 1941.

————. *How to Develop a Good Memory.* New York: Simon and Schuster, 1951.

ROTH, D. M. *Roth Memory Course.* Rolston Publishing Co., 1918, 1955.

WEINLAND, J. D. *How to Improve Your Memory.* New York: Barnes and Noble, 1957.

YOUNG, M. N. *Bibliography of Memory.* Philadelphia: Chilton, 1961.

————, and W. B. GIBSON. *How to Develop an Exceptional Memory.* Philadelphia: Chilton, 1962.

13

*Another potential practical and direct application of labora-
tory research is discussed by Thom Verhave in the next article.
This fascinating account of the use of trained pigeons on an assembly line
needs no further introduction.*

the pigeon as
a quality-control inspector [1]

THOM VERHAVE

Many of the operations involved in the
quality-control inspection of commercial
products consist of monotonous checking
jobs performed by human operators. In
addition to monotony, these (usually visual)
inspection jobs have several other characteristics in common: (*a*) They require little
if any manual skill or dexterity, (*b*) they
require good visual acuity, (*c*) they require
a capacity for color vision, and (*d*) they
are extremely difficult to automate. There
is, however, an organic device which has
the following favorable properties: (*a*) an
average life span of approximately 10–15
years (Levi, 1963), (*b*) an extreme flexibility in adjusting to its environment as

[1] Opinions and conclusions contained in this
article are those of the author. They are not to be
construed as necessarily reflecting the views or the
endorsement of either the pharmaceutical industry or any pigeon.

I am indebted to John E. Owen, my former
collaborator, for a critical reading of this paper,
which saved me from many errors due to faulty
memory.

Reprinted from *American Psychologist*, 1966,
21: 109–115, by permission of the author and
publisher. Copyright © 1966 by the American
Psychological Association.

well as an enormous learning ability (Ferster and Skinner, 1957; Smee, 1850), (*c*) a
visual acuity as good as the human eye
(Reese, 1964), (*d*) color vision (Reese,
1964). The price for one such device is
only (approximately) $1.50; its name: *Co-
lumba livia domestica* or the pigeon.

Because of the characteristics listed
above it is quite feasible to train pigeons
to do all the visual checking operations involved in commercial manufacture. What
follows is a brief account of an exploratory
attempt to put the above suggestion into
actual practice (Verhave, 1959). This paper
is written partially in self-defense: Stories
about the pill-inspecting pigeons have circulated for many years—many versions containing gross inaccuracies.

In July of 1955 I was employed as a
"psychopharmacologist" at one of the larger
pharmaceutical companies. The main purpose of the laboratory was to develop and
evaluate techniques for the experimental
analysis of the effects of drugs on the behavior of animals.

Sometime, probably early in 1958, I
finally took the tour of the plant, which is
mandatory for all new employees. During
the all-day tour of the extensive research

and manufacturing facilities, I ran into the (gelatin) drug-capsule facilities. The capsules are manufactured by several very large and extremely complex machines, which together have a maximum production capacity of approximately 20,000,000 capsules per day. All of the capsules, which are made in a large number of sizes, and colors, are visually inspected. This job was done by a contingent of about 70 women. After inspection the capsules go to other machines which fill them automatically with the appropriate pharmaceuticals. The capsules are inspected in batches. The number of caps in a batch depends on the volume or size of the capsule: the larger the capsule size the smaller the number in a batch to be inspected. All of the capsules in a particular batch are of the same shape, size, and color. A big reservoir with a funnel drops the capsules at a fixed rate on an endless moving belt. The inspector, or "capsule sorter" as she is called, is located in front of the moving belt which is illuminated from underneath. She "pattern scans" the capules as they move by and picks up and throws out all "skags." A skag is a discard capsule because it is off color, has a piece of gelatin sticking out, or has a dent in it. This also includes all double-cap capsules. When the capsule comes to the capsule sorter, it is already closed by putting two halves, a cap and a body, together. This step was already performed by the production machine. Sometimes, however, during transportation or in storage a second cap (the larger half of a capsule) is put on top of an already capped capsule (a cap and body may vibrate apart and a loose cap may then slide over the body of another already capped capsule). Such a "double-cap skag" produces problems later on in the filling machine. After inquiry, I was told that the double-cap skag is also one of the more difficult types to spot.

The sorters (all female) are paid off on a group-bonus schedule employing "error cost." After the inspection of a batch is completed, a supervisor (usually also fe-

male) scoops a ladleful of inspected capsules out of the barrel in which they were collected. The types of skag defects are categorized and the inspector can allow up to three or four of the more minor imperfections per sample before a batch is rejected. If she finds more than the allowed number of skags in the sample ladled from the batch, the inspector has to reinspect the entire batch of capsules. She is thus likely to reduce her bonus pay for the day since it depends partially on her own inspection output.

To come back to the main story: On seeing those women and their simple monotonous task, and knowing about Skinner's "Pigeons in a Pelican" (1960, 1965), I said to myself, "Hell, a pigeon can do that!" Sometime later, I mentioned my birdbrain idea to a friend and fellow scientist in the physiochemistry department who also supervised the electronics shop which supported the research division. He almost fell out of his chair and choked in a fit of laughter. However, after the joke had worn off, we talked more seriously about my odd notion, especially after I told him about Project ORCON (organic control—Skinner, 1960, 1965). Eventually the director of research and I talked about it. It so happened that I had come up with my suggestion at an opportune time. The company had recently spent a considerable sum of money on a machine constructed by an outside engineering firm designed to inspect automatically for double caps. It did not work. After some deliberation the director of research gave me the go-ahead to build a demonstration and tryout setup. With the able help and splendid cooperation of the instrument-shop people, under the direction of my friend of the physiochemistry department, a demonstration apparatus was built. The result of our labor is shown in Figures 1, 2, 3, and 4. Figure 1 provides a general overview of the entire apparatus except the endless belt-driving mechanism, a close-up of which is given in Figure 2. Figure 3 gives a top view of the "business

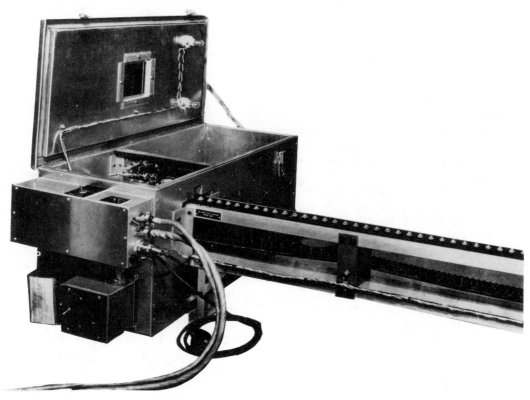

figure 1 *General overview of pill-inspection apparatus (except endless belt-driving mechanism).*

figure 2 *Close-up of endless belt-driving mechanism of pill-inspection apparatus.*

figure 3   Pill-inspection apparatus: top view of work space.

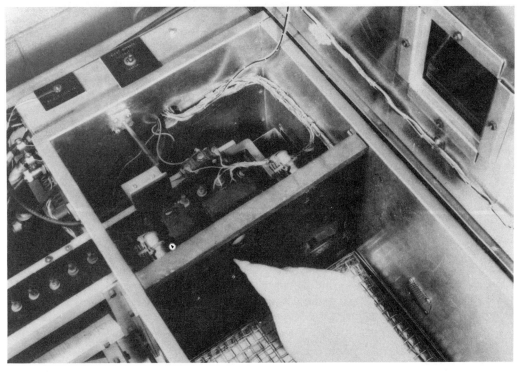

figure 4   Pill-inspection apparatus: pigeon at work.

end" of the pigeon's work space, and Figure 4 shows one of the birds in action.

While the apparatus was being designed and built, I had plenty of opportunity to consider varying aspects of the discrimination-training problems I would be faced with. The first decision to be made was which particular "skag" problem to tackle first. I obtained samples of various sized capsules of different colors. It was tempting to tackle the most troublesome problem first: the double-cap skag, especially those involving small capsules of colorless and transparent gelatin. On the actual inspection line these were the most difficult to spot. After playing around with different ways of presenting these capsules to a pigeon behind a modified pigeon key, a simple solution to the double-cap problem was discovered by accident. One of the minor problems to be solved was the lighting of the capsules presented behind the key. I discovered that by shining a narrow beam of light at the proper angle on a three-dimensional transparent curved surface, one obtains a focal point inside the object. (The tops and bottoms of all capsules are either round or oval.) In the case of a double-cap skag, one gets two clearly distinct focal points in slightly different positions. So, even in the case of the transparent double-cap capsule, all a pigeon had to do was to discriminate between one versus two bright spots of light inside the curious objects behind his key: no problem! [2]

For the purpose of working out the details of the actual training and work procedure, however, I decided to take the simplest discrimination problem possible. I chose a simple color discrimination: white versus red capsules. Two naive birds were selected for inspection duty. For one bird the red capsules were arbitrarily defined as skags ($S^\triangle$). For the other bird, the white capsules were given the same status.

As is clear from Figure 4, there were two pigeon keys. One key was actually a small transparent window, the other was opaque. The capsules could be brought into view behind the transparent key one by one at a maximum rate of about two per second. After a preliminary training phase, the birds were run as follows: A single peck on the weakly illuminated opaque key would (a) momentarily (.5 second) turn off the light behind the transparent key, and (b) weakly illuminate the window key to an extent insufficient to see much of the capsule in place behind it.

Next, a single peck on the now weakly lit window key would turn on a bright and narrow beam of light which clearly illuminated the capsule. The capsules were individually mounted in small and hollow bottletops glued onto the metal plates of the endless belt (see Figures 2, 3, 4). If the bird now pecked three more times on the window key with the new illuminated capsule exposed to view, a brief tone would sound. Next came the moment of decision. If the capsule exposed to view was judged to be a skag, the bird was required to make two more pecks on the window key. This would (a) turn off the beam of light illuminating the capsule, (b) move up the next capsule, and (c) produce food by way of the automatic hopper on a fixed-percentage basis (usually 100 per cent). However, if the capsule was considered to be acceptable, the bird indicated this by changing over to the opaque key. A peck on this key would also (a) turn off the beam of light behind the other key (window), and (b) move up the next capsule. It would not, however, produce reinforcement.

A bird, then, determined his own inspection rate. A peck on the opaque key would initiate an inspection cycle. However, reinforcement came only after making the appropriate number of pecks on the window key in case of a true skag only. Skags occurred rarely; they made up 10 per cent of all the capsules on the belt. Wrong pecks, either false alarms or misses, did not

---

[2] The opaque, single-color double cap may still be a difficult discrimination problem, even for a pigeon.

get reinforced, and produced a blackout (Ferster, 1954) of 30 seconds. The results were very encouraging: Both birds inspected on a 99 per cent correct basis within 1 week of daily discrimination training. The director of the pharmacology division, my immediate superior, who had watched the entire project with serious misgiving since its inception (he was sincerely afraid I was making a fool of myself), was delighted. In his immediate enthusiasm he called the director of research, who came over for a look. One week later the vice presidents as well as the president of the company had been given a demonstration. Everybody, including my immediate associates and co-workers, was greatly excited. The situation, as Skinner had previously discovered in a similar situation (Skinner, 1960), was a great source for jokes. There was talk about a new company subsidiary: "Inspection, Inc.!" (Company slogan: "It's for the birds!")

There were some sobering thoughts, however. One of them concerned the staggering problem of the logistics involved in getting pigeons to inspect as many as 20,000,000 separate objects each day. Although this problem did not seem insoluble to me, the details of the various possible approaches to a solution were never worked out.

After the company president had watched my feathered pupils perform, he congratulated me on my achievement. I was subsequently informed that serious consideration would be given to the further use and development of the method. I was also told that I could expect a visit from the chairman of the board and his brother, both elder statesmen of the company, who made all final policy decisions of importance. During their brief visit to the laboratory, one of them raised the question of possible adverse publicity. What about the Humane Society, and more important, suppose salesmen from other pharmaceutical houses would tell doctors not to buy any of our company's products: "Who would trust

medicine inspected by pigeons?!" I suggested that the use of pigeons was incidental, and that, for example, one could use hawks just as well; after all, what is better than a hawk's eye? This suggestion produced a wan smile.

One other problem that was brought up raised the question of the pigeons coming in contact with what was being inspected. The competition could well choose to ignore the mechanical details of the situation and exploit the more distasteful but imaginary possibilities. Even though the birds would only see the capsules at a distance through a window, the first mental picture [3] is usually one of a pigeon "manually" (proboscically?) sorting capsules, a thought no doubt repulsive to many people, especially to those who already have an aversion to birds as such.

After a brief stay, and a polite pat on the back, my distinguished visitors left.

Three weeks went by without any further word from HUM (Higher-Up-Management—Verhave, 1961). I concluded that probably meant that my pigeons were finished. I was right. Sometime later I was so informed. Through the grapevine I learned that the board of directors had voted 13 to 1 not to continue to explore the use of animals for quality-control inspection. The one "yes" vote presumably came from the director of research who initially had given me the green light for the preliminary demonstration.

There is one further amusing tale to the story: The company did try to patent my inspection method. The poor lawyer assigned to the case almost developed a nervous breakdown. It turned out to be "unpatentable" because, as the lawyers of the patent office put it (so succinctly), the method involved "a mental process" which is unpatentable in principle.[4] I tried to pin

[3] If a behaviorist may be excused for using such illegitimate terms . . .

[4] On this point, I may refer the reader to a recent article in *Science* by J. H. Munster, Jr., and Justin C. Smith (1965).

my lawyer friends down on what they meant by "a mental process." I suggested that the pigeon was merely an organic computor. However, I got nowhere. Lawyers apparently want no part of either physicalism or behaviorism.

So much as far as my own story is concerned. My efforts stimulated another exploratory attempt by my friend William Cumming, of Columbia University, who trained pigeons to inspect diodes. Brief descriptions of his work can be found in an article by Ferster and Ferster (1962), an anonymous (1959) article in *Factory*, and a recent article in *The Atlantic Monthly* by R. J. Herrnstein (1965).

One problem not yet touched on deserves some discussion. In the demonstration apparatus the capsules were coded as to whether they were acceptable or skags. In this way the automatic programing (relay) circuit could set up and enforce the appropriate discriminatory behavior of the birds. However, on an actual inspection line, this aspect of the training procedure could no longer be maintained. There would be no way of knowing which capsules are skags except by actual inspection. Consequently on a real inspection line there would be no way of knowing when to reward or not to reward the animal inspector! As a result, due to the lack of differential reward, the animal's discriminations would rapidly deteriorate.[5] There are two solutions. I discarded the first and most obvious one because it seemed mechanically cumbersome and not as interesting as the other solution.

The first solution would involve the use of known skags. A certain percentage of the capsules inspected would consist of such labeled duds, and be used to check up on the discriminatory behavior of the birds. This is similar to the use of catch tests in human psychophysical experiments.

This solution to the problem of guaranteeing that the animal inspector conforms to the values of his human employers makes it necessary to determine what minimum percentage of the objects inspected have to be planted skags in order to keep the inspecting behavior at an acceptable level of reliability.[6]

As a solution to the conformity-enforcement problem, however, this general solution is expensive and awkward. The on-line inspection equipment would need special machinery to insert in a random manner a fixed percentage of "stool-pigeon skags" and after inspection remove them again automatically for later reuse. The slightest observable difference between the "planted" objects and the other ones would lead to the development of a conditional discrimination (Lashley, 1938), and reintroduce the problem one set out to solve initially.

The second solution is simpler from a purely mechanical point of view. It also is of more theoretical or philosophical interest.

Briefly, it would involve the use of a minimum of two animals to simultaneously inspect each object. Initially, each animal would be trained to inspect capsules by using a training apparatus such as the one I had already constructed. In this apparatus all the capsules would be labeled as to whether they were skags or not and thus control the reward circuit.

After the desired discriminatory performance was well established the two birds would be removed to the on-line inspection situation. From then on the birds would only be rewarded if they *both* agreed on whether a particular object was a skag or not. Such an agreement-contingency setup would most likely be quite adequate to maintain the desired behavior. There is, of course, the possibility that both birds would indeed, once in a while, agree to treat a

---

[5] Skinner, in his World War II project to train pigeons to home missiles, did not face this problem. His birds were meant to "extinguish" after a brief period of duty.

[6] This question was investigated experimentally by Cumming.

skag as an acceptable object. However, the probability of this happening for any particular object on a particular inspection trial is the product of the error frequencies (the probability of such an error) of each bird. If, therefore, each bird independently has an error frequency as high as 1 out of 100, the probability of both birds being wrong but still rewarded would be 1 out of 10,000! Hooking additional animals into the agreement-contingency circuit would make the possibility of the development of a "multiple folly" [7] very unlikely.

The solution is of some philosophical interest because it makes the pigeon observers act according to Charles Pierce's (1923, orig. publ. 1878) pragmatic theory of truth: "The opinion which is fated to be ultimately agreed to by all who investigate, is what is meant by the truth, and the object represented in this opinion is real" (pp. 56–57). It also appears to me that the agreement-contingency type of arrangement provides a basic paradigm for the experimental analysis of social behavior, a terra incognita so far hardly even explored by a systematic experimental investigation (Verhave, 1966).

In conclusion, let me point out that the idea of using trained animals for the dubious purposes of Homo sapiens is very old indeed. Since antiquity man has domesticated many animals. It seems an obvious development to apply our modern knowledge of behavior theory to the task of training some of our animal companions for the performance of various sophisticated tasks (Clarke, 1958; Herrnstein, 1965).

The obstacle in the way of such developments is not our ignorance of behavior, though it is still large, but mainly, it seems, the obstinate belief of man in his intellectual superiority over other creatures as well as a generalized fear of the imagined consequences of novel developments.

[7] "folie a deux, trois, . . . n."

REFERENCES

ANONYMOUS. This inspector is a bird. *Factory,* 1959 (Dec.), 219–221.

CLARKE, A. C. Our dumb colleagues. *Harper's Magazine,* 1958, **216,** 32–33.

FERSTER, C. B. Use of the blackout in the investigation of temporal discrimination in fixed-interval reinforcement. *Journal of Experimental Psychology,* 1954, **47,** 69–74.

————, and B. F. SKINNER. *Schedules of reinforcement.* New York: Appleton-Century-Crofts, 1957.

FERSTER, MARILYN B., and C. B. FERSTER. Animals as workers. *New Scientist,* 1962, **15,** 497–499.

HERRNSTEIN, R. J. In defense of bird brains. *Atlantic Monthly,* 1965 (Sept.), **216,** 101–104.

LASHLEY, K. S. Conditional reactions in the rat. *Journal of Psychology,* 1938, **6,** 311–324.

LEVI, W. M. *The pigeon.* (Rev. ed.) Sumter, S. C.: Levi Publishing Company, 1963.

MUNSTER, J. H., JR., and J. C. SMITH. The care and feeding of intellectual property. *Science,* 1965, **148,** 739–743.

PEIRCE, C. How to make our ideas clear. (Orig. publ. 1878) In M. R. Cohen (Ed.), *Chance, love and logic.* New York: Harcourt, Brace, 1923.

REESE, E. P. *Experiments in operant behavior.* New York: Appleton-Century-Crofts, 1964.

SKINNER, B. F. Pigeons in a pelican. *American Psychologist,* 1960, **15,** 28–37.

————. Stimulus generalization in an operant: A historical note. In D. I. Mostofsky (Ed.), *Stimulus generalization.* Stanford: Stanford Univer. Press, 1965.

SMEE, A. *Instinct and reason.* London: Reeve, Benham & Reeve, 1850.

VERHAVE, T. Recent developments in the experimental analysis of behavior. *Proceedings of the Eleventh Research Conference, American Meat Institute Foundation,* 1959, Mar., 113–116.

————. Is the system approach of engineering psychology applicable to social organizations? *Psychological Record,* 1961, **11,** 69–86.

————. *The experimental analysis of behavior: Selected readings.* New York: Appleton-Century-Crofts, 1966.

UNIT

IV

motivation

14

The topic of motivation has had a stormy history in experimental psychology. For years, research attention was directed almost exclusively to the so-called "primary drives" (e.g., hunger, thirst, sex, avoidance of pain) which had their origins in the tissue needs of the organism. According to a strict interpretation of this view, all motivated behavior is derived from these biological needs. However, in the last 20 years research on motives that are not based on physiological needs has increased considerably. In the following paper, William N. Dember describes several experiments which indicate the importance of stimulus change, novelty, and complexity for human and animal behavior. He also sketches a motivational model developed in close collaboration with Robert W. Earl. The Dember-Earl model is offered as representative of those new approaches to motivation which stress "information processing," rather than stimulus intensity, as their key theoretical concept.

the new look in motivation

WILLIAM N. DEMBER

About a decade and a half ago, when I began graduate training in psychology, one of the most exciting research topics concerned the effects on perception of motivational and cognitive variables. For example, evidence was presented that showed recognition thresholds for words to be affected by the motivational significance of the words; thus, words with positive or pleasant connotations might have lower thresholds—that is, be correctly recognized at a shorter presentation duration—than neutral words, whereas the recognition of negatively toned or taboo words required longer durations of presentation than those needed for the recognition of neutral words. Other research showed the perceived size of an object to

be related to its value. Thus, children tended to overestimate the size of coins relative to discs of neutral value, and poor children were more subject to this type of error than were rich children. By now, a host of such studies has been conducted; with each passing year the methodology employed gets a little more sophisticated and the results a little more equivocal. But that is a different story.[1] The point for the present purpose is to note that this approach to the study of perception—which became known as the New Look in Perception—emphasized the interaction between processes which psychologists had in general hitherto been careful to keep in separate conceptual categories, and, in the textbooks in separate chapters.

To speak of a New Look implies an "old

Reprinted from *American Scientist*, 1965, **53**: 409–427, by permission of the author and publisher. Copyright © 1965 by the Society of the Sigma Xi.

[1] For a review of this literature, see Dember (1960).

look." In the case of perception the old look was one in which the variables influencing perception were thought to reside in two sources: (1) the physical stimulus and (2) the sensory system, consisting of receptor organ, afferent nerve and subcortical and cortical sensory projection areas. The New Look in Perception was not antineurophysiology; rather, it postulated kinds of interactions within the nervous system that were more elaborate and diffuse than those allowed for in the classical neurophysiology and neuroanatomy of the nineteenth century. Interestingly enough, direct evidence for some of the neural mechanisms consistent with the New Look has been reported, as, for example, in the discovery of the cortical priming function of the reticular arousal system.[2]

Let me make one last remark about the New Look in Perception before I turn to its analogue in motivation. And that is to note that the New Look was not entirely new. Similar ideas had been proposed earlier by such diverse theorists as Freud and John Dewey. What made the New Look novel was its attempt at empirical verification of its postulates.

the new look in motivation

What about the New Look in Motivation? From the sense of my previous remarks you might anticipate, first of all, that the New Look in Motivation will be characterized by an emphasis on *interaction* between motivational and perceptual and cognitive processes. Secondly, you might expect to hear something about the "old look" in motivation. Finally, you should not be surprised to learn that the New Look in Motivation has a long history of its own, and that what might better be called the "latest new look" is characterized not so much by its theoretical postulates as by its attempts at empirical verification.

[2] See, for example, Samuels (1959).

Now, rather than elaborate on these ideas at this point, I would prefer to defer their discussion until later, and launch immediately into a description of some of my own research experience in this area.

alternation behavior

Let me begin where I began—with a phenomenon called "alternation behavior." This behavior has been studied almost exclusively in rats, but has also been observed in other species, including man. It can be described very simply with the aid of the first figure.

Figure 1 depicts in plan view a piece of apparatus that is popular among those who investigate the behavior of rats. It is called a T-maze, and consists of: a starting alley; a choice-point region; and two goal arms. Frequently, guillotine doors are located at the juncture of the goal arms and the choice-point so that once the rat has entered an arm it can be prevented from leaving that arm until the experimenter is ready to remove it from the maze. Depending on the purpose of a particular experiment, the goal arms may be kept identical in stimulus properties, or specific differences between them may be introduced, as, for example, by painting one arm black and the other white. For the experiments which

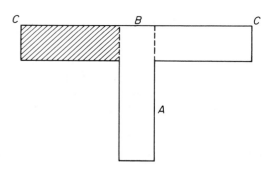

figure 1   The T-maze, consisting of (A) starting alley, (B) choice-point, and (C) goal arms. The dashed lines indicate guillotine doors, which can be lowered to prevent retracing.

I will first describe, let us assume that the left arm is black and the right arm is white.

The T-maze is typically used in studying *learning* in the rat, and usually in the following manner. The rat is first deprived of some commodity to establish a state of physiological need and a concomitant state of "psychological drive"; for example, a schedule of food deprivation might be instituted in order to make the rat hungry. Then the rat is introduced into the T-maze; at the end of one of the goal arms a bit of food is located. If the rat enters that arm, it is allowed to eat the food and is then removed from the maze. Such "trials" are repeated until the rat has reached a criterion performance level—perhaps entering the proper arm on 10 successive trials.

Such a problem, though it may seem simple to us, will usually not be solved immediately by the rat. Indeed, it may take 20 or 30 trials before criterion is reached. The gradual improvement in performance that occurs over trials, as evidenced by the behavior of a large group of rats, is considered to reveal the gradual establishment of a habit. One can then study the variables that influence habit acquisition; for example, strength of hunger drive during training, amount and quality of the drive-reducing commodity (i.e., the reward or reinforcement), the distribution of training trials, and a host of other variables, limited only by the imagination and ingenuity of the experimenter.

Now, in pursuing such an experiment about 30 years ago, Wayne Dennis (1935) noticed something unexpected. He had assumed, along with other researchers, that the acquisition of the habit—say, of always turning right in the maze—was superimposed on an initially random process. That is, the rat's behavior on the first few trials at least was expected to be unsystematic. But Dennis found it to be quite the contrary. In particular, on examining the records of the early trials, he discovered the phenomenon of *alternation*: that is, if a rat made a right turn, for example, on the first

trial, the probability was high that it would turn left on the second trial. Incidentally, this will happen, on the early trials, even if the rat finds food on the first trial. Thus, the behavioral stereotypy which emerges during the course of learning is superimposed on an already existing and strong tendency toward behavioral variability, and variability that is *systematic*, not random.

What Dennis did next, as any good scientist would, was to put aside his investigation of learning and to explore the alternation phenomenon. I have reviewed his and other work on alternation elsewhere (Dember, 1961; Dember and Fowler, 1958) and will not burden you with the details of all those investigations. What is significant for this presentation is the assumption that Dennis made about *what* the rat was alternating with respect to. According to Dennis, the rat was alternating with respect to the *maze arms*.

What other possibilities might there be? When an animal is observed entering the black goal arm, one could describe that bit of behavior by reference to the arm, as Dennis did, by saying that the rat entered the *black* arm, or the arm on the left, or perhaps the arm oriented toward the west. All such statements focus on the part of his environment with which the rat's behavior brings him into contact. A different kind of assertion would focus on the behavioral act itself, and say that the animal made a left-turning *response*.

If, on the next trial, the rat alternates, one could say, again with Dennis, that the rat was alternating with respect to maze arms (he went into the black arm on the first trial, and into the white arm on the second). Or, from the other point of view, one could say that having made a left-turning response on the first trial (which happened to bring the rat into the black arm), the rat alternated by way of a right-turning response on the second trial (which happened to bring him into the white arm).

Dennis's view, which sees alternation as stimulus-alternation, not only has historical priority; it also would seem the more natural of the two accounts. Strangely enough, however, the response-alternation point of view was the one that prevailed.

This happened, and quite obviously to one who is familiar with American psychology, because there existed a dominant behavior theory which had the concepts available to allow the deduction of response-alternation, i.e., Hull's (1943) learning theory. Within Hull's theory is contained the concept of "reactive inhibition"; it is the function of the concept of reactive inhibition [3] to account for the process of experimental extinction and related phenomena—that is, the process whereby the animal stops making a learned response when that response is no longer followed by reward. In essence, reactive inhibition is a hypothetical quantity which grows each time a particular response is made. The size of the increment to reactive inhibition is a direct function of the amount of effort required to make the response and also a function of how many times the response has been made. An additional property of reactive inhibition is that it spontaneously dissipates over time. The behavioral effect of reactive inhibition is to decrease the tendency to make the response that gave rise to it. If you think of reactive inhibition as a fatigue-like state, its properties and effects may become more readily apparent.

The application of Hull's reactive inhibition concept to the case of alternation behavior is straightforward. Whenever a response is made—say, a left turn in a T-maze —a certain quantity of left-turning, reactive inhibition is built up. Given a second trial, the animal will be somewhat less inclined than previously to make that response, and given no other compelling tendency to turn left, it will turn right by default, and thus will alternate. In these terms, alternation reflects the animal's attempt to minimize the aversive consequences of its own responding. At this point, one might wonder

why an animal behaves at all—why make that first left turn or the second right turn? Why not stay put in the starting alley? The answer, I believe, from the Hullian point of view is that the animal *would* be entirely quiescent were it not for the behavior-arousing physiological drives. That answer, by the way, expresses the essence of the "old look" in motivation, whether it be the version of the animal psychologists, such as Hull, or of the classical Freudian psychoanalysts.[4]

To continue with the alternation story, recall that two accounts of alternation have been proposed, which we will refer to as the *stimulus-alternation* hypothesis and the *response-alternation* hypothesis. The response-alternation hypothesis was for several decades the generally accepted account largely because of its nice fit within Hullian theory, but also because it allowed for some testable derivations that were empirically confirmed. For example, the response-alternation hypothesis predicts decreasing probability of alternation with increasing time between the two trials; it predicts increasing probability of alternation with increases in the number of forced turns to one side of the maze prior to a free-choice trial. These and other predictions were confirmed, lending additional credence to the response-alternation hypothesis, but also additional impact to the experiments next to be described.

Since the conflicting hypotheses were designed to account for the same phenomenon—i.e., alternation in the T-maze—any attempt to choose between them must necessarily be based on some variation from the standard procedure. A beautiful set of experiments was finally conducted by Murray Glanzer (1953a,b) that permitted a clear choice between the opposing hypotheses.

Glanzer's theoretical position was derived from Dennis's. It asserted that alternation

---

[3] An additional concept, conditioned inhibition, is necessary for a complete account of the extinction process.

[4] Robert White (1959) has most clearly drawn the parallel between motivational concepts, old and new, in academic psychology and psychoanalytic theory.

occurred with respect to environmental stimuli, not to the rat's own prior responses. According to the theory, any time an organism is exposed to a stimulus, a quantity, called "stimulus satiation," is built up which has the effect of decreasing the probability that the organism will respond to that stimulus on future occasions. Note that this postulate is *formally* just like the reactive inhibition postulate in Hullian theory. Indeed, Glanzer has endowed stimulus satiation with all the properties of reactive inhibition; for example, it accumulates with increasing exposure to a stimulus; it spontaneously dissipates in time, and so forth. As a result, Glanzer's theory can predict equally as well as Hull's the outcome of the experiments mentioned earlier relating to the interval between trials, number of forced turns in the goal arm, and so on.

Beyond this, Glanzer devised some situations for which the two theories make opposing predictions. One of these situations made use of a cross-shaped maze, as depicted in Figure 2. On a given trial, the maze is used as a T, with one of the two possible starting alleys blocked off at the choice-point. The two trials which any animal runs, however, are made from opposite starting alleys. For example, if on trial-1 a rat is started from the south starting alley, it will start its second trial from the north.

Now, consider the rat who, starting from the south, turns right on the first trial. According to reactive inhibition theory it should make a left-turning response on the second trial, regardless of the alley into which that response takes it. But, to alternate responses in the cross-maze, the animal must repeat maze arms.

According to satiation theory, that same animal, having been exposed to the white arm on the first trial, should avoid that arm on the second trial, and therefore should enter the black arm, even though that means repeating its previous right-turning response. The experiment suggested by these arguments was done and clearly confirmed Glanzer's prediction. The rats were

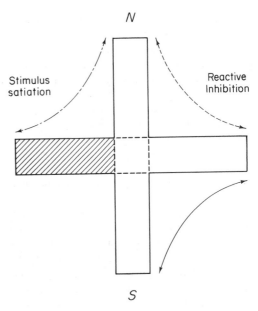

figure 2 *The cross-maze. The solid arrow represents the behavior of an animal on trial-one. Behavior predicted on trial-two is represented by broken arrows, one for the reactive-inhibition prediction, the other for the satiation prediction.*

stimulus alternaters, not response alternaters.

A second, and equally elegant experiment, was conducted, based on the following argument. According to the Hullian theory, reactive inhibition following a response dissipates over time. Thus, if a rat makes a right turn and is then confined in the maze arm instead of being immediately removed, the reactive inhibition generated on the first trial should decrease in amount. A second trial, following a long delay in the maze arm, should be less likely to exhibit the alternation tendency than an immediate second trial. In addition, it should not matter where the rat spends its time during the delay. A long wait between trials outside the maze should have the same effect on probability of alternation as a long delay within the maze arm.

From the point of view of satiation theory, it matters considerably where the rat spends its time, but matters little how it got there. Indeed, a long delay in a maze arm is really a longer than usual exposure to the to-be-satiated stimulus: the longer the exposure, the greater the satiation; the greater the satiation, the greater the probability of alternation. Thus, rats delayed in the maze arm should alternate more than rats given an immediate second trial, and rats delayed in the maze arm should alternate more than rats given an equally long delay outside the maze. Again, the data clearly confirmed Glanzer's predictions. Rats are stimulus alternaters, not response alternaters.

The dramatic success of Glanzer's satiation theory made it worthy of further inspection and test. One such test, the first of the studies in which I was directly involved, examined the validity of the assumption that exposure to a stimulus *per se* is a sufficient condition for inducing alternation behavior (Walker, *et al.*, 1955). For these experiments a simple modification was made in the standard procedure: instead of walking into one of the goal arms on the "exposure" trial, rats were *placed* in the arm by the experimenter. After an appropriate length of exposure, the animals were removed from the arm and given an immediate free-choice trial. Several variations of this procedure were run, but in no case was there any evidence that this "passive exposure" to the goal arm stimuli had an effect on the rats' subsequent behavior. At that point it looked as though alternation depended on the rats' making an active choice on the first trial.

Several years after those initial failures to find alternation following passive exposure, the effect was obtained in experiments by Glanzer, by myself, and by others. Why those earlier studies did not reveal the effect remains a mystery.[5] In a way, however, that failure was fortunate, for it led to a pair of new experiments which are of great

[5] The mystery may have been cleared up, and indeed the whole problem of alternation behavior reopened, by an exciting group of experiments recently reported as a doctoral dissertation by Robert Douglas (1964).

significance, at least for purposes of this presentation.

response to change

The first of the pair was based on the following argument. In the previous passive exposure experiments the animals were not in direct contact with the stimuli at the juncture of the choice-point and the goal arm. But that is the place at which the choice was to be made on the second trial. Thus, it would seem a fairer test of satiation theory if the first trial were so designed that the rat's exposure to the goal arm stimuli occurred within a context that included the choice-point region.

That argument was translated into an experiment (Kivy, Earl, and Walker, 1956) for which the standard T-maze was modified slightly by employing transparent glass doors instead of the usual opaque doors to block off the goal arms from the choice-point. These glass doors were already in place when the exposure trial began. When the rats were introduced into the starting alley, they could wander up to the choice-point and peer through the glass doors into the goal arms, but could not enter either arm on that trial. What the rat saw on the exposure trial was two goal arms of the same brightness, either both black or both white. The animals were given lengthy exposure trials to assure adequate satiation; they were then taken out of the maze, the glass doors were removed, and one of the goal arms was changed in brightness.

The design of the experiment is given in Figure 3. It was expected that if Glanzer's theory were correct, and if this version of the passive exposure procedure were the appropriate one, then those rats exposed to black goal arms on the first trial would enter the white arm on the second trial, and *vice versa*. And that is exactly what happened.

Before discussing the second experiment of this pair, let me recall a comment I made

Maze arm

	Left	Right
Exposure	W(B)	W(B)
Test	B(W)	W(B)

figure 3 *Design of the Kivy, Earl, and Walker experiment. On the exposure trial, the arms of the T-maze are both black or both white and the rat views them through glass partitions; on the test trial, the animal can choose between a black and a white arm.*

earlier about Glanzer's theory—that it was formally identical with the reactive inhibition theory, with the exception of the assumed source of the alternation tendency. The formal identity that I referred to was related to the postulates about the growth and decay of the inhibiting quantity. But there is another way in which the two theories are identical: for both, alternation behavior represents an *avoidance* response. For both, the animal does what it does on trial-two because it cannot do what it did on trial-one. Hull's rat turns left because, in some sense, it is "tired of making right turns"; Glanzer's rat enters the black arm because it "can't stand seeing whiteness," not because it finds the black arm attractive.[6]

Now, during the time when we were working on these studies with Professor Walker, Robert Earl and I were beginning to develop some theoretical ideas about motivation which I intend to discuss more fully a little later. These ideas were stimulated in large part by the work I have been describing, but they also derived from a variety of other sources, including our own introspections. One notion we had was that it was inappropriate to consider the

choices an animal or a person makes to be determined exclusively by avoidance tendencies. This might prevail in some instances, but there must also be cases in which an alternative is chosen because it has positive valence, and positive in an absolute, not just a relative sense.

To develop this idea further, it was necessary to specify the properties of a stimulus object that would make it attractive to a given individual. In somewhat different language, our task was to specify the properties of what the learning theorists variously called "goal objects," "incentives," or "rewards." Within classical motivation theory, such objects were characterized either by their ability to reduce a physiological need or by their having been associated with such need-reducing objects. The former class constituted the so-called *primary rewards*, the latter class, the *secondary* or *acquired* rewards. Between them, the primary and secondary rewards comprised the entire set of goal objects.

Now, it was our notion—and not ours alone, of course [7]—that this conceptualization of motivation and reward was incomplete; that there were goal objects other than those that reduced physiological need states. Moreover, we believed that the slack could not adequately be taken up by reference to a vaguely specified set of acquired rewards.

Let me postpone completion of this level of discussion and return temporarily to the real world of rats and mazes, beginning with another brief look at Figure 3, in which the Kivy experiment is diagrammed. While that experiment was designed as a test of Glanzer's satiation theory and the results fit the satiation prediction, an alternative interpretation of what was going on in that experiment could be offered. It was my thought that what the rat was doing

[6] For a newer and more sophisticated analysis of alternation theories than the one offered here, see O'Connell (1965).

[7] We were working within a tradition begun in recent decades by, among many others, Berlyne (1954, 1960), Harlow (1953), and Nissen (1954), and continued most recently by Munsinger and Kessen (1964), and Walker (1964).

when it entered the white arm, after having been exposed to two black arms, was not avoiding further exposure to blackness; rather, on approaching the choice-point and noting a marked change in one of the goal arms—for example, the one changed from black to white—the rat responded to the change by entering the changed arm and exploring it. I refer to this interpretation as the *response-to-change* hypothesis.

But an alternative interpretation is not worth much if all it can do is predict experimental results that have already been obtained. To be taken seriously it must make unique predictions and preferably predictions that are opposite to those derived from the original theoretical position. What can the response-to-change hypothesis predict that will differentiate it from the satiation hypothesis?

As so often happens, the answer to that question came by way of a mistake I made while describing the Kivy experiment to a psychology class. What I did, in effect, was to reverse the stimulus conditions that prevailed in the Kivy experiment; my erroneous description would be represented by the diagram in Figure 4. Here, on the exposure trial the two arms are different—one black and one white, and on the test trial they are of the same brightness, both black or both white. My initial response to the error in presentation was to apologize to the class, erase the mistake from the black-board, and do it properly. Several hours later, while I was perseverating on this error, it struck me that my erroneous diagram provided the design for an experiment that would answer the question: how can the response-to-change hypothesis be differentiated from the satiation hypothesis? What would each of the two hypotheses predict were the experiment diagrammed in Figure 4 actually run?

First consider the satiation hypothesis. On the exposure trial, the animal is satiated for black and for white; on the test trial it is offered a choice between, say, two black arms. The satiation induced on the exposure trial would not bias it against either the black arm on the left or the black arm on the right. In short, the choices made by a group of rats should be distributed independently of the rats' satiation experience.

The response-to-change hypothesis makes a different prediction. The rat which saw black on the left and white on the right on the exposure trial and is then faced with two black arms on the test trial should be attracted to the *changed* arm—in this case the black arm that used to be white; that is, the arm on the right.

The experiment suggested by this analysis was run (Dember, 1956), using the Kivy apparatus and generally following his procedures except for the configuration of the stimuli on the two trials. The rats' behavior conformed to the response-to-change prediction, and this result has since been replicated by other investigators.

The outcome of this experiment greatly encouraged Robert Earl and me to pursue the theoretical developments that we had been working on. Rather than dwell further on the details of where the ideas came from, I propose at this point to sketch the product of this thinking, which took the form of both some general hypotheses about motivation (that we called the Theory of Choice) and some specific experimental tests of these hypotheses.

Maze arm

	Left	Right
Exposure	B(W)	W(B)
Test	W(B)	W(B)

figure 4 *Design of the Response-to-Change experiment. Conditions are just the reverse of those in the Kivy, et al., experiment.*

the theory of choice [8]

From the experiments that I have described, from many that I do not have time to mention, and from the set of observations which form the base of those nonexperimental approaches to knowledge about man and his motives—such as philosophy and art—it is clear that the direction of an individual's behavior is at least partly under the control of the stimulus objects and events surrounding him. It is clear also that one need not be suffering from physiological imbalance, or anticipating that state, to become interested in those external objects; it is clear that these objects of interest need not be potential restorers of physiological balance, nor even associated with such servants of the homeostatic process, in order to exert powerful impact on the individual's behavior.

What are these objects and events? For a rat, a change in the brightness of a goal arm in a T-maze; for a monkey, a toy railroad train running on a table top; for a human baby, a rattle, its own fingers, plastic birdies swinging on a mobile over its crib; for the human adult, a painting, a puzzle, a pin-ball machine, a poem (I am tempted to add "a partridge in a pear tree," perhaps to preserve the alliteration, but maybe also because it typifies a class of objects, characterized by incongruity, that has considerable impact on the direction of behavior).

I have used the word incongruity; the items in the preceding list call to mind other terms, such as novelty, complexity, movement, uncertainty, ambiguity, and so on. There are specific objects and events, impinging on specific individuals at particular moments which might best be labeled by one of these terms, rather than another. For example, the rat entering the changed goal arm is responding to novelty;

[8] The theory is presented more formally and in greater detail in Dember and Earl (1957), Earl (1957, 1961), and Musselman (1963).

the toy railroad train is characterized, for the monkey, by movement; the puzzle by uncertainty, and so on. Rather than dwell on these fine distinctions, the Theory of Choice seizes on what they appear to have in common, as objects or events, and on the way that they influence behavior.

As objects or events, the items in the list share the property of being bearers of *information*. I use the word in the technical sense of Information Theory; these are objects or events which are unexpected, nonredundant, and which, when they occur, therefore reduce uncertainty. With regard to the perceiving individual, these highly informative objects or events have the effect of arousing his interest, directing his attention, consuming his time and energy— at least if he is free to let them.

The Theory of Choice asserts, then, that every object (let us drop the word, event, for convenience) can be assigned an information value, or a "complexity value," as the theory was originally proposed; moreover, the theory asserts that the complexity of an object is a motivationally crucial property of that object, so long as that object is functioning as a goal object, and not simply as a means to another end.

The next step in the development of the theory is hard to convey clearly without a lot of attendant discussion. It asserts that each individual can also be assigned a "complexity value." What we have in mind here is that for each individual there is some highest level of complexity, in the range of objects that he might encounter, which he is equipped to deal with comfortably and effectively. The individual's complexity level is called his "ideal."

Some objects would *for him* be excessively complex; some would be too simple; some would be just right, as the baby bear's bed was for Goldilocks. Objects that are too simple elicit boredom if they are unavoidable; objects that are too complex elicit fear, anger, and sometimes rage if one is forced to maintain contact with them.

Quite obviously, then, if the individual is free to choose, he will prefer to encounter objects of a complexity level that matches his own. He will *select* them from among others if they are made available to him; he will *seek* them out if they are absent; he will *work* for them; and he will even *learn* what he must do in order to obtain them, all of these (select, seek, work, learn) behaviors that in classical motivation theory serve as indicators of the presence of a primary or secondary reward.

While the theory expects that the individual will maintain considerable contact with objects of ideal complexity in preference to objects of much lower or higher complexity, it also recognizes that nonideal objects will also be sampled by the individual. Indeed, it seems to be the case, as evidenced by some results that Earl (1957) obtained in his doctoral dissertation, that the modal amount of time goes not to the ideal stimulus, but to one that is just a little more complex than the ideal.

We refer to that object as a "pacer," and attribute to it a special function. It is the pacer, if one is available, that enables the individual to change his ideal. As he maintains active contact with the pacer and eventually masters it, his own level of complexity grows, and he is ready for a new pacer and eventually a still higher ideal.

Of course pacers are not always available, and there are probably some neurophysiological limits to perceptual and cognitive growth, but, in general, the theory takes the optimistic position that under the proper circumstances an individual's complexity level can keep increasing and that learning can be achieved neither as a boring chore nor as a fearful burden. Indeed, the New Look in Motivation—of which the Theory of Choice is but a glance —has already invaded the classroom, or so I gather from a recent article by Robert Gross published in the *New York Times*

Magazine, for Sunday, September 6, 1964. The article is about innovations in teaching techniques, and in one brief paragraph the author says

. . . Another element is a new consensus on motivation. Cumulative evidence from many sources—animal experiments, studies of how children learn, everyday observations of the way they really behave—has shown up the inadequacies of old notions of motivation, based on reward and punishment, by demonstrating that human beings are born with the desire to know, the urge to explore and to master their environment, to achieve. . . .

The ideas contained within the Theory of Choice are not especially novel. As I implied earlier, they can be found in the writings of many authors. For example, I was both dismayed and delighted to discover some very similar notions in the works of Herbert Spencer and Thomas Brown, two nineteenth-century philosopher-psychologists. The major innovation provided by the theory—I said this also about the New Look in Perception—is its attempt at empirical verification, which in turn implies an attempt at operational definition of its concepts, such as complexity, pacer, etc., and a related concern for measurement.

some tests of the theory

A brief account of two experiments will serve to illustrate both the problem of measuring the concepts of the theory and the beginning steps that have been taken to solve that problem. In addition, the two experiments will reveal how the theory can be generalized to cover the phylogenetic range from rats to college students and stimulus materials ranging from visual patterns to poetry.

The theory was first tested in an experiment with rats (Dember, Earl, and Paradise, 1957). A new piece of apparatus was constructed, the figure-8 maze, as illustrated in Figure 5. The rat, after several

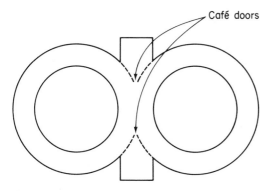

Café doors

figure 5 *The figure-8 maze. The rat is placed in one of the boxes at the juncture of the two loops, and enters the maze by pushing through one-way café doors.*

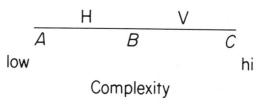

figure 6 *Two stimuli, H and V, and three hypothetical rats, arranged according to their complexity values. See text for explanation.*

days of taming, was introduced into the maze and then left there for about an hour. One loop of the figure-8 was lined with horizontal black and white stripes; the other loop was lined with vertically oriented stripes. The two loops were equal in total brightness. However, as the rat moved through the vertically striped loop, it experienced more changes in illumination than it did when moving through the horizontally striped loop. We assumed that, for the rat, the greater the number of illumination changes, the greater the perceptual complexity. Note that our assessment of the relative complexity of the two alternatives was based on intuitive judgment, and though derived from many years of intimate contact with rats, our judgment is ideally no substitute for a more direct measurement.

Now, the theory enabled the following prediction: any change in the rat's preference for one of the loops, as indexed by the amount of time it spent in each loop over two consecutive daily one-hour sessions, would be in the direction *from less complex to more complex.* The basis of this prediction can be shown with the help of Figure 6. The rat that enters the maze with an ideal at C would have an initial preference for the more complex, i.e., the vertically striped, loop and would maintain that

preference, as long as it kept behaving in the situation. Rats entering at A would initially prefer the less complex loop; in the course of sampling both loops, however, their ideals might grow until they are close enough to the complexity of the vertically striped alternative so that it became preferred. Once that happened, if it did, a fixed preference for the more complex loop would be evidenced. Rats entering with ideals at B might initially prefer either H or V, depending on which of the two they were closer to, but if their preference changed, once again the change could occur only from H to V.

The data collected from 17 rats conformed very well to the prediction, but the sample was small and the procedure somewhat informal, to be excused on the grounds that this was a "pilot study." Therefore, a second experiment was conducted, with a neater procedure—for example, 5 daily sessions were conducted rather than just 2—and with a change in the patterns lining the two loops. In this case, the horizontally striped loop was contrasted with a plain black loop for half the rats and a plain white loop for the other half. Here the intuitive judgment about which was the more complex seemed less equivocal; clearly the horizontally striped loop was now functioning as the more complex alternative. The same prediction was made— any change in preference would be from the less to the more complex loop, i.e., from plain to horizontally striped, but not *vice versa*—and again was convincingly verified in the data.

The theory so far has been successful with rats, but what about people? I have already mentioned Earl's doctoral dissertation, in which the subjects were 12-year-old children, and the stimulus materials were puzzles which the children were allowed to work on. I am also aware of an attempt by some colleagues at the University of Chicago to run (literally) children in a human-size version of the figure-8 maze, complete with horizontally and vertically striped loops. There the results were a bit messy, but they probably should have been.

Closer to home is an experiment conducted by Richard Kammann (1964) as his doctoral dissertation at the University of Cincinnati. This is the study in which the stimulus material was poetry.

I think it is clear that the physiological-need approach to motivation would be hard pressed to predict which of a set of poems would be preferred by college students. What can the Theory of Choice, as a representative of the New Look in Motivation, contribute to this problem?

A poem, like any other stimulus, has a complexity value, which is the resultant of a whole set of formal, or structural properties of the elements of the poem—for example, its meter, rhyme scheme, etc.—as well as semantic properties, relating to the meanings of individual words and phrases. Also contributing to the complexity of a poem is the ambiguity of its total message —the meanings of the individual words may be clear, but the poet's intent may not. In addition to these formal and nonformal sources of complexity is the factor of familiarity. It seems reasonable to anticipate that even the initially most complex poem would lose in complexity as it became more and more familiar to, and better and better understood by, a particular reader. "A rose is a rose is a rose" is a very unlikely sequence of words, but not to someone who has heard that line a few times. This last consideration suggests that it might be futile to attempt an assessment of the complexity of a given poem without interposing the intended reader of that poem. In short, he is the one who should, in effect, tell us how complex that poem is for him. But how might that be done?

One could try a direct approach and simply ask subjects to rate poems according to their complexity. This seemed too simple-minded, however, and while it might work, its usefulness would appear limited. A somewhat less direct approach to measuring poem complexity was sought by Dr. Kammann and found in what is referred to as the Cloze technique.

Suppose I show you the letters CINCINNAT__, with a blank space for a final letter, and I ask you to guess what single letter belongs in that space. I believe you would have little difficulty in correctly guessing the appropriate letter. It is really terribly redundant, and I am sure that a piece of mail addressed to the city of "Cincinnat" would not be delayed any longer than usual.

Suppose, however, at the opposite extreme, I randomly selected a sequence of 9 letters and asked you what the 10th should be; the redundancy of that last letter, and hence its predictability by you, would be greatly reduced.

We could play the same game with sequences of words, deleting say every fourth word in a passage and asking people to fill in the blanks. Their ability to make correct guesses surely would reflect the internal redundancies within the word sequence. This, in essence, is the Cloze technique. It was developed, incidentally, as a measure of readability to compete with the popular Flesch count.

Dr. Kammann saw in the Cloze technique a possible way of measuring the complexity of a poem. He argued that the higher the Cloze score associated with a given poem—the greater the number of blanks properly filled in by a subject, or group of subjects—the less complex it was as a total stimulus object.

The rest should now be obvious. A set of 15 poems was selected, which seemed *a*

A_____, a ringing health, _____the king
of_____our hearts to-day! _____what proud song
_____ follow on the_____, nor do him_____?
Unless the sea_____harp, each mirthful_____
Woven of the_____of the nights_____Spring,
And Dawn_____lonely listener, glad_____grave
With colours_____ the sea-shell_____the wave
In_____eye and cheek, _____is none to_____!

Drink to him, _____men upon an _____peak
Brim one_____cup of crimson _____,
And into it_____ one pure cold_____ of snow,
Then_____it up, too_____to speak
And_____— to the mountains, _____on glittering line,
_____away into the_____-glow.

figure 7   One of the unclozed poems (for the Eightieth Birthday of George Meredith) used in the poetry experiment. The deleted words, in order are: health, unto, all, But, should, thought, wrong, were, string, lightning, of, the, and, of, and, brightening, there sing, as, Alpine, immortal, wine, drop, crust, hold, rapturously, drink, line, surging, sunset.

priori to cover a wide range of complexity values. Every fourth word was deleted from each of the poems, beginning with the second word, and these "unclozed" poems were given to college students, whose task it was to guess what word belonged in each blank space. One such fragmented poem is shown in Figure 7.

On the basis of the subjects' performance, the poems could then be ranked according to their complexity. At a later date, these same subjects were given the intact poems and asked, among other tasks, to rate them on a good-bad scale and to indicate which they would like to have the opportunity to memorize, to hear discussed by an expert, etc.

Among the many interesting results that were obtained, the two most pertinent were that the poems of intermediate complexity were given the highest "goodness" ratings and that the subjects' own ability to guess the missing words in all the poems—what one might call the subjects' "clozability" score—was highly correlated with the complexity of the poems they said they would prefer to memorize and hear discussed by an expert.

This brief description fails to do justice to a very complex and clever piece of work, but it does indicate a promising approach

to the measurement of the concepts in the theory. In addition, it may suggest the scope of coverage that the theory is seeking. In this latter respect, the theory is quite representative of those that comprise the New Look in Motivation.

BIBLIOGRAPHY

BERLYNE, D. E. A theory of human curiosity. *Brit. J. Psychol.*, 1954, **45**, 180–191.

————. *Conflict, arousal, and curiosity.* New York: McGraw-Hill, 1960.

DEMBER, W. N. Response by the rat to environmental change. *J. comp. physiol. Psychol.*, 1956, **49**, 93–95.

————. *The psychology of perception.* New York: Holt, 1960.

————. Alternation behavior. In D. W. Fiske and S. R. Maddi (Eds.), *Functions of varied experience.* Homewood, Ill.: Richard D. Irwin and The Dorsey Press, Inc., 1961.

————, and R. W. EARL. Analysis of exploratory, manipulative, and curiosity behavior. *Psychol. Rev.*, 1957, **64**, 91–96.

————, and N. PARADISE. Response by rats to differential stimulus complexity. *J. comp. physiol. Psychol.*, 1957, **50**, 514–518.

DEMBER, W. N., and H. FOWLER. Spontaneous alternation behavior. *Psychol. Bull.*, 1958, **55**, 412–428.

DENNIS, W. A comparison of the rat's first and second explorations of a maze unit. *Amer. J. Psychol.*, 1935, **47**, 488–490.

DOUGLAS, R. J. An analysis of spontaneous alternation cues. Unpublished doctoral dissertation, Univ. of Michigan, 1964.

EARL, R. W. Problem solving and motor skill behaviors under conditions of free-choice. Unpublished doctoral dissertation, Univ. of Michigan, 1957.

————. *A theory of stimulus selection.* Human Factors Section, Hughes Ground Systems, Special Document SD 61–132, 1961.

GLANZER, M. Stimulus satiation: An explanation of spontaneous alternation and related phenomena. *Psychol. Rev.*, 1953a, **60**, 257–268.

————. The role of stimulus satiation in spontaneous alternation. *J. exp. Psychol.*, 1953b, **45**, 387–393.

HARLOW, H. F. Mice, monkeys, men, and motives. *Psychol. Rev.*, 1953, **60**, 23–32.

HULL, C. L. *Principles of behavior*. New York: Appleton-Century-Crofts, 1943.

KAMMANN, R. Cognitive complexity and preferences in poetry. Unpublished doctoral dissertation, Univ. of Cincinnati, 1964.

KIVY, P. N., R. W. EARL, and E. L. WALKER. Stimulus context and satiation. *J. comp. physiol. Psychol.*, 1956, **49**, 90–92.

MUNSINGER, H., and W. KESSEN. Uncertainty, structure, and preference. *Psychol. Monographs*, 1964, **78** (No. 9, Whole No. 586).

MUSSELMAN, D. R. Free choice behavior as a function of stimulus changes along three dimensions of complexity. Unpublished doctoral dissertation, Claremont Graduate School, 1963.

NISSEN, H. W. The nature of the drive as innate determinant of behavioral organization.

In M. R. Jones (Ed.), *Nebraska symposium on motivation*. Lincoln, Nebr.: Univ. of Nebraska Press, 1954.

O'CONNELL, R. H. Trials with tedium and titillation. *Psychol. Bull.*, 1965, **63**, 170–179.

SAMUELS, INA. Reticular mechanisms and behavior. *Psychol. Bull.*, 1959, **56**, 1–25.

WALKER, E. L. Psychological complexity as a basis for a theory of motivation and choice. In D. Levine (Ed.), *Nebraska symposium on motivation: 1964*. Lincoln: Univ. of Nebraska Press, 1964.

———, W. N. DEMBER, R. W. EARL, S. E. FLIEGE, and A. J. KAROLY. Choice alternation: II. Exposure to stimulus or stimulus and place without choice. *J. comp. physiol. Psychol.*, 1955, **48**, 24–28.

WHITE, R. W. Motivation reconsidered: the concept of competence. *Psychol. Rev.*, 1959, **66**, 297–333.

15

All living organisms tend to function so as to maintain the various physiological systems in a balanced condition and the behavior which results is referred to as "motivated." But as Dember has argued (in Chapter 14), much behavior, particularly that of human beings, cannot be accounted for solely in terms of these physiological models. A very powerful motive in man apparently results from certain cognitive imbalances or inconsistencies which continually occur. In the next article, Robert Zajonc discusses three of the major theories which have guided research on this problem. Although the theories originally dealt with problems in attitude change, there have been more recent attempts to extend and apply the models to such diverse topics as animal learning, physiological motivation, international conflict behavior, and interpersonal perception.

the concepts of balance, congruity, and dissonance

ROBERT B. ZAJONC

Common to the concepts of balance, congruity, and dissonance is the notion that thoughts, beliefs, attitudes, and behavior tend to organize themselves in meaningful and sensible ways.[1] Members of the White Citizens Council do not ordinarily contrib-ute to NAACP. Adherents of the New Deal seldom support Republican candidates. Christian Scientists do not enroll in medical schools. And people who live in glass houses apparently do not throw stones. In this respect the concept of consistency underscores and presumes human *rationality*. It holds that behavior and attitudes are not only consistent to the objective observer, but that individuals try to appear consistent to themselves. It assumes that inconsistency is a noxious state setting up pressures to eliminate it or reduce it. But in the *ways* that consistency in human behavior and attitudes is achieved we see rather often a striking lack of rationality. A heavy smoker cannot readily accept evidence relating cancer to smoking [2]; a socialist, told that Hoover's endorsement of certain polit-

---

[1] The concepts of balance, congruity, and dissonance are due to Heider, Osgood and Tannenbaum, and Festinger, respectively. (F. Heider, "Attitudes and Cognitive Organization," *Journal of Psychology*, Vol. 21, 1946, pp. 107–112. C. E. Osgood and P. H. Tannenbaum, "The Principle of Congruity in the Prediction of Attitude Change," *Psychological Review*, Vol. 62, 1955, pp. 42–55. L. Festinger, *A Theory of Cognitive Dissonance*, New York, Harper & Row, 1957.) For purposes of simplicity we will subsume these concepts under the label of consistency.

Reprinted from *Public Opinion Quarterly*, 1960, **24**: 280–296, by permission of the author and publisher. Copyright © 1960 by Columbia University Press.

[2] Festinger, *op. cit.*, pp. 153–156.

ical slogans agreed perfectly with his own, calls him a "typical hypocrite and a liar." [3] Allport illustrates this irrationality in the following conversation:

Mr. X: The trouble with Jews is that they only take care of their own group.

Mr. Y: But the record of the Community Chest shows that they give more generously than non-Jews.

Mr. X: That shows that they are always trying to buy favor and intrude in Christian affairs. They think of nothing but money; that is why there are so many Jewish bankers.

Mr. Y: But a recent study shows that the per cent of Jews in banking is proportionally much smaller than the per cent of non-Jews.

Mr. X: That's just it. They don't go in for respectable business. They would rather run night clubs.[4]

Thus, while the concept of consistency acknowledges man's rationality, observation of the means of its achievement simultaneously unveils his irrationality. The psychoanalytic notion of rationalization is a literal example of a concept which assumes both rationality and irrationality—it holds, namely, that man strives to understand and justify painful experiences and to make them sensible and rational, but he employs completely irrational methods to achieve this end.

The concepts of consistency are not novel. Nor are they indigenous to the study of attitudes, behavior, or personality. These concepts have appeared in various forms in almost all sciences. It has been argued by some that it is the existence of consistencies in the universe that made science possible, and by others that consistencies in the universe are a proof of divine power.[5] There

is, of course, a question of whether consistencies are "real" or mere products of ingenious abstraction and conceptualization. For it would be entirely possible to categorize natural phenomena in such a haphazard way that instead of order, unity, and consistency, one would see a picture of utter chaos. If we were to eliminate one of the spatial dimensions from the conception of the physical world, the consistencies we now know and the consistencies which allow us to make reliable predictions would be vastly depleted.

The concept of consistency in man is, then, a special case of the concept of universal consistency. The fascination with this concept led some psychologists to rather extreme positions. Franke, for instance, wrote,

. . . the unity of a person can be traced in each instant of his life. There is nothing in character that contradicts itself. If a person who is known to us seems to be incongruous with himself that is only an indication of the inadequacy and superficiality of our previous observations.[6]

This sort of hypothesis is, of course, incapable of either verification or disproof and therefore has no significant consequences.

Empirical investigations employing the concepts of consistency have been carried out for many years. Not until recently, however, has there been a programmatic and systematic effort to explore with precision and detail their particular consequences for behavior and attitudes. The greatest impetus to the study of attitudinal consistency was given recently by Festinger and his students. In addition to those already named, other related contributions in this area are those of Newcomb, who introduced the concept of "strain toward symmetry," [7] and of Cartwright and Harary, who ex-

[3] H. B. Lewis, "Studies in the Principles of Judgments and Attitudes: IV, The Operation of 'Prestige Suggestion,'" *Journal of Social Psychology*, Vol. 14, 1941, pp. 229–256.

[4] G. W. Allport, *The Nature of Prejudice*, Reading, Mass., Addison-Wesley, 1954.

[5] W. P. Montague, *Belief Unbound*, New Haven, Conn., Yale University Press, 1930, pp. 70–73.

[6] R. Franke, "Gang und Character," *Beihefte, Zeitschrift für angewandte Psychologie*, No. 58, 1931, p. 45.

[7] T. M. Newcomb, "An Approach to the Study of Communicative Acts," *Psychological Review*, Vol. 60, 1953, pp. 393–404.

pressed the notions of balance and symmetry in a mathematical form.[8] These notions all assume inconsistency to be a painful or at least psychologically uncomfortable state, but they differ in the generality of application. The most restrictive and specific is the principle of congruity, since it restricts itself to the problems of the effects of information about objects and events on the attitudes toward the source of information. The most general is the notion of cognitive dissonance, since it considers consistency among any cognitions. In between are the notions of balance and symmetry, which consider attitudes toward people and objects in relation to one another, either within one person's cognitive structure, as in the case of Heider's theory of balance, or among a given group of individuals, as in the case of Newcomb's strain toward symmetry. It is the purpose of this paper to survey these concepts and to consider their implications for theory and research on attitudes.

the concepts of balance and strain toward symmetry

The earliest formalization of consistency is attributed to Heider,[9] who was concerned with the way relations among persons involving some impersonal entity are cognitively experienced by the individual. The consistencies in which Heider was interested were those to be found in the ways people view their relations with other people and with the environment. The analysis was limited to two persons, labeled P and O, with P as the focus of the analysis and with O representing some other person, and to one impersonal entity, which could be a physical object, an idea, an event, or the like, labeled X. The object of Heider's inquiry was to discover how relations

among P, O, and X are organized in P's cognitive structure, and whether there exist recurrent and systematic tendencies in the way these relations are experienced. Two types of relation, liking (L) and so-called U, or unit, relations (such as possession, cause, similarity, and the like) were distinguished. On the basis of incidental observations and intuitive judgment, probably, Heider proposed that the person's (P's) cognitive structure representing relations among P, O, and X are either what he termed "balanced" or "unbalanced." In particular, he proposed, "In the case of three entities, a balanced state exists if all three relations are positive in all respects or if two are negative and one positive." Thus a balanced state is obtained when, for instance, P likes O, P likes X, and O likes X; or when P likes O, P dislikes X, and O dislikes X; or when P dislikes O, P likes X, and O dislikes X (see Figure 1). It should be noted

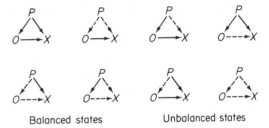

Balanced states   Unbalanced states

figure 1 *Examples of balanced and unbalanced states according to Heider's definition of balance. Solid lines represent positive, and broken lines negative, relations.*

that within Heider's conception a relation may be either positive or negative; degrees of liking cannot be represented. The fundamental assumption of balance theory is that an unbalanced state produces tension and generates forces to restore balance. This hypothesis was tested by Jordan.[10] He

---

[8] D. Cartwright and F. Harary, "Structural Balance: A Generalization of Heider's Theory," *Psychological Review,* Vol. 63, 1956, pp. 277–293.

[9] Heider, *op. cit.*

[10] N. Jordan, "Behavioral Forces That Are a Function of Attitudes and of Cognitive Organization," *Human Relations,* Vol. 6, 1953, pp. 273–287.

presented subjects with hypothetical situations involving two persons and an impersonal entity to rate for "pleasantness." Half the situations were by Heider's definition balanced and half unbalanced. Jordan's data showed somewhat higher unpleasantness ratings for the unbalanced than the balanced situations.

Cartwright and Harary [11] have cast Heider's formulation in graph-theoretical terms and derived some interesting consequences beyond those stated by Heider. Heider's concept allows either a balanced or an unbalanced state. Cartwright and Harary have constructed a more general definition of balance, with balance treated as a matter of degree, ranging from 0 to 1. Furthermore, their formulation of balance theory extended the notion to any number of entities, and an experiment by Morrissette [12] similar in design to that of Jordan obtained evidence for Cartwright and Harary's derivations.

A notion very similar to balance was advanced by Newcomb in 1953.[13] In addition to substituting A for P, and B for O, Newcomb took Heider's notion of balance out of one person's head and applied it to communication among people. Newcomb postulates a "strain toward symmetry" which leads to a communality of attitudes of two people (A and B) oriented toward an object (X). The strain toward symmetry influences communication between A and B so as to bring their attitudes toward X into congruence. Newcomb cites a study in which a questionnaire was administered to college students in 1951 following the dismissal of General MacArthur by President Truman. Data were obtained on students' attitudes toward Truman's decision and their perception of the attitudes of their closest friends. Of the pro-Truman subjects 48 said that their closest friends favored

Truman and none that their closest friends were opposed to his decision. Of the anti-Truman subjects only 2 said that their friends were generally pro-Truman and 34 that they were anti-Truman. In a longitudinal study, considerably more convincing evidence was obtained in support of the strain-toward-symmetry hypothesis. In 1954 Newcomb set up a house at the University of Michigan which offered free rent for one semester for seventeen students who would serve as subjects. The residents of the house were observed, questioned, and rated for four to five hours a week during the entire semester. The study was then repeated with another set of seventeen students. The findings revealed a tendency for those who were attracted to one another to agree on many matters, including the way they perceived their own selves and their ideal selves, and their attractions for other group members. Moreover, in line with the prediction, these similarities, real as well as perceived, seemed to increase over time.[14]

Newcomb also cites the work of Festinger and his associates on social communication [15] in support of his hypothesis. Festinger's studies on communication have clearly shown that the tendency to influence other group members toward one's own opinion increases with the degree of attraction. More recently Burdick and Burnes reported two experiments in which measures of skin resistance (GSR) were obtained as an index of emotional reaction in the presence of balanced and unbalanced situations.[16] They observed significant differences in skin resistance depending on

[14] T. M. Newcomb, "The Prediction of Interpersonal Attraction," *American Psychologist*, Vol. 11, 1956, pp. 575–586.

[15] L. Festinger, K. Back, S. Schachter, H. H. Kelley, and J. Thibaut, *Theory and Experiment in Social Communication*, Ann Arbor, Mich., University of Michigan, Institute for Social Research, 1950.

[16] H. A. Burdick and A. J. Burnes, "A Test of 'Strain toward Symmetry' Theories," *Journal of Abnormal and Social Psychology*, Vol. 57, 1958, pp. 367–369.

[11] Cartwright and Harary, *op. cit.*

[12] J. Morrissette, "An Experimental Study of the Theory of Structural Balance," *Human Relations*, Vol. 11, 1958, pp. 239–254.

[13] Newcomb, *op. cit.*

whether the subjects agreed or disagreed with a "well-liked experimenter." In the second experiment Burdick and Burnes found that subjects who liked the experimenter tended to change their opinions toward greater agreement with his, and those who disliked him, toward greater disagreement. There are, of course, many other studies to show that the attitude toward the communicator determines his persuasive effectiveness. Hovland and his co-workers have demonstrated these effects in several studies.[17] They have also shown, however, that these effects are fleeting; that is, the attitude change produced by the communication seems to dissipate over time. Their interpretation is that over time subjects tend to dissociate the source from the message and are therefore subsequently less influenced by the prestige of the communicator. This proposition was substantiated by Kelman and Hovland,[18] who produced attitude changes with a prestigeful communicator and retested subjects after a four-week interval with and without reminding the subjects about the communicator. The results showed that the permanence of the attitude change depended on the association with the source.

In general, the consequences of balance theories have up to now been rather limited. Except for Newcomb's longitudinal study, the experimental situations dealt mostly with subjects who responded to hypothetical situations, and direct evidence is scarce. The Burdick and Burnes experiment is the only one bearing more directly on the assumption that imbalance or asymmetry produces tension. Cartwright and Harary's mathematization of the concept of balance should, however, lead to impor-

tant empirical and theoretical developments. One difficulty is that there really has not been a serious experimental attempt to *disprove* the theory. It is conceivable that some situations defined by the theory as unbalanced may in fact remain stable and produce no significant pressures toward balance. Festinger once inquired in a jocular mood if it followed from balance theory that since he likes chicken, and since chickens like chicken feed, he must also like chicken feed or else experience the tension of imbalance. While this counter-example is, of course, not to be taken seriously, it does point to some difficulties in the concepts of balance. It is not clear from Heider's theory of balance and Newcomb's theory of symmetry what predictions are to be made when attraction of both P and O toward X exists but when the origin and nature of these attractions are different. In other words, suppose both P and O like X but for different reasons and in entirely different ways, as was the case with Festinger and the chickens. Are the consequences of balance theory the same then as in the case where P and O like X for the same reasons and in the same way? It is also not clear, incidentally, what the consequences are when the relation between P and O is cooperative and when it is competitive. Two men vying for the hand of the same fair maiden might experience tension whether they are close friends or deadly enemies.

In a yet unpublished study conducted by Harburg and Price at the University of Michigan, students were asked to name two of their best friends. When those named were of opposite sexes, subjects reported they would feel uneasy if the two friends liked one another. In a subsequent experiment subjects were asked whether they desired their good friend to like, be neutral to, or dislike one of their strongly disliked acquaintances, and whether they desired the disliked acquaintance to like or dislike the friend. It will be recalled that in either case a balanced state obtains only if the two persons are negatively related to one

17 C. I. Hovland, I. L. Janis, and H. H. Kelley, *Communication and Persuasion: Psychological Studies of Opinion Change*, New Haven, Conn., Yale University Press, 1953.

18 H. C. Kelman and C. I. Hovland, "'Reinstatement' of the Communicator in Delayed Measurement of Opinion Change," *Journal of Abnormal and Social Psychology*, Vol. 48, 1953, pp. 327–335.

another. However, Harburg and Price found that 39 per cent desired their friend to be liked by the disliked acquaintance, and only 24 per cent to be disliked. Moreover, faced with the alternative that the disliked acquaintance dislikes their friend, 55 per cent as opposed to 25 per cent expressed uneasiness. These results are quite inconsistent with balance theory. Although one may want one's friends to dislike one's enemies, one may not want the enemies to dislike one's friends. The reason for the latter may be simply a concern for the friends' welfare.

Osgood and Tannenbaum's principle of congruity

The principle of congruity, which is in fact a special case of balance, was advanced by Osgood and Tannenbaum in 1955.[19] It deals specifically with the problem of *direction* of attitude change. The authors assume that "judgmental frames of reference tend toward maximal simplicity." Thus, since extreme "black-and-white," "all-or-nothing" judgments are simpler than refined ones, valuations tend to move toward extremes or, in the words of the authors, there is "a continuing pressure toward polarization." Together with the notion of maximization of simplicity is the assumption of identity as being less complex than the discrimination of fine differences. Therefore, related "concepts" will tend to be evaluated in a similar manner. Given these assumptions, the principle of congruity holds that when change in evaluation or attitude occurs it always occurs in the direction of increased congruity with the prevailing frame of reference. The paradigm of congruity is that of an individual who is confronted with an assertion regarding a particular matter about which he believes and feels in a certain way, made by a person toward whom

[19] Osgood and Tannenbaum, *op. cit.*

he also has some attitude. Given that Eisenhower is evaluated positively and freedom of the press also positively, and given that Eisenhower (+) comes out in favor of freedom of the press (+), congruity is said to exist. But given that the *Daily Worker* is evaluated negatively, and given that the *Daily Worker* (−) comes out in favor of freedom of the press (+), incongruity is said to exist. Examples of congruity and incongruity are shown in Figure 2. The dia-

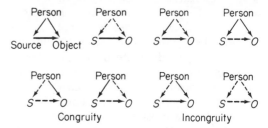

figure 2   *Examples of congruity and incongruity. Heavy lines represent assertions, light lines attitudes. Solid heavy lines represent assertions which imply a positive attitude on the part of the source, and broken heavy lines negative attitudes. Solid light lines represent positive, and broken light lines negative, attitudes.*

gram shows the attitudes of a given individual toward the source and the object of the assertion. The assertions represented by heavy lines imply either positive or negative attitudes of the source toward the object. It is clear from a comparison of Figures 1 and 2 that in terms of their formal properties, the definitions of balance and congruity are identical. Thus, incongruity is said to exist when the attitudes toward the source and the object are similar and the assertion is negative, or when they are dissimilar and the assertion is positive. In comparison, unbalanced states are defined as having either one or all negative relations, which is of course equivalent to the above. To the extent that the person's attitudes are congruent with those implied in the assertion, a stable state exists. When the attitudes toward the person and the assertion are incongruent, there will be a tendency to change the attitude toward the person and the object of the assertion in the direction of increased congruity. Tannenbaum obtained measures on 405 college students regarding their attitudes toward labor leaders, the *Chicago Tribune*, and Senator Robert Taft as sources, and toward legalized gambling, abstract art, and accelerated college programs as objects. Some time after the attitude scores were obtained, the subjects were presented with "highly realistic" newspaper clippings involving assertions made by the various sources regarding the concepts. In general, when the original attitudes toward the source and the concept were both positive and the assertion presented in the newspaper clippings was also positive, no significant attitude changes were observed in the results. When the original attitudes toward the source and the concept were negative and the assertion was positive, again no changes were obtained. As predicted, however, when a positively valued source was seen as making a positive assertion about a negatively valued concept, the attitude toward the source became less favorable, and toward the concept more favorable. Conversely, when a negatively valued source was seen as making a positive assertion about a positively valued concept, attitudes toward the source became more favorable and toward the concept less favorable. The entire gamut of predicted changes was confirmed in Tannenbaum's data; it is summarized in the accompanying table, in which the direction of change is represented by either a plus or a minus sign, and the extent of change by either one or two such signs.

A further derivation of the congruity principle is that incongruity does not invariably produce attitude change, but that it may at times lead to incredulity on the part of the individual. When confronted by an assertion which stands in an incongruous relation to the person who made it, there will be a tendency not to believe that the

change of attitude toward the source and the object when positive and negative assertions are made by the source

original attitude toward the source	positive assertion about an object toward which the attitude is		negative assertion about an object toward which the attitude is	
	positive	negative	positive	negative
	change of attitude toward the source			
Positive	+	− −	− −	+
Negative	+ +	−	−	+ +
	change of attitude toward the object			
Positive	+	+ +	− −	−
Negative	− −	−	+	+ +

person made the assertion, thus reducing incongruity.

There is a good deal of evidence supporting Osgood and Tannenbaum's principle of congruity. As early as 1921, H. T. Moore had subjects judge statements for their grammar, ethical infringements for their seriousness, and resolutions of the dominant seventh chord for their dissonance.[20] After two and one-half months the subjects returned and were presented with judgments of "experts." This experimental manipulation resulted in 62 per cent reversals of judgments on grammar, 50 per cent of ethical judgments, and 43 per cent of musical judgments. And in 1935 in a study on a similar problem of prestige suggestion, Sherif let subjects rank sixteen authors for their literary merit.[21] Subsequently, the subjects were given sixteen passages presumably written by the various authors previously ranked. The subjects were asked to rank-order the passages for literary merit. Although in actuality *all* the passages were written by Robert Louis Ste-

[20] H. T. Moore, "The Comparative Influence of Majority and Expert Opinion," *American Journal of Psychology*, Vol. 32, 1921, pp. 16–20.
[21] M. Sherif, "An Experimental Study of Stereotypes," *Journal of Abnormal and Social Psychology*, Vol. 29, 1935, pp. 371–375.

venson, the subjects were able to rank the passages. Moreover, the correlations between the merit of the author and the merit of the passage ranged from between .33 to .53. These correlations are not very dramatic, yet they do represent some impact of attitude toward the source on attitude toward the passage.

With respect to incredulity, an interesting experiment was conducted recently by Jones and Kohler in which subjects learned statements which either supported their attitudes or were in disagreement with them.[22] Some of the statements were plausible and some implausible. The results were rather striking. Subjects whose attitudes favored segregation learned plausible pro-segregation statements and implausible anti-segregation statements much more rapidly than plausible anti-segregation and implausible pro-segregation statements. The reverse was of course true for subjects whose attitudes favored desegregation.

While the principle of congruity presents no new ideas, it has a great advantage over the earlier attempts in its precision. Osgood and Tannenbaum have formulated the principle of congruity in quantitative terms allowing for precise predictions regarding the extent and direction of attitude change —predictions which in their studies were fairly well confirmed. While balance theory allows merely a dichotomy of attitudes, either positive or negative, the principle of congruity allows refined measurements using Osgood's method of the semantic differential.[23] Moreover, while it is not clear from Heider's statement of balance in just what direction changes will occur when an unbalanced state exists, such predictions can be made on the basis of the congruity principle.

Festinger's theory
of cognitive dissonance

Perhaps the largest systematic body of data is that collected in the realm of Festinger's dissonance theory. The statement of the dissonance principle is simple. It holds that two elements of knowledge ". . . are in dissonant relation if, considering these two alone, the obverse of one element would follow from the other." [24] It further holds that dissonance ". . . being psychologically uncomfortable, will motivate the person to try to reduce dissonance and achieve consonance" and ". . . in addition to trying to reduce it, the person will actively avoid situations and information which would likely increase the dissonance." [25] A number of rather interesting and provocative consequences follow from Festinger's dissonance hypothesis.

First, it is predicted that all decisions or choices result in dissonance to the extent that the alternative not chosen contains positive features which make it attractive also, and the alternative chosen contains features which might have resulted in rejecting it. Hence after making a choice people seek evidence to confirm their decision and so reduce dissonance. In the Ehrlich experiment cited by Cohen in this issue [of *Public Opinion Quarterly*] the finding was that new car owners noticed and read ads about the cars they had recently purchased more than ads about other cars.[26]

Post-decision dissonance was also shown to result in a change of attractiveness of the alternative involved in a decision. Brehm had female subjects rate eight appliances for desirability.[27] Subsequently,

[22] E. E. Jones and R. Kohler, "The Effects of Plausibility on the Learning of Controversial Statements," *Journal of Abnormal and Social Psychology*, Vol. 57, 1958, pp. 315–320.

[23] C. E. Osgood, "The Nature and Measurement of Meaning," *Psychological Bulletin*, Vol. 49, 1952, pp. 197–237.

[24] Festinger, *op. cit.*, p. 13.

[25] *Ibid.*, p. 3.

[26] D. Ehrlich, I. Guttman, P. Schönbach, and J. Mills, "Post-decision Exposure to Relevant Information," *Journal of Abnormal and Social Psychology*, Vol. 54, 1957, pp. 98–102.

[27] J. Brehm, "Post-decision Changes in the Desirability of Alternatives," *Journal of Abnormal and Social Psychology*, Vol. 52, 1956, pp. 384–389.

the subjects were given a choice between two of the eight products, given the chosen product, and after some interpolated activity (consisting of reading research reports about four of the appliances) were asked to rate the products again. Half the subjects were given a choice between products which they rated in a similar manner, and half between products on which the ratings differed. Thus in the first case higher dissonance was to be expected than in the second. The prediction from dissonance theory that there should be an increase in the attractiveness of the chosen alternative and decrease in the attractiveness of the rejected alternative was on the whole confirmed. Moreover, the further implication was also confirmed that the pressure to reduce dissonance (which was accomplished in the above experiment by changes in attractiveness of the alternatives) varies directly with the extent of dissonance.

Another body of data accounted for by the dissonance hypothesis deals with situations in which the person is forced (either by reward or punishment) to express an opinion publicly or make a public judgment or statement which is contrary to his own opinions and beliefs. In cases where the person actually makes such a judgment or expresses an opinion contrary to his own as a result of a promised reward or threat, dissonance exists between the knowledge of the overt behavior of the person and his privately held beliefs. Festinger also argues that in the case of noncompliance dissonance will exist between the knowledge of overt behavior and the anticipation of reward and punishment.

An example of how dissonance theory accounts for forced-compliance data is given by Brehm.[28] Brehm offered prizes to eighth-graders for eating disliked vegetables and obtained measures of how well the children liked the vegetables. Children who ate the vegetables increased their liking for them. Of course, one might argue that a simpler explanation of the results is that the attractiveness of the prize generalized to the vegetable, or that, even more simply, the vegetables increased in utility because a reward came with them. However, this argument would also lead one to predict that the increment in attraction under such conditions is a *direct* function of the magnitude of the reward. Dissonance theory makes the opposite prediction, and therefore a test of the validity of the two explanations is possible. Data collected by Festinger and Carlsmith[29] and by Aronson and Mills[30] support the dissonance point of view. In Festinger and Carlsmith's experiment subjects were offered either $20 or $1 for telling someone that an experience which had actually been quite boring had been rather enjoyable and interesting. When measures of the subjects' private opinions about their actual enjoyment of the task were taken, those who were to be paid only $1 for the false testimony showed considerably higher scores than those who were to be paid $20. Aronson and Mills, on the other hand, tested the effects of negative incentive. They invited college women to join a group requiring them to go through a process of initiation. For some women the initiation was quite severe, for others it was mild. The prediction from dissonance theory that those who had to undergo severe initiation would increase their attraction for the group more than those having no initiation or mild initiation was borne out.

A third set of consequences of the theory of dissonance deals with exposure to information. Since dissonance occurs between cognitive elements, and since information

[28] J. Brehm, "Increasing Cognitive Dissonance by a *Fait Accompli*," *Journal of Abnormal and Social Psychology*, Vol. 58, 1959, pp. 379–382.

[29] L. Festinger and J. M. Carlsmith, "Cognitive Consequences of Forced Compliance," *Journal of Abnormal and Social Psychology*, Vol. 58, 1959, pp. 203–210.

[30] E. Aronson and J. Mills, "The Effect of Severity of Initiation on Liking for a Group," *Journal of Abnormal and Social Psychology*, Vol. 59, 1959, pp. 177–181.

may lead to change in these elements, the principle of dissonance should have a close bearing on the individual's commerce with information. In particular, the assumption that dissonance is a psychologically uncomfortable state leads to the prediction that individuals will seek out information reducing dissonance and avoid information increasing it. The study on automobile-advertising readership described above is a demonstration of this hypothesis.[31] In another study Mills, Aronson, and Robinson gave college students a choice between an objective and an essay examination.[32] Following the decision, the subjects were given articles about examinations presumably written by experts, and they were asked if they would like to read them. In addition, in order to vary the intensity of dissonance, half the subjects were told that the examination counted 70 per cent toward the final grade, and half that it counted only 5 per cent. The data were obtained in the form of rankings of the articles for preference. While there was a clear preference for reading articles containing positive information about the alternative chosen, no significant selective effects were found when the articles presented arguments against the given type of examination. Also, the authors failed to demonstrate effects relating selectivity in exposure to information to the magnitude of dissonance, in that no significant differences were found between subjects for whom the examination was quite important (70 per cent of the final grade) and those for whom it was relatively unimportant (5 per cent of the final grade).

Festinger was able to account for many other results by means of the dissonance principle, and in general his theory is rather successful in organizing a diverse body of empirical knowledge by means of a limited number of fairly reasonable assumptions. Moreover, from these reasonable assumptions dissonance theory generated several nontrivial and nonobvious consequences. The negative relationship between the magnitude of incentive and attraction of the object of false testimony is not at all obvious. Also not obvious is the prediction of an increase in proselytizing for a mystical belief following an event that clearly contradicts it. Festinger, Riecken, and Schachter studied a group of "Seekers"—people who presumably received a message from outer space informing them of an incipient major flood.[33] When the flood failed to materialize on the critical date, instead of quietly withdrawing from the public scene, as one would expect, the "Seekers" summoned press representatives, gave extended interviews, and invited the public to visit them and be informed of the details of the whole affair. In a very recent study by Brehm, a "nonobvious" derivation from dissonance theory was tested.[34] Brehm predicted that when forced to engage in an unpleasant activity, an individual's liking for this activity will increase more when he receives information essentially berating the activity than when he receives information promoting it. The results tended to support Brehm's prediction. Since negative information is said to increase dissonance, and since increased dissonance leads to an increased tendency to reduce it, and since the only means of dissonance reduction was increasing the attractiveness of the activity, such an increase would in fact be expected.

conclusions

The theories and empirical work dealing with consistencies are mainly concerned

[31] Ehrlich *et al., op. cit.*

[32] J. Mills, E. Aronson, and H. Robinson, "Selectivity in Exposure to Information," *Journal of Abnormal and Social Psychology*, Vol. 59, 1959, pp. 250–253.

[33] L. Festinger, J. Riecken, and S. Schachter, *When Prophecy Fails*, Minneapolis, University of Minnesota Press, 1956.

[34] J. W. Brehm, "Attitudinal Consequences of Commitment to Unpleasant Behavior," *Journal of Abnormal and Social Psychology*, Vol. 60, 1960, pp. 379–383.

with intra-individual phenomena, be it with relationships between one attitude and another, between attitudes and values, or information, or perception, or behavior, or the like. One exception is Newcomb's concept of "strain toward symmetry." Here the concern is primarily with the interplay of forces among individuals which results in uniformities or consistencies among them. There is no question that the concepts of consistency, and especially the theory of cognitive dissonance, account for many varied attitudinal phenomena. Of course, the various formulations of consistency do not pretend, nor are they able, to account completely for the phenomena they examine. Principles of consistency, like all other principles, are prefaced by the *ceteris paribus* preamble. Thus, when other factors are held constant, then the principles of consistency should be able to explain behavior and attitudes completely. But the question to be raised here is just what factors must be held constant and how important and significant, relative to consistency, are they.

Suppose a man feels hostile toward the British and also dislikes cricket. One might be tempted to conclude that if one of his attitudes were different he would experience the discomfort of incongruity. But there are probably many people whose attitudes toward the British and cricket are incongruent, although the exact proportions are not known and are hardly worth serious inquiry. But if such an inquiry were undertaken it would probably disclose that attitudes depend largely on the conditions under which they have been acquired. For one thing, it would show that the attitudes depend at least to some extent on the relationship of the attitude object to the individual's needs and fears, and that these may be stronger than forces toward balance. There are in this world things to be avoided and feared. A child bitten by a dog will not develop favorable attitudes toward dogs. And no matter how much he likes Popeye you can't make him like spinach,

although according to balance theory he should.

The relationship between attitudes and values or needs has been explored, for instance, in *The Authoritarian Personality*, which appeared in 1950.[35] The authors of this work hypothesized a close relationship between attitudes and values on the one hand and personality on the other. They assumed that the ". . . convictions of an individual often form a broad and coherent pattern, as if bound together by a mentality or spirit." They further assumed that ". . . opinions, attitudes, and values depend on human needs and since personality is essentially an organization of needs, then personality may be regarded as a determinant of ideological preference." Thus the *Authoritarian Personality* approach also stresses consistency, but while the concepts of congruity, balance, and dissonance are satisfied with assuming a general tendency toward consistency, the *Authoritarian Personality* theory goes further in that it holds that the dynamic of consistency is to be found in personality, and it is personality which gives consistency meaning and direction. Attitudes and values are thus seen to be consistent among themselves and with one another because they are both consistent with the basic personality needs, and they are consistent with needs because they are determined by them.

The very ambitious research deriving from the *Authoritarian Personality* formulation encountered many difficulties and, mainly because of serious methodological and theoretical shortcomings, has gradually lost its popularity. However, some aspects of this general approach have been salvaged by others. Rosenberg, for instance, has shown that attitudes are intimately related to the capacity of the attitude object to be instrumental to the attainment of the

[35] T. W. Adorno, E. Frenkel-Brunswik, D. J. Levinson, and R. N. Sanford, *The Authoritarian Personality*, New York, Harper, 1950.

individual's values.[36] Carlson went a step further and has shown that, if the perceived instrumentality of the object with respect to a person's values and needs is changed, the attitude itself may be modified.[37] These studies, while not assuming a general consistency principle, illustrate a special instance of consistency, namely that between attitudes and utility, or instrumentality of attitude objects, with respect to the person's values and needs.

The concepts of consistency bear a striking historical similarity to the concept of vacuum. According to an excellent account by Conant,[38] for centuries the principle that nature abhors a vacuum served to account for various phenomena, such as the action of pumps, behavior of liquids in joined vessels, suction, and the like. The strength of everyday evidence was so overwhelming that the principle was seldom questioned. However, it was known that one cannot draw water to a height of more than 34 feet. The simplest solution of this problem was to reformulate the principle to read that "nature abhors a vacuum below 34 feet." This modified version of *horror vacui* again was satisfactory for the phenomena it dealt with, until it was discovered that "nature abhors a vacuum below 34 feet only when we deal with water." As Torricelli has shown, when it comes to mercury "nature abhors a vacuum below 30 inches." Displeased with the crudity of a principle which must accommodate numerous exceptions, Torricelli formulated the notion that it was the pressure of air acting upon the surface of the liquid which was responsible for the height to which one could draw liquid by the action of pumps. The 34-foot limit represented the weight

[36] M. J. Rosenberg, "Cognitive Structure and Attitudinal Affect," *Journal of Abnormal and Social Psychology*, Vol. 53, 1956, pp. 367–372.

[37] E. R. Carlson, "Attitude Change through Modification of Attitude Structure," *Journal of Abnormal and Social Psychology*, Vol. 52, 1956, pp. 256–261.

[38] James B. Conant, *On Understanding Science*, New Haven, Conn., Yale University Press, 1947.

of water which the air pressure on the surface of earth could maintain, and the 30-inch limit represented the weight of mercury that air pressure could maintain. This was an entirely different and revolutionary concept, and its consequences had drastic impact on physics. Human nature, on the other hand, is said to abhor inconsistency. For the time being the principle is quite adequate, since it accounts systematically for many phenomena, some of which have never been explained and all of which have never been explained by one principle. But already today there are exceptions to consistency and balance. Some people who spend a good portion of their earnings on insurance also gamble. The first action presumably is intended to protect them from risks, the other to expose them to risks. Almost everybody enjoys a magician. And the magician only creates dissonance—you see before you an event which you know to be impossible on the basis of previous knowledge—the obverse of what you see follows from what you know. If the art of magic is essentially the art of producing dissonance, and if human nature abhors dissonance, why is the art of magic still flourishing? If decisions are necessarily followed by dissonance, and if nature abhors dissonance, why are decisions ever made? Although it is true that those decisions which would ordinarily lead to great dissonance take a very long time to make, they are made anyway. And it is also true that human nature does not abhor dissonance absolutely, as nature abhors a vacuum. Human nature merely avoids dissonance, and it would follow from dissonance theory that decisions whose instrumental consequences would not be worth the dissonance to follow would never be made. There are thus far no data to support this hypothesis, nor data to disprove it.

According to Conant, *horror vacui* served an important purpose besides explaining and organizing some aspects of physical knowledge. Without it the discomfort of "exceptions to the rule" would never have been felt, and the important developments in theory might have been delayed considerably. If a formulation has then a virtue in being wrong, the theories of consistency do have this virtue. They do organize a large body of knowledge. Also, they point out exceptions, and thereby they demand a new formulation. It will not suffice simply to reformulate them so as to accommodate the exceptions. I doubt if Festinger would be satisfied with a modification of his dissonance principle which would read that dissonance, being psychologically uncomfortable, leads a person to actively avoid situations and information which would be likely to increase the dissonance, except when there is an opportunity to watch a magician. Also, simply to disprove the theories by counterexamples would not in itself constitute an important contribution. We would merely lose explanations of phenomena which had been explained. And it is doubtful that the theories of consistency could be rejected simply *because* of counterexamples. Only a theory which accounts for all the data that the consistency principles now account for, for all the exceptions to those principles, and for all the phenomena which these principles should now but do not consider, is capable of replacing them. It is only a matter of time until such a development takes place.

16

*Although Dember (Chapter 14) and others have called atten-
tion to intrinsically motivated behavior, they would not deny
the importance of behavioral research on the biological drives. Among the
latter, hunger has probably been the most widely studied. In the next article,
Philip Teitelbaum summarizes some of the innovative techniques which have
been used to investigate the physiological mechanisms underlying eating behavior.*

"appetite"

PHILIP TEITELBAUM

Many of the scientific concepts we use in
dealing with natural phenomena are based
on earlier approaches to those phenomena.
As new techniques are developed, our ideas
often have to be revised to encompass the
new information obtained. This paper ex-
amines briefly the trends in the development of the concepts of hunger, appetite,
and the regulation of food intake. . . .
[I]t is time to re-evaluate them in the light
of a behavioral analysis of feeding.[1]

the early conception of hunger

The early scientific attempts to understand
normal and deranged feeding may be labeled as psychological. They were based
on the study of man and focused on the

[1] The research reported in this paper was supported by funds from the National Science Foundation. An excellent history of research on hunger
and thirst has been published by Rosenzweig
(1962).

psychological aspects of eating: the unpleasant sensations of hunger and the
pleasure obtained from food during and
after a meal.

For example, in 1765, Albrecht von Haller wrote,

We are induced to take food, both from the
sense of pain which we call hunger, and from
that of the pleasure imparted by the sense of
taste. The first of these proceeds undoubtedly
from the folds of the stomach, which possess
great sensibility, being rubbed against each
other, by the peristaltic motion, and by the
pressure of the diaphragm and abdominal
muscles, so that naked nerves being rubbed
against naked nerves excite an intolerable degree of pain. Thus man is both effectually ad-
monished of the dangers of abstinence, and
excited to procure food by his labours [1765,
pp. 313–314].

According to von Haller, the second inducement to feed depends on the pleasure
of eating. This aspect of hunger has often
been called appetite, and includes the eager
anticipation of food based on the memories
of past pleasures. Some authors have considered it merely a weaker, initial phase
of hunger, but many have agreed that it

differs in being a pleasant aspect of the urge to eat (Carlson, 1916). But pleasant or unpleasant, by this view the psychological sensations of appetite and hunger are understood to cause feeding. In the same way, satiety, the sense of repletion and satisfaction that accompany a full stomach and a good meal, puts an end to feeding.

The physiological basis of behavior involved in feeding was therefore naturally believed to depend upon those organs responsible for the sensation of hunger and satiety. There was controversy over whether these sensations resided peripherally, in local organs such as the stomach (v. Haller, 1765, pp. 313–314); centrally, in a "hunger center" in the nervous system (Magendie, 1836, pp. 29–30; Schiff, 1867, pp. 29–57); or (because nervous centers were later believed to be unaffected by humoral changes, and inactive except when aroused by peripheral stimulation) generally, in nerve endings in cells throughout the body (Roux, 1897, pp. 409–455). But the physiologists were unanimous in their belief that the causes of feeding were those of sensation and motivation: the urge to eat was based on the gnawing unpleasant sensations of hunger and the delightful pleasures of eating and satiety.

the physiological study of feeding

A major change in the conceptualization of the behavior that governs food intake occurred after the nineteenth century. Based on the development of experimentation as a means of understanding natural phenomena, the science of physiology arose as the study of experimental medicine. Great experimenters like Flourens (1842) and Magendie (1836, pp. 29–30) developed techniques for experimentation on animals. They continually battled to prove that the phenomena of life are amenable to fruitful scientific study, remaining in constant opposition to the vitalist position that life is by its very nature unsusceptible to experi-

mental analysis. The greatest step was taken by Claude Bernard (1878, pp. 111–124), who explained the mysterious ability of living systems to remain independent of many environmental changes that were known to determine the chemical and physical reactions of nonliving matter. He formulated the concept of the constancy of the internal environment—the idea that many of the body's activities serve to regulate within a narrow range the properties of the blood and other fluids that bathe all the cells of the body in the constant environment essential to their well-being, and thereby make them independent of many changes in the external environment. He was the first to point out that the behaviors involved in breathing, heat production and loss, drinking, and eating are all regulated to maintain the constancy of the internal environment.

This concept of homeostatic regulation was very fruitfully applied to the study of feeding and drinking in animals by the great French physiologist, André Mayer (1901; Gasnier and Mayer, 1939, pp. 145–214). The earlier concepts of hunger and satiety, urges to eat and the pleasures of eating had been derived from psychological observation of people, and were of little value for the study of animals. Experimental analysis, however, had to be performed on animals and no techniques existed that could measure the psychological aspects of their feeding. All that could be observed was their behavior; all that could be measured was the amount they ate; no other reliable estimates could be made of their hunger or of their enjoyment of food. Although he was highly appreciative of the importance of the psychological urges to eat and drink, Mayer found it useful at that stage of the problem to study feeding in terms of the regulation of food intake—the short-term variation of the amount eaten daily to adjust caloric intake in the face of changes in bodily activity, in environmental temperature, and in the energy value of food. By showing that body weight and individual tissue reserves were maintained precisely for long periods of time and were readjusted after depletion by starvation, he also demonstrated the existence of long-term regulation of body weight (Gasnier and Mayer, 1939, pp. 145–214).

The concept of regulation thus recast the problem of understanding feeding. The question now became: how does the machinery of the body regulate food intake?

The answers lay readily at hand. In order to explain similarities in animal and human behavior without having to endow animals with souls, Descartes (1664, pp. 130–132) had conceived of the reflex—that quality of the nervous system that enabled the body to respond to a stimulus automatically and appropriately without purposiveness, consciousness, pleasure, or pain.

Robert Whytt (1763) and Marshall Hall (1833, pp. 635–655) had demonstrated the existence of reflexes in the spinal cord. Sherrington (1906) had elaborated many of their properties and had shown that they could be integrated into complex patterns of behavior at higher levls of the nervous system. The regulation of food intake could thus be understood in principle as the end result of homeostatic reflexes, which, in response to changes in the internal environment due to lack of food, caused eating.

The path of research on this problem was therefore clear: isolate the reflexes involved in the regulation of food intake to determine the nature of the control mechanisms and map out the pathways in the nervous system to find out where and how these reflexes are integrated. There seemed to be no need to study the psychological aspects of feeding, since these were merely conscious correlates of regulatory mechanisms, not causal determinants of that regulation.

Many lines of evidence fit in with this point of view. Cannon and Washburn (1912, pp. 441–454) demonstrated that the conscious sensations of hunger pangs are closely correlated with increased periods of gastric motility. Bulatao and Carlson (1924, pp. 107–115) showed that low blood sugar increases gastric contractions, whereas hyperglycemia inhibits them. Jean Mayer, the son of André Mayer, pointed out that the level of blood sugar alone cannot account for the ravenous appetite seen in diabetic patients. However, if one measures glucose uptake in the body, as revealed by the difference between the sugar level in the arterial blood entering an organ and the sugar content in the venous blood leaving it, then there is a very close correlation with hunger and satiety. Hungry people (both diabetic and normal) showed very low glucose uptake values, whereas after eating these values are quite high. Mayer therefore postulated the existence of glucoreceptors which would monitor the level of glucose utilization and suggested that these receptors, perhaps located in the hypothalamus, could serve in the "glucostatic" regulation of daily food intake (1952, pp. 43–49, 1955, pp. 15–43). John Brobeck was struck by the amount of evidence showing that animals and people eat more in the cold and less when the temperature is warm. He reasoned that the main function of eating is to provide energy intake sufficient to compensate for the energy expended in maintaining body temperature and in performing daily activities. In a sense, "animals eat to keep warm." Therefore, it would seem that the "thermostatic" regulation of food intake must be controlled by thermoreceptors (1948, pp. 545–552, 1960, pp. 439–466).

Work on the nervous pathways involved in the regulation of food intake has proceeded with an accelerating pace since the demonstration by Hetherington and Ranson (1939, pp. 465–466) that the obesity seen in people with pituitary tumors (Fröhlich's syndrome) can be produced in animals by discrete lesions in the ventromedial nuclei of the hypothalamus. The earlier work of Cannon (1929) on the expression of emotions, and that of Bard (1939, pp. 190–218) on such emotional and instinctive patterns as rage and sexual behavior, had clearly shown the importance of the hypothalamus in the integration of these behavioral patterns. It was, therefore, reasonable to expect that the regulation of food intake might be integrated in the hypothalamus. Brobeck, Tepperman, and Long in 1943 (pp. 831–853) showed that the obesity resulting from ventromedial hypothalamic lesions in rats was caused by overeating, not by any disturbance in metabolism or utilization of food. Anand and Brobeck in 1951 (pp. 123–140) discovered that small lesions in the lateral hypothalamus of rats and cats would produce the opposite effect —refusal to eat and death from starvation. They realized that these two antagonistic feeding mechanisms—a lateral, excitatory, "feeding" system held in check by a medial, inhibitory, "satiety" system—are sufficient to achieve the homeostatic regulation of food intake. In a very striking parallel to the control of respiration by the integration in the medulla of breathing reflexes, hypothalamic integration of feeding reflexes could produce the regulation of food intake (Brobeck, 1957, pp. 565–574).

Direct evidence for the existence of the receptors involved in homeostatic feeding reflexes has been recently found. Paintal (1954, pp. 255–270) has located stretch receptors responding to gastric distension in the stomach and has traced their pathways in the vagus nerve. Sharma, Anand, Dua, and Singh (1961, pp. 593–598) have shown that gastric distension produces increased activity of cells in the ventromedial nucleus of the hypothalamus. Increased activity of this satiety center is also produced by hyperglycemia (Anand, Dua, and Singh, 1961, pp. 54–59). Temperature receptors that control feeding also exist in the hypothalamus. Andersson and Larsson (1961, pp. 75–89) showed that local cooling of the hypothalamus elicits feeding, whereas local warming inhibits it.

Thus, the feeding mechanism is well worked out. As pointed out by Anand (1961, pp. 677–708) in a recent review, reflexes involved in feeding are integrated

in the hypothalamus. Bodily states associated with lack of food, such as increased gastric motility, decreased blood sugar utilization, and decreased body temperature all act to increase the activity of the lateral "feeding center." Changes associated with repletion, such as gastric distension, increased blood sugar utilization, and a rise in body temperature, cause an increase in the activity of the ventromedial "satiety center" which inhibits the "feeding center" and stops the behavior involved in eating. The psychological correlates of these reflexes—the urges and pleasures of hunger and satiety—are epiphenomena of the regulation of food intake; they accompany regulation, but do not cause it.

It was with this point of view that my colleagues and I started working on the disturbances in the regulation of food intake shown by animals with hypothalamic damage. However, the more we worked, the more difficult it became to reconcile the aberrations in feeding behavior with the concept of reflex regulation of food intake.

An animal that overeats after hypothalamic lesions is called hyperphagic. Shortly after medial hypothalamic damage, the animal eats two to three times as much as normal and gains weight rapidly. This is the dynamic phase of hypothalamic hyperphagia. As shown in Figure 1, such animals become quite fat. Once obese, a static phase

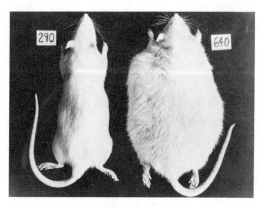

figure 1   Hypothalamic obese female rat (right) compared with its normal control.

ensues, in which the weight levels off at a high plateau and the animal's food intake drops back to only slightly more than normal. As shown in Figure 2, when their diet is diluted with non-nutritive cellulose, normal animals increase their intake to maintain caloric regulation. Even at 50 and 75 per cent dilution, when tremendous bulk has to be eaten to get an adequate amount of food, normal animals will still eat appreciable quantities. In contrast, hyperphagic animals do not increase their intake when the diet is mixed with cellulose. Although they eat two to three times as much of the ordinary diet, they refuse to overeat when the food contains as little as 25 per cent cellulose. This finicky eating is particularly marked in obese hyperphagic animals, which eat little or nothing for a week at a time and lose a great deal of weight. Making the diet slightly bitter by adding one part of quinine sulphate to eight hundred parts of food will also completely prevent them from eating, although normal animals remain unaffected. However, if one sweetens the diet by mixing equal parts of dextrose and food, then static hyperphagic animals which had ceased overeating and

had leveled off in weight show dynamic hyperphagia all over again. They overeat vigorously and become more obese than they had been before (Teitelbaum, 1955, pp. 156–163). Actually, hyperphagic animals can regulate their caloric intake. If, instead of a dry, solid diet, a liquid diet is used, and is diluted with water, they eat more and regulate their food intake quite well (Williams and Teitelbaum, 1959, pp. 458–465). They maintain their excessive level of caloric intake. But what kind of homeostatic control can be so sensitive to the taste and texture of the diet? What homeostatic mechanism will allow the animal to be a complete glutton if the food tastes good and yet will let him starve if the food tastes at all bad?

A similar phenomenon can be seen in animals with lateral hypothalamic lesions. Such animals are typically active and alert and are capable of chewing and swallowing, but they do not eat or drink and will starve to death in the face of food and water. Nevertheless, as my colleagues and I have shown, if these animals are kept alive by tube-feeding, they eventually recover (Teitelbaum and Stellar, 1954, pp.

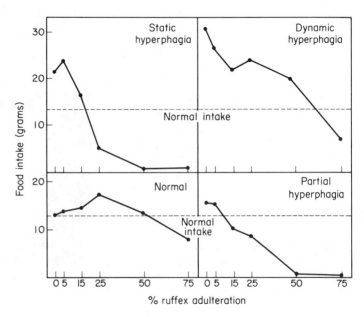

figure 2 Food intake of normal and hyperphagic animals when offered a diet mixed with non-nutritive cellulose. (From Teitelbaum, 1955.)

894–895), and their recovery yields a great deal of information about the nature of the deficits produced by the lesions (Teitelbaum and Epstein, 1962, pp. 74–90). Long before they accept ordinary food and water, they can be induced to eat appreciable quantities by offering them wet and palatable foods such as milk chocolate, wet cookies, and egg-nog liquid diets. However, they do not eat enough to stay alive. It is as though they are drawn to the food by appetite, not driven to it by hunger. Even after they have recovered their capacity to regulate their food intake (as demonstrated by their increased intake of a liquid diet when it is diluted with water), when subsequently offered only their ordinary dry diet and water they refuse to eat or drink and starve to death (Williams and Teitelbaum, 1959, pp. 458–465). Once again, palatability controls regulation.

What does the taste of food provide that is essential to the regulation of food intake? Can an animal regulate his caloric intake in the absence of taste? We first tried to answer this question by cutting the nerves that mediate taste. However, as Richter (1956, pp. 577–629) has pointed out, it is extremely difficult to do so. In the rat, he found taste buds present even after combined section of the chorda tympani, glossopharyngeal, and the pharyngeal branch of the vagus nerves. Pfaffmann (1952, pp. 393–400) has shown that only partial loss of taste results from combined removal of the chorda tympani and glossopharyngeal nerves. When the pharyngeal branch of the vagus is also removed, severe impairment of chewing and swallowing can result, with complications arising from the aspiration of food during feeding. It is difficult to measure the regulation of food intake in such a preparation.

Therefore, instead of removing the sense of taste surgically, we decided to by-pass it. My colleague, Dr. Alan N. Epstein, devised a permanently implanted gastric tube for the rat (1960, pp. 497–498). This is shown in Figure 3. A slender polyethylene tube is

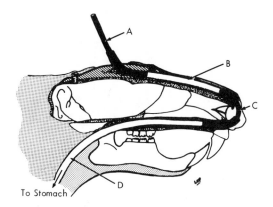

figure 3   The course of the nasopharyngeal gastric tube shown in a schematic drawing of a midsagittal section of the rat's head. (From Epstein and Teitelbaum, 1962.)

slipped into the rat's nostril, through the nasopharynx, into the esophagus, and down into the stomach. The outer end of the tube is brought under the skin of the snout and scalp to the top of the skull where it is anchored firmly by screws and dental cement. Water or liquid food can now be pumped directly into the animal's stomach, thus completely by-passing the nasal and oropharyngeal receptors for taste and smell. By training the rat to press a lever to inject a liquid diet directly into its own stomach, we can study the regulation of food intake in the absence of taste and smell and without even the consummatory acts of chewing and swallowing. This arrangement is shown in Figure 4.

The rat is first taught to press a bar for the delivery of fluid into a cup in its cage. It ingests the fluid by mouth. Then the pump is connected to the animal's gastric tube so that when it presses the bar food is delivered into its stomach. A watertight swivel joint (Epstein and Teitelbaum, 1962, pp. 171–172) coupled between the animal's gastric tube and the pump allows him to spend day and night in the cage. The joint swivels with the animal and prevents its movement around the cage from kinking the delivery tube. The rat can there-

figure 4   Schematic drawing of the apparatus for intragastric self-injection by the rat. (From Epstein and Teitelbaum, 1962.)

fore feed itself whenever it wishes without tasting or even eating the food.

DOES REGULATION CONTINUE IN THE ABSENCE OF TASTE?

As Epstein and I (1962, pp. 753–759) have shown in Figure 5, a normal rat when switched from oral to intragastric feeding maintains normal intake and weight. He doubles his intake when the diet is diluted 50 per cent with water and regulates his caloric intake precisely in response to sudden halving or doubling of the size of the individual stomach loads by adjusting the number of loads taken. If we make the animal press not once, but as many as thirty-six times for each gastric injection, he does so and achieves normal intake.

The hyperphagic animal, however, is much more drastically affected by the absence of taste and smell. As shown in Fig-

ure 6, a dynamic hyperphagic animal, when pressing a bar six times to obtain two and a half milliliters of a liquid diet delivered into his food cup, eats the diet avidly and presses the bar many times to obtain sixty milliliters of food in a day. This is almost twice the normal intake and is typical of the excessive oral intake seen in dynamic hyperphagic animals. When the diet is delivered directly into his stomach, however, the hyperphagic animal refuses to press the bar frequently enough to obtain sufficient food. It was only after seven days of semistarvation that he began to regulate his intake intragastrically (McGinty, Epstein, and Teitelbaum, in preparation). In our experience, many of these hyperphagic animals will go for long periods in the absence of taste without regulating their intake and, although we have not permitted it, I believe some would even starve to death under this regime. However, if we merely provide a sweet taste along with the food in the stomach, such a starving animal will work vigorously, regulate his intake perfectly, and gain weight very rapidly. As shown in Figure 7, merely delivering one-tenth of a milliliter of 0.1 per cent sodium saccharine solution into the animal's food cup at the same time that the liquid diet is delivered intragastrically, transforms this animal from an apathetic starving one into a vigorous hyperphagic. How does taste accomplish this transformation?

In an operant situation, when an animal uses an arbitrary act (like pressing a bar) to obtain food, we say that food is a reinforcing stimulus. We say that the reinforcement maintains his operant behavior, because without it the animal fails to work. As shown very clearly by the experiment just described, the taste of food is a powerful reinforcement. It maintains the operant behavior necessary to achieve caloric regulation of food intake. Without it, the hyperphagic animal fails to regulate his food intake. An animal must work to regulate his food intake, just as he must work to get food in a bar-pressing situation. The same

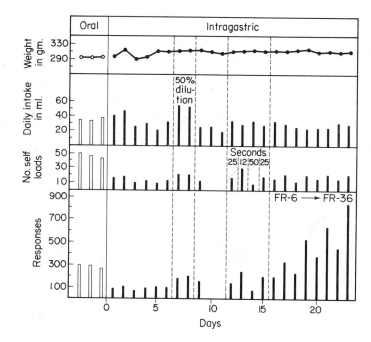

figure 5 Body weight, daily food intake, the number of self-loads, and the number of daily responses during three days of oral food intake and twenty-five days of intragastric intake in the normal rat. (From Epstein and Teitelbaum, 1962.)

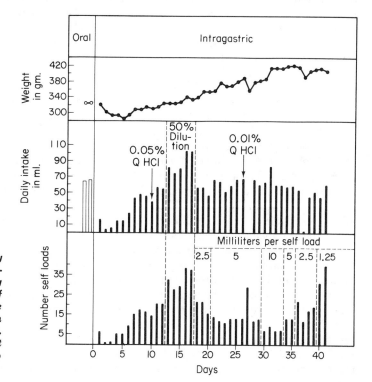

figure 6 Body weight, daily food intake, the number of self-loads, and the number of daily responses during two days of oral food intake and forty-one days of intragastric intake in the dynamic hyperphagic rat. On day 27, the pump was shut off and the animal received no food.

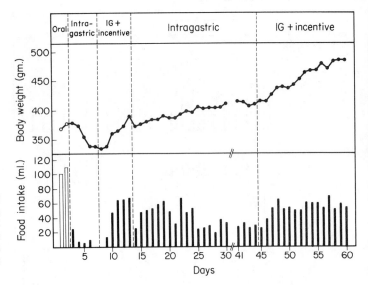

figure 7   Body weight and daily food intake of a dynamic hyperphagic rat under conditions of oral intake, intragastric self-injection, and intragastric self-injection with a saccharin taste incentive.

variables that influence operant behavior control the regulation of food intake.

Clearly this does not fit the concept of the reflex regulation of food intake. A reflex is a built-in fixed response to a particular kind of stimulus. A knee-jerk, for instance, is an automatic fixed response to a tap of the patellar tendon. Such an act can occur in an animal that is asleep or unconscious, or in a spinal animal in which no impulses reach or descend from the brain. The act can be completely involuntary and can occur without the animal being aware of it.

An operant response is a much more complicated kind of behavior (Teitelbaum, 1966). It is a voluntary act which the animal uses to obtain a reinforcement. The act is completely arbitrary—we could as readily have trained the animal to pull a string, bob his head, or dance around the cage if we so chose. Actually, in any operant situation, the response and the reinforcement are both arbitrary and bear no fixed built-in relationship to each other. We arrange the animal's motivational state so that a given stimulus is reinforcing. Then we train him to use an arbitrary response to obtain the reinforcement. We deprive him of food and teach him that each time he presses the

bar, food will be delivered. This is what is common to all operant situations: the animal works for a reinforcement appropriate to his motivational state. The same is true of the regulations of food intake: the animal works to obtain food when he is hungry.

Therefore, there are at least two kinds of homeostatic regulatory mechanisms: reflexes and behavioral regulations. Reflexes, such as those involved in control of heart rate, blood pressure, and respiration go on automatically, without awareness, whether the animal is unconscious or awake. Behavioral regulations, on the other hand, can occur only when the animal is awake; they require motivated, directed behavior to achieve the necessary regulation. Feeding, drinking, and many aspects of temperature regulation are such behavioral regulations. They are motivated acts and are governed by the same variables that govern operant behavior.

These ideas are not new. Curt Richter (1942, pp. 63–103) has been speaking of behavioral regulations for many years. Edward F. Adolph (1947, pp. 110–125) has often described caloric regulations as the urge to eat. André Mayer (1901) vividly described the overwhelming urge to drink.

These behavioral scientists have always been impressed by motivational control of the regulation of food intake. But, as I have pointed out, much of the recent work on the regulation of food intake has emphasized the hypothalamic control of feeding. In an attempt to be parsimonious, many neurophysiologists have restricted their thinking to the concept of automatic reflex regulations, whereas the behavioral variables and the neurophysiological mechanisms that control food-getting are those of motivated behavior and are not reflexes. That is why taste is so important in the caloric regulation of animals with hypothalamic lesions. Taste is a powerful reinforcement that maintains behavior involved in feeding (Pfaffmann, 1960, pp. 253–268; Teitelbaum and Epstein, 1962, pp. 74–90). It is a psychic energizer that increases the urge to eat. Wherever motivation for food is impaired, the pleasure provided by the taste of food is necessary for caloric regulation.

In a sense, we have come full-circle in our study of feeding. Psychological observations on the sensation of hunger in human beings gave way to the study of caloric regulation in animals. The behavioral analysis of disturbed regulations in animals has led to a renewed emphasis on the urge to eat and the reinforcements provided by food. In this way the old concept proves to be the most modern—for a more complete understanding of the regulation of food intake, we must return to the study of hunger and appetite.

In closing, I can only marvel at the apt statement of the famed French gastronome, Brillat-Savarin, who, in 1825 (p. 107), when describing the virtues of gourmandism, the habitual preference for that which gratifies the organ of taste, wrote,

Morally considered, [gourmandism] denotes implicit obedience to the commands of the Creator, Who, when He bade us eat that we might live, gave us the inducement of appetite, the encouragement of taste, and the reward of pleasure.

BIBLIOGRAPHY

ADOLPH, EDWARD F. 1947. "Urges to Eat and Drink in Rats." *Amer. Jour. Physiol.*, **151**: pp. 110–125.

ANAND, BAL K. 1961. "Nervous Regulation of Food Intake." *Physiol. Rev.*, **41**: pp. 677–708.

———, and JOHN R. BROBECK. 1951. "Hypothalamic Control of Food Intake." *Yale Jour. Biol. Med.*, **24**: pp. 123–140.

ANAND, BAL K., SHEEL DUA, and BALDEV SINGH. 1961. "Electrical Activity of the Hypothalamic 'Feeding Centres' Under the Effect of Changes in Blood Chemistry." *EEG clin. Neurophysiol.*, **13**: pp. 54–59.

ANDERSSON, BENGT, and BÖRJE LARSSON. 1961. "Influence of Local Temperature Changes in the Preoptic Area and Rostral Hypothalamus on the Regulation of Food and Water Intake." *Acta physiol. scand.*, **52**: pp. 75–89.

BARD, PHILIP. 1939. "Central Nervous Mechanisms for Emotional Behavior Patterns in Animals." *Res. Publ. Ass. Nerv. Ment. Dis.* **19**: pp. 190–213.

BERNARD, CLAUDE. 1878. *Leçons sur les Phénomènes de la Vie Communs aux Animaux et aux Vegetaux* (Paris: Baillière et Fils) **1**: pp. 111–124.

BRILLAT-SAVARIN, JEAN A. 1960. *The Physiology of Taste* (New York: Dover Publications, Inc. Republication of the translation first published by Peter Davies Limited and Doubleday and Company, Inc., in 1925 from the original published in 1825), p. 107.

BROBECK, JOHN R. 1948. "Food Intake as a Mechanism of Temperature Regulation." *Yale Jour. Biol. Med.*, **20**: pp. 545–552.

———. 1957. "Neural Control of Hunger, Appetite, and Satiety." *Yale Jour. Biol. Med.* **29**: pp. 565–574.

———. 1960. "Food and Temperature." *Recent Progress in Hormone Research*, **16**: pp. 439–466.

———, JAY TEPPERMAN, and CYRIL N. H. LONG. 1943. "Experimental Hypothalamic Hyperphagia in the Albino Rat." *Yale Jour. Biol. Med.*, **15**: pp. 831–853.

BULATAO, E., and ANTON J. CARLSON. 1924. "Influence of Experimental Changes in Blood Sugar Level on Gastric Hunger Contractions." *Amer. Jour. Physiol.*, **69**: pp. 107–115.

CANNON, WALTER B. 1929. *Bodily Changes in Pain, Hunger, Fear and Rage* (New York: Appleton-Century).

———, and A. L. WASHBURN. 1912. "An Explanation of Hunger." *Amer. Jour. Physiol.*, **29**: pp. 441–454.

CARLSON, ANTON J. 1916. *The Control of Hunger in Health and Disease* (Chicago, Ill.: The University of Chicago Press).

DESCARTES, RENÉ. 1664. *Traité de l'Homme* (v. 11, Republished in French by Adams, Charles and Paul Tannery, 1909. *Oevres de Descartes,* Paris: Leopold Cerf.), pp. 130–132.

EPSTEIN, ALAN N. 1960. "Water Intake Without the Act of Drinking." *Science*, **131**: pp. 497–498.

———, and PHILIP TEITELBAUM. 1962a. "A Watertight Swivel Joint Permitting Chronic Injection into Moving Animals. *Jour. Appl. Physiol.*, **17**: pp. 171–172.

———. 1962b. "Regulation of Food Intake in the Absence of Taste, Smell, and Other Oro-Pharyngeal Sensations." *Jour. Comp. Physiol. Psychol.*, **55**: pp. 753–759.

FLOURENS, MARIE-JEAN-PIERRE. 1842. *Recherches Experimentales sur les Propriétés et les Fonctions du Système Nerveux, dans les Animaux Vertébrés* (2nd ed. Paris).

GASNIER, A., and ANDRÉ MAYER. 1939. "Recherches sur la Regulation de la Nutrition." *Ann. physiol. Physicochim. Biol.*, **15**: pp. 145–214.

HALL, MARSHALL. 1833. "The Reflex Function of the Medulla Oblongata and the Medulla Spinalis." *Phil. Trans., The Royal Society*, **123**, 1–2: pp. 635–655.

HETHERINGTON, ALBERT W., and STEPHEN W. RANSON. 1939. "Experimental Hypothalam-ico-Hypophysial Obesity in the Rat." *Proc. Soc. Exp. Biol., N.Y.*, **41**: pp. 465–466.

MAGENDIE, FRANCOIS. 1836. *Précis Élémentaire de Physiologie* (2nd v., 4th ed., Paris: Mequignon-Marvis, Père et Fils), pp. 29–30.

MAYER, ANDRÉ. 1901. *Essai sur la Soif* (Paris: Felix Alcan, Éditeur. Coulommiers; Imprimerie Paul Brodard).

MAYER, JEAN. 1952. "The Glucostatic Theory of Regulation of Food Intake and the Problem of Obesity." *Bull. N.E. Med. Cen.*, **14**: pp. 43–49.

———. 1955. "Regulation of Energy Intake and the Body Weight: The Glucostatic Theory and the Lipostatic Hypothesis." *Ann. N.Y. Acad. Sci.*, **63**: pp. 15–43.

McGINTY, DENNIS J., ALAN N. EPSTEIN, and PHILIP TEITELBAUM. "Intragastric Regulation of Food Intake in Hypothalamic Hyperphagic Rats." (Manuscript in preparation.)

PAINTAL, A. S. 1954. "A Study of Gastric Stretch Receptors. Their Role in the Peripheral Mechanism of Satiation of Hunger and Thirst." *Jour. Physiol.*, **126**: pp. 255–270.

PFAFFMANN, CARL. 1952. "Taste Preference and Aversion Following Lingual Denervation." *Jour. Comp. Physiol. Psychol.*, **45**: pp. 393–400.

———. 1960. "The Pleasures of Sensation." *Psychol. Rev.*, **67**: pp. 253–268.

RICHTER, CURT P. 1942–1943. "Total Self-Regulatory Functions in Animals and Human Beings." *Harvey Lect.*, **38**: pp. 63–103.

———. 1956. "'Salt Appetite of Mammals: Its Dependence on Instinct and Metabolism." Autuori, M., *et al.* In *L'Instinct dans le Comportement des Animaux et de l'Homme* (Paris: Masson et Cie.), pp. 577–629.

ROSENZWEIG, MARK R. 1962. "The Mechanisms of Hunger and Thirst." In Postman, Leo (ed.), *Psychology in the Making* (New York: Alfred A. Knopf), pp. 73–143.

ROUX, JOANNY. 1897. "La Faim, Étude Psycho-Physiologique." *Bulletin de la Société d'Anthropologie de Lyon*, **16**: pp. 409–455.

SCHIFF, M. MAURICE. 1867. *Leçons sur la Physiologie de la Digestion* (Florence and Turin: Hermann Loescher), pp. 29–57.

SHARMA, KAMAL N., BAL K. ANAND, SHEEL DUA, and BALDEV SINGH. 1961. "Role of Stomach in Regulation of Activities of Hypothalamic Feeding Centers." *Amer. Jour. Physiol.*, **201**: pp. 593–598.

SHERRINGTON, CHARLES S. 1906. *The Integrative Action of the Nervous System* (New Haven: Yale Univ. Press, issued as a Yale Paperbound, 1961). Originally published in New York: Charles Scribner's Sons, 1906.

TEITELBAUM, PHILIP. 1955. "Sensory Control of Hypothalamic Hyperphagia." *Jour. Comp. Physiol. Psychol.*, **48**: pp. 156–163.

———. "The Use of Operant Methods in the Assessment and Control of Motivational States." In Werner K. Honig (ed), *Operant Behavior: Areas of Research and Applica-*

tion (New York: Appleton-Century-Crofts, 1966), pp. 565–608.

————, and ALAN N. EPSTEIN. 1962. "The Lateral Hypothalamic Syndrome: Recovery of Feeding and Drinking after Lateral Hypothalamic Lesions." *Psychol. Rev.*, **69:** pp. 74–90.

————. 1963. "The Role of Taste and Smell in the Regulation of Food and Water Intake." In Yngve Zotterman (ed.), *Olfaction and Taste* (Oxford: Pergamon Press, Ltd.), pp. 347–360.

TEITELBAUM, PHILIP, and ELIOT STELLAR. 1954. "Recovery From the Failure to Eat Produced by Hypothalamic Lesions." *Science,* **120:** pp. 894–895.

VON HALLER, ALBRECHT. 1803. *First Lines of Physiology* (Troy, N.Y.: O. Penniman and Company. Translation from the Third Latin Edition published in 1765), pp. 313–314.

WHYTT, ROBERT. 1763. *Essay on the Vital and Other Involuntary Motions of Animals* (2nd ed., Edinburgh: John Balfour).

WILLIAMS, DAVID R., and PHILIP TEITELBAUM. 1959. "Some Observations on the Starvation Resulting From Lateral Hypothalamic Lesions." *Jour. Comp. Physiol. Psychol.,* **52:** pp. 458–465.

17

Obesity is a major health problem in the United States. Although there are many metabolic disorders which may contribute to obesity, most people are obese simply because they overeat. In the next paper, Stanley Schachter describes his recent research which points to the possibility that normal and obese subjects use different kinds of information in regulating food intake. People of normal weight appear to eat in quantities appropriate to their state of physiological need, but obese subjects seem to be overdependent on cognitive, situational, and palatability factors in determining their food intake. The research also surprisingly suggests that even though obese subjects overeat, they do not do so because they are excessively hungry.

obesity and eating

STANLEY SCHACHTER

Current conceptions of hunger control mechanisms indicate that food deprivation leads to various peripheral physiological changes such as modification of blood constituents, increase in gastric motility, changes in body temperature, and the like. By means of some still debated mechanism, these changes are detected by a hypothalamic feeding center. Presumably some or all facets of this activated machinery lead the organism to search out and consume food. There appears to be no doubt that peripheral physiological changes and activation

of the hypothalamic feeding center are inevitable consequences of food deprivation. On the basis of current knowledge, however, one may ask, when this biological machinery is activated, do we necessarily describe ourselves as hungry, and eat? For most of us raised on the notion that hunger is the most primitive of motives, wired into the animal and unmistakable in its cues, the question may seem far-fetched, but there is increasing reason to suspect that there are major individual differences in the extent to which these physiological changes are associated with the desire to eat.

On the clinical level, the analyst Hilde Bruch[1] has observed that her obese patients literally do not know when they are physiologically hungry. To account for this observation she suggests that, during childhood, these patients were not taught to discriminate between hunger and such states as fear, anger, and anxiety. If this is so, these people may be labeling almost any

This article is based on a speech delivered at a conference entitled "Biology and Behavior: Neurophysiology and Emotion," held at the Rockefeller University, New York, on 10 December 1965, under the sponsorship of the Russell Sage Foundation and the Rockefeller University. Much of the research described in this article was supported by grants G23758 and GS732 from the National Science Foundation.

[1] H. Bruch, *Psychiat. Quart.*, **35** (1961), 458.

state of arousal "hunger," or, alternatively, labeling no internal state "hunger."

If Bruch's speculations are correct, it should be anticipated that the set of physiological symptoms which are considered characteristic of food deprivation are not labeled "hunger" by the obese. In other words the obese literally may not know when they are physiologically hungry. For at least one of the presumed physiological correlates of food deprivation, this does appear to be the case. In an absorbing study, Stunkard [2] has related gastric motility to self-reports of hunger in 37 obese subjects and 37 subjects of normal size. A subject, who had eaten no breakfast, came to the laboratory at 9 A.M.; he swallowed a gastric balloon, and for 4 hours Stunkard continuously recorded gastric motility. Every 15 minutes the subject was asked if he was hungry. He answered "yes" or "no," and that is all there was to the study. We have, then, a record of the extent to which a subject's self-report of hunger corresponds to his gastric motility. The results show (1) that obese and normal subjects do not differ significantly in degree of gastric motility, and (2) that, when the stomach is not contracting, the reports of obese and normal subjects are quite similar, both groups reporting hunger roughly 38 percent of the time. When the stomach is contracting, however, the reports of the two groups differ markedly. For normal subjects, self-report of hunger coincides with gastric motility 71 percent of the time. For the obese, the percentage is only 47.6. Stunkard's work seems to indicate that obese and normal subjects do not refer to the same bodily state when they use the term *hunger*.

effects of food deprivation and fear

If this inference is correct, we should anticipate that, if we were to directly manipulate

gastric motility and the other symptoms that we associate with hunger, we would, for normal subjects, be directly manipulating feelings of hunger and eating behavior. For the obese there would be no correspondence between manipulated internal state and eating behavior. To test these expectations, Goldman, Gordon, and I [3] performed an experiment in which bodily state was manipulated by two means—(1) by the obvious technique of manipulating food deprivation, so that some subjects had empty stomachs and others had full stomachs before eating; (2) by manipulating fear, so that some subjects were badly frightened and others were quite calm immediately before eating. Carlson [4] has indicated that fear inhibits gastric motility; Cannon [5] also has demonstrated that fear inhibits motility, and has shown that it leads to the liberation, from the liver, of sugar into the blood. Hypoglycemia and gastric contractions are generally considered the chief peripheral physiological correlates of food deprivation.

Our experiment was conducted under the guise of a study of taste. A subject came to the laboratory in mid-afternoon or evening. He had been called the previous evening and asked not to eat the meal (lunch or dinner) preceding his appointment at the laboratory. The experiment was introduced as a study of "the interdependence of the basic human senses—of the way in which the stimulation of one sense affects another." Specifically, the subject was told that this study would be concerned with "the effects of tactile stimulation on the way things taste."

It was explained that all subjects had been asked not to eat a meal before coming to the laboratory because "in any scientific experiment it is necessary that the subjects

[2] A. Stunkard, *Psychosomat. Med.*, **21** (1959), 281; and idem and C. Koch, *Arch. Genet. Psychiat.*, **11** (1964), 74.

[3] S. Schachter, R. Goldman, and A. Gordon, *J. Personality Soc. Psychol.*, **10** (1968), 91.

[4] A. J. Carlson, *Control of Hunger in Health and Disease* (Chicago: Univ. of Chicago Press, 1916).

[5] W. B. Cannon, *Bodily Changes in Pain, Hunger, Fear and Rage* (New York: Appleton, 1915).

be as similar as possible in all relevant ways. As you probably know from your own experience," the experimenter continued, "an important factor in determining how things taste is what you have recently eaten." The introduction over, the experimenter then proceeded as follows.

For the "full stomach" condition he said to the subject, "In order to guarantee that your recent taste experiences are similar to those of other subjects who have taken part in this experiment, we should now like you to eat exactly the same thing they did. Just help yourself to the roast beef sandwiches on the table. Eat as much as you want— till you're full."

For the "empty stomach" condition, the subjects, of course, were not fed.

Next, the subject was seated in front of five bowls of crackers and told, "We want you to taste five different kinds of crackers and tell us how they taste to you." The experimenter then gave the subject a long set of rating scales and said, "We want you to judge each cracker on the dimensions (salty, cheesy, garlicky, and so on) listed on this sheet. Taste as many or as few of the crackers of each type as you want in making your judgments; the important thing is that your ratings be as accurate as possible."

Before permitting the subject to eat, the experimenter continued with the next stage of the experiment—the manipulation of fear.

"As I mentioned," he said, "our primary interest in this experiment is the effect of tactile stimulation on taste. Electric stimulation is the means we use to excite your skin receptors. We use this method in order to carefully control the amount of stimulation you receive."

For the "low fear" condition the subject was told, "For the effects in which we are interested, we need to use only the lowest level of stimulation. At most you will feel a slight tingle. Probably you will feel nothing at all. We are only interested in the effect of very weak stimulation."

For the "high fear" condition the experi-

menter pointed to a large black console loaded with electrical junk and said, "That machine is the one we will be using. I am afraid that these shocks will be painful. For them to have any effect on your taste sensations, the voltage must be rather high. There will, of course, be no permanent damage. Do you have a heart condition?" A large electrode connected to the console was then attached to each of the subject's ankles, and the experimenter concluded, "The best way for us to test the effect of tactile stimulation is to have you rate the crackers now, before the electric shock, and then rate them again, after the shock, to see what changes in your ratings the shock has made."

The subject then proceeded to taste and rate crackers for 15 minutes, under the impression that this was a taste test; meanwhile we were simply counting the number of crackers he ate.[6] We then had measures of the amounts eaten by subjects who initially had either empty or full stomachs and who were initially either frightened or calm. There were, of course, two types of subjects; obese subjects (from 14 percent to 75 percent overweight) and normal subjects (from 8 percent underweight to 9 percent overweight).

To review expectations: If we were correct in thinking that the obese do not label as hunger the bodily states associated with food deprivation, then our several experimental manipulations should have had no effects on the amount eaten by obese subjects; on the other hand, the eating behavior of normal subjects should have directly paralleled the effects of the manipulations on bodily state.

It will be a surprise to no one to learn, from Figure 1, that the normal subjects ate considerably fewer crackers when their stomachs were full than when their stom-

[6] It is a common belief among researchers in the field of obesity that the sensitivity of their fat subjects makes it impossible to study their eating behavior experimentally—hence this roundabout way of measuring eating; the subjects in this study are taking a "taste test," not "eating."

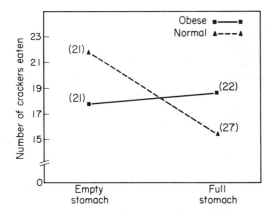

figure 1 Effects of preliminary eating on the amounts eaten during the experiment by normal and obese subjects. Numbers in parentheses are numbers of subjects.

achs were empty. The results for obese subjects stand in fascinating contrast. They ate as much—in fact, slightly more—when their stomachs were full as when they were empty (interaction $P < .05$). Obviously the actual state of the stomach has nothing to do with the eating behavior of the obese.

In Figure 2, pertaining to the effect of fear, we note an analogous picture. Fear markedly decreased the number of crackers the normal subjects ate but had no effect on the number eaten by the obese (interaction $P < .01$). Again, there was a small, though

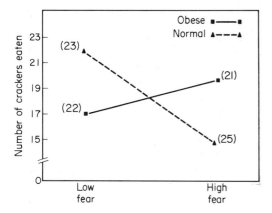

figure 2 Effects of fear on the amounts eaten by normal and obese subjects. Numbers in parentheses are numbers of subjects.

nonsignificant, reversal: the fearful obese ate slightly more than the calm obese.

It seems clear that the set of bodily symptoms the subject labels "hunger" differs for obese and normal subjects. Whether one measures gastric motility, as Stunkard did, or manipulates it, as I assume my co-workers and I have done, one finds, for normal subjects, a high degree of correspondence between the state of the gut and eating behavior and, for obese subjects, virtually no correspondence. While all of our manipulations have had a major effect on the amounts eaten by normal subjects, nothing that we have done has had a substantial effect on the amounts eaten by obese subjects.

effects of the circumstances of eating

With these facts in mind, let us turn to the work of Hashim and Van Itallie [7] of the Nutrition Clinic, St. Luke's Hospital, New York City. Their findings may be summarized as follows: virtually everything these workers do seems to have a major effect on the eating behavior of the obese and almost no effect on the eating behavior of the normal subject.

These researchers have prepared a bland liquid diet similar to commercial preparations such as vanilla-flavored Nutrament or Metrecal. The subjects are restricted to this monotonous diet for periods ranging from a week to several months. They can eat as much or as little of it as they want. Some of the subjects get a pitcher full and pour themselves a meal any time they wish. Other subjects are fed by a machine which delivers a mouthful every time the subject presses a button. With either feeding technique, the eating situation has the following characteristics. (1) The food itself is unappealing. (2) Eating is entirely self-determined: whether or not the subject eats,

[7] S. A. Hashim and T. B. Van Itallie, *Ann. N.Y. Acad. Sci.*, **131** (1965), 654.

how much he eats, and when he eats are matters decided by him and no one else. Absolutely no pressure is brought to bear to limit his consumption. (3) The eating situation is devoid of any social or domestic trappings. It is basic eating; it will keep the subject alive, but it's not much fun.

To date, six grossly obese and five normal individuals have been subjects in these studies. In Figure 3 the eating curves for a typical pair of subjects over a 21-day period are plotted. Both subjects were healthy people who lived in the hospital during the entire study. The obese subject was a 52-year-old woman, 5 feet 3 inches (1.6 meters) tall, who weighed 307 pounds (138 kilograms) on admission. The normal subject was a 30-year-old male, 5 feet 7 inches tall, who weighed 132 pounds.

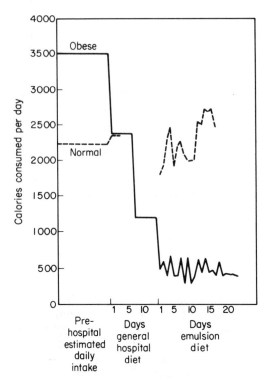

figure 3   *The effects of an emulsion diet on the amounts eaten by an obese and a normal subject.*

The subject's estimated daily caloric intake before entering the hospital (as determined from a detailed interview) is plotted at the left in Figure 3. Each subject, while in the hospital but before entering upon the experimental regime, was fed a general hospital diet. The obese subject was placed on a 2400-calorie diet for 7 days and a 1200-calorie diet for the next 8 days. As may be seen in Figure 3, she ate everything on her tray throughout this 15-day period. The normal subject was placed on a 2400-calorie diet for 2 days, and he too ate everything.

With the beginning of the experiment proper, the difference in the eating behavior of the two subjects was dramatic and startling. The food consumption of the obese subject dropped precipitately the moment she entered upon the experimental regime, and it remained at an incredibly low level for the duration of the experiment. This effect is so dramatic that the weight of one obese subject who took part in the experiment for 8 months dropped from 410 to 190 pounds. On the other hand, the food consumption of the normal subject of Figure 3 dropped slightly on the first 2 days, then returned to a fairly steady 2300 grams or so of food a day. The curves for these two subjects are typical. Each of the six obese subjects has manifested this marked and persistent decrease in food consumption during the experiment; each of the normal subjects has steadily consumed about his normal amount of food.

Before suggesting possible interpretations, I should note certain marked differences between these two groups of subjects. Most important, the obese subjects had come to the clinic for help in solving their weight problem and were, of course, motivated to lose weight. The normal subjects were simply volunteers. Doubtless this difference could account for the observed difference in eating behavior during the experiment, and until obese volunteers, unconcerned with their weight, are used as subjects in similar studies, we cannot be sure of the interpretation of this phenomenon. However, I think we should not, solely on grounds of methodological fastidiousness, dismiss these findings. It was concern with weight that brought these obese subjects to the clinic. Each of them, before entering the hospital and while in the hospital before being put on the experimental diet, was motivated to lose weight. Yet, despite this motivation, none of these subjects had been capable of restricting his diet at home, and each of them, when fed the general hospital diet, had eaten everything on his tray. Only when the food was dull and the act of eating was self-initiated and devoid of any ritual trappings did the obese subject, motivated or not, severely limit his consumption.

internal and external control

On the one hand, then, our experiments indicate virtually no relationship between internal physiological state and the eating behavior of the obese subject; on the other hand, these case studies seem to indicate a close tie between the eating behavior of the obese and what might be called the circumstances of eating. When the food is dull and the eating situation is uninteresting, the obese subject eats virtually nothing. For the normal subject, the situation is just the reverse: his eating behavior seems directly linked to his physiological state but is relatively unaffected by the external circumstances or the ritual associated with eating.

Given this set of facts it seems clear that eating is triggered by different sets of stimuli in obese and normal subjects. Indeed, there is growing reason to suspect that the eating behavior of the obese is relatively unrelated to any internal state but is, in large part, under external control, being initiated and terminated by stimuli external to the organism. Let me give a few examples. A person whose eating behavior is under external control will stroll by a pastry shop, find the food in the window

irresistible, and, even if he has recently eaten, go in and buy something. He will pass by a hamburger stand, smell the broiling meat, and, even though he has just eaten, buy a hamburger. Obviously such external factors—smell, sight, taste, other people's actions—to some extent affect anyone's eating. However, in normal individuals such external factors interact with internal state. They may affect what, where, and how much the normal individual eats, but they do so chiefly when he is in a state of physiological hunger. For the obese, I suggest, internal state is irrelevant and eating is determined largely by external factors.

This hypothesis obviously fits the data presented here, as well it should, since it is an *ad hoc* construction designed specifically to fit these data. Let us see, then, what independent support there is for the hypothesis, and where the hypothesis leads.

effects of manipulating time

Among the multitude of external food-relevant cues, one of the most intriguing is the passage of time. Everyone "knows" that 4 to 6 hours after eating his last meal he should eat his next one. Everyone "knows" that, within narrow limits, there are set times for eating regular meals. We should, then, expect that if we manipulate time we should be able to manipulate the eating behavior of the obese subjects. In order to do this, Gross and I [8] simply gimmicked two clocks so that one ran at half normal speed and the other, at twice normal speed. A subject arrives at 5:00 P.M., ostensibly to take part in an experiment on the relationship of base levels of autonomic reactivity to personality factors. He is ushered into a windowless room containing nothing but electronic equipment and a clock. Electrodes are put on his wrists, his watch is removed "so that it will not get

[8] S. Schachter and L. Gross, *J. Personality Soc. Psychol.*, **10** (1968), 98.

gummed up with electrode jelly," and he is connected to a polygraph. All this takes 5 minutes, and at 5:05 he is left alone, with nothing to do for a true 30 minutes, while ostensibly we are getting a record of galvanic skin response and cardiac rate in a subject at rest. There are two experimental conditions. In one, the experimenter returns after a true 30 minutes and the clock reads 5:20. In the other, the clock reads 6:05, which is normal dinner time for most subjects. In both cases the experimenter is carrying a box of crackers and nibbling a cracker as he comes into the room; he puts the box down, invites the subject to help himself, removes the electrodes from the subject's wrists, and proceeds with personality testing for exactly 5 minutes. This done, he gives the subject a personality inventory which he is to complete and leaves him alone with the box of crackers for another true 10 minutes. There are two groups of subjects—normal and obese—and the only datum we collect is the weight of the box of crackers before and after the subject has had a chance at it.

If these ideas on internal and external controls of eating behavior are correct, normal subjects, whose eating behavior is presumably linked to internal state, should be relatively unaffected by the manipulation and should eat roughly the same number of crackers regardless of whether the clock reads 5:20 or 6:05. The obese, on the other hand, whose eating behavior is presumably under external control, should eat very few crackers when the clock reads 5:20 and a great many crackers when it reads 6:05.

The data of Figure 4 do indeed indicate that the obese subjects eat almost twice as many crackers when they think the time is 6:05 as they do when they believe it to be 5:20. For normal subjects, the trend is just the reverse (interaction $P = .002$)—an unanticipated finding but one which seems embarrassingly simple to explain, as witness the several normal subjects who thought the time was 6:05 and politely refused the

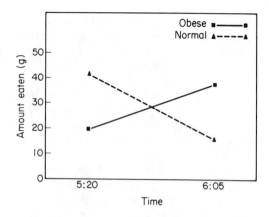

figure 4 The effects of manipulation of time on the amounts eaten by obese and normal subjects.

crackers, saying, "No thanks, I don't want to spoil my dinner." Obviously cognitive factors affected the eating behavior of both the normal and the obese subjects, but there was a vast difference. While the manipulation of the clock served to trigger or stimulate eating among the obese, it had the opposite effect on normal subjects, most of whom at this hour were, we presume, physiologically hungry, aware that they would eat dinner very shortly, and unwilling to spoil their dinner by filling up on crackers.

effects of taste

In another study, Nisbett[9] examined the effects of taste on eating behavior. Nisbett reasoned that taste, like the sight or smell of food, is essentially an external stimulus to eating. Nisbett, in his experiment, also extended the range of weight deviation by including a group of underweight subjects as well as obese and normal subjects. His purpose in so doing was to examine the hypothesis that the relative potency of external versus internal controls is a dimension directly related to the degree of overweight. If the hypothesis was correct, he reasoned, the taste of food would have the

[9] R. E. Nisbett, *J. Personality Soc. Psychol.*, **10** (1968), 107.

greatest impact on the amounts eaten by obese subjects and the least impact on the amounts eaten by underweight subjects. To test this, Nisbett had his subjects eat as much as they wanted of one of two kinds of vanilla ice cream; one was a delicious and expensive product, the other an acrid concoction of cheap vanilla and quinine which he called "vanilla bitters." The effects of taste are presented in Figure 5, in which the subjects' ratings of how good or bad the ice cream is are plotted against the amount eaten. As may be seen in Figure 5, when the ice cream was rated "fairly good" or better, the obese subjects ate considerably more than the normal subjects did; these, in turn, ate more than the underweight subjects did. When the ice cream was rated "not very good" or worse, the ordering tended to reverse: the underweight subjects ate more than either the normal or the obese subjects. This experiment, then, in-

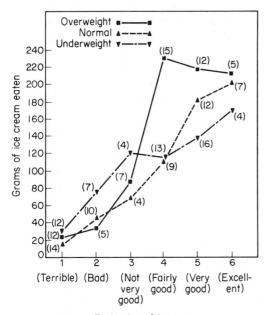

figure 5 *The effects of food quality on the amounts eaen by obese, normal and underweight subjects. Numbers in parentheses are numbers of subjects.*

dicates that the external, or at least non-visceral, cue *taste* does have differential effects on the eating behavior of underweight, normal, and obese subjects.

The indications, from Nisbett's experiment, that the degree of dependence on external cues relative to internal cues varies with deviation from normal weight are intriguing, for, if further work supports this hypothesis, we may have the beginnings of a plausible explanation of why the thin are thin and the fat are fat. We know from Carlson's work [10] that gastric contractions cease after a small amount of food has been introduced into the stomach. To the extent that such contractions are directly related to the hunger "experience"—to the extent that a person's eating is under internal control—he should "eat like a bird," eating only enough to stop the contractions. Eating beyond this point should be a function of external cues—the taste, sight, and smell of food. Individuals whose eating is externally controlled, then, should find it hard to stop eating. This hypothesis may account for the notorious "binge" eating of the obese [11] or the monumental meals described in loving detail by students [12] of the great, fat gastronomic magnificoes.

This rough attempt to explain why the obese are obese in itself raises intriguing questions. For example, does the external control of eating behavior inevitably lead to obesity? It is evident, I believe, that not only is such a linkage logically not inevitable but that the condition of external control of eating may in rare but specifiable circumstances lead to emaciation. A person whose eating is externally controlled should eat and grow fat when food-related cues are abundant and when he is fully aware of them. However, when such cues are lacking or when for some reason, such as withdrawal or depression, the individual is un-

[10] Carlson, *op. cit.*

[11] A. Stunkard, *Amer. J. Psychiat.*, **118** (1961), 212.

[12] L. Beebe, *The Big Spenders* (Garden City, N. Y.: Doubleday, 1966).

aware of the cues, the person under external control would, one would expect, not eat, and, if the condition persisted, would grow "concentration-camp" thin. From study of the clinical literature one does get the impression that there is an odd but distinct relationship between obesity and extreme emaciation. For example, 11 of 21 subjects of case studies discussed by Bliss and Branch in *Anorexia Nervosa* [13] were, at some time in their lives, obese. In the case of eight of these 11 subjects, anorexia was preceded and accompanied by either marked withdrawal or intense depression. In contrast, intense attacks of anxiety or nervousness (states which our experiment [14] suggests would inhibit eating in normal individuals) seem to be associated with the development of anorexia among most of the ten subjects who were originally of normal size.

At this point, these speculations are simply idea-spinning—fun, but ephemeral. Let us return to the results of the studies described so far. These can be quickly summarized as follows.

1. Physiological correlates of food deprivation, such as gastric motility, are directly related to eating behavior and to the reported experience of hunger in normal subjects but unrelated in obese subjects.[15]
2. External or nonvisceral cues, such as smell, taste, the sight of other people eating, and the passage of time, affect eating behavior to a greater extent in obese subjects than in normal subjects.[16]

obesity and fasting

Given these basic facts, their implications have ramifications in almost any area pertaining to food and eating, and some of our

studies have been concerned with the implications of these experimental results for eating behavior in a variety of nonlaboratory settings. Thus, Goldman, Jaffa, and I [17] have studied fasting on Yom Kippur, the Jewish Day of Atonement, on which the orthodox Jew is supposed to go without food for 24 hours. Reasoning that, on this occasion, food-relevant external cues are particularly scarce, one would expect obese Jews to be more likely to fast than normal Jews. In a study of 296 religious Jewish college students (defined as Jewish college students who had been to a synagogue at least once during the preceding year on occasions other than a wedding or a bar mitzvah), this proves to be the case, for 83.3 percent of obese Jews fasted, as compared with 68.8 percent of normal Jews ($P < .05$).

Further, this external-internal control schema leads to the prediction that fat, fasting Jews who spend a great deal of time in the synagogue on Yom Kippur will suffer less from fasting than fat, fasting Jews who spend little time in the synagogue. There should be no such relationship for normal fasting Jews. Obviously, there will be far fewer food-related cues in the synagogue than on the street or at home. Therefore, for obese Jews, the likelihood that the impulse to eat will be triggered is greater outside of the synagogue than within it. For normal Jews, this distinction is of less importance. In or out of the synagogue, stomach pangs are stomach pangs. Again, the data support the expectation. When the number of hours in the synagogue is correlated with self-ratings of the unpleasantness of fasting, for obese subjects the correlation is $-.50$, whereas for normal subjects the correlation is only $-.18$. In a test of the difference between correlations, $P = .03$. Obviously, for the obese, the more time the individual spends in the synagogue, the less of an ordeal fasting is. For normals, the number of hours in the

[13] E. L. Bliss and C. H. Branch, *Anorexia Nervosa* (New York: Hoeber, 1960).

[14] Schachter, Goldman, and Gordon, *op. cit.*

[15] *Ibid.*; and Koch, *op. cit.*

[16] Hashim and Van Itallie, *op. cit.*; Schachter and Gross, *op. cit.*; and Nisbett, *op. cit.*

[17] R. Goldman, M. Jaffa, and S. Schachter, *J. Personality Soc. Psychol.*, **10** (1968), 117.

synagogue has little to do with the difficulty of the fast.

obesity and choice of eating place

In another study [18] we examined the relationship of obesity to choice of eating places. From Nisbett's findings on taste, it seemed a plausible guess that the obese would be more drawn to good restaurants and more repelled by bad ones than normal subjects would be. At Columbia, students have the option of eating in the university dining halls or in any of the many restaurants that surround the campus. At Columbia, as probably at every similar institution in the United States, students have a low opinion of the institution's food. If a freshman elects to eat in a dormitory dining hall, he may, if he chooses, join a prepayment food plan at the beginning of the school year. Any time after 1 November he may, by paying a penalty of $15, cancel his food contract. If we accept prevailing campus opinion of the institution's food as being at all realistically based, we should anticipate that those for whom taste or food quality is most important will be the most likely to let their food contracts expire. Obese freshmen, then, should be more likely to drop out of the food plan than normal freshmen. Again, the data support the expectation: 86.5 percent of fat freshmen cancel their contracts as compared with 67.1 percent of normal freshmen ($P < .05$). Obesity does to some extent serve as a basis for predicting who will choose to eat institutional food.

obesity and adjustments to new eating schedules

In the final study in this series [19] we examined the relationship of obesity to the difficulty of adjusting to new eating schedules imposed by time-zone changes. This study involved an analysis of data collected by the medical department of Air France in a study of physiological effects of time-zone changes on 236 flight personnel assigned to the Paris–New York and Paris–Montreal flights. Most of these flights leave Paris around noon, French time; fly for approximately 8 hours; and land in North America sometime between 2:00 and 3:00 P.M., Eastern time. Flight-crew members eat lunch shortly after takeoff and, being occupied with landing preparations, are not served another meal during the flight. They land some 7 hours after their last meal, at a time that is later than the local lunch hour and earlier than the local dinner time.

Though this study was not directly concerned with eating behavior, the interviewers systematically noted all individuals who volunteered the information that they "suffered from the discordance between their physiological state and meal time in America." [20] One would anticipate that the fatter individuals, being sensitive to external cues (local meal hours) rather than internal ones, would adapt most readily to local eating schedules and be least likely to complain of the discrepancy between American meal times and physiological state.

Given the physical requirements involved in the selection of aircrews, there are, of course, relatively few really obese people in this sample. However, the results of Nisbett's experiment [21] indicate that the degree of reliance on external relative to internal cues may well be a dimension which varies with the degree of deviation from normal weight. It seems reasonable, then, to anticipate that, even within a restricted sample, there will be differences in response between the heavier and the lighter members of the sample. This is the case. In comparing the 101 flight personnel who are

---

[18] *Ibid.*
[19] *Ibid.*

[20] J. Lavernhe and E. Lafontaine (Air France), personal communication.
[21] *Op. cit.*

overweight (0.1 to 29 percent overweight) with the 135 who are not overweight (0 to 25 percent underweight), we find that 11.9 percent of the overweight complain as compared with 25.3 percent of the non-overweight ($P < .01$). It does appear that the fatter were less troubled by the effects of time changes on eating than the thinner flyers.[22]

These persistent findings that the obese are relatively insensitive to variations in the physiological correlates of food deprivation but highly sensitive to environmental, food-related cues is, perhaps, one key to un-

[22] Obviously, I do not mean to imply that the *only* explanation of the results of these three non-laboratory studies lies in this formulation of the external-internal control of eating behavior. These studies were deliberately designed to test implications of this general schema in field settings. As with any field research, alternative explanations of the findings are legion, and, within the context of any specific study, impossible to rule out. Alternative formulations of this entire series of studies are considered in the original papers. (See Schachter, Goldman, and Gordon, *op. cit.*; Schachter and Gross, *op. cit.*; Nisbett, *op. cit.*; and Goldman, Jaffa, and Schachter, *op. cit.*)

derstanding the notorious long-run ineffectiveness of virtually all attempts to treat obesity.[23] The use of anorexigenic drugs such as amphetamine or of bulk-producing, nonnutritive substances such as methyl cellulose is based on the premise that such agents dampen the intensity of the physiological symptoms of food deprivation. Probably they do, but these symptoms appear to have little to do with whether or not a fat person eats. Restricted, low-calorie diets should be effective just so long as the obese dieter is able to blind himself to food-relevant cues or so long as he exists in a world barren of such cues. In the Hashim and Van Itallie study,[24] the subjects did, in fact, live in such a world. Restricted to a Metrecal-like diet and to a small hospital ward, all the obese subjects lost impressive amounts of weight. However, on their return to normal living, to a man they returned to their original weights.

[23] A Stunkard and M. McLaren-Hume, *Arch. Internal Med.*, 103 (1959), 79; A. R. Feinstein, *J. Chronic Diseases*, 11 (1960), 349.

[24] *Op. cit.*

18

Although many psychologists, psychiatrists, and psychoanalysts have placed considerable emphasis on the analysis of dream content in the assessment and treatment of personality disorders, it was not until recently that "dreaming" became the subject of extensive laboratory research. The joint occurrence of certain physiological events and subjective reports of dreaming provide investigators with the important tools necessary to determine the onset, duration, and frequency of dreams. Furthermore, by awakening subjects at the appropriate time, scientists can now obtain immediate dream reports, thereby minimizing forgetting and distortion; moreover, through the awakening technique, the effects of dream deprivation on behavior can also be assessed. In the next article, Milton Kramer briefly describes some of the new approaches to the psychology and physiology of dreaming.

paradoxical sleep

MILTON KRAMER

Throughout the ages man has been intrigued with the dream, that peculiar mental content that pervades his sleep each night. Physicians also have been interested in the dream, for many reasons. It has been suggested that the dream is the sane man's psychosis and that a study of the dream would help to unravel the mystery of psychosis, since hallucinated visual and auditory experiences are accepted as valid in both conditions. Patients' frequent complaints of sleep disturbances have been related to disturbing dreams, and if the dream could be altered by medical or psychologic treatment, the physician might be

Adapted from a presentation before the Eleventh National Medicinal Chemistry Symposium, Laval University, Quebec.

Reprinted from *Post Graduate Medicine*, April, 1969, **45**: 157–161, by permission of the author and publisher. Copyright © 1969 by McGraw-Hill Book Company, Inc.

able to treat insomnia more effectively. A study of dreams also provides the physician with a significant insight into the psychology of men, which can assist in the psychologic understanding and treatment of his patients.

The absence of technics for signaling the occurrence of the dream had been one of the more serious obstacles to its study. Aserinsky and Kleitman's discovery in 1953 that dreaming sleep is accompanied by an observable phenomenon, conjugate rapid eye movement (REM), made it possible to study the process of dreaming with objective methods and to recover dream content almost at will. The availability of an objective indicator of dreaming has led to the elaboration of the sleep-dream cycle and to the detailed study of the paradoxical phase of sleep, in which each of us "turns on" four to six times a night without the assistance of psychedelic drugs.

We experience a state of total activation,

of which the dream is the psychologic concomitant, about every 90 minutes during a night of sleep. The most frequently used of the 23 names assigned to this recurring period of activation are paradoxical sleep, dreaming sleep, emergent stage I, D state, REM state, and third organismic state. This peculiar recurring condition during sleep is characterized by conjugate rapid eye movements, autonomic irregularities in the cardiovascular and respiratory systems, elevated brain temperature, decreased postural muscle tone, penile erections, and a low-voltage fast electroencephalogram free of spindling. These dreaming episodes comprise 20 to 25 percent of the night's sleep in the young adult. They begin one to two hours after the onset of sleep, are each 15 to 60 minutes' duration, and become longer and more dreamlike as the night progresses. Subjects more often report dreaming when awakened from these periods than when awakened from other phases of sleep.

During paradoxical sleep the organism is neither awake nor asleep but is in some state in which functional relationships are uniquely integrated. The arousal threshold of the organism is generally higher during this REM state than during the other sleep phases. Yet the pattern of neuronal firing during this state is that of neither non-REM sleep nor waking, but is more like that of some hyper-alert state or seizurelike condition.

Both phylogenetic and ontogenetic studies support the concept that the dreaming phase of sleep is a third state of the organism, separate from both the waking state and nondreaming sleep. The REM state has been found in all mammalian species from the mouse to the elephant. It also has been observed in birds and probably in reptiles. The ontogenetic development of paradoxical sleep in the life cycle of a given species is remarkably consistent. The very young of any species spends far more time in REM sleep than does the adult. In the human life cycle the newborn spends 50 percent of its sleep in the REM

state while the aged person spends only 13 to 18 percent of his sleep in this state. The REM state is closely related to the waking state and it is at the expense of the REM state that waking develops, with the superimposition of the 24-hour rest-activity cycle, since the amount of time spent in non-REM sleep changes little with age.

mechanisms of REM cycle

How is such a basic, ubiquitous and recurrent state controlled? The periodicity of the sleep-dream cycle is under the control of nuclei in the pons, which have both anterior and posterior connections. Transection, coagulation and stimulation technics have shown that the anterior firing of the nucleus pontis caudalis accounts for the cortical desynchronization, the low-voltage fast electroencephalogram, which characterizes paradoxical sleep, while the posterior firing of a nucleus located in the roof of the fourth ventricle, the locus ceruleus, accounts for the motor inhibition that occurs during the REM state. The refractory period that follows electric stimulation of these nuclei has led investigators to explore the possibility that neurohumoral mechanisms are involved in the initiation and control of paradoxical sleep.

Cholinergic and adrenergic neurohumoral mechanisms are involved in the control of the REM-non-REM cycle. Special roles have been suggested for serotonin, norepinephrine and gamma aminobutyric acid, which have been shown experimentally to function as neuromodulators, if not neurotransmitters, in initiating the REM state.

The most promising hypothesis concerned with the neurochemical regulation of the REM cycle involves the interrelated effects of serotonin, norepinephrine and acetylcholine. This hypothesis states that increased "free" serotonin, or more probably a balance of serotonin and norepinephrine, in certain brain areas produces a tendency toward REM periods. When a certain level of serotonin is reached, it triggers a release of acetylcholine, which discharges the REM period, during which serotonin is metabolized, probably by mono-amine oxidase.

The hormonal secretions of the anterior and posterior pituitary gland and the gonads stimulate or prolong the REM cycle. The relationship of REM cycle length to the metabolic rate and the evidence for increased metabolic expenditure during the REM state strongly suggest a role for thyroid hormone in the process of paradoxical sleep.

significance of REM state

The question arises as to the possible adaptive significance of paradoxical sleep to the organism. The functions which have been suggested for the REM state, none of which explains all of what is known and many of which are complementary rather than contradictory to one another, may be grouped under three headings: input theories, output theories, and theories that the function of REM sleep, at least in the adult human, is to permit psychologic dreaming to occur.

The input theories contend that REM sleep may permit (1) the periodic awakening of the organism to scan a potentially dangerous environment (a phylogenetic theory), (2) the reorganization of neuronal firing patterns that have become disorganized during non-REM sleep, (3) the periodic recovery from the sensory deprivation of deep sleep, or (4) the endogenous in utero stimulation of the developing nervous system to assist in the maturation and maintenance of function until external stimulation is available post partum (an ontogenetic theory).

The output theories maintain that the REM-state function may allow (1) the elimination of endogenous metabolites (such as serotonin) that have accumulated during the waking state and non-REM

sleep, (2) the discharge of instinctual or drive energies (Freudian theory), (3) the discarding of unneeded information gathered during the day, or (4) the transference of recent memories to long-term memory systems.

The psychologic dreaming theories maintain that the REM state may permit (1) a disguised gratification of wishes (Freud), (2) the availability of the more universal truths of the unconscious (Jung), (3) a rehearsal for the events of waking life (Adler), or (4) the solution and integration of current emotional problems (French).

In pursuing the issue of the functional significance of the REM state, efforts have been made to deprive men and animals of this state by awakening them whenever they enter it. Depriving both men and animals of paradoxical sleep leads to an increased frequency of awakenings, to the onset of the REM-state electroencephalographic pattern immediately on returning to sleep, and on recovery nights to an almost quantitative increase in the percentage of the night's sleep spent in the REM phase.

In REM-deprived animals drive-oriented behavior (oral, aggressive and sexual) is intensified and thus may terminate in death. In some humans, REM-state deprivation leads to increased anxiety, irritability, hostility, appetite and difficulty in remembering, concentrating and motor coordination. These deprived subjects have a heightened susceptibility to hallucinations after photic stimulation. Subjects totally deprived of sleep report after 120 hours, especially at night, the cyclical intensification of hallucinations and delusions at about 90-minute intervals. Possibly, the hallucination is the breakthrough of the dream into waking life.

effects of drugs on dreams

If hallucinations are the breakthrough of dreams into waking life, it is intriguing to explore the effects of hallucination-stimulating drugs, such as the psychotogens (LSD) or alcohol, on the REM state, as well as the effects of the so-called antihallucinogenics such as the tranquilizers. In this attempt, one must focus on studies that have examined both the physiologic (dream time) and psychologic (dream content) effects of drugs on dreams.

The reports of the effects of drugs on REM time include an examination of the effects of psychotropics, psychotogens, alcohol, stimulants and depressants. With the possible exception of reserpine, chlordiazepoxide hydrochloride (LIBRIUM®), and related compounds (and one study of a tranylcypromine [PARNATE®] addict), all studies on the psychotropics, including major and minor tranquilizers and various types of antidepressants, report a decrease in REM time associated with taking these drugs. The work on the psychotogens is inconclusive, with a trend suggesting they cause an increase in REM time. Chronic alcoholics have shown extreme increases in REM time while having delirium tremens. Reports on such stimulants and depressants as caffeine, amphetamine, barbiturates and the opium derivatives generally show a decrease in REM time or no effect at all.

It has been aptly observed, "If we don't keep our attention on the psychology of the dream, we might find out a lot of biology without knowing what it is the biology of." The studies of the effects on dream content of various drugs have been extremely limited. Imipramine, an antidepressant, has been reported to stimulate the expression of hostility in the dreams of normal persons. In dreams of depressed patients, imipramine tends initially to increase hostility and anxiety, but taken on a long-term basis it tends to decrease hostility and anxiety and increase sexuality and motility. Meprobamate has been observed to lead to an increase in motility in dreams, phenobarbital to an increase in homosexuality, and prochlorperazine to an increase in heterosexuality. In general, drugs cause dreams that reflect an increase in anxiety and dependency and a decrease in intimacy.

recovering dream content

A technic that detects the time of dreaming has contributed to our understanding of the psychology of the dream. It should be recognized that although mental content can be recovered from the non-REM phase of sleep, the dream as an intense, elaborated visual experience is most generally associated with the REM state. We have learned that the later in an REM period or the later in the night the dream collection is made, the more visual and vivid is the dream report. The peripheral manifestations of paradoxical sleep (eye and limb movements) are indeed related to the content of the dream. The recall of dreams is higher if (1) a person is awakened from or just after an REM period, (2) he is awakened suddenly rather than gradually, and (3) he is stimulated to recall his dreams.

Interestingly, some emotional theme related to the previous day's experience rather than the experience itself is recalled in dreams. Tactile, auditory and visual stimuli presented concurrently with dreaming are incorporated 10 to 25 percent of the time. Tactile stimuli are the easiest and visual stimuli are the most difficult to incorporate into the dream content. Meaningful insights into personality-coping patterns can be gained from studying the interrelationships of the multiple dreams of a single night. However, because of difficulties in collecting the dream reports, the dream content of psychotic patients has only begun to be systematically examined.

comment

Recent work on paradoxical sleep has stimulated a renewed interest in dreams. The delineation of a basic biologic cycle with a precise anatomic center and numerous neurohumoral and hormonal interrelationships has aroused hopes that a significant neurophysiologic basis for understanding nighttime and perhaps also daytime hallucinated states has at long last been realized. However, just as poetry will never be completely understood in electrophysical terms, dreams cannot be explained solely from a description of eye movements and activated REM-state electroencephalograms. We may some day have a biochemistry of dreaming but never of dreams.

REFERENCES

1. DEMENT, W. C. Psychophysiology of sleep and dreams. In S. Arieti (Editor), *American Handbook of Psychiatry*. New York: Basic Books, Inc., 1966, Vol. 3, pp. 290–332.
2. HARTMANN, E. *The Biology of Dreaming.* Springfield, Ill.: Charles C Thomas, Publisher, 1967.
3. KETY, S. S., E. V. EVARTS, and H. L. WILLIAMS, Eds. Sleep and altered states of consciousness. *Res. Publ. Ass. Res. Nerv. Ment. Dis.*, 1967, **45**.
4. KLEITMAN, N. *Sleep and Wakefulness.* Chicago: University of Chicago Press, 1963.
5. KRAMER, M., et al. Pharamcology of dreaming. In C. J. Martin and B. Kisch (Editors). *Enzymes in Mental Health*. Philadelphia: J. P. Lippincott Company, 1966, pp. 102–116.
6. KRAMER, M., Ed. *Dream Psychology and the New Biology of Dreaming.* Springfield, Ill.: Charles C Thomas, Publisher, 1970.
7. SNYDER, F. The organismic state associated with dreaming. In N. S. Greenfield and W. C. Lewis (Editors). *Psychoanalysis and Current Biological Thought*. Madison, Wis.: University of Wisconsin Press, 1965, pp. 275–315.
8. WITKIN, H. A., and H. B. LEWIS, Eds. *Experimental Studies of Dreaming.* New York: Random House, Inc., 1967.

UNIT

V

emotion

19

For several years, Harry F. Harlow and his associates have been separating infant monkeys from their natural mothers in order to determine the effects of early rearing conditions, such as maternal deprivation, on later intellectual, social, sexual, and emotional behavior. The results of some early experiments, which indicated that the physical characteristics of the surrogate (artificial mother) may be important in later development, led Harlow to postulate a need for "contact-comfort." In the next article Harlow and Suomi report their most recent findings on the effects of early infantile experiences on the development of affection in monkeys.

nature of love—simplified [1]

HARRY F. HARLOW

STEPHEN J. SUOMI

The cloth surrogate and its wire surrogate sibling (see Figure 1) entered into scientific history as of 1958 (Harlow, 1958). The cloth surrogate was originally designed to test the relative importance of body contact in contrast to activities associated with the breast, and the results were clear beyond all expectation. Body contact was of overpowering importance by any measure taken, even contact time, as shown in Figure 2.

However, the cloth surrogate, beyond its power to measure the relative importance of a host of variables determining infant affection for the mother, exhibited another surprising trait, one of great independent usefulness. Even though the cloth mother was inanimate, it was able to impart to its infant such emotional security that the infant would, in the surrogate's presence, explore a strange situation and manipulate available physical objects (see Figure 3), or animate objects (see Figure 4). Manipulation of animate objects leads to play if these animate objects are age-mates, and play is the variable of primary importance in the development of normal social, sexual, and maternal functions, as described by Harlow and Harlow (1965). It is obvious that surrogate mothers, which are more docile and manipulative than real monkey mothers, have a wide range of experimental uses.

[1] This research was supported by United States Public Health Service Grants MH-11894 and FR-0167 from the National Institutes of Health to the University of Wisconsin Primate Laboratory and Regional Primate Research Center, respectively.

simplified surrogate

Although the original surrogates turned out to be incredibly efficient dummy mothers,

figure 1 *Cloth and wire surrogate mothers.*

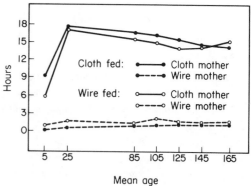

figure 2 *Contact time to cloth and wire surrogate.*

they presented certain practical problems. The worst of the problems was that of cleanliness. Infant monkeys seldom soil their real mothers' bodies, though we do not know how this is achieved. However, infant monkeys soiled the bodies of the original cloth surrogates with such efficiency and enthusiasm as to present a health problem and, even worse, a financial problem resulting from laundering. Furthermore, we believed that the original cloth surrogate was too steeply angled and thereby relatively inaccessible for

cuddly clinging by the neonatal monkey.

In the hope of alleviating practical problems inherent in the original cloth surrogate, we constructed a family of simplified surrogates. The simplified surrogate is mounted on a rod attached to a lead base 4 inches in diameter, angled upward at 25°, and projected through the surrogate's body for 4 inches, so that heads may be attached if desired. The body of the simplified surrogate is only 6 inches long, 2½ inches in diameter, and stands approximately 3 inches off the ground. Figure 5 shows an original

figure 3 *Infant monkey security in presence of cloth surrogate.*

of smaller body and decreased angle of inclination. Infant monkeys do soil the simplified surrogate, but the art and act of soiling is very greatly reduced. Terry cloth slipcovers can be made easily and relatively cheaply, alleviating, if not eliminating, laundry problems. Thus, the simplified surrogate is a far more practical dummy mother than the original cloth surrogate.

surrogate variables

LACTATION

Although the original surrogate papers (Harlow, 1958; Harlow and Zimmermann, 1959) were written as if activities associated with the breast, particularly nursing, were of no importance, this is doubtlessly incorrect. There were no statistically significant differences in time spent by the babies on the lactating versus nonlactating cloth surrogates and on the lactating versus nonlactating wire surrogates, but the fact is that there were consistent preferences for both the cloth and the wire lactating surrogates and that these tendencies held for both the situations of time on surrogate and frequency of surrogate preference when the infant was exposed to a fear stimulus. Thus,

figure 4   Infant play in presence of surrogate.

cloth surrogate and simplified surrogate placed side by side.

As can be seen in Figure 6, infants readily cling to these simplified surrogates

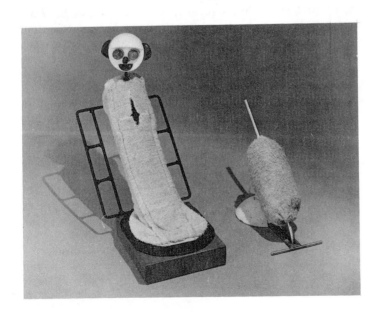

figure 5 Original surrogate and simplified surrogate.

figure 6   Infant clinging to simplified surrogate.

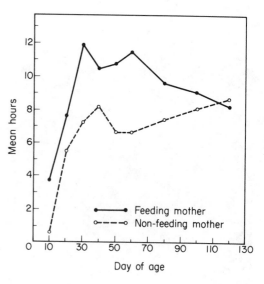

figure 7   Infant preference for lactating cloth surrogate.

if one can accept a statistically insignificant level of confidence, consistently obtained from four situations, one will properly conclude that nursing is a minor variable but one of more than measurable importance operating to bind the infant to the mother.

To demonstrate experimentally that activities associated with the breasts were variables of significant importance, we built two sets of differentially colored surrogates, tan and light blue; and using a 2 × 2 Latin square design, we arranged a situation such that the surrogate of one color lactated and the other did not. As can be seen in Figure 7, the infants showed a consistent preference for the lactating surrogate when contact comfort was held constant. The importance of the lactational variable probably decreases with time. But at least we had established the hard fact that hope springs eternal in the human breast and even longer in the breast, undressed.

FACIAL VARIABLES

In the original surrogates we created an ornamental face for the cloth surrogate and a simple dog face for the wire surrogate. I was working with few available infants and against time to prepare a presidential address for the 1958 American Psychological Association Convention. On the basis of sheer intuition, I was convinced that the

ornamental cloth-surrogate face would become a stronger fear stimulus than the dog face when fear of the unfamiliar matured in the monkeys from about 70 to 110 days (Harlow and Zimmermann, 1959; Sackett, 1966). But since we wanted each surrogate to have an identifiable face and had few infants, we made no effort to balance faces by resorting to a feebleminded 2 × 2 Latin square design.

Subsequently, we have run two brief unpublished experiments. We tested four rhesus infants unfamiliar with surrogate faces at approximately 100 days of age and found that the ornamental face was a much stronger fear stimulus than the dog face. Clearly, the early enormous preference for the cloth surrogate over the wire surrogate was not a function of the differential faces. Later, we raised two infants on cloth and two on wire surrogates, counterbalancing the ornamental and dog faces. Here, the kind of face was a nonexistent variable. To a baby all maternal faces are beautiful. A mother's face that will stop a clock will not stop an infant.

The first surrogate mother we constructed came a little late, or phrasing it another way, her baby came a little early. Possibly her baby was illegitimate. Certainly it was her first baby. In desperation we gave the mother a face that was nothing but a round wooden ball, which displayed no trace of shame. To the baby monkey this featureless face became beautiful, and she frequently caressed it with hands and legs, beginning around 30–40 days of age. By the time the baby had reached 90 days of age we had constructed an appropriate ornamental cloth-mother face, and we proudly mounted it on the surrogate's body. The baby took one look and screamed. She fled to the back of the cage and cringed in autistic-type posturing. After some days of terror the infant solved the medusa-mother problem in a most ingenious manner. She revolved the face 180° so that she always faced a bare round ball! Furthermore, we could rotate the maternal face dozens of times and within an hour or so the infant would turn it around 180°. Within a week the baby resolved her unfaceable problem once and for all. She lifted the maternal head from the body, rolled it into the corner, and abandoned it. No one can blame the baby. She had lived with and loved a faceless mother, but she could not love a two-faced mother.

These data imply that an infant visually responds to the earliest version of mother he encounters, that the mother he grows accustomed to is the mother he relies upon. Subsequent changes, especially changes introduced after maturation of the fear response, elicit this response with no holds barred. Comparisons of effects of baby-sitters on human infants might be made.

BODY-SURFACE VARIABLES

We have received many questions and complaints concerning the surrogate surfaces, wire and terry cloth, used in the original studies. This mountain of mail breaks down into two general categories: that wire is aversive, and that other substances would be equally effective if not better than terry cloth in eliciting a clinging response.

The answer to the first matter in question is provided by observation: Wire is not an aversive stimulus to neonatal monkeys, for they spend much time climbing on the sides of their hardware-cloth cages and exploring this substance orally and tactually. A few infants have required medical treatment from protractedly pressing their faces too hard and too long against the cage sides. Obviously, however, wire does not provide contact comfort.

In an attempt to quantify preference of various materials, an exploratory study [2] was performed in which each of four infants was presented with a choice between surrogates covered with terry cloth versus rayon, vinyl, or rough-grade sandpaper. As shown in Figure 8, the infants demonstrated a clear preference for the cloth surrogates, and no significant preference difference between the other body surfaces. An extension of this study is in progress in which an attempt is being made to further quantify and rank order the preference for these materials by giving infants equal exposure time to all four materials.

[2] We wish to thank Carol Furchner, who conducted this experiment and the described experiment in progress.

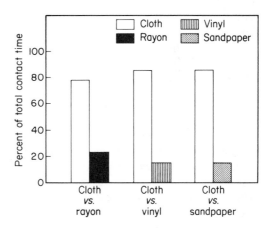

figure 8   *Effect of surface on surrogate contact.*

MOTION VARIABLES

In the original two papers, we pointed out that rocking motion, that is, proprioceptive stimulation, was a variable of more than statistical significance, particularly early in the infant's life, in binding the infant to the mother figure. We measured this by comparing the time the infants spent on two identical planes, one rocking and one stationary (see Figure 9) and two identical cloth surrogates, one rocking and one stationary (see Figure 10).

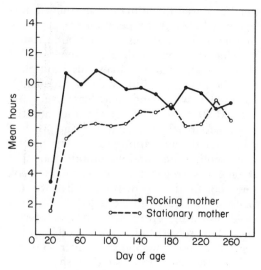

figure 10   *Infant contact to stationary and rocking surrogates.*

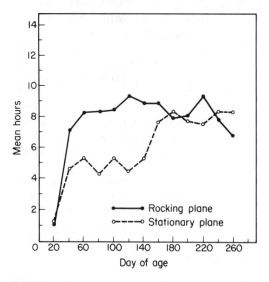

figure 9   *Infant contact to stationary and rocking planes.*

increasing age this difference decreased, and at approximately 15 days the preference reversed. In a second experiment, we used two differentially colored cloth surrogates and heated one and not the other. The infants preferred the hot surrogate, but frequently contacted the room-temperature surrogate for considerable periods of time.

More recently, a series of ingenious studies on the temperature variable has been conducted by Suomi, who created hot- and cold-running surrogates by adaptation of

TEMPERATURE VARIABLES

To study another variable, temperature, we created some "hot mamma" surrogates. We did this by inserting heating coils in the maternal bodies that raised the external surrogate body surface about 10° F. In one experiment, we heated the surface of a wire surrogate and let four infant macaques choose between this heated mother and a room-temperature cloth mother. The data are presented in Figure 11. The neonatal monkeys clearly preferred the former. With

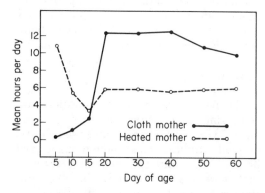

figure 11   *Infant contact to heated-wire and room-temperature cloth surrogates.*

the simplified surrogate. These results are important not only for the information obtained concerning the temperature variable but also as an illustration of the successful experimental use of the simplified surrogate itself.

The surrogates used in these exploratory studies were modifications of the basic simplified surrogate, designed to get maximum personality out of the minimal mother. One of these surrogates was a "hot mamma," exuding warmth from a conventional heating pad wrapped around the surrogate frame and completely covered by a terry cloth sheath. The other surrogate was a cold female; beneath the terry cloth sheath was a hollow shell within which her life fluid—cold water—was continuously circulated. The two surrogates are illustrated in Figure 12, and to the untrained observer they look remarkably similar. But looks can be deceiving, especially with females, and we felt that in these similar-looking surrogates we had really simulated the two extremes of womanhood—one with a hot body and no head, and one with a cold shoulder and no heart. Actually, this is an exaggeration, for the surface temperature of the hot surrogate was only 7° F. above room temperature, while the surface temperature of the cold surrogate was only 5° F. below room temperature.

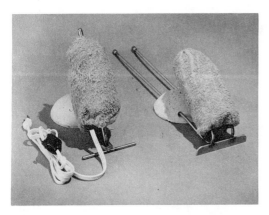

figure 12   Warm (left) and cold simplified surrogates.

In a preliminary study, we raised one female infant from Day 15 on the warm surrogate for a period of four weeks. Like all good babies she quickly and completely became attached to her source of warmth, and during this time she exhibited not only a steadily increasing amount of surrogate contact but also began to use the surrogate as a base for exploration (see Figure 13). At the end of this four-week period, we decided that our subject had become spoiled enough and so we replaced the warm surrogate with the cold version for one week. The infant noticed the switch within two minutes, responding by huddling in a corner and vocalizing piteously. Throughout the week of bitter maternal cold, the amount of surrogate contact fell drastically; in general, the infant avoided the surrogate in her feeding, exploratory, and sleeping behaviors. Feeling somewhat guilty, we switched surrogates once more for a week and were rewarded for our efforts by an almost immediate return to previously high levels of surrogate contact. Apparently, with heart-warming heat, our infant was capable of forgiveness, even at this tender age. At this point, we switched the two surrogates daily for a total two weeks, but by this time the infant had accepted the inherent fickle nature of her mothers. On the days that her surrogate was warm, she clung tightly to its body, but on the days when the body was cold, she generally ignored it, thus providing an excellent example of naive behaviorism.

With a second infant we maintained this procedure but switched the surrogates, so that he spent four weeks with the cold surrogate, followed by one week with the warm, an additional week with the cold, and finally a two-week period in which the surrogates were switched daily. This infant became anything but attached to the cold surrogate during the initial four-week period, spending most of his time huddling in the corner of his cage and generally avoiding the surrogate in his exploratory behavior (see Figure 14). In succeeding

figure 13   Infant clinging to and exploring from warm simplified surrogate.

weeks, even with the warm surrogate, he failed to approach the levels of contact exhibited by the other infant to the cold surrogate. Apparently, being raised with a cold mother had chilled him to mothers in general, even those beaming warmth and comfort.

Two months later both infants were exposed to a severe fear stimulus in the presence of a room-temperature simplified surrogate. The warm-mother infant responded to this stimulus by running to the surrogate and clinging for dear life. The cold-mother infant responded by running the other way and seeking security in a

corner of the cage. We seriously doubt that this behavioral difference can be attributed to the sex difference of our subjects. Rather, this demonstration warmed our hopes and chilled our doubts that temperature may be a variable of importance. More specifically, it suggested that a simple linear model may not be adequate to describe the effects of temperature differences of surrogates on infant attachment. It is clear that warmth is a variable of major importance, particularly in the neonate, and we hazard the guess that elevated temperature is a variable of importance in the operation of all the affectional systems: maternal, mother-in-

figure 14   Typcial infant reactions to cold simplified surrogate.

fant, possibly age-mate, heterosexual, and even paternal.

prospectives

Recently we have simplified the surrogate mother further for studies in which its only function is that of providing early social support and security to infants. This super-simplified surrogate is merely a board 1½ inches in diameter and 10 inches long with a scooped-out, concave trough having a maximal depth of ¾ inch. As shown in Figure 15, the supersimplified surrogate has an angular deviation from the base of less than 15°, though this angle can be increased by the experimenter at will. The standard cover for this supremely simple surrogate mother is a size 11, cotton athletic sock, though covers of various qualities, rayon, vinyl (which we call "linoleum lover"), and sandpaper, have been used for experimental purposes.

Linoleum lover, with you I am through
The course of smooth love never runs true.

figure 15   The supersimplified surrogate.

This supersimplified mother is designed to attract and elicit clinging responses from the infant during the first 15 days of the infant's life.

We have designed, but not yet tested, a swinging mother that will dangle from a frame about 2 inches off the floor and have a convex, terry cloth or cotton body surface. Observations of real macaque neonates and mothers indicate that the infant, not the mother, is the primary attachment object even when the mother locomotes, and that this swinging mother may also elicit infantile clasp and impart infant security very early in life. There is nothing original in this day and age about a swinger becoming a mother, and the only new angle, if any, is a mother becoming a swinger.

Additional findings, such as the discovery that six-month social isolates will learn to cling to a heated simplified surrogate, and that the presence of a surrogate reduces clinging among infant-infant pairs, have substantiated use of the surrogate beyond experiments for its own sake. At present, the heated simplified surrogate is being utilized as a standard apparatus in studies as varied as reaction to fear, rehabilitation of social isolates, and development of play. To date, additional research utilizing the cold version of the simplified surrogate has been far more limited, possibly because unused water faucets are harder to obtain than empty electrical outlets. But this represents a methodological, not a theoretical problem, and doubtlessly solutions will soon be forthcoming.

It is obvious that the surrogate mother at this point is not merely a historical showpiece. Unlike the proverbial old soldier, it it far from fading away. Instead, as in the past, it continues to foster not only new infants but new ideas.

REFERENCES

HARLOW, H. F. The nature of love. *American Psychologist*, 1958, 13, 673–685.

————, and M. K. Harlow. The affectional systems. In A. M. Schrier, H. F. Harlow, & F. Stollnitz (Eds.), *Behavior of nonhuman primates*. Vol. 2. New York: Academic Press, 1965.

Harlow, H. F., and R. R. Zimmermann. Af-
fectional responses in the infant monkey. *Science*, 1959, **130**, 421–432.

Sackett, G. P. Monkeys reared in visual isolation with pictures as visual input: Evidence for an innate releasing mechanism. *Science*, 1966, **154**, 1468–1472.

20

We are all aware that various physiological changes occur during states of emotional arousal. The nature of the relationship between emotion and bodily processes, however, has been the subject of considerable debate among various theorists. At one extreme is the position that different physiological activation patterns result from different emotional states; other theories have postulated that the specific pattern of physiological activation determines the particular emotion experienced. The innovative research of Stanley Schachter and his associates indicates that neither of these models of emotion is adequate: an individual's emotional behavior and the emotional experience which he reports seem to depend upon a generalized state of physiological arousal, the specific social situation, and the subject's understanding of his physiological condition.

on the assumption of "identity" in psychopharmacology [1]

STANLEY SCHACHTER

Though we rarely bother to make the matter explicit, the assumption of an identity between a physiological state and a psychological or behavioral event is implicit in much, though certainly not all, of contemporary work in the human aspects of psychopharmacology. Simply put, much of this work seems to proceed on the assumption that there is a simple, one-to-one relationship between a biochemical change or a physiological process and a specific behavior. In philosopher's jargon, it is as if we

[1] Much of the research described in this paper was supported by Grant MH 05203 from the National Institute of Mental Health, United States Public Health Service and by Grant G 23758 from the National Science Foundation.

Reprinted from Symposium on Medical Aspects of Stress in the Military Climate, April 22–24, 1964, Walter Reed Army Institute of Research, Washington, D.C., by permission of the author.

assumed that physiological state is an "unconditionally sufficient condition" to account for a psychological event.

Such an assumption has, of course, been enormously fruitful in many areas of purely biological and medical research. Spirochetes cause syphilis. If we kill the spirochete, we cure syphilis. An iodine-deficient diet leads to colloid goiters; if we repair the deficiency, we repair the goiter. As we move from the world of purely medical and physiological research, however, the assumption of such an "identity" seems to become more and more troublesome and is, I suspect, the chief reason that it sometimes seems the rule rather than the exception in psychopharmacology to find a single drug proven in a variety of studies to have blatantly opposite behavioral effects. LSD, for example, has been proved to be a hallucinogenic and a non-hallucinogenic, to be a euphoriant, a depressant and to have no effects on mood at all.

This nightmarish pattern of conflicting and non-replicable results is one that is familiar to anyone who has delved into the literature on behavioral or "emotional" effects of many of the so-called psychotropic drugs. This is not, however, a pattern that is limited only to the exotic drugs; even as familiar an agent as adrenalin has a similarly depressing history. Many years ago the endocrinologist, Marañon (5) injected several hundred of his patients with adrenalin and then asked them to introspect. Some of his subjects simply described their physical symptoms and reported no emotional effects at all; others described their feelings in a fashion that Marañon labeled the "cold" or "as if" emotions, that is, they made statements such as "I feel as if I were afraid" or "as if I were awaiting a great happiness." Still other subjects described themselves as feeling genuine emotions. Of those who noted any emotional effects at all, some described themselves as feeling anxious, some as angry, some as euphoric. In short, adrenalin, producing almost identical physiological effects in most of these subjects, produced a wide diversity of self-reports of feeling states.

This state of affairs is, I suspect, inevitable and will remain puzzling and depressing just so long as we persist in the assumption of an identity between the physiological and the psychological effects of a drug. If we do, my guess is that we will be just about as successful at deriving predictions about complex behavior from a knowledge of biochemical and physiological conditions as we would be at predicting the destination of a moving automobile from an exquisite knowledge of the workings of the internal combustion engine and of petroleum chemistry.

If we are eventually to make sense of this area, we will, I believe, be forced to adopt a set of concepts with which most physiologically inclined scientists feel somewhat uncomfortable and ill-at-ease for they are concepts which are, at present, difficult to physiologize about or to reify. We will be forced to examine a subject's perception of his bodily state and his interpretation of it in terms of his immediate situation and his past experience. We will be forced to deal with concepts about perception, about cognition, about learning, and about the social situation.

In order to avoid any misunderstanding let me make completely explicit that I am most certainly not suggesting that such notions as perception and cognition do not have physiological correlates. I am suggesting that at present we know virtually nothing about these physiological correlates but that we can and must use such non-physiologically anchored concepts if we are to make headway in understanding the relationship of complex behavioral patterns to physiological and biochemical processes.

To move from generalities, let us consider the effects of adrenalin or epinephrine. We know that an injection of ½ cc. of a 1:1000 solution of epinephrine causes an increase in heart rate, a marked increase in systolic blood pressure, a redistribution of blood with a cutaneous decrease and a muscle and cerebral blood flow increase. Blood sugar and lactic acid concentrations increase and respiration rate increases slightly. As far as the human subject is concerned the major subjective symptoms are palpitation, slight tremor, and sometimes a feeling of flushing and accelerated breathing.

These are some of the measured physiological effects of an injection of epinephrine. In and of themselves are such bodily changes pleasant or unpleasant? Given these symptoms should the subject describe himself as angry, or as anxious, or as manic or euphoric or simply as sick? From the results of the Marañon study and its several replications (3, 4) any of these self-descriptions are possible. How can we make coherent sense of such findings?

Several years ago, bemused by such results, my colleagues and I undertook a program of research on the interaction of physiological and cognitive determinants of emotional state. This program was based on speculation about an, at that time, hypothetical event. Imagine a subject whom one somehow managed covertly to inject with adrenalin, or to feed a sympathomimetic agent such as ephedrine. Such a subject would become aware of palpitations, tremor, etc., and at the same time would be utterly unaware of why he felt this way. What would be the consequences of such a state?

In other contexts (6) I have suggested that precisely this condition would lead to the arousal of evaluative needs; that is, pressures would operate on such an individual to understand and evaluate his bodily feelings. His bodily state roughly resembles the condition in which it has been at times of emotional excitement. How would he label his present feelings? I would suggest that such an individual would label his bodily feelings in terms of the situation in which he finds himself. Should he at the time be watching a horror film, he would probably decide that he was badly frightened. Should he be with a beautiful woman, he might decide that he was wildly in love or sexually excited. Should he be in an argument, he might explode in fury and hatred. Or, should the situation be completely inappropriate he would decide that he was excited or upset by something that had recently happened, or, I suppose, that he was sick. In any case, it is my basic assumption that the labels one attaches to a bodily state, how one describes his feelings, are a joint function of such cognitive factors and of a state of physiological arousal.

This line of thought, then, leads to the following propositions: (1) Given a state of physiological arousal for which an individual has no immediate explanation, he will "label" this state and describe his feelings in terms of the cognitions available to him. To the extent that cognitive factors are potent determiners of emotional states, it could be anticipated that precisely the same state of physiological arousal could be labeled "joy" or "fury" or any of a great

diversity of emotional labels depending on the cognitive aspects of the situation. (2) Given a state of physiological arousal for which an individual has a completely appropriate explanation (e.g., "I feel this way because I have just received an injection of adrenalin"), no evaluative needs will arise and the individual is unlikely to label his feelings in terms of the alternative cognitions available. (3) Given the same cognitive circumstances, the individual will react emotionally or describe his feelings as emotions only to the extent that he experiences a state of physiological arousal.

The experimental test of these propositions requires (1) the experimental manipulation of a state of physiological arousal or sympathetic activation; (2) the manipulation of the extent to which the subject has an appropriate or proper explanation of his bodily state; and (3) the creation of situations from which explanatory cognitions may be derived.

In order to satisfy these requirements, Jerome Singer and I (8) constructed an experiment [2] which was cast in the framework of a study of the effects of vitamin supplements on vision. As soon as a subject arrived, he was told: "In this experiment we would like to make various tests of your vision. We are particularly interested in how a vitamin compound called Suproxin affects the visual skills. If you agree to take part in the experiment, we would like to give you an injection of Suproxin."

If a subject agreed (and all but one of 185 subjects did), he received an injection of one of two forms of Suproxin—placebo or epinephrine. We have then two groups of subjects—placebo subjects on whom the injection can have no possible effect and epinephrine subjects who, within a few

---

[2] For purposes of brevity the description of this experiment does not include details of all of the conditions in this study. The chief omission is a description of a control condition introduced to evaluate alternative interpretations of the data. The interested reader is referred to the original paper by Schachter and Singer (8).

minutes after injection, will become aware of the full battery of sympathomimetic symptoms.

In order to manipulate the extent to which subjects had a proper explanation of their bodily state, subjects who received epinephrine received one of two types of instructions:

1. *Informed Subjects:* Before receiving the injection such subjects were told: "I should also tell you that some of our subjects have experienced side effects from the Suproxin. These side effects will only last for 15 or 20 minutes. What will probably happen is that your hand will start to shake, your heart will start to pound and your face may get warm and flushed."

These subjects, then, are told precisely what they will feel and why they will feel it. For such subjects, then, evaluative needs are low. They have an exact explanation for their bodily feelings and cognitive or situational factors should have no effect on how the subject labels his feelings.

2. *Uninformed Subjects:* Such subjects are told that the injection will have no side effects at all. These subjects then will experience a state of sympathetic arousal but have no experimenter-provided explanation for why they feel the way they do. Evaluative needs then should be high and cognitive-situational factors should have maximal effect on how such a subject labels his bodily state.

Finally, in order to expose subjects to situations from which they might derive explanatory cognitions relevant to their bodily state immediately after injection, subjects were placed in one of two situations:

1. *Euphoria.* In this situation, a subject was placed alone in a room with a stooge who had been introduced as a fellow subject and who, following a completely standardized routine, acted in a manic-euphoric fashion doing such things as flying paper airplanes, hula-hooping and the like, keeping up all the while a standard patter and atempting occasionally to induce the subject to join the fray.

2. *Anger.* In this situation, a subject was asked to fill out a long, infuriatingly personal questionnaire asking such questions as:

"With how many men (other than your father) has your mother had extra-marital relationships?"
4 and under____: 5–9____: 10 and over____.

Filling in the questionnaire alongside the subject was a stooge, again presumably a fellow subject, who volubly grew more and more irritated at the questionnaire, finally in a rage ripping the thing up and slamming it to the floor while biting out, "I'm not wasting any more time. I'm getting my books and leaving"—and stamping out of the room.

In both situations, an observer, through a one-way mirror, systematically recorded the behavior of the subject in order to provide indices of the extent to which the subject joined in the stooge's mood. Finally, once these rigged situations had run their course, the experimenter returned and with a plausible pretext, asked the subject to fill out a series of standardized scales designed to measure the intensity of anger or euphoria.

We have then a set of experimental conditions in which we are simultaneously manipulating the degree of sympathetic arousal and the extent to which subjects understand why they feel as they do and measuring the impact of these variations on the extent to which the subject catches the mood of a situation rigged in one set of conditions to induce euphoria and in another set of conditions to induce anger. From the line of thought that generated this study, it should be anticipated that subjects injected with epinephrine and told that there would be no side effects should catch the mood of the rigged situation to a greater extent than either subjects who had been injected with placebo or subjects who had been injected with epinephrine and given a completely appropriate explanation of what they would feel and why.

Examining first the results of the euphoria conditions, we find that this is exactly the case. The uninformed epinephrine subjects, those who had been told that there would be no side effects, tend to catch the stooge's mood with alacrity; they join the stooge's whirl of activity and invent new manic activities of their own. In marked contrast, the informed epinephrine subjects and the placebo subjects who give no indication of autonomic arousal tend to simply sit and stare at the subject in mild disbelief. The relevant data are reported in detail elsewhere. For present purposes it should suffice simply to note that these differences between conditions are large and statistically significant on both observational and self-report measures of mood.

In the anger conditions, the pattern of results is precisely the same. Uninformed epinephrine subjects grow openly annoyed and irritated while placebo and informed epinephrine subjects maintain their equanimity. The evidence is good, then, in support of our basic propositions. Given a state of physiological arousal for which a subject has no ready explanation, he proves readily manipulable into the disparate states of euphoria and anger. Given an identical physiological state for which the subject has an appropriate explanation, his mood is almost untouched by the rigged situation.

Such results are not limited to the states of anger and euphoria. In still other experiments enploying somewhat similar techniques and comparisons, we have been readily able to manipulate uninformed epinephrine subjects into amusement as measured by laughter at a slapstick movie (9) and into fearful or anxious states (7).

In sum, precisely the same physiological state, an epinephrine-induced state of sympathetic arousal, can be manifested as anger, euphoria, amusement, fear or, as in the informed subjects, as no mood or emotional state at all. Such results are virtually incoherent if we persist in the assumption of an identity between physiological and psychological states but fall neatly into place if we specify the fashion in which cognitive and physiological factors interact. With the addition of cognitive propositions we are able to specify and manipulate the conditions under which an injection of epinephrine will or will not lead to an emotional state and to predict what emotion will result.

Though the experiments I have described have all involved injections of epinephrine, my basic assumptions, as worded, clearly imply applicability to bodily states other than the epinephrine-induced state of sympathetic activation. If these ideas are correct, it should be expected that any novel bodily state will give rise to pressures to decide what is felt, to decide how these feelings are to be labeled and, perhaps, to decide whether these feelings are pleasant or unpleasant ones. Though I know of no experiments directly designed to test these ideas for states other than that induced by epinephrine, the extensive literature on the effects of drugs provides constant hints and bits of data which suggest that these ideas do have wide applicability.

As an example, let us consider the effects of smoking marihuana. Following the pharmacological texts, marihuana is to some extent sympathomimetic and produces in addition the following effects—hunger, ataxia, vertigo, tinnitus, hyper-reflexia, increased sensitivity to touch, pressure, pain and taste stimuli and nystagmus on lateral gaze. Given these physiological changes we may ask, as we did for adrenalin, how is the marihuana user to label his feelings? Given such symptoms should the smoker describe himself as "high" or as "sick"?

In an absorbing study of 50 marihuana users, the sociologist Becker (1) reports an invariable sequence in learning to use marihuana for pleasure. Once he has learned the techniques of smoking, the smoker must learn to label his physiological symptoms as being "high." In Becker's words,

. . . being high consists of two elements; the presence of symptoms caused by marihuana use and the recognition of these symptoms and their connection by the user with his use of the drug. It is not enough, that is, that the effects be present; they alone do not automatically provide the experience of being high. The user must be able to point them out to himself and consciously connect them with his having smoked marihuana before he can have this experience. Otherwise, regardless of the actual effects produced, he considers that the drug has had no effect on him.

An example of learning that he is high is provided by this quotation from a novice who gets high for the first time only after he learns that intense hunger is one consequence of smoking marihuana:

"They were just laughing the hell out of me because like I was eating so much. I just scoffed [ate] so much food, and they were just laughing at me, you know. Sometimes I'd be looking at them, you know, wondering why they're laughing, you know, not knowing what I was doing. (Well, did they eventually tell you why they were laughing?) Yeah, yeah, I come back, 'Hey, man, what's happening?' and all of a sudden I feel weird, you know. 'Man, you're on you know. You're on pot (high on marihuana).' I said, 'No, am I?' Like I don't know what's happening."

Obviously, this is an instance where the novice must literally learn to notice his feelings and connect them with marihuana. After a user has been made aware of his symptoms and has learned that what he is feeling is being "high," Becker notes that one further step is necessary for continued use of the drug:

He must learn to enjoy the effects he has just learned to experience. Marihuana-produced sensations are not automatically or necessarily pleasurable. The taste for such experience is a socially acquired one, not different in kind from acquired tastes for oysters or dry martinis. The user feels dizzy, thirsty; his scalp tingles; he misjudges time and distances, and so on. Are these things pleasurable? He isn't sure. If he is to continue marihuana use, he must decide that they are. Otherwise, getting high, while a real enough experience, will be an unpleasant one he would rather avoid.

Becker supports this analysis with numerous instances of novice smokers being taught, in social interaction, that their feelings were pleasant.

This study, then, indicates that new marihuana users must be taught to notice and identify what they feel, must be taught to label the state as "high" and must be taught that the state is "pleasant." The marihuana-induced state of feelings appears to be another instance of a bodily state which takes its meaning and labels in good part from cognitive and social factors.

I would guess that the labels and hedonic valuation attached to an amazing variety of bodily conditions, drug-induced or not, are cognitively determined. Obviously, there are limits. It is unlikely that anyone with undiagnosed peritonitis could ever be convinced that he was euphoric, "high" or anything but deathly ill. I suspect, though, that the limits are astonishingly wide. Vomiting to us may seem unpleasant, but to a banqueting Roman gourmet, it may have been one of the exquisite pleasures.

One final item: my basic point in this paper is more than a simple methodological plea that we take account of cognitive and situational factors in evaluating the effects of a drug. The assumption of the cognitive determination of the labeling of bodily states has on its own a number of surprising implications and does lead to a new approach to some very old phenomena. If it is correct that the labels attached to feeling states are cognitively, situationally, or socially determined, it becomes a distinct possibility that an uncommon or inappropriate label can be attached to a feeling state. Where such is the case, we may anticipate bizarre and pathological behavior.

As an example of this possibility, consider the state of hunger. We are so accustomed to think of hunger as a primary motive, wired into the animal and unmistakable in its cues, that even the possibility that an organism would be incapable of correctly labeling the state seems too far-fetched to credit. The physiological changes accompanying food deprivation seem distinct, identifiable, and invariant. Yet even a moment's consideration will make it clear that attaching the label "hunger" to this set of bodily feelings and behaving accordingly, is a learned, socially determined cognitive act. Consider the neonate. Wholly at the mercy of its feelings, when uncomfortable, or in pain, or frightened, or hungry, it screams. Whether it is comforted, or soothed, or fondled, or fed has little to do with the state of its own feelings but depends entirely on the ability and willingness of its mother or nurse to recognize the proper cues. If she is experienced, she will comfort the baby when he is frightened, soothe him when he is chafed, feed him when he is hungry, and so on. If inexperienced, her behavior may be completely inappropriate to the child's state. Most commonly, perhaps, the compassionate but bewildered mother will feed her child at any sign of distress.

It is precisely this state of affairs that the analyst Hilde Bruch (2) suggests is at the heart of chronic obesity. Such cases she describes as characterized by a confusion between intense emotional states and hunger. During childhood these patients, she presumes, have not been taught to discriminate between hunger and such states as fear, anger, and anxiety. If correct, these people are, in effect, labeling a state of sympathetic activation as hunger.

If Bruch's speculation is correct, it might be anticipated that the obese will literally not know when they are physiologically hungry. They should not, then, label as "hunger" the set of physiological symptoms which are considered characteristic of this state. Astonishingly, this appears to be exactly the case. In an absorbing study, Stunkard (10) has related gastric motility to self-reports of hunger in 17 obese and 18 normal women. Over a 4-hour experimental session he obtained continuous measures of gastric motility by use of a gastric balloon.

Every 15 minutes, subjects were asked whether or not they were hungry. For the normals, the self-report of hunger coincided perfectly with gastric motility an average of 74 percent of the time. For the obese, the coincidence was only 38 percent. Though other interpretations are possible, it would certainly seem that the obese do not label the physiological symptoms of gastric motility as hunger.[3]

REFERENCES

1. BECKER, H. S. Becoming a Marihuana User. *Amer. J. Sociol.*, **59**: 235–242, 1953.
2. BRUCH, HILDE. Transformation of Oral Impulses in Eating Disorders: A Conceptual Approach. *Psychiat. Quart.*, **35**: 458–481, 1961.
3. CANTRIL, H., and W. A. HUNT. Emotional Effects Produced by the Injection of Adrenalin. *Amer. J. Psychol.*, **44**: 300–307, 1932.
4. LANDIS, C., and W. A. HUNT. Adrenalin and Emotion. *Psychol. Rev.*, **39**: 467–485, 1932.
5. MARAÑON, G. Contribution à l'étude de l'action émotive de l'adrénaline. *Revue Française D'endocrinologia*, **2**: 301–325, 1924.
6. SCHACTER, S. *The Psychology of Affiliation.* Stanford, Calif.: Stanford University Press, 1959.
7. ———, and B. LATANÉ. Crime, Cognition and the Autonomic Nervous System. Mimeograph, 1964.
8. SCHACTER, S., and J. SINGER. Cognitive, Social and Physiological Determinants of Emotional State. *Psychol. Rev.*, **69**: 379–399, 1962.
9. SCHACTER, S., and L. WHEELER. Epinephrine, Chlorpromazine, and Amusement. *J. Abnorm. & Soc. Psychol.*, **65**: 121–128, 1962.
10. STUNKARD, A. Obesity and the Denial of Hunger. *Psychosom. Med.*, **21**: 281–289, 1959.

[3] [See Schachter's 1968 study, "Obesity and Eating," reprinted in this volume on pp. 188–198.]

UNIT

VI

language

21

In the historically oriented paper that follows, James J. Jenkins suggests that the fields of psychology and linguistics are changing and that the nature of the relevant theories is altering. The arguments developed here apply to all higher mental processes (and perhaps to all behavior), and therefore the controversies are fundamental and the debates spirited.

the nature of psychological theory[1]

JAMES J. JENKINS

There is a wealth of evidence that the established theoretical positions in psychology are currently under serious attack. This is dramatically demonstrated in Dixon and Horton's book, *Verbal Behavior and General Behavior Theory* (1968). The conference reported in that book was to have been a straightforward attempt to relate the experimental and theoretical work in verbal behavior research to general learning theory, the dominant theoretical area of American psychology. Instead of a quiet scholarly exploration, however, the result was more like a pitched battle. Traditional associative learning theory was attacked violently; defectors from the established positions gave testimony to new faiths; and revolutionary credos were shouted at conference table and dinner table alike.

One way to understand what was happening at the Dixon-Horton conference is to examine the nature of psychological theory as it has been and to ask what its nature may be in the future. The present paper attempts to perform this service from the vantage point of one who has been "converted" and who sees much of the uproar of the current day as a consequence, in part at least, of the revolution in modern linguistics. Preliminary to the effort, however, it will be useful to dwell momentarily on the question of why the nature of psychological theory is not automatically made clear by the definition of the word psychology itself.

[1] The view expressed here is the product of many interactions with friends and colleagues. I am particularly indebted to Jerry Fodor, Donald Foss, Terry Halwes and Robert Shaw. Frank Kessel made helpful suggestions about the form and content of the paper. Much of this material is drawn from a discussion in Dixon and Horton (1968) and a symposium at the Midwestern Psychological Association in May, 1967. The preparation of this paper was supported by the Center for Research in Human Learning, University of Minnesota, through grants from the National Institute of Child Health and Human Development (HD-01136), the National Science Foundation (GS-1761) and the Graduate School of the University of Minnesota.

defining psychology

Unfortunately for this approach, it is not an easy matter to define any field of science. I find it hard to think of a completely neutral definition of "psychology" and efforts to do so have convinced me that the term cannot be given any serious definition prior to theoretical or metatheoretical commitments. Even a superficial study of the history of our field reveals that what we mean by "psychology" changes, depending on both the historical period in which one finds himself and the geographical location in which he speaks. Historical periods appear to have contracted for certain obligations as to what it is that the science is about, including border agreements with adjacent sciences; and particular schools, areas of the country, nationalities and hemispheres seem to have markedly different biases.

For western Europe at the turn of the century, the consensus seems to have been that psychology was the study of the structure of the mind through the study of the contents of consciousness. It was an empirical (or perhaps better, experimental) science which was largely concerned with a mapping of "experience" onto the physically described world. Its classic problem had to do with the observation of mental events and it struggled with a set of pertinent "crucial" issues (imageless thought, determining tendencies, Act Psychology, etc.).

In a brief, vigorous revolution this schema was overthrown by American Behaviorism. (This is true at least insofar as the majority of the practicing academic psychologists were concerned. The older adherents of the previous school who did not mend their ways either quietly moved on into chairmanships and deanships or simply grew old and died.) The important thing to note, of course, is not just that introspection went out, that "observers" were replaced by "subjects," that animal psychology blossomed or that conditioning was

"in." The important thing to note is that *what psychology was* changed. *The* question now became: How do stimuli come to control responses? Higher mental processes were declared "out of bounds" or were permitted "in bounds" only under great restrictions and with the proviso that they must be defined in such a way as to be reducible to assemblies of elementary stimuli and responses (whether observed or unobserved). Peripheralism, environmentalism, objectivism and reflexology all became part and parcel of the basic assumptions and ground rules that controlled psychology.[2]

A radical change in the nature of the field is not the peculiar property of psychology as an underdeveloped and immature science. Indeed, this kind of restructuring and revision is typical of the sciences whose histories have been studied. The myth of the slow, steady, unidirectional accumulation of knowledge is just that: a myth.

---

[2] Robert I. Watson (1967) argues that psychology has not yet risen to the status of having a *paradigm* as the older and more mature sciences have. He believes that in the absence of universal agreement about the nature of a contentual model for the science, we can only speak of *prescriptions* or themes which characterize the orientation or attitude of the psychologist-scientist with respect to a set of dimensions, such as determinism-indeterminism, empiricism-rationalism, functionalism-structuralism and the like. While recognizing the reasons for his choice and the undoubted absence of a universal definition of psychology, I think it is more descriptive to take the view that there was a paradigm of American Behaviorism and that it replaced its academically accepted predecessor, Structuralism. If one prefers to think in terms of "bundles of prescriptions" as Watson does, I cannot see that it would be objectionable. The point I want to stress is that for the psychologist in training at the typical American institution, the nature of the science was radically altered. Problems changed, experimentation changed, crucial issues changed and, ultimately, what one could publish in a psychological journal changed. On the other hand, the shift from Behaviorism to Neo-behaviorism to Neo-neo-behaviorism does not represent such a change in either paradigmatic terms or in terms of the bundle of prescriptions represented.

Thomas Kuhn (1962) in his book, *The Structure of Scientific Revolutions,* asserts that revolution is the ordinary pattern of scientific development rather than the exceptional case. He points out that "normal science" operates within a *paradigm,* that is, a set of rules and examples which serve to tell the practitioner how to identify a legitimate problem in the science, what counts as an explanation, which constructs are viewed as elementaries, and so on. When the science is put under great pressure in terms of its failures and inadequacies, it becomes ripe for revolution. Then, if some counter view is available, it may be called upon to restructure the field. Under such a restructuring, the old problems may be lost; crucial issues may be viewed as irrelevant; new issues, some of which are not even expressible under the old view, may claim attention. If the new view wins in the resulting struggle, the field is reorganized; the textbooks rewritten; the old disputes ignored in favor of the new; and the entire change is made to look as if it were an inevitable development of orderly progress in the science.

Joseph Schwab (1964) makes the same point when he contrasts "stable enquiry" with "fluid enquiry." Stable inquiry usually corresponds within its own invisible limits to the usual "rules" of scientific method within its discipline. But in fluid inquiry, says Schwab, all the rules seem to be suspended; the sources of ideas and hypotheses may shift radically; the justifications employed may be markedly different; the talents required of the investigators change; and there is little of the traditional kind of work performed. He points out that a special part of the work of such a time consists of "the political-rhetorical-scientific hard work of obtaining acceptance of a new conceptual scheme by one's fellow scientists."

As is suggested by the discourse thus far, I think that the paradigm in psychology is in the process of change and that there are hints of a new paradigm coming that may be powerful enough to displace the current one. This paper is, then, one of the attempts on the political-rhetorical side to get this conception before you. It is precisely because the nature of psychology itself is at issue that we cannot get any guidance from the exercise of trying to find a definition for the term.

psychology of language

What happened at the Dixon-Horton conference should be viewed in the light of the history of the psychology of language for it is obvious that the struggle at the conference pitted the psychologists of language against the traditionalists in learning theory, both those working with verbal behavior and those working with other behaviors. As the above section suggests, it was inevitable that there should be deep disagreements and misunderstandings. Proponents of "the establishment" felt that their positions were distorted and caricatured. Opponents felt that "the establishment" was being evasive and blind. Both groups, while trying to avoid doing so, played with the treacherous tactic of telling the other just how one ought to do science. Because this is a good instance of our current problem, my remarks are focussed on the recent histories of psychology and linguistics and the prescriptive tendencies of psychologists and linguists.

In the 1930's and 40's, psychology was shaken with furious debates about what was and what was not "scientific" in psychology. Advocates were outrageously prescriptive. Their debates seemed to serve the purpose of keeping the majority of psychologists "in line." Behaviorism, positivism and operationalism were firmly set as dominant views that were basic to the existence of psychology. At many schools, graduate students were given the "correct" view and carefully inoculated with the proper philosophical serum against the "incorrect" views.

During the same period the linguists were impressed with similar strong views about the philosophy of science. The great American linguist, Bloomfield (1933), for example, instructed linguists in scientific materialism and warned them not to have anything to do with mentalism and with psychologists. Thus, though they held the same scientific biases, linguists remained psychologically innocent except for naive behaviorism of the 1920's and psychologists remained ignorant of the development of concepts of linguistic structure. With few exceptions, psychologists at the beginning of this period treated language as a "word heap." Psychological theories of meaning were (and for the most part still are) theories about the reference relation—a kind of linkage between single words and the world. With increasing sophistication, psychologists progressed toward models which considered language as consisting of strings of words (the "information theory" approach), or, alternatively, as composed of whole utterances which were relatively unanalyzed.

In the early 1950's, the great meeting of the fields of linguistics and psychology took place under the gentle guidance of the Social Science Research Council (see Osgood and Sebeok, 1954). I remember quite well the fervor with which we were informed by some of the leading linguists of the day that linguistics was virtually a "closed book," "the most nearly complete of the social sciences," the "most objective of all behavioral disciplines." In a class on grammar one could hear the astonishing claim that in principle one could feed an appropriately programmed computer the phonetic transcription of a large corpus and the computer would produce the phonemics, morphemics and syntax of the language. It was also explained that in practice "short cuts" (such as pair tests and knowledge of meanings) were used to achieve this but that they could always be replaced by completely objective discovery techniques that

produced the correct set of concepts for the language.

The psychologist, green with envy, confessed that he had not yet reached such a state of perfection but felt that he was on the way. We were encouraged by the obvious success of the simple, operational, positivistic approach of the linguist and determined to continue our pursuit of the same tactics. The psychologist had a nice theory that made contiguity and succession the key ingredients and the linguist had just the data to show that that was the right approach. All that remained was to bridge the gap between the linguists' putatively perfect analysis and the psychologists' entirely adequate theory.

It turned out that bridging the gap was no great problem. Item-and-arrangement grammars and psychological mediation theory were seen to be variations of the same line of thought. The linguist looks at the distribution of an item in the corpus and if he finds another item that is distributed in the same environments, he knows that it is the same item (or belongs to the same class of items). To the psychologist, items which follow the same kinds of items or precede the same kinds of items are equivalent responses and equivalent stimuli; if they are not at the outset, they become so via mediation (see Jenkins, 1965; Jenkins and Palermo, 1964). Psychological theory and linguistic procedures meshed nicely. The only sad note in this little story is that by the time the bridge was completed, someone had dynamited the structure at the linguistic end.

the new linguistics

Though many of us read Chomsky's *Syntactic Structures* when it first appeared in 1957, I think most of us failed to appreciate what was in store. We felt that transformations were appealing devices that we would have to give some thought to as soon as we had worked out the basic problem of the item-and-arrangement grammar. We failed to realize that a fundamentally new approach to grammar had been presented and that a "generative grammar" was a quite different kind of object from the old "descriptive grammar," exemplifying a different approach to science and making radically different claims. In short, a revolution of the sort described by Kuhn was taking place; a new paradigm was emerging.

As the consequences of the linguistic revolution became clearer, the psychologist's position became more and more painful. Having worked hard to build his bridge to linguistics, he was disappointed to be told that the discipline was now quite different in important ways. His pain was not eased by the charge that he had been wasting his time by trying to do what he felt he had just done. What the linguist was saying was that language, the object he was describing in a new way, was a fundamentally different kind of thing from what the psychologist thought it was. The linguist also insisted that language required a fundamentally different kind of machinery than the old view implied. In short, he was saying, no amount of revision, patching, or adding *neo-* before the name of the psychological theory was going to make it work. The psychologist asked what kind of model, written in the surface language alone, might be adequate to describe language and the new linguist replied "None!" The linguist went on to add that he had a formal proof that natural language could not be produced by a left-to-right Markov process—just the sort of machinery that the psychologist had tried to use. The linguist then turned to a set of persuasive intuitive arguments. He pointed out that many sentences were ambiguous. This, he said, showed that one string at the surface level could represent several different underlying strings or "bases" and that people were somehow able to "recover" or understand those multiple meanings. Here was a one-

to-many mapping which would defeat any attempt to use a simple discovery procedure at the surface level. Conversely, different sentences at the surface level could be seen to be closely related in meaning as if they related to some fundamental string at the underlying level. These constitute instances of many-to-one mappings whose relationship had to be teased out and expressed. Further, it was clear that many sentences shared "structural similarities" that were not shown in surface identities of word sequences nor in relating to the same underlying string. These examples showed the importance of abstract terms and levels of representation between the final surface representation and the deepest underlying representation. Further, it was argued that these levels were "known" to the speakers in some sense. All of these arguments were illustrated by the linguist with sets of English sentences that provided instances of his claim.

As an aside it must be said that psychologists need some coaching concerning the use of arguments by example and illustration. Each example is supposed to be an instance of a whole class of such behaviors. One is supposed to twist and turn and examine each such example until he is sure that he understands the implication. Psychologists often complain that the linguists use the same example over and over again—as if there were only a few instances of the distinctions they have in mind. This criticism misses the mark. The same example is used repeatedly because it serves as a familiar label for the distinction being made. For example, I can say, "We are running a discrimination test on the 'growling of lions' versus 'raising of flowers' difference" and everybody who is "in" is supposed to know that means we are testing sentences that differ in the base structure though there is no difference in the derived sentence structure. But one does not conclude because of the labels that there is only a single pair of sentences being examined. In fact, just the opposite is intended. Similarly, when the linguist says "The boy hit the ball" and "The ball was hit by the boy" are related sentences, implying that there is an abstract level at which the two sentences are represented in the same way, he also means to imply that this relation holds for some indefinitely large number of pairs of sentences. The sentences are obviously different at the physical level but the theory of the language must show the equivalence of active sentences to their appropriate passives at some abstract level.

In a different way, the ambiguous sentence furnishes a compelling argument. The traditional references to "The shooting of the hunters was dreadful" or to "Flying planes may be dangerous" or "They are cooking apples" serve to direct your attention to the fact that some sentences (an indefinitely large number) can be understood in more than one way. What does it mean to take a sentence in two ways? It presumably means that there are ways that you can "see" that stimulus as the outcome of two different derivations. The stimulus is *in some sense* two different things. Specifying exactly *in what sense* the stimulus is two different things demands descriptions that are deep enough and complex enough to relate the surface structure to deep structure with clear derivations. This demands levels of abstraction that can be connected with overlapping or identical outcomes onto the surface level. How one recognizes this possibility when confronted with the surface level alone is indeed a formidable puzzle for the psychologist.

Another interesting variation is the case, where, though the physical product is different, the sentences may be seen to be "the same" at a low level of abstraction. And, at still more abstract levels, they may be seen to be different again. Here the canonical examples are: "The growling of lions is unpleasant" and "The raising of flowers is difficult." Clearly the words are different and the messages are different. However,

it is easy to see that the sequence of form classes is identical, and at that level of abstraction the sentences are the same. Another and deeper look, however, shows that the sentences must differ in some more fundamental sense. "Lions growl" is permissible but "Flowers raise" is not. The illustration is intended to lead you to the conclusion that two vast sets of sentences differ in exactly the same way. Then, when you encounter the sentence "The shooting of the hunters was dreadful," you may recognize that you put first one of these derivations on it and then the other. The ambiguous case is thus the case where these two families of sentences fuse into identical words at the surface level.

Sentence examples are used by the linguist to indicate the unlimited numbers of cases where (1) the same structure of the obvious stimulus is mapped on different derivations, (2) different structures in the obvious stimuli map on to the same basic strings, and (3) different structures in the obvious stimuli map on to the same abstract structure and then diverge again. The way to make clear what one is talking about is to specify exactly what is meant when one talks about these various abstract levels. That, of course, is the purpose of a grammar. When someone asks about the nature of the stimulus, you can tell him at each level of representation what it is that you are talking about.

implications for psychology

The psychologist can, of course, choose one level of representation and never move away from it. To some reasonable extent he can get away with this strategy. But he must be willing to be told that he is not studying some general case of language behavior. Language behavior is not *at* a particular level. It is the entire representation involved at all levels of description. It can be *represented* at each of those levels but it cannot be identified with any one level.

Notice that the implications of this kind

of thinking are far-reaching. This analysis implies that there are no simple ways to treat the surface level to make it yield up the deeper levels in any automatic fashion. If one takes the large corpus in a fine phonetic transcription and puts it in the computer for analysis, all one can expect to get is confetti. If the psychologist picks one level and sticks to it, he will never see the rest of language behavior and he is going to have to solve some very funny problems, like accounting for data that are the same when there is no reason to suppose that they should be the same, and data that are different when there is no reason to suppose that they should be different. Such a decision puts one in the world of Alice's white knight in *Through the Looking Glass*, wandering about in a two-dimensional world and trying to explain the unfathomable events of the three-dimensional world that intersects his plane of observation. The notions of deep structure and abstract equivalence that the linguist brings to us are important notions for all psychologists, not just those interested in language. My feeling is that psychologists of this generation must give them careful and attentive hearings.

Similarly, this conception of language has many important practical consequences. It helps explain, for example, why it is that we have failed to build a reading machine for the blind. If language is regarded as a collection of diverse, arbitrary sounds that have some simple invariance, then it should be easy to build a machine to read aloud. We should be able to get letters in a book to make distinctive sounds when scanned with light rays. When we have done that we should have a bookreader that anyone could be trained to listen to. Sad experience convinces us that this approach does not work. The newer conception of language suggests that the nature of language is different from the simple model, and the research of the Haskins Laboratories shows that the notions of simple invariance have to be replaced with a variety of many-to-

one and one-to-many mappings. The same set of reasons explains why it is that we do not yet have the voice typewriter that has so often been promised. And the prospect of high-quality, automatic machine translation of language has shifted from something that was to be achieved "tomorrow" to something that may well be impossible in our lifetimes.

Psychologists who work on verbal learning have often shown reluctance to study learning tasks that involve complex relationships. We would like to have situations in which there is no question concerning the units that the subject is employing and the ways in which he employs them, but we also know that we have not been able to find such a case. Subjects persist in trying to do more than we want them to do; as a result we have had to concern ourselves with response integration, stimulus differentiation, response differentiation, stimulus and response classes, selective fractionation of the stimulus, segmentation of the response, etc. If we present the subject with textual material, we face the problem that he may have perfect recall of the content but not of the form, i.e., he gives us a good paraphrase. Our inability to handle this kind of complexity drives us back to observations that we can call "more objective" but we must note that our retreat does not remove the importance or relevance of the original problem. We must not let trivial objectivity act to redefine the field of acceptable problems.

I used to ask myself the question, "What is *the* unit of language behavior?" I have folders full of notes on that question. I now believe that the reason these notes never led to anything is that this is the wrong kind of question to ask about complexly organized behavior. If we were omniscient and knew all that there was to know about language behavior all the way from the semantic structures down through the syntactics, the phrase structures, the transformations, the terminal strings, the mapping of strings into symbols, symbols into motor commands driving the articulators, the effects of the articulators on the air flow, the acoustic effects impinging on someone else's ear, etc., it would not occur to us to ask what *the* unit of behavior was supposed to be. We would know, I presume, that the behavior could be represented at any level and at that level we would know what kinds of units or structures were appropriate to that representation; and, importantly, we would know how these were constrained by adjacent levels.

A simple example of linguistic constraint is found in our own invention: the nonsense syllable. If one tries to account for the meaningfulness of patterns of consonant-vowel-consonant in English, it is difficult to make sense of the data without taking "the right kind" of constraints into consideration. Raw frequency of letters or sounds is of little use. For example, one must attend to syllable boundaries and the differing effects of initial and final position. In the interpretation of a graphic symbol one must ask what the context is (e.g., C before O is /k/ but C before E is /s/; however C in final position is k in both cases). If one permits one's self to look both up and down the hierarchy, it is possible to make sense of the otherwise mystifying difference in C-V-C nonsense syllables.

Similarly, if we are interested in observing how a skilled reader reads a sentence, we find him responding to many cues that are not represented in any simple way in the material before him. We can *hear* stress, intonation and pauses in his sentences which he (and we) arrange to get in the right linguistic places, but we will not find much in the way of cues in the written material to explain this behavior. Similarly, he will be able to provide paraphrases and rereadings which must look for their explanation even further up the hierarchy of the sentence but which are not present in any direct way in the surface structure or the symbols on the page. In these cases it is manifestly irrelevant to ask what is *the* unit of language.

experimentation

This leads me naturally into the issue of experimentation and its purpose in the framework described. The investigator must ask himself what it is that he wants to find out via an experiment. If he is interested in what the subject *will do*, that is one kind of problem. The questions are phrased, "What does the subject do under conditions X, Y, and Z?" But, if he wants to know what the subject *can do*, it should be clear that this is a different kind of question. In this case, one is presumably trying to ask a question about the subject's capacity under the most favorable circumstances that can be provided.

In the research that we are trying to do in our laboratories at Minnesota at the present time, we are interested for the most part in the second kind of question. For that reason some of our experiments look unconventional. We know that the subject brings all kinds of special self-instructions to the laboratory with him. If we want him to sort sentences into active and passive sentence types, we will have to wait for him to sort through all manner of semantic groupings (pleasant-unpleasant, animate-inanimate, happy-sad, common-uncommon, etc.), and obvious physical properties (order, length, position, etc.), before he arrives at grammatical sorts at all. However, if the experimenter keeps rejecting sorts that the subject makes, the subject will, in over half the cases, eventually get to the one wanted —actives *vs.* passives. This kind of experiment is rich in information about what the subject *does do*, but that is not ordinarily what we want to know. We want to know whether he *can* sort active and passive sentences. A very simple thing to do is to ask him; it is surprising how fast one can cover the ground in that way.

As an aside, it is of some interest to note that many of our psychological friends regard this kind of experimentation as unethical, immoral or simply nonscientific. They seem to believe (perhaps on some kind of analogue from animal psychology) that one must make the subject guess what the experimenter wants or that one must show that the behavior is some kind of automatic consequence of a reinforcement program, to have the experiment "count" as real psychology. I think this is a confusion concerning the purpose of such experimentation. An error on the other side is to assume that if one does not get the desired behavior under verbal instruction, it is not part of the capacity of the subject, i.e., anything a subject "knows" should be available to verbal command. This view is equally naive of course. Many subjects make fine discriminations for which they have no verbal labels or even incorrect labels. To expect them to respond appropriately to the experimenter's words alone is wildly optimistic. Often instruction, practice and training are necessary before a fair test can be made.

Particularly with problems concerning the linguistic system where so much of the subject's skill and knowledge is below the level of awareness, the questions of what constitutes appropriate and adequate instruction are thorny ones. An instance is furnished by a study that we have recently completed (see Jenkins, Foss, and Greenberg, 1968). Subjects were presented with a six-pair paired-associate list to learn. The list was systematically structured from a linguistic point of view. The stimuli were unvoiced stops (PA, KA, TA, etc.), and the responses were the appropriately matched voiced stops (BA, GA, DA, etc.). If subjects are merely instructed to learn this set of pairs in the usual fashion, the systematic arrangement of the pairs confers no advantage over a list that is nonsystematically arranged. This shows that this variable *under these conditions* does not influence what a subject *does do*. If, however, we inject more information into the instructions by telling the subject that there is a system in the arrangement, the learning is faster. If we also add that it has something to do with the way the syllables sound,

however, there is no added advantage. If, on the other hand, we add, "Pay attention to what your mouth is doing" (omitting reference to sound), subjects show markedly faster learning. Interestingly enough, though the instruction to "pay attention to your mouth" helps engage the appropriate system of regularities, many of the subjects report at the end that they were helped by the fact that the syllables "sounded alike." In this case it is clear that the capacity of the subject can be brought to bear on this problem by a specific instruction which at the end he may not even acknowledge that he used. In the various conditions of this experiment we have a series of lessons concerning the difference between can-do and does-do experiments and the tricky business of finding ways to instruct subjects which will, in fact, engage the capabilities that we believe can be brought to bear on the task.

the nature of psychological theory

If one looks in a textbook, one usually finds that the purpose of a theory is to "predict, control and explain" something or it is to "describe and classify" some set of "objects," or it is some combination of these. However, it is an old observation that any particular science takes what it can get from its theories and feels lucky to get that. The theory of evolution fails most of the "tests" of a theory but it is a powerful, influential and important theory nonetheless. Astronomical theory has been theory ever since it accepted the constraint that what one said about the heavens had to be responsive to some aspects of the data available in the sky. The lack of control and the existing errors of prediction did not disqualify the theory as a theory; they merely showed its limits and its deficiencies.

In the most general sense, the business of a theory is to explain something, to deepen our understanding of events, processes, regularities, objects, etc. Perhaps the word *understanding* is the key. It implies familiarity, insight, comprehension and knowledge. Prediction and control may be much more a function of our technology and resources than of our understanding of our subject matter. In some cases they may be dependent on events and processes in other domains that are not themselves understood or for which data are not available. But *explanation* and *understanding* must be available to us if we are to talk of theory at all. To the extent description and classification are essential to explanation, they must be included here also, of course.

It should be noted that many disciplines (technologies) can proceed with little or no theory if prediction and control are the only goals. Most of the "useful" contributions of psychology to our present-day society depend largely on observed but unexplained collections of facts about relationships between performances. Such contributions are very important, of course, and such a technology is of great value, but, obviously, it must not be confused with psychological theory.

Given that a theory is to yield explanation and understanding, what is it that we as psychologists are to explain? If we take the linguistic examples above seriously, it is apparent that we should try to avoid the pitfalls of attempting to describe the nature of our units and the form of our analysis in advance. It seems much more profitable to turn toward a new version of an older question: What is the nature of the organism that behaves? Are there ways in which we can use the analysis of behavior and behavior products to lead us to an understanding of the nature of man? Can we build a theory, or more properly *a set of theories*, of psychological man?

Notice that the emphasis here is shifted back to theories of the organism or, more radically, theories of the mind, rather than stopping with models of the behavior itself, which has been one of our more popularly

claimed goals. I think we may be encouraged to ask such questions again after all these years of neglect; encouraged not just by our own yearnings for "something better" but encouraged by recent advances in technology and recent advances in mathematics.

Our major source of support comes from a curious place, the modern digital computer. Since the middle ages, men have drawn inspiration for their psychologies from their machines. It was fashionable at one time to compare animals to clock-work toys and music boxes; at another time it was tempting to make the inner world Newtonian as the outer world appeared to be. In the time of Thorndike and Watson, the telephone switchboard was the latest delight. In the servo-mechanism period, Watt's governor and the lowly thermostat assumed popular importance.

While such fashions are obviously not to be trusted in any naive way, they do tell us something about the search for models and man's tendency to investigate complex phenomena by modeling some abstraction in a simpler form. Much of the time this activity is simple metaphorical play, but one must not underestimate the usefulness of the procedure in general. Under the right circumstances such models become important means for advancing thinking in the subject matter. A wind tunnel is merely an analogue device, a toy pretending to be a full-scale model, but it has made major contributions to science and technology. A map of Capetown is not Capetown, but it may be a useful model from which to educe new relationships which can be verified by actual explorations. One must know and respect the senses in which a representation is intended, of course; the texture of the map paper is not supposed to be a representation of any property of the city, for instance.

The digital computer has returned to us a host of questions which psychologists and philosophers had thrown out as illegal.

When man's behavior was described as "purposive," or "striving toward something," or "trying to do something," one was warned in stern tones that such a description was teleological and therefore forbidden. Now, however, purposive machines are commonplace and it seems difficult to remember why we felt that we could not use such obviously mechanistic devices as those involved in the programming of a computer. Similarly, we were told that we were not to consider a human being as a series of persons, particularly that there should be no "little man in the head" because that would lead to an infinite regress. I find it pleasant to dwell upon the "executive" portion of our modern computers which monitors and evaluates other portions of the machine and its overall progress and which gets along perfectly well without an infinite regress.

Most importantly, we have seen the incredibly rapid development of new languages and new branches of mathematics concerned with problems of automata which can be directly related to the puzzles facing the psychologist who is trying to understand the structure of behavior by attempting to model the organism.

As I see it, much of the argument between the old approach and the new hinges on whether one wants to develop a psychology which at some point has a mysterious box labeled "organism" or "human being" or whether one wants to go ahead and analyze that portion of the system too. I am sure that it is possible to develop a technology to shape or control a piece of behavior without asking much about what is in the box. For some problems in education and therapy, technology is exactly what we most need. However, I think that I want something different as a scientist; I want to *understand* psychological man. I will even grant that this may not do much for the technology that society needs. That is not my task. Understanding and explanation themselves are adequate goals for me

at this time; and, while I will bet that in the long run they will make better prediction and control possible, I do not think that they need to be justified on that ground.

an example

A charming and intriguing example of the role of theory in deepening our understanding and knowledge is found in the persistent puzzle of the great English monument, Stonehenge. In the midst of the Salsbury plain, this "circle" of enormous hand-hewn monoliths confronts the visitor. Geographical and geological study make it clear that the assembly of the structure was a staggering feat of engineering since none of the materials are native to the immediate vicinity. The size and shape of the blocks indicate that a large number of men, at least some of whom were highly skilled, were employed for many years over the course of three centuries in its construction, suggesting that this was of general importance to an entire community. The monument poses a set of questions which cannot be answered directly: Why was it built? What was it supposed to be? What is its purpose? None of these questions is answered by a straightforward description of the site as a physical object nor is there any way to know which portions of such a description are "interesting" and which portions are irrelevant and accidental.

For the last three years, the monument has received renewed attention because an astronomer, Gerald Hawkins (1965), formulated a rich theory about the purpose of Stonehenge and pursued it vigorously. Given that one has a theory, he can presumably distinguish between the accidental and the relevant features of the monument and can begin to seek confirmation or disconfirmation of his notions by relating these features to other phenomena.

Hawkins' theory held that intelligent, widely traveled and (for their time) technologically sophisticated people built Stonehenge to be used as an astronomical observatory and computer. This is a theory only in that it specifies a few abstract notions. To bring it "down to earth" it was necessary to get these notions related to clear instances of events. Hawkins asked what kinds of astronomical information would have been important to such a people who might need both navigational and seasonal agricultural information. He took as "clear cases" the maximal and minimal declinations of the sun and the moon, the planets and the brightest of the fixed stars. Given that he had these classes of events, his task was to get the monument to generate them. Since he was not the original builder, of course, he had to work backwards. Employing ancillary sciences he reconstructed a precise diagram of the points and edges of the monument as they must have been originally. Archeologists dated the various features of the monument. Then with the aid of modern computers he reconstructed the visible sky for the appropriate period in time (1500 B.C.) and for the appropriate location on earth. This reconstruction was further corrected for parallax, atmospheric refraction and assumed horizon line. Finally he brought together the data for the observation points, the apertures and the optical appearance of the celestial events of presumed significance and examined them for correspondence. In short, Hawkins built an elaborate theoretical and constructual network to provide the basis for identifying confirmatory evidence *if* it existed.

Hawkins' studies rejected completely the role of the planets and the stars but confirmed and reconfirmed the importance of the sun and the moon. Careful analysis yielded overwhelming evidence that this enormous device could have indeed been used as a precise calendar, quartering the year with great exactness and providing counting points sufficient to keep track of events of importance between quarters. Following a hint from an historian from the first century before the Christian era, Hawkins found that Stonehenge provided

sufficient information to predict eclipses of the sun and the moon. Indeed, his study yielded the suggestion that these ancient astronomers had information about eclipse cycles only recently rediscovered. In addition, when the key points of the monument were determined in accordance with his theory, its very location was seen to have been determined for important astronomical reasons since the latitudinal location of the monument makes possible regularity and symmetry of the physical design features which would not have been possible if the site were moved even as little as thirty miles away.

Hawkins went on to show that this theory receives further support from other related stone circles of the same historical period in England, Scotland and continental Europe. One can account for the respects in which these other structures differ from Stonehenge as they do, given that the astronomical theory is correct. The overall result is that we must agree that Stonehenge has been explained in a deep and powerful sense. We can now understand Stonehenge in a different, more elegant and more beautiful way than we did when it was described only as a collection of physical properties.

I think this analogy is important and instructive in many ways which cannot be developed in detail here. It is worth much thought and reflection. Surely Hawkins' situation is unusual. It is as if he were presented with a portion of an automaton and asked "What did it do?," "What was it for?" His problem was to devise a theory of its use, its function and to show how to make it run. He had to find "clear cases" that it should be able to generate if his theory was correct. The selection of those cases and the confirmation of the salient instances required the help of many sister sciences, arts and technologies. Only when the whole network was woven together was it possible to evaluate it and pass judgment on it.

It is further important to note that Hawkins and the original builders of Stonehenge shared two important sources of knowledge. They were human beings and they knew a common core of astronomy. Without the first sharing, there is no reason to suppose Hawkins would even have had the theory at all. Without the second sharing, there would have been no way to validate it.

Our task is different from Hawkins' in that we don't begin with an automaton, we begin with some of the behavior functions, i.e., with the "clear cases" that we want to understand. Our task is to develop a rich enough and tight enough description of those cases that we know in relevant abstraction and in specific detail what it is we are trying to explain. Then, finally, we have to develop the structure of a machine which can generate the events we want to explain and which will match the other known characteristics of human beings. When we have reached that point, then, indeed, can we talk about understanding and real explanation.

REFERENCES

BLOOMFIELD, L. *Language.* New York: Holt, Rinehart & Winston, 1933.

CHOMSKY, N. *Syntactic structures.* The Hague: Mouton, 1957.

DIXON, T. R., and D. L. HORTON. *Verbal be-havior and general behavior theory.* Englewood Cliffs, N.J.: Prentice-Hall, 1968.

HAWKINS, G. S. *Stonehenge decoded.* Garden City, N.Y.: Doubleday, 1965.

JENKINS, J. J. Mediation theory and grammatical behavior. In S. Rosenberg (Ed.), *Directions in psycholinguistics.* New York: Macmillan, 1965, pp. 66–96.

———, D. J. Foss, and J. H. GREENBERG. Phonological distinctive features as cues in learning. *Journal of Experimental Psychology,* 1968, **77**, 200–205.

JENKINS, J. J., and D. S. PALERMO. Mediation processes and the acquisition of linguistic structure. In U. Bellugi and R. W. Brown (Eds.), The acquisition of language. *Monographs of the Society for Research in Child Development,* 1964, Serial No. 92, **29**, No. 1, 79–92.

KUHN, T. S. *The structure of scientific revolutions.* Chicago: University of Chicago Press, 1962.

OSGOOD, C. E., and T. A. SEBEOK. Psycholinguistics: A survey of theory and research problems. Supplement to the *Journal of Abnormal and Social Psychology,* 1954, p. 203.

SCHWAB, J. J. Structure of the natural sciences. In G. W. Ford and L. Pugno (Eds.), *The structure of knowledge and the curriculum.* Chicago: Rand McNally & Co., 1964.

WATSON, R. I. Psychology: A prescriptive science. *American Psychologist,* 1967, **22**, 435–443.

22

Most theories of language acquisition and development have been based, appropriately, on observations of human subjects. The authors of the next article, R. Allen Gardner and Beatrice T. Gardner, suggest that future analyses of language may have to be broadened to include aspects of communication with other species. While the Gardners, at this point, are not particularly concerned with the issue of whether sign language in chimpanzees is "really language," their initial demonstrations of two-way communication between man and chimpanzee may eventually result in a reformulation of our current notions about language, a form of behavior almost universally considered to be unique to human beings.

teaching sign language to a chimpanzee

R. ALLEN GARDNER

BEATRICE T. GARDNER

The extent to which another species might be able to use human language is a classical problem in comparative psychology. One approach to this problem is to consider the nature of language, the processes of learning, the neural mechanisms of learning and of language, and the genetic basis of these mechanisms, and then, while recognizing certain gaps in what is known about these factors, to attempt to arrive at an answer by dint of careful scholarship.[1] An alternative approach is to try to teach a form of human language to an animal. We chose the latter alternative and, in June 1966, began training an infant female chimpanzee, named Washoe, to use the gestural language of the deaf. Within the first 22 months of training it became evident that we had been correct in at least one major aspect of method, the

The research described in this article has been supported by National Institute of Mental Health grants MH-12154 and MH-34953 (Research Scientist Development Award to B. T. Gardner) and by National Science Foundation grant GB-7432. We acknowledge a great debt to the personnel of the Aeromedical Research Laboratory, Holloman Air Force Base, whose support and expert assistance effectively absorbed all of the many difficulties attendant upon the acquisition of a wild-caught chimpanzee. We are also grateful to Dr. Frances L. Fitz-Gerald of the Yerkes Regional Primate Research Center for detailed advice on the care of an infant chimpanzee. Drs. Emanual Berger of Reno, Nevada, and D. B. Olsen of the University of Nevada have served as medical consultants, and we are grateful to them for giving so generously of their time and medical skills. The faculty of the Sarah Hamilton Fleischmann School of Home Economics, University of Nevada, has generously allowed us to use the facilities of their experimental nursery school on weekends and holidays.

Reprinted from *Science*, 1969, *165*: 664–672, by permission of the authors and publisher. Copyright © 1969 by the American Association for The Advancement of Science.

[1] See, for example, E. H. Lenneberg, *Biological Foundations of Language* (New York: Wiley, 1967).

use of a gestural language. Additional aspects of method have evolved in the course of the project. These and some implications of our early results can now be described in a way that may be useful in other studies of communicative behavior. Accordingly, in this article we discuss the considerations which led us to use the chimpanzee as a subject and American Sign Language (the language used by the deaf in North America) as a medium of communication; describe the general methods of training as they were initially conceived and as they developed in the course of the project; and summarize those results that could be reported with some degree of confidence by the end of the first phase of the project.

preliminary considerations

THE CHIMPANZEE AS A SUBJECT

Some discussion of the chimpanzee as an experimental subject is in order because this species is relatively uncommon in the psychological laboratory. Whether or not the chimpanzee is the most intelligent animal after man can be disputed; the gorilla, the orangutan, and even the dolphin have their loyal partisans in this debate. Nevertheless, it is generally conceded that chimpanzees are highly intelligent, and that members of this species might be intelligent enough for our purposes. Of equal or greater importance is their sociability and their capacity for forming strong attachments to human beings. We want to emphasize this trait of sociability; it seems highly likely that it is essential for the development of language in human beings, and it was a primary consideration in our choice of a chimpanzee as a subject.

Affectionate as chimpanzees are, they are still wild animals, and this is a serious disadvantage. Most psychologists are accustomed to working with animals that have been chosen, and sometimes bred, for docility and adaptability to laboratory procedures. The difficulties presented by the wild nature of an experimental animal must not be underestimated. Chimpanzees are also very strong animals; a full-grown specimen is likely to weigh more than 120 pounds (55 kilograms) and is estimated to be from three to five times as strong as a man, pound-for-pound. Coupled with the wildness, this great strength presents serious difficulties for a procedure that requires interaction at close quarters with a free-living animal. We have always had to reckon with the likelihood that at some point Washoe's physical maturity will make this procedure prohibitively dangerous.

A more serious disadvantage is that human speech sounds are unsuitable as a medium of communication for the chimpanzee. The vocal apparatus of the chimpanzee is very different from that of man.[2] More important, the vocal behavior of the chimpanzee is very different from that of man. Chimpanzees do make many different sounds, but generally vocalization occurs in situations of high excitement and tends to be specific to the exciting situations. Undisturbed, chimpanzees are usually silent. Thus, it is unlikely that a chimpanzee could be trained to make refined use of its vocalizations. Moreover, the intensive work of Hayes and Hayes[3] with the chimpanzee Viki indicates that a vocal language is not appropriate for this species. The Hayeses used modern, sophisticated, psychological methods and seem to have spared no effort to teach Viki to make speech sounds. Yet in 6 years Viki learned only four sounds that approximated English words.[4]

Use of the hands, however, is a prominent feature of chimpanzee behavior; manipulatory mechanical problems are their forte. More to the point, even caged, labora-

[2] A. L. Bryan, *Curr. Anthropol.*, 4 (1963), 297.
[3] K. J. Hayes and C. Hayes, *Proc. Amer. Phil. Soc.*, **95** (1951), 105.
[4] K. J. Hayes, personal communication. Dr. Hayes also informed us that Viki used a few additional sounds which, while not resembling English words, were used for specific requests.

tory chimpanzees develop begging and similar gestures spontaneously,[5] while individuals that have had extensive contact with human beings have displayed an even wider variety of communicative gestures.[6] In our choice of sign language we were influenced more by the behavioral evidence that this medium of communication was appropriate to the species than by anatomical evidence of structural similarity between the hands of chimpanzees and of men. The Hayeses point out that human tools and mechanical devices are constructed to fit the human hand, yet chimpanzees have little difficulty in using these devices with great skill. Nevertheless, they seem unable to adapt their vocalizations to approximate human speech.

Psychologists who work extensively with the instrumental conditioning of animals become sensitive to the need to use responses that are suited to the species they wish to study. Lever-pressing in rats is not an arbitrary response invented by Skinner to confound the mentalists; it is a type of response commonly made by rats when they are first placed in a Skinner box. The exquisite control of instrumental behavior by schedules of reward is achieved only if the original responses are well chosen. We chose a language based on gestures because we reasoned that gestures for the chimpanzee should be analogous to bar-pressing for rats, key-pecking for pigeons, and babbling for humans.

AMERICAN SIGN LANGUAGE

Two systems of manual communication are used by the deaf. One system is the manual alphabet, or finger spelling, in which

configurations of the hand correspond to letters of the alphabet. In this system the words of a spoken language, such as English, can be spelled out manually. The other system, sign language, consists of a set of manual configurations and gestures that correspond to particular words or concepts. Unlike finger spelling, which is the direct encoding of a spoken language, sign languages have their own rules of usage. Word-for-sign translation between a spoken language and a sign language yields results that are similar to those of word-for-word translation between two spoken languages: the translation is often passable, though awkward, but it can also be ambiguous or quite nonsensical. Also, there are national and regional variations in sign languages that are comparable to those of spoken languages.

We chose for this project the American Sign Language (ASL), which, with certain regional variations, is used by the deaf in North America. This particular sign language has recently been the subject of formal analysis.[7] The ASL can be compared to pictograph writing in which some symbols are quite arbitrary and some are quite representational or iconic, but all are arbitrary to some degree. For example, in ASL the sign for "always" is made by holding the hand in a fist, index finger extended (the pointing hand), while rotating the arm at the elbow. This is clearly an arbitrary representation of the concept "always." The sign for "flower," however, is highly iconic; it is made by holding the fingers of one hand extended, all five fingertips touching (the tapered hand), and touching the fingertips first to one nostril then to the other, as if sniffing a flower. While this is an iconic sign for "flower," it is only one of a number of conventions by which the concept "flower" could be iconically represented;

[5] R. M. Yerkes, *Chimpanzees* (New Haven: Yale Univ. Press, 1943).

[6] K. J. Hayes and C. Hayes, in *The Non-Human Primates and Human Evolution*, J. A. Gavan, Ed. (Detroit: Wayne Univ. Press, 1955), p. 110; W. N. Kellogg and L. A. Kellogg, *The Ape and the Child* (New York: Hafner, 1967; originally published New York: McGraw-Hill, 1933); W. N. Kellogg, *Science,* 162 (1968), 423.

[7] W. C. Stokoe, D. Casterline, C. G. Croneberg, *A Dictionary of American Sign Language* (Washington, D.C.: Gallaudet College Press, 1965); E. A. McCall, doctoral thesis, University of Iowa (1965).

it is thus arbitrary to some degree. Undoubtedly, many of the signs of ASL that seem quite arbitrary today once had an iconic origin that was lost through years of stylized usage. Thus, the signs of ASL are neither uniformly arbitrary nor uniformly iconic; rather the degree of abstraction varies from sign to sign over a wide range. This would seem to be a useful property of ASL for our research.

The literate deaf typically use a combination of ASL and finger spelling; for purposes of this project we have avoided the use of finger spelling as much as possible. A great range of expression is possible within the limits of ASL. We soon found that a good way to practice signing among ourselves was to render familiar songs and poetry into signs; as far as we can judge, there is no message that cannot be rendered faithfully (apart from the usual problems of translation from one language to another). Technical terms and proper names are a problem when first introduced, but within any community of signers it is easy to agree on a convention for any commonly used term. For example, among ourselves we do not finger-spell the words *psychologist* and *psychology*, but render them as "think doctor" and "think science." Or, among users of ASL, "California" can be finger-spelled but is commonly rendered as "golden playland." (Incidentally, the sign for "gold" is made by plucking at the earlobe with thumb and forefinger, indicating an earring—another example of an iconic sign that is at the same time arbitrary and stylized.)

The fact that ASL is in current use by human beings is an additional advantage. The early linguistic environment of the deaf children of deaf parents is in some respects similar to the linguistic environment that we could provide for an experimental subject. This should permit some comparative evaluation of Washoe's eventual level of competence. For example, in discussing Washoe's early performance with deaf parents we have been told that many

of her variants of standard signs are similar to the baby-talk variants commonly observed when human children sign.

WASHOE

Having decided on a species and a medium of communication, our next concern was to obtain an experimental subject. It is altogether possible that there is some critical early age for the acquisition of this type of behavior. On the other hand, newborn chimpanzees tend to be quite helpless and vegetative. They are also considerably less hardy than older infants. Nevertheless, we reasoned that the dangers of starting too late were much greater than the dangers of starting too early, and we sought the youngest infant we could get. Newborn laboratory chimpanzees are very scarce, and we found that the youngest laboratory infant we could get would be about 2 years old at the time we planned to start the project. It seemed preferable to obtain a wild-caught infant. Wild-caught infants are usually at least 8 to 10 months old before they are available for research. This is because infants rarely reach the United States before they are 5 months old, and to this age must be added 1 or 2 months before final purchase and 2 or 3 months for quarantine and other medical services.

We named our chimpanzee Washoe for Washoe County, the home of the University of Nevada. Her exact age will never be known, but from her weight and dentition we estimated her age to be between 8 and 14 months at the end of June 1966, when she first arrived at our laboratory. (Her dentition has continued to agree with this initial estimate, but her weight has increased rather more than would be expected.) This is very young for a chimpanzee. The best available information indicates that infants are completely dependent until the age of 2 years and semidependent until the age of 4; the first signs of sexual maturity (for example, menstruation, sexual swelling) begin to appear at about 8 years, and full adult growth is reached between the ages of 12 and 16.[8] As for the complete lifespan, captive specimens have survived for well over 40 years. Washoe was indeed very young when she arrived; she did not have her first canines or molars, her hand-eye coordination was rudimentary, she had only begun to crawl about, and she slept a great deal. Apart from making friends with her and adapting her to the daily routine, we could accomplish little during the first few months.

LABORATORY CONDITIONS

At the outset we were quite sure that Washoe could learn to make various signs in order to obtain food, drink, and other things. For the project to be a success, we felt that something more must be developed. We wanted Washoe not only to ask for objects but to answer questions about them and also to ask us questions. We wanted to develop behavior that could be described as conversation. With this in mind, we attempted to provide Washoe with an environment that might be conducive to this sort of behavior. Confinement was to be minimal, about the same as that of human infants. Her human companions were to be friends and playmates as well as providers and protectors, and they were to introduce a great many games and activities that would be likely to result in maximum interaction with Washoe.

In practice, such an environment is readily achieved with a chimpanzee; bonds of warm affection have always been established between Washoe and her several human companions. We have enjoyed the interaction almost as much as Washoe has, within the limits of human endurance. A number of human companions have been enlisted to participate in the project and

[8] J. Goodall, in *Primate Behavior*, I. DeVore, Ed. (New York: Holt, Rinehart & Winston, 1965), p. 425; A. J. Riopelle and C. M. Rogers, in *Behavior of Nonhuman Primates*, A. M. Schrier, H. F. Harlow, F. Stollnitz, Eds. (New York: Academic Press, 1965), p. 449.

relieve each other at intervals, so that at least one person would be with Washoe during all her waking hours. At first we feared that such frequent changes would be disturbing, but Washoe seemed to adapt very well to this procedure. Apparently it is possible to provide an infant chimpanzee with affection on a shift basis.

All of Washoe's human companions have been required to master ASL and to use it extensively in her presence, in association with interesting activities and events and also in a general way, as one chatters at a human infant in the course of the day. The ASL has been used almost exclusively, although occasional finger spelling has been permitted. From time to time, of course, there are lapses into spoken English, as when medical personnel must examine Washoe. At one time, we considered an alternative procedure in which we would sign and speak English to Washoe simultaneously, thus giving her an additional source of informative cues. We rejected this procedure, reasoning that, if she should come to understand speech sooner or more easily than ASL, then she might not pay sufficient attention to our gestures. Another alternative, that of speaking English among ourselves and signing to Washoe, was also rejected. We reasoned that this would make it seem that big chimps talk and only little chimps sign, which might give signing an undesirable social status.

The environment we are describing is not a silent one. The human beings can vocalize in many ways, laughing and making sounds of pleasure and displeasure. Whistles and drums are sounded in a variety of imitation games, and hands are clapped for attention. The rule is that all meaningful sounds, whether vocalized or not, must be sounds that a chimpanzee can imitate.

training methods

IMITATION

The imitativeness of apes is proverbial, and rightly so. Those who have worked closely with chimpanzees have frequently remarked on their readiness to engage in visually guided imitation. Consider the following typical comment of Yerkes:

Chim and Panzee would imitate many of my acts, but never have I heard them imitate a sound and rarely make a sound peculiarly their own in response to mine. As previously stated, their imitative tendency is as remarkable for its specialization and limitations as for its strength. It seems to be controlled chiefly by visual stimuli. Things which are seen tend to be imitated or reproduced. What is heard is not reproduced. Obviously an animal which lacks the tendency to reinstate auditory stimuli—in other words to imitate sounds—cannot reasonably be expected to talk. The human infant exhibits this tendency to a remarkable degree. So also does the parrot. If the imitative tendency of the parrot could be coupled with the quality of intelligence of the chimpanzee, the latter undoubtedly could speak.[9]

In the course of their work with Viki, the Hayeses devised a game in which Viki would imitate various actions on hearing the command "Do this." [10] Once established, this was an effective means of training Viki to perform actions that could be visually guided. The same method should be admirably suited to training a chimpanzee to use sign language; accordingly we have directed much effort toward establishing a version of the "Do this" game with Washoe. Getting Washoe to imitate us was not difficult, for she did so quite spontaneously, but getting her to imitate on command has been another matter altogether. It was not until the 16th month of the project that we achieved any degree of control over Washoe's imitation of gestures. Eventually we got to a point where she would imitate a simple gesture, such as pulling at her ears, or a series of such gestures—first we make a gesture, then she imitates, then we make a second gesture, she imitates the second

gesture, and so on—for the reward of being tickled. Up to this writing, however, imitation of this sort has not been an important method for introducing new signs into Washoe's vocabulary.

As a method of prompting, we have been able to use imitation extensively to increase the frequency and refine the form of signs. Washoe sometimes fails to use a new sign in an appropriate situation, or uses another, incorrect sign. At such times we can make the correct sign to Washoe, repeating the performance until she makes the sign herself. (With more stable signs, more indirect forms of prompting can be used—for example, pointing at, or touching, Washoe's hand or a part of her body that should be involved in the sign; making the sign for "sign," which is equivalent to saying "Speak up"; or asking a question in signs, such as "What do you want?" or "What is it?") Again, with new signs, and often with old signs as well, Washoe can lapse into what we refer to as poor "diction." Of course, a great deal of slurring and a wide range of variants are permitted in ASL as in any spoken language. In any event, Washoe's diction has frequently been improved by the simple device of repeating, in exaggeratedly correct form, the sign she has just made, until she repeats it herself in more correct form. On the whole, she has responded quite well to prompting, but there are strict limits to its use with a wild animal —one that is probably quite spoiled, besides. Pressed too hard, Washoe can become completely diverted from her original object; she may ask for something entirely different, run away, go into a tantrum, or even bite her tutor.

Chimpanzees also imitate, after some delay, and this delayed imitation can be quite elaborate.[11] The following is a typical example of Washoe's delayed imitation. From the beginning of the project she was bathed regularly and according to a standard routine. Also, from her 2nd month with

---

[9] R. M. Yerkes and B. W. Learned, *Chimpanzee Intelligence and Its Vocal Expression* (Baltimore: William & Wilkins, 1925), p. 53.

[10] K. J. Hayes and C. Hayes, *J. Comp. Physiol. Psychol.,* **45** (1952), 450.

[11] *Ibid.*

us, she always had dolls to play with. One day, during the 10th month of the project, she bathed one of her dolls in the way we usually bathed her. She filled her little bathtub with water, dunked the doll in the tub, then took it out and dried it with a towel. She has repeated the entire performance, or parts of it, many times since, sometimes also soaping the doll.

This is a type of imitation that may be very important in the acquisition of language by human children, and many of our procedures with Washoe were devised to capitalize on it. Routine activities—feeding, dressing, bathing, and so on—have been highly ritualized, with appropriate signs figuring prominently in the rituals. Many games have been invented which can be accompanied by appropriate signs. Objects and activities have been named as often as possible, especially when Washoe seemed to be paying particular attention to them. New objects and new examples of familiar objects, including pictures, have been continually brought to her attention, together with the appropriate signs. She likes to ride in automobiles, and a ride in an automobile, including the preparations for a ride, provides a wealth of sights that can be accompanied by signs. A good destination for a ride is a home or the university nursery school, both well stocked with props for language lessons.

The general principle should be clear: Washoe has been exposed to a wide variety of activities and objects, together with their appropriate signs, in the hope that she would come to associate the signs with their referents and later make the signs herself. We have reason to believe that she has come to understand a large vocabulary of signs. This was expected, since a number of chimpanzees have acquired extensive understanding vocabulary of spoken words.[12] The understanding vocabulary that Washoe has acquired, however, consists of signs that a chimpanzee can imitate.

[12] C. J. Warden and L. H. Warner, *Quart. Rev. Biol.*, 3 (1928), 1.

Some of Washoe's signs seem to have been originally acquired by delayed imitation. A good example is the sign for "toothbrush." A part of the daily routine has been to brush her teeth after every meal. When this routine was first introduced Washoe generally resisted it. She gradually came to submit with less and less fuss, and after many months she would even help or sometimes brush her teeth herself. Usually, having finished her meal, Washoe would try to leave her highchair; we would restrain her, signing "First, toothbrushing, then you can go." One day, in the 10th month of the project, Washoe was visiting the Gardner home and found her way into the bathroom. She climbed up on the counter, looked at our mug full of toothbrushes, and signed "toothbrush." At the time, we believed that Washoe understood this sign but we have not seen her use it. She had no reason to ask for the toothbrushes, because they were well within her reach, and it is most unlikely that she was asking to have her teeth brushed. This was our first observation, and one of the clearest examples, of behavior in which Washoe seemed to name an object or an event for no obvious motive other than communication.

Following this observation, the toothbrushing routine at mealtime was altered. First, imitative prompting was introduced. Then as the sign became more reliable, her rinsing-mug and toothbrush were displayed prominently until she made the sign. By the 14th month she was making the "toothbrush" sign at the end of meals with little or no prompting; in fact she has called for her toothbrush in a peremptory fashion when its appearance at the end of a meal was delayed. The "toothbrush" sign is not merely a response cued by the end of a meal; Washoe retained her ability to name toothbrushes when they were shown to her at other times.

The sign for "flower" may also have been acquired by delayed imitation. From her first summer with us, Washoe showed a great interest in flowers, and we took advantage of this by providing many flowers and pictures of flowers accompanied by the appropriate sign. Then one day in the 15th month she made the sign, spontaneously, while she and a companion were walking toward a flower garden. As in the case of "toothbrush," we believed that she understood the sign at this time, but we had made no attempt to elicit it from her except by making it ourselves in appropriate situations. Again, after the first observation, we proceeded to elicit this sign as often as possible by a variety of methods, most frequently by showing her a flower and giving it to her if she made the sign for it. Eventually the sign became very reliable and could be elicited by a variety of flowers and pictures of flowers.

It is difficult to decide which signs were acquired by the method of delayed imitation. The first appearance of these signs is likely to be sudden and unexpected; it is possible that some inadvertent movement of Washoe's has been interpreted as meaningful by one of her devoted companions. If the first observer were kept from reporting the observation and from making any direct attempts to elicit the sign again, then it might be possible to obtain independent verification. Quite understandably, we have been more interested in raising the frequency of new signs than in evaluating any particular method of training.

BABBLING

Because the Hayeses were attempting to teach Viki to speak English, they were interested in babbling, and during the first year of their project they were encouraged by the number and variety of spontaneous vocalizations that Viki made. But, in time, Viki's spontaneous vocalizations decreased further and further to the point where the Hayeses felt that there was almost no vocal babbling from which to shape spoken language. In planning this project we expected a great deal of manual "babbling," but during the early months we observed very

little behavior of this kind. In the course of the project, however, there has been a great increase in manual babbling. We have been particularly encouraged by the increase in movements that involve touching parts of the head and body, since these are important components of many signs. Also, more and more frequently, when Washoe has been unable to get something that she wants, she has burst into a flurry of random flourishes and arm-waving.

We have encouraged Washoe's babbling by our responsiveness; clapping, smiling, and repeating the gesture much as you might repeat "goo goo" to a human infant. If the babbled gesture has resembled a sign in ASL, we have made the correct form of the sign and have attempted to engage in some appropriate activity. The sign for "funny" was probably acquired in this way. It first apeared as a spontaneous babble that lent itself readily to a simple imitation game—first Washoe signed "funny," then we did, then she did, and so on. We would laugh and smile during the interchanges that she initiated, and initiate the game ourselves when something funny happened. Eventually Washoe came to use the "funny" sign spontaneously in roughly appropriate situations.

Closely related to babbling are some gestures that seem to have appeared independently of any deliberate training on our part, and that resemble signs so closely that we could incorporate them into Washoe's repertoire with little or no modification. Almost from the first she had a begging gesture—an extension of her open hand, palm up, toward one of us. She made this gesture in situations in which she wanted aid and in situations in which we were holding some object that she wanted. The ASL signs for "give me" and "come" are very similar to this, except that they involve a prominent beckoning movement. Gradually Washoe came to incorporate a beckoning wrist movement into her use of this sign. In Table 1 we refer to this sign as "come-gimme." As Washoe has come to use

table 1

Signs used reliably by chimpanzee Washoe within 22 months of the beginning of training. The signs are listed in the order of their original appearance in her repertoire (see text for the criterion of reliability and for the method of assigning the date of original appearance).

signs	description	context
Come-gimme	Beckoning motion, with wrist or knuckles as pivot.	Sign made to persons or animals, also for objects out of reach. Often combined: "come tickle," "gimme sweet," etc.
More	Fingertips are brought together, usually overhead. (Correct ASL form: tips of the tapered hand touch repeatedly.)	When asking for continuation or repetition of activities such as swinging or tickling, for second helpings of food, etc. Also used to ask for repetition of some performance, such as a somersault.
Up	Arm extends upward, and index finger may also point up.	Wants a lift to reach objects such as grapes on vine, or leaves; or wants to be placed on someone's shoulders; or wants to leave potty-chair.
Sweet	Index or index and second fingers touch tip of wagging tongue. (Correct ASL form: index and second fingers extended side by side.)	For dessert; used sponstaneously at end of meal. Also, when asking for candy.
Open	Flat hands are placed side by side, palms down, then drawn apart while rotated to palms up.	At door of house, room, car, refrigerator, or cupboard; on containers such as jars; and on faucets.
Tickle	The index finger of one hand is drawn across the back of the other hand. (Related to ASL "touch.")	For tickling or for chasing games.
Go	Opposite of "come-gimme."	While walking hand-in-hand or riding on someone's shoulders. Washoe usually indicates the direction desired.
Out	Curved hand grasps tapered hand; then tapered hand is withdrawn upward.	When passing through doorways; until recently, used for both "in" and "out." Also, when asking to be taken outdoors.
Hurry	Open hand is shaken at the wrist. (Correct ASL form: index and second fingers extended side by side.)	Often follows signs such as "come-gimme," "out," "open," and "go," particularly if there is a delay before Washoe is obeyed. Also, used while watching her meal being prepared.
Hear-listen	Index finger touches ear.	For loud or strange sounds: bells, car horns, sonic booms, etc. Also, for asking someone to hold a watch to her ear.
Toothbrush	Index finger is used as brush, to rub front teeth.	When Washoe has finished her meal, or at other times when shown a toothbrush.
Drink	Thumb is extended from fisted hand and touches mouth.	For water, formula, soda pop, etc. For soda pop, often combined with "sweet."
Hurt	Extended index fingers are jabbed toward each other. Can be used to indicate location of pain.	To indicate cuts and bruises on herself or on others. Can be elicited by red stains on a person's skin or by tears in clothing.
Sorry	Fisted hand clasps and unclasps at shoulder. (Correct ASL form: fisted hand is rubbed over heart with circular motion.)	After biting someone, or when someone has been hurt in another way (not necessarily by Washoe). When told to apologize for mischief.

signs	*description*	*context*
Funny	Tip of index finger presses nose, and Washoe snorts. (Correct ASL form: index and second fingers used; no snort.)	When soliciting interaction play, and during games. Occasionally, when being pursued after mischief.
Please	Open hand is drawn across chest. (Correct ASL form: fingertips used, and circular motion.)	When asking for objects and activities. Frequently combined: "Please go," "Out, please," "Please drink."
Food-cat	Several fingers of one hand are placed in mouth. (Correct ASL form: fingertips of tapered hand touch mouth repeatedly.)	During meals and preparation of meals.
Flower	Tip of index finger touches one or both nostrils. (Correct ASL form: tips of tapered hand touch first one nostril, then the other.)	For flowers.
Cover-blanket	Draws one hand toward self over the back of the other.	At bedtime or naptime, and, on cold days, when Washoe wants to be taken out.
Dog	Repeated slapping on thigh.	For dogs and for barking.
You	Index finger points at a person's chest.	Indicates successive turns in games. Also used in response to questions such as "Who tickle?" "Who brush?"
Napkin-bib	Fingertips wipe the mouth region.	For bib, for washcloth, and for Kleenex.
In	Opposite of "out."	Wants to go indoors, or wants someone to join her indoors.
Brush	The fisted hand rubs the back of the open hand several times. (Adapted from ASL "polish.")	For hairbrush, and when asking for brushing.
Hat	Palm pats top of head.	For hats and caps.
I-me	Index finger points at, or touches, chest.	Indicates Washoe's turn, when she and a companion share food, drink, etc. Also used in phrases, such as "I drink," and in reply to questions such as "Who tickle?" (Washoe: "you"); "Who I tickle?" (Washoe: "Me").
Shoes	The fisted hands are held side by side and strike down on shoes or floor. (Correct ASL form: the side of the fisted hands strike against each other.)	For shoes and boots.
Smell	Palm is held before nose and moved slightly upward several times.	For scented objects: tobacco, perfume, sage, etc.
Pants	Palms of the flat hands are drawn up against the body toward waist.	For diapers, rubber pants, trousers.
Clothes	Fingertips brush down the chest.	For Washoe's jacket, nightgown, and shirts; also for our clothing.
Cat	Thumb and index finger grasp cheek hair near side of mouth and are drawn outward (representing cat's whiskers).	For cats.
Key	Palm of one hand is repeatedly touched with the index finger of the other. (Correct ASL form: crooked index finger is rotated against palm.)	Used for keys and locks and to ask us to unlock a door.
Baby	One forearm is placed in the crook of the other, as if cradling a baby.	For dolls, including animal dolls such as a toy horse and duck.
Clean	The open palm of one hand is passed over the open palm of the other.	Used when Washoe is washing, or being washed, or when a companion is washing hands or some other object. Also used for "soap."

it, the sign is not simply a modification of the original begging gesture. For example, very commonly she reaches forward with one hand (palm up) while she gestures with the other hand (palm down) held near her head. (The result resembles a classic fencing posture.)

Another sign of this type is the sign for "hurry," which, so far, Washoe has always made by shaking her open hand vigorously at the wrist. This first appeared as an impatient flourish following some request that she had made in signs; for example, after making the "open" sign before a door. The correct ASL for "hurry" is very close, and we began to use it often, ourselves, in appropriate contexts. We believe that Washoe has come to use this sign in a meaningful way, because she has frequently used it when she, herself, is in a hurry—for example, when rushing to her nursery chair.

INSTRUMENTAL CONDITIONING

It seems intuitively unreasonable that the acquisition of language by human beings could be strictly a matter of reiterated instrumental conditioning—that a child acquires language after the fashion of a rat that is conditioned, first, to press a lever for food in the presence of one stimulus, then to turn a wheel in the presence of another stimulus, and so on until a large repertoire of discriminated responses is acquired. Nevertheless, the so-called "trick vocabulary" of early childhood is probably acquired in this way, and this may be a critical stage in the acquisition of language by children. In any case, a minimal objective of this project was to teach Washoe as many signs as possible by whatever procedures we could enlist. Thus, we have not hesitated to use conventional procedures of instrumental conditioning.

Anyone who becomes familiar with young chimpanzees soon learns about their passion for being tickled. There is no doubt that tickling is the most effective reward that we have used with Washoe. In the early months, when we would pause in our tickling, Washoe would indicate that she wanted more tickling by taking our hands and placing them against her ribs or around her neck. The meaning of these gestures was unmistakable, but since we were not studying our human ability to interpret her chimpanzee gestures, we decided to shape an arbitrary response that she could use to ask for more tickling. We noted that, when being tickled, she tended to bring her arms together to cover the place being tickled. The result was a very crude approximation of the ASL sign for "more" (see Table 1). Thus, we would stop tickling and then pull Washoe's arms away from her body. When we released her arms and threatened to resume tickling, she tended to bring her hands together again. If she brought them back together, we would tickle her again. From time to time we would stop tickling and wait for her to put her hands together by herself. At first, any approximation to the "more" sign, however crude, was rewarded. Later, we required closer approximations and introduced imitative prompting. Soon, a very good version of the "more" sign could be obtained, but it was quite specific to the tickling situation.

In the 6th month of the project we were able to get "more" signs for a new game that consisted of pushing Washoe across the floor in a laundry basket. In this case we did not use the shaping procedure but, from the start, used imitative prompting to elicit the "more" sign. Soon after the "more" sign became spontaneous and reliable in the laundry-basket game, it began to appear as a request for more swinging (by the arms) —again, after first being elicited with imitative prompting. From this point on, Washoe transferred the "more" sign to all activities, including feeding. The transfer was usually spontaneous, occurring when there was some pause in a desired activity or when some object was removed. Often we ourselves were not sure that Washoe wanted "more" until she signed to us.

The sign for "open" had a similar history. When Washoe wanted to get through a door, she tended to hold up both hands and pound on the door with her palms or her knuckles. This is the beginning position for the "open" sign (see Table 1). By waiting for her to place her hands on the door and then lift them, and also by imitative prompting, we were able to shape a good approximation of the "open" sign, and would reward this by opening the door. Originally she was trained to make this sign for three particular doors that she used every day. Washoe transferred this sign to all doors; then to containers such as the refrigerator, cupboards, drawers, briefcases, boxes, and jars; and eventually—an invention of Washoe's—she used it to ask us to turn on water faucets.

In the case of "more" and "open" we followed the conventional laboratory procedure of waiting for Washoe to make some response that could be shaped into the sign we wished her to acquire. We soon found that this was not necessary; Washoe could acquire signs that were first elicited by our holding her hands, forming them into the desired configuration, and then putting them through the desired movement. Since this procedure of guidance is usually much more practical than waiting for a spontaneous approximation to occur at a favorable moment, we have used it much more frequently.

results

VOCABULARY

In the early stages of the project we were able to keep fairly complete records of Washoe's daily signing behavior. But, as the amount of signing behavior and the number of signs to be monitored increased, our initial attempts to obtain exhaustive records became prohibitively cumbersome. During the 16th month we settled on the following procedure. When a new sign was introduced we waited until it had been reported by three different observers as having occurred in an appropriate context and spontaneously (that is, with no prompting other than a question such as "What is it?" or "What do you want?"). The sign was then added to a checklist in which its occurrence, form, context, and the kind of prompting required were recorded. Two such checklists were filled out each day, one for the first half of the day and one for the second half. For a criterion of acquisition we chose a reported frequency of at least one appropriate and spontaneous occurrence each day over a period of 15 consecutive days.

In Table 1 we have listed 30 signs that met this criterion by the end of the 22nd month of the project. In addition, we have listed four signs ("dog," "smell," "me," and "clean") that we judged to be stable, despite the fact that they had not met the stringent criterion before the end of the 22nd month. These additional signs had, nevertheless, been reported to occur appropriately and spontaneously on more than half of the days in a period of 30 consecutive days. An indication of the variety of signs that Washoe used in the course of a day is given by the following data: during the 22nd month of the study, 28 of the 34 signs listed were reported on at least 20 days, and the smallest number of different signs reported for a single day was 23, with a median of 29.[13]

The order in which these signs first appeared in Washoe's repertoire is also given in Table 1. We considered the first appearance to be the date on which three different observers reported appropriate and spontaneous occurrences. By this criterion, 4 new signs first appeared during the first 7 months, 9 new signs during the next 7 months, and 21 new signs during the next 7 months. We chose the 21st month rather than the 22nd month as the cutoff for this tabulation so that no signs would be in-

[13] The development of Washoe's vocabulary of signs is being recorded on motion-picture film. At the time of this writing, 30 of the 34 signs listed in Table 1 are on film.

cluded that do not appear in Table 1. Clearly, if Washoe's rate of acquisition continues to accelerate, we will have to assess her vocabulary on the basis of sampling procedures. We are now in the process of developing procedures that could be used to make periodic tests of Washoe's performance on samples of her repertoire. However, now that there is evidence that a chimpanzee can acquire a vocabulary of more than 30 signs, the exact number of signs in her current vocabulary is less significant than the order of magnitude—50, 100, 200 signs, or more—that might eventually be achieved.

DIFFERENTIATION

In Table 1, column 1, we list English equivalents for each of Washoe's signs. It must be understood that this equivalence is only approximate, because equivalence between English and ASL, as between any two human languages, is only approximate, and because Washoe's usage does differ from that of standard ASL. To some extent her usage is indicated in the column labeled "Context" in Table 1, but the definition of any given sign must always depend upon her total vocabulary, and this has been continually changing. When she had very few signs for specific things, Washoe used the "more" sign for a wide class of requests. Our only restriction was that we discouraged the use of "more" for first requests. As she acquired signs for specific requests, her use of "more" declined until, at the time of this writing, she was using this sign mainly to ask for repetition of some action that she could not name, such as a somersault. Perhaps the best English equivalent would be "do it again." Still, it seemed preferable to list the English equivalent for the ASL sign rather than its current referent for Washoe, since further refinements in her usage may be achieved at a later date.

The differentiation of the signs for "flower" and "smell" provides a further il-

lustration of usage depending upon size of vocabulary. As the "flower" sign became more frequent, we noted that it occurred in several inappropriate contexts that all seemed to include odors; for example, Washoe would make the "flower" sign when opening a tobacco pouch or when entering a kitchen filled with cooking odors. Taking our cue from this, we introduced the "smell" sign by passive shaping and imitative prompting. Gradually Washoe came to make the appropriate distinction between "flower" contexts and "smell" contexts in her signing, although "flower" (in the single-nostril form) (see Table 1) has continued to occur as a common error in "smell" contexts.

TRANSFER

In general, when introducing new signs we have used a very specific referent for the initial training—a particular door for "open," a particular hat for "hat." Early in the project we were concerned about the possibility that signs might become inseparable from their first referents. So far, however, there has been no problem of this kind: Washoe has always been able to transfer her signs spontaneously to new members of each class of referents. We have already described the transfer of "more" and "open." The sign for "flower" is a particularly good example of transfer, because flowers occur in so many varieties, indoors, outdoors, and in pictures, yet Washoe uses the same sign for all. It is fortunate that she has responded well to pictures of objects. In the case of "dog" and "cat" this has proved to be important because live dogs and cats can be too exciting, and we have had to use pictures to elicit most of the "dog" and "cat" signs. It is noteworthy that Washoe has transferred the "dog" sign to the sound of barking by an unseen dog.

The acquisition and transfer of the sign for "key" illustrates a further point. A great many cupboards and doors in Washoe's quarters have been kept secure by small padlocks that can all be opened by the same simple key. Because she was immature and awkward, Washoe had great difficulty in learning to use these keys and locks. Because we wanted her to improve her manual dexterity, we let her practice with these keys until she could open the locks quite easily (then we had to hide the keys). Washoe soon transferred this skill to all manner of locks and keys, including ignition keys. At about the same time, we taught her the sign for "key," using the original padlock keys as a referent. Washoe came to use this sign both to name keys that were presented to her and to ask for the keys to various locks when no key was in sight. She readily transferred the sign to all varieties of keys and locks.

Now, if an animal can transfer a skill learned with a certain key and lock to new types of key and lock, it should not be surprising that the same animal can learn to use an arbitrary response to name and ask for a certain key and then transfer that sign to new types of keys. Certainly, the relationship between the use of a key and the opening of locks is as arbitrary as the relationship between the sign for "key" and its many referents. Viewed in this way, the general phenomenon of transfer of training and the specifically linguistic phenomenon of labeling become very similar, and the problems that these phenomena pose for modern learning theory should require similar solutions. We do not mean to imply that the problem of labeling is less complex than has generally been supposed; rather, we are suggesting that the problem of transfer of training requires an equally sophisticated treatment.

COMBINATIONS

During the phase of the project covered by this article we made no deliberate attempts to elicit combinations or phrases, although we may have responded more readily to strings of two or more signs than to single signs. As far as we can judge, Washoe's early use of signs in strings was spontaneous. Almost as soon as she had eight or ten signs in her repertoire, she began to use them two and three at a time. As her repertoire increased, her tendency to produce strings of two or more signs also increased, to the point where this has become a common mode of signing for her. We, of course, usually signed to her in combinations, but if Washoe's use of combinations has been imitative, then it must be a generalized sort of imitation, since she has invented a number of combinations, such as "gimme tickle" (before we had ever asked her to tickle us), and "open food drink" (for the refrigerator—we have always called it the "cold box").

Four signs—"please," "come-gimme," "hurry," and "more"—used with one or more other signs, account for the largest share of Washoe's early combinations. In general, these four signs have functioned as emphasizers, as in "please open hurry" and "gimme drink please."

Until recently, five additional signs—"go," "out," "in," "open," and "hear-listen"—accounted for most of the remaining combinations. Typical examples of combinations using these four are, "go in" or "go out" (when at some distance from a door), "go sweet" (for being carried to a raspberry bush), "open flower" (to be let through the gate to a flower garden), "open key" (for a locked door), "listen eat" (at the sound of an alarm clock signaling meal-time), and "listen dog" (at the sound of barking by an unseen dog). All but the first and last of these six examples were inventions of Washoe's. Combinations of this type tend to amplify the meaning of the single signs used. Sometimes, however, the function of these five signs has been about the same as that of the emphasizers, as in "open out" (when standing in front of a door).

Toward the end of the period covered in this article we were able to introduce the pronouns "I-me" and "you," so that combinations that resemble short sentences have begun to appear.

concluding observations

From time to time we have been asked questions such as, "Do you think that Washoe has language?" or "At what point will you be able to say that Washoe has language?" We find it very difficult to respond to these questions because they are altogether foreign to the spirit of our research. They imply a distinction between one class of communicative behavior that can be called language and another class that cannot. This in turn implies a well-established theory that could provide the distinction. If our objectives had required such a theory, we would certainly not have been able to begin this project as early as we did.

In the first phase of the project we were able to verify the hypothesis that sign language is an appropriate medium of two-way communication for the chimpanzee. Washoe's intellectual immaturity, the continuing acceleration of her progress, the fact that her signs do not remain specific to their original referents but are transferred spontaneously to new referents, and the emergence of rudimentary combinations all suggest that significantly more can be accomplished by Washoe during the subsequent phases of this project. As we proceed, the problems of these subsequent phases will be chiefly concerned with the technical business of measurement. We are now developing a procedure for testing Washoe's ability to name objects. In this procedure, an object or a picture of an object is placed in a box with a window. An observer, who does not know what is in the box, asks Washoe what she sees through the window. At present, this method is limited to items that fit in the box; a more ingenious method will have to be devised for other items. In particular, the ability to combine and recombine signs must be tested. Here, a great deal depends upon reaching a stage at which Washoe produces an extended series of signs in answer to questions. Our hope is that Washoe can be brought to the point where she describes events and situations to an observer who has no other source of information.

At an earlier time we would have been more cautious about suggesting that a chimpanzee might be able to produce extended utterances to communicate information. We believe now that it is the writers—who would predict just what it is that no chimpanzee will ever do—who must proceed with caution. Washoe's accomplishments will probably be exceeded by another chimpanzee, because it is unlikely that the conditions of training have been optimal in this first attempt. Theories of language that depend upon the identification of aspects of language that are exclusively human must remain tentative until a considerably larger body of intensive research with other species becomes available.

summary

We set ourselves the task of teaching an animal to use a form of human language. Highly intelligent and highly social, the chimpanzee is an obvious choice for such a study, yet it has not been possible to teach a member of this species more than a few spoken words. We reasoned that a spoken language, such as English, might be an inappropriate medium of communication for a chimpanzee. This led us to choose American Sign Language, the gestural system of communication used by the deaf in North America, for the project.

The youngest infant that we could obtain was a wild-born female, whom we named Washoe, and who was estimated to be between 8 and 14 months old when we began our program of training. The laboratory conditions, while not patterned after those of a human family (as in the studies of Kellogg and Kellogg and of Hayes and Hayes), involved a minimum of confinement and a maximum of social interaction with human companions. For all practical purposes, the only verbal communication was in ASL, and the chimpanzee was maximally exposed to the use of this language by human beings.

It was necessary to develop a rough-and-ready mixture of training methods. There was evidence that some of Washoe's early signs were acquired by delayed imitation of the signing behavior of her human companions, but very few if any, of her early signs were introduced by immediate imitation. Manual babbling was directly fostered and did increase in the course of the project. A number of signs were introduced by shaping and instrumental conditioning. A particularly effective and convenient method of shaping consisted of holding Washoe's hands, forming them into a configuration, and putting them through the movements of a sign.

We have listed more than 30 signs that Washoe acquired and could use spontaneously and appropriately by the end of the 22nd month of the project. The signs acquired earliest were simple demands. Most of the later signs have been names for objects, which Washoe has used both as demands and as answers to questions. Washoe readily used noun signs to name pictures of objects as well as actual objects and has frequently called the attention of her companions to pictures and objects by naming them. Once acquired, the signs have not remained specific to the original referents but have been transferred spontaneously to a wide class of appropriate referents. At this writing, Washoe's rate of acquisition of new signs is still accelerating.

From the time she had eight or ten signs in her repertoire, Washoe began to use them in strings of two or more. During the period covered by this article we made no deliberate effort to elicit combinations other than by our own habitual use of strings of signs. Some of the combined forms that Washoe has used may have been imitative, but many have been inventions of her own. Only a small proportion of the possible combinations have, in fact, been observed. This is because most of Washoe's combinations include one of a limited group of signs that act as combiners. Among the signs that Washoe has recently acquired are the pronouns "I-me" and "you." When these occur in combinations the result resembles a short sentence. In terms of the eventual level of communication that a chimpanzee might be able to attain, the most promising results have been spontaneous naming, spontaneous transfer to new referents, and spontaneous combinations and recombinations of signs.

UNIT

intelligence

23 *The history of psychology is littered with written documents
arguing that intelligence is determined by hereditary factors
or by environmental events. This nature-nurture controversy, as it has been
called, has more recently been abandoned in favor of a realistic approach to
the concept of intelligence which allows for the contribution of both genetic
and experiential factors. In the next article, Jane W. Kessler discusses research
on those aspects of intellectual ability which are affected by the experiential
influences.*

environmental components of measured intelligence

JANE W. KESSLER

The fact that there are significant individual differences in intelligence is undisputed, and no one advances a single-cause explanation for this fact. It is customary to speak of intelligence as the product of the interaction of environment and genetic potentiality. A small minority of psychologists, for example, Burt and R. B. Cattell, prefer to restrict the term intelligence to inborn capacity. Objection to this view is taken on the basis that inborn capacity is of necessity a hypothetical construct, something which can be inferred but never directly measured. Even before birth, there are factors operating to influence the genetic potential, and it is several years *after* birth and exposure to environment before one can get reliable measures of intelligence. For these reasons, among others, it is impossible to measure inborn potential. Intel-

Reprinted from *The School Review*, 1965, 73: 339–353, by permission of the author and publisher. Copyright © 1965 by The University of Chicago Press.

ligence is better and more commonly used to describe mental functioning which can be observed in home life, at school, at work, and which is sampled by standardized psychological tests.

Since the genetic components of intellectual ability have been well covered in other articles, this paper attempts an analysis of four factors which can be subsumed under the broad heading of "environment": (1) prenatal and paranatal conditions; (2) early maternal care; (3) sociocultural influences; and (4) individual personality characteristics. The paper concludes with a discussion of the validity of IQ tests and the proper use of their results.

environment

PRENATAL AND PARANATAL CONDITIONS

At birth babies are already different. Experimental studies of such behavior as spontaneous motor activity in the first week

259

of life [1] and changes in skin temperature and cardiac rate in response to stimulation in three-day-old neonates [2] show differences falling into the normal distribution curve. Although heredity undoubtedly contributes a large share to these constitutional differences, the effects of the fetal environment and process of birth are perhaps equally important. Ashley-Montagu reviewed the many kinds of prenatal influences possible and concluded, contrary to the traditional view, that the placenta is apparently a highly permeable filter through which almost anything can be transferred to the fetus.[3] Abundant evidence has shown the effects of maternal nutrition upon the physical development of the fetus. There is also some evidence to show that the intelligence of the offspring, as measured by performance in later life, may be affected by the mother's nutrition during pregnancy. Harrell, Woodyard, and Gates reported the results of a study in Kentucky and Virginia concerning the influence of vitamin supplementation of the diets of pregnant and lactating women on the intelligence quotients obtained by their children at three to four years of age.[4] A statistically significant difference of 3.7 points was found between the Binet IQ's of the children whose mothers had had the vitamin supplements and those children whose mothers had received placebos during pregnancy and lactation. Since inadequate maternal nutrition is more prevalent in conditions of poverty, this provides a partial explanation for the lower

mean IQ's in children from poor socioeconomic backgrounds.

Another possible influence on fetal reactions and development is the mother's emotional state. Sontag noted that bodily movements of fetuses increased several hundred per cent while their mothers were undergoing emotional stress.[5] When the mother's emotional upset lasted several weeks, fetal activity continued at an exaggerated level throughout the entire period. Other more recent studies have confirmed the general idea that the mother's emotional attitudes are reflected in the newborn.[6] It is hard to evaluate the long-range effects of prenatal influences because of the overlay of later events, but it was Sontag's contention that prolonged maternal emotional stress during pregnancy may have enduring consequences for the child.

Pasamanick and his co-workers have reported a number of retrospective investigations in which the pregnancy and birth histories of children with physical and mental problems are compared with the early case histories of "normal" children. They concluded that there is a continuum of reproductive casualty resulting from prematurity and complications of pregnancy. In the extreme, these complications resulted in death, but there were many survivors with lesser degrees of brain damage who subsequently developed a series of disorders extending from cerebral palsy, epilepsy, and mental retardation through all types of behavioral and learning disabilities.[7] An important part of the Pasamanick studies is the association of pregnancy ab-

[1] E. D. Brownfield, "An Investigation of the Activity and Sensory Responses of Healthy, Newborn Infants" (unpublished doctoral dissertation, Cornell University, 1956).

[2] Julius Richmond and Seymour Lustman, "Autonomic Function in the Neonate: Implications for Psychosomatic Theory," *Psychosomatic Medicine,* XVII (1955), 269–75.

[3] M. F. Ashley-Montagu, *Prenatal Influences* (Springfield, Ill.: Charles C Thomas, 1962).

[4] Ruth Flinn Harrell, Ella Woodyard, and Arthur I. Gates, *The Effect of Mothers' Diets on the Intelligence of the Offspring* (New York: Teachers College Press, 1955), VII.

[5] L. S. Sontag, "The Significance of Fetal Environmental Differences," *American Journal of Obstetrics and Gynecology,* XLII (1941), 996–1003.

[6] A. S. Davids and M. Talmadge, "Anxiety, Pregnancy, and Childbirth Abnormalities," *Journal of Consulting Psychology,* XXV (1961), 74–77.

[7] B. Pasamanick and H. Knobloch, "Epidemiologic Studies on the Complications of Pregnancy and the Birth Process," in G. Caplan, *Prevention of Mental Disorders in Children* (New York: Basic Books, 1961).

normalities with certain life experiences related to socioeconomic status. It is not only possible, but highly probable, that the poor physical health and stressful emotional state of the pregnant mother in economically deprived circumstances put her baby at a significant disadvantage from the moment he is born.

EARLY MATERNAL CARE

The lasting importance of the maternal care provided the baby in the first years of life is highlighted by noting the serious consequences of deprivation. The publication which most forcefully draws attention to this is that of Bowlby.[8] Bowlby reviews direct studies of the development of children living in institutions and hospitals, retrospective studies investigating the early histories of adolescents or adults who developed psychological problems, and follow-up studies of children who had no consistent mother figure during the first year. The most frequently quoted follow-up study is that of Goldfarb[9] in which he compared fifteen adolescents, who had lived in an institution for the first three or four years of life, with fifteen adolescents, supposedly of similar genetic background, who had lived in foster homes since infancy. The mean Wechsler IQ of the institution children was 72.4 and of the group living in foster homes, 95.4. Along with the mental retardation of the "ex-institution" children, there were distinct emotional trends; chiefly, the absence of a normal capacity for inhibition. The institution group showed extremely difficult behavior with symptoms of hyperactivity, restlessness, inability to concentrate, and unmanageability. Furthermore, they seemed to have no genuine attachments to people although they were in-

discriminately and insatiably demanding of affection.

A more recent study of infants in institutions was made by Provence and Lipton.[10] They examined 75 children placed in an institution, 75 children with similar backgrounds placed in foster homes, and 75 children who remained with their own families. Although there were individual differences, the institutional children were significantly retarded in general development compared to both other groups. Language development was the first area revealing retardation, and it showed the greatest amount of retardation. It also took a longer period of family living for significant improvement to take place.

Studies with animal subjects also show that early experience influences adult problem-solving capacity. A classic experiment relating to this ability is that of Thompson and Heron who used dogs as subjects.[11] Some were reared under isolation in laboratory cages from the time of weaning to eight months of age. Their litter mates were reared for this same period in homes as pets. The cage-reared and pet-reared dogs were put together in a dog pasture for ten months; then, at eighteen months of age, their ability to solve mazes was tested. The pet-reared dogs were clearly superior to their cage-reared litter mates, indicating the permanent importance of the environmental differences in their early infancy.

In the face of such clear evidence concerning the effects of maternal care deprivation, the amount of misunderstanding has been surprising. First, some clinicians understood "maternal deprivation" to include *any* separation of the infant from the mother. This is not true; it is only prolonged separation with inadequate substi-

[8] John Bowlby, "Maternal Care and Mental Health" (World Health Organization Monograph, Series No. 2, 1951).

[9] W. Goldfarb, "The Effects of Early Institutional Care on Adolescent Personality," *Journal of Experimental Education,* XII (1943), 106–29.

[10] Sally Provence and Rose C. Lipton, *Infants in Institutions* (New York: International Universities Press, 1962).

[11] W. R. Thompson and W. Heron, "The Effects of Restricting Early Experience on the Problem-solving Capacity of Dogs," *Canadian Journal of Psychology,* VIII (1954), 17–31.

tute mother care for which serious consequences may be expected. Second, many have thought that the dire consequences were inevitable and universal; that all children undergoing early institutionalization or other sorts of gross maternal deprivation develop an "affectionless character" or suffer retarded mental development. This is also untrue; but the fact that there are differences in vulnerability does not destroy the causal connections. In physical medicine not every individual exposed to a particular virus falls ill of the disease. Third, the inference has been made by some that every child of psychopathic disposition or with mental retardation has had this pathogenic experience in infancy. This also is not logical; many kinds of pathogenic factors can have the same end result. In this respect there is a difference between physical and mental illnesses. Physical illnesses are likely to be more specific in their symptomatology and be the result of more specific antecedent conditions. Psychological problems are less sharply delineated and may result from multiple rather than single causes.

Oversimplification of the maternal deprivation concept has had its effects on clinical opinion and practice. Concern about maternal care tends to exaggerate the role of the mother in the development of any and all psychological difficulties of her children. Prevention is conceived solely in terms of maternal love and attention, and the cause of psychological difficulties is automatically attributed to "maternal rejection." Another misinterpretation has arisen from the issue of the possible irreversibility of damage done by early deprivation. Somehow the evidence showing the lasting effects of early deprivation despite improved environmental opportunities has been taken by some to mean that the personality is fixed by the age of three years and that no further changes are possible. On the basis of common sense and ordinary observation, this stand is obviously untenable. In normal development, the child of three years is reasonably plastic, having a potential for a great deal of further learning and development. It is only in abnormal conditions that the capacity for change is lost. A child who has been exposed to pathogenic deprivation and reacted to it in a sensitive way is in some ways "scarred for life." Depending on circumstances and the endowment of the child, these scars may be barely noticeable or may be severely handicapping. But the results of the special conditions of maternal deprivation cannot be generalized to children under normal environmental conditions.

In terms of clinical practice, Prugh and Harlow object to the current tendency to believe that separation of the child from his mother is to be avoided at all costs.[12] They point out that there can be "masked deprivation" where the infant's needs are unfulfilled even though he remains at home. After clinical study of the parents of mentally retarded children who were in the IQ range from 50 to 80 and had no history of birth injury or demonstrable organic pathology, Goshen suggests that mental retardation can occur as the by-product of certain types of maternal attitudes.[13] Specifically, he suggests that neurotic maternal attitudes which are characterized by a failure to stimulate and evoke meaningful signals during critical periods of life can result in the child's failure to grasp the significance of language. This failure may proceed to a state recognizable as mental retardation. Goshen was concerned with mothers who were ordinarily capable and conscientious but temporarily unable to give more than perfunctory physical care to their infants. He concluded with the excellent recommendation that "when a mother develops a deep psychological de-

[12] Dane G. Prugh and Robert G. Harlow, "Masked Deprivation in Infants and Young Children," in *Deprivation of Maternal Care: A Reassessment of Its Effects* (Geneva: World Health Organization, "Public Health Papers," No. 14, 1962).

[13] Charles E. Goshen, "Mental Retardation and Neurotic Maternal Attitudes," *Archives of General Psychiatry*, IX (1963), 168–75.

pression during the first year of a child's life, it would seem to be an urgent necessity to place the child in the care of a healthy adult until the mother comes out of the depression." [14]

There is nothing mystical about the importance of "mother love" in the first year of life. Biological motherhood does not guarantee maternal devotion, and the baby will accept a substitute mother if one is provided. It is not the existence of the person that counts, but the part that she plays in the infant's daily life. The relationship with a single person is the key factor in the infant's development. The gratifications provided by the mother draw the baby's attention to the outside world and serve as a bridge to other objects external to himself. After the baby has come to know her and to attach some importance to her, he becomes aware of her absences, and this helps him in differentiating between self and not-self. Inevitably, the mother frustrates the baby at times, and this adds further impetus to the baby's drive to gain independence and control over the outside world. By virtue of the coincidence of neural maturational changes, the baby acquires at the same time new powers of perception, memory, discrimination, motor coordination, and imitation which create some new problems for him, but, at the same time, new ways of solving them. Thus, we see that during the first year the baby is normally in an ideal educational situation where ability, opportunity, and motivation combine in the service of a common goal—development.

SOCIOCULTURAL INFLUENCES

Although there is some connection between low socioeconomic status and (a) poor prenatal condition and (b) inadequate maternal care in the first year of life, the impact of these conditions on mental development is even greater at later ages. For

many years there has been cogent evidence attesting to the effects of environment on measured intelligence. Skeels and Dye showed that the IQ's of retarded children in institutions could be raised by "differential stimulation" [15]; Skodak and Skeels studied the effects of adoptive homes in raising IQ's [16]; and Klineberg reported the effect of environment on Negro children who had moved from the South. [17] The lowest scores were obtained by the groups most recently arrived from the South, with a close correlation between the length of time lived in New York and intelligence test scores. The improvement seemed to take place almost entirely in the first five or six years; those children who had lived in New York for a longer period showed little further improvement, and those Negroes who had moved to the North were, as a group, approximately at the average of the whole Negro school population of their original home cities.

Other studies, conversely, show the deteriorating effect of cultural impoverishment. Gordon, for instance, studied a group of children who grew up on canal boats in England. [18] At young ages, the average IQ of these children was about 90 (low average) but when the children were older the IQ dropped consistently, so that in their teens it was well below the average for the general population. Sherman and Key studied some communities located in

[15] H. M. Skeels and H. B. Dye, "A Study of the Effects of Differential Stimulation on Mentally Retarded Children," *Proceedings of the American Association for Mental Deficiency*, XLIV (1939), 114–36.

[16] M. Skodak and H. M. Skeels, "A Final Follow-up Study of One Hundred Adopted Children," *Journal of Genetic Psychology*, LXXV (1949), 85–125.

[17] O. Klineberg, *Negro Intelligence and Selective Migration* (New York: Columbia University Press, 1935).

[18] H. Gordon, "Mental and Scholastic Tests among Retarded Children: An Enquiry into the Effects of Schooling on the Various Tests," *Education Pamphlets*, Board of Education, London, No. 44 (1923).

[14] *Ibid.*, p. 174.

Appalachia and reported similar findings.[19] The lowering of IQ in the older children was related to the varying degrees of isolation and opportunities for schooling that were provided in the areas studied. This is similar to the "cumulative deficit phenomenon" recently described by Deutsch as taking place between the first- and fifth-grade years in lower-class children attending New York City schools.[20]

Although the importance of environment on measured intelligence has been well substantiated for some period of time, very little was done with this knowledge. Attempts were made to construct "culture-free" tests of intelligence to get at the "underlying potential" but none was successful. For example, Rosenblum, Keller, and Papania tried the Davis-Eells ("Culture-Fair") test with a group of mentally handicapped school-aged boys of lower social-class standing and found that the mean score was not significantly higher than the mean IQ's obtained on the Binet, which is highly verbal in content.[21] The authors commented that, though the Davis-Eells test may not contain culturally biased items, the conditions under which the test was administered cannot be said to have been completely free of middle-class overtones. Although it was presented to the children as a series of games, the children were not fooled and revealed by their comments that they knew from the outset that they were taking a test. A "good" test-taking attitude is dependent on cultural factors insofar as the child has been schooled to think it is important and profitable to try to do one's best.

In the 1960's, many people began to take a new, hard look at the old knowledge. The new questions asked were, "In what ways does culture affect intelligence?" and "What can be done about it?" It was soon obvious that many children came to school ill-prepared for academic work, and attention was focused on the preschool years. The role of maturation in early child development was re-examined. The work of Gesell and his colleagues provided normative pictures of children at different ages and stressed the orderly sequence of behavioral changes with increasing age. The developmental principles that Gesell offered as explanations were couched in terms of embryology[22] and stressed *intrinsic* factors rather than external, environmental factors. His dictum that "training does not transcend maturation"[23] implied a passive approach to early child care. Not only was early training considered futile, it was viewed as dangerous to "pressure" a child before he reached the point of optimum "readiness." According to this philosophy the young child should be left alone as much as possible in order that intrinsic growth processes take their natural course of progression.

In some quarters there was question about this assumption of automatic growth in the young child. For one thing, the observations of the results of early maternal deprivation indicated the importance of the environment in stimulating and supporting the very beginnings of mental development. Animal experiments showed permanent loss of function without proper stimulation. By keeping chimpanzee babies in

[19] M. Sherman and C. B. Key, "The Intelligence of Isolated Mountain Children," *Child Development*, III (1932), 279–90.

[20] Martin Deutsch, "Facilitating Development in the Preschool Child: Social and Psychological Perspectives," *Merrill-Palmer Quarterly*, X (1964), 249–63.

[21] Sidney Rosenblum, James E. Keller, and Ned Papania, "Davis-Eells ('Culture-Fair') Test Performance of Lower Class Retarded Children," *Journal of Consulting Psychology*, XIX (1955), 51–54.

[22] A. Gesell, *Infant Development: The Embryology of Early Human Behavior* (New York: Harper & Bros., 1932).

[23] A. Gesell, "The Developmental Psychology of Twins," in Carl Murchison (ed.), *Handbook of Child Psychology* (Worcester, Mass.: Clark University Press, 1931), p. 189.

total darkness for varying lengths of time, Riesen and others found that certain anatomical structures of the retina were permanently damaged.[24] With a very different approach, namely, the study of mental development in young children in normal circumstances, Piaget came to the similar conclusion that nothing was so automatic that it did not require practice. Talking about the sucking reflex, Piaget stated that only practice leads to normal functioning.[25]

That is the first aspect of accommodation: contact with the object modified, in a way, the activity of the reflex, and, even if this activity were oriented hereditarily to such contact, the latter is no less necessary to the consolidation of the former. This is how certain instincts are lost or certain reflexes cease to function normally, due to the lack of a suitable environment.[26]

The new thought that "readiness" is in part an acquisition of experience rather than solely a development of time prompted an analysis of the environmental conditions in which culturally disadvantaged children spent their first five years. Even more specifically, attention was drawn to the role of social class in language development (Deutsch).[27] Children in the lower socioeconomic groups start to talk, on the average, at a later age than do children in higher socioeconomic groups. In the lower income groups, verbal productions from the child are likely to be ignored as of little value. It is regarded as more important that the child take care of himself and achieve independence from the mother as early as possible so she can turn her attention to other babies, earn extra money, or maintain the household. In contrast, parents of middle and high socioeconomic status are more likely to talk to their children and to listen with pride and pleasure to what their children have to say. Irwin demonstrated that talking *to* children from an early age (twelve months and up) increases the verbal productivity of the child.[28] He explained this in two ways. First, in classical learning terms, a certain behavior, that is, verbalization, is positively rewarded by the mother's attention. Second, in psychodynamic terms, the child normally identifies with his mother, and if she talks, so does he.

There have been efforts to pinpoint the language deficiencies prevailing in lower-class families. Errors in enunciation and grammatical syntax have been analyzed. Perhaps even more important than the quality of language is its use. John and Goldstein report that children from low-income homes have relatively little opportunity to engage in active dialogue when learning labels,[29] and Bernstein points out that in poorer homes language is used in a restrictive fashion rather than in an explanatory one.[30] If the child asks for something, the parental response is an abbreviated acknowledgment rather than a complete sentence or thought which elaborates on the child's utterance. The feedback does not provide the child with more information than that with which he started. The parents, setting little store by words, are content with approximations and imprecise labels where "flower" covers "tree,"

24 A. H. Riesen, "Plasticity of Behavior: Psychological Aspects" in H. F. Harlow and C. N. Woolsey (eds.), *Biological and Biochemical Bases of Behavior* (Madison: University of Wisconsin Press, 1958), pp. 425–50.

25 J. Piaget, *The Origin of Intelligence in the Child,* trans. Margaret Cook (New York: International Universities Press, 1952).

26 *Ibid.,* p. 30.

27 M. Deutsch, "The Role of Social Class in Language Development and Cognition" (Institute for Developmental Studies, Department of Psychiatry, New York Medical College, April, 1964) (mimeographed).

28 O. C. Irwin, "Infant Speech: The Effect of Systematic Reading of Stories," *Journal of Speech and Hearing Research* (1960), pp. 187–90.

29 V. P. John and L. S. Goldstein, "The Social Context of Language Acquisition," *Merrill-Palmer Quarterly,* X (1964), 265–76.

30 Basil Bernstein, "Language and Social Class," *British Journal of Sociology* (1960), 271–76.

"bush," "weed," and so on. As pointed out by John and Goldstein,[31] it is only by corrective feedback that the child learns that a "dog" is not a horse or cat or some other four-legged object (discrimination). By the same process he learns that "dog" is not only the white Spitz but also the black police dog, the brown stuffed animal, and the picture of "Spot" in a book.

There are many theories regarding the intimate connections between language and thought. Piaget emphasizes the importance of language in the socialization process. Progression from primitive modes of thinking requires that the child become aware of himself as thinking, feeling, seeing, hearing, from a point of view unique to himself. He needs a dual perspective whereby he not only perceives reality but is aware of himself perceiving and is thus able, within limits, to discount and compensate for his own biases, blind spots, and restricted vision. He can only require his kind of awareness of self in contrast to something else, namely, the point of view of others. To see the world as it appears to someone else can only be done through the medium of language.

Intelligence, just because it undergoes a gradual process of socialization, is enabled through the bond established by language between thoughts and words to make an increasing use of concepts; whereas autism, just because it remains individual, is still tied to imagery, to organic activity, and even to organic movements. The mere fact, then, of telling one's thought, of telling it to others, or of keeping silence and telling it only to oneself must be of enormous importance to the fundamental structure and functioning of thought in general, and of child logic in particular.[32]

Others have studied children's ability to solve complex problems as related to the use they make of language in verbal mediation. Jensen defines verbal mediation as "verbal behavior which facilitates further

learning, which controls behavior and which permits the development of conceptual thinking." [33] It appears that children who receive insufficient verbal stimulation in early childhood develop deficiencies not only in spoken language but also in verbal mediational behavior so that they are handicapped in the concept formation and problem-solving abilities required in the school learning situation.

The facts about early language development and later intellectual ability have given renewed impetus to preschool education. Hunt has proposed preschool enrichment as an antidote for cultural deprivation and social disadvantage.[34] In accordance with these new ideas, preschools in underprivileged, urban neighborhoods have been mushrooming in an effort to fill in the gaps, particularly in language, which are left by the parents. One hopes that the parents will not be forgotten in all the flurry. It is unlikely that the preschool teacher can equal the parent as an identification figure for the child. It would be profitable to give the parents the opportunity to identify with the teacher so that the parents in turn can serve as models for the child and support the educational efforts.

INDIVIDUAL PERSONALITY CHARACTERISTICS

The influence of sociocultural factors on intelligence development is usually considered in terms of group trends with little attention to the individual variations. The emphasis is on environmental conditions insofar as they provide the child with an opportunity to learn. There is less thought given to the role of motivation for learning; there is an assumption that if the proper opportunities are provided at the crucial

---

[31] *Op. cit.*

[32] Piaget, *Language and Thought of the Child* (New York: Meridian Press, 1955), p. 64.

[33] A. Jensen, "Learning in the Pre-School Years," *Journal of Nursery Education* (January, 1963), 133–39.

[34] J. McV. Hunt, "The Psychological Basis for Using Pre-School Enrichment as an Antidote for Cultural Deprivation," *Merrill-Palmer Quarterly,* X (1964), 209–48.

times, the child will "naturally" seize upon these opportunities because of some intrinsic growth motivation. In Hunt's words,

the problem for a teacher endeavoring to keep children interested in intellectual growth is one of providing circumstances so matched, or mismatched, to those with which her pupils are already familiar that an interesting and attractive challenge is continually provided.[35]

Hunt feels that there is a "kind of intrinsic motivation which is inherent in information processing and action" and that "an opportunity to see and hear a variety of things is more important than the fate of instinctual needs and impulses." [36]

There is a tendency for exciting new ideas to be taken as a replacement for what went before. There is no fundamental conflict between the psychoanalytic ideas concerning the transformation of basic drives in the stimulation of intelligence and Hunt's suggestions regarding the importance of environmental stimulation for promoting intelligence. Early maternal deprivation has its devastating effect on intelligence not only because of lack of environmental stimulation but also because of the lack of emotional attachments. To put it simply, the child must care for a person before he really cares about things. Without an emotional attachment he tends to be either apathetic and disinterested in his environment, or he takes an obsessive interest in objects and things excluding those stimulations emanating from people. Such an exclusion has a disastrous effect on language development and eventually on the whole of mental development. This distortion is seen most clearly in autistic children, though other forms of childhood psychosis also block intellectual development as a by-product of the disturbed social relationships. Without help on the social score, these children are unable to take advantage of environmental opportunities for learning

and remain fixed at primitive levels of thinking.

There are less pathological conditions where one also sees the interaction of personality factors and the development of intelligence. Learning requires activity, and if the parents keep the child dependent and in a state of enforced passivity, mental growth is often stunted as a consequence. An interesting study that corroborates this thesis was done by Sontag, Baker, and Nelson.[37] They compared the personalities of children who showed increases or decreases in measured intelligence over a period of years. According to their observations, the "passive, infantile dependent pattern" led to a decreasing level of Binet performance, whereas, "aggressive, self-reassuring mastery of tasks, competitive independent patterns" led to progressively advanced performance. Child therapists (for instance, Sperry, Ulrich, and Staver [38]) have noticed that therapy for learning problems is more effective with aggressive children than with passive, compliant children. Regardless of socioeconomic status, the drive for mastery is not the same in all children. This may in part be determined by inborn constitution, but it is also affected by parental attitudes toward the child's early strivings for independence and autonomy.

A second important connecting link between personality and intelligence is the fate of early childhood curiosity. During the age period of one to two years, curiosity finds expression primarily through physical acts. From the age of two years on, curiosity becomes increasingly intellectual. Although curiosity is generally thought of as a desirable characteristic, this holds true only for impersonal topics. Questions about God,

[37] L. S. Sontag, C. T. Baker, and V. P. Nelson, "Personality as a Determinant of Performance," *American Journal of Orthopsychiatry*, XXV (1955), 555–62.

[38] B. Sperry, D. N. Ulrich, and Nancy Staver, "The Relation of Motility to Boys' Learning Problems," *American Journal of Orthopsychiatry*, XXVIII (1958), 640–46.

[35] *Ibid.*, p. 234.
[36] *Ibid.*, p. 242.

death, sex differences, the origin of babies are often shunted aside by the nervous parent. Individual families may have special secrets which are constantly in evidence, but which at the same time are taboo for discussion. Forbidden secrets exist in families of all cultural descriptions but are perhaps more frequent in disorganized families of low socioeconomic level. For instance, a family forced to make repeated, surreptitious moves in order to "jump the rent" will not prepare the child in advance or explain it after the move. If the child cannot ask (and receive an answer) about such vital questions as to where he will sleep, where is Daddy, who is that man (or woman), he is not going to venture questions about the moon and the stars. Anxiety is one powerful incentive for wonderment. The child wants to know what is going to happen and why, in order to avoid surprises and prepare himself. If curiosity does not help to relieve anxiety, it has little value. Curiosity cannot be compartmentalized or restricted only to safe subjects.

A corollary to this problem of forbidden curiosity is the problem of forbidden knowledge. By independent observation the child may learn something about which he later feels guilty or anxious. Inner conflict may motivate the child to repress or hide his knowledge from others. This is one of the dynamic mechanisms involved in the oft-quoted case of "pseudo-imbecility" published by Mahler.[39] Many times the repressed or hidden knowledge is of a sexual nature because sexuality is commonly an emotionally charged topic, though any subject can be equally taboo in specific family circumstances. In these cases where the retardation is a defense against the anxiety of knowing, the child acts out the aphorism, "Where ignorance is bliss, it's folly to be wise."

There are many other possible points of connection between personality and mental

development based on the mechanism of displacement. For example, conflicts in infantile feeding experiences do not inevitably result in symptoms of an oral nature only. Eating is a form of incorporation, a process of taking in from the outside world. Difficulties in taking in by mouth may spread to the perceptual processes of taking in through the eyes and ears. The possible connection is shown in everyday idioms such as "drinking in with the eyes," "devouring the sight," "digesting information," "a voracious reader," "hunger for knowledge," and so on. There is more than a similarity in process. The carry-over from eating to learning may stem from the repetition of a specific interpersonal relationship as well. A child who has been fed against his will, for instance, is likely to have residual feelings about superior, strong persons who force things on him. Learning requires the gracious acceptance of someone's superiority (at least on a pro tem basis) and can be blocked by unconscious feelings against someone who knows more than the learner. The neurotic children in whom eating conflicts have been displaced to the intellectual sphere, show poor absorption, appear not to understand what they are taught, and seem to forget from one time to the next.[40]

Another kind of displacement is from genital conflicts. Here the child's major concern is with the genital differences between the sexes and his feelings about his own genital adequacy. Visual experience is important in learning about the sex difference. Jarvis, in an article on visual problems in reading disabilities, linked neurotic conflicts in looking with fantasies which deny the fact of castration in women.[41] A child warding off the anxiety caused by looking

[40] B. Sperry, Nancy Staver, and Harold Mann, "Destructive Fantasies in Certain Learning Difficulties," *American Journal of Orthopsychiatry,* XXII (1952), 356–66.
[41] Vivian Jarvis, "Clinical Observations on the Visual Problem in Reading Disability," *Psychoanalytic Study of the Child,* Vol. XIII (New York: International Universities Press, 1958).

[39] Margaret S. Mahler, "Pseudo-Imbecility: A Magic Cap of Indivisibility," *Psychoanalytic Quarterly,* XI (1942), 149–64.

at one thing avoids looking at anything with close attention. For example, at the age levels of four and a half and five years, there are several items on the Stanford-Binet test which require comparison of visually presented objects in terms of their likenesses and differences. Occasionally a child will refuse to look at them, saying flatly, "They are all the same." If a child will not look for fear of seeing differences, he will have considerable difficulty in learning to read.

One could give other examples where the acquisition, retention, and/or demonstration of knowledge are blocked because of anxiety about one or another aspect of "knowing." When stupidity serves a defensive purpose to reduce anxiety, the child is immune to environmental stimulation no matter how well it is planned. Throughout a child's life there is constant interaction between mental and emotional development, and difficulties on the one side usually affect the other. Under normal conditions there is no incompatibility; affective and cognitive lines of development proceed together. In the absence of conflict there is indeed pleasure in "knowing" because it gives a sense of mastery and relieves the anxiety of helplessness.

measurement of intellectual functioning

In talking about intelligence and the factors that influence its development, it is important to consider how intelligence is measured. Intelligence is judged by overt behavior. Some use diffuse standards of "adaptive" behavior, such as getting along well with people and meeting the demands of school and work. Quantification of individual differences, however, demands the use of more limited, rigid criteria provided by intelligence-test performance. As measuring tools, IQ tests have much less reliability than tools of physical measurements. The probabilities of IQ changes over a period

of time have been well researched. Pinneau prepared a series of tables which give the changes in Binet IQ's in individuals tested and retested at various ages.[42] One study showed that in a group of children first tested at six years and retested at twelve years, 50 per cent showed IQ changes of 8 points or more, with 25 per cent changing 13 points or more. The accumulation of such figures has completely destroyed the myth of IQ constancy. The changes are in part errors of measurement, and in part changes in the individual being tested.

The changes in the person can come about for many reasons. The opportunities the child has for experience is one possible causal factor. Psychologists do not hesitate to say that intelligence tests measure the results of learning and that no sharp distinction can be made between intelligence and attainment. In the words of Cureton:

It is obvious that every test of intelligence, as well as every test of school achievement, is a measure of a set of developed abilities. The difference lies in the choice of abilities to be measured and in the method of devising items to measure them. The general intelligence test, as its name implies, tries to measure general ability. To do this, it must include a variety of mental tasks, including samples of the more important types of mental operations and of symbolic content. The achievement test, on the contrary, limits the range of sampling to a relatively narrow and specific set of abilities. The symbolic content covered is fairly definite, and the range of mental operations called for is well-defined and not extremely extensive.[43]

More recently, Vernon arrived at a similar conclusion. "There is no essential difference between the acquisition of, say, reading skills and the acquisition of reasoning or other capacities which would be conven-

---

[42] Samuel Pinneau, *Changes in Intelligence Quotient* (Boston, Mass.: Houghton Mifflin Co., 1961).

[43] E. E. Cureton, "The Accomplishment Quotient Technique," *Journal of Experimental Education*, V (1937), 315–26.

tionally regarded as part of intelligence." [44]

Environment is filtered through the individual's screen of perceptual styles, interests, ego ideals, and prejudices. Neurotic conflicts with their subsequent defenses, characterological traits, and specific anxieties all affect efficiency of intellectual functioning, sometimes serving to heighten it. It has been proposed that intelligence be regarded as a dynamic aspect of personality, and suggestions have been made regarding the analysis of intelligence-test behavior for such personality features as "coping styles." [45]

Considering errors of measurement and the effects of learning and personality on intelligence-test scores, one can appreciate that we are very far from measuring anything like "inborn potential." This does not render the intelligence test meaningless. The intelligence test is useful for short-range predictions of scholastic ability. The

[44] P. E. Vernon, *Intelligence and Attainment Tests* (New York: Philosophical Library, 1960), p. 39.

[45] A. E. Moriarty, "Coping Patterns of Preschool Children in Response to Intelligence Test Demands," *Genetic Psychology Monographs,* LXIV, No. 1 (1961), 3–127.

score is not an attribute of the child; by itself it does not explain why the child is the way he is. A good intelligence test gives important information about present functioning. When combined with an evaluation of the history and total situation of the child, it may provide the basis for remediation of deprivation and/or psychological conflict. The information from careful tests should not be brushed aside as irrelevant because it is environmentally produced. The term "pseudo-retardation" is a misnomer in that it implies retardation on a familial or organic basis. "Pseudo-retardation" may be less permanent but it is no less real at the moment. Intelligence tests (assuming that they have been carefully administered) are valid in describing present level, which is of necessity the starting point for therapists or teachers. Just as a child cannot jump from primer reading to Shakespeare, he cannot jump from magical thinking to an understanding of the principle of number equations. IQ results cannot be projected backward to evaluate genetic potentiality nor can they be projected into the future to determine the ceiling of achievement possibilities. It is quite sufficient that they be used for current planning.

24

*The widespread use of intelligence tests (and other psycho-
metric instruments) for making important decisions about people has been strongly attacked from time to time. Although the criticisms have
frequently been valid, more often they have been based on various misunderstandings concerning the intended purposes of the tests. Indeed, sometimes the
concern has been inappropriately directed at the tests rather than at those
individuals who misuse the instruments. In the next article, Alexander G. Wes-
man discusses some of the controversial issues concerning intelligence tests and
their practical importance and then makes an appeal for increased and more
effective communication between the psychologists who administer tests and
interpret their scores and the general public.*

intelligent testing [1]

ALEXANDER G. WESMAN

The nature of intelligence has been a favor-
ite subject for contemplation and disputa-
tion for centuries—perhaps from the dawn
of man as Homo sapiens. The topic is being
studied and debated today by educators,
sociologists, geneticists, neurophysiologists,
and biochemists, and by psychologists
specializing in various branches of the discipline. Despite this attention and effort,
however—or perhaps *because* of it—there
appears to be no more general agreement
as to the nature of intelligence or the most
valid means of measuring intelligence than
was the case 50 years ago. Concepts of intelligence and the definitions constructed to
enunciate these concepts abound by the
dozens, if not indeed by the hundreds.

[1] Presidential Address presented to Division 5
at the meeting of the American Psychological Association, Washington, D.C., September 1967.

Reprinted from *American Psychologist*, 1968,
23: 267–274, by permission of the author and publisher. Copyright © 1968 by the American Psychological Association.

With so many diverse definitions of intelligence, it is perhaps not surprising that
we cannot agree on how to measure intelligence. It is my conviction that much of the
confusion which plagued us in the past,
and continues to plague us today, is attributable to our ignoring two propositions
which should be obvious:

1. Intelligence is an attribute, not an entity.
2. Intelligence is the summation of the learning experiences of the individual.

We have all too often behaved as though
intelligence is a physical substance, like a
house or an egg crate composed of rooms
or cells; we might better remember that it
is no more to be reified than attributes like
beauty, or speed, or honesty. There are
objects which are classifiable as beautiful;
there are performances which may be characterized as speedy; there are behaviors
which display honesty. Each of these is
measurable, with greater or lesser objec-

tivity. Because they can be measured, however, does not mean they are substances. We may agree with E. L. Thorndike that if something exists it can be measured; we need not accept the converse notion that if we can measure something it has existence as a substance.

Intelligence as here defined is a summation of learning experiences. The instances in which intelligent behavior is observed may be classified in various ways that appear to be logical or homogeneous, but they are individual instances all the same. Each instance represents a response the organism has learned; each learned response in turn predisposes the organism for learning additional responses which permit the organism to display new acts of intelligent behavior.

For our present purposes, it matters little whether we are more comfortable with stimulus-response bonds, with experience-producing drives, with imprinting, or with neuropsychological explanations of *how* or *why* learning occurs; whatever the learning theory, the fundamental principle is universal. We start with an organism which is subject to modification by interaction with the environment; as a product of that interaction, the organism has been modified. Further interaction involves a changed organism—one which is ready to interact with its environment in a new way.

Organisms may differ from one another in their susceptibility to modification. One organism may need a more potent stimulus to trigger reaction to the environment than does another. A particular organism may respond to a given class of stimuli more readily than it does to other kinds of stimuli. Organisms may differ from one another in their readiness to respond to different classes of stimuli. There may be important differences in the ability of organisms to modify their behavior in effective ways as a result of experience.

We may develop and investigate hypotheses as to whether such differences in response as are displayed arise from variations in neurological endowment or in conducive environment. All that we can be sure of, at least as of now, is that what we are dealing with is a response-capable organism which has been exposed to environmental stimuli, has interacted in some way with those stimuli, and has been modified thereby.

The bits or modules which constitute intelligence may be information or may be skill; i.e., they may be content or process. Furthermore, they are multidimensional, and some modules may have more dimensions than do others. Each module is subject to essential change as the individual is exposed to further learning experiences. Each act of learning serves to create new modules, change the existing ones, or both. Modules are not independent; rather, they may overlap with several or many other modules; thus, they are complex both in their number of dimensions and in their interrelationships. Even early percepts are rarely if ever simple. A toy ball when first seen has at least size, shape, and color; if it is touched, it has texture and hardness as well. Accordingly, few if any modules of learning are truly simple.

The whole of a person's intelligence at any given moment may well be thought of as an amorphous mass—not a regular geometric figure. Within this mass, modules may cluster with greater or lesser permanence, and may be organized along principles of relatedness. Thus, word knowledge may form a cluster—but the words of which one has knowledge will be components of other clusters as well. A pencil is an object one writes with; it has shape in common with other objects, it has function in common with pens and crayons, it produces color of varying intensity, it has a number property, it is usually associated with paper. The learned module "pencil" may thus be part of many clusters.

One need not posit that a learning module is permanent. It could, presumably, disappear entirely, although far more often we would expect it to undergo essential change by taking on a more complex character. This model does assume that higher learning depends so intimately and essentially on certain previous learnings that the more complex modules cannot exist without the antecedent modules from which they grew. For example, if the ability to subtract numbers should disappear, the ability to do long division could not remain unaffected. Thus, retention of learning is integral to the concept here proposed.

The simple-minded conceptualization outlined above may have horrified those of my colleagues who are even moderately sophisticated with respect to modern learning theories. To those colleagues I apologize, but I also beg their indulgence. Oversimplified as the conceptualization undoubtedly is, I believe it does no *essential* violence to any current theory; it has, I hope, the virtue of permitting a view of the organization of intelligence, and of the nature of the testing of intelligence, which may prove illuminating for several issues which confront us.

issue I: the classification of ability tests into aptitude, achievement, and intelligence measures

As soon as we have agreed that what we know and what we can do intellectually is learned, the artificiality of the above classification becomes self-evident. Historically, we have recognized that what achievement tests measure is what the examinee has learned. We have been less ready to accord similar recognition to intelligence tests. In their case, we have too often behaved as though what these tests measure is somehow independent of the learning phenomenon. We have played the role of Aladdin seeking a magical lamp, complete with a genie ready to spring forth with full power to accomplish all sorts of wondrous things. We have pondered wistfully on the number of critical issues that would be resolved if we could only somehow measure "intelligence" separately from "achievement."

We have been similarly unrealistic in treating the concept of "aptitude." Our textbooks enunciate the distinction that ap-

titude tests measure what the individual *can* learn, while achievement tests measure what he *has* learned. Some of our leading theorists aggravate the confusion by ignoring the implications of their special use of the term. "Aptitude" is typically used in laboratory learning experiments as a matching or otherwise controlling variable; it is employed to assure that groups to be compared start the experiment as equal in initial ability. One gets a strong impression that the aptitude instrument is perceived as measuring the innate potential of the individual as distinguished from what is to be achieved (i.e., learned) in the experimental process. If learning theorists recognize that what they are calling "aptitude" (or, for that matter, "intelligence") is "previously learned" (as, clearly, at least some of them do), the artificiality of the distinction between "aptitude" or "intelligence" and "achievement" should be eminently apparent.

I wish that at least a few of my psychometric colleagues would leave off searching for *the* structure of intelligence, and devote their wisdom and energy to learning more about the learning process, and to teaching learning theorists about testing. I am convinced that both specialties would profit immeasurably from the cooperative enterprise. It is my strong impression that the inattention of the psychometrician to the facts of learning is matched fully by the unsophisticated treatment accorded to testing by many learning theorists.

All ability tests—intelligence, aptitude, and achievement—measure what the individual *has* learned—and they often measure with similar content and similar process. Let us take, for example, an item [2] such as this: A square and a rectangle have the same perimeter. The square has an area of 10,000 square feet. The rectangle has an area of 9,324 square feet. What are the dimensions of the rectangle?

[2] This item was proposed by G. K. Bennett in another context as an example of an arithmetic problem which might be correctly answered by any of several methods.

This item would clearly be deemed appropriate whether it appeared in an achievement test in high school mathematics, a test of aptitude for mathematics, or the numerical portion of an "intelligence" test. I submit that a great many items can readily fit any of the three categories.

Such justification as we have for our labeling system resides entirely in the *purpose* for which the test is used, not in the test document itself. If our intent is to discover how much the examinee has learned in a particular area, such as a school course, we may select items which probe for the distinctive learnings the schooling was intended to stimulate. We label the test an "achievement" test. If our intent is to predict what success an individual is likely to attain in learning a new language, or a new job, we seek those specific previous learnings the possession of which bodes favorably for that future learning, and we label the test an "aptitude" test or a "special aptitude test." If our intent is to predict future acquisition of learning over broad areas of environmental exposure, we seek those previous learnings the possession of which will be relevant to as many, and as important, future learning situations as we can anticipate. This test we label an "intelligence" test. The selection of test items or sample tasks for the three purposes may or may not differ; but in each instance what is measured is what was previously learned. We are not measuring different abilities; we are merely attending to different criteria. It is the *relevance* of the learnings we select for investigation that largely determines how we name our test, and whether we will succeed in our purpose.

issue II: the utility of culture-free and culture-fair tests

The notion of relevance of previous learnings leads naturally to a consideration of some follies we have committed in the search for culture-free or culture-fair instruments. I do not wish to impugn the high social motives which stimulate the search for such devices; I do wish to question that such a search, in its usual setting, is sensible. A culture-free test would presumably probe learnings which had not been affected by environment; this is sheer nonsense. A culture-fair test attempts to select those learnings which are common to many cultures. In the search for experiences which are common to several different cultures or subcultures, the vital matter of relevance of the learning for our purpose is subordinated or ignored.

The implicit intent in the attempt to create culture-free or culture-fair tests is somehow to measure intelligence without permitting the effects of differential exposure to learning to influence scores. This contains the tacit assumption that "native intelligence" lies buried in pure form deep in the individual, and needs only to be uncovered by ingenious mining methods. If we recognize that intelligence comprises learning experiences, it becomes clear that our attempts are not ingenious, but ingenuous.

It is true that we can probe learnings that have occurred in nonverbal, nonnumerical domains. This means only that we can test selected aspects of intelligence. The question immediately arises of the relevance of these special domains to the kinds of learnings we will want to predict. The measurement purpose for which culture-fair tests are ordinarily developed is that of predicting academic or industrial performance. Most academic courses and most industrial jobs involve some use of verbal abilities. Since further learning is conditioned by relevant past learning, the individual who has developed more of the prerequisite ability inevitably has an advantage over the individual with less of the prerequisite ability. If we wish to predict whether an individual will profit appreciably from additional exposure to learning, our best predictor must be a measure which appraises what prerequisite learning he has acquired heretofore. Appropriate verbal abilities are more relevant to the largely verbal learning we usually wish to predict than other abilities are.

It has on occasion been suggested that tests be developed which sample the verbal skills or factual information which are peculiar to a given subculture. Such tests are proposed as a "fairer" measure of the "intelligence," or readiness to learn, of the members of that subculture. The response to this proposal is "readiness to learn *what?*" If our purpose is to distinguish members of that subculture from their peers with respect to how much of that special culture they have assimilated, such a test might well be useful. If, as is more likely the case, we wish to predict future learnings of the content of the more general culture (e.g., the so-called white, middle-class culture such as typifies what the majority of our schools are organized to transmit), tests designed for the subculture will be less relevant than those which sample from the general culture. This is not intended to imply that the members of the subculture *could* not learn what the schools as constituted are offering. It does emphasize that, at the moment at which we make our appraisal, what the individual has already learned from the general culture domain is the most significant information as to what he is then ready to learn. The less relevant the previous learnings we appraise, the more hazardous must be our predictions of future learnings.

As long as our educational system and our general culture are dependent on conventional verbal abilities, those who aspire to progress in that system and that culture will need to command those abilities. In a verbal society, verbal competence cannot sensibly be ignored.

issue III: is "verbal ability" synonymous with "intelligence"?

To say that we cannot afford to ignore learnings in relevant verbal areas when we are appraising "intelligence" does not imply that *only* the verbal domain is important. The development of tests of "general mental ability" which sample only the verbal domain implies that since verbal tests predict school criteria best, it is unnecessary to attend to other cognitive abilities the student has developed; in other words, that, in effect, "verbal ability" is synonymous with "intelligence." It would be most unfortunate if, consciously or unconsciously, we adopted this too narrow perspective.

That verbal tests are typically good predictors of grades in many academic courses is undeniable. *Why* this is the case warrants some thought. Is it because all, or even most, of what constitutes "intelligence" is represented by verbal ability? Certainly the chief symbol system of our society is verbal. Even when we deal with numerical, spatial, or figural problems we often transform them to verbal expressions. It is one thing, however, to recognize the involvement of verbal abilities in all kinds of learning experiences and quite another to grant them exclusive sovereignty over learning domains. Many domains require the possession of other abilities as well, but our appraisal methods are often inadequate to reveal that need. Because it is easier to employ verbal criteria, or more convenient— or because we have given insufficient thought to criterion validity—we predetermine the finding that verbal abilities dominate the scene.

A particularly revealing demonstration of this phenomenon came to the attention of the authors of the Differential Aptitude Tests some years ago. Grades in an auto mechanics course were found to be better predicted by the Verbal Reasoning test of the DAT than by the Mechanical Reasoning test. We had the unusual good fortune of having access to further information about the course. We discovered that early in the course the teacher had been called from the room for almost a half-hour. In his absence, the students had disobeyed his instructions not to fool around with the automobile motors. To let the punishment fit the crime, he conducted the rest of the course almost entirely by lecturing, giving the students minimum opportunity for actually working with the engines. That grades in a course taught by lecture and evaluated by a written test should be best predicted by a verbal test is not too surprising!

An illustration such as the above should force us to stop and think. As we study tables replete with validity coefficients, how many of those coefficients represent similar instances? As we develop hypotheses as to the importance of particular aspects of intelligence, how well do we understand the *criteria* which gave rise to the coefficients on which our hypotheses are based? Would the use of more valid criteria in courses for which curricular goals transcend verbal skills have produced similar data, or different? Would the admittedly broad pervasiveness of verbal skills seem quite so broad if more appropriate measures of learning were employed? If we remain complacent about criteria composed largely of behaviors from the verbal domain, we are unlikely to see the relevance of other abilities.

In his APA presidential address in 1964, McNemar paid flattering attention to the Differential Aptitude Tests; he quite accurately reported that the verbal tests were most frequently the best predictors of course grades. The data he cited certainly supported the point he was making: Verbal tests predict grades in many academic courses. What might well have been added was recognition that the nature of our educational criteria exaggerates the real importance of verbal skills. If (and it is hoped *when*) grades or other criterion statements become more content valid, the relevance of a number of other skills will be more demonstrable.

Industry has perforce learned this lesson. Few mechanical apprentices are selected solely, or even primarily, because they can describe a process, rather than perform it. The military has learned that the ability to diagnose a malfunctioning torpedo is poorly demonstrated by verbal exposition, but well demonstrated by a work sample requiring actual mechanical repairs. It is to be hoped that education will increasingly become more realistic with respect to what *its* criteria *should* be.

issue IV: the growth and decline of "intelligence"

So preoccupied have we been with reifying intelligence as some mystical substance that we have too often neglected to take a common-sense look at what intelligence tests measure. We find ourselves distressed at our failure to predict with satisfactory accuracy the intelligence test scores of a teen-ager from his intelligence test scores as an infant. Why should this occasion surprise, let alone distress? If we look inside the tests, it should be obvious that the kinds of learnings we typically appraise at the earlier ages bear little resemblance, and may have little relevance, to the kinds of learnings we appraise later.

At the earlier age levels, we have typically tested for such characteristics as motor dexterity, perception, and similar features of physical development. When intellectual concepts become available for testing as baby grows to infant, to child, to teen-ager, we change the focus of our testing from the physical domains to the cognitive—we appraise knowledge, concept formation, and reasoning.

It is possible that future research will disclose that possession of certain physical abilities or tendencies is prerequisite to the development of concept formation, and that earlier possession of these characteristics will foretell the future intellectual development of the individual. Interesting and promising research now being conducted is directed toward this goal. It is my opinion that, because learning experiences vary so from one child to another, there is some practical limit beyond which we will be unable to predict, however penetrating our research. In any event, we would do well at this moment to recognize that since we are measuring in different ability domains at infant and school-age levels, we should not expect good prediction from one level to the other—and we should certainly not behave as though the data permitted confident prediction.

At the other end of the age spectrum we have, with similar lack of insight, proceeded to corollary errors. We have accepted the gloomy dictum that once we have passed the age of 18, or 25, or 35, we have passed our peak; from that age, our ability to learn declines. Our texts are peppered with charts showing that depressing downhill slide. What is the basis for this widely accepted conclusion? The principal basis is that when we apply our conventional measures of intelligence to older people, we find that average scores decrease. We have implicitly accepted the idea that intelligence is defined by what is measured by these particular intelligence tests. If, however, we return to our previous formulation of intelligence as what we know in a wide variety of domains, and hence as a base for what we can learn at a given moment, our perspective changes. We then proceed to compare what the intelligence tests measure with the kinds of learning individuals have engaged in from age 30 or 40 on. The relevance of the tests, except perhaps as measures of retention, is seen as increasingly remote with each passing year. Most individuals have not failed to learn more with added years of life. Their learnings have occurred in areas (science, business, politics, psychology, psychometrics), often relatively specialized, which are not measured by conventional intelligence tests.

It is true that new learnings of adults occur in such a variety of endeavors that it would be virtually impossible to find a common core on which all could be examined. We should not, however, pretend we do not suffer this psychometric disability;

we should not continue to use less relevant measures to support deceptive graphs and curves of the decline of "intelligence." We might better recognize the limitations of our measure, until such time as we can devise relevant measures of the significant learnings which do occur. For the present, we can conclude only that with each passing decade older people do less well on tests designed for younger adults.

issue V: the search for purity

A discussion of the nature of intelligence, and of intelligent testing, should not ignore the topic of factor analysis. It is a method which has influenced test construction and test selection. It is a technique which has stimulated the promulgation of theories of the structure of intellect.

The history of psychometrics gives evidence that each new major technique has attained a heyday of popularity, during which unrealistic hopes led to unbridled use. In the 1920s and 1930s, Pearson product-moment coefficients held the stage; everybody seemed to be correlating everything with everything else with wild abandon. We appear, in more recent times, to have been engaging in factor analysis with almost equal frenzy. With so much activity going on, it is perhaps to be expected that some studies, and some conclusions, would be characterized more by enthusiasm than by wisdom.

To criticize factor analysis as a procedure because individuals have misled themselves through its use would be very silly indeed. Among the benefits it has provided are the ability to summarize vast masses of data, and to facilitate the organization of information in a way that inspires, and then leads to investigation of interesting and often fruitful research hypotheses. At the same time, we need not believe that the power of the tool assures the validity of the product. Some of the conclusions which have been drawn, some attitudes which have been adopted, and some theories which have occasionally been treated as though they were established fact might well be exposed to scrutiny.

There have been instances in which a test battery was chosen for practical use *because* it had its origins in a program of factorial research. Presumably, the rationale was that such a battery consists of relatively "pure" tests, and would show near-zero intercorrelation among the tests; it would therefore be more efficient than a battery of similar measures not derived from factorial studies. If this rationale survived empirical study, it would still not of itself be adequate justification for selecting one set of tests rather than another. Efficiency is certainly desirable—but *validity* is *crucial*. How tests were constructed is interesting and even germane; how they *work* is the critical issue.

Let us return, however, to the rationale. Is the leap from "factorial origin" to "purity" defensible? The "pure" tests developed in psychometric laboratories often do correlate very little with one another. To some degree, at least, this low correlation is frequently ascribable to the unreliability of short, experimental tests, or to restriction in range of the various abilities of the subject, or both. For exploratory and research purposes, these conditions represent a reasonable situation. Practical test use situations are something else again.

When batteries of reliable tests with factorial ancestry, and batteries testing in similar domains but not factor oriented, are given to the same students, the within-battery intercorrelation of scores is ordinarily of about the same order. For example, with one ninth-grade group of boys, the average inter-*r* among the Differential Aptitude Tests was .37; for the same group, the average inter-*r* of the Primary Mental Abilities Tests was .36. Similar results were obtained in a comparison of the DAT and the General Aptitude Test Battery scores for a twelfth-grade group. Thus, there was little evidence of greater "purity" in the

factorially derived batteries than in the DAT, which were not so derived. (In the everyday world, it appears, "purity" is all too likely to be an illusion.) Accordingly, we would be well advised when choosing tests for practical use to concentrate on how they work, not on how they were built.

Let us now turn briefly to the role of factor analysis as a stimulator of hypotheses concerning the structure of intellect. Its influence has often seemed to be not so much mathematicodeductive as mathematicoseductive! The power of the method as a way of manipulating great masses of data appears all too often to have led us astray. Even our more eminent protagonists of the technique have not always appeared immune. When expounding on the theory of factor analysis, experts almost invariably agree that factors are merely descriptive categories; they are not functional entities. But when engaged in interpreting the factors which have emerged from their studies, some analysts apparently succumb to the mystic charm of rotating axes and perceive entities which, they have told us, do not exist. The lure of the temptation to discover a psychological structure analogous to the periodic table of the elements is too powerful to resist. We then hear of "primary mental abilities" or are shown "the three faces of intellect." Though the authors of such creations have sometimes demonstrated in other writings that they well understand the difference between the reality of descriptive categories and the illusion of underlying entities, some of their disciples and many of their readers seem less clear in their perception.

If we accept the thesis that the modules or bits which constitute intelligence are themselves complex, a combination of such modules can hardly be expected to be simple or "pure." A 6-year-old who assembles three alphabet blocks to spell out "cat" has employed, at a minimum, verbal and spatial skills; if he is aware that there are three blocks or letters, he has engaged in numerical perception as well. The ability to perform the task has required cognition, memory, convergent thinking, and evaluation. The product is figural, symbolic, and semantic. All this, and we have not yet taken into account such considerations as the motor-manipulative activity, the perception of color, the earlier learning experiences which enabled him to perform the task successfully, or the imagery which the concept "cat" induces in him. We, as analysts, may choose to attend to only a single aspect of the behavior—but the behavior itself remains multifaceted and complex. To assume that we can abstract from a host of such activities a pure and simple entity is to ignore the psychological meaning of intelligent behavior.

Let us continue to explore, by all means available to us (including factor analysis) the nature of man's abilities. Let us *not* assume that the results of research obtained under closely managed conditions in the laboratory will hold true as realities in day-to-day situations. Let us not unwittingly forget that the descriptive categories we adopt for convenience in communication do not have real existence as ultimate psychological entities.

conclusion

To what view of a structure of intellect am I led by the ideas I have enunciated here? Essentially, I believe intelligence is *un*structured. I believe that it is differently comprised in every individual—the sum total of all the learning experiences he has uniquely had up to any moment in time. Such structure as we perceive is structure which we have imposed. We can so select samples of previous learnings to examine as to reveal a general factor, or group factors, or specifics. We can sample from domains that are relatively homogeneous and apply labels such as verbal, numerical, spatial; we can sample from a wider variety of learnings, and apply labels such as "general mental ability" or, simply, "intelligence."

There are many bases on which we may choose which kinds of learnings we will sample. The most reasonable basis, I believe, is that of predictive purpose. Those previous learnings should be probed which are most relevant to the particular future learnings we wish to predict. In addition to criterion—or, more likely, *criteria*—relevance, the principles of band width and fidelity (as enunciated by Cronbach and Gleser) might well serve as guides. If we are interested in forecasting narrow-band criteria, selection of highly homogeneous, directly relevant behaviors is indicated. If we are interested in a wide range of criteria, we have at least two options: we may choose to select small samples from widely scattered domains—as in a Binet, a Wechsler, or a broader gauge instrument still to be devised—or examine more intensively with several narrower gauge tests, as in the Differential Aptitude Tests. The broader gauge instruments will offer economy, but lesser fidelity for selected criteria. The narrower gauge instruments will be longer and more time consuming—but the possibility of more direct relevance to one or more particular criteria should permit higher fidelity.

The critical issue, then, is not which approach measures intelligence—each of them does, in its own fashion. No approach save sampling from every domain in which learnings have occurred—an impossible task—fully measures intelligence. The question is rather which approach provides the most useful information for the various purposes we wish the test to serve. Recognition that what we are measuring is what the individual has learned, and composing our tests to appraise *relevant* previous learnings, will yield the most useful information. We, and those who utilize the results of our work—educators, personnel men, social planners—face problems for which intelligence test data are relevant, and sometimes crucial. We must remember, and we must teach, what out test scores really reflect. The measurement of intelligence is not, and has not been, a matter of concern only to psychology. It has always been, and continues to be, an influence on educational and social programs. If we are to avert uninformed pressures from government agencies, from school administrators, from the courts, and indeed from psychologist colleagues, we must understand and we must broadly communicate what these scores truly represent. Only then can we who build tests and they who use them properly claim that we are indeed engaged in intelligent testing.

UNIT

VIII

personality

25 *There is considerable interest and debate concerning the potential impact of the mass media, particularly television, on immediate behavior and later personality development in children. It is tempting to speculate about the influence of exposure to violence and aggression, but it is quite another thing to evaluate the effects of this exposure in controlled experimental situations. In recent years, Albert Bandura and his associates have been carrying on just such studies with considerable success. In the article which follows, Bandura discusses some of his early findings as well as the rationale and theoretical interpretations of this work.*

the role of modeling processes in personality development[1]

ALBERT BANDURA

I remember reading a story reported by Professor Mowrer about a lonesome farmer who decided to get a parrot for company. After acquiring the bird, the farmer spent many long evenings teaching the parrot the phrase, "Say Uncle." Despite the devoted tutoral attention, the parrot proved totally unresponsive and finally the frustrated

[1] The experiments reported in this paper were supported in part by research grants M-1734, M-4398, and M-5316 from the National Institute of Health, Public Health Service, and the Lewis S. Haas Child Development Research Fund, Stanford University.

The author wishes to express his appreciation to the many students who assisted in various phases of this research. I am also grateful to Edith Dowley, Director, Marilyn Haley and Patricia Rowe Webster, Head Teachers, Stanford University Nursery Schools, for their aid in arranging the research facilities.

farmer got a stick and struck the parrot on the head after each refusal to produce the desired phrase.

But the visceral method proved no more effective than the cerebral one, so the farmer grabbed his feathered friend and tossed him in the chicken house. A short time later the farmer heard a loud commotion in the chicken house and upon investigation found that the parrot was pummeling the startled chickens on the head with a stick and shouting, "Say Uncle! Say Uncle!" While this story is not intended as an introduction to a treatise on parrot-training practices, it provides a graphic illustration of the process of social learning that I shall discuss in this paper.

One can distinguish two kinds of processes by which children acquire attitudes, values, and patterns of social behavior. First, there is learning that occurs on the basis of direct tuition or instrumental training. In this form of learning, parents and other socializing agents are relatively explicit about what they wish the child to learn and attempt to shape his behavior

through rewarding and punishing consequences.

Although a certain amount of socialization of a child takes place through such
direct training, personality patterns are primarily acquired through the child's active
imitation of parental attitudes and behavior, most of which the parents have never
directly attempted to teach. Indeed, parental modeling behavior may often counteract the effects of their direct training.
When a parent punishes his child physically for having aggressed toward peers, for
example, the intended outcome of this training is that the child should refrain from
hitting others. The child, however, is also
learning from parental demonstration how
to aggress physically and this imitative
learning may provide the direction for the
child's behavior when he is similarly frustrated in subsequent social interactions.

Research bearing on modeling processes
demonstrates that, unlike the relatively slow
process of instrumental training, when a
model is provided, patterns of behavior are
rapidly acquired in large segments or in
their entirety (Bandura, 1962). The pervasiveness of this form of learning is also
clearly evident in naturalistic observations
of children's play in which they frequently
reproduce the entire parental role, including the appropriate mannerisms, voice in-
flections, and attitudes, much to the parents'
surprise and embarrassment. Although the
process whereby a person reproduces the
behavior exhibited by real-life or symbol-
ized models is generally "labeled" identification" in theories of personality, I shall employ the term imitation or modeling because
it encompasses the same behavioral phenomenon and it avoids the elusiveness and
surplus meanings that have come to be associated with the former concept.

Let us now consider a series of experiments that both illustrates the process of
learning through imitation and identifies
some of the factors which serve to enhance
or to reduce the occurrence of imitative
behavior.

transmission of aggression

One set of experiments was designed primarily to determine the extent to which
aggression can be transmitted to children
through exposure to aggressive adult models (Bandura, Ross, and Ross, 1961). One
group of children observed an aggressive
model who exhibited relatively novel forms
of physical and verbal aggression toward a
large inflated plastic doll; a second group
viewed the same model behave in a very
subdued and inhibited manner, while children in a control group had no exposure
to any models. Half the children in each of
the experimental conditions observed models of the same sex as themselves and the
remaining children in each group witnessed
opposite-sex models.

This investigation was later extended
(Bandura, Ross, and Ross, 1963a) in order
to compare the effects of real-life and film-
mediated or televised aggressive models on
children's behavior. Children in the human
film-aggression group viewed a movie showing the same adults who had served as
models in the earlier experiment portraying
the novel aggressive acts toward the inflated doll. Children in the cartoon-aggres-
sion group saw a film projected on a glass
lenscreen in a television console. In this film
a female model was costumed as a cat and
exhibited aggressive behavior toward a
plastic doll. After exposure to their respective models all children, including those in
the control group, were mildly frustrated
and tested for the amount of imitative and
nonimitative aggression.

The results of these experiments leave
little doubt that exposure to aggressive
models heightens children's aggressive responses to subsequent frustration. As shown
in Figure 1, children who observed the aggressive models exhibited approximately
twice as much aggression as did subjects in
the nonaggressive model group or the control group. In addition, children who witnessed the subdued nonaggressive model
displayed the inhibited behavior charac-

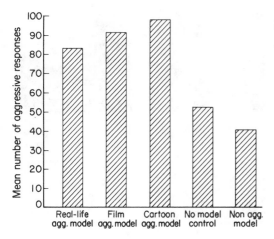

figure 1 Mean number of aggressive responses performed by children in each of five groups.

teristic of their model and expressed significantly less aggression than the control children.

Some evidence that the influence of models is partly determined by the sex appropriateness of their behavior is provided by the finding that the aggressive male model was a more powerful stimulus for aggression than the aggressive female model. Some of the children, particularly the boys, commented spontaneously on the fact that the female model's behavior was out of character (e.g., "That's no way for a lady to behave. Ladies are supposed to act like ladies . . .").

In contrast, aggression by the male model was generally viewed as appropriate and approved by both the boys ("Al's a good socker, he beat up Bobo. I want to sock like Al.") and the girls ("That man is a strong fighter. He punched and punched, and he could hit Bobo right down to the floor and if Bobo got up he said, 'Punch your nose.' He's a good fighter like Daddy.").

Furthermore, the data reveal that aggressive models are highly influential not only in reducing children's inhibitions over aggression, but also in shaping the form of their behavior. Children who observed the

aggressive models displayed a great number of precisely imitative aggressive acts, whereas such responses rarely occurred in either the nonaggressive model group or the control group. Illustrations of the way many of the children become virtual carbon copies of their models are presented in Figure 2. The top frames show the female model performing four novel aggressive responses; the lower frames depict a boy and a girl reproducing the behavior of the female model whom they had observed in the film presentation.

Although the children were somewhat less inclined to imitate precisely the cartoon character than the real-life aggressive model, all three experimental conditions—real-life, film-mediated, and cartoon-aggressive models—produced equivalent increases in overall aggressive behavior based on a variety of measures of both imitative and nonimitative aggression.

The finding that film-mediated models are as effective as real-life models in eliciting and transmitting aggressive responses indicates that televised models may serve as important sources of behavior and can no longer be ignored in conceptualizations of personality development. Indeed, most youngsters probably have more exposure to prestigeful televised male models than to their own fathers. With further advances in mass media and audiovisual technology, models presented pictorially, mainly through television, are likely to play an increasingly influential role in shaping personality patterns and in modifying attitudes and social norms.

It has been widely assumed on the basis of psychoanalytic theory and other hydraulic energy models of personality that children's vicarious participation in film-mediated aggression or the direct expression of aggressive behavior will serve to discharge "pent-up energies" and affects. Guided by this catharsis hypothesis, many parents, educators, and mental health workers encourage hyperaggressive children to participate in aggressive recreational activities,

figure 2 Photographs of two children exhibiting precise imitation of the female model whom they had previously observed on film.

to view highly aggressive televised programs, and to aggress in psychotherapeutic playrooms and other permissive settings.

In contrast to this "drainage" view, social learning theory (Bandura and Walters, 1963) would predict that the provision of aggressive models and the inadvertent positive reinforcement of aggression, which inevitably occurs during the encouragement of cathartic expressions, are exceedingly effective procedures for enhancing aggressive response tendencies. It is not surprising, therefore, that studies in which children or adolescents have been exposed to film-mediated aggressive models (Bandura, Ross, and Ross, 1961, 1963a,b; Hartmann, 1965; Lovaas, 1961; Mussen and Rutherford, 1961; Siegel, 1959; Walters, Llewellyn-Thomas, and Acker, 1962) have uniformly demonstrated that vicarious participation in aggressive activity increases, rather than decreases, aggressive behavior.

On the other hand, providing aggressive children with examples of alternative, constructive ways of coping with interpersonal frustration has been found to be highly successful in modifying aggressive-domineering personality patterns (Chittenden, 1942). Additional comparisons of social-learning theory and the traditional approaches to personality development will be presented later.

modification of fears through modeling

Results of a recent study (Bandura, Grusec, and Menlove, 1967a) disclose that well-established fears and inhibitions can be effectively eliminated by having fearful children observe a graduated sequence of modeling activities beginning with presentations that are easily tolerated. Nursery school children who were fearful of dogs, as revealed by parental ratings and an actual test of dog-avoidance behavior, participated in eight brief sessions in which they observed a fearless peer model exhibit progressively longer, closer, and more intimate interactions with a dog. In order to assess both the generality and the stability of treatment effects, the children were re-administered tests for avoidance behavior toward two dogs following completion of the treatment series and approximately one month later. In the initial tasks, the dog was enclosed in a playpen and the children were asked to walk up and look down at the dog, to touch her fur, and to pet her. Following assessment of avoidance of the dog in the playpen, the children were instructed to remove her from the pen, to walk her on a leash, and to pet her. In subsequent tasks the children were asked to remain alone in the room with the animal and to feed her dog biscuits. The final and most difficult set of tasks required the children to climb into the playpen with the dog, to pet her,

and to remain alone in the room with her under the confining conditions.

The modeling treatment proved surprisingly effective in reducing the children's fears. Indeed, two-thirds of the children overcame their fear of dogs completely, as shown in the fact that they were willing to remain alone in the room confined with the dog in the playpen. These favorable outcomes are largely corroborated by a second experiment (Bandura and Menlove, 1967b) in which fearful children observed similar modeled performances in filmed presentations, while others, assigned to a control group, watched some entertaining movies. In addition, at the completion of the experiment, the control children, whose fear of dogs remained unchanged, were shown the therapeutic films. Their inhibitions were substantially reduced. The increased boldness of one of the control children who had been subsequently treated is portrayed in Figure 3. The top frames show the model's

figure 3   Photographs of two children exhibiting reduced fear of dogs following observation of a fearless peer model.

dauntless behavior; the lower frames depict the girl's fearless interaction with the two canine research assistants.

The influential role of modeling processes in personality development is further revealed by studies demonstrating that children adopt, through observation of behavior exemplified by adults and peers, relatively complex attributes including standards of achievement and self-evaluation (Bandura, Grusec, and Menlove, 1967b; Bandura and Kupers, 1964; Bandura and Whalen, 1966; Mischel and Liebert, 1966), patterns of emotional responsivity (Bandura and Rosenthal, 1966), syntactic styles (Bandura and Harris, 1966), moral judgmental orientations (Bandura and McDonald, 1963), and patterns of self-gratification (Bandura and Mischel, 1965).

It is apparent that children do not reproduce the personality characteristics of every model with whom they come into contact, nor do they imitate every element of behavior exhibited even by models whom they may have selected as their primary sources of social behavior. The experiments discussed in the remaining sections of this paper are mainly concerned with some of the psychological variables determining the selection of models and the degree to which their behavior will be emulated.

response consequences to the model

The manner in which rewarding or punishing consequences to the model's behavior influences imitation is demonstrated in an experiment in which nursery school children observed either an aggressive model rewarded, an aggressive model punished, or had no exposure to the models (Bandura, Ross, and Ross, 1963b). The models were two adults, and the film presented to the children was projected into a television console. In the aggression-rewarded condition, Rocky, the aggressive model, appropriates all of Johnny's attractive play possessions and tasty foodstuffs through aggressive-domineering means. The film shown to the children in the aggression-punished condition was identical with that shown to the aggression-rewarded group except for a slight rearrangement of the film sequence so that the aggression exhibited by Rocky resulted in his being severely punished by Johnny. Following exposure to the models the children were tested for the incidence of post-exposure aggressive behavior. Children who observed Rocky's aggressive behavior rewarded readily imitated his physical and verbal aggression, whereas children who saw him punished exhibited relatively little imitative behavior and did not differ from a group of control children who had no exposure to the models.

At the conclusion of the experiment each child was asked to evaluate the behavior of Rocky and Johnny and to select the character he preferred to emulate. These data yielded some interesting and surprising findings. As might be expected, children who observed Rocky's aggressive behavior punished both failed to reproduce his behavior and rejected him as a model for emulation. On the other hand, when Rocky's aggression was highly successful in amassing rewarding resources, he was chosen by most of the children as the preferred model for imitation. The surprising finding, however, is that without exception these children were highly critical of his behavior (e.g., "Rocky is harsh" . . . "Rough and bossy" . . . "Mean" . . . "Wicked" . . . "He whack people" . . .).

It was evident from the children's comments that the successful payoff of aggression rather than its intrinsic desirability served as the primary basis for emulation (e.g., "Rocky beat Johnny and chase him and get all the good toys" . . . "He came and snatched Johnny's toys. Get a lot of toys". . .). The children resolved the conflict by derogating the unfortunate victim, apparently as justification for Rocky's exploitive-assaultive behavior. They criticized

Johnny for his inability to control Rocky ("He's a cry baby. Didn't know how to make Rocky mind"), for his miserliness ("If he'd shared right in the beginning, Rocky might have played nice"), and generally described him as "Sulky," "Mean," and "Sort of dumb."

This study clearly demonstrates the way in which rewarding consequences to the model may outweigh the value systems of observers—children readily adopted successful modeling behavior even though they had labeled it objectionable, morally reprehensible, and publicly had criticized the model for engaging in such behavior.

In many televised and other mass media presentations antisocial models amass considerable rewarding resources through devious means but are punished following the last commercial on the assumption that the punishment ending will erase or counteract the learning of the model's antisocial behavior. The findings of an experiment by Bandura in 1965 reveal that although punishment administered to a model tends to inhibit children's performance of the modeled behavior, it has virtually no influence on the occurrence of imitative learning. In this experiment children observed a film-mediated aggressive model who was severely punished in one condition, generously rewarded in a second condition, and received no response-consequences to the model in the third condition.

Consistent with the findings cited earlier, a post-exposure test of imitative behavior showed that children who observed the punished model performed significantly fewer imitative responses than children in the model-rewarded and the no-consequences groups. Children in all three groups were then offered attractive incentives contingent on their reproducing the model's behavior. The introduction of the rewards completely wiped out the previously observed performance differences, revealing an equivalent amount of learning among the children in the model-rewarded, model-punished, and the no-consequences groups.

Moreover, girls had acquired approximately as much imitative aggression as did the boys.

It might be concluded from these findings that exposure of children to punished antisocial or other types of models is likely to result in little overt imitative behavior. Nevertheless, the observed behavior is learned and may be exhibited on future occasions given appropriate instigation, the instruments necessary for performing the imitative acts, and the prospect of sufficiently attractive positive rewards contingent on the successful execution of the behavior.

nurturance

The role of nurturance in facilitating imitative learning has been emphasized in most theories of identification. Through the repeated association of the parent's behavior and attributes with warm, rewarding, and affectionately demonstrative caretaking activities, it is assumed that the parent's behavioral characteristics gradually take on positive value for the child. Consequently, the child is motivated to reproduce these positively valenced attributes in his own behavior.

Some empirical support for the nurturance hypothesis is provided in an experiment in which the quality of the rewarding interaction between a female model and nursery school children was systematically varied (Bandura and Huston, 1961). With one group of children the model behaved in a warm and rewarding manner, while a second group of children experienced a distant and nonnurturant relationship with the model. Following the experimental social interactions the model and the children played a game in which the model exhibited a relatively novel pattern of verbal and motor behavior and the number of imitative responses performed by the children was recorded.

Children who had experienced the rewarding interaction with the model displayed substantially more imitative behavior than did children with whom the same adult had interacted in a nonrewarding way. Exposure to a model possessing rewarding qualities not only elicited precisely imitative verbal responses but also increased the level of nonimitative verbalization. These results are essentially in agreement with those of Milner (1951), who found that children receiving high reading readiness scores had more verbal and affectionately demonstrative maternal models than children in the low reading ability group.

The importance of attaching positive valence to the activities and behavior which the parent or teacher wishes the child to reproduce is dramatically illustrated in a case report by Mowrer (1960). A 2-year-old girl, who suffered from an auditory defect, was seriously retarded in language development, a condition that resulted primarily from her refusal to wear a hearing aid. In analyzing the mother-child verbal interaction, it became readily apparent that the girl was hearing only language responses of high amplitude which the mother uttered in a raised voice during disciplinary interventions. Considering the repeated association of the mother's verbal behavior with negative emotional experiences, it was not surprising that the child refused to wear a hearing aid and exhibited little interest in, or desire for, vocalization.

The mother was instructed to follow a remedial program in which she deliberately and frequently associated her vocalizations with highly positive experience and refrained from using language punitively. Within a brief period of time the child began to show an active interest in the mother's verbalizations, was quite willing to wear the hearing aid, and made rapid progress in her language development.

In discussions of the process of education and socialization, considerable emphasis is generally placed on direct training procedures. As the above case illustrates,

however, the attachment of positive valence to modeling behavior may be an important precondition for the occurrence of social learning. Indeed, once the behavior in question has acquired positive properties, the child is likely to perform in the absence of socializing agents and externally administered rewards.

social power

In the studies to which reference has been made, children were exposed to only a single model. During the course of social development, however, children have extensive contact with multiple models, particularly family members, who may differ widely in their behavior and in their relative influence. Therefore, a further study, designed to test several different theories of identificatory learning, utilized three-person groups representing prototypes of the nuclear family (Bandura, Ross, and Ross, 1963c).

In one condition of the experiment an adult assumed the role of controller of highly rewarding resources including attractive play material, appetizing foods, and high-status objects. Another adult was the recipient of these resources, while the child, a participant observer in the triad, was essentially ignored. In a second condition, one adult controlled the resources; the child, however, was the recipient of the positive resources, while the other adult was assigned a subordinate and powerless role.

An adult male and female served as models in each of the triads. For half the boys and girls in each condition, the male model controlled and dispensed the rewarding resources, simulating the husband-dominant home; for the remaining children, the female model mediated the positive resources as in the wife-dominant home. Following the experimental social interactions the adult models exhibited divergent patterns of behavior in the presence of the child, and measures were obtained of the degree to which the child subsequently patterned his behavior after that of the models.

According to the status-envy theory of identification proposed by Whiting (1959, 1960), where a child competes unsuccessfully with an adult for affection, attention, food, and care, the child will envy the consumer adult and consequently identify with him. This theory represents an extension of the psychoanalytic defensive identification hypothesis that identification is the outcome of rivalrous interaction between the child and the parent who occupies an envied consumer status. In contrast to the status-envy hypothesis, the social power theory of identification (Maccoby, 1959; Mussen and Distler, 1960) predicts that children will reproduce more of the behavior of the adult who controls positive resources than that of the powerless adult model.

The results of this experiment reveal that children tend to identify with the source of rewarding power rather than with the competitor for the rewards. In both experimental triads, regardless of whether the rival adult or the children themselves were the recipients of the rewarding resources, the model who possessed rewarding power was imitated to a considerably greater extent than was the competitor or the ignored model. Moreover, power inversions on the part of the male and female models produced cross-sex imitation, particularly in girls. These findings suggest that the distribution of rewarding power within the family may play an important role in the development of both appropriate and deviant sex-role behavior.

Although the children adopted many of the characteristics of the model who possessed rewarding power they also reproduced some of the response patterns exhibited by the model who occupied a subordinate role. The children's behavior represented a synthesis of behavioral elements selected from both models, and since the specific admixture of elements varied from child to child, they displayed quite different patterns of imitative behavior. Thus, within one family even same-sex siblings may exhibit different personality characteristics, owing to their having selected for imitation different elements of their parents' attitudes and behavior. Paradoxical as it may seem, it is possible to achieve considerable innovation through selective imitation.

social learning, psychoanalytic, and stage theories of personality

It was pointed out in preceding sections of this paper that laboratory data have failed to support predictions derived from several widely accepted psychoanalytic principles of personality development. Research generated by social learning theory also raises some questions about the validity of stage theories that typically depict the developmental process as involving a relatively spontaneous emergence of age-specific modes of behavior as the child passes from one stage to another. According to Piaget's theory of moral development (1948), for example, one can distinguish two clearcut stages of moral orientations demarcated from each other at approximately seven years of age.

In the first stage, defined as objective morality, children judge the gravity of a deviant act in terms of the amount of material damages and disregard the intention of the action. By contrast, during the second or subjective morality stage, children judge conduct in terms of its intent rather than its material consequences. The sequence and timing of these stages are presumably predetermined and, consequently, young children are incapable of adopting a subjective orientation, while objective moral judgments are rarely encountered in older children.

However, in an experiment designed to study the influence of models in transmitting and modifying children's moral judgments (Bandura and McDonald, 1963), objective and subjective moral judgments were found to exist together rather than as successive developmental stages. The vast majority of young children were capable of exercising subjective judgments and most of the older children displayed varying degrees of objective morality.

Children who exhibited predominantly objective and subjective moral orientations were then selected and exposed to adult models who consistently expressed moral judgments that were counter to the children's orientations. The provision of models was highly effective in altering the children's moral judgments. Objective children modified their moral orientations toward subjectivity and, similarly, subjective children became considerably more objective in their judgmental behavior. Furthermore, the children maintained their altered orientations in a new test situation in the absence of the models.

A second study (Bandura and Mischel, 1965), utilizing a similar design, demonstrates that other personality characteristics generally viewed as predetermined age-specific phenomena can also be altered through the application of appropriate social learning principles. Children who showed decided preferences for either immediate or delayed gratification observed adult models who displayed a self-gratification pattern opposite to the children's dominant tendencies. It was found that high-delay children increased their preference for immediate but less valued rewards after having witnessed models favoring immediate gratification; conversely, children who had exhibited a marked disposition toward immediate gratification increased their willingness to wait for more highly valued rewards following exposure to models exemplifying high-delay behavior.

Despite the voluminous clinical and theoretical literature pertaining to child development, the available body of empirically verified knowledge is comparatively meager. The recent years, however, have witnessed a new direction in theorizing about the developmental process which has generated considerable laboratory research within the framework of social learning theory. These studies are beginning to yield relatively unambiguous statements about the influence of particular antecedent events on the behavior and attitudes of children. This approach evidently holds promise of providing both more reliable guidelines for educational practice and the type of evidence necessary for discarding procedures that prove to be ineffective in, or even a hindrance to, the successful realization of desired developmental, educational, and psychotherapeutic objectives.

REFERENCES

BANDURA, A. Social learning through imitation. In M. R. Jones (Ed.), *Nebraska Symposium on Motivation*. Lincoln: Univ. of Nebraska Press, 1962, 211–269.

————. Influence of models' reinforcement contingencies on the acquisition of imitative responses. *J. pers. soc. Psychol.*, 1965, **1**, 589–595.

————, JOAN E. GRUSEC, and FRANCES L. MENLOVE. Vicarious extinction of avoidance behavior. *J. pers. soc. Psychol.*, 1967a, **5**, 16–23.

————. Some social determinants of self-monitoring reinforcement systems. *J. pers. soc. Psychol.*, 1967b, **5**, 449–455.

BANDURA, A., and MARY B. HARRIS. Modification of syntactic style. *J. exper. child Psychol.*, 1966, 341–352.

BANDURA, A., and ALETHA C. HUSTON. Identification as a process of incidental learning. *J. abnorm. soc. Psychol.*, 1961, **63**, 311–318.

BANDURA, A., and CAROL J. KUPERS. The transmission of patterns of self-reinforcement through modeling. *J. abnorm. soc. Psychol.*, 1964, **69**, 1–9.

BANDURA, A., and F. J. McDONALD. The influence of social reinforcement and the behavior of models in shaping children's moral judgments. *J. abnorm. soc. Psychol.*, 1963, **67**, 274–281.

BANDURA, A., and FRANCES L. MENLOVE. Psychotherapeutic application of symbolic modeling. Unpublished manuscript, Stanford Univ., 1967.

BANDURA, A., and W. MISCHEL. Modification of self-imposed delay of reward through exposure to live and symbolic models. *J. pers. soc. Psychol.*, 1965, **2**, 698–705.

BANDURA, A., and T. L. ROSENTHAL. Vicarious classical conditioning as a function of arousal level. *J. pers. soc. Psychol.*, 1966, **3**, 54–62.

BANDURA, A., DOROTHEA ROSS, and SHEILA A. ROSS. Transmission of aggression through imitation of aggressive models. *J. abnorm. soc. Psychol.*, 1961, **63**, 575–582.

———. Imitation of film-mediated aggressive models. *J. abnorm. soc. Psychol.*, 1963a, **66**, 3–11.

———. Vicarious reinforcement and imitative learning. *J. abnorm. soc. Psychol.*, 1963b, **67**, 601–607.

———. A comparative test of the status envy, social power, and secondary reinforcement theories of identificatory learning. *J. abnorm. soc. Psychol.*, 1963c, **67**, 527–534.

BANDURA, A., and R. H. WALTERS. *Social Learning and Personality Development.* New York: Holt, Rinehart & Winston, 1963.

BANDURA, A., and CAROL K. WHALEN. The influence of antecedent reinforcement and divergent modeling cues on patterns of self-reward. *J. pers. soc. Psychol.*, 1966, **3**, 54–62.

CHITTENDEN, GERTRUDE E. An experimental study in measuring and modifying assertive behavior in young children. *Monogr. Soc. Res. child Develpm.*, 1942, **7** (Serial No. 31).

HARTMANN, D. The influence of symbolically modeled instrumental aggression and pain cues on the disinhibition of aggressive behavior. Unpublished doctoral dissertation, Stanford Univ., 1965.

LOVAAS, O. I. Effect of exposure to symbolic aggression on aggressive behavior. *Child Develpm.*, 1961, **32**, 37–44.

MACCOBY, ELEANOR E. Role-taking in childhood and its consequences for social learning. *Child Develpm.*, 1959, **30**, 239–252.

MILNER, ESTHER. A study of the relationship between reading readiness and patterns of parent-child interaction. *Child Develpm.*, 1951, **22**, 95-112.

MISCHEL, W., and R. M. LIEBERT. Effects of discrepancies between observed and imposed reward criteria on their acquisition and transmission. *J. pers. soc. Psychol.*, 1966, **3**, 45–53.

MOWRER, O. H. *Learning Theory and the Symbolic Processes.* New York: John Wiley, 1960.

MUSSEN, P., and L. M. DISTLER. Child-rearing antecedents of masculine identification in kindergarten boys. *Child Develpm.*, 1960, **31**, 89–100.

MUSSEN, P., and E. RUTHERFORD. Effects of aggressive cartoons on children's aggressive play. *J. abnorm. soc. Psychol.*, 1961, **62**, 461–464.

PIAGET, J. *The Moral Judgment of the Child.* New York: The Free Press, 1948.

SIEGEL, ALBERTA E. Film-mediated fantasy aggression and strength of aggressive drive. *Child Develpm.*, 1956, **27**, 365–378.

WALTERS, R. H., E. LLEWELLYN-THOMAS, and C. W. ACKER. Enhancement of punitive behavior by audio-visual displays. *Science*, 1962, **136**, 872–873.

WHITING, J. W. M. Sorcery, sin, and the superego. In M. R. Jones (Ed.), *Nebraska Symposium on Motivation.* Lincoln: Univ. of Nebraska Press, 1959, 174–195.

———. Resource mediation and learning by identification. In I. Iscoe & H. W. Stevenson (Eds.), *Personality Development in Children.* Austin: Univ. of Texas Press, 1960, 112–126.

Laboratory studies of behavior are gradually providing us with the ability to predict, modify, and control the behavior of human subjects. Certainly the process of psychotherapy may be considered a form of behavior control and modification. In this selection, Frederick Kanfer discusses some of the ethical issues to be considered in determining the types of behavior which we might attempt to change and the specific techniques to be used in the actual modification process.

issues and ethics in behavior manipulation [1]

FREDERICK H. KANFER

Whenever a science is ready to apply its principles or methods to the control of man's social and physical environment, public attention demands that the consequences of such application be carefully examined. This scrutiny often results in argumentative debates and emotional alignment of the public vis-à-vis the science, its contents and its practitioners. The merciless beam of the public spotlight has by no means been confined to psychology. In our own time chemistry, physics and biology have repeatedly provided discoveries which the public viewed and discussed with alarm. Public concern usually declined gradually as scientific contributions were absorbed into the social fabric. Nevertheless, the vigor of recent public reactions to progress in the study and control of human behavior has taken our academically-minded science by surprise. Perhaps the sudden widespread concern with test makers, public opinion swayers, and adjustment manipulators simply indicates that psychology finally may have something to offer which has applicability in everyday life. The hope for eventual development of the psychology of behavioral control also raises the problem of the ethics of manipulating the behavior of another person. The most surprising aspect of the psychologist's dilemma posed by this problem is its recency. After all, the manipulation of behavior reportedly first took place when Eve whetted Adam's appetite in the Garden of Eden. For centuries the issues of morality and the control of one human being over another either have been kept separated or, in fact, combined in such absurd fashion that the most cruel methods of control were perpetrated under the guise of morality. The slaughter

[1] An earlier version of this paper was presented at a symposium of the Indiana Psychological Association in Indianapolis, April 1960. The revised paper was written in conjunction with research supported by Research grant MH 06922–03 from the National Institute of Mental Health, United States Public Health Service.

during the crusades, the elimination of witchcraft, the conquest of the American Indian, the "liberation" of Europe by the Nazis represent a few choice historical examples of human misbehavior and the use of the ultimate in behavior control through physical force and extermination. By comparison, the minor infraction committed currently when a psychotherapist subtly alters a neurotic patient's value system or his social behavior patterns seems rather mild. Nevertheless, numerous recent popular articles and books reflect the increasing public concern with the use of psychological methods in education, in industry, in the treatment of the mentally ill, and in politics.

The purpose of this paper is to discuss several issues concerning use of psychological principles in the manipulation of human behavior. These issues may arise in the context of psychology practiced in the clinic, in industry, by the military, or by governments. This paper will focus on behavior control by psychotherapy. The issues concern: (1) the methods of control, (2) the domain of controlled behavior, and (3) the selection of ends for which control is exercised.

control by reward versus punishment

With regard to the "psychology of behavior control" (Krasner, 1962a) in the clinic, the current sensitivity to the ethical issues stems largely from an increased proficiency in the control of behavior, and especially from a fear of one special kind of manipulation.[2] In the past, efforts toward improving control over adult behavior have mainly been directed at finding better

[2] While skeptics can point to evidence of current ignorance of even the most common determinants of individual behavior, few will doubt that rapid progress has been made in the last decade. We assume here that modification of individual behavior is feasible, though all the necessary controlling variables are not yet known.

methods of aversive control, e.g., by threat, coercion, or physical force. Currently, there is a tendency toward increasing use of control by positive reinforcement in all areas of life. This shift to promised rewards, and seductions rather than coercion represents, in our opinion, the pith of public concern. In his discussion of methods used by controlling agencies, Skinner (1953) suggests that government, law, and religion mainly use practices of threat of punishment, withdrawal of positive reinforcers, or presentation of negative reinforcers to achieve obedience. Further, with use of these methods by social agencies the usual "effect of group control is in conflict with a strong primarily reinforced behavior of the individual" (Skinner, 1953, p. 327). In contrast, economic control, education, and psychotherapy rely more heavily on positive reinforcement. Recently, control by positive reinforcement has been used extensively in programs of "ideological totalism" (Lifton, 1961). In practice such control is heightened when used only after achievement of complete control over the individual's environment and thought processes by force. As in laboratory animals, positive reinforcement is most effective following severe deprivation. If such deprivations can be created in human groups, success in behavior control should be markedly enhanced for the possessor of the positive reinforcers. The deliberate application of methods reserved earlier mostly for education, work achievement, child rearing and therapy, in politics and government represents a major innovation. Coupled with extension from control over individuals to control over groups, this advance in control techniques raises serious public concern. The shift in methods of control is illustrated in the history of psychotherapy by the progress from straitjackets, padded cells, and beatings to therapeutic communities, insight therapy, and counter-conditioning.

It is interesting to speculate why control by positive reinforcement might be more dangerous than control by coercion. Manipulation by aversive control creates its own hazards. The person under aversive control usually knows it. He suffers pain, experiences humiliation, anger, or other emotional discomfort. It is also likely that aversive control inevitably breeds attempts at counter-control. Even in the young child the first response to being slapped is to try to slap back. Aversive control thus motivates behavior aimed at reducing such control by annoying, teasing, or destroying the controller. Further, aversive control is difficult to maintain by a small group. To use force effectively you have to be bigger, stronger, or more numerous than your adversary. Thus aversive control by an individual over a large group, or by a small minority is doomed to failure in the long run. Finally, as Skinner (1953) has indicated, aversive control affects only public behavior. It is of limited use in "thought control" because a person can escape some aversive consequences by thinking silently or by nonconforming behavior in his private experiences.

In contrast, manipulation by positive control produces none of these disturbing by-products. By definition these methods use reinforcing stimuli which have the inherent potential for increasing or maintaining behaviors which procure these stimuli. People respond in blind faith to reward, to promises, and to reassurances. Large-scale use of these methods, however, has not concerned people because the age-old deceptions of the Pied Piper have been assumed to be sufficiently transparent to allow most adults to recognize them as false promises and to resist temptation by persuasion. Recently, Browning's Pied Piper of Hamlin has become more sophisticated. He has put on the disguise of a gray flannel suit, of a human relationship expert, a psychotherapist, or a friendly interrogator in a prison camp. His pipe has turned into other instruments promising such sweet things as affection and happiness to a juvenile delinquent, money-back guaranteed satisfaction with soaps and cereals, or a

political paradise for the masses, all without pain, coercion, or physical violence. This increased professionalism and sophistication in the application of psychological principles has caused uneasiness to the public because the methods have lost some of their transparency and amateurish quality. Although there is contradictory experimental evidence on the question of behavioral modification without awareness (Eriksen, 1962; Kanfer and Marston, 1961), these studies also clearly indicate that Ss cannot verbalize all aspects of the controlling stimuli which affect their behavior.

Certainly, the increase in psychological sophistication has also made it easier for the controller to disguise his own motives in order to mislead Ss of his controlling influence. In addition, he can manipulate conditions which would make positive reinforcement more effective. Frank (1961) makes this point in discussing the methods of thought reform: "[T]he essence of the relationship is that the persuader invests great effort to bring about changes in the sufferer's bodily state or attitudes that he regards as beneficial . . . [and the setting] . . . occurs in the context of hope and potential support from the persuader and the group" (1961, p. 95). Since our democratic principles also uphold the right of consent of the governed, any use of control resulting in a change of behavior without S's awareness of the methods of influence and the intent of his controllers would be ethically objectionable to our society. Even though these emphases placed upon self-control, self-government, and self-determination are accepted by our culture and its scientist members, a deterministic behavioral psychology cannot disavow its implication that behavior is controlled by an organism's previous history and its environment, regardless of its ability to describe verbally these controlling variables. Regardless of ethic or social interest the fiction of the complete Rational Man as the captain of his own destiny, is as naive to behavioristic psychology as it was to Freudian psychoanalysis (although for different reasons).

In psychotherapy, social pressures or other devices attempting to manipulate the patient's behavior by coercion are rarely used as a primary method of control. Therapeutic operations are more likely to stress positive goals, to reduce tensions, to reinforce and strengthen new behaviors. The therapist is, of course, at an additional disadvantage in the use of aversive controls. When the therapist acts as a noxious stimulus the patient can counter by "resistance," by failing to keep his appointments, or by leaving the field altogether. Patients under strong aversive control by parental pressure or by court order are notoriously poor risks for psychotherapy.

control of private experiences

The inevitability of mutual influence in a clinical relationship is well documented by recent research and some of its implications have been discussed by Krasner (1962a).

What are some of the features then which make the psychotherapeutic interaction or other similar relationships especially suited for the manipulation or control of behavior?

One factor is the distress and discomfort of the patient. The social role of the patient has been described by Parsons (Parsons and Fox, 1958). In our society the sick person can claim certain privileges. It is assumed that he is not responsible for his incapacity, and his state of sickness exempts him from his normal social obligations. In turn, it is understood that he will attempt to get well and that he has an obligation to seek help and cooperate with others who treat him. As Parsons states, the latter implies a dependency of the sick person on the healer. The act of coming for help signifies the patient's realization that he cannot cope with the problem and that he wishes another person to take responsibility for treating it. This dependency status should tend to increase the effectiveness of

the therapist's reinforcing operations (cf., research on the role of dependency, prestige, and other therapist-patient variables in verbal conditioning; Greenspoon, 1962; Krasner, 1962b).

A second feature concerns the *content* of the interactions. Most psychologists agree that the specific content of the patient's verbalizations in psychotherapy is far less important than was believed by earlier theorists. One common element in all therapeutic interactions is the therapist's insistence that the patient talk about those private experiences, fears, attitudes, and beliefs which are usually not shared with other people. Recent reviews by William Sargant (1957), Jerome Frank (1961) and Robert Lifton (1961) of methods of persuasion, thought reform, and therapy all suggest that the most successful methods of behavior manipulation, including magic, religion, and political coercion, share the requirement that the person publicly expose at least some of his privately held beliefs and attitudes. This accessibility to personal and private behavior, in turn, makes the person more vulnerable to control. The more behavior is exposed to the controlling agent the easier it is to set up conditions which modify behavior. Lifton (1961) points out that the admissions of guilt over minimal crimes against the state in Chinese "brainwashing" camps and universities provide the opportunity for the controller to reinforce such self-accusing behavior, to promise relief from guilt by self-punishing procedures and generally to weaken existing behavior and introduce new responses.

Privacy, the inaccessibility of much personal behavior in a democratic society, probably represents the bulwark of democracy because it allows for variability, and for divergence of attitudes and beliefs. What is jealously guarded as a right to privacy in everyday life is, in fact, surrendered in the psychotherapeutic hour. The consequences of this making accessible of the patient's private experiences have been discussed elsewhere (Kanfer, 1961). The potentials for controlling important behavioral sequences, usually not subject to control by direct social reinforcement, increase very much the extent of the therapist's influence.

metavalues and personal values

Clinicians are beginning to accept the thesis that the therapist's value system tends to affect the direction of the patient's change in treatment (Rosenthal, 1955; Schrier, 1953). Among the many problems raised by this recognition are the methods of handling valued material (e.g., Ellis, 1962; Meehl, 1959; Segal, 1959), and the ethical implications of the intrusion of personal values into psychotherapy (Weisskopf-Joelson, 1953; Williamson, 1958). Existential analysis (Weisskopf-Joelson, 1958) assumes that the purpose of treatment is the realization of creative and attitudinal values and this school frankly admits its value-orientation.

Although the term "value" is difficult to define, two separate aspects relating to the problem of control in psychotherapy are worthy of mention.

There are clear-cut rules for many behaviors which are common to practically all members of a given culture. These rules are usually also accepted by the therapist and his client. We will call these *metavalues* (cultural values). In addition, there is a variety of situations in which several alternate behaviors and goal hierarchies are equally tolerated by society but which differ in the degree to which they lead to satisfaction in the individual. These alternatives are determined primarily by the individual's past experience. We shall call these alternatives *personal values*. Complications arise both in the patient's value system and in the psychotherapy relationship because of the inconsistencies between metavalues and personal values. Interpretation of the cultural metavalues further

varies as a function of membership in a subgroup such as a socioeconomic, religious, or geographic affiliation. The outcome of therapy should provide a wider choice of alternative behaviors for the patient with the only restriction that the new behaviors must also be compatible with the metavalues of the patient's cultural environment. The problem lies mainly in producing those changes which lead to socially acceptable behavior even while they result in sweeping changes in the life pattern of the patient. For example, therapists generally do not disagree whether to manipulate behavior which may avert a suicide, but they *do* disagree whether a client's vocational or marital choice should be modified. In complete absence of standards for such personal and private modes of behavior the therapist's judgments are based mainly on his theoretical orientation, on his own experiences and on his own personal values. These therapist experiences then become the standards for selecting the goals for a particular patient in psychotherapy.[3]

In most cases the neurotic patient can be of little help in deciding what personal values need changing and what range of alternatives would be tolerated both by him and by his environment. When a patient *is* able to do this, the therapist's job does not involve the problem of values. The patient might indicate that he wishes to improve his study habits or seek technical help in making a vocational choice. In these cases technical skills by the psychologist may be applied directly to a problem with an outcome defined clearly by the client himself. Unfortunately, therapists sometimes become suspicious even in these cases and the desirability of the patient's stated goal is often

---

[3] If all mental health workers were to share a single set of values their influence would carry with it the same dangers as any system of total control. A requirement of strict conformity to the mores and values set up by the therapist's model of behavior is also tantamount to the complete subservience imposed by totalistic control systems.

questioned by therapists from the viewpoint of their own personal value systems. Endowed with a tradition of depth-probing, many a therapist is tempted to substitute his own goal for that of the patient. Instead of rendering technical assistance in a circumscribed area, the therapist may then attempt to change the patient's total pattern of living.

rules for control

The most heated arguments are generated by the question, "Who establishes the legitimacy of means and ends in behavioral control?" The writer does not presume to have a solution to this question, but wishes to present a few thoughts designed to stimulate further debate.

The APA attempted to indicate the limitations of appropriate means and ends for psychological practice in its early code of ethics (1953). Principle 1.12–1 (p. 7) reads in part: "[T]he psychologist's ultimate allegiance is to society, and his professional behavior should demonstrate awareness of his social responsibilities. The welfare of the profession and of the individual psychologist are clearly subordinate to the welfare of the public." Further, Principle 1.13–1 (p. 10): "The psychologist should express in his professional behavior a firm commitment to those values which lie at the foundation of a democratic society, such as freedom of speech, freedom of research, and respect for the integrity of the individual." While these statements arouse the unqualified support of all good psychologists, they do not help to resolve the conflict inherent in the problem of treating neurotic patients. On the one hand, as citizens in a democratic society, psychologists believe that every person has the right to make his own free choice about his way of life. One the other hand, as professionals they also recognize that people who are in difficulties should be helped and choices must often be made for them. The clinical psychologist is an expert in assessing and

modifying human behavior by virtue of his training. Regardless of the limitations of psychological theories and methods, psychologists constitute a profession (some say the only profession) which offers extensive training in behavior theory and in methods used to assist people with psychological problems. Therefore, the psychologist is better prepared to apply his knowledge than the layman.[4] However, as noted above, there is a difference between competence in bringing about behavioral changes and in judging the desirability of the behavior and the value system to be substituted. The clinician cannot accept sole responsibility for judging the adequacy of the individual's value system, nor can he become the ultimate interpreter of cultural meta-values to the patient by psychotherapy or education. In clinical practice, the patient, his social milieu and other significant persons in his life must all be considered in selecting appropriate goals for therapy.

Nor can psychology be held responsible for the application of its principles and methods by social agencies or industry in the fields of government, economics, or education. Decisions concerning the legitimacy of means and ends in use of behavioral control methods are no more the responsibility of the psychologist than is the question whether to use atomic weapons in a war in the area of competence of the physicist, or the decision to adopt sterilization procedures with some humans in the domain of the biologist. In the absence of any specific mandate from the social community through its legal, political, religious, or social agencies psychologists will continue to use methods of control which are sometimes not acceptable to the public and use these for purposes about which there is some debate.

---

[4] We recognize that personality variables as yet unexplored may be important determinants of therapist effectiveness. But no scientifically grounded profession can fail to assume that additional didactic training is a necessary, if not sufficient, condition for practice.

There has already been some indication that psychological knowledge is gradually becoming incorporated into the legal system, providing some standards of behavior which are more consistent with our knowledge of man than many current laws. There is, however, a considerable lag between mores and their incorporation into the legal structure of a society. During this lag professional groups will have to provide leadership in working out rules which describe the goals for which individual human behavior may be manipulated, and the restrictions upon methods under which this purpose is to be accomplished.

When the psychologist leaves his immediate work setting, his conduct falls under the rules by which other social groups operate. A social scientist who publicly gives opinions about the implications of behavior control techniques for international politics, education, or consumer behavior must expect the same treatment as other public figures who champion controversial issues. It is probably this change in the accustomed reaction from student or patient audiences which has made psychologists so reluctant to participate in public debate and to provide information and guidance to social groups. An additional problem, of course, lies in the thin line of distinction between fact and opinion, between researcher and reformer.

From these considerations it seems that several specific contributions can be made by psychologists to further public recognition of the social implications of recent advances in psychology.

1. In their role as scientists, continuing research on behavioral control methods and on factors limiting their effects to special circumstances should provide clearer understanding of the extent of the problem in practical situations. Research findings already exist which tend to suggest that total behavioral control requires a totally controlled environment; that verbal (and attitudinal) behavior can be influenced by a variety of variables toward maximal or min-imal change; and that self-control training can modify the effect of incentives, thereby reducing greatly the utility of many conditioning procedures. Knowledge of these factors should permit a better estimate of the actual threat inherent in practical methods to which objections are currently raised. If recently described methods turn out to be no more effective than previous controlling devices, or if easy countermeasures are available, no further concern or action would be warranted.

2. With no special prerogatives to dictate to society the rules by which its members should be educated, controlled, or changed, psychologists as educated citizens can make a contribution as resource persons to established social agencies. These activities demand of the consultant that he explicitly distinguish between facts, interpretation of facts, and his personal opinion.

3. Our discussion suggests that continued public awareness of the growing effectiveness of psychological techniques may present the best safeguards against their misapplication. Ultimately, the products of any science become public property and only the informed public can wisely regulate their use.

4. If psychologists have a service to perform in society's effort to evaluate itself, it is the scientific analysis of current psychological practices, embedded in our social matrix. Among those are many which appear to have relevance to the control of *individual* behavior, i.e., practices in education, in law-enforcement, in treatment of emotional adjustment, in consumer persuasion, and in industrial personnel procedures. Contributions to each of these fields lie not only in suggestions for changes but also in a thorough analysis of the present practices and their consequences.

REFERENCES

ELLIS, A. *Reason and Emotion in Psychotherapy.* New York: Lyle Stuart, 1962.

ERIKSEN, C. W. (Ed.) *Behavior and Awareness.* Durham: Duke University Press, 1962.

FRANK, J. D. *Persuasion and Healing: A Comparative Study of Psychotherapy.* Baltimore: Johns Hopkins Press, 1961.

GREENSPOON, J. "Verbal Conditioning and Clinical Psychology." In A. J. Bachrach (Ed.), *Experimental Foundations of Clinical Psychology.* New York: Basic Books, 1962, pp. 510–553.

KANFER, F. H. "Comments on Learning in Psychotherapy," *Psychol. Rep.,* 1961, 9, 681–699.

———, and A. R. MARSTON. "Verbal Conditioning, Ambiguity and Psychotherapy," *Psychol. Rep.,* 1961, 9, 461–475.

KRASNER, L. "Behavior Control and Social Responsibility," *Amer. Psychologist,* 1962a, 17, 199–204.

———. "The Therapist as a Social Reinforcement Machine." In H. Strupp and L. Luborsky (Eds.), *Research in Psychotherapy.* Washington: APA, 1962b, pp. 61–95.

LIFTON, R. J. *Thought Reform and the Psychology of Totalism.* New York: Norton, 1961.

MEEHL, P. E. "Some Technical and Axiological Problems in the Therapeutic Handling of Religious and Valuational Material," *J. counsel. Psychol.,* 1959, 6, 255–259.

PARSONS, T., and R. Fox. "Illness, Therapy and the Modern Urban Family." In E. G. Jaco (Ed.), *Patients, Physicians and Illness.* New York: The Free Press, 1958, pp. 234–245.

ROSENTHAL, D. "Changes in Some Moral Values Following Psychotherapy," *J. consult. Psychol.,* 1955, 19, 431–436.

SARGANT, W. *Battle for the Mind: A Physiology of Conversion and Brainwashing.* Garden City, N.Y.: Doubleday, 1957.

SCHRIER, H. "The Significance of Identification in Therapy," *Amer. J. Orthopsychiat.,* 1953, 23, 585–604.

SEGAL, S. J. "The Role of the Counselor's Religious Values in Counseling," *J. counsel. Psychol.,* 1959, 6, 270–274.

SKINNER, B. F. *Science and Human Behavior.* New York: Macmillan, 1953.

WEISSKOPF-JOELSON, E. "Some Suggestions Concerning Weltanschauung and Psychotherapy," *J. abnorm. soc. Psychol.,* 1953, 48, 601–604.

———. "Logotherapy and Existential Analysis," *Acta Psychother., psychosomat. Orthopaed.,* 1958, 6, 193–204.

WILLIAMSON, E. G. "Value Orientation in Counseling," *Personnel Guid. J.,* 1958, 36, 520–528.

27

When one considers the strong differences of opinion about the use of marihuana and related psychoactive drugs, it is appalling that so few of the arguments (on both sides) are based on reliable evidence. In the next article Weil, Zinberg, and Nelsen discuss some of the methodological problems with the older research on the effects of marihuana. Their own recent research and conclusions concerning the physiological and psychological effects of the drug are then discussed in considerable detail. The student should be aware that the new results reported here are from a small sample of subjects who were studied for a relatively short period of time, using a limited range of drug dosages. Although the results are certainly important, a responsible scientist would not yet make sweeping generalizations from them. The article does indicate that careful research is both warranted and feasible and that behavioral scientists have an important role in such investigations.

clinical and psychological effects of marihuana in man

ANDREW T. WEIL

NORMAN E. ZINBERG

JUDITH M. NELSEN

In the spring of 1968 we conducted a series of pilot experiments on acute marihuana intoxication in human subjects. The study

This work was conducted in the Behavioral Pharmacology Laboratory of the Boston University School of Medicine, sponsored and supported by its division of psychiatry, in part through PHS grants MH12568, MH06795-06, MH7753-06, and MH33319, and the Boston University Medical Center. The authors thank Dr. P. H. Knapp and Dr. C. Kornetsky of the Boston University School of Medicine, Department of Psychiatry and Pharmacology, for consistent support and excellent advice, and J. Finkelstein of New York City for his support at a crucial time.

was not undertaken to prove or disprove popularly held convictions about marihuana as an intoxicant, to compare it with other drugs, or to introduce our own opinions. Our concern was simply to collect some long overdue pharmacological data. In this article we describe the primitive state of knowledge of the drug, the research problems encountered in designing a replicable study, and the results of our investigations.

Marihuana is a crude preparation of flowering tops, leaves, seeds, and stems of female plants of Indian hemp *Cannabis sativa* L.; it is usually smoked. The intoxicating constituents of hemp are found in the sticky resin exuded by the tops of the plants, particularly the females. Male plants produce some resin but are grown mainly for hemp fiber, not for marihuana. The resin itself, when prepared for smoking or eating, is known as "hashish." Various *Cannabis* preparations are used as intoxicants throughout the world; their potency varies directly with the amount of resin present.[1] Samples of American marihuana differ greatly in pharmacological activity, depending on their composition (tops contain most resin; stems, seeds, and lower leaves least) and on the conditions under which the plants were grown. In addition, different varieties of *Cannabis* probably produce resins with different proportions of constituents.[2] Botanists feel that only one species of hemp exists, but work on the phytochemistry of the varieties of this species is incomplete.[3] Chronic users claim that samples of marihuana differ in quality of effects as well as in potency; that some types cause a preponderance of physical symptoms, and that other types tend to cause greater distortions of perception or of thought.

Pharmacological studies of *Cannabis* indicate that the tetrahydrocannabinol fraction of the resin is the active portion. In 1965, Mechoulam and Gaoni[4] reported the first total synthesis of $(-)$ Δ^1-*trans*-tetrahydrocannabinol (THC), which they called "the psychotomimetically active constituent of hashish (marihuana)." Synthetic THC is now available for research in very limited supply.

In the United States, the use of *Cannabis* extracts as therapeutics goes back to the 19th century, but it was not until the 1920's that use of marihuana as an intoxicant by

migrant Mexican laborers, urban Negroes, and certain Bohemian groups caused public concern.[5] Despite increasingly severe legal penalties imposed during the 1930's, use of marihuana continued in these relatively small populations without great public uproar or apparent changes in numbers or types of users until the last few years. The fact that almost none of the studies devoted to the physiological and psychological effects of *Cannabis* in man was based on controlled laboratory experimentation escaped general notice. But with the explosion of use in the 1960's, at first on college campuses followed by a spread downward to secondary schools and upward to a portion of the established middle class, controversy over the dangers of marihuana generated a desire for more objective information about the drug.

Of the three known studies on human subjects performed by Americans, the first [6] was done in the Canal Zone with 34 soldiers; the consequences reported were hunger and hyperphagia, loss of inhibitions, increased pulse rate with unchanged blood pressure, a tendency to sleep, and unchanged performance of psychological and neurological tests. Doses and type of marihuana were not specified.

The second study, known as the 1944 LaGuardia Report,[7] noted that 72 prisoners, 48 of whom were previous *Cannabis* users, showed minimum physiological responses, but suffered impaired intellectual functioning and decreased body steadiness, especially well demonstrated by nonusers after high doses. Basic personality structures remained unchanged as subjects reported feelings of relaxation, disinhibition, and self-confidence. In that study, the drug was administered orally as an extract. No

---

[1] R. J. Bouquet, *Bull. Narcotics*, **2** (1950), 14.

[2] F. Korte and H. Sieper, in *Hashish: Its Chemistry and Pharmacology*, G. E. W. Wolstenholme and J. Knight, Eds. (Boston: Little, Brown, 1965), pp. 15–30.

[3] Task Force on Narcotics and Drug Abuse, the President's Commission on Law Enforcement and the Administration of Justice, *Task Force Report: Narcotics and Drug Abuse* (1967), p. 14.

[4] R. Mechoulam, and Y. Gaoni, *J. Amer. Chem. Soc.*, **67** (1965), 3273.

[5] *Task Force Report, op. cit.*

[6] See J. F. Siler, W. L. Sheep, L. B. Bates, G. F. Clark, G. W. Cook, and W. A. Smith, *Mil. Surg.* (November 1933), pp. 269–280.

[7] Mayor's Committee on Marihuana, *The Marihuana Problem in the City of New York*, 1944.

controls were described, and doses and quality of marihuana were unspecified.

Williams *et al.* in 1946 [8] studied a small number of prisoners who were chronic users; they were chiefly interested in effects of long-term smoking on psychological functioning. They found an initial exhilaration and euphoria which gave way after a few days of smoking to indifference and lassitude that somewhat impaired performance requiring concentration and manual dexterity. Again, no controls were provided.

Predictably, these studies, each deficient in design for obtaining reliable physiological and psychological data, contributed no dramatic or conclusive results. The 1967 President's Commission on Law Enforcement and the Administration of Justice decribed the present state of knowledge by concluding [9]: ". . . no careful and detailed analysis of the American experience [with marihuana] seems to have been attempted. Basic research has been almost nonexistent. . . ." Since then, no other studies with marihuana itself have been reported, but in 1967 Isbell [10] administered synthetic THC to chronic users. At doses of 120 μg/kg orally or 50μg/kg by smoking, subjects reported this drug to be similar to marihuana. At higher doses (300 to 400 μg/kg orally or 200 to 250 μg/kg by smoking) psychotomimetic effects occurred in most subjects. This synthetic has not yet been compared with marihuana in nonusers or given to any subjects along with marihuana in double-blind fashion.

Investigations outside the United States have been scientifically deficient, and for the most part have been limited to anecdotal and sociological approaches.[11] So far

as we know, our study is the first attempt to investigate marihuana in a formal double-blind experiment with the appropriate controls. It is also the first attempt to collect basic clinical and psychological information on the drug by observing its effects on marihuana-naive human subjects in a neutral laboratory setting.

research problems

That valid basic research on marihuana is almost nonexistent is not entirely accounted for by legislation which restricts even legitimate laboratory investigations or by public reaction sometimes verging on hysteria. A number of obstacles are intrinsic to the study of this drug. We now present a detailed description of our specific experimental approach, but must comment separately on six general problems confronting the investigator who contemplates marihuana research.

1. Concerning the route of administration, many pharmacologists dismiss the possibility of giving marihuana by smoking because, they say, the dose cannot be standardized.[12] We consider it not only possible, but important to administer the drug to humans by smoking rather than by the oral route for the following reasons. (i) Smoking is the way nearly all Americans use marihuana. (ii) It is possible to have subjects smoke marihuana cigarettes in such a way that drug dosage is reasonably uniform for all subjects. (iii) Standardization of dose is not assured by giving the drug orally because little is known about gastrointestinal absorption of the highly water-insoluble cannabinols in man.

[8] E. G. Williams, C. K. Himmelsbach, A. Winkler, D. C. Ruble, and B. J. Lloyd, *Public Health Rep.*, 61 (1946), 1059.

[9] *Task Force Report, op. cit.*

[10] H. Isbell, *Psychopharmacologia*, 11 (1967), 184.

[11] I. C. Chopra and R. N. Chopra, *Bull. Narcotics*, 9 (1957), 4; F. Ames, *J. Ment. Sci.*, 104 (1958), 972; C. J. Miras, in *Hashish: Its Chemistry and Pharmacology*, G. E. W. Wolstenholme and

J. Knight, Eds. (Boston: Little, Brown, 1965), pp. 37–47; and J. M. Watt, in *Hashish: Its Chemistry and Pharmacology*, G. E. W. Wolstenholme and J. Knight, Eds. (Boston: Little, Brown, 1965), pp. 54–66.

[12] AMA Council on Mental Health, *J. Amer. Med. Ass.*, 204 (1968), 1181.

(iv) There is considerable indirect evidence from users that the quality of the intoxication is different when marihuana or preparations of it are ingested rather than smoked. In particular, ingestion seems to cause more powerful effects, more "LSD-like" effects, longer-lasting effects, and more hangovers.[13] Further, marihuana smokers are accustomed to a very rapid onset of action due to efficient absorption through the lungs, whereas the latency for onset of effects may be 45 or 60 minutes after ingestion. (v) There is reported evidence from experiments with rats and mice that the pharmacological activities of natural hashish (not subjected to combustion) and hashish sublimate (the combustion products) are different.[14]

2. Until quite recently, it was extremely difficult to estimate the relative potencies of different samples of marihuana by the techniques of analytical chemistry. For this study, we were able to have the marihuana samples assayed spectrophotometrically[15] for THC content. However, since THC has not been established as the sole determinant of marihuana's activity, we still feel it is important to have chronic users sample and rate marihuana used in research. Therefore, we assayed our material by this method as well.

3. One of the major deficiencies in previous studies has been the absence of negative control or placebo treatments, which we consider essential to the design of this kind of investigation. Because marihuana smoke has a distinctive odor and taste, it is difficult to find an effective placebo for use with chronic users. The problem is much less difficult with nonusers. Our solution to this dilemma was the use of portions of male hemp stalks,[16] devoid of THC, in the placebo cigarettes.

4. In view of the primitive state of knowledge about marihuana, it is difficult to predict which psychological tests will be sensitive to the effects of the drug. The tests we chose were selected because, in addition to being likely to demonstrate effects, they have been used to evaluate many other psychoactive drugs. Of the various physiological parameters available, we chose to measure (i) heart rate, because previous studies have consistently reported increases in heart rate after administration of marihuana[17]; (ii) respiratory rate, because it is an easily measured vital sign, and depression has been reported[18]; (iii) pupil size, because folklore on effects of marihuana consistently includes reports of pupillary dilatation, although objective experimental evidence of an effect of the drug on pupils has not been sought; (iv) conjunctival appearance, because both marihuana smokers and eaters are said to develop red eyes[19]; and (v) blood sugar, because hypoglycemia has been invoked as a cause of the hunger and hyperphagia commonly reported by marihuana users, but animal and human evidence of this effect is contradictory.[20] (The LaGuardia Report, quoted by Jaffe in Goodman and Gilman[21] described hyperglycemia as an effect of acute intoxication.) We did not measure blood pressure because previous studies have failed to demonstrate any consistent effect on blood pressure in man, and

[16] We thank R. H. Pace and E. H. Hall of the Peter J. Schweitzer Division of the Kimberly-Clark Corp. for supplying placebo material.

[17] For example, Siler *et al., op. cit.*

[18] Miras, *op. cit.*; and S. Garattini, in *Hashish: Its Chemistry and Pharmacology*, G. E. W. Wolstenholme and J. Knight, Eds. (Boston: Little, Brown, 1965), pp. 70–78.

[19] Miras, *ibid.*

[20] *The Marihuana Problem in . . . New York*; Ames; and Miras; all *op. cit.*

[21] J. H. Jaffee, in *The Pharmacological Basis of Therapeutics*, L. S. Goodman and A. Gilman, Eds. (New York: Macmillan, 3rd ed., 1965), pp. 299–301.

[13] Watt, *op. cit.*; and G. Joachimoglu, in *Hashish: Its Chemistry and Pharmacology*, G. E. W. Wolstenholme and J. Knight, Eds. (Boston: Little, Brown, 1965), pp. 2–10.

[14] Joachimoglu, *ibid.*

[15] We thank M. Lerner and A. Bober of the U.S. Customs Laboratory, Baltimore, for performing this assay.

we were unwilling to subject our volunteers to a nonessential annoyance.

5. It is necessary to control set and setting. "Set" refers to the subject's psychological expectations of what a drug will do to him in relation to his general personality structure. The total environment in which the drug is taken is the setting. All indications are that the form of marihuana intoxication is particularly dependent on the interaction of drug, set, and setting. Because of recent increases in the extent of use and in attention given this use by the mass media, it is difficult to find subjects with a neutral set toward marihuana. Our method of selecting subjects (described below), at the least, enabled us to identify the subjects' attitudes. Unfortunately, too many researchers have succumbed to the temptation to have subjects take drugs in "psychedelic" environments or have influenced the response to the drug by asking questions that disturb the setting. Even a question as simple as, "How do you feel?" contains an element of suggestion that alters the drug-set-setting interaction. We took great pains to keep our laboratory setting neutral by strict adherence to an experimental timetable and to a prearranged set of conventions governing interactions between subjects and experimenters.

6. Medical, social, ethical, and legal concerns about the welfare of subjects are a major problem in a project of this kind. Is it ethical to introduce people to marihuana? When can subjects safely be sent home from the laboratory? What kind of follow-up care, if any, should be given? These are only a few specific questions with which the investigator must wrestle. Examples of some of the precautions we took are as follows. (i) All subjects were volunteers. All were given psychiatric screening interviews and were clearly informed that they might be asked to smoke marihuana. All nonusers tested were persons who had reported that they had been planning to try marihuana. (ii) All subjects were driven home by an experimenter; they agreed not to engage in unusual activity or operate machinery until the next morning and to report any unusual, delayed effects. (iii) All subjects agreed to report for follow-up interviews 6 months after the experiment. Among other things, the check at 6 months should answer the question whether participation in the experiment encouraged further drug use. (iv) All subjects were protected from possible legal repercussions of their participation in these experiments by specific agreements with the Federal Bureau of Narcotics, the Office of the Attorney General of Massachusetts, and the Massachusetts Bureau of Drug Abuse and Drug Control.[22]

subjects

The central group of subjects consisted of nine healthy, male volunteers, 21 to 26 years of age, all of whom smoked tobacco cigarettes regularly but had never tried marihuana previously. Eight chronic users of marihuana also participated, both to "assay" the quality of marihuana received from the Federal Bureau of Narcotics and to enable the experimenters to standardize the protocol, using subjects familiar with their responses to the drug. The age range for users was also 21 to 26 years. They all smoked marihuana regularly, most of them every day or every other day.

The nine "naive" subjects were selected after a careful screening process. An initial pool of prospective subjects was obtained by placing advertisements in the student newspapers of a number of universities in the Boston area. These advertisements sought "male volunteers, at least 21 years old, for psychological experiments." After

[22] We thank E. L. Richardson, Attorney General of the Commonwealth of Massachusetts for permitting these experiments to proceed and N. L. Chayet for legal assistance. We do not consider it appropriate to describe here the opposition we encountered from governmental agents and agencies and from university bureaucracies.

nonsmokers were eliminated from this pool, the remaining volunteers were interviewed individually by a psychiatrist who determined their histories of use of alcohol and other intoxicants as well as their general personality types. In addition to serving as a potential screening technique to eliminate volunteers with evidence of psychosis, or of serious mental or personality disorder, these interviews served as the basis for the psychiatrist's prediction of the type of response an individual subject might have after smoking marihuana. (It should be noted that no marihuana-naive volunteer had to be disqualified on psychiatric grounds.) Only after a prospective subject passed the interview was he informed that the "psychological experiment" for which he had volunteered was a marihuana study. If he consented to participate, he was asked to sign a release, informing him that he would be "expected to smoke cigarettes containing marihuana or an inert substance." He was also required to agree to a number of conditions, among them that he would "during the course of the experiment take no psychoactive drugs, including alcohol, other than those drugs administered in the course of the experiment."

It proved extremely difficult to find marihuana-naive persons in the student population of Boston, and nearly 2 months of interviewing were required to obtain nine men. All those interviewed who had already tried marihuana volunteered this information quite freely and were delighted to discuss their use of drugs with the psychiatrist. Nearly all persons encountered who had not tried marihuana admitted this somewhat apologetically. Several said they had been meaning to try the drug but had not got around to it. A few said they had no access to it. Only one person cited the current laws as his reason for not having experimented with marihuana. It seemed clear in the interviews that many of these persons were actually afraid of how they might react to marihuana; they therefore welcomed a chance to smoke it under medi-

cal supervision. Only one person (an Indian exchange student) who passed the screening interview refused to participate after learning the nature of the experiment.

The eight heavy users of marihuana were obtained with much less difficulty. They were interviewed in the same manner as the other subjects and were instructed not to smoke any marihuana on the day of their appointment in the laboratory.

Subjects were questioned during screening interviews and at the conclusion of the experiments to determine their knowledge of marihuana effects. None of the nine naive subjects had ever watched anyone smoke marihuana or observed anyone high on marihuana. Most of them knew of the effects of the drug only through reports in the popular press. Two subjects had friends who used marihuana frequently; one of these (No. 4) announced his intention to "prove" in the experiments that marihuana really did not do anything; the other (No. 3) was extremely eager to get high because "everyone I know is always talking about it very positively."

setting

Greatest effort was made to create a neutral setting. That is, subjects were made comfortable and secure in a pleasant suite of laboratories and offices, but the experimental staff carefully avoided encouraging any person to have an enjoyable experience. Subjects were never asked how they felt, and no subject was permitted to discuss the experiment with the staff until he had completed all four sessions. Verbal interactions between staff and subjects were minimum and formal. At the end of each session, subjects were asked to complete a brief form asking whether they thought they had smoked marihuana that night; if so, whether a high dose or a low dose; and how confident they were of their answers. The experimenters completed similar forms on each subject.

marihuana

Marihuana used in these experiments was of Mexican origin, supplied by the Federal Bureau of Narcotics.[23] It consisted of finely chopped leaves of *Cannabis,* largely free of seeds and stems. An initial batch, which was judged to be of low potency by the experimenters on the basis of the doses needed to produce symptoms of intoxication in the chronic users, was subsequently found to contain only 0.3 percent of THC by weight. A second batch, assayed at 0.9 percent THC, was rated by the chronic users to be "good, average" marihuana, neither exceptionally strong nor exceptionally weak compared to their usual supplies. Users consistently reported symptoms of intoxication after smoking about 0.5 gram of the material with a variation of only a few puffs from subject to subject. This second batch of marihuana was used in the experiments described below; the low dose was 0.5 gram, and the high dose was 2.0 grams.

All marihuana was administered in the form of cigarettes of standard size made with a hand-operated rolling machine. In any given experimental session, each person was required to smoke two cigarettes in succession (Table 1).

Placebo material consisted of the chopped outer covering of mature stalks of male hemp plants; it contained no THC. All cigarettes had a tiny plug of tobacco at one end and a plug of paper at the other end so that the contents were not visible. The length to which each cigarette was to be smoked was indicated by an ink line. Marihuana and placebos were administered to the naive subjects in double-blind fashion. Scented aerosols were sprayed in the laboratory before smoking, to mask the odor of marihuana. The protocol during an experimental session was as follows. The sessions began at approximately 5.30 P.M.

time	procedure
0:00	Physiological measurements; blood sample drawn
0:05	Psychological test battery No. 1 (base line)
0:35	Verbal sample No. 1
0:40	Cigarette smoking
1:00	Rest period
1:15	Physiological measurements; blood sample drawn
1:20	Psychological test battery No. 2
1:50	Verbal sample No. 2
1:55	Rest period (supper)
2:30	Physiological measurements
2:35	Psychological test battery No. 3
3:05	End of testing

table 1

composition of the dose. The placebo cigarette consisted of placebo material, tobacco filler, and mint leaves for masking flavor. The low dose was made up of marihuana, tobacco filler, and mint leaves. The high dose consisted of marihuana and mint leaves.

dose	marihuana in each cigarette (g)	total dose marihuana (2 cigarettes) (g)	approximate dose THC
Placebo	–	–	–
Low	0.25	0.5	4.5 mg
High	1.0	2.0	18 mg

[23] We thank D. Miller and M. Seifer of the Federal Bureau of Narcotics (now part of the Bureau of Narcotics and Dangerous Drugs, under the Department of Justice) for help in obtaining marihuana for this research.

experimental sessions

Chronic users were tested only on high doses of marihuana with no practice sessions. Each naive subject was required to come to four sessions, spaced about a week apart. The first was always a practice session, in which the subject learned the proper smoking technique and during which he became thoroughly acquainted with the tests and the protocol. In the practice session, each subject completed the entire protocol, smoking two hand-rolled tobacco cigarettes. He was instructed to take a long puff, to inhale deeply, and to maintain inspiration for 20 seconds, as timed by an experimenter with a stopwatch. Subjects were allowed 8 to 12 minutes to smoke each of the two cigarettes. One purpose of this practice smoking was to identify and eliminate individuals who were not tolerant to high doses of nicotine, thus reducing the effect of nicotine on the variables measured during subsequent drug sessions.[24] A surprising number (five) of volunteers who had described themselves in screening interviews as heavy cigarette smokers, "inhaling" up to two packs of cigarettes a day, developed acute nicotine reactions when they smoked two tobacco cigarettes by the required method. Occurrence of such a reaction disqualified a subject from participation in the experiments.

In subsequent sessions, when cigarettes contained either drug or placebo, all smoking was similarly supervised by an experimenter with a stopwatch. Subjects were not permitted to smoke tobacco cigarettes while the experiment was in progress. They were assigned to one of the three treatment groups listed in Table 2.

physiological and psychological measures

The physiological parameters measured were heart rate, respiratory rate, pupil size, blood glucose level, and conjunctival vascular state. Pupil size was measured with a millimeter rule under constant illumination with eyes focused on an object at constant distance. Conjunctival appearance was rated by an experienced experimenter for dilation of blood vessels on a 0 to 4 scale with ratings of 3 and 4 indicating "signifi-

[24] The doses of tobacco in placebo and low-dose cigarettes were too small to cause physiological changes in subjects who qualified in the practice session.

table 2

order of treatment

| group | drug session | | |
	1	2	3
I	High	Placebo	Low
II	Low	High	Placebo
III	Placebo	Low	High

cant" vasodilatation. Blood samples were collected for immediate determinations of serum glucose and for the serum to be frozen and stored for possible future biochemical studies. Subjects were asked not to eat and not to imbibe a beverage containing sugar or caffeine during the 4 hours preceding a session. They were given supper after the second blood sample was drawn.

The psychological test battery consisted of (i) the Continuous Performance Test (CPT)—5 minutes; (ii) the Digit Symbol Substitution Test (DSST)—90 seconds; (ii) CPT with strobe light distraction—5 minutes;(iv) self-rating bipolar mood scale —3 minutes; and (v) pursuit rotor—10 minutes.

The Continuous Performance Test was designed to measure a subject's capacity for sustained attention.[25] The subject was placed in a darkened room and directed to watch a small screen upon which six letters of the alphabet were flashed rapidly and in random order. The subject was instructed to press a button whenever a specified critical letter appeared. The number of letters presented, correct responses, and errors of commission and omission were counted over the 5-minute period. The test was also done with a strobe light flickering at 50 cycles per second. Normal subjects make no or nearly no errors on this test

[25] K. E. Rosvold, A. F. Mirsky, I. Sarason, E. D. Bransome, and L. H. Beck, J. Consult. Psychol., 20 (1956), 343; A. F. Mirsky and P. V. Cardon, Electroencephalogr. Clin. Neurophysiol., 14 (1962), 1; C. Kornetsky and G. Bain, Psychopharmacologia, 8 (1965), 277.

either with or without strobe distraction; but sleep deprivation, organic brain disease, and certain drugs like chlorpromazine adversely affect performance. Presence or absence of previous exposure to the task has no effect on performance.

The Digit Symbol Substitution Test is a simple test of cognitive function (see Figure 1). A subject's score was the number of correct answers in a 90-second period. As in the case of the CPT, practice should have little or no effect on performance.

The self-rating bipolar mood scale used in these experiments was one developed by Smith and Beecher [26] to evaluate subjective effects of morphine. By allowing subjects to rate themselves within a given category of moods, on an arbitrary scale from + 3 to − 3, it minimizes suggestion and is thus more neutral than the checklists often employed in drug testing.

[26] G. M. Smith and H. K. Beecher, *J. Pharmacol.*, **126** (1959), 50.

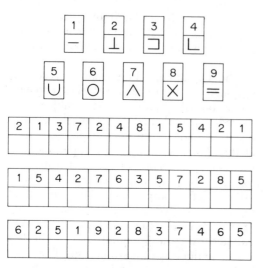

figure 1 *This is a sample of the Digit Symbol Substitution Test as used in these studies. On a signal from the examiner the subject was required to fill as many of the empty spaces as possible with the appropriate symbols. The code was always available to the subject during the 90-second administration of the test. [This figure appeared originally in Psychopharmacologia, 5 (1964), 164.]*

The pursuit rotor measures muscular coordination and attention. The subject's task was to keep a stylus in contact with a small spot on a moving turntable. In these experiments, subjects were given ten 30-second trials in each battery. The score for each trial was total time in contact with the spot. There is a marked practice effect on this test, but naive subjects were brought to high levels of performance during their practice session, so that the changes due to practice were reduced during the actual drug sessions. In addition, since there was a different order of treatments for each of the three groups of naive subjects, any session-to-session practice effects were minimized in the statistical analysis of the pooled data.

At the end of the psychological test battery, a verbal sample was collected from each subject. The subject was left alone in a room with a tape recorder and instructions to describe "an interesting or dramatic experience" in his life until he was stopped. After exactly 5 minutes he was interrupted and asked how long he had been in the recording room. In this way, an estimate of the subject's ability to judge time was also obtained.

results

1. *Safety of marihuana in human volunteers.* In view of the apprehension expressed by many persons over the safety of administering marihuana to research subjects, we wish to emphasize that no adverse marihuana reactions occurred in any of our subjects. In fact, the five acute nicotine reactions mentioned earlier were far more spectacular than any effects produced by marihuana.

In these experiments, observable effects of marihuana were maximum at 15 minutes after smoking. They were diminished between 30 minutes and 1 hour, and they were largely dissipated 3 hours after the end of smoking. No delayed or persistent effects beyond 3 hours were observed or reported.

2. *Intoxicating properties of marihuana in a neutral setting.* With the high dose of marihuana (2.0 grams), all chronic users became "high" [27] by their own accounts and in the judgment of experimenters who had observed many persons under the influence of marihuana. The effect was consistent even though prior to the session some of these subjects expressed anxiety about smoking marihuana and submitting to tests in a laboratory.

On the other hand, only one of the nine naive subjects (No. 3) had a definite "marihuana reaction" on the same high dose. He became markedly euphoric and laughed continuously during his first battery of tests after taking the drug. Interestingly, he was the one subject who had expressed his desire to get high.

3. *Comparison of naive and chronic user subjects.* Throughout the experiments it was apparent that the two groups of subjects reacted differently to identical doses of marihuana. We must caution, however, that our study was designed to allow rigorous statistical analysis of data from the naive group—it was not designed to permit formal comparison between chronic users and naive subjects. The conditions of the experiment were not the same for both groups: the chronic users were tested with the drug on their first visit to the laboratory with no practice and were informed that they were to receive high doses of marihuana. Therefore, differences between chronic and naive groups reported below—although statistically valid—must be regarded as trends to be confirmed or rejected by additional experiments.

4. *Recognition of marihuana versus placebo.* All nine naive subjects reported that they had not been able to identify the taste or smell of marihuana in the experimental cigarettes. A few subjects remarked that they noticed differences in the taste of the three sets of cigarettes but could not interpret the differences. Most subjects found the pure marihuana cigarettes (high dose) more mild than the low dose or placebo cigarettes, both of which contained tobacco.

The subjects' guesses of the contents of cigarettes for their three sessions are presented in Table 3. It is noteworthy that one

table 3

subjects' appraisal of the dose

| actual dose | guessed dose | | | fraction correct |
	placebo	low	high	
Placebo	8	1		8/9
Low	3	6		6/9
High	2	6	1	1/9

of the two subjects who called the high dose a placebo was the subject (No. 4) who had told us he wanted to prove that marihuana really did nothing. There were three outstanding findings: (i) most subjects receiving marihuana in either high or low dose recognized that they were getting a drug; (ii) most subjects receiving placebos recognized that they were receiving placebos; (iii) most subjects called their high dose a low dose, but none called his low dose a high dose, emphasizing the unimpressiveness of their subjective reactions.

5. *Effect of marihuana on heart rate.* The mean changes in heart rate from baseline rates before smoking the drug to rates at 15 and 90 minutes after smoking marihuana and placebo (Table 4) were tested for significance at the .05 level by an analysis of variance; Tukey's method was applied for all possible comparisons (Table 5). In the naive subjects, marihuana in low dose or high dose was followed by increased heart rate 15 minutes after smoking, but the effect was not demonstrated to be dose-dependent. The high dose caused a statistically greater increase in the heart rates of chronic users than in those of the naive subjects 15 minutes after smoking.

---

[27] We will attempt to define the complex nature of a marihuana high in a subsequent paper discussing the speech samples and interviews.

table 4

Change in heart rate (beat/min) after smoking the best material. Results are recorded as a change from the base line 15 minutes and 90 minutes after the smoking session.

subject	15 minutes			90 minutes		
	placebo	low	high	placebo	low	high
			Naive subjects			
1	+16	+20	+16	+20	− 6	− 4
2	+12	+24	+12	− 6	+ 4	− 8
3	+ 8	+ 8	+26	− 4	+ 4	+ 8
4	+20	+ 8	0	0	+20	− 4
5	+ 8	+ 4	− 8	0	+22	− 8
6	+10	+20	+28	−20	− 4	− 4
7	+ 4	+28	+24	+12	+ 8	+18
8	− 8	+20	+24	− 3	+ 8	−24
9	0	+20	+24	+ 8	+12	0
Mean	+ 7.8	+16.9	+16.2	+ 0.8	+ 7.6	− 2.9
S.E.	2.8	2.7	4.2	3.8	3.2	3.8
			Chronic subjects			
10			+32			+ 4
11			+36			−
12			+20			+36
13			+ 8			+12
14			+32			+ 4
15			+54			−
16			+24			+12
17			+60			+22
Mean			+33.2			+15.0
S.E.			6.0			5.0

table 5

Significance of differences (at the .05 level) in heart rate. Results of Tukey's test for all possible comparisons.

comparison	15 minutes	90 minutes
Low dose versus placebo	Significant	Significant
High dose versus placebo	Significant	Not significant
Low dose versus high dose	Not significant	Significant
Chronic users versus high dose	Significant	Significant

Two of the chronic users had unusually low resting pulse rates (56 and 42), but deletion of these two subjects (No. 11 and No. 15) still gave a significant difference in mean pulse rise of chronic users compared to naives. Because the conditions of the sessions and experimental design were not identical for the two groups, we prefer to report this difference as a trend that must be confirmed by further studies.

6. *Effect of marihuana on respiratory rate.* In the naive group, there was no change in respiratory rate before and after smoking marihuana. Chronic users showed a small but statistically significant increase in respiratory rate after smoking, but we do not regard the change as clinically significant.

7. *Effect of marihuana on pupil size.*

There was no change in pupil size before and after smoking marihuana in either group.

8. *Effect of marihuana on conjunctival appearance.* Significant reddening of conjunctivae due to dilatation of blood vessels occurred in one of nine subjects receiving placebo, three of nine receiving the low dose of marihuana, and eight of nine receiving the high dose. It occurred in all eight of the chronic users receiving the high dose and was rated as more prominent in them. The effect was more pronounced 15 minutes after the smoking period than 90 minutes after it.

9. *Effect of marihuana on blood sugar.* There was no significant change in blood sugar levels after smoking marihuana in either group.

10. *Effect of marihuana on the Continuous Performance Test.* Performance on the CPT and on the CPT with strobe distraction was unaffected by marihuana for both groups of subjects.

11. *Effect of marihuana on the Digit Symbol Substitution Test.* The significance of the differences in mean changes of scores at the .05 level was determined by an analysis of variance by means of Tukey's method for all possible comparisons. Results of these tests are summarized in Tables 6 and 7.

The results indicate that: (i) Decrements in performance of naive subjects

table 6

Significance of differences (at the .05 level) for the Digit Symbol Substitution Test. Results of Tukey's test for all possible comparisons.

comparison	15 minutes	90 minutes
Low dose versus placebo	Significant	Significant
High dose versus placebo	Significant	Significant
Low dose versus high dose	Significant	Not significant
Chronic users versus high dose	Significant	Significant

following low and high doses of marihuana were significant at 15 and 90 minutes after smoking. (ii) The decrement following marihuana was greater after high dose than after low dose at 15 minutes after taking the drug, giving preliminary evidence of a dose-response relationship. (iii) Chronic users started with good baseline performance and improved slightly on the DSST after smoking 2.0 grams of marihuana, whereas performance of the naive subjects was grossly impaired. Experience with the DSST suggests that absence of impairment in chronic users cannot be accounted for solely by a practice effect. Still, because of the different procedures employed, we prefer to report this difference as a trend.

12. *Effect of marihuana on pursuit rotor performance.* This result is presented in Table 8. Again applying Tukey's method in an analysis of variance, we tested differences in mean changes in scores (Table 9). Decrements in performance of naive subjects after both low and high doses of marihuana were significant at 15 and 90 minutes. This effect on performance followed a dose-response relation on testing batteries conducted at both 15 minutes and 90 minutes after the drug was smoked.

All chronic users started from good baselines and improved on the pursuit rotor after smoking marihuana. These data are not presented, however, because it is probable that the improvement was largely a practice effect.

13. *Effect of marihuana on time estimation.* Before smoking, all nine naive subjects estimated the 5-minute verbal sample to be 5 ± 2 minutes. After placebo, no subject changed his guess. After the low dose, three subjects raised their estimates to 10 ± 2 minutes, and after the high dose, four raised their estimates.

14. *Subjective effects of marihuana.* When questioned at the end of their participation in the experiment, persons who had never taken marihuana previously reported minimum subjective effects after

table 7

Digit Symbol Substitution Test. Change in scores from base line (number correct) 15 and 90 minutes after the smoking session.

subject	15 minutes			90 minutes		
	placebo	low	high	placebo	low	high
			Naive subjects			
1	− 3	0	+ 5	− 7	+ 4	+ 8
2	+10	−8	−17	− 1	−15	− 5
3	− 3	+6	− 7	−10	+ 2	− 1
4	+ 3	−4	− 3	0	− 7	0
5	+ 4	+1	− 7	+ 6	0	− 8
6	− 3	−1	− 9	+ 3	− 5	−12
7	+ 2	−4	− 6	+ 3	− 5	− 4
8	− 1	+3	+ 1	+ 4	+ 4	− 3
9	− 1	−4	− 3	+ 6	− 1	−10
Mean	+ 0.9	−1.2	− 5.1	+ 0.4	− 2.6	− 3.9
S.E.	1.4	1.4	2.1	1.9	2.0	2.0
			Chronic users			
10			− 4			−16
11			+ 1			+ 6
12			+11			+18
13			+ 3			+ 4
14			− 2			− 3
15			− 6			
16			− 4			+ 8
17			+ 3			
Mean			+ 0.25			+ 2.8
S.E.			1.9			4.7

table 8

Pursuit rotor (naive subjects). Changes in scores (averages of ten trials) from base line (seconds).

subject	15 minutes			90 minutes		
	placebo	low	high	placebo	low	high
1	+1.20	−1.04	−4.01	+1.87	−1.54	−6.54
2	+0.89	−1.43	−0.12	+0.52	+0.44	−0.68
3	+0.50	−0.60	−6.56	+0.84	−0.96	−4.34
4	+0.18	−0.11	+0.11	+0.06	+1.95	−1.37
5	+3.20	+0.39	+0.13	+2.64	+3.33	+0.34
6	+3.45	−0.32	−3.46	+2.93	+0.22	−2.26
7	+0.81	+0.48	−0.79	+0.63	+0.16	−0.52
8	+1.75	−0.39	−0.92	+2.13	+0.40	+1.02
9	+3.90	−1.94	−2.60	+3.11	−0.97	−3.09
Mean	+1.8	−0.6	−2.0	+1.6	+0.3	−1.9
S.E.	0.5	0.3	0.8	0.4	0.5	0.8

table 9

Significance of differences (at the .05 level) for the pursuit rotor. Results of Tukey's test for all possible comparisons, 15 and 90 minutes after the smoking session.

comparison	15 minutes	90 minutes
Low dose versus placebo	Significant	Significant
High dose versus placebo	Significant	Significant
Low dose versus high dose	Significant	Significant

smoking the drug, or, more precisely, few effects like those commonly reported by chronic users. Nonusers reported little euphoria, no distortion of visual or auditory perception, and no confusion. However, several subjects mentioned that "things seemed to take longer." Below are examples of comments by naive subjects after high doses.

Subject 1: "It was stronger than the previous time (low dose) but I really didn't think it could be marihuana. Things seemed to go slower."

Subject 2: "I think I realize why they took our watches. There was a sense of the past disappearing as happens when you're driving too long without sleeping. With a start you wake up to realize you were asleep for an instant; you discover yourself driving along the road. It was the same tonight with eating a sandwich. I'd look down to discover I'd just swallowed a bite but I hadn't noticed it at the time."

Subject 6: "I felt a combination of being almost-drunk and tired, with occasional fits of silliness—not my normal reaction to smoking tobacco."

Subject 8: "I felt faint briefly, but the dizziness went away, and I felt normal or slightly tired. I can't believe I had a high dose of marihuana."

Subject 9: "Time seemed very drawn out. I would keep forgetting what I was doing, especially on the continuous performance test,

but somehow every time an "X" (the critical letter) came up, I found myself pushing the button."

After smoking their high dose, chronic users were asked to rate themselves on a scale of 1 to 10, 10 representing "the highest you've ever been." All subjects placed themselves between 7 and 10, most at 8 or 9. Many of these subjects expressed anxiety at the start of their first battery of tests after smoking the drug when they were feeling very high. Then they expressed surprise during and after the tests when they judged (correctly) that their performance was as good as or better than it had been before taking the drug.

15. The effect of marihuana on the self-rating mood scale, the effect of marihuana on a 5-minute verbal sample, and the correlation of personality type with subjective effects of marihuana will be reported separately.

discussion

Several results from this study raise important questions about the action of marihuana and suggest directions for future research. Our finding that subjects who were naive to marihuana did not become subjectively "high" after a high dose of marihuana in a neutral setting is interesting when contrasted with the response of regular users who consistently reported and exhibited highs. It agrees with the reports of chronic users that many, if not most, people do not become high on their first exposure to marihuana even if they smoke it correctly. This puzzling phenomenon can be discussed from either a physiological or psychosocial point of view. Neither interpretation is entirely satisfactory. The physiological hypothesis suggests that getting high on marihuana occurs only after some sort of pharmacological sensitization takes place. The psychosocial interpretation is that repeated exposure to marihuana reduces psychological inhibition, as part of, or as the result of a learning process.

Indirect evidence makes the psychological hypothesis attractive. Anxiety about drug use in this country is sufficiently great to make worthy of careful consideration the possibility of an unconscious psychological inhibition or block on the part of naive drug takers. The subjective responses of our subjects indicate that they had imagined a marihuana effect to be much more profoundly disorganizing than what they experienced. For example, subject No. 4, who started with a bias against the possibility of becoming high on marihuana, was able to control subjectively the effect of the drug and report that he had received a placebo when he had actually gotten a high dose. As anxiety about the drug is lessened with experience, the block may decrease, and the subject may permit himself to notice the drug's effects.

It is well known that marihuana users, in introducing friends to the drug, do actually "teach" them to notice subtle effects of the drug on consciousness.[28] The apparently enormous influence of set and setting on the form of the marihuana response is consistent with this hypothesis, as is the testimony of users that, as use becomes more frequent, the amount of drug required to produce intoxication decreases— a unique example of "reverse tolerance." (Regular use of many intoxicants is accompanied by the need for increasing doses to achieve the same effects.)

On the other hand, the suggestion arising from this study that users and nonusers react differently to the drug, not only subjectively but also physiologically, increases the plausibility of the pharmacological-sensitization hypothesis. Of course, reverse tolerance could equally well be a manifestation of the sensitization.

It would be useful to confirm the suggested differences between users and non-

users and then to test in a systematic manner the hypothetical explanations of the phenomenon. One possible approach would be to continue to administer high doses of marihuana to the naive subjects according to the protocol described. If subjects begin reporting high responses to the drug only after several exposures, in the absence of psychedelic settings, suggestions, or manipulations of mood, then the likelihood that marihuana induces a true physiological sensitization or that experience reduces psychological inhibitions, permitting real drug effects to appear, would be increased. If subjects fail to become high, we could conclude that learning to respond to marihuana requires some sort of teaching or suggestion.

An investigation of the literature of countries where anxieties over drug use are less prominent would be useful. If this difference between responses of users and nonusers is a uniquely American phenomenon, a psychological explanation would be indicated, although it would not account for greater effects with smaller doses after the initial, anxiety-reducing stage.

One impetus for reporting the finding of differences between chronic and naive subjects on some of the tests, despite the fact that the experimental designs were not the same, is that this finding agrees with the statements of many users. They say that the effects of marihuana are easily suppressed—much more so than those of alcohol. Our observation, that the chronic users after smoking marihuana performed on some tests as well as or better than they did before taking the drug, reinforced the argument advanced by chronic users that maintaining effective levels of performance for many tasks—driving, for example [29]— is much easier under the influence of marihuana than under that of other psycho-

---

[28] H. S. Becker, *Outsiders: Studies in the Sociology of Deviance* (New York: Macmillan, 1963), chap. 3.

[29] Although the motor skills measured by the pursuit rotor are represented in driving ability, they are only components of that ability. The influence of marihuana on driving skill remains an open question of high medico-legal priority.

active drugs. Certainly the surprise that the chronic users expressed when they found they were performing more effectively on the CPT, DSST, and pursuit rotor tests than they thought they would is remarkable. It is quite the opposite of the false sense of improvement subjects have under some psychoactive drugs that actually impair performance.

What might be the basis of this suppressibility? Possibly, the actions of marihuana are confined to higher cortical functions without any general stimulatory or depressive effect on lower brain centers. The relative absence of neurological—as opposed to psychiatric—symptoms in marihuana intoxication suggests this possibility.[30]

Our failure to detect any changes in blood sugar levels of subjects after they had smoked marihuana forces us to look elsewhere for an explanation of the hunger and hyperphagia commonly reported by users. A first step would be careful interviewing of users to determine whether they really become hungry after smoking marihuana or whether they simply find eating more pleasurable. Possibly, the basis of this effect is also central rather than due to some peripheral physiological change.

Lack of any change in pupil size of subjects after they had smoked marihuana is an enlightening finding especially because so many users and law-enforcement agents firmly believe that marihuana dilates pupils. (Since users generally observe each other in dim surroundings, it is not surprising that they see large pupils.) This negative finding emphasizes the need for data from carefully controlled investigations rather than from casual observation or anecdotal reports in the evaluation of marihuana. It also agrees with the findings of others that synthetic THC does not alter pupil size.[31]

Finally, we would like to comment on the fact that marihuana appears to be a relatively mild intoxicant in our studies. If these results seem to differ from those of earlier experiments, it must be remembered that other experimenters have given marihuana orally, have given doses much higher than those commonly smoked by users, have administered potent synthetics, and have not strictly controlled the laboratory setting. As noted in our introduction, more powerful effects are often reported by users who ingest preparations of marihuana. This may mean that some active constituents which enter the body when the drug is ingested are destroyed by combustion, a suggestion that must be investigated in man. Another priority consideration is the extent to which synthetic THC reproduces marihuana intoxication— a problem that must be resolved before marihuana research proceeds with THC instead of the natural resin of the whole plant.

The set, both of subjects and experimenters, and the setting must be recognized as critical variables in studies of marihuana. Drug, set, and setting interact to shape the form of a marihuana reaction. The researcher who sets out with prior conviction that hemp is psychotomimetic or a "mild hallucinogen" is likely to confirm his conviction experimentally,[32] but he would probably confirm the opposite hypothesis if his bias were in the opposite direction. Precautions to insure neutrality of set and setting, including use of a double-blind procedure as an absolute minimum, are vitally important if the object of investigation is to measure real marihuana-induced responses.

conclusions

1. It is feasible and safe to study the effects of marihuana on human volunteers who smoke it in a laboratory.

---

[30] Williams *et al.*, *op. cit.*

[31] Isbell, *op. cit.*; and L. E. Hollister, R. K. Richards, and H. K. Gillespie, in preparation.

[32] Ames, *op. cit.*

2. In a neutral setting persons who are naive to marihuana do not have strong subjective experiences after smoking low or high doses of the drug, and the effects they do report are not the same as those described by regular users of marihuana who take the drug in the same neutral setting.
3. Marihuana-naive persons do demonstrate impaired performance on simple intellectual and psychomotor tests after smoking marihuana; the impairment is dose-related in some cases.
4. Regular users of marihuana do get high after smoking marihuana in a neutral setting but do not show the same degree of impairment of performance on the tests as do naive subjects. In some cases, their performance even appears to improve slightly after smoking marihuana.
5. Marihuana increases heart rate moderately.
6. No change in respiratory rate follows administration of marihuana by inhalation.
7. No change in pupil size occurs in short-term exposure to marihuana.
8. Marihuana administration causes dilatation of conjunctival blood vessels.
9. Marihuana treatment produces no change in blood sugar levels.
10. In a neutral setting the physiological and psychological effects of a single, inhaled dose of marihuana appear to reach maximum intensity within one-half hour of inhalation, to be diminished after 1 hour, and to be completely dissipated by 3 hours.

UNIT

IX

social psychology

28

A recent series of experiments by Bibb Latané and John M. Darley provide a good example of the potential role that basic behavioral research may play in the understanding of significant social problems. In the following selection Latané and Darley describe some of the variables which may determine when an innocent bystander will become "involved" in a stranger's problem. One of the dramatic and unexpected findings is that the probability of involvement decreases as the number of bystanders increases.

bystander "apathy" [1]

BIBB LATANÉ

JOHN M. DARLEY

> Do the work that's nearest
>   Though it's dull at whiles,
> Helping, when you meet them,
>   Lame dogs over stiles.

In the century since it was written, this minor bit of exhortatory doggerel has become sheer camp. We have become too sophisticated to appreciate the style—many believe that we have become too cynical to appreciate the moral. Working at dull tasks is now taken as a sign of dullness,

[1] The experiments reported in this paper were supported by National Science Foundation grants GS1238 and GS1239 and were conducted while the authors were at Columbia University and New York University, respectively. Their . . . book on this research (Latané and Darley, *The Unresponsive Bystander*, Appleton-Century-Crofts, 1970) won the 1968 Socio-Psychological Prize awarded by the American Association for the Advancement of Science and the Century Psychology Prize for 1968.

Reprinted from *American Scientist*, 1969, **57**: 244–268, by permission of the authors and publisher. Copyright © 1969 by the Society of the Sigma Xi.

and helping lame dogs is no longer much in vogue. At least, that is the impression we get from the newspapers.

On a March night in 1964, Kitty Genovese was set upon by a maniac as she came home from work at 3 A.M. Thirty-eight of her Kew Gardens neighbors came to their windows when she cried out in terror—none came to her assistance. Even though her assailant took over half an hour to murder her, no one even so much as called the police.

This story became the journalistic sensation of the decade. "Apathy," cried the newspapers. "Indifference," said the columnists and commentators. "Moral callousness," "dehumanization," "loss of concern for our fellow man," added preachers, professors, and other sermonizers. Movies, television specials, plays, and books explored this incident and many more like it. Americans became concerned about their lack of concern.

But can these epithets be correct? We think not. Although it is unquestionably true that witnesses in such emergencies have often done nothing to save the victims, "apathy," "indifference," and "unconcern" are not entirely accurate descriptions of their reactions. The 38 witnesses to Kitty Genovese's murder did not merely look at the scene once and then ignore it. Instead they continued to stare out their windows at what was going on. Caught, fascinated, distressed, unwilling to act but unable to turn away, their behavior was neither helpful nor heroic; but it was not indifferent or apathetic either.

Actually, it was like crowd behavior in many other emergency situations; car accidents, drownings, fires, and attempted suicides all attract substantial numbers of people who watch the drama in helpless fascination without getting directly involved in the action. Are these people alienated and indifferent? Are the rest of us? Obviously not. It seems only yesterday we were being called overconforming. But why, then, don't we act?

There are certainly strong forces leading us to act. Empathy or sympathy, innate or learned, may cause us to share, at least in part, a victim's distress. If intervention were easy, most of us would be willing to relieve our own discomfort by alleviating another's suffering. As Charles Darwin put it some years ago,

As man is a social animal it is almost certain that . . . he would, from an inherited tendency, be willing to defend, in concert with others, his fellow men; and be ready to aid them in any way, which did not interfere too greatly with his own welfare or his own strong desires.

Even if empathy or sympathy were not strong enough to lead us to help in emergencies, there are a variety of social norms which suggest that each of us has a responsibility to each other, and that help is the proper thing to do. "Do unto others as you would have them do unto you," we hear from our earliest years. Although norms such as these may not have much influence on our behavior in specific situations, they may imbue us with a general predisposition to try to help others.

Indeed, in many non-emergency situations, people seem surprisingly willing to share their time and money with others. According to the Internal Revenue Service, Americans contribute staggering sums to a great variety of charitable organizations each year. Even when tax deductions don't fan the urge to help, people still help others. When Columbia students asked 2,500 people on the streets of New York for 10¢ or 20¢, over half of these people gave it.

If people are so willing to help in non-emergency situations, they should be even more willing to help in emergencies when the need is so much greater. Or should they? Emergencies differ in many ways from other types of situations in which people need help, and these differences may be important. The very nature of an emergency implies certain psychological consequences.

characteristics of emergencies

Perhaps the most distinctive characteristic of an emergency is that it involves threat or harm. Life, well-being, or property is in danger. Even if an emergency is successfully dealt with, nobody is better off afterwards than before. Except in rare circumstances, the best that can be hoped for if an emergency occurs is a return to the status quo. Consequently, there are few positive rewards for successful action in an emergency. At worst, an emergency can claim the lives not only of those people who were initially involved in it, but also of anybody who intervenes in the situation. This fact puts pressures on individuals to ignore a potential emergency, to distort their perceptions of it, or to underestimate their responsibility for coping with it.

The second important feature of an emergency is that it is an unusual and rare event. Fortunately, although he may read about them in newspapers, or watch fictionalized accounts on television, the average person probably will encounter fewer than half a dozen serious emergencies in his lifetime. Unfortunately when he does encounter one, he will have had little direct personal experience in handling such a situation. Unlike the stereotyped patterns of his everyday behavior, an individual facing an emergency is untrained and unrehearsed.

In addition to being rare, emergencies differ widely, one from another. There are few common requirements for action between a drowning, a fire, or an automobile accident. Each emergency presents a different problem, and each requires a different type of action. Consequently, unlike other rare events, our culture provides us with little secondhand wisdom about how to deal with emergencies. An individual may cope with the rare event of a formal dinner party by using manners gleaned from late night Fred Astaire movies, but the stereotypes that the late movies provide for dealing with emergencies are much less accurate. "Charge!" "Women and children first!" "Quick, get lots of hot water and towels." This is about the extent of the advice offered for dealing with emergencies and it is singularly inappropriate in most specific real emergency situations.

The fourth basic characteristic of emergencies is that they are unforeseen. They "emerge," suddenly and without warning. Being unexpected, emergencies must be handled without the benefit of forethought and planning and an individual does not have the opportunity to think through in advance what course of action he should take when faced with an emergency. He must do his thinking in the immediacy of the situation, and has no opportunity to consult others as to the best course of action or to alert others who are especially equipped to deal with emergencies. The individual confronted with an emergency is thrown on his own resources. We have already seen that he does not have much in the way of practical responses or cultural stereotypes to fall back upon.

A final characteristic of an emergency is that it requires instant action. It represents a pressing necessity. If the emergency is not dealt with immediately, the situation will deteriorate. The threat will transform itself into damage; the harm will continue or spread. There are urgent pressures to deal with the situation at once. The requirement for immediate action prevents the individual confronted with an emergency from leisurely considering the possible courses of action open to him. It forces him to come to a decision before he has had time to consider his alternatives. It places him in a condition of stress.

The picture we have drawn is a rather grim one. Faced with a situation in which there is no benefit to be gained for himself, unable to rely on past experience, on the experience of others, or on forethought and planning, denied the opportunity to consider carefully his course of action, the bystander to an emergency is in an unenviable position. It is perhaps surprising that anyone should intervene at all.

a model of the intervention process

If an individual is to intervene in an emergency, he must make not just one, but a *series* of decisions. Only one particular set of choices will lead him to take action in the situation. Let us now consider the behavioral and cognitive processes that go on in an individual who is in the vicinity of an emergency. What must he do and decide before he actually intervenes? These may have important implications for predicting whether an individual will act.

Let us suppose that an emergency is actually taking place. A middle-aged man, walking down the street, has a heart attack. He stops short, clutches his chest, and staggers to the nearest building wall, where he slowly slumps to the sidewalk in a sitting position. What is the likelihood with which a passerby will come to his assistance? First, the bystander has to *notice* that something is happening. The external event has to break into his thinking and intrude itself on his conscious mind. He must tear himself away from his private thoughts or from the legs of the pretty girl walking down the street ahead of him and pay attention to this unusual event.

Once the person is aware of the event as something to be explained, it is necessary that he *interpret* the event. Specifically, he must decide that there is something wrong, that this ambiguous event is an emergency. It may be that the man slumped on the sidewalk is only a drunk, beyond any assistance that the passerby can give him. If the bystander decided that something is indeed wrong, he must next decide that he has a *responsibility* to act. Perhaps help is on the way or perhaps someone else might be better qualified to help. Even in an emergency, it is not clear that everybody should immediately intrude himself into the situation.

If the person does decide that he should help, he must decide what *form of assistance* he can give. Should he rush in directly and try to help the victim or should he detour by calling a doctor or the police? Finally, of course, he must decide how to *implement* his choice and form of intervention. Where is the nearest telephone? Is there a hospital nearby? At this point, the person may finally begin to act in the situation. The socially responsible act is the end point of a series of decisions that the person makes.

Obviously, this model is too rational. It seems unlikely that a bystander will run through the series of choice points in a strictly logical and sequential order. Instead, he may consider two or three of them simultaneously and "try on" various decisions and their consequences before he finally arrives at his overall assessment of the situation. Since he has no commitment to any intermediary decision until he has taken final action, he may cycle back and forth through the decision series until he comes up with a set which serves both his needs and the needs of "reality."

Second, the bystander in an emergency is not a detached and objective observer. His decisions have consequences for himself just as much as for the victim. Unfortunately, however, the rewards and penalties for action and inaction are biased in favor of inaction. All the bystander has to gain from intervention is a feeling of pride and the chance to be a hero. On the other hand, he can be made to appear a fool, sued, or even attacked and wounded. By leaving the situation, he has little to lose but his self-respect. There are strong pressures against deciding that an event is an emergency.

Intervention, then, requires choosing a single course of action through a rather complex matrix of possible actions. The failure to intervene may result from failing to notice an event, failing to realize that the event is an emergency, failing to feel personally responsible for dealing with the emergency, or failing to have sufficient skill to intervene.

social determinants of bystander intervention: I

Most emergencies are, or at least begin as, ambiguous events. A quarrel in the street may erupt into violence, but it may be simply a family argument. A man staggering about may be suffering a coronary or an onset of diabetes; he may simply be drunk. Smoke pouring from a building may signal a fire; on the other hand, it may be simply steam or airconditioner vapor. Before a bystander is likely to take action in such ambiguous situations, he must first define the event as an emergency and decide that intervention is the proper course of action.

In the course of making these decisions, it is likely that an individual bystander will be considerably influenced by the decisions he perceives other bystanders to be taking. If everyone else in a group of on-lookers seems to regard an event as non-serious and the proper course of action as non-intervention, this consensus may strongly affect the perceptions af any single individual and inhibit his potential intervention.

The definitions that other people hold may be discovered by discussing the situation with them, but they may also be inferred from their facial expressions or their behavior. A whistling man with his hands in his pockets obviously does not believe he is in the midst of a crisis. A bystander who does not respond to smoke obviously does not attribute it to fire. An individual, seeing the inaction of others, will judge the situation as less serious than he would if alone.

But why should the others be inactive? Unless there were some force inhibiting responses on the part of others, the kind of social influence process described would, by itself, only lead to a convergence of attitudes within a group. If each individual expressed his true feelings, then, even if each member of the group were entirely guided by the reactions of the others, the group should still respond with a likelihood equal to the average of the individuals.

An additional factor is involved, however. Each member of a group may watch the others, but he is also aware that others are watching him. They are an audience to his own reactions. Among American males, it is considered desirable to appear poised and collected in times of stress. Being exposed to the public view may constrain the actions and expressions of emotion of any individual as he tries to avoid possible ridicule and embarrassment. Even though he may be truly concerned and upset about the plight of a victim, until he decides what to do, he may maintain a calm demeanor.

The constraints involved with being in public might in themselves tend to inhibit action by individuals in a group, but in conjunction with the social influence process described above, they may be expected to have even more powerful effects. If each member of a group is, at the same time, trying to appear calm and also looking around at the other members to gauge their reactions, all members may be led (or misled) by each other to define the situation as less critical than they would if alone. Until someone acts, each person sees only other non-responding bystanders, and is likely to be influenced not to act himself. A state of "pluralistic ignorance" may develop.

It has often been recognized (Brown, 1954, 1965) that a crowd can cause contagion of panic, leading each person in the crowd to over-react to an emergency to the detriment of everyone's welfare. What we suggest here is that a crowd can also force inaction on its members. It can suggest, implicitly but strongly, by its passive behavior that an event is not to be reacted to as an emergency, and it can make any individual uncomfortably aware of what a fool he will look for behaving as if it is.

This line of thought suggests that individuals may be less likely to intervene in an emergency if they witness it in the presence of other people than if they see it alone. It suggests that the presence of other people may lead each person to interpret the situation as less serious, and less demanding of action than he would if alone. The presence of other people may alter each bystander's perceptions and interpretations of the situation. We suspect that the presence of other people may also affect each individual's assessment of the rewards and costs involved in taking action, and indeed we will discuss this possibility in some detail later. First, however, let us look at evidence relevant to this initial process. The experiments reported below were designed to test the line of thought presented above.

EXPERIMENT 1: WHERE THERE'S SMOKE, THERE'S (SOMETIMES) FIRE [2]

In this experiment we presented an emergency to individuals either alone, in the presence of two passive others (confederates of the experimenter who were instructed to notice the emergency but remain indifferent to it), or in groups of three. It was our expectation that individuals faced with the passive reactions of the confederates would be influenced by them and thus less likely to take action than single subjects. We also predicted that the constraints on behavior in public combined with social influence processes would lessen the likelihood that members of three-person groups would act to cope with the emergency.

Male Columbia students living in campus residences were invited to an interview to discuss "some of the problems involved in life at an urban university." As they sat in a small room waiting to be called for the interview and filling out a preliminary questionnaire, they faced an ambiguous but potentially dangerous situation as a stream of smoke began to puff into the room through a wall vent. Some subjects filled out the questionnaire and were exposed to this potentially critical situation while alone. Others were part of three-person groups consisting of one subject and two confederates acting the part of naive subjects. The confederates attempted to avoid conversation as much as possible. Once the smoke had been introduced, they stared at it briefly, made no comment, but simply shrugged their shoulders, returned to the questionnaires

and continued to fill them out, occasionally waving away the smoke to do so. If addressed, they attempted to be as uncommunicative as possible and to show apparent indifference to the smoke. "I dunno," they said, and no subject persisted in talking. In a final condition, three naive subjects were tested together. In general, these subjects did not know each other, although in two groups, subjects reported a nodding acquaintance with another subject. Since subjects arrived at slightly different times and since they each had individual questionnaires to work on, they did not introduce themselves to each other, or attempt anything but the most rudimentary conversation.

As soon as the subjects had completed two pages of their questionnaires, the experimenter began to introduce the smoke through a small vent in the wall. The "smoke" was finely divided titanium dioxide produced in a stoppered bottle and delivered under slight air pressure through the vent. It formed a moderately fine-textured but clearly visible stream of whitish smoke. For the entire experimental period, the smoke continued to jet into the room in irregular puffs. By the end of the experimental period, vision was obscured in the room by the amount of smoke present.

All behavior and conversation was observed and coded from behind a one-way window (largely disguised on the subject's side by a large sign giving preliminary instructions). When and if the subject left the experimental room and reported the smoke, he was told that the situation "would be taken care of." If the subject had not reported the smoke within six minutes of the time he first noticed it, the experiment was terminated.

The typical subject, when tested alone, behaved very reasonably. Usually, shortly after the smoke appeared, he would glance up from his questionnaire, notice the smoke, show a slight but distinct startle reaction, and then undergo a brief period of indecision, and perhaps return briefly

[2] A more detailed report of this experiment is given in B. Latané and J. M. Darley, Group inhibition of bystander intervention in emergencies, *Journal of Personality and Social Psychology*, 1968, **10**: 215–221.

to his questionnaire before again staring at the smoke. Soon, most subjects would get up from their chairs, walk over to the vent, and investigate it closely, sniffing the smoke, waving their hands in it, feeling its temperature, etc. The usual Alone subject would hesitate again, but finally walk out of the room, look around outside, and, finding somebody there, calmly report the presence of the smoke. No subject showed any sign of panic; most simply said, "There's something strange going on in there, there seems to be some sort of smoke coming through the wall. . . ." The median subject in the Alone condition had reported the smoke within two minutes of first noticing it. Three-quarters of the 24 people run in this condition reported the smoke before the experimental period was terminated.

The behavior of subjects run with two passive confederates was dramatically different; of ten people run in this condition, only one reported the smoke. The other nine stayed in the waiting room as it filled up with smoke, doggedly working on their questionnaires and waving the fumes away from their faces. They coughed, rubbed their eyes, and opened the window—but they did not report the smoke. The difference between the response rate of 75 per cent in the Alone condition and 10 per cent in the Two Passive Confederates condition is highly significant ($p < .002$ by Fisher's Exact test, two-tailed).

Because there are three subjects present and available to report the smoke in the Three Naive Bystander condition as compared to only one subject at a time in the Alone condition, a simple comparison between the two conditions is not appropriate. On the one hand, we cannot compare speeds in the Alone condition with the average speed of the three subjects in a group, since, once one subject in a group had reported the smoke, the pressure on the other two disappeared. They legitimately could feel that the emergency had been handled, and that any action on their part would be redundant and potentially confusing. Therefore, we used the speed of the *first* subject in a group to report the smoke as our dependent variable. However, since there were three times as many people available to respond in this condition as in the Alone condition, we would expect an increased likelihood that at least one person would report the smoke by chance alone. Therefore, we mathematically created "groups" of three scores from the Alone condition to serve as a baseline.[3]

In contrast to the complexity of this procedure, the results were quite simple. Subjects in the Three Naive Bystander condition were markedly inhibited from reporting the smoke. Since 75 per cent of the Alone subjects reported the smoke, we would expect over 98 per cent of the three-person groups to include at least one reporter. In fact, in only 38 per cent of the eight groups in this condition did even one person report ($p < .01$). Of the twenty-four people run in these eight groups, only one person reported the smoke within the first four minutes before the room got noticeably unpleasant. Only three people reported the smoke within the entire experimental period. Social inhibition of reporting was so strong that the smoke was reported quicker when only one person saw it than when groups of three were present ($p < .01$).

Subjects who had reported the smoke were relatively consistent in later describing their reactions to it. They thought the smoke looked somewhat "strange," they were not sure exactly what it was or whether it was dangerous, but they felt it was unusual enough to justify some examination. "I wasn't sure whether it was a fire, but it looked like something was wrong." "I thought it might be steam, but

[3] The formula for calculating the expected proportion of groups in which at least one person will have acted by a given time is $1 - (1 - p)^n$ where p is the proportion of single individuals who act by that time and n is the number of persons in the group.

it seemed like a good idea to check it out."

Subjects who had not reported the smoke also were unsure about exactly what it was, but they uniformly said that they had rejected the idea that it was a fire. Instead, they hit upon an astonishing variety of alternative explanations, all sharing the common characteristic of interpreting the smoke as a nondangerous event. Many thought the smoke was either steam or airconditioning vapors, several thought it was smog, purposely introduced to simulate an urban environment, and two (from different groups) actually suggested that the smoke was a "truth gas" filtered into the room to induce them to answer the questionnaire accurately (surprisingly, they were not disturbed by this conviction). Predictably, some decided that "it must be some sort of experiment" and stoically endured the discomfort of the room rather than overreact.

Despite the obvious and powerful report-inhibiting effect of other bystanders, subjects almost invariably claimed that they had paid little or no attention to the reactions of the other people in the room. Although the presence of other people actually had a strong and pervasive effect on the subjects' reactions, they were either unaware of this or unwilling to admit it.

The results of this study clearly support the predictions. Individuals exposed to a room filling with smoke in the presence of passive others themselves remained passive, and groups of three naive subjects were less likely to report the smoke than solitary bystanders. Our predictions were confirmed—but this does not necessarily mean that our explanation for these results is the correct one. As a matter of fact several alternatives are available.

Two alternative explanations stem from the fact that the smoke represented a possible danger to the subject himself as well as to others in the building. Subjects' behavior might have reflected their fear of fire, with subjects in groups feeling less threatened by the fire than single subjects

and thus less concerned to act. It has been demonstrated in studies with humans (Schachter, 1959) and with rats (Latané, 1969; Latané and Glass, 1968) that togetherness reduces fear, even in situations where it does not reduce danger. In addition, subjects may have felt that the presence of others increased their ability to cope with fire. For both these reasons, subjects in groups may have been less afraid of fire and thus less likely to report the smoke than solitary subjects.

A similar explanation might emphasize, not fearfulness, but the desire to hide fear. To the extent that bravery or stoicism in the face of danger or discomfort is a socially desirable trait (as it appears to be for American male undergraduates), we might expect individuals to attempt to appear more brave or more stoic when others are watching than when they are alone. It is possible that subjects in the Group conditions saw themselves as engaged in a game of "Chicken," and thus did not react.

Although both of these explanations are plausible, we do not think that they provide an accurate account of subjects' thinking. In the postexperimental interviews, subjects claimed, *not* that they were unworried by the fire or that they were unwilling to endure the danger; but rather that they had decided that there was no fire at all and the smoke was caused by something else. They failed to act because they thought there was no reason to act. Their "apathetic" behavior was reasonable —given their interpretation of the circumstances.

EXPERIMENT 2: A LADY IN DISTRESS [4]

Although it seems unlikely that the group inhibition of bystander intervention

[4] A more detailed description of this experiment is given in B. Latané and J. Rodin, A Lady in distress: Inhibiting effects of friends and strangers on bystander intervention, *Journal of Experimental Social Psychology*, 1969, **5**: 189–202.

observed in Experiment 1 can be attributed entirely to the fact that smoke represents a danger to the individual bystander, it is certainly possible that this is so. Experiment 2 was designed to see whether similar group inhibition effects could be observed in situations where there is no danger to the individual himself for not acting. In addition, a new variable was included: whether the bystanders knew each other.

Male Columbia undergraduates waited either alone, with a friend, or with a stranger to participate in a market research study. As they waited, they heard someone fall and apparently injure herself in the room next door. Whether they tried to help, and how long they took to do so were the main dependent variables of the study. Subjects were telephoned and offered $2 to participate in a survey of game and puzzle preferences conducted at Columbia by the Consumer Testing Bureau (CTB), a market research organization. Each person contacted was asked to find a friend who would also be interested in participating. Only those students who recommended friends, and the friends they suggested, were used as subjects.

Subjects were met at the door by the market research representative, an attractive young woman, and taken to the testing room. On the way, they passed the CTB office and through its open door they were able to see a desk and bookcases piled high with papers and filing cabinets. They entered the adjacent testing room which contained a table and chairs and a variety of games, and they were given a preliminary background information and game preference questionnaire to fill out. The representative told subjects that she would be working next door in her office for about 10 minutes while they completed the questionnaires, and left by opening the collapsible curtain which divided the two rooms. She made sure that subjects were aware that the curtain was unlocked and easily opened and that it provided a means of entry to her office. The respresentative

stayed in her office, shuffling papers, opening drawers, and making enough noise to remind the subjects of her presence. Four minutes after leaving the testing area, she turned on a high fidelity stereophonic tape recorder.

The emergency. If the subject listened carefully, he heard the representative climb up on a chair to reach for a stack of papers on the bookcase. Even if he were not listening carefully, he heard a loud crash and a scream as the chair collapsed and she fell to the floor. "Oh, my God, my foot . . . I . . . can't move . . . it. Oh . . . my ankle," the representative moaned. "I . . . can't get this . . . thing . . . off me." She cried and moaned for about a minute longer, but the cries gradually got more subdued and controlled. Finally, she muttered something about getting outside, knocked over the chair as she pulled herself up, and thumped to the door, closing it behind her as she left. The entire incident took 130 seconds.

The main dependent variable of the study, of course, was whether the subjects took action to help the victim and how long it took him to do so. There were actually several modes of intervention possible: a subject could open the screen dividing the two rooms, leave the testing room and enter the CTB · office by the door, find someone else, or, most simply, call out to see if the representative needed help. Four experimental conditions were run. In one condition (Alone, $n = 26$) each subject was by himself in the testing room while he filled out the questionnaire and heard the fall. In a second condition (Stooge, $n = 14$), a stranger, actually a confederate of the experimenter, was also present. The confederate had instructions to be as passive as possible and to answer questions put to him by the subjects with a brief gesture or remark. During the emergency, he looked up, shrugged his shoulders, and continued working on his questionnaire. Subjects in the third condition (Strangers, $n = 20$ pairs) were placed in the testing room in pairs. Each subject in the pair was unacquainted with the other before entering the room and they were not introduced. Only one subject in this condition spontaneously introduced himself to the other. In a final condition (Friends, $n = 20$ pairs), pairs of friends overheard the incident together.

Mode of intervention. Across all experimental groups, the majority of subjects who intervened did so by pulling back the room divider and coming into the CTB office (61 per cent). Few subjects came the round-about way through the door to offer their assistance (14 per cent), and a surprisingly small number (24 per cent) chose the easy solution of calling out to offer help. No one tried to find someone else to whom to report the accident. Since experimental conditions did not differ in the proportions choosing various modes of intervention, the comparisons below will deal only with the total proportions of subjects offering help.

Alone vs. stooge conditions. Seventy per cent of all subjects who heard the accident while alone in the waiting room offered to help the victim before she left the room. By contrast the presence of a non-responsive bystander markedly inhibited helping. Only 7 per cent of subjects in the Stooge condition intervened. These subjects seemed upset and confused during the emergency and frequently glanced at the passive confederate who continued working on his questionnaire. The difference between the Alone and Stooge response rates is, of course, highly significant ($p < .001$).

Alone vs. two strangers. Since 70 per cent of Alone subjects intervened, we should expect that at least one person in 91 per cent of all two-person groups would offer help if members of a pair had no influence upon each other. In fact, members did influence each other. In only 40 per cent of the groups did even one person offer help to the injured woman. Only 8

subjects of the 40 who were run in this condition intervened. This response rate is significantly below the hypothetical baseline ($p < .001$). Social inhibition of helping was so strong, that the victim was actually aided more quickly when only one person heard her distress than when two did ($p < .01$).

Strangers vs. stooge. The response rate in the Two Strangers condition appears to be somewhat higher than the 7 per cent rate in the Stooge condition. Making a correction similar to that used for the Alone scores, the expected response rate based on the Stooge condition is 13 per cent. This is significantly lower than the response rate in the Strangers condition ($p < .05$).

Alone vs. two friends. Pairs of friends often talked about the questionnaire before the accident, and sometimes discussed a course of action after the fall. Even so, in only 70 per cent of the pairs did even one person intervene. While, superficially, this appears as high as the Alone condition, there must again be a correction for the fact that twice as many people are free to act. When compared to the 91 per cent hypothetical base rate, friends do inhibit each other from intervening ($p < .10$). They were also slower to intervene than would be expected from the Alone condition ($p < .05$).

Friends vs. strangers. Although pairs of friends were inhibited from helping when compared to the Alone condition, they were significantly faster to intervene than were pairs of strangers ($p < .01$). The median latency of the first response from pairs of friends was 36 seconds; the median pair of strangers did not respond at all within the arbitrary 130-second duration of the emergency.

Subjects who intervened usually claimed that they did so either because the fall sounded very serious or because they were uncertain what had occurred and felt they should investigate. Many talked about intervention as the "right thing to do" and asserted they would help again in any situation.

Many of the non-interveners also claimed that they were unsure what had happened (59 per cent), but had decided that it was not too serious (46 per cent). A number of subjects reported that they thought other people would or could help (25 per cent), and three said they refrained out of concern for the victim—they did not want to embarrass her. Whether to accept these explanations as reasons or rationalizations is moot—they certainly do not explain the differences among conditions. The important thing to note is that non-interveners did not seem to feel that they had behaved callously or immorally. Their behavior was generally consistent with their interpretation of the situation. Subjects almost uniformly claimed that, in a "real" emergency, they would be among the first to help the victim.

Interestingly, when subjects were asked whether they had been influenced by the presence of action of their coworkers, they were either unwilling or unable to report that they had. Subjects in the passive confederate condition reported, on the average, that they were "very little" influenced by the stooge. Subjects in the Two Strangers condition claimed to have been only "a little bit" influenced by each other, and friends admitted to "moderate" influence. Put another way, only 14 per cent, 30 per cent, and 70 per cent of the subjects in these three conditions admitted to at least a "moderate" degree of influence. These claims, of course, run directly counter to the experimental results, in which friends were the least inhibited and subjects in the Stooge condition most inhibited by the other's actions.

These results strongly replicate the findings of the Smoke study. In both experiments, subjects were less likely to take action if they were in the presence of passive confederates than if they were alone, and in both studies, this effect showed up even when groups of naive subjects were tested together. This congruence of findings from different experimental settings supports the validity and generality of the phenomenon: it also helps rule out a variety of alternative explanations suitable to either situation alone. For example, the possibility that smoke may have represented a threat to the subject's personal safety and that subjects in groups may have had a greater concern to appear "brave" than single subjects does not apply to the present experiment. In the present experiment, non-intervention cannot signify bravery. Comparison of the two experiments also suggests that the absolute number of non-responsive bystanders may not be a critical factor in producing social inhibition of intervention. One passive confederate in the present experiment was as effective as two in the smoke study; pairs of strangers in the present study inhibited each other as much as did trios in the former study.

How can we account for the differential social inhibition caused by friends and strangers? It may be that people are less likely to fear possible embarrassment in front of friends than before strangers, and that friends are less likely to misinterpret each other's inaction than are strangers. If so, social influence should be less likely to lead friends to decide there is no emergency than strangers. When strangers overheard the accident, they seemed noticeably concerned but confused. Attempting to interpret what they had heard and to decide upon a course of action, they often glanced furtively at one another, apparently anxious to discover the other's reaction yet unwilling to meet eyes and betray their own concern. Friends, on the other hand, seemed better able to convey their concern nonverbally, and often discussed the incident and arrived at a mutual plan of action. Although these observations are admittedly impressionistic, they are consistent with other data. During the emergency, a record was kept of whether the bystanders engaged in conversation. Unfortunately, no attempt was made to code the amount or content of what was said, but it is possible to determine if there was any talking at all. Only 29 per cent of subjects attempted any conversation with the stooge; while 60 per cent of the pairs of strangers engaged in some conversation, it was mostly desultory and often unrelated to the accident. Although the latter rate seems higher than the former, it really is not, since there are two people free to initiate a conversation rather than just one. Friends, on the other hand, were somewhat more likely to talk than strangers—85 per cent of the pairs did so. Friends, then, may show less mutual inhibition than strangers because they are less likely to develop a state of "pluralistic ignorance."

These first experiments show that in two, widely different types of emergency settings, the presence of other people inhibits intervention. Subjects were less likely to report a possible fire when together than alone, and they were less likely to go to the aid of the victim of an accident when others were present. Is this a general effect? Will it apply to all types of emergency? Are there situations in which the presence of other people might actually facilitate bystander intervention? One possible set of circumstances in which we might expect social facilitation of intervention is when an emergency is caused by a villain. People who fail to intervene in real emergencies sometimes claim they were afraid of the consequences of intervention—afraid of direct attack, afraid of later retribution, afraid of having to go to court. In situations involving a villain, even if one person is afraid to take action, the presence of other people as potential risk-sharing allies might embolden him to intervene. Under these circumstances, there might actually be a group facilitation of intervention. To test this possibility, two Columbia undergradu-

ates, Paul Bonnarigo and Malcolm Ross, turned to a life of crime.

EXPERIMENT 3: THE CASE OF THE STOLEN BEER

The Nu-Way Beverage Center in Suffern, New York, is a discount beer store. It sells beer and soda by the case, often to New Jerseyans who cross the state line to find both lowered prices and a lowered legal drinking age. During the spring of 1968 it was the scene of a minor crime wave—within one two-week period, it was robbed 96 times. The robbers followed much the same modus operandi on each occasion. Singly or in a pair, they would enter the store and ask the cashier at the checkout counter "What is the most expensive imported beer that you carry?" The cashier, in cahoots with the robbers, would reply "Lowenbrau. I'll go back and check how much we have." Leaving the robbers in the front of the store, the cashier would disappear into the rear to look for the Lowenbrau. After waiting for a minute, the robbers would pick up a case of beer near the front of the store, remark to nobody in particular, "They'll never miss this," walk out of the front door, put the beer in their car, and drive off. On 46 occasions, one robber carried off the theft; on 46 occasions, two robbers were present.

The robberies were always staged when there were either one or two people in the store, and the timing was arranged so that the one or both customers would be at the checkout counter at the time when the robbers entered. On 46 occasions, one customer was at the checkout counter during the theft; on 46 occasions, two customers were present. Although occasionally the two customers had come in together, more usually they were strangers to each other. Sixty-one per cent of the customers were male, 39 per cent female. Since the checkout counter was about 20 feet from the front door, since the theft itself took less than a minute, and since the robbers were both husky young men, nobody tried directly to prevent the theft. There were, however, other courses of intervention available.

When the cashier returned from the rear of the store, he went to the checkout counter and resumed waiting on the customers there. After a minute, if nobody had spontaneously mentioned the theft, he casually inquired, "Hey, what happened to that man (those men) who was (were) in here? Did you see him (them) leave?" At this point the customer could either report the theft, say merely that he had seen the man or men leave, or disclaim any knowledge of the event whatsoever. Overall, 20 per cent of the subjects reported the theft spontaneously, and 51 per cent of the remainder reported it upon prompting. Since the results from each criterion followed an identical pattern, we shall indicate only the total proportion of subjects in each condition who reported the theft, whether spontaneously or not.

↳ *Results.* Whether there were one or two robbers present made little difference. Customers were somewhat but not significantly more likely to report the theft if there were two robbers (69 per cent) than if there was only one (52 per cent). Sex also made no difference; females were as likely to report as males. The number of customers, on the other hand, made a big difference. Thirty-one of the 48 single customers, or 65 per cent, mentioned the theft. From this, we would expect that 87 per cent of the two-person groups would include at least one reporter. In fact, in only 56 per cent of the two-person groups did even one person report the theft ($p < .01$). Social inhibition of reporting was so strong that the theft was actually somewhat (though not significantly) less likely to be reported when two people saw it than when only one did.

In three widely differing situations the same effect has been observed. People are less likely to take a socially responsible action if other people are present than if they are alone. This effect has occurred in a situation involving general danger, in a situation where someone has been the victim of an accident, and in a situation involving one or more villains. The effect holds in real life as well as in the laboratory, and for members of the general population as well as college students. The results of each of these three experiments clearly support the line of theoretical argument advanced earlier. When bystanders to an emergency can see the reactions of other people, and when other people can see their own reactions, each individual may, through a process of social influence, be led to interpret the situation as less serious than he would if he were alone, and consequently be less likely to take action.

social determinants of bystander intervention: II

So far we have devoted our attention exclusively to one stage of our hypothesized model of the intervention process: noticing the situation and interpreting it. Once an individual has noticed an emergency and interpreted it as being serious, he still has to decide what, if anything, he will do about it. He must decide that he has a responsibility to help, and that there is some form of assistance that he is in a position to give. He is faced with the choice of whether he himself will intervene. His decision will presumably be made in terms of the rewards and costs of the various alternative courses of action open to him.

In addition to affecting the interpretations that he places on a situation, the presence of other people can also alter the rewards and costs facing an individual bystander. Perhaps most importantly, the presence of other people can alter the cost of not acting. If only one bystander is present at an emergency, he carries all of the responsibility for dealing with it; he will feel all of the guilt for not acting; he will bear all of any blame others may level for non-intervention. If others are present, the onus of responsibility is diffused, and the individual may be more likely to resolve his conflict between intervening and not intervening in favor of the latter alternative.

When only one bystander is present at an emergency, if help is to come it must be from him. Although he may choose to ignore them (out of concern for his personal safety, or desire "not to get involved"), any pressures to intervene focus uniquely on him. When there are several observers present, however, the pressures to intervene do not focus on any one of the observers; instead the responsibility for intervention is shared among all the onlookers and is not unique to any one. As a result, each may be less likely to help.

Potential blame may also be diffused. However much we wish to think that an individual's moral behavior is divorced from considerations of personal punishment or reward, there is both theory and evidence to the contrary. It is perfectly reasonable to assume that, under circumstances of group responsibility for a punishable act, the punishment or blame that accrues to any one individual is often slight or nonexistent.

Finally, if others are known to be present, but their behavior cannot be closely observed, any one bystander may assume that one of the other observers is already taking action to end the emergency. If so, his own intervention would only be redundant—perhaps harmfully or confusingly so. Thus, given the presence of other onlookers whose behavior cannot be observed, any given bystander can rationalize his own inaction by convincing himself that "somebody else must be doing something."

These considerations suggest that, even when bystanders to an emergency cannot see or be influenced by each other, the more bystanders who are present, the less likely any one bystander would be to intervene and provide aid. To test this suggestion, it would be necessary to create an emergency situation in which each subject is blocked from communicating with others to prevent his getting information about their behavior during the emergency. Experiment 4 attempted to fulfill this requirement.

EXPERIMENT 4: A FIT TO BE TRIED [5]

Procedure. Thirteen male and 104 female students in introductory psychology courses at New York University were recruited to take part in an unspecified experiment as part of their class requirement. When a subject arrived in the laboratory, he was ushered into an individual room from which a communication system would enable him to talk to the other participants (who were actually figments of the tape recorder). Over the intercom, the subject was told that the experimenter was concerned with the kinds of personal problems faced by normal college students in a high-pressure, urban environment, and that he would be asked to participate in a discussion about these problems. To avoid possible embarrassment about discussing personal problems with strangers, the experimenter said, several precautions would be taken. First, subjects would remain anonymous, which was why they had been placed in individual rooms rather than face-to-face. Second, the experimenter would not listen to the initial discussion himself, but would only get the subjects' reactions later by questionnaire.

The plan for the discussion was that each person would talk in turn for two minutes, presenting his problems to the

[5] Portions of these results have been reported in J. M. Darley and B. Latané, Bystander intervention in emergencies: Diffusion of responsibility, *Journal of Personality and Social Psychology*, 1968, 8: 377–383.

group. Next, each person in turn would comment on what others had said, and finally there would be a free discussion. A mechanical switching device regulated the discussion, switching on only one microphone at a time.

The emergency. The discussion started with the future victim speaking first. He said he found it difficult to get adjusted to New York and to his studies. Very hesitantly and with obvious embarrassment, he mentioned that he was prone to seizures, particularly when studying hard or taking exams. The other people, including the one real subject, took their turns and discussed similar problems (minus the proneness to seizures). The naive subject talked last in the series, after the last prerecorded voice.

When it was again the victim's turn to talk, he made a few relatively calm comments, and then, growing increasingly loud and incoherent, he continued:

I er um I think I I need er if if could er er somebody er er er er er er er give me a little er give me a little help here because er I er I'm er er h-h-having a a a a real problem er right now and I er if somebody could help me out it would it would er er s-s-sure be sure be good . . . because er there er er a cause I er I uh I've got a a one of the er sei————er er things coming on and and and I could really er use some help so if somebody would er give me a little h-help uh er-er-er-er-er c-could somebody er er help er uh uh uh (choking sounds) . . . I'm gonna die er er I'm . . . gonna die er help er er seizure er (chokes, then quiet).

The major independent variable of the study was the number of people the subject believed also heard the fit. The subject was led to believe that the discussion group was one of three sizes: a two-person group consisting of himself and the victim; a three-person group consisting of himself, the victim and one other person; or a six-person group consisting of himself, the victim, and four other persons.

Varying the kind of bystanders present

at an emergency as well as the number of bystanders should also vary the amount of responsibility felt by any single bystander. To test this, several variations of the three-person group were run. In one three-person condition, the other bystander was a female; in another, a male; and in a third, a male who said that he was a premedical student who occasionally worked in the emergency wards at Bellevue Hospital.

Subjects in the above conditions were female college students. To test whether there are sex differences in the likelihood of helping, males drawn from the same subject pool were tested in the three-person, female bystander condition.

Two final experimental variations concerned acquaintanceship relationships between the subject and other bystanders and between the subject and the victim. In one of these conditions, female subjects were tested in the three-person condition, but were tested with a friend that they had been asked to bring with them to the laboratory. In another, subjects were given prior contact with the victim before being run in the six-person group. Subjects underwent a very brief "accidental" encounter with an experimental confederate posing as the future victim. The two met for about a minute in the hall before the experiment began. During this time, they chatted about topics having nothing to do with the experiment.

The major dependent variable of the experiment was the time elapsed from the start of the victim's seizure until the subject left her experimental cubicle. When the subject left her room, she saw the experiment's assistant seated at the end of the hall, and invariably went to the assistant to report the seizure. If six minutes elapsed without the subject's having emerged from her room, the experiment was terminated.

Ninety-five per cent of all the subjects who ever responded did so within the first half of the time available to them. No subject who had not reported within three minutes after the fit ever did so. This suggests that even had the experiment been allowed to run for a considerably longer period of time, few additional subjects would have responded.

Eighty-five per cent of the subjects who thought they alone knew of the victim's plight reported the seizure before the victim was cut off; only 31 per cent of those who thought four other bystanders were present did so. Every one of the subjects in the two-person condition, but only 62 per cent of the subjects in the six-person condition ever reported the emergency. To do a more detailed analysis of the results, each subject's time score was transformed into a "speed" score by taking the reciprocal of the response time in seconds and multiplying by 100. Analysis of variance of these speed scores indicates that the effect of group size was highly significant ($p < .01$), and all three groups differed significantly one from another ($p < .05$).

Effect of group composition and sex of the subject. Several variations of the three-person group were run. In one pair of variations, the female subject thought the other bystander was either male or female; in another, she thought the other bystander was a premedical student who worked in the emergency ward at Bellevue Hospital. These variations in the sex and medical competence of the other bystander had no important or detectable effect on speed of response. Subjects responded equally frequently and fast whether the other bystander was female, male, or medically experienced.

Coping with emergencies is often thought to be the duty of males, especially when there are females present, but there was no evidence that this is the case in this study. Male subjects responded to the emergency with almost exactly the same speed as did females.

Effects of friendship and prior acquaintance. Friends responded considerably differently from strangers in the three-person condition. When two friends were each aware of the victim's distress, even though they could not see or be seen by each other, they responded significantly faster than subjects in the other three-person groups. In fact, the average speed of response by subjects who thought their friend was also present was not noticeably different from the average speed of response in the two-person condition, where subjects believed that they alone were aware of the emergency. This suggests that responsibility does not diffuse across friends.

The effects of prior acquaintance with the victim were also strong. Subjects who had met the victim, even though only for less than a minute, were significantly faster to report his distress than other subjects in the six-person condition. Subjects in this condition later discussed their reactions to the situation. Unlike subjects in any other group, some of those who had accidentally met the victim-to-be later reported that they had actually *pictured* him in the grip of the seizure. Apparently, the ability to *visualize* a specific, concrete, distressed individual increases the likelihood of helping that person.

Subjects, whether or not they intervened, believed the fit to be genuine and serious. "My God, he's having a fit," many subjects said to themselves (and we overheard via their microphones). Others gasped or simply said, "Oh." Several of the male subjects swore. One subject said to herself, "It's just my kind of luck, something has to happen to me!" Several subjects spoke aloud of their confusion about what course of action to take: "Oh, God, what should I do?"

When those subjects who intervened stepped out of their rooms, they found the experiment's assistant down the hall. With some uncertainty but without panic, they reported the situation. "Hey, I think Number 1 is very sick. He's having a fit or something." After ostensibly checking on the situation, the experimenter returned to report that "everything is under control."

The subjects accepted these assurances with obvious relief.

Subjects who failed to report the emergency showed few signs of the apathy and indifference thought to characterize "unresponsive bystanders." When the experimenter entered her room to terminate the situation, the subject often asked if the victim were all right. "Is he being taken care of?" "He's all right, isn't he?" Many of these subjects showed physical signs of nervousness; they often had trembling hands and sweating palms. If anything, they seemed more emotionally aroused than did the subjects who reported the emergency.

Why, then, didn't they respond? It is not our impression that they had decided *not* to respond. Rather, they were still in a state of indecision and conflict concerning whether to respond or not. The emotional behavior of these non-responding subjects was a sign of their continuing conflict; a conflict that other subjects resolved by responding.

The fit created a conflict situation of the avoidance-avoidance type. On the one hand, subjects worried about the guilt and shame they would feel if they did not help the person in distress. On the other hand, they were concerned not to make fools of themselves by overreacting, not to ruin the ongoing experiment by leaving their intercoms and not to destroy the anonymous nature of the situation, which the experimenter had earlier stressed as important. For subjects in the two-person condition, the obvious distress of the victim and his need for help were so important that their conflict was easily resolved. For the subjects who knew that there were other bystanders present, the cost of not helping was reduced and the conflict they were in was more acute. Caught between the two negative alternatives of letting the victim continue to suffer, or the costs of rushing in to help, the non-responding bystanders vacillated between them rather than choosing not to respond. This distinction may be academic for the victim, since he got no help in either case, but it is an extremely important one for understanding the causes of bystanders' failures to help.

Although the subjects experienced stress and conflict during the emergency, their general reactions to it were highly positive. On a questionnaire administered after the experimenter had discussed the nature and purpose of the experiment, every single subject found the experiment either "interesting" or "very interesting" and was willing to participate in similar experiments in the future. All subjects felt they understood what the experiment was all about and indicated they thought the deceptions were necessary and justified. All but one felt they were better informed about the nature of psychological research in general.

We asked all subjects whether the presence or absence of other bystanders had entered their minds during the time that they were hearing the seizure. We asked the question every way we knew how: subtly, directly, tactfully, bluntly, and the answer was always the same. Subjects had been aware of the presence of other bystanders in the appropriate conditions, but they did not feel that they had been influenced in any way by their presence. As in our previous experiments, this denial occurred in the face of results showing that the presence of others did affect helping.

social determinants of bystander intervention: III

We have suggested two distinct processes which might lead people to be less likely to intervene in an emergency if there are other people present than if they are alone. On the one hand, we have suggested that the presence of other people may affect the interpretations each bystander puts on an ambiguous emergency situation. If other people are present at an emergency, each bystander will be guided by their apparent reactions in formulating his own impressions. Unfortunately, their apparent reactions may not be a good indication of their true feelings. It is possible for a state of "pluralistic ignorance" to develop, in which each bystander is led by the *apparent* lack of concern of the others to interpret the situation as being less serious than he would if alone. To the extent that he does not feel the situation is an emergency, of course, he will be unlikely to take any helpful action.

Even if an individual does decide that an emergency is actually in process and that something ought to be done, he still is faced with the choice of whether he himself will intervene. Here again, the presence of other people may influence him—by reducing the costs associated with non-intervention. If a number of people witness the same event, the responsibility for action is diffused, and each may feel less necessity to help.

Both the "social influence" and the "diffusion of responsibility" explanations seem valid, and there is no reason why both should not be jointly operative. Neither alone can account for all the data. For example, the diffusion explanation cannot account for the significant difference in response rate between the Strangers and Stooge conditions in Experiment 2. There should be equal diffusion in either case. This difference can more plausibly be attributed to the fact that strangers typically did not show such complete indifference to the accident as did the stooge. The diffusion process also does not seem applicable to the results of Experiment 1. Responsibility for protecting oneself from fire should not diffuse. On the other, hand "social influence" processes cannot account for results in Experiment 4. Subjects in that experiment could not communicate with each other and thus could not be influenced by each other's reactions.

Although both processes probably operate, they may not do so at the same time. To the extent that social influence leads an individual to define the situation as non-

serious and not requiring action, his responsibility is eliminated, making diffusion unnecessary. Only if social influence is unavailable or unsuccessful in leading subjects to misinterpret a situation, should diffusion play a role. Indirect evidence supporting this analysis comes from observation of non-intervening subjects in the various emergency settings. In settings involving face-to-face contact, as in Experiments 1 and 2, non-interveners typically redefined the situation and did not see it as a serious emergency. Consequently, they avoided the moral choice of whether or not to take action. During the post-experimental interviews, subjects in these experiments seemed relaxed and assured. They felt they had behaved reasonably and properly. In Experiment 4, on the other hand, face-to-face contact was prevented, social influence could not help subjects define the situation as non-serious, and they were faced with the moral dilemma of whether to intervene. Although the imagined presence of other people led many subjects to delay intervention, their conflict was exhibited in the post-experimental interviews. If anything, subjects who did not intervene seemed more emotionally aroused than did subjects who reported the emergency.

The results of these experiments suggest that social inhibition effects may be rather general over a wide variety of emergency situations. In four different experiments, bystanders have been less likely to intervene if other bystanders are present. The nature of the other bystander seems to be important: a non-reactive confederate provides the most inhibition, a stranger provides a moderate amount, and a friend, the least. Overall, the results are consistent with a multiprocess model of intervention; the effect of other people seems to be mediated both through the interpretations that bystanders place on the situation, and through the decisions they make once they have come up with an interpretation.

"There's safety in numbers," according to an old adage, and modern city dwellers seem to believe it. They shun deserted streets, empty subway cars, and lonely walks in dark parks, preferring instead to go where others are or to stay at home. When faced with stress, most individuals seem less afraid when they are in the presence of others than when they are alone. Dogs are less likely to yelp when they face a strange situation with other dogs; even rats are less likely to defecate and freeze when they are placed in a frightening open field with other rats.

A feeling so widely shared should have some basis in reality. Is there safety in numbers? If so, why? Two reasons are often suggested: Individuals are less likely to find themselves in trouble if there are others about, and even if they do find themselves in trouble, others are likely to help them deal with it. While it is certainly true that a victim is unlikely to receive help if nobody knows of his plight, the experiments above cast doubt on the suggestion that he will be more likely to receive help if more people are present. In fact, the opposite seems to be true. A victim may be more likely to get help, or an emergency be reported, the fewer people who are available to take action.

Although the results of these studies may shake our faith in "safety in numbers," they also may help us begin to understand a number of frightening incidents where crowds have listened to, but not answered, a call for help. Newspapers have tagged these incidents with the label "apathy." We have become indifferent, they say, callous to the fate of suffering others. Our society has become "dehumanized" as it has become urbanized. These glib phrases may contain some truth, since startling cases such as the Genovese murder often seem to occur in our large cities, but such terms may also be misleading. Our studies suggest a different conclusion. They suggest that situational factors, specifically factors involving the immediate social environment, may be of greater importance in determining an individual's reaction to an emer-

gency than such vague cultural or personality concepts as "apathy" or "alienation due to urbanization." They suggest that the failure to intervene may be better understood by knowing the relationship among bystanders rather than that between a bystander and the victim.

Our results may explain why the failure to intervene seems to be more characteristic of large cities than rural areas. Bystanders to urban emergencies are more likely to be, or at least to think they are, in the presence of other bystanders than witnesses of non-urban emergencies. Bystanders to urban emergencies are less likely to know each other or to know the victim than are witnesses of non-urban emergencies. When an emergency occurs in a large city, a crowd is likely to gather; the crowd members are likely to be strangers; and it is likely that no one will be acquainted with the victim. These are exactly the conditions that made the helping response least likely in our experiments.

In a less sophisticated era, Rudyard Kipling prayed "That we, with Thee, may walk uncowed by fear or favor of the crowd; that, under Thee, we may possess man's strength to comfort man's distress." It appears that the latter hope may depend to a surprising extent upon the former.

REFERENCES

BROWN, R. W. Mass Phenomena. In Lindzey, G. (ed.) *Handbook of Social Psychology,* Vol. 2. Cambridge: Addison-Wesley, 1954.

————. *Social Psychology.* New York: The Free Press, 1965.

DARLEY, J. M., and B. LATANÉ. Bystander intervention in emergencies: Diffusion of responsibility. *Journal of Personality and Social Psychology,* 1968, **8**, 377–383.

LATANÉ, B. Gregariousness and fear in laboratory rats. *Journal of Experimental Social Psychology,* 1969, **5**, 61–69.

————, and J. M. DARLEY. Group inhibition of bystander intervention in emergencies. *Journal of Personality and Social Psychology,* 1968, **10**, 215–221.

LATANÉ, B., and D. C. GLASS. Social and non-social attraction in rats. *Journal of Personality and Social Psychology*, 1968, 9, 142–146.

LATANÉ, B., and J. RODIN. A lady in distress: Inhibiting effects of friends and strangers on bystander intervention. *Journal of Experimental Social Psychology*, in press.

SCHACHTER, S. *The Psychology of Affiliation.* Stanford: Stanford University Press, 1959.

29

In the next paper, Stanley Milgram discusses some recent research which nicely complements the previous paper on bystander apathy. Milgram formulates some theoretical notions which attempt to relate the individual's experience and behavior to the physical-demographic environment in which he lives. The analysis which follows may provide a starting point for defining the role of the experimental social psychologist in activities such as community planning, urban renewal, race relations, and environmental control.

the experience of living in cities

STANLEY MILGRAM

When I first came to New York it seemed like a nightmare. As soon as I got off the train at Grand Central I was caught up in pushing, shoving crowds on 42nd Street. Sometimes people bumped into me without apology; what really frightened me was to see two people literally engaged in combat for possession of a cab. Why were they so rushed? Even drunks on the street were bypassed without a glance. People didn't seem to care about each other at all.

This statement represents a common reaction to a great city, but it does not tell the whole story. Obviously cities have great appeal because of their variety, eventful-

This article is based on an address given on 2 September 1969 at the 77th annual meeting of the American Psychological Association, in Washington, D.C. Barbara Bengen worked closely with me in preparing the present version of this article. I thank Dr. Gary Winkel, editor of *Environment and Behavior,* for useful suggestions and advice.

ness, possibility of choice, and the stimulation of an intense atmosphere that many individuals find a desirable background to their lives. Where face-to-face contacts are important, the city offers unparalleled possibilities. It has been calculated by the Regional Plan Association [1] that in Nassau County, a suburb of New York City, an individual can meet 11,000 others within a 10-minute radius of his office by foot or car. In Newark, a moderate-sized city, he can meet more than 20,000 persons within this radius. But in midtown Manhattan he can meet fully 220,000. So there is an order-of-magnitude increment in the communication possibilities offered by a great city. That is one of the bases of its appeal and, indeed, of its functional necessity. The city provides options that no other social arrangement permits. But there is a negative side also, as we shall see.

Granted that cities are indispensable in complex society, we may still ask what con-

[1] *New York Times* (15 June 1969).

tribution psychology can make to understanding the experience of living in them. What theories are relevant? How can we extend our knowledge of the psychological aspects of life in cities through empirical inquiry? If empirical inquiry is possible, along what lines should it proceed? In short, where do we start in constructing urban theory and in laying out lines of research?

Observation is the indispensable starting point. Any observer in the streets of midtown Manhattan will see (i) large numbers of people, (ii) a high population density, and (iii) heterogeneity of population. These three factors need to be at the root of any sociopsychological theory of city life, for they condition all aspects of our experience in the metropolis. Louis Wirth,[2] if not the first to point to these factors, is nonetheless the sociologist who relied most heavily on them in his analysis of the city. Yet, for a psychologist, there is something unsatisfactory about Wirth's theoretical variables. Numbers, density, and heterogeneity are demographic facts but they are not yet psychological facts. They are external to the individual. Psychology needs an idea that links the individual's *experience* to the demographic circumstances of urban life.

One link is provided by the concept of overload. This term, drawn from systems analysis, refers to a system's inability to process inputs from the environment because there are too many inputs for the system to cope with, or because successive inputs come so fast that input A cannot be processed when input B is presented. When overload is present, adaptations occur. The

system must set priorities and make choices. A may be processed first while B is kept in abeyance, or one input may be sacrificed altogether. City life, as we experience it, constitutes a continuous set of encounters with overload, and of resultant adaptations. Overload characteristically deforms daily life on several levels, impinging on role performance, the evolution of social norms, cognitive functioning, and the use of facilities.

The concept has been implicit in several theories of urban experience. In 1903 Georg Simmel[3] pointed out that, since urban dwellers come into contact with vast numbers of people each day, they conserve psychic energy by becoming acquainted with a far smaller proportion of people than their rural counterparts do, and by maintaining more superficial relationships even with these acquaintances. Wirth[4] points specifically to "the superficiality, the anonymity, and the transitory character of urban social relations."

One adaptive response to overload, therefore, is the allocation of less time to each input. A second adaptive mechanism is disregard of low-priority inputs. Principles of selectivity are formulated such that investment of time and energy are reserved for carefully defined inputs (the urbanite disregards the drunk sick on the street as he purposefully navigates through the crowd). Third, boundaries are redrawn in certain social transactions so that the overloaded system can shift the burden to the other party in the exchange; thus, harried New York bus drivers once made change for customers, but now this responsibility has been shifted to the client, who must have the exact fare ready. Fourth, reception is blocked off prior to entrance into a system; city dwellers increasingly use

---

[2] L. Wirth, *Amer. J. Soc.*, 44 (1938), 1. Wirth's ideas have come under heavy criticism by contemporary city planners, who point out that the city is broken down into neighborhoods, which fulfill many of the functions of small towns. See, for example, H. J. Gans, *People and Plans: Essays on Urban Problems and Solutions* (New York: Basic Books, 1968); J. Jacobs, *The Death and Life of Great American Cities* (New York: Random House, 1961); G. D. Suttles, *The Social Order of the Slum* (Chicago: Univ. of Chicago Press, 1968).

[3] G. Simmel, *The Sociology of Georg Simmel*, K. H. Wolff, Ed. (New York: Macmillan, 1950) [English translation of G. Simmel, *Die Grosstadte und das Geistesleben Die Grossstadt* (Dresden: Jansch, 1903)].

[4] *Op. cit.*

unlisted telephone numbers to prevent individuals from calling them, and a small but growing number resort to keeping the telephone off the hook to prevent incoming calls. More subtly, a city dweller blocks inputs by assuming an unfriendly countenance, which discourages others from initiating contact. Additionally, social screening devices are interposed between the individual and environmental inputs (in a town of 5000 anyone can drop in to chat with the mayor, but in the metropolis organizational screening devices deflect inputs to other destinations). Fifth, the intensity of inputs is diminished by filtering devices, so that only weak and relatively superficial forms of involvement with others are allowed. Sixth, specialized institutions are created to absorb inputs that would otherwise swamp the individual (welfare departments handle the financial needs of a million individuals in New York City, who would otherwise create an army of mendicants continuously importuning the pedestrian). The interposition of institutions between the individual and the social world, a characteristic of all modern society, and most notably of the large metropolis, has its negative side. It deprives the individual of a sense of direct contact and spontaneous integration in the life around him. It simultaneously protects and estranges the individual from his social environment.

Many of these adaptive mechanisms apply not only to individuals but to institutional systems as well, as Meier [5] has so brilliantly shown in connection with the library and the stock exchange.

In sum, the observed behavior of the urbanite in a wide range of situations appears to be determined largely by a variety of adaptations to overload. I now deal with several specific consequences of responses to overload, which make for differences in the tone of city and town.

[5] R. L. Meier, *A Communications Theory of Urban Growth* (Cambridge, Mass.: M.I.T. Press, 1962).

social responsibility

The principal point of interest for a social psychology of the city is that moral and social involvement with individuals is necessarily restricted. This is a direct and necessary function of excess of input over capacity to process. Such restriction of involvement runs a broad spectrum from refusal to become involved in the needs of another person, even when the person desperately needs assistance, through refusal to do favors, to the simple withdrawal of courtesies (such as offering a lady a seat, or saying "sorry" when a pedestrian collision occurs). In any transaction more and more details need to be dropped as the total number of units to be processed increases and assaults an instrument of limited processing capacity.

The ultimate adaptation to an overloaded social environment is to totally disregard the needs, interests, and demands of those whom one does not define as relevant to the satisfaction of personal needs, and to develop highly efficient perceptual means of determining whether an individual falls into the category of friend or stranger. The disparity in the treatment of friends and strangers ought to be greater in cities than in towns; the time allotment and willingness to become involved with those who have no personal claim on one's time is likely to be less in cities than in towns.

BYSTANDER INTERVENTION IN CRISES

The most striking deficiencies in social responsibility in cities occur in crisis situations, such as the Genovese murder in Queens. In 1964, Catherine Genovese, coming home from a night job in the early hours of an April morning, was stabbed repeatedly, over an extended period of time. Thirty-eight residents of a respectable New York City neighborhood admit to having witnessed at least a part of the attack, but none went to her aid or called the police until after she was dead. Milgram and Hollander, writing in *The Nation*,[6] analyzed the event in these terms:

Urban friendships and associations are not primarily formed on the basis of physical proximity. A person with numerous close friends in different parts of the city may not know the occupant of an adjacent apartment. This does not mean that a city dweller has fewer friends than does a villager, or knows fewer persons who will come to his aid; however, it does mean that his allies are not constantly at hand. Miss Genovese required immediate aid from those physically present. There is no evidence that the city had deprived Miss Genovese of human associations, but the friends who might have rushed to her side were miles from the scene of her tragedy.

Further, it is known that her cries for help were not directed to a specific person; they were general. But only individuals can act, and as the cries were not specifically directed, no particular person felt a special responsibility. The crime and the failure of community response seem absurd to us. At the time, it may well have seemed equally absurd to the Kew Gardens residents that not one of the neighbors would have called the police. A collective paralysis may have developed from the belief of each of the witnesses that someone else must surely have taken that obvious step.

Latané and Darley [7] have reported laboratory approaches to the study of bystander intervention and have established experimentally the following principle: the larger the number of bystanders, the less the likelihood that any one of them will intervene in an emergency. Gaertner and Bickman [8] of The City University of New York have extended the bystander studies to an examination of help across ethnic lines. Blacks and whites, with clearly identifiable ac-

cents, called strangers (through what the caller represented as an error in telephone dialing), gave them a plausible story of being stranded on an outlying highway without more dimes, and asked the stranger to call a garage. The experimenters found that the white callers had a significantly better chance of obtaining assistance than the black callers. This suggests that ethnic allegiance may well be another means of coping with overload: the city dweller can reduce excessive demands and screen out urban heterogeneity by responding along ethnic lines; overload is made more manageable by limiting the "span of sympathy."

In any quantitative characterization of the social texture of city life, a necessary first step is the application of such experimental methods as these to field situations in large cities and small towns. Theorists argue that the indifference shown in the Genovese case would not be found in a small town, but in the absence of solid experimental evidence the question remains an open one.

More than just callousness prevents bystanders from participating in altercations between people. A rule of urban life is respect for other people's emotional and social privacy, perhaps because physical privacy is so hard to achieve. And in situations for which the standards are heterogeneous, it is much harder to know whether taking an active role is unwarranted meddling or an appropriate response to a critical situation. If a husband and wife are quarreling in public, at what point should a bystander step in? On the one hand, the heterogeneity of the city produces substantially greater tolerance about behavior, dress, and codes of ethics than is generally found in the small town, but this diversity also encourages people to withhold aid for fear of antagonizing the participants or crossing an inappropriate and difficult-to-define line.

Moreover, the frequency of demands present in the city gives rise to norms of noninvolvement. There are practical limi-

6 S. Milgram and P. Hollander, *Nation*, **25** (1964), 602.

7 B. Latané and J. Darley, *Amer. Sci.*, **57** (1969), 244 [p. 321 in this volume].

8 S. Gaertner and L. Bickman (Graduate Center, The City University of New York), unpublished research.

tations to the Samaritan impulse in a major city. If a citizen attended to every needy person, if he were sensitive to and acted on every altruistic impulse that was evoked in the city, he could scarcely keep his own affairs in order.

WILLINGNESS TO TRUST AND ASSIST STRANGERS

We now move away from crisis situations to less urgent examples of social responsibility. For it is not only in situations of dramatic need but in the ordinary, everyday willingness to lend a hand that the city dweller is said to be deficient relative to his small-town cousin. The comparative method must be used in any empirical examination of this question. A commonplace social situation is staged in an urban setting and in a small town—a situation to which a subject can respond by either extending help or withholding it. The responses in town and city are compared.

One factor in the purported unwillingness of urbanites to be helpful to strangers may well be their heightened sense of physical (and emotional) vulnerability—a feeling that is supported by urban crime statistics. A key test for distinguishing between city and town behavior, therefore, is determining how city dwellers compare with town dwellers in offering aid that increases their personal vulnerability and requires some trust of strangers. Altman, Levine, Nadien, and Villena [9] of The City University of New York devised a study to compare the behaviors of city and town dwellers in this respect. The criterion used in this study was the willingness of householders to allow strangers to enter their home to use the telephone. The student investigators individually rang doorbells, explained that they had misplaced the address of a friend nearby, and asked to use the phone. The investigators (two males

[9] D. Altman, M. Levine, M. Nadien, J. Villena (Graduate Center, The City University of New York), unpublished research.

and two females) made 100 requests for entry into homes in the city and 60 requests in the small towns. The results for middle-income housing developments in Manhattan were compared with data for several small towns (Stony Point, Spring Valley, Ramapo, Nyack, New City, and West Clarkstown) in Rockland County, outside of New York City. As Table 1 shows, in all cases

table 1

percentage of entries achieved by investigators for city and town dwellings (see text)

	entries achieved (%)	
experimenter	city *	small town †
Male		
No. 1	16	40
No. 2	12	60
Female		
No. 3	40	87
No. 4	40	100

* Number of requests for entry, 100.
† Number of requests for entry, 60.

there was a sharp increase in the proportion of entries achieved by an experimenter when he moved from the city to a small town. In the most extreme case the experimenter was five times as likely to gain admission to homes in a small town as to homes in Manhattan. Although the female experimenters had notably greater success both in cities and in towns than the male experimenters had, each of the four students did at least twice as well in towns as in cities. This suggests that the city-town distinction overrides even the predictably greater fear of male strangers than of female ones.

The lower level of helpfulness by city dwellers seems due in part to recognition of the dangers of living in Manhattan, rather than to mere indifference or coldness. It is significant that 75 percent of all the city respondents received and answered messages by shouting through closed doors and by peering out through peepholes; in the towns, by contrast, about 75 percent of the respondents opened the door.

Supporting the experimenters' quantitative results was their general observation that the town dwellers were noticeably more friendly and less suspicious than the city dwellers. In seeking to explain the reasons for the greater sense of psychological vulnerability city dwellers feel, above and beyond the differences in crime statistics, Villena [10] points out that, if a crime is committed in a village, a resident of a neighboring village may not perceive the crime as personally relevant, though the geographic distance may be small, whereas a criminal act committed anywhere in the city, though miles from the city-dweller's home is still verbally located within the city; thus, Villena says, "the inhabitant of the city possesses a larger vulnerable space."

CIVILITIES

Even at the most superficial level of involvement—the exercise of everyday civilities—urbanites are reputedly deficient. People bump into each other and often do not apologize. They knock over another person's packages and, as often as not, proceed on their way with a grumpy exclamation instead of an offer of assistance. Such behavior, which many visitors to great cities find distasteful, is less common, we are told, in smaller communities, where traditional courtesies are more likely to be observed.

In some instances it is not simply that, in the city, traditional courtesies are violated; rather, the cities develop new norms of noninvolvement. These are so well defined and so deeply a part of city life that *they* constitute the norms people are reluctant to violate. Men are actually embarrassed to give up a seat on the subway to an old woman; they mumble "I was getting off anyway," instead of making the

[10] *Ibid.*

gesture in a straightforward and gracious way. These norms develop because everyone realizes that, in situations of high population density, people cannot implicate themselves in each others' affairs, for to do so would create conditions of continual distraction which would frustrate purposeful action.

In discussing the effects of overload I do not imply that at every instant the city dweller is bombarded with an unmanageable number of inputs, and that his responses are determined by the excess of input at any given instant. Rather, adaptation occurs in the form of gradual evolution of norms of behavior. Norms are evolved in response to frequent discrete experiences of overload; they persist and become generalized modes of responding.

OVERLOAD ON COGNITIVE CAPACITIES: ANONYMITY

That we respond differently toward those whom we know and those who are strangers to us is a truism. An eager patron aggressively cuts in front of someone in a long movie line to save time only to confront a friend; he then behaves sheepishly. A man is involved in an automobile accident caused by another driver, emerges from his car shouting in rage, then moderates his behavior on discovering a friend driving the other car. The city dweller, when walking through the midtown streets, is in a state of continual anonymity vis-à-vis the other pedestrians.

Anonymity is part of a continuous spectrum ranging from total anonymity to full acquaintance, and it may well be that measurement of the precise degrees of anonymity in cities and towns would help to explain important distinctions between the quality of life in each. Conditions of full acquaintance, for example, offer security and familiarity, but they may also be stifling, because the individual is caught in a web of established relationships. Conditions of complete anonymity, by contrast, provide freedom from routinized social ties, but they may also create feelings of alienation and detachment.

Empirically one could investigate the proportion of activities in which the city dweller or the town dweller is known by others at given times in his daily life, and the proportion of activities in the course of which he interacts with individuals who know him. At his job, for instance, the city dweller may be known to as many people as his rural counterpart. However, when he is not fulfilling his occupational role—say, when merely traveling about the city—the urbanite is doubtless more anonymous than his rural counterpart.

Limited empirical work on anonymity has begun. Zimbardo [11] has tested whether the social anonymity and impersonality of the big city encourage greater vandalism than do small towns. Zimbardo arranged for one automobile to be left for 64 hours near the Bronx campus of New York University and for a counterpart to be left for the same number of hours near Stanford University in Palo Alto. The license plates on the two cars were removed and the hoods were opened, to provide "releaser cues" for potential vandals. The New York car was stripped of all movable parts within the first 24 hours, and by the end of 3 days was only a hunk of metal rubble. Unexpectedly, however, most of the destruction occurred during daylight hours, usually under the scrutiny of observers, and the leaders in the vandalism were well-dressed, white adults. The Palo Alto car was left untouched.

Zimbardo attributes the difference in the treatment accorded the two cars to the "acquired feelings of social anonymity provided by life in a city like New York," and he supports his conclusions with several other anecdotes illustrating casual, wanton vandalism in the city. In any comparative study of the effects of anonymity

in city and town, however, there must be satisfactory control for other confounding factors: the large number of drug addicts in a city like New York; the higher proportion of slum-dwellers in the city; and so on.

Another direction for empirical study is investigation of the beneficial effects of anonymity. The impersonality of city life breeds its own tolerance for the private lives of the inhabitants. Individuality and even eccentricity, we may assume, can flourish more readily in the metropolis than in the small town. Stigmatized persons may find it easier to lead comfortable lives in the city, free of the constant scrutiny of neighbors. To what degree can this assumed difference between city and town be shown empirically? Judith Waters,[12] at The City University of New York, hypothesized that avowed homosexuals would be more likely to be accepted as tenants in a large city than in small towns, and she dispatched letters from homosexuals and from normal individuals to real estate agents in cities and towns across the country. The results of her study were inconclusive. But the general idea of examining the protective benefits of city life to the stigmatized ought to be pursued.

ROLE BEHAVIOR IN CITIES AND TOWNS

Another product of urban overload is the adjustment in roles made by urbanites in daily interactions. As Wirth has said [13]: "Urbanites meet one another in highly segmental roles. . . . They are less dependent upon particular persons, and their dependence upon others is confined to a highly fractionalized aspect of the other's round of activity." This tendency is particularly noticeable in transactions between customers and individuals offering professional or sales services. The owner of a country store has time to become well acquainted with his dozen-or-so daily cus-

---

[11] P. G. Zimbardo, paper presented at the Nebraska Symposium on Motivation (1969).

[12] J. Waters (Graduate Center, The City University of New York), unpublished research.

[13] *Op. cit.*

tomers, but the girl at the checkout counter of a busy A & P, serving hundreds of customers a day, barely has time to toss the green stamps into one customer's shopping bag before the next customer confronts her with his pile of groceries.

Meier, in his stimulating analysis of the city,[14] discusses several adaptations a system may make when confronted by inputs that exceed its capacity to process them. Meier argues that, according to the principle of competition for scarce resources, the scope and time of the transaction shrink as customer volume and daily turnover rise. This, in fact, is what is meant by the "brusque" quality of city life. New standards have developed in cities concerning what levels of services are appropriate in business transactions (see Figure 1).

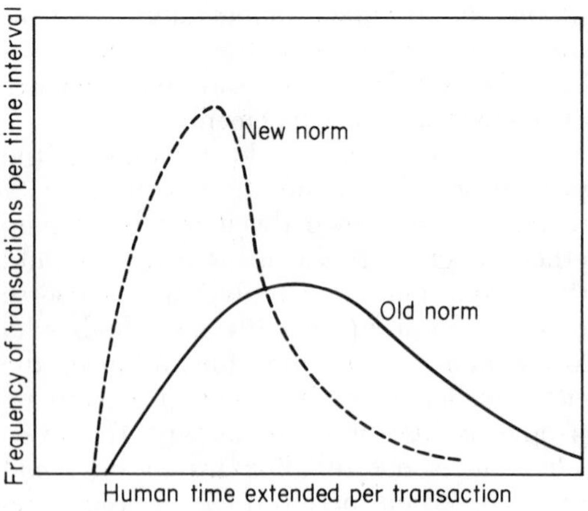

McKenna and Morgenthau,[15] in a seminar at The City University of New York, devised a study (i) to compare the willingness of city dwellers and small-town dwellers to do favors for strangers that entailed expenditure of a small amount of time and slight inconvenience but no personal vulnerability, and (ii) to determine whether the more compartmentalized, transitory relationships of the city would make urban salesgirls less likely than small-town salesgirls to carry out, for strangers, tasks not related to their customary roles.

To test for differences between city dwellers and small-town dwellers, a simple experiment was devised in which persons from both settings were asked (by telephone) to perform increasingly onerous favors for anonymous strangers.

Within the cities (Chicago, New York, and Philadelphia), half the calls were to housewives and the other half to salesgirls in women's apparel shops; the division was the same for the 37 small towns of the

14 *Op. cit.*
15 W. McKenna and S. Morgenthau (Graduate Center, The City University of New York), unpublished research.

figure 1   *Changes in the demand for time for a given task when the overall transaction frequency increases in a social system. [Reprinted from R. L. Meier,* A Communications Theory of Urban Growth *(Cambridge, Mass.: The M.I.T. Press, 1962), by permission. Copyright © 1962 by The M.I.T. Press.]*

study, which were in the same states as the cities. Each experimenter represented herself as a long-distance caller who had, through error, been connected with the respondent by the operator. The experimenter began by asking for simple information about the weather for purposes of travel. Next the experimenter excused herself on some pretext (asking the respondent to "please hold on"), put the phone down for almost a full minute, and then picked it up again and asked the respondent to provide the phone number of a hotel or motel in her vicinity at which the experimenter might stay during a forthcoming visit. Scores were assigned the subjects on the basis of how helpful they had been. McKenna summarizes her results in this manner:

People in the city, whether they are engaged in a specific job or not, are less helpful and informative than people in small towns; . . . People at home, regardless of where they live, are less helpful and informative than people working in shops.

However, the absolute level of cooperativeness for urban subjects was found to be quite high, and does not accord with the stereotype of the urbanite as aloof, self-centered, and unwilling to help strangers. The quantitative differences obtained by McKenna and Morgenthau are less great than one might have expected. This again points up the need for extensive empirical research in rural-urban differences, research that goes far beyond that provided in the few illustrative pilot studies presented here. At this point we have very limited objective evidence on differences in the quality of social encounters in city and small town.

But the research needs to be guided by unifying theoretical concepts. As I have tried to demonstrate, the concept of overload helps to explain a wide variety of contrasts between city behavior and town behavior: (i) the differences in role enactment (the tendency of urban dwellers to deal with one another in highly segmented, functional terms, and of urban sales personnel to devote limited time and attention to their customers); (ii) the evolution of urban norms quite different from traditional town values (such as the acceptance of noninvolvement, impersonality, and aloofness in urban life); (iii) the adaptation of the urban dweller's cognitive processes (his inability to identify most of the people he sees daily, his screening of sensory stimuli, his development of blasé attitudes toward deviant or bizarre behavior, and his selectivity in responding to human demands); and (iv) the competition for scarce facilities in the city (the subway rush; the fight for taxis; traffic jams; standing in line to await services). I suggest that contrasts between city and rural behavior probably reflect the responses of similar people to very different situations, rather than intrinsic differences in the personalities of rural and city dwellers. The city is a situation to which individuals respond adaptively.

further aspects of urban experience

Some features of urban experience do not fit neatly into the system of analysis presented thus far. They are no less important for that reason. The issues raised next are difficult to treat in quantitative fashion. Yet I prefer discussing them in a loose way to excluding them because appropriate language and data have not yet been developed. My aim is to suggest how phenomena such as "urban atmosphere" can be pinned down through techniques of measurement.

THE "ATMOSPHERE" OF GREAT CITIES

The contrast in the behavior of city and town dwellers has been a natural starting point for urban social scientists. But even among great cities there are marked differences in "atmosphere." The tone, pacing, and texture of social encounters are different in London and New York, and many persons willingly make financial sacrifices for the privilege of living within a specific urban atmosphere which they find pleasing or stimulating. A second perspective in the study of cities, therefore, is to define exactly what is meant by the atmosphere of a city and to pinpoint the factors that give rise to it. It may seem that urban atmosphere is too evanescent a quality to be reduced to a set of measurable variables, but I do not believe the matter can be judged before substantial effort has been made in this direction. It is obvious that any such approach must be comparative. It makes no sense at all to say that New York is "vibrant" and "frenetic" unless one has some specific city in mind as a basis of comparison.

In an undergraduate tutorial that I conducted at Harvard University some years ago, New York, London, and Paris were selected as reference points for attempts to measure urban atmosphere. We began with a simple question: Does any consensus exist about the qualities that typify given cities? To answer this question one could undertake a content analysis of travel-book, literary, and journalistic accounts of cities. A second approach, which we adopted, is to ask people to characterize (with descriptive terms and accounts of typical experiences) cities they have lived in or visited. In advertisements placed in the *New York Times* and the *Harvard Crimson* we asked people to give us accounts of specific incidents in London, Paris, or New York that best illuminated the character of that particular city. Questionnaires were then developed, and administered to persons who were familiar with at least two of the three cities.

Some distinctive patterns emerged.[16] The distinguishing themes concerning New York, for example, dealt with its diversity, its great size, its pace and level of activity, its cultural and entertainment opportunities, and the heterogeneity and segmentation ("ghettoization") of its population. New York elicited more descriptions in terms of physical qualities, pace, and emotional impact than Paris or London did, a fact which suggests that these are particularly important aspects of New York's ambiance.

A contrasting profile emerges for London; in this case respondents placed far greater emphasis on their interactions with the inhabitants than on physical surroundings. There was near unanimity on certain themes: those dealing with the tolerance and courtesy of London's inhabitants. One respondent said:

When I was 12, my grandfather took me to the British Museum . . . one day by tube and recited the *Aeneid* in Latin for my benefit. . . . He is rather deaf, speaks very loudly and it embarrassed the hell out of me, until I realized that nobody was paying any attention. Londoners are extremely worldly and tolerant.

[16] N. Abuza (Harvard University), "The Paris-London-New York Questionnaires," unpublished.

In contrast, respondents who described New Yorkers as aloof, cold, and rude referred to such incidents as the following:

I saw a boy of 19 passing out anti-war leaflets to passersby. When he stopped at a corner, a man dressed in a business suit walked by him at a brisk pace, hit the boy's arm, and scattered the leaflets all over the street. The man kept walking at the same pace down the block.

We need to obtain many more such descriptions of incidents, using careful methods of sampling. By the application of factor-analytic techniques, relevant dimensions for each city can be discerned.

The responses for Paris were about equally divided between responses concerning its inhabitants and those regarding its physical and sensory attributes. Cafés and parks were often mentioned as contributing to the sense that Paris is a city of amenities, but many respondents complained that Parisians were inhospitable, nasty, and cold.

We cannot be certain, of course, to what degree these statements reflect actual characteristics of the cities in question and to what degree they simply tap the respondents' knowledge of widely held preconceptions. Indeed, one may point to three factors, apart from the actual atmospheres of the cities, that determine the subjects' responses.

1. A person's impression of a given city depends on his implicit standard of comparison. A New Yorker who visits Paris may well describe that city as "leisurely," whereas a compatriot from Richmond, Virginia, may consider Paris too "hectic." Obtaining reciprocal judgment, in which New Yorkers judge Londoners, and Londoners judge New Yorkers, seems a useful way to take into account not only the city being judged but also the home city that serves as the visitor's base line.

2. Perceptions of a city are also affected by whether the observer is a tourist, a newcomer, or a longer-term resident. First, a tourist will be exposed to features of the

city different from those familiar to a long-time resident. Second, a prerequisite for adapting to continuing life in a given city seems to be the filtering out of many observations about the city that the newcomer or tourist finds particularly arresting; this selective process seems to be part of the long-term resident's mechanism for coping with overload. In the interest of psychic economy, the resident simply learns to tune out many aspects of daily life. One method for studying the specific impact of adaptation on perception of the city is to ask several pairs of newcomers and old-timers (one newcomer and one old-timer to a pair) to walk down certain city blocks and then report separately what each has observed.

Additionally, many persons have noted that when travelers return to New York from an extended sojourn abroad they often feel themselves confronted with "brutal ugliness" [17] and a distinctive, frenetic atmosphere whose contributing details are, for a few hours or days, remarkably sharp and clear. This period of fresh perception should receive special attention in the study of city atmosphere. For, in a few days, details which are initially arresting become less easy to specify. They are assimilated into an increasingly familiar background atmosphere which, though important in setting the tone of things, is difficult to analyze. There is no better point at which to begin the study of city atmosphere than at the moment when a traveler returns from abroad.

3. The popular myths and expectations each visitor brings to the city will also affect the way in which he perceives it.[18] Sometimes a person's preconceptions about a city are relatively accurate distillations of its character, but preconceptions may also reinforce myths by filtering the visitor's preceptions to conform with his ex-

pectations. Preconceptions affect not only a person's perceptions of a city but what he reports about it.

The influence of a person's urban base line on his perceptions of a given city, the differences between the observations of the long-time inhabitant and those of the newcomer, and the filtering effect of personal expectations and stereotypes raise serious questions about the validity of travelers' reports. Moreover, no social psychologist wants to rely exclusively on verbal accounts if he is attempting to obtain an accurate and objective description of the cities' social texture, pace, and general atmosphere. What he needs to do is to devise means of embedding objective experimental measures in the daily flux of city life, measures that can accurately index the qualities of a given urban atmosphere.

experimental comparisons of behavior

Roy Feldman [19] incorporated these principles in a comparative study of behavior toward compatriots and foreigners in Paris, Athens, and Boston. Feldman wanted to see (i) whether absolute levels and patterns of helpfulness varied significantly from city to city, and (ii) whether inhabitants in each city tended to treat compatriots differently from foreigners. He examined five concrete behavioral episodes, each carried out by a team of native experimenters and a team of American experimenters in the three cities. The episodes involved (i) asking natives of the city for street directions; (ii) asking natives to mail a letter for the experimenter; (iii) asking natives if they had just dropped a dollar bill (or the Greek or French equivalent) when the money actually belonged to the experimenter himself; (iv) deliberately overpaying for goods in a store to see if the cashier would correct the mistake

[17] P. Abelson, *Science*, **165** (1969), 853.
[18] See A. L. Strauss, Ed., *The American City: A Sourcebook of Urban Imagery* (Chicago: Aldine, 1968).

[19] R. E. Feldman, *J. Personality Soc. Psychol.*, **10** (1968), 202.

and return the excess money; and (v) determining whether taxicab drivers overcharged strangers and whether they took the most direct route available.

Feldman's results suggest some interesting contrasts in the profiles of the three cities. In Paris, for instance, certain stereotypes were borne out. Parisian cab drivers overcharged foreigners significantly more often than they overcharged compatriots. But other aspects of the Parisians' behavior were not in accord with American preconceptions: in mailing a letter for a stranger, Parisians treated foreigners significantly better than Athenians or Bostonians did, and, when asked to mail letters that were already stamped, Parisians actually treated foreigners better than they treated compatriots. Similarly, Parisians were significantly more honest than Athenians or Bostonians in resisting the temptation to claim money that was not theirs, and Parisians were the only citizens who were more honest with foreigners than with compatriots in this experiment.

Feldman's studies not only begin to quantify some of the variables that give a city its distinctive texture but they also provide a methodological model for other comparative research. His most important contribution is his successful application of objective, experimental measures to everyday situations, a mode of study which provides conclusions about urban life that are more pertinent than those achieved through laboratory experiments.

tempo and pace

Another important component of a city's atmosphere is its tempo or pace, an attribute frequently remarked on but less often studied. Does a city have a frenetic, hectic quality, or is it easygoing and leisurely? In any empirical treatment of this question, it is best to start in a very simple way. Walking speeds of pedestrians in different cities and in cities and towns should be measured and compared. William Ber-

kowitz [20] of Lafayette College has undertaken an extensive series of studies of walking speeds in Philadelphia, New York, and Boston, as well as in small and moderate-sized towns. Berkowitz writes that "there does appear to be a significant linear relation between walking speed and size of municipality, but the absolute size of the difference varies by less than 10 percent."

Perhaps the feeling of rapid tempo is due not so much to absolute pedestrian speeds as to the constant need to dodge others in a large city to avoid collisions with other pedestrians. (One basis for computing the adjustments needed to avoid collisions is to hypothesize a set of mechanical manikins sent walking along a city street and to calculate the number of collisions when no adjustments are made. Clearly, the higher the density of manikins the greater the number of collisions per unit of time, or, conversely, the greater the frequency of adjustments needed in higher population densities to avoid collisions.)

Patterns of automobile traffic contribute to a city's tempo. Driving an automobile provides a direct means of translating feelings about tempo into measurable acceleration, and a city's pace should be particularly evident in vehicular velocities, patterns of acceleration, and latency of response to traffic signals. The inexorable tempo of New York is expressed, further, in the manner in which pedestrians stand at busy intersections, impatiently awaiting a change in traffic light, making tentative excursions into the intersection, and frequently surging into the street even before the green light appears.

visual components

Hall has remarked [21] that the physical layout of the city also affects its atmos-

20 W. Berkowitz, personal communication.
21 E. T. Hall, *The Hidden Dimension* (Garden City, N.Y.: Doubleday, 1966).

phere. A gridiron pattern of streets gives the visitor a feeling of rationality, orderliness, and predictability but is sometimes monotonous. Winding lanes or streets branching off at strange angles, with many forks (as in Paris or Greenwich Village), create feelings of surprise and esthetic pleasure, while forcing greater decision-making in plotting one's course. Some would argue that the visual component is all-important—that the "look" of Paris or New York can almost be equated with its atmosphere. To investigate this hypothesis, we might conduct studies in which only blind, or at least blindfolded, respondents were used. We would no doubt discover that each city has a distinctive texture even when the visual component is eliminated.

sources of ambiance

Thus far we have tried to pinpoint and measure some of the factors that contribute to the distinctive atmosphere of a great city. But we may also ask, Why do differences in urban atmosphere exist? How did they come about, and are they in any way related to the factors of density, large numbers, and heterogeneity discussed above?

First, there is the obvious factor that, even among great cities, populations and densities differ. The metropolitan areas of New York, London, and Paris, for example, contain 15 million, 12 million, and 8 million persons, respectively. London has average densities of 43 persons per acre, while Paris is more congested, with average densities of 114 persons per acre.[22] Whatever characteristics are specifically attributable to density are more likely to be pronounced in Paris than in London.

A second factor affecting the atmosphere of cities is the source from which the populations are drawn.[23] It is a charac-

22 P. Hall, *The World Cities* (New York: McGraw-Hill, 1966).
23 R. E. Park, E. W. Burgess, and R. D. McKenzie, *The City* (Chicago: Univ. of Chicago Press, 1967), pp. 1–45.

teristic of great cities that they do not reproduce their own populations, but that their numbers are constantly maintained and augmented by the influx of residents from other parts of the country. This can have a determining effect on the city's atmosphere. For example, Oslo is a city in which almost all of the residents are only one or two generations removed from a purely rural existence, and this contributes to its almost agricultural norms.

A third source of atmosphere is the general national culture. Paris combines adaptations to the demography of cities *and* certain values specific to French culture. New York is an admixture of American values and values that arise as a result of extraordinarily high density and large population.

Finally, one could speculate that the atmosphere of a great city is traceable to the specific historical conditions under which adaptations to urban overload occurred. For example, a city which acquired its mass and density during a period of commercial expansion will respond to new demographic conditions by adaptations designed to serve purely commercial needs. Thus, Chicago, which grew and became a great city under a purely commercial stimulus, adapted in a manner that emphasizes business needs. European capitals, on the other hand, incorporate many of the adaptations which were appropriate to the period of their increasing numbers and density. Because aristocratic values were prevalent at the time of the growth of these cities, the mechanisms developed for coping with overload were based on considerations other than pure efficiency. Thus, the manners, norms, and facilities of Paris and Vienna continue to reflect esthetic values and the idealization of leisure.

cognitive maps of cities

When we speak of "behavioral comparisons" among cities, we must specify which parts of the city are most relevant for sampling purposes. In a sampling of "New Yorkers," should we include residents of Bay Ridge or Flatbush as well as inhabitants of Manhattan? And, if so, how should we weight our sample distribution? One approach to defining relevant boundaries in sampling is to determine which areas form the psychological or cognitive core of the city. We weight our samples most heavily in the areas considered by most people to represent the "essence" of the city.

The psychologist is less interested in the geographic layout of a city or in its political boundaries than in the cognitive representation of the city. Hans Blumenfeld [24] points out that the perceptual structure of a modern city can be expressed by the "silhouette" of the group of skyscrapers at its center and that of smaller groups of office buildings at its "subcenters" but that urban areas can no longer, because of their vast extent, be experienced as fully articulated sets of streets, squares, and space.

In *The Image of the City*,[25] Kevin Lynch created a cognitive map of Boston by interviewing Bostonians. Perhaps his most significant finding was that, while certain landmarks, such as Paul Revere's house and the Boston Common, as well as the paths linking them, are known to almost all Bostonians, vast areas of the city are simply unknown to its inhabitants.

Using Lynch's technique, Donald Hooper [26] created a psychological map of New York from the answers to the study questionnaire on Paris, London, and New York. Hooper's results were similar to those of Lynch: New York appears to have a

dense core of well-known landmarks in midtown Manhattan, surrounded by the vast unknown reaches of Queens, Brooklyn, and the Bronx. Times Square, Rockefeller Center, and the Fifth Avenue department stores alone comprise half the places specifically cited by respondents as the haunts in which they spent most of their time. However, outside the midtown area, only scattered landmarks were recognized. Another interesting pattern is evident: even the best-known symbols of New York are relatively self-contained, and the pathways joining them appear to be significant on the map.

The psychological map can be used for more than just sampling techniques. Lynch [27] argues, for instance, that a good city is highly "imageable," having many known symbols joined by widely known pathways, whereas dull cities are gray and nondescript. We might test the relative "imagibility" of several cities by determining the proportion of residents who recognize sampled geographic points and their accompanying pathways.

If we wanted to be even more precise we could construct a cognitive map that would not only show the symbols of the city but would measure the precise degree of cognitive significance of any given point in the city relative to any other. By applying a pattern of points to a map of New York City, for example, and taking photographs from each point, we could determine what proportion of a sample of the city's inhabitants could identify the locale specified by each point (see Figure 2). We might even take the subjects blindfolded to a point represented on the map, then remove the blindfold and ask them to identify their location from the view around them.

One might also use psychological maps to gain insight into the differing perceptions of a given city that are held by mem-

[24] H. Blumenfeld, in *The Quality of Urban Life* (Beverly Hills, Calif.: Sage, 1969).

[25] K. Lynch, *The Image of the City* (Cambridge, Mass.: M.I.T. and Harvard Univ. Press, 1960).

[26] D. Hooper (Harvard University), unpublished.

[27] *Op. cit.*

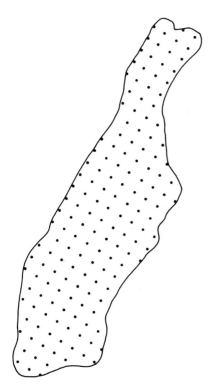

figure 2   To create a psychological map of Manhattan, geographic points are sampled, and, from photographs, the subjects attempt to identify the location of each point. To each point a numerical index is assigned indicating the proportion of persons able to identify its location.

immediate neighborhood in which they are raised. In adolescence, however, the field of knowledge of the white teen-ager probably undergoes rapid enlargement; he learns of opportunities in midtown and outlying sections and comes to see himself as functioning in a larger urban field. But the process of ghettoization, to which the black teen-ager is subjected, may well hamper the expansion of his sense of the city. These are speculative notions, but they are readily subject to precise test.

conclusion

I have tried to indicate some organizing theory that starts with the basic facts of city life: large numbers, density, and heterogeneity. These are external to the individual. He experiences these factors as overloads at the level of roles, norms, cognitive functions, and facilities. These overloads lead to adaptive mechanisms which create the distinctive tone and behaviors of city life. These notions, of course, need to be examined by objective comparative studies of cities and towns.

A second perspective concerns the differing atmospheres of great cities, such as Paris, London, and New York. Each has a distinctive flavor, offering a differentiable quality of experience. More precise knowledge of urban atmosphere seems attainable through application of the tools of experimental inquiry.

bers of its cultural subgroups, and into the manner in which their perceptions may change. In the earlier stages of life, whites and Negroes alike probably have only a limited view of the city, centering on the

30 *The experiment described in the following article was the first in a series of studies carried out by Stanley Milgram which deal with the subject of voluntary obedience to authority. The results were as unexpected as they were frightening. Essentially, Milgram found that a substantial number of paid volunteer subjects would deliver strong, painful electrical shock to another individual in spite of the victim's strong protests.*

Although the experiments were originally designed to shed light on the Nazi personality, Milgram indicates that blind obedience to authority is not necessarily limited to a few national groups.

behavioral study of obedience [1]

STANLEY MILGRAM

Obedience is as basic an element in the structure of social life as one can point to. Some system of authority is a requirement of all communal living, and it is only the man dwelling in isolation who is not forced to respond, through defiance or submission, to the commands of others. Obedience, as a determinant of behavior, is of particular relevance to our time. It has been reliably established that from 1933–45 millions of innocent persons were systematically slaughtered on command. Gas chambers were built, death camps were guarded, daily quotas of corpses were produced with the same efficiency as the manufacture of appliances. These in-

[1] This research was supported by a grant (NSF G-17916) from the National Science Foundation. Exploratory studies conducted in 1960 were supported by a grant from the Higgins Fund at Yale University. The research assistance of Alan C. Elms and Jon Wayland is gratefully acknowledged.

Reprinted from *Journal of Abnormal and Social Psychology*, 1963, 67: 371–378, by permission of the author and publisher. Copyright © 1963 by the American Psychological Association.

humane policies may have originated in the mind of a single person, but they could only be carried out on a massive scale if a very large number of persons obeyed orders.

Obedience is the psychological mechanism that links individual action to political purpose. It is the dispositional cement that binds men to systems of authority. Facts of recent history and observation in daily life suggest that for many persons obedience may be a deeply ingrained behavior tendency, indeed, a prepotent impulse overriding training in ethics, sympathy, and moral conduct. C. P. Snow (1961) points to its importance when he writes:

When you think of the long and gloomy history of man, you will find more hideous crimes have been committed in the name of obedience than have ever been committed in the name of rebellion. If you doubt that, read William Shirer's *Rise and Fall of the Third Reich*. The German Officer Corps were brought up in the most rigorous code of obedience . . . in the name of obedience they were party to, and assisted in, the most wicked large-scale action in the history of the world [p. 24].

While the particular form of obedience dealt with in the present study has its antecedents in these episodes, it must not be thought all obedience entails acts of aggression against others. Obedience serves numerous productive functions. Indeed, the very life of society is predicated on its existence. Obedience may be ennobling and educative and refer to acts of charity and kindness, as well as to destruction.

GENERAL PROCEDURE

A procedure was devised which seems useful as a tool for studying obedience (Milgram, 1961). It consists of ordering a naive subject to administer electric shock to a victim. A simulated shock generator is used, with 30 clearly marked voltage levels that range from 15 to 450 volts. The instrument bears verbal designations that range from Slight Shock to Danger: Severe Shock. The responses of the victim, who is a trained confederate of the experimenter, are standardized. The orders to administer shocks are given to the naive subject in the context of a "learning experiment" ostensibly set up to study the effects of punishment on memory. As the experiment proceeds the naive subject is commanded to administer increasingly more intense shocks to the victim, even to the point of reaching the level marked Danger: Severe Shock. Internal resistances become stronger, and at a certain point the subject refuses to go on with the experiment. Behavior prior to this rupture is considered "obedience," in that the subject complies with the commands of the experimenter. The point of rupture is the act of disobedience. A quantitative value is assigned to the subject's performance based on the maximum intensity shock he is willing to administer before he refuses to participate further. Thus for any particular subject and for any particular experimental condition the degree of obedi-

ence may be specified with a numerical value. The crux of the study is to systematically vary the factors believed to alter the degree of obedience to the experimental commands.

The technique allows important variables to be manipulated at several points in the experiment. One may vary aspects of the source of command, content and form of command, instrumentalities for its execution, target object, general social setting, etc. The problem, therefore, is not one of designing increasingly more numerous experimental conditions, but of selecting those that best illuminate the *process* of obedience from the socio-psychological standpoint.

RELATED STUDIES

The inquiry bears an important relation to philosophic analyses of obedience and authority (Arendt, 1958; Friedrich, 1958; Weber, 1947), an early experimental study of obedience by Frank (1944), studies in "authoritarianism" (Adorno, Frenkel-Brunswik, Levinson, and Sanford, 1950; Rokeach, 1961), and a recent series of analytic and empirical studies in social power (Cartwright, 1959). It owes much to the long concern with *suggestion* in social psychology, both in its normal forms (e.g., Binet, 1900) and in its clinical manifestations (Charcot, 1881). But it derives, in the first instance, from direct observation of a social fact; the individual who is commanded by a legitimate authority ordinarily obeys. Obedience comes easily and often. It is a ubiquitous and indispensable feature of social life.

method

SUBJECTS

The subjects were 40 males between the ages of 20 and 50, drawn from New Haven and the surrounding communities. Subjects were obtained by a newspaper advertisement and direct mail solicitation. Those who responded to the appeal believed they were to participate in a study of memory and learning at Yale University. A wide range of occupations is represented in the sample. Typical subjects were postal clerks, high school teachers, salesmen, engineers, and laborers. Subjects ranged in educational level from one who had not finished elementary school, to those who had doctorate and other professional degrees. They were paid $4.50 for their participation in the experiment. However, subjects were told that payment was simply for coming to the laboratory, and that the money was theirs no matter what happened after they arrived. Table 1 shows

table 1

distribution of age and occupational types in the experiment

occupations	20–29 years N	30–39 years N	40–50 years N	percentage of total (occupations)
Workers, skilled and unskilled	4	5	6	37.5
Sales, business, and white-collar	3	6	7	40.0
Professional	1	5	3	22.5
Percentage of total (age)	20	40	40	

Note.—Total N = 40.

the proportion of age and occupational types assigned to the experimental condition.

PERSONNEL AND LOCALE

The experiment was conducted on the grounds of Yale University in the elegant interaction laboratory. (This detail is relevant to the perceived legitimacy of the experiment. In further variations, the ex-

periment was dissociated from the university, with consequences for performance.) The role of experimenter was played by a 31-year-old high school teacher of biology. His manner was impassive, and his appearance somewhat stern throughout the experiment. He was dressed in a gray technician's coat. The victim was played by a 47-year-old accountant, trained for the role; he was of Irish-American stock, whom most observers found mild-mannered and likeable.

PROCEDURE

One naive subject and one victim (an accomplice) performed in each experiment. A pretext had to be devised that would justify the administration of electric shock by the naive subject. This was effectively accomplished by the cover story. After a general introduction on the presumed relation between punishment and learning, subjects were told:

But actually, we know *very little* about the effect of punishment on learning, because almost no truly scientific studies have been made of it in human beings.

For instance, we don't know how *much* punishment is best for learning—and we don't know how much difference it makes as to who is giving the punishment, whether an adult learns best from a younger or an older person than himself—or many things of that sort.

So in this study we are bringing together a number of adults of different occupations and ages. And we're asking some of them to be teachers and some of them to be learners.

We want to find out just what effect different people have on each other as teachers and learners, and also what effect *punishment* will have on learning in this situation.

Therefore, I'm going to ask one of you to be the teacher here tonight and the other one to be the learner.

Does either of you have a preference?

Subjects then drew slips of paper from a hat to determine who would be the teacher and who would be the learner in the experiment. The drawing was rigged so that the naive subject was always the teacher and the accomplice always the learner. (Both slips contained the word "Teacher.") Immediately after the drawing, the teacher and learner were taken to an adjacent room and the learner was strapped into an "electric chair" apparatus.

The experimenter explained that the straps were to prevent excessive movement while the learner was being shocked. The effect was to make it impossible for him to escape from the situation. An electrode was attached to the learner's wrist, and electrode paste was applied "to avoid blisters and burns." Subjects were told that the electrode was attached to the shock generator in the adjoining room.

In order to improve credibility the experimenter declared, in response to a question by the learner: "Although the shocks can be extremely painful, they cause no permanent tissue damage."

Learning task. The lesson administered by the subject was a paired-associate learning task. The subject read a series of word pairs to the learner, and then read the first word of the pair along with four terms. The learner was to indicate which of the four terms had originally been paired with the first word. He communicated his answer by pressing one of four switches in front of him, which in turn lit up one of four numbered quadrants in an answer-box located atop the shock generator.

Shock generator. The instrument panel consists of 30 lever switches set in a horizontal line. Each switch is clearly labeled with a voltage designation that ranges from 15 to 450 volts. There is a 15-volt increment from one switch to the next going from the left to right. In addition, the following verbal designations are clearly indicated for groups of four switches going from left to right: Slight Shock, Moderate Shock, Strong Shock, Very Strong Shock, Intense Shock, Extreme Intensity Stock, Danger: Severe Shock. (Two switches after this last designation are simply marked XXX.)

Upon depressing a switch: a pilot light corresponding to each switch is illuminated in bright red; an electric buzzing is heard; an electric blue light, labeled "voltage energizer," flashes; the dial on the voltage meter swings to the right; various relay clicks are sounded.

The upper left-hand corner of the generator is labeled Shock Generator, Type ZLB, Dyson Instrument Company, Waltham, Mass. Output 15 Volts–450 Volts.

Details of the instrument were carefully handled to insure an appearance of authenticity. The panel was engraved by precision industrial engravers, and all components were of high quality. No subject in the experiment suspected that the instrument was merely a simulated shock generator.[2]

Sample shock. Each naive subject is given a sample shock on the shock generator, prior to beginning his run as teacher. This shock is always 45 volts, and is applied by pressing the third switch of the generator. The shock is applied to the wrist of the naive subject, and has its source in a 45-volt battery wired into the generator. This further convinces the subject of the authenticity of the generator.

Shock instructions. The subject is told to administer a shock to the learner each time he gives a wrong response. Moreover —and this is the key command—the subject is instructed to "move one level higher on the shock generator each time the

[2] A related technique, making use of a shock generator, was reported by Buss (1961) for the study of aggression in the laboratory. Despite the considerable similarity of technical detail in the experimental procedures, both investigators proceeded in ignorance of the other's work. Milgram provided plans and photographs of his shock generator, experimental procedure, and first results in a report to the National Science Foundation in January 1961. This report received only limited circulation. Buss reported his procedure 6 months later, but to a wider audience. Subsequently, technical information and reports were exchanged. The present article was first received in the Editor's office on December 27, 1961; it was resubmitted with deletions on July 27, 1962.

learner flashes a wrong answer." He is also instructed to announce the voltage level before administering a shock. This serves to continually remind subjects of the increasing intensity of shocks administered to the learner.

Preliminary and regular run. Pretests revealed that the procedure of reading words and administering shocks requires some practice before it can be handled smoothly. Therefore, immediately preceding the regular run, the teacher is given a preliminary series of 10 words to read to the learner. There are 3 neutral words in the practice series (i.e., words that the learner answers correctly), so that shocks are administered for 7 of the words, with the maximum shock at 105 volts (moderate shock). Almost all subjects master the procedure by the time the preliminary run is over.

Subjects are then presented with a second list, and are told that the procedure is the same as for the first list; the experimenter adds, however:

When you get to the bottom of the list, repeat it over again, and continue giving shocks, until the learner has learned all the pairs correctly.

The experimenter instructs the subject to,

start from 15 volts and increase the shock level one step each time the learner gives a wrong answer.

Feedback from the victim. In all conditions the learner gives a predetermined set of responses to the word pair test, based on a schedule of approximately three wrong answers to one correct answer. In the present experimental condition no vocal response or other sign of protest is heard from the learner until Shock Level 300 is reached. When the 300-volt shock is administered, the learner pounds on the wall of the room in which he is bound to the electric chair. The pounding can be heard by the subject. From this point on, the learner's answers no longer appear on the four-way panel.

At this juncture, subjects ordinarily turn to the experimenter for guidance. The experimenter instructs the subject to treat the absence of a response as a wrong answer, and to shock the subject according to the usual schedule. He advises the subjects to allow 5–10 seconds before considering no response as a wrong answer, and to increase the shock level one step each time the learner fails to respond correctly. The learner's pounding is repeated after the 315-volt shock is administered; afterwards he is not heard from, nor do his answers reappear on the four-way signal box.

Experimenter feedback. At various points in the experiment the subject may turn to the experimenter for advice on whether he should continue to administer shocks. Or he may indicate that he does not wish to go on. It was important to standardize the experimenter's responses to these inquiries and reactions.

If the subject indicated his unwillingness to go on, the experimenter responded with a sequence of "prods," using as many as necessary to bring the subject into line.

Prod 1: Please continue, *or* Please go on.
Prod 2: The experiment requires that you continue.
Prod 3: It is absolutely essential that you continue.
Prod 4: You have no other choice, you *must* go on.

The prods were always made in sequence: Only if Prod 1 had been unsuccessful, could Prod 2 be used. If the subject refused to obey the experimenter after Prod 4, the experiment was terminated. The experimenter's tone of voice was at all times firm, but not impolite. The sequence was begun anew on each occasion that the subject balked or showed reluctance to follow orders.

Special prods. If the subject asked if the learner was liable to suffer permanent physical injury, the experimenter said:

Although the shocks may be painful, there is

no permanent tissue damage, so please go on. [Followed by Prods 2, 3, and 4 if necessary.]

If the subject said that the learner did not want to go on, the experimenter replied:

Whether the learner likes it or not, you must go on until he has learned all the word pairs correctly. So please go on. [Followed by Prods 2, 3, and 4 if necessary.]

DEPENDENT MEASURES

The primary dependent measure for any subject is the maximum shock he administers before he refuses to go any further. In principle this may vary from 0 (for a subject who refuses to administer even the first shock) to 30 (for a subject who administers the highest shock on the generator). A subject who breaks off the experiment at any point prior to administering the thirtieth shock level is termed a *defiant* subject. One who complies with experimental commands fully, and proceeds to administer all shock levels commanded, is termed an *obedient* subject.

Further records. With few exceptions, experimental sessions were recorded on magnetic tape. Occasional photographs were taken through one-way mirrors. Notes were kept on any unusual behavior occurring during the course of the experiments. On occasion, additional observers were directed to write objective descriptions of the subjects' behavior. The latency and duration of shocks were measured by accurate timing devices.

Interview and dehoax. Following the experiment, subjects were interviewed; open-ended questions, projective measures, and attitude scales were employed. After the interview, procedures were undertaken to assure that the subject would leave the laboratory in a state of well being. A friendly reconciliation was arranged between the subject and the victim, and an effort was made to reduce any tensions that arose as a result of the experiment.

PRELIMINARY NOTIONS

Before giving an account of the experimental results, it is instructive to consider how persons predict others will perform when commanded to administer powerful shocks to another person. Fourteen Yale seniors, all psychology majors, were provided with a detailed description of the experimental situation. They were asked to reflect carefully on it, and to predict the behavior of 100 hypothetical subjects. More specifically, they were instructed to plot the distribution of obedience of "100 Americans of diverse occupations, and ranging in age from 20 to 50 years," who were placed in the experimental situation.

There was considerable agreement among the respondents on the expected behavior of hypothetical subjects. All respondents predicted that only an insignificant minority would go through to the end of the shock series. (The estimates ranged from 0 to 3 per cent; i.e., the most "pessimistic" member of the class predicted that of 100 persons, 3 would continue through to the most potent shock available on the shock generator—450 volts.) The class mean was 1.2 per cent. The question was also posed informally to colleagues of the author, and the most general feeling was that few if any subjects would go beyond the designation Very Strong Shock.

RESULT OF EXPERIMENT I

Subjects accept situation. With few exceptions subjects were convinced of the reality of the experimental situation, that they were administering shocks to another person, and the most potent shocks were extremely painful. In the post-experimental interview subjects were asked: "How painful to the learner were the last few shocks that you administered to him?" Subjects were instructed to indicate their answers on a printed 14-point scale ranging from "Not at all painful" to "Extremely painful." The modal response was 14 (Extremely painful) with the mean at 13.42.

Signs of extreme tension. Many subjects showed signs of nervousness in the experimental situation, and especially upon administering the more powerful shocks. In a large number of cases the degree of tension reached extremes that are rarely seen in sociopsychological laboratory studies. Subjects were observed to sweat, tremble, stutter, bite their lips, groan, and dig their fingernails into their flesh. These were characteristic rather than exceptional responses to the experiment.

One sign of tension was the regular occurrence of nervous laughing fits. Fourteen of the 40 subjects showed definite signs of nervous laughter and smiling. The laughter seemed entirely out of place, even bizarre. Full-blown, uncontrollable seizures were observed for 3 subjects. On one occasion we observed a seizure so violently convulsive that it was necessary to call a halt to the experiment. The subject, a 46-year-old encyclopedia salesman, was seriously embarrassed by his untoward and uncontrollable behavior. In the post-experimental interviews subjects took pains to point out that they were not sadistic types, and that the laughter did not mean they enjoyed shocking the victim.

Distribution of scores. It had been conjectured that persons would not, in general, agree to administer shocks beyond the level designated as Very Strong Shock. The distribution of maximum shocks for this experiment is shown in Table 2. The obtained distribution of scores deviates radically from the prediction.

Upon command of the experimenter, each of the 40 subjects went beyond the expected breakoff point. No subject stopped prior to administering Shock Level 20. (At this level—300 volts—the victim kicks on the wall and no longer provides answers to the teacher's multiple-choice questions.)

table 2

distribution of breakoff points

verbal designation and voltage indication	number of subjects for whom this was maximum shock
Slight Shock	
15	0
30	0
45	0
60	0
Moderate Shock	
75	0
90	0
105	0
120	0
Strong Shock	
135	0
150	0
165	0
180	0
Very Strong Shock	
195	0
210	0
225	0
240	0
Intense Shock	
255	0
270	0
285	0
300	5
Extreme Intensity Shock	
315	4
330	2
345	1
360	1
Danger: Severe Shock	
375	1
390	0
405	0
420	0
XXX	
435	0
450	26

Of the 40 subjects, 5 refused to obey the experimental commands beyond the 300-volt level. Four more subjects administered one further shock, and then refused to go on. Two broke off at the 330-volt level, and 1 each at 345, 360, and 375 volts. Thus a total of 14 subjects defied the experimenter. It is instructive to reprint their remarks at the point of defiance, as transcribed from the tape recordings:

[0124] I think he's trying to communicate, he's knocking. . . . Well it's not fair to shock the guy . . . these are terrific volts. I don't think this is very humane. . . . Oh, I can't go on with this; no, this isn't right. It's a hell of an experiment. The guy is suffering in there. No, I don't want to go on. This is crazy. [Subject refused to administer more shocks.]

[0123] He's banging in there, I'm gonna chicken out. I'd like to continue, but I can't do that to a man. . . . I'm sorry I can't do that to a man. I'd hurt his heart. You take your check. . . . No really, I couldn't do it.

These subjects were frequently in a highly agitated and even angered state. Sometimes, verbal protest was at a minimum, and the subject simply got up from his chair in front of the shock generator, and indicated that he wished to leave the laboratory.

Of the 40 subjects, 26 obeyed the orders of the experimenter to the end, proceeding to punish the victim until they reached the most potent shock available on the shock generator. At that point, the experimenter called a halt to the session. (The maximum shock is labeled 450 volts, and is two steps beyond the designation: Danger: Severe Shock.) Although obedient subjects continued to administer shocks, they often did so under extreme stress. Some expressed reluctance to administer shocks beyond the 300-volt level, and displayed fears similar to those who defied the experimenter; yet they obeyed.

After the maximum shocks had been delivered, and the experimenter called a halt to the proceedings, many obedient subjects heaved sighs of relief, mopped their brows, rubbed their fingers over their eyes, or nervously fumbled cigarettes. Some shook their heads, apparently in regret. Some subjects had remained calm throughout the experiment, and displayed only minimal signs of tension from beginning to end.

discussion

The experiment yielded two findings that were surprising. The first finding concerns the sheer strength of obedient tendencies manifested in this situation. Subjects have learned from childhood that it is a fundamental breach of moral conduct to hurt another person against his will. Yet, 26 subjects abandon this tenet in following the instructions of an authority who has no special powers to enforce his commands. To disobey would bring no material loss to the subject; no punishment would ensue. It is clear from the remarks and outward behavior of many participants that in punishing the victim they are often acting against their own values. Subjects often expressed deep disapproval of shocking a man in the face of his objections, and others denounced it as stupid and senseless. Yet the majority complied with the experimental commands. This outcome was surprising from two perspectives: first, from the standpoint of predictions made in the questionnaire described earlier. (Here, however, it is possible that the remoteness of the respondents from the actual situation, and the difficulty of conveying to them the concrete details of the experiment, could account for the serious underestimation of obedience.)

But the results were also unexpected to persons who observed the experiment in progress, through one-way mirrors. Observers often uttered expressions of disbelief upon seeing a subject administer more powerful shocks to the victim. These persons had a full acquaintance with the details of the situation, and yet systematically underestimated the amount of obedience that subjects would display.

The second unanticipated effect was the extraordinary tension generated by the procedures. One might suppose that a subject would simply break off or continue as his conscience dictated. Yet, this is very far from what happened. There were striking reactions of tension and emotional strain. One observer related:

I observed a mature and initially poised businessman enter the laboratory smiling and confident. Within 20 minutes he was reduced to a twitching, stuttering wreck, who was rapidly approaching a point of nervous collapse. He constantly pulled on his earlobe, and twisted his hands. At one point he pushed his fist into his forehead and muttered: "Oh God, let's stop it." And yet he continued to respond to every word of the experimenter, and obeyed to the end.

Any understanding of the phenomenon of obedience must rest on an analysis of the particular conditions in which it occurs. The following features of the experiment go some distance in explaining the high amount of obedience observed in the situation.

1. The experiment is sponsored by and takes place on the grounds of an institution of unimpeachable reputation, Yale University. It may be reasonably presumed that the personnel are competent and reputable. The importance of this background authority is now being studied by conducting a series of experiments outside of New Haven, and without any visible ties to the university.

2. The experiment is, on the face of it, designed to attain a worthy purpose—advancement of knowledge about learning and memory. Obedience occurs not as an end in itself, but as an instrumental element in a situation that the subject construes as significant and meaningful. He may not be able to see its full significance, but he may properly assume that the experimenter does.

3. The subject perceives that the victim has voluntarily submitted to the authority system of the experimenter. He is not (at first) an unwilling captive impressed for involuntary service. He has taken the trouble to come to the laboratory presum-

ably to aid the experimental research. That he later becomes an involuntary subject does not alter the fact that, initially, he consented to participate without qualification. Thus he has in some degree incurred an obligation toward the experimenter.

4. The subject, too, has entered the experiment voluntarily, and perceives himself under obligation to aid the experimenter. He has made a commitment, and to disrupt the experiment is a repudiation of this initial promise of aid.

5. Certain features of the procedure strengthen the subject's sense of obligation to the experimenter. For one, he has been paid for coming to the laboratory. In part this is canceled out by the experimenter's statement that:

Of course, as in all experiments, the money is yours simply for coming to the laboratory. From this point on, no matter what happens, the money is yours.[3]

6. From the subject's standpoint, the fact that he is the teacher and the other man the learner is purely a chance consequence (it is determined by drawing lots) and he, the subject, ran the same risk as the other man in being assigned the role of learner. Since the assignment of positions in the experiment was achieved by fair means, the learner is deprived of any basis of complaint on this count. (A similar situation obtains in Army units, in which—in the absence of volunteers—a particularly dangerous mission may be assigned by drawing lots, and the unlucky soldier is expected to bear his misfortune with sportsmanship.)

7. There is, at best, ambiguity with regard to the prerogatives of a psychologist and the corresponding rights of his subject. There is a vagueness of expectation concerning what a psychologist may require of his subject, and when he is overstepping

---

[3] Forty-three subjects, undergraduates at Yale University, were run in the experiment without payment. The results are very similar to those obtained with paid subjects.

acceptable limits. Moreover, the experiment occurs in a closed setting, and thus provides no opportunity for the subject to remove these ambiguities by discussion with others. There are few standards that seem directly applicable to the situation, which is a novel one for most subjects.

8. The subjects are assured that the shocks administered to the subject are "painful but not dangerous." Thus they assume that the discomfort caused the victim is momentary, while the scientific gains resulting from the experiment are enduring.

9. Through Shock Level 20 the victim continues to provide answers on the signal box. The subject may construe this as a sign that the victim is still willing to "play the game." It is only after Shock Level 20 that the victim repudiates the rules completely, refusing to answer further.

These features help to explain the high amount of obedience obtained in this experiment. Many of the arguments raised need not remain matters of speculation, but can be reduced to testable propositions to be confirmed or disproved by further experiments.[4]

The following features of the experiment concern the nature of the conflict which the subject faces.

10. The subject is placed in a position in which he must respond to the competing demands of two persons: the experimenter and the victim. The conflict must be resolved by meeting the demands of one or the other; satisfaction of the victim and the experimenter are mutually exclusive. Moreover, the resolution must take the form of a highly visible action, that of continuing to shock the victim or breaking off the experiment. Thus the subject is forced into a public conflict that does not permit any completely satisfactory solution.

11. While the demands of the experimenter carry the weight of scientific authority, the demands of the victim spring

from his personal experience of pain and suffering. The two claims need not be regarded as equally pressing and legitimate. The experimenter seeks an abstract scientific datum; the victim cries out for relief from physical suffering caused by the subject's actions.

12. The experiment gives the subject little time for reflection. The conflict comes on rapidly. It is only minutes after the subject has been seated before the shock generator that the victim begins his protests. Moreover, the subject perceives that he has gone through but two-thirds of the shock levels at the time the subject's first protests are heard. Thus he understands that the conflict will have a persistent aspect to it, and may well become more intense as increasingly more powerful shocks are required. The rapidity with which the conflict descends on the subject, and his realization that it is predictably recurrent may well be sources of tension to him.

13. At a more general level, the conflict stems from the opposition of two deeply ingrained behavior dispositions: first, the disposition not to harm other people, and second, the tendency to obey those whom we perceive to be legitimate authorities.

REFERENCES

ADORNO, T., ELSE FRENKEL-BRUNSWIK, D. J. LEVINSON, and R. N. SANFORD. *The authoritarian personality.* New York: Harper, 1950.

ARENDT, H. What was authority? In C. J. Friedrich (Ed.), *Authority.* Cambridge: Harvard Univer. Press, 1958, pp. 81–112.

BINET, A. *La suggestibilité.* Paris: Schleicher, 1900.

BUSS, A. H. *The psychology of aggression.* New York: Wiley, 1961.

CARTWRIGHT, S. (Ed.) *Studies in social power.* Ann Arbor: University of Michigan Institute for Social Research, 1959.

CHARCOT, J. M. *Oeuvres complètes.* Paris: Bureaux du Progrès Médical, 1881.

FRANK, J. D. Experimental studies of personal pressure and resistance. *J. gen. Psychol.,* 1944, **30**, 23–64.

[4] A series of recently completed experiments employing the obedience paradigm is reported in Milgram (1964).

FRIEDRICH, C. J. (Ed.) *Authority.* Cambridge: Harvard Univer. Press, 1958.

MILGRAM, S. Dynamics of obedience. Washington: National Science Foundation, 25 January 1961. (Mimeo)

————. Some conditions of obedience and disobedience to authority. *Hum. Relat.,* **18,** 1964, 57–76.

ROKEACH, M. Authority, authoritarianism, and conformity. In I. A. Berg & B. M. Bass (Eds.), *Conformity and deviation.* New York: Harper, 1961, pp. 230–257.

SNOW, C. P. Either-or. *Progressive,* 1961 (Feb.), 24.

WEBER, M. *The theory of social and economic organization.* Oxford: Oxford Univer. Press, 1947.